China's
Middle East
Diplomacy

China's
Middle East
Diplomacy

The Belt and Road Strategic Partnership

MORDECHAI CHAZIZA

sussex
ACADEMIC
PRESS
Brighton • Chicago • Toronto

2 4 6 8 10 9 7 5 3 1

First published in 2020 in Great Britain by
SUSSEX ACADEMIC PRESS
P.O. Box 139
Eastbourne BN24 9BP

Distributed in North America by
SUSSEX ACADEMIC PRESS
Independent Publishers Group
814 N. Franklin Street
Chicago, IL 60610

British Library Cataloguing in Publication Data
A CIP catalogue record for this book is available from the British Library.

Library of Congress Cataloging-in-Publication Data
To be applied for.

Hardcover ISBN 978-1-78976-056-9

Typeset and designed by Sussex Academic Press, Brighton & Eastbourne.
Printed and bound by CPI Group (UK) Ltd, Croydon, CR0 4YY

Contents

Preface

The Chinese partnership diplomacy along with the Belt and Road Initiative (BRI) countries has been more widely reviewed and discussed in the last year since my previous book that analyzes the synergy between the new Silk Road strategy and the emerging partnerships between the People's Republic of China (PRC) and the Persian Gulf region.[1] Of course, I feel honored and gratified that the book has had an impact and contribution to public discourse. That is why I decided to expand the book's thesis to the Middle East region to examine whether the synergy between the Chinese partnership diplomacy and the new Silk Road strategy is much wider than the Gulf countries. The new book also presents up-to-date material of China's relations with the Gulf states.

The Middle East geographical and political area is subject to different country inclusion interpretations that have changed over time and reflect complex and multifaceted circumstances involving conflict, religion, ethnicity, and language. PRC considers most Arab League member countries (as well as Israel, Turkey, and Iran) as representing the Middle East. The Ministry of Foreign Affairs and official Chinese publications refer to this region as *Xiya beifei* (West Asia and North Africa). The Middle East includes the following sixteen countries: Bahrain, Egypt, Iran, Iraq, Israel, Palestine, Jordan, Kuwait, Lebanon, Oman, Qatar, Saudi Arabia, Syria, Turkey, United Arab Emirates, and Yemen. Outside of Asia-Pacific, the Middle East is likely the most critical region of the world for China. PRC designated the Middle East as a 'neighbor' region, which indicates that the Middle East now falls into China's top priority geostrategic zone.[2]

China's BRI is one of the most ambitious infrastructure projects in modern history and has the potential to reconfigure and optimize global trade routes. The Middle East is situated at the heart of Beijing's new Silk Road strategy. The BRI aims to deepen and expand links between Asia, the Middle East, Europe, and Africa by recreating the ancient Silk Road trade routes through both land and sea. The Middle East occupies a strategic geographical position at the intersection of both a land-based (Silk Road Economic Belt) and a maritime component (the 21st Century Maritime Silk Road Initiative). It sits at the juncture of Asia, Africa, and Europe and has vital maritime chokepoints (Strait of Hormuz, Strait of Bab-al-Mandab, and the Suez Canal) that are critical for the global energy transport system and the connectivity BRI framework. Hence, the Middle East has critical importance for the maritime trade route, as much of the various straits, sea routes, and many hubs and offshoots run through the region.

In recent years, partnership diplomacy has become a primary foreign policy tool for the Chinese government. Since the end of the Cold War, the number of partnerships has steadily increased, PRC has established partnerships with 78 countries and five regional organizations (African Union, Arab Union, ASEAN, CELAC, and EU), which is 45 percent of the 174 countries that have formal diplomatic ties with China. In addition to its comprehensiveness, the network also consists of different stratifications, going from regular partnership to a comprehensive strategic partnership.[3]

In the Middle East, China partnership diplomacy includes fifteen relationships, spread across the eastern Mediterranean, the Gulf, and the Red Sea, which fall into four broad categories in line with their importance. The first category comprises comprehensive strategic partnerships with Egypt, Iran, Saudi Arabia, and the UAE). The second includes an innovative comprehensive partnership with Israel and a strategic cooperative relationship with Turkey (the latter being inferior to a strategic partnership). The third covers strategic partnerships with several midsized countries: Iraq, Jordan, Kuwait, Oman, and Qatar. The fourth comprises a relationship with the smaller states: Bahrain, Lebanon, Syria, and Yemen.

This book adopts the BRI as a framework for analyzing China–Middle East relations by examining China's growing presence in fifteen countries in the Middle East, and explores the significance of the PRC's strategic partnerships with the regional countries in the context of the BRI framework, as well as the increasing mutual interdependency between both sides in various sectors such as energy, construction, and infrastructure building, political ties, trade and investments, financial integration, people-to-people bond, and defense ties. A stable Middle East region is vital for China's sustainable growth and continued prosperity. As the world's largest oil consumer with an ambition to expand its economic and arguably political influences, it is predictable that the Middle East's geostrategic location and holdings of most of the world's known energy resources make it indispensable to the BRI.

China–U.S.–Middle East Relations in the Coronavirus Era

The Middle East was already plagued by war, famine, and death in the form of civil wars. The outbreak of the coronavirus added pestilence to this trio and makes for a long-term toxic mix. In December 2019, a mysterious outbreak of infectious disease emerged in the central Chinese city of Wuhan (Hubei Province); cases soon began to surface in other Chinese cities. The World Health Organization (WHO) declared the novel coronavirus (冠状病毒) – now officially designated as 'COVID-19' – to be a pandemic (a disease that is spreading in multiple countries around the world at the same time). It has spread far beyond China's borders and is now present in 213 other countries and territories around the world. The outbreak has become a major international health crisis, with official figures indicating over six million cases of infection worldwide and nearly 375,000 deaths.[1] However, the actual figures may be far higher due to the under-reporting of the infection rate and death toll in many countries.[2] (All figures cited in this text are correct as of June 1, 2020.)

Owing to its geographical location and centrality to Eurasian trade networks, the Middle East has historically been a conduit for the spread of pandemics. The COVID-19 pandemic is the second coronavirus outbreak that affects the Middle East region (a large family of viruses including the common cold, Severe Acute Respiratory Syndrome, SARS, and Middle East Respiratory Syndrome, MERS–CoV). The MERS virus was first reported in Saudi Arabia in 2012 (more than 2,000 cases) and has since spread to several other Arabian Peninsula countries, as well as the United States. More than 800 people have died from the MERS virus as of 2020.[3]

In the first months of the coronavirus outbreak, the Middle East rapidly became the second largest hotspot for the novel coronavirus outbreak after China. All the countries in the region have confirmed cases of the virus. The COVID-19 continues to spread across the Middle East, with official figures indicating over 557,014 cases of infection, 156,477 active cases, and nearly 14,116 reported deaths, as of early June 2020.[4] Compared to America, Europe, or Africa, the number of cases of infection and reported deaths in the Middle East is significantly lower. However, the real number is likely to be higher, as there is no reliable reporting from Syria, Yemen, Egypt, Iraq, or Iran because of conflict, official denial, or both.

The UAE was the first Middle East country to report a coronavirus-positive case. However, the most significant number of infections and fatalities are in Turkey, followed by Iran (151,466 cases of infection, 24,821 active cases, and nearly 8,000 deaths) and Saudi Arabia (85,261 cases of infection, 22,316 active cases, and nearly 550 deaths) in coronavirus cases. Turkey is the country with the ninth highest number of reported COVID-19 cases after the USA, Spain, Russia, the UK, Italy, Brazil, France, and Germany, being the first in the Middle East region (163,942 cases of infection, 31,429 active cases and nearly 4,540 deaths).[5]

The vast majority of countries in the region have closed schools and universities, stopped football league matches from taking place, canceled cultural events of world importance (the Qatar Grand Prix and the Ultra festival in the UAE), and suspended all commercial flights until further notice, while other countries are imposing bans on citizens traveling to specific countries in order to stop the spread of the coronavirus. Moreover, bars and cafes are shut, mosque attendance and traditional religious events have been canceled, and religious sites have been closed (The Al-Aqsa Mosque in Jerusalem, the Church of the Nativity in Bethlehem, and the Shiite Muslim shrine in Karbala, Iraq). There is fear that coronavirus has infiltrated a main pilgrimage route in the Middle East, which could lead the deadly pathogen to multiply in vulnerable refugee populations, causing unprecedented public health crises across the region.[6] The ability to contain the virus depends on the strength of the government effectiveness and public health systems of the Middle East countries, which is sorely lacking except perhaps in Israel.

Even before the coronavirus pandemic upended the world, U.S.–China relations had entered a particularly mistrustful and combative period. Since taking office, the Trump administration has openly stated that Great Power competition was the defining feature of the age, and the contest with China was at the heart of U.S. global strategy.[7] President Trump launched a trade war with Beijing and sought to decouple aspects of U.S. economic interdependence with China. China's actions (militarily fortifying artificial islands in the South China Sea, acting assertively in the East China Sea, curtailing promised freedoms in Hong Kong, and the mistreatment of Muslim Uighurs in Xinjiang) also increased tensions between the two powers.[8]

The COVID-19 pandemic has created a human catastrophe not seen outside wartime. Nevertheless, rather than being a reason for both powers to come together, the virus has been an accelerant in their hostilities. Washington's resentment toward Beijing has increased dramatically, stoked by the Trump administration's explicit efforts to pin the blame for all aspects of the coronavirus on China. President Donald Trump posted a tweet on March 16, 2020, that the COVID-19 is a "Chinese virus",[9] and during a press conference two days later, defended the term ("because it comes from China").[10] He continued to reiterate this for some time, but then pulled back from associating the novel coronavirus with China.[11] Secretary of State Mike Pompeo has criticized China's coronavirus response as a "classic Communist disinformation effort" and for working "to make sure the world didn't learn in a timely fashion" about the virus outbreak.[12]

According to an internal Chinese report, Beijing faces a rising wave of hostility in the wake of the coronavirus outbreak that could tip relations with the United States into a confrontation (relations were already tricky before the virus appeared and the COVID-19 crisis has made them worse). The report concluded that global anti-China sentiment is at its highest since the 1989 Tiananmen Square crackdown. As a result, the PRC faces a wave of anti-China sentiment led by the United States in the aftermath of the pandemic. It is no exaggeration to confirm that some political and military elements of the Chinese state feel the necessity to prepare for armed confrontation between the two global powers.[13]

All of this indicates that the infectious disease will not transform relations between the two global powers positively, but rather accelerate the competition and distrust between them. However, although the relationship between the United States and China has deteriorated significantly (the friction is principally symbolic), it is not yet irretrievably so. In the Middle East context, and indeed in the context of the present analysis, we must ask: What are the virus's implications for China's regional partnership network? It is too early to determine how the coronavirus outbreak will play out, how it will end, and how it will impact the economic growth and stability in the Middle East in the longer term. And, of course, how the virus will impact the overall China–Middle East relationship – bearing in mind how the Middle East and Persian Gulf are choke points in China's ability to trade with the world.

1   The data is updated as of June 1, 2020, https://www.worldometers.info/coronavirus/.
2   "COVID-19 coronavirus pandemic," *Worldometer*, March 23, 2020, https://www.worldometers.info/coronavirus/.
3   "Middle East Respiratory Syndrome (MERS)," *Centers for Disease Control and Prevention (CDC)*, August 2, 2019, https://www.cdc.gov/coronavirus/mers/index.html.
4   The data is updated as of June 1, 2020, https://www.worldometers.info/coronavirus/.
5   The data is updated as of June 1, 2020, https://www.worldometers.info/coronavirus/.
6   Liz Sly, "The Middle East is already wracked by war. Now it must confront the coronavirus, too," *The Washington Post*, March 17, 2020, https://www.washingtonpost.com/world/middle_east/the-middle-east-is-already-wracked-by-war-now-it-must-confront-coronavirus-too/2020/03/16/a233d2b0-62f8-11ea-8a8e-5c5336b32760_story.html.
7   "National Security Strategy of the United States of America," The White House, December 2017, https://www.whitehouse.gov/wp-content/uploads/2017/12/NSS-Final-12-18-2017-0905.pdf.
8   Nick Bisley, "US–China relations were already heated. Then coronavirus threw fuel on the flames," *The Conversation*, May 12, 2020, https://theconversation.com/us-china-relations-were-already-heated-then-coronavirus-threw-fuel-on-the-flames-137886.
9   Kimmy Yam, "Trump tweets about coronavirus using the term 'Chinese Virus'," *NBC News*, March 17, 2020, https://www.nbcnews.com/news/asian-america/trump-tweets-about-coronavirus-using-term-chinese-virus-n1161161.
10   Christopher Britom, "President Trump uses term "Chinese virus" to describe coronavirus, prompting a backlash," *CBS News*, March 19, 2020, https://www.cbsnews.com/news/president-trump-coronavirus-chinese-virus-backlash/.
11   Maegan Vazquez, "Trump says he's pulling back from calling novel coronavirus the 'China virus'," *CNN*, March 24, 2020, https://edition.cnn.com/2020/03/24/politics/donald-trump-pull-back-coronavirus-chinese-virus/index.html.
12   Andrew O'Reilly, "Pompeo blasts China for suppressing coronavirus information, call it a 'classic Communist disinformation effort'," *Fox News*, May 3, 2020, https://www.foxnews.com/politics/pompeo-blasts-china-for-suppressing-coronavirus-information-call-it-a-classic-communist-disinformation-effort.
13   "Exclusive: Internal Chinese report warns Beijing faces Tiananmen-like global backlash over virus," *Reuters*, May 4, 2020 , https://www.reuters.com/article/us-health-coronavirus-china-sentiment-ex/exclusive-internal-chinese-report-warns-beijing-faces-tiananmen-like-global-backlash-over-virus- ...

Acknowledgments

I wish to thank my parents, Abraham and Phoebe Chaziza, for their love and encouragement. I am most grateful to my family – my wife Revital and my beloved kids, Hillel, Agam, and Yarden – for their unwavering faith in me and their constant support and understanding. I have also benefited from the experience and wisdom of my editor, Sharon Blass. The work on the book was supported by the Ashkelon Academic College, Israel.

List of Abbreviations

Asian Infrastructure Investment Bank (AIIB)
Arabian Travel Market (ATM)
Belt and Road Initiative (BRI)
Baku-Tbilisi-Kars (BTK)
Bank of China (BOC)
China Arab Exchange Association (CAFA)
China–Arab States Cooperation Forum (CASCF)
China Civil Engineering Construction Corporation (CCECC)
China-Central-West Asia Economic Corridor (CCWAEC)
China Council to Promote International Trade (CCPIT)
China Development Bank (CDB)
China Fortune Land Development Company (CFLD)
Chinese Harbor State Company (CHEC)
China's Ministry of Commerce (MOC)
China's National Aero-Technology Import and Export Corporation (CATIC)
China National Nuclear Corporation (CNNC)
China National Petroleum Corporation (CNPC)
China Nuclear Engineering Corporation (CNEC)
China Ocean Shipping Company (COSCO)
China–Pakistan Economic Corridor (CPEC)
Chinese People's Association for Friendship with Foreign Countries (CPAFFC)
China Precision Machinery Import-Export Corporation (CPMIEC)
China Railway Construction Corporation (CRCC)
China State Construction Engineering Corporation (CSCEC)
Conference on Interaction and Confidence Building in Asia (CICA)
Energy Information Administration (EIA)
Foreign Direct Investment (FDI)
Forum on China-Africa Cooperation (FOCAC)
Gulf Cooperation Council (GCC)
Industrial Commercial Bank of China (ICBC)
International Energy Agency (IEA)
Jebel Ali Free Zone (JAFZA)
Joint Comprehensive Plan of Action (JCPOA)
Khalifa Industrial Zone Abu Dhabi (KIZAD)
Liquefied Natural Gas (LNG)

Memorandum of Understanding (MoU)
Middle East and North Africa (MENA)
Mohammed bin Salman al-Saud (MBS)
National Bureau of Statistics (NBS)
One Belt, One Road (OBOR)
Organization of the Petroleum Exporting Countries (OPEC)
People's Liberation Army Navy (PLAN)
People's Republic of China (PRC)
Qatar Investment Authority (QIA)
Shanghai Cooperation Organization (SCO)
Sea Lines of Communication (SLOC)
Shanghai International Port Group (SIPG)
Silk Road Economic Belt (SREB)

Introduction

In recent years, the People's Republic of China (PRC) has significantly increased its economic and diplomatic engagement with the Middle East. China's involvement spans multiple dimensions, including trade and investment, the energy sector, military cooperation, and diplomatic activity. Outside of Asia-Pacific, the Middle East (West Asia) is the most critical region of the world for China.[1] Connecting China through the Suez Canal to the Mediterranean and Europe, the Middle East is a unique geostrategic location for Beijing, a critical source of much-needed energy resources, and an area of expanding economic ties. In turn, Middle Eastern countries see Beijing as the most important world capital after Washington because of China's considerable economic power.

The 'Middle East' as a geographical and political area is subject to different interpretations of country inclusion that have changed over time and reflect complex and multifaceted circumstances involving conflict, religion, ethnicity, and language. China considers most Arab League member countries (as well as Turkey and Iran) as representing the 'Middle East'. The PRC's Ministry of Foreign Affairs and official Chinese publications refer to this region as *Xiya beifei* (West Asia and North Africa).[2] This study uses the phrase 'Middle East' or simply 'the region'. The Middle East includes the following sixteen countries: Bahrain, Egypt, Iran, Iraq, Israel, Palestine, Jordan, Kuwait, Lebanon, Oman, Qatar, Saudi Arabia, Syria, Turkey, United Arab Emirates, and Yemen.

China's economic relationship with the Middle East region gained a higher profile with the official launch of its One Belt, One Road Initiative (OBOR) in 2013 – a name changed in 2016 to the Belt and Road Initiative (BRI). At the Third Plenary Session of the 18th Central Committee of Communist Party in China, Beijing designated the Middle East as a 'neighbor' region, which indicates that the Middle East now falls into China's top priority geostrategic zone.[3] China has officially made clear that it sees the Middle East as an intrinsic part of the BRI and has ramped up its investments in the region accordingly. Most of China's trade and investment in the region involves the Middle East countries, focusing on energy, infrastructure construction, and investment in nuclear power, new energy sources, agriculture, and finance.

In the past two decades, substantial changes have been seen in the global economy and geopolitical trends, with the rise of the PRC on the global and regional stage. These developments are creating new opportunities for the Middle East countries, as they look to diversify or rebuild their economy, increase trade, and seek investment opportunities in emerging markets. They also want to promote the BRI and incorporate it into their national development plan. This is a growing tendency among the regional countries that want to benefit from China's favorable business conditions, expertise, and experience, in its rapid path to economic development.

The relative decline of US hegemony and power in the Middle East and the emergence of a risen China that seeks significant roles in the region might affect the stability of power balance.[4] Within this context, Middle East countries have started seeking ways to invest in stronger ties with the PRC, as well as with other powers, to strengthen their position in an increasingly vulnerable geopolitical balance of power. Some of the countries are determined to preserve their strategic alliance with the United States but are also seeking to hedge themselves against the threats that are emanating from regional crises or power competition to guarantee their security in the future.[5]

Since the announcement of China's Silk Road Economic Belt and 21st Century Maritime Silk Road, the Middle East states have become a crucial hub in the successful implementation of the BRI due to their geostrategic location that links China to Middle Eastern, African, and European markets. At the same time, their vast hydrocarbon reserves are an essential factor in driving the development projects that comprise the Silk Road. Sino–Middle East cooperation can, therefore, be expected to expand as China's footprint expands across the Indian Ocean. At the same time, BRI cooperation builds upon bilateral relationships that China and the Middle East countries have been developing over the past decades.

This book adopts the BRI as a framework for analyzing China–Middle East relations. It examines China's growing presence in 15 countries in the Middle East and explores the significance of the PRC's strategic partnerships with the regional countries in the context of the BRI framework, as well as the increasing mutual interdependency between both sides in various sectors, such as energy, construction, and infrastructure building, political ties, trade and investments, financial integration, people-to-people bonds, and defense ties. A stable Middle East region is vital for China's sustainable growth and continued prosperity. As the world's largest oil consumer with an ambition to expand its economic and arguably political influences, it is predictable that the Middle East's geostrategic location and holdings of most of the world's known energy resources make it indispensable to the BRI.[6]

One Belt, One Road Initiative (BRI)

China's most significant twenty-first-century diplomatic and economic activity is the launching of the Silk Road initiative. The BRI is the sprawling framework of trade and commercial ties between China and various world regions that have become the flagship foreign policy of the Xi administration. The BRI primarily seeks to open up new markets and secure global supply chains to help generate sustained Chinese economic growth and, thereby, contribute to social stability at home.[7]

The BRI (一带一路), the most ambitious geo-economic vision in recent history, has both a land-based and a maritime component: the maritime element is the 21st century Maritime Silk Road Initiative (21世纪海上丝绸之路), and the land-based equivalent is the Silk Road Economic Belt (丝绸之路经济带). The different sub-branches of the Silk Road Economic Belt (a series of land-based infrastructure projects including roads, railways, and pipelines) and the 21st Century Maritime Silk Road (made up of ports and coastal development) would create a multi-national network connecting China to Europe and Africa via the Middle East. This will facilitate trade, improve access to foreign energy resources, and give China access to new markets. The two schemes are inseparable, and the PRC has set as its goal their parallel implementation.[8]

The Belt and Road Initiative is a developing economic trade network planned to stretch from China to Europe. The BRI provides two pathways for connecting China with Eurasia. The Silk Road Economic Belt (SREB), the one garnering the most attention, is an overland route that begins in Central China, moves through Xinjiang and China's western region into Central Asia, across the Middle East, and terminates in Europe. The SREB will have two main corridors, with several offshoots and hub cities. It would begin in Xi'an, capital of Shaanxi province in western China, and continue west, crossing Central Asia, the Middle East, possibly Russia, and finally end in Europe. The 21st Century Maritime Silk Road (MSRI) has one primary sea corridor, also with many hubs and offshoots. The MSRI would start in China's southeastern ports, travel along the coast of Southeast Asia, around India, connect with the Persian Gulf, and end in the Mediterranean Sea.[9]

The BRI will require cooperation and agreements with over a dozen states along the route, greatly expanding not only China's economic connections to these regions but also its political relationships. This, in turn, will expand China's sphere of influence into areas traditionally under the purview of other great powers. The plan progresses through a multitude of projects in stages, including roadways, bridges, telecommunication networking structures, pipelines, etc. The BRI emphasizes certain countries, namely Pakistan, Myanmar, Iran, and Kazakhstan, but includes virtually all of the countries that are considered part of China's Eurasian west.[10]

China's BRI – previously called 'One Belt, One Road' – has been designed by PRC as its new guiding economic and foreign policy framework with a focus on its direct neighborhood at its southern and western borders, but also reaching out to the Persian Gulf, Africa, and Europe. However, the BRI is not just a strategy to enhance PRC's commercial, trade, and other economic interests. The BRI was designed as a multi-purpose umbrella for the PRC's comprehensive economic, domestic and foreign policy development to increase its geo-economic and geopolitical influence and is a vehicle to open markets, expand export overcapacities, generate employment, reduce regional inequalities, promote political stability and security through development as well as prosperity, and to restore Chinese spheres of influence in the Eurasian land-mass and beyond.[11]

The scope of the BRI is broad, covering more than 72 countries along six economic corridors. The BRI's six main economic corridors include the New Eurasian Land Bridge, the China-Central Asia-West Asia Economic Corridor; the China–Pakistan Economic Corridor; the Bangladesh–China–Myanmar Economic Corridor; the China–Mongolia–Russia Economic Corridor, and the China–Indochina Peninsula Economic Corridor. The BRI covers two-thirds of the world's population, 40 percent of the global gross national product, and an estimated 75 percent of known energy reserves.[12] Thus, this great ambition will require significant resources – technological, human, financial and political – that must be garnered globally to realize the vision, as the BRI will run through Asia, Africa, and Europe and will directly link the East Asian economies to the West Asian and further to the European economies.[13]

The total cost of this initiative has always been in debate. According to some estimates, $8 trillion will be invested in the initiative.[14] Nevertheless, the global infrastructure investment needed to support the currently expected rates of economic growth is between $3.3 trillion and $6.3 trillion annually.[15] According to the chief economist of the Bank of China, Beijing's outbound direct investment in the BRI will reach $300 billion by 2030.[16] Furthermore, BRI has the potential to establish a new order not only in Eurasia but in the entire international system as well.[17]

The BRI fits China's economic, security, military, and diplomatic strategy as well as its long-term strategic requirements. In the 21st century, the PRC has emerged as the world's top trading nation; hence it needs to ensure that it has timely, efficient, and secure access to markets and resources, and therefore facilitation of trade and investment is one key focus. Also, it should not be surprising that securing conventional and renewable energy and resources is another focus for China. Once completed, the BRI will provide land-based and sea-based alternatives, not just for PRC accessing the continents but also access for other countries to China. Transport link is a critical consideration for China, as it is vulnerable to choke points along its sea route. Such threats would be mitigated once land-based alternatives, including railroads, highways, and communication links are in place.[18]

PRC's involvement in infrastructure developments globally already goes beyond officially designated BRI and China-funded projects. Chinese contractors are involved in projects outside China at various stages of development, with a total value of $1.1 trillion. In the Middle East and North Africa (MENA), the value of projects in which Chinese contractors are involved totals $227 billion.[19] Chinese firms have also established more than 50 economic and trade zones in more than 30 countries.[20] In the past five years, nearly one hundred Chinese state-owned enterprises carried out a total of 3,116 investment projects in BRI countries.[21]

According to data provided by China's Ministry of Commerce (MoC), the trade volume between the PRC and countries along the BRI totaled $1.3 trillion in 2018. This marked a year-on-year growth of 16.3 percent, 3.7 percentage points higher than PRC's trade growth in 2018. That is, China exported goods worth $704.73 billion to BRI countries last year, up 10.9 percent year on year, while importing goods from them worth $563.07 billion, increasing 23.9 percent year on year. Chinese firms invested $15.64 billion in non-financial sectors in BRI countries last year, up 8.9 percent year on year, while receiving investments from them totaling $6.08 billion, up 11.9 percent.[22]

By the end of March 2019, the Chinese government had signed 173 cooperation agreements with 125 countries and 29 international organizations on Belt and Road cooperation, a large number of cooperation projects have been launched, and a general connectivity framework has been put in place.[23] The total trade between PRC and other BRI countries has exceeded $6 trillion, and Beijing's investment in these countries has surpassed $80 billion. The 82 cooperation parks jointly built by China and other participating countries have created more than $2 billion in tax revenue and about 300,000 jobs for host countries. According to the latest studies by the World Bank and other international institutions, BRI cooperation will cut the costs of global trade by 1.1 percent to 2.2 percent, and those of trade along with the China-Central Asia-West Asia Economic Corridor by 10.2 percent, and will contribute at least 0.1 percent of global growth in 2019.[24]

The Belt and Road Initiative and the Middle East

In the last decade, and especially in the aftermath of the so-called Arab Spring in 2011, coupled with China's more active and assertive foreign policy after Xi Jinping became president in 2013, China has increasingly become involved in the Middle East region, especially in the Persian Gulf. Almost all states in the region are looking to China as a promising market and a provider of investment and finance without the political conditionalities about democracy and human rights that Western countries and institutions try to insist on. Of course, PRC has been economically active in the Middle East, especially in the Persian Gulf, for more than three decades, but its engagement has increased substantially along with its economic growth and its more assertive position in the global economy.

The economic relationships between China and the Middle Eastern nations have thickened, including finance and investment, to complement the increasingly robust trade component, and not surprisingly, interests have consequently become more complex. Chinese leaders increasingly see the Middle East as a strategically important region, and Middle Eastern politicians increasingly look east when contemplating their long-term interests. The BRI is creating more opportunities for cooperation, and China–Middle East nexus is becoming an essential geopolitical axis in understanding Eurasian international affairs.

PRC's policy toward the Middle East has to be defined in a complex regional context, a context involving plenty of local rivalries and serious major power competition.[25] The Chinese policy intends to maintain a balance among several priorities that may sometimes be in conflict or tension. First, maintain mutual respect between China and each of the regional states, its territorial integrity and sovereignty, and mutual non-interference in each other's internal affairs. Second, maintain a peaceful and stable international environment for advancing China's modernization drive, promoting development, and improving its people's livelihood.[26]

Third, maintain a peaceful environment in the Middle East, in line with the above, to protect PRC's regional interests. Fourth, preserve good relations with all countries in the region, and finally, avoid a major confrontation with the U.S. while limiting its regional hegemony and promoting regional as well as global multi-polarity.[27] Based on this policy, China seeks to strengthen the mutual interdependency with the countries in the region in various sectors such as energy, and investments in construction and infrastructure projects and to leverage its economic capabilities to realize the successful implementation of the BRI.

The Middle East is the region bringing together the land and maritime Silk Road, coupled with its unique geographical location and diverse and complex humanitarian, religious, and ethnic factors, notably with an increasingly significant role played by the energy sector. As an energy-rich zone, it plays a decisive role in the process of building the BRI. This region also plays a prominent role in security coordination, economic cooperation, and cultural exchanges under the BRI framework. Thus, the Chinese government should pay close attention to the role of the Middle East region in the construction of its Belt and Road vision.[28]

In the second decade of the 21st century, the Middle East represents four major priorities for China's foreign policy. Foremost among these priorities is the criticality of the region as a source of imported energy and an essential region for Chinese trade and investment. As the world's largest consumer of energy overall and the second-largest importer of crude oil, safeguarding a stable flow of crude oil from the region is a paramount concern.[29] In 2019, roughly half (44.8 percent) of Chinese imported crude oil originates from nine Middle Eastern countries.[30]

Second, the region is also a crucial part of China's BRI, especially for its 21st Century Maritime Silk Road component. In the past, the Middle East was considered by Beijing a peripheral and relatively insignificant region of the world. In contrast, now the Middle East is considered a vital geostrategic global crossroads, and the PRC's most famous region beyond its own Asia Pacific neighborhoods for the realization of the BRI. Third, Beijing views the Middle East as an arena of great power competition in which a rising power such as China must be seen as a player.[31]

Finally, the PRC has vital security interests in the Middle East: concerns regarding the spread of terrorism and extremist ideology from the Middle East and its impact on Uighur separatism.[32] China fears that Chinese Uighurs fighting alongside al-Qaeda and ISIS in Syria may leave the fighting and attempt to return to China. As they return, they may bring a newly Islamized narrative and motivation, which will pose a challenge to Xinjiang's social stability and economic development.[33]

The Middle East is also situated at the heart of China's BRI where not only do the three continents of Asia, Africa, and Europe meet, but the five seas of the Mediterranean, Red Sea, Arabian Sea, Caspian Sea, and the Black Sea also converge there; and it is adjacent to the four maritime strategic channels of Bosporus, Dardanelles, Bab el-Mandeb, and Hormuz. The Gulf countries can be referred to as the core of the region since they are the most influential countries in the Middle East. The advantageous location, the unique endowment of natural resources, and the vast industrialization potential make the Gulf regions of supreme strategic importance to the implementation of the BRI.[34]

The Levant region also is of vital importance to China for several reasons: first, it supplies over 18 percent of the PRC's total import of crude petroleum. Second, it is the top destination for Chinese investment in the Middle East, with investment concentrated particularly in high-tech and the oil and gas sectors. Third, it is an essential destination for Chinese exports. Finally, it is geographically situated at the heart of the proposed BRI, with routes connecting Asia to Africa, Europe, and the Mediterranean. The Levant offers an alternative route through the Suez Canal to the Mediterranean Sea through the China–Central Asia–West Asia economic corridor. Beijing has been able to successfully develop friendly relations with countries of this region, while avoiding complex political or geopolitical disputes, e.g., the Palestine–Israel conflict, the war in Syria, and the conflict in Lebanon.[35]

The BRI called for "policy coordination, facilities connectivity, unimpeded trade, financial integration, and people-to-people bonds to make complementary use of participating countries' unique resource advantages through multilateral mechanisms and multilevel platforms".[36] It lies at the core of the PRC's diplomatic encounter with Middle East countries. Chinese officials have repeatedly emphasized that through the BRI, China and countries of the region will be able to develop mutually beneficial relations. As a result, the Beijing new Silk Road strategy will provide new momentum for the Middle East region's economic transformation. Despite challenges, risks can be turned into opportunities, as long as China faces up to them squarely and responds positively.

The Belt and Road Initiative and the Persian Gulf region

Economic and energy interests have brought China to the Persian Gulf, but the BRI and emerging expertise in constructing new cities and infrastructure have made the PRC a likely long-term partner in regional development. In March 2015, the Chinese government published a report: "Vision and Actions on Jointly Building the SREB and the MSRI". This report describes plans for how the SREB will link the PRC with the Persian Gulf and the Mediterranean Sea through Central Asia and West Asia, and how the MSRI will connect China with Europe through the South China Sea and the Indian Ocean. This means the Persian Gulf region will serve as a hub of the two routes, entailing many added economic benefits. Furthermore, Gulf countries could benefit not only from the BRI's focus on improved transportation across Eurasia, providing an alternative route for exports to Asia that avoids the bottlenecks of the Strait of Hormuz, but from greater affluence and stability in Central Asia.[37]

The BRI has become the main focus of strategic and economic engagement between the PRC and countries in the Gulf region. The Gulf Cooperation Council (GCC) countries (Saudi Arabia, United Arab Emirates, Qatar, Kuwait, Bahrain, and Oman), plus Iran and Iraq, are 'natural cooperative partners' in the Belt and Road construction in an essential geographical area which is difficult to bypass.[38] Thus, the Gulf countries are important key partners and will play significant roles in the successful implementation of the BRI due to their geostrategic location, a vast reserve of oil and gas, the fast and steady growth of the economy of the region with the rapid expansion of the market for consumer and merchandise goods, of which China has plenty.

The PRC increasingly attempts to engage with the Persian Gulf through two multilateral mechanisms. First, China–Arab States Cooperation Forum (CASCF), which was launched in 2004 in Cairo. In June 2014, at the sixth Ministerial Conference of the CASCF, President Xi Jinping proposed the establishment of a '1+2+3' pattern of cooperation: energy cooperation as the core; then infrastructure construction plus trade and investment facilitation as two wings; and three new areas of high-tech cooperation (nuclear energy, space satellites, and other new energy initiatives). According to the Chinese President, in the next ten years, these efforts will increase the bilateral trade volume from $240 billion of 2013 to $600 billion. The second mechanism is China-GCC Strategic Dialogue, initiated in 2010 and targeted at building a strategic partnership. While both sides agreed to accelerate the pace of establishing a free trade area, China asserted its desire to play a more active role in regional affairs.[39]

Energy is at the heart of the growing links between the PRC and the Persian Gulf, which centers on the crude oil and petrochemical industries. The significance of a strong relationship between China and the region is founded on energy (although it extends to other commodities). China is highly dependent upon oil and gas imports, principally from the Persian Gulf and Africa, which are carried mainly by tankers over sea lines of communication (SLOCs) and run through maritime chokepoints. Beijing's dependence on crude oil imports from the Persian Gulf, a leading oil-producing region, has been increasing gradually since 1993 when it became a net importer of oil.[40]

According to data from the General Administration of Customs, the PRC's crude oil imports in 2019 surged 9.5 percent from a year earlier, setting a record for a 17th straight year. The annual increase equates to 882,000 bpd in incremental purchases, largely because of demand from new plants that added 900,000 bpd to China's oil-processing capacity. Last year, China imported a record 506 million tonnes of crude oil. That is equivalent to 10.12 million barrels per day (bpd). Meanwhile, natural gas imports, including fuel supplied as liquefied natural gas (LNG) and via pipeline, were 9.45 million tonnes. Imports 2019 expanded 6.9 percent to 96.56 million tonnes, with the annual growth slowing from 31.9 percent recorded for 2018.[41]

Currently, almost half of the PRC's oil imports are sourced from the Middle East, principally from the Persian Gulf. An energy imports cut-off enforced during hostile conditions could trigger a rapid collapse of China's economy and paralyze its military forces. Hence the BRI and especially the Gulf Pearl Chain would be a breakthrough to reduce its dependence on SLOCs on one side and increase economic and regional integration as it would connect West Asia with Southeast and East Asia, which would be a win-win situation for all the partners.[42]

Connectivity, as the basis of the BRI, aims at linking land, sea, air, and cyberspace environments of countries along the routes. Through six major economic corridors,

China will be closely connected with Europe, Africa, and the rest of Asia. While the Gulf states are well funded and in urgent need of infrastructure construction, China's experience and technology accumulated in its development process could offer vital assistance. At present, Chinese enterprises have actively participated in the above projects and other infrastructures such as ports, docks, industrial parks, and oil pipelines.[43]

However, the aims to increase the PRC's access to the Persian Gulf's energy resources and connect Beijing's economy with those of the Middle East, Central Asia, and eventually Europe through massive infrastructure building could be severely affected by the instability generated in the region's hotspots (e.g., Yemen, Iraq, Syria, and Qatar) or geopolitical rivalry (e.g., Iran and Saudi Arabia). Such regional instability presents a formidable obstacle to the BRI's strategic design, as it undermines connectivity, threatens infrastructure projects, and makes an economic corridor through the volatile Middle East to the markets of developed Europe less viable.[44]

The GCC, accordingly, has mixed feelings about China's Belt and Road ambitious project. Though the Persian Gulf is not directly along BRI's trade routes, the GCC states have high economic and geopolitical stakes in the PRC's planned economic corridor. They have much to gain from BRI as the initiative aims to enhance Beijing's diplomatic and economic relations with these countries. However, there are concerns about the initiative's geopolitical implications because Iran will likely achieve significant gains from it since it plays a vital role in the BRI. The implementation of the BRI will undoubtedly enhance Iran's position in the tumultuous Middle East's unstable geopolitical order. Ultimately, however, despite the challenges and risks that the new Silk Road has to offer to the region, the Gulf States are focused on ways to maximize the benefits they reap from this ambitious initiative. These countries have to balance their increasingly important relationship with China against the ways the BRI concomitantly threatens their relations with major external powers or empowers their rivals.[45]

In the end, the PRC and the Gulf States are at Asia's eastern and western ends, respectively, linked by the ancient Silk Road across the Gobi desert. The BRI has become the main focus of strategic cooperation between the two sides. The Gulf States are natural cooperative partners in the BRI,[46] in an essential geographical area challenging to bypass. Although the political and security situation in the Gulf region is complicated and unpredictable, presenting challenges to the implementation of the BRI, there remains room for the PRC to turn around the situation of West Asia and to seize this opportunity, circumventing possible risks and enhancing pragmatic cooperation under the BRI.

China's Partnership Diplomacy

In recent years, partnership diplomacy has become a primary foreign policy tool for the Chinese government. The concept of 'partnership' emerged within Chinese diplomacy after the end of the Cold War and continues to flourish. Beijing established its first strategic partnership with Brazil in 1993. Since then, building strategic partnerships has become one of the most important dimensions of Chinese diplomacy.[47] Since then, the number of partnerships has steadily increased, reaching 81 in 2016,[48] Moreover, as of today, ten of the fifteen states in the Middle East have established a comprehensive strategic partnership or strategic partnership with China.

China partnership diplomacy includes a scale of relations, ranging from a friendly cooperative partnership at the bottom to a comprehensive strategic partnership at the high end.[49] Each of the five categories of relations features specific priorities, signaling the level of importance Beijing attaches to that particular state. According to Chinese levels of Strategic Partnerships diplomacy (from highest to lowest): *Comprehensive Strategic Partnership* (全面战略伙伴关系) is the full pursuit of cooperation and development on regional and international affairs. *Strategic Partnership* (战略伙伴关系) coordinates more closely on regional and international affairs, including military. *Comprehensive Cooperative Partnership* (全面合作伙伴关系) maintains the sound momentum of high-level exchanges, enhanced contacts at various levels, and increased mutual understanding on issues of common interest. *Cooperative Partnership* (合作夥伴關係) develops cooperation on bilateral issues, based on mutual respect and benefit. *Friendly Cooperative Partnership* (友好合作关) strengthens cooperation on bilateral issues such as trade.[50]

An analysis of the PRC's practice of strategic partnership diplomacy yields a four-point description, calling them a commitment to: build stable bilateral relationships without targeting a third state; promote deep economic engagement; focus on cooperation in areas of mutual interests while not focusing on domestic affairs of potential disagreement; routinize official visits and military exchanges.[51] Taken together, these provide a useful framework for understanding China's choice to use strategic partnership diplomacy.

The post-Cold War unipolarity has provided the PRC (a rising power) with a unique strategic opportunity to develop power and influence in the Middle East without facing overt challenges from the United States. Balancing against Washington during the unipolar era would not advance Beijing's interests, but at the same time, neither would "bandwagoning" nor neutrality. Dynamic balancing is too risky, and bandwagoning or neutrality is not consistent with Chinese ambitions.[52] Instead, the PRC has taken advantage of the relative stability provided by U.S. dominance to develop strong ties with strategically important states in the Middle East (e.g., Iran, Egypt, Turkey, United Arab Emirates, and Saudi Arabia). These relations have been built mostly on economic foundations, but as they become increasingly multifaceted, there is a corresponding growth of strategic considerations.

In the competitive Middle East dominated by Washington, Beijing has had to build a regional presence that does not alienate the U.S. or any Middle East states while pursuing its interests. Strategic partnership diplomacy has provided the space to methodically build up its economic relations while the U.S. security umbrella provides a low-cost entry into the region. Beginning with trade, economic ties became increasingly multifaceted and sophisticated, incorporating finance and investment. The relationships with the Middle East states have progressed beyond the economic to include political and security objectives, but in a way that has consistently allowed the PRC the flexibility of being everyone's friend in the competitive regional environment.[53]

During his first European trip as Chinese premier, Wen Jiabao defined the key features of a comprehensive strategic partnership as follows: "By 'comprehensive', it means that the cooperation should be all-dimensional, wide-ranging and multi-layered. It covers economic, scientific, technological, political and cultural fields, contains both bilateral and multilateral levels, and is conducted by both governments and non-governmental groups. By 'strategic', it means that the cooperation should be long-term and stable, bearing on the larger picture of China–EU relations. It transcends the differences in ideology and social system and is not subjected to the impacts of individual events that occur from time to time. By 'partnership', it means that the cooperation should be equal-footed, mutually beneficial, and win-win. The two sides should base themselves on mutual respect and mutual trust, endeavor to expand converging interests and seek common ground on the major issues while shelving differences on the minor ones."[54]

China's Middle East partnership diplomacy

In the Middle East, the PRC's regional partnerships differ from those of the U.S. or Western alliances. Beijing seeks flexible political cooperation based on free political bonds, while the US or Western alliances often target external enemies based on defense treaties. China believes that whereas alliances can potentially expose states to a high degree of risk, partnerships are perceived as more interest-driven and flexible relations; the partnership denotes a shared commitment to managing unavoidable conflicts so that they can continue to work together on vital areas of common interest.[55]

Since 2013, the PRC has gradually constructed a multidimensional global partnership network that involves great powers, neighboring countries, developing countries, and regional organizations. These layered partnerships are interlinked and mutually reinforcing. China's involvement in the Middle East is a crucial component of its global partnership network. These fifteen relationships, spread across the eastern Mediterranean, the Gulf, and the Red Sea, fall into four broad categories in line with their importance. The first category comprises comprehensive strategic partnerships with Egypt, Iran, Saudi Arabia, and the United Arab Emirates (UAE). The second includes an innovative, comprehensive partnership with Israel and a strategic cooperative relationship with Turkey (the latter being inferior to a strategic partnership). The third covers strategic partnerships with several midsized countries: Iraq, Jordan, Kuwait, Oman, and Qatar. The fourth comprises a relationship with the smaller states: Bahrain, Lebanon, Syria, and Yemen.

Governments in the Middle East generally welcome partnerships with China because they claim, it treats them as equals rather than junior partners or colonial proxies. Combined with its policy of non-interference in other states' internal affairs, nonalignment, and refusal to engage in proxy wars, Beijing has stayed on good terms with all conflicting parties (including Iran–Saudi Arabia, Arab countries/ Palestine-Israel, and the crisis in Lebanon, Syria, and Yemen) because its partnerships do not harm or provoke third parties.[56]

Almost all of the strategic partnership agreements that the PRC has signed with countries in the Middle East came about in the past decade (the one with Egypt, signed in 1999, is the sole exception). Relationships can be upgraded depending upon the progress made, as in the case of the UAE, with which China established a strategic partnership in January 2012.[57] During President Xi's state visit in July 2018, the relationship was elevated to a comprehensive strategic partnership, demonstrating that it was a central pillar of China's Middle East policy.[58] In contrast, when Qatari Emir Hamdan Al Thani visited Beijing in January 2019, the PRC did not upgrade the relationship but rather stated that it wanted to continue working with the framework established in the strategic partnership of 2014. This signaled China's perception of Qatar as being less crucial to its interests than the UAE. Coinciding with the expansion of the BRI, this flurry of diplomatic activity indicates that Chinese leaders increasingly perceive the Middle East as relevant to their political and strategic goals.[59]

The PRC's partnership diplomacy in the Middle East began when China and Egypt established a strategic partnership in 1999, the first strategic cooperative with an Arab and Middle East country.[60] In the Persian Gulf, the UAE was the first state that established a strategic partnership in January 2012. Since then, every state in the Gulf except Bahrain (which has a friendly cooperative partnership status) has signed either a strategic or comprehensive strategic partnership with China (see Table 1). A key integral feature of the BRI is the designation of specific countries along the Silk Road routes as strategic partners. Unlike the U.S., China does not have security alliances, but in lieu thereof does have intimate diplomatic relations with all the Middle Eastern countries, which are labeled strategic partnerships. Such partnerships are predicated more on trade and economic relations, rather than on security cooperation.

Table 1 China's Partnerships with the Middle Eastern Countries

State	AIIB	MoU on BRI	Level of Partnership	Total Trade with China ($B)
Egypt	+	+	CSP (2014)	13.2
Saudi Arabia	+	+	CSP (2016)	77.9
Iran	+	+	CSP (2016)	22.9
UAE	+	+	CSP (2018)	48.6
Israel	+	+	ICP (2017)	14.7
Turkey	+	+	SCR (2010)	20.7
Jordan	+	+	SP (2015)	4
Qatar	+	-	SP (2014)	11.1
Iraq	+	+	SP (2015)	33.2
Oman	+	+	SP (2018)	22.5
Kuwait	+	+	SP (2018)	17.2
Bahrain	+	+	FCR (2013)	1.6
Lebanon	+	+	DR (1971)	1.7
Syria	–	–	DR (1956)	1.3
Yemen	–	–	DR (1958)	3.8

CSP Comprehensive Strategic Partnership.
ICP Innovative Comprehensive Partnership.
SCR Strategic Cooperative Relationship.
SP Strategic Partnership.
FCR Friendly Cooperative Relations.
DR Diplomatic Relations.

This growing diplomatic attention to the region can be attributed to several factors. First, Chinese trade with the Middle East has sharply increased in recent years, making the country the region's largest trade partner. The two sides have deepened cooperation in the fields of energy, trade, project contracting, and investment. According to China Customs Statistics (export-import), China-Middle Eastern countries' trade volume increased to $294.4 billion by 2019 up from $227 billion in 2018.[61]

In 2016, China became the largest extra-regional source of Foreign Direct Investment (FDI) in the Middle East and since then has steadily grown.[62] According to the *China Global Investment Tracker*, PRC investments, and construction in the Middle Eastern states from 2013 to 2019 reached $93.3 billion. Most of the Chinese investments are in the energy sector ($52.8 billion) real estate ($18.4 billion), the transport sector ($18.6 billion), and utilities ($5.9 billion).[63] This is important for the Middle Eastern countries as they are all under pressure to create more diverse economies, and so are embarking upon massive infrastructure and construction projects. Chinese firms are uniquely well-positioned to take advantage of this, with a competitive approach to infrastructure development driving much of its BRI.[64]

Second, the PRC remains a major buyer of oil and natural gas from the Middle Eastern exporters. The Middle East accounts for more than 40 percent of China's oil imports and is also a key supplier of the country's liquefied natural gas. In 2019, the value of crude oil imported into China totaled $238.7 billion (20.2 percent of total crude oil imports). Forty-three countries supplied crude petroleum oil to China, but close to half (44.8 percent) of Chinese imported crude oil originates from just nine Middle Eastern nations, and six Persian Gulf states are among the top 15 crude oil suppliers to Beijing. This energy relationship is set to continue since the Middle Eastern exporters look to East Asia in general and China in particular as a reliable long-term energy export market, with the International Energy Agency (IEA) expecting Beijing to double its oil imports from the region by 2035.[65]

Third, the implementation of the BRI is the critical factor that underscores the increasingly strategic component of Beijing partnership diplomacy with the Middle Eastern countries. The $1 trillion BRI, put forward in October 2013 by Chinese President Xi Jinping, seeks to connect Beijing to the global market by linking Asia and Europe via a set of land and maritime trade routes. The concept had been taking shape for several years and has now become a cornerstone of President Xi's foreign policy. This is extending Chinese influence and interests far beyond its traditional East Asia sphere. With the Middle East's unique geostrategic location connecting several important states and regions in the BRI, the PRC places a premium on region stability, evident in the fact that ten of fifteen regional states have the two highest levels of partnership diplomacy with China (e.g., six states with strategic partnership and four states with comprehensive strategic partnership) and one state at the level of an innovative comprehensive partnership.[66]

Moreover, Chinese companies are operating in the Middle East, often focusing on projects that lend themselves to the BRI goal of connectivity. Ports and industrial parks have been central to such cooperation, as they create an economic chain that links China to the Gulf, the Arabian Sea, the Red Sea, and the Mediterranean. These connectivity projects include United Arab Emirates' Khalifa Port, Oman's Duqm Port, Saudi Arabia's Jizan Port, Egypt's Port Said, and Israel's Ashdod and Haifa ports. Chinese companies are also likely to play a significant role in reconstruction projects in Iraq, Syria, Lebanon, and Yemen. The Gulf monarchies have been significant sources of infrastructure construction contracts for Chinese companies, such as those for Qatar's Lusail Stadium, Saudi Arabia's Yanbu Refinery, and the highspeed rail line that connects Jeddah with Mecca and Medina.[67]

Finally, in the wake of Arab uprisings and the civil wars, the Middle Eastern countries were pressured into rebuilding their economy or boosting economic growth to maintain social stability. To this end, they have been actively rolling out plans for long-term development for rehabilitation and encouraging economic growth, and comprehensive and upgraded Chinese engagement will provide the impetus for it. In this way, there is a common interest for the PRC and Middle Eastern countries to integrate and synergize the BRI with major initiatives of future-oriented reforms for national rejuvenation (e.g., Saudi Arabia's Vision 2030, UAE's Vision 2021, Jordan Vision 2025, Turkey Middle Corridor, Egypt's Vision 2030 and Suez Canal Corridor Development Project, Oman's Vision 2020, Kuwait's Vision 2035, and Qatar's and Bahrain's respective Vision 2030s).[68]

China's comprehensive strategic partnerships, the highest level in its hierarchy of diplomatic relations, with the Middle Eastern countries (e.g., Egypt, Iran, UAE or Saudi Arabia) includes three essential components: high levels of political trust, dense economic ties, and good relations in other sectors, such as cultural exchanges. Beyond the structure of the bilateral relationship, the state's stature in global affairs is an important consideration; Beijing only considers this level of partnership with states that play an essential role in international economics and politics, as well as being an indispensable partner in the Middle East for the realization of the BRI.[69] It is also commonplace to upgrade the strategic partnership to a comprehensive one a few years after its launch. Usually, a solid record of cooperation can be widely seen as a blessing for further upgrading the partnership or a good omen for initiating similar partnerships.[70]

Given these requirements, it is unlikely that other relationships with Middle Eastern countries would be elevated to a comprehensive strategic partnership. For example, PRC–Qatar relations are quite dense but not at the same level as the UAE or Saudi Arabia, and given Qatar's ongoing dispute with the fellow members of the GCC, it is more likely that Beijing will not allow the relationship to elevate to a comprehensive strategic partnership.[71] Oman's relations with the PRC are also deep, and the Duqm port project indicates a more strategic direction. Economically, however, Oman is less important to China, making it an unlikely candidate. Iraq also does not meet any of the three conditions, and because Bahrain has no existing formal partnership with the PRC and bilateral trade is negligible, there is no chance that it will be considered.[72] Moreover, while there are some positive developments in the Ankara-Beijing strategic partnership framework, there are also some problematic issues (e.g., the Uyghur problem) that hinder improving and upgrading the relationship.

The PRC has four principal comprehensive strategic partnerships in the Middle East: Egypt, Saudi Arabia, the UAE, and Iran. Saudi Arabia is China's largest trading partner in West Asia, and Beijing is the Kingdom's largest trading partner worldwide. Chinese construction companies have been playing a growing role in developing Saudi infrastructure; meanwhile, the Kingdom has been especially eager to build refineries and petrochemical production facilities in China that are specially tailored to use Saudi grades of crude oil. The Kingdom seems to be developing China as a hedge against a decline in Western oil consumption, and also a hedge against Western discomfort with authoritarianism within Saudi Arabia.[73] The PRC is also the UAE's largest trading partner, and Dubai Port is a vital global shipping and logistics hub for Chinese goods. More than 200,000 Chinese nationals live in the UAE, which is emerging as an ideal regional hub for Chinese traders seeking proximity to overseas markets. The UAE sees a leading role for itself in the PRC's BRI, building on what is already a robust trading relationship.[74]

The Chinese–Egyptian relations are one of the most important bilateral relations axes in the MENA. Egypt has emerged as a crucial component of the MSRI due to its unique geographical strategic position as the main transit point between the Indian Ocean and the Mediterranean Sea.[75] Egypt also has many valuable features: a unique geographic location which makes it the meeting point of the Arab World, Africa, Asia, and Europe through the Mediterranean Sea and the Red Sea and a unique civilization and culture, with a longstanding history and interactions throughout millennia with the ancient empires. All these features help Egypt to have a global outreach, which contributes excellent value to China's BRI and enable Egypt to play a vital role in the world with China as a strategic partner.[76]

However, and perhaps most importantly, Iran (along with Turkey) has a unique geographical and communication status in West Asia, in that it is connected to South and Central Asia, the Middle East, and Europe through both land and sea routes. Access points at the Persian Gulf, the Gulf of Oman, and the Caspian Sea combine to make Iran one of the critical centerpieces of the BRI. China is Iran's biggest trading partner and leading buyer of Iranian oil; Iran is a promising market for Chinese investment projects, as well as an important provider of energy. Iran is critical to China's ability to realize the BRI network to connect Asia, Europe, and Africa.[77]

The PRC's partnership diplomacy will continue to be an important instrument in China's Middle East foreign policy in the years ahead. At the same time, China's presence in the region will require a more overarching strategic design and more sophisticated diplomatic tactics. China will need to be more proactive and creative in mobilizing strategic partnerships as a policy instrument, together with other diplomatic tools, for the successful implementation of its BRI.

Summary

This book examines the PRC's relationship with the Middle Eastern nations based on a two-dimensional approach: the new Silk Road strategy and the strategic partnership diplomacy between them. China's levels of interdependence with these states under consideration have increased dramatically in recent years, spanning a wide range of interests (e.g., energy security, trade cooperation, and infrastructure construction). Light will be shed on the complexities and challenges of the PRC's BRI to reveal how the synergy between the new Silk Road strategy and the local, national development plan, or post-conflict reconstruction process will shape the Middle East in the future. The balance of global politics will be critically affected by these powerful emerging partnerships and the convergence of interests.

The PRC's Middle East partnership diplomacy has provided a platform for deepening and expanding the cooperation between China and the countries of the region under the framework of the BRI. Since 1999, China has forged special political relations with every state in the Middle East, except countries engaged in civil war (e.g., Lebanon, Syria, and Yemen), which has signed either a strategic or comprehensive strategic partnership. There is a clear and direct connection between the PRC's emerging partnerships with the Middle Eastern countries and the implementation of the new Silk Road strategy. Therefore, the key to understanding China's upgraded involvement in the Middle East must be in the context of the successful implementation of the BRI. The new Silk Road strategy is an essential guide for China–Middle Eastern countries' partnership diplomacy since the region holds a unique position in the PRC's new policy framework.

The central thesis to be presented in the chapters that follow is that the Middle East region has a significant and unique role in the successful implementation of China's new Silk Road strategy, as well as the emerging partnerships between them. These partnerships help the PRC to achieve effective management and control the flow of its energy, goods, or product needs, and to open new markets and trade routes. Beijing has been mostly successful in employing strategic partnerships, a prominent instrument in its limited diplomatic toolkit, to guarantee integration between the national development plans of the Gulf monarchies or post-conflict economic reconstruction process (e.g., Iraq, Iran, Lebanon, Syria, and Yemen), and China's Belt and Road vision.

Such national development and post-conflict economic reconstruction plans have converged with China's BRI under common economic interests and a development path that complements each other, and their strategic synergy will bring new opportunities for both sides. As a result, the realization of the BRI strategy will provide new momentum for the economic transformation/economic growth of the Middle Eastern nations. The implementation of the new Silk Road strategy will unleash a regional infrastructure boom by connecting trade paths across Europe and Central Asia as well as sea routes between Southeast Asia and Africa.

Although various studies have analyzed the political, economic, cultural, and military relations between China and the Middle East in recent years,[78] only a few relate to the emerging strategic partnerships between China and the Middle Eastern countries.[79] The studies that analyzed relations between China and the region preferred to focus mainly on key areas that include energy security, political relations, trade ties, cultural relations, security coordination, and arms sales.[80] Some of these studies also focused on the wave of uprisings that has engulfed the Arab world since 2011;[81] others have chosen to examine the relations between the Gulf monarchies and external powers;[82] yet others have analyzed the evolution of Sino–GCC relations.[83] But few studies have analyzed the mutual effect of China's Belt and Road strategy on all the Middle Eastern countries.[84] The present study, therefore, presents a comprehensive analysis of the mutual influence of China's new Silk Road strategy on emerging partnerships in the Middle East.

1 | Turkey

Turkey is a Middle Eastern country, an emerging power, a member of OECD and NATO, a quasi-member of the European Union (EU), an Islamic country, as well as a Turkic-speaking country that has a close relationship with Central Asia. As one of the leading powers in the Middle East region, Ankara also has a vital part to play in China's Belt and Road Initiative (BRI) which aims to build links between East Asia, Central Asia, West Asia, Africa, and Europe both overland and by sea.

The triangle of the Middle East, Europe, and Central Asia are unique, and these three regions are all of important practical significance to promote the new Silk Road initiative.[1] Turkey's position at the crossroads of the Middle East, South Caucasus, Eastern Mediterranean, and Europe makes it a key geographical location for the BRI. As the gateway to the Middle East, Central Asia, and North Africa, Turkey has a central position in the implementation of the BRI in terms of land, sea, and air transportation, and thus has the potential to determine the trajectory of Beijing's future policy as it seeks to connect China to Europe.[2] Up to now, several agreements have been signed by Beijing and Ankara within the BRI concerning the development of railway infrastructure, the use of ports, and the creation of highway connections.

Relations between the People's Republic of China (PRC) and Ankara have always had their ups and downs. When they established diplomatic relations in 1971, they made no effort to deepen their relationship, and yet, in October 2010 they elevated their relationship to a strategic partnership.[3] In recent years, China–Turkey relations have been growing steadily with frequent high-level exchanges, ever deeper economic and trade cooperation, colorful cultural and people-to-people exchanges, and close communication and coordination on international and regional issues. Turkey and China are making efforts to improve their relations on a long-term basis, and the BRI is considered a useful instrument to this end.

For Ankara, the BRI is an opportunity to strengthen its geopolitical importance, to diversify its economy and decrease its dependency on the West, and to consolidate its position as a global player.[4] The new Silk Road initiative is also a promising opportunity for Turkey to strengthen its economic, social, and political relations and to find alternative alliances to the West-centric trade system by looking for opportunities eastwards. More important, Turkey has viewed China as an important opportunity for rapid economic development. The biggest challenge the Turkish government faces is how to put the sluggish economy back on a steady growth track. Cooperation between China and Turkey under the framework of the BRI could help Ankara to overcome many of its difficulties and attract the foreign investments that it so badly needs.[5]

For the PRC, Turkey is an important regional actor in terms of its geographical location connecting the continents of Asia and Europe, in terms of its stability as compared with its Middle Eastern and Caucasus neighbors, and in terms of its willingness to play an active role within the BRI. With regard to cultural interaction, Turkey has significant inroads and influence because of its Turkic cultural identity and impact on other Turkic states, especially in Central Asia.[6] In terms of commerce, Turkey, albeit with its ambivalent relations with the European Union, could be an essential springboard for Chinese companies to enter the European market as well as an essential platform attracting global investment and trade communication. Turkey has a unique location advantage: the area surrounding Turkey covers dozens of countries, with a population of some 1.5 billion, and a GDP of about $25 trillion.[7]

The main argument presented here is that Beijing's strategic partnership framework with Turkey is based on shared or mutual complementary economic and commercial interests, especially to integrate Turkey's Middle Corridor vision into the BRI, two grand schemes that envisage trans-continental integration. These two ambitious infrastructure development plans – Ankara's Middle Corridor initiative and China's Belt and Road vision – were developed independently of one another, yet have converged on a common economic development path. Their synergetic strategy will bring new opportunities for both sides.

The Middle Corridor

Turkey's vision of connecting with its civilizational cousins in Central Asia and further afield with China, thus pioneering a new East–West trading route through the middle of Eurasia (hence the name), perfectly complements the goals of Beijing's BRI. Its core aim is to extend the railway line that originates from Turkish territory to Central Asia (Kazakhstan, Turkmenistan, etc.) via Transcaucasia (Georgia and Azerbaijan).[8] The Middle Corridor is a multi-transportation route that connects this huge country from the Mediterranean in the West, the Black Sea to the North, and through to the Caspian in the East. The Middle Corridor was designed to provide an alternative to the northern routes of the New Silk Road, which sends cargo through Russia, Kazakhstan, and Belarus, to enter Europe at the border with Poland. The Middle Corridor runs from China to Kazakhstan, Azerbaijan, and Georgia to Turkey, thus providing another gateway to Europe via the Black Sea.

Ankara's main objectives in launching this initiative are to create a belt of prosperity in the region, encourage people-to-people contacts (which is of deep socio-cultural significance since its countrymen are related by ethnicity, language, and history to all of Central Asia's indigenous people, apart from the Tajik), reinforce the sense of regional ownership, connecting Europe to Asia – notably the Caucasus, Central Asia, East Asia, and South Asia, create connectivity between the East-West corridor and the North–South corridor, expand markets and create large economic scales, and provide a concrete contribution to the development of regional cooperation in Eurasia.[9]

Turkey's Middle Corridor could be dovetailed with the BRI (allowing flexibility and if necessary, bypassing Russia) to improve Turkey's infrastructure. This, in turn, will help Ankara stimulate its economy and attract more capital, as well as make it a more valuable bridge between Asia and Europe. In November 2015 Beijing and Ankara signed the "Memorandum of Understanding (MoU) on aligning the BRI and the Middle Corridor initiative to strengthen their cooperation within the BRI.[10] Turkey regards the BRI positively, seeing it as complementary to its own Middle Corridor initiative to create a rail and road network along the ancient Silk Road from Turkey through the Caucasus and Central Asia to China. As Turkish President Recep Tayyip Erdoğan said: "There is a natural harmony between our Middle Corridor Initiative and China's BRI. This harmony allows us to cooperate with China in large geographies such as Central Asia and Africa."[11]

Turkey and the Belt and Road Initiative

China's strategic partnerships with Ankara include seven significant areas for cooperation within the new Silk Road initiative. These areas are policy coordination, connectivity, trade and investments, energy cooperation, financial integration, military ties, and people-to-people bonds. However, each country views the BRI framework according to its perspective and the consequences for its national interests and international status. Therefore, the two countries have very different perceptions about optimal ways of implementing the vision.

Policy coordination

As part of China's strategic partnership with Turkey, promoting political cooperation between countries, creating mechanisms for dialogue and consensus-building on global and regional issues, developing shared interests, deepening political trust, and reaching a new consensus on cooperation, are vital to integrate the Middle Corridor into the BRI framework.[12]

Relations between Turkey and the PRC started gradually, developing from the 1980s with the opening up of both countries. The reciprocal high-level visits between the two states helped to create this strategic cooperation relationship. In October 2010, during Chinese Premier Wen Jiabao's visit to Turkey, Ankara and Beijing agreed to establish the strategic cooperative relations that deepen the economic and political ties of two states.[13] The high-level visits continued at the presidential level between 2012 and 2019, and at the ministerial level in 2016, 2017, and 2018 periodically.

Sino–Turkish relations have become more dynamic, especially during the President Xi Jinping era. In February 2012, Xi first visited Turkey as Vice President to attend the China–Turkey Economic and Trade Cooperation Forum in Istanbul.[14] In April 2012, Prime Minister Erdoğan reciprocated Xi's visit, traveling to China, which constituted the first visit at the prime ministerial level after 27 years.[15] In July 2015, Turkey President Erdoğan visited China and met with President Xi Jinping.[16] The two presidents also met on the margins of the G20 summit in Antalya (November 2015),[17] in Hangzhou (September 2016),[18] at the Belt and Road Summit in Beijing (May 2017),[19] the G20 Leaders' Summit in Buenos Aires (November 2018),[20] the 10th BRICS summit in Johannesburg (July 2018),[21] and during Turkish President

Erdoğan's official visit to China (July 2019).[22] Over the years, many consultation mechanisms have been established at different levels with China to discuss bilateral as well as regional and global issues. Ministers of Foreign Affairs of Turkey and China, Mevlüt Çavuşğlu and Wang Yi met in Ankara (November 2016),[23] in Beijing (August 2017),[24] and in Bangkok (July 2019),[25] within the framework of the Foreign Ministerial Consultation Mechanism, Turkish Foreign Minister Çavu Oğlu paid a working visit to China on June 2018.[26] In October, President Erdoğan appointed his Chief Advisor, Abdülkadir Emin Önen, as Ambassador to China. The selection of his Chief Advisor Önen is a clear sign that President Erdoğan wants to develop a direct channel to Beijing and a closer relationship with the Chinese leadership.[27]

In March 2011, Turkey applied to receive the status of Dialogue Partnership in the Shanghai Cooperation Organization (SCO), founded in 2001, of which China is the most influential member. and on June 2012 the SCO approved Turkey's application. (Dialogue partners are entitled to take part in ministerial-level and some other meetings of the SCO, but do not have voting rights.) Since 2013, Ankara has expressed interest in obtaining observer status or even joining the SCO as a full member.[28] In November 2016, President Erdoğan was quoted by the *Hürriyet* newspaper as saying that Turkey did not need to join the EU "at all costs," and could instead join the Shanghai Five, which "will enable Turkey to act with much greater ease."[29]

In May 2017, the Chinese ambassador to Turkey, Yu Hongyang, said to *Anadolu Agency* that Beijing would be willing to discuss Turkey joining the six-nation bloc with other member states. "Turkey has reached the position of being a dialogue partner of the organization by attending the activities of the SCO in recent years. China, which understands Turkey's intention of becoming a member of the SCO, is ready for Turkey's membership . . . in consultation with other member countries."[30] Nevertheless, Beijing still views Turkey's SCO ambitions with caution. China's stance on Ankara's role in the SCO is also likely to become more firm as its relationship with Turkey evolves.

The past two years have witnessed a real and profound improvement in the relations between the two countries; trade is flourishing, more Chinese investment is flowing into the Turkish economy, and there is a stronger and more constructive dialogue between the two sides. The subsequent blossoming of Ankara's relations with China has occurred against the backdrop of Turkey's apparent strategic estrangement from the West. Indeed, since the failed military coup of July 2016, Turkey's relations with the West are at an all-time low.[31] Some observers have seen in the improvement in the bilateral relationship a sign of Turkey's increasing estrangement from the Western bloc as it seeks to diversify relations.

Nevertheless, China cannot replace its alliance with the U.S. or relations with the EU. Turkey has strong and mutually beneficial economic and military relations with the West. Despite sharing growing strategic interests with China, Ankara remains militarily and economically much more closely integrated with the West (a member of OECD and NATO), if not even dependent. Turkey's economy is so strongly anchored in the West that it is simply impossible to replace the latter with China. In 2018. Turkey was the fifth-largest partner for EU exports of goods (77.3 billion, 4 percent) and the sixth-largest partner for EU imports of goods (76.1, 4 percent),[32] whereas the figure for Asia was 24.9 percent.[33] Thus, Turkey cannot replace the West with China as its major partner. Instead, Ankara wants to diversify its economic relationships around the globe to support its development.[34]

Beijing's increasing emergence as an economic actor in the region primarily drives the relations between the two countries and Turkey's desire to benefit from Chinese capital and technology, as well as affording it a certain degree of leverage vis-à-vis the West. For instance, Turkey President Erdoğan's last meeting with Chinese President Xi in July 2019 was more about economics and diversifying relations, and not part of a strategic shift to the East.[35] For Turkey, Beijing's importance is primarily economic. In the short run, as the economy continues to sail through turbulent waters, and with the lira having sunk to historic lows against major international currencies, securing external financing is crucial for Ankara. In the long term, Turkey is getting closer to Beijing because it needs partners for its rapid economic development, and China as a major player in the global economy is a natural choice for this.[36]

At the heart of Turkey's longer-term vision for a more productive economic relationship with China lies the BRI. The new Silk Road project will ensure the improvement of economic relations between the two countries; it also requires strategic cooperation and partnership relations in terms of realizing the project and establishing the required infrastructure.[37] In recent years, both countries explicitly stated their enthusiasm to collaborate and promote the new Silk Road project. In July 2015, President Xi said he highly values China–Turkey relations and is willing to work with President Erdoğan to translate bilateral friendship into mutual trust and to open new chapters in promoting the China–Turkey strategic cooperative relationship.[38]

In November 2015, Chinese President Xi met with the Turkish President Erdoğan in Antalya ahead of the G20 Summit. During the meeting, President Xi emphasized that China and Turkey would improve strategic communication and that both sides would provide policy support to each other within the framework of BRI. Both countries would take advantage of the Silk Road Infrastructure Fund and the Asian Infrastructure Investment Bank (AIIB) to create a new form of cooperation. President Erdoğan said Turkey values its friendship with China and is willing to cooperate with China within the framework of the BRI, as it welcomes infrastructure investment from Chinese companies. After the meeting, both countries signed an MoU to promote the BRI, and the inking of several cooperative deals to cover fields including infrastructure, entry-exit inspection, and quarantine.[39]

In September 2016, President Xi Jinping met President Erdoğan who was in China for the G20 Hangzhou Summit. Xi emphasized that both countries should explore concrete cooperation means and projects to link the "BRI" with the "Middle Corridor" initiative and thus make substantial progress in practical cooperation in infrastructure construction, energy, inspection, and quarantine, and other fields.[40]

In May 2017, President Erdoğan, in the Belt and Road Forum in Beijing, emphasized that Turkey is an indispensable partner with China and will play a key role in the BRI as the country is the geographical and cultural bridge link with East and West. The Turkish President also pledged that as an indispensable participant, Turkey is providing strong support to Beijing's initiative to revive the ancient Silk Road.[41]

In July 2018, President Xi and President Erdoğan met on the sidelines of the 10th BRICS summit in Johannesburg, South Africa. According to the Chinese President, the China–Turkey strategic cooperative relationship has seen smooth development in recent years with the progress achieved in cooperation in various fields, and Beijing is willing to make joint efforts with Turkey to refresh and further promote bilateral cooperation, as natural partners in the joint construction of the BRI. President Erdoğan said that the Turkish side supports the joint construction of the Belt and Road, opposes protectionism and stands for free trade, Turkey is willing to boost communication and coordination with China in international affairs.[42]

In November 2018, the two presidents held talks on the sidelines of the G20 summit in Buenos Aires. President Xi urged the two countries to strengthen coordination and cooperation, share development opportunities, and meet challenges and risks together, cooperating with Turkey to jointly oppose protectionism and unilateralism and safeguard the common interest of emerging market economies. President Erdoğan said that the Turkish side looks forward to carrying out closer high-level exchanges with China and is ready to deepen cooperation with China in areas such as trade and economy, investment, aviation, and tourism within the BRI framework.[43]

In July 2019, during an official visit in China, Turkish President Erdoğan said, "I believe that both countries have great potential for strengthening the cooperation."[44] In an interview with Chinese news agency *Xinhua*, the Turkish president emphasized the importance of bilateral relations within the framework of China's BRI. "We are on the same page regarding President Xi's approach to the initiative, which is not only to improve transport and communication networks, to construct trade corridors and to harmonize trade policies and development strategies but also to boost cultural and human ties in this framework."[45]

In a separate article in *Global Times*, Erdoğan wrote, "We are pleased to see that the BRI has emerged as the greatest development project of the 21st century encompassing over 100 nations and international organizations – all in line with President Xi's vision. The Middle Corridor, an initiative led by Turkey, lies at the heart of the BRI. It is an important component of the project, which links Turkey to Georgia and Azerbaijan via rail, crosses the Caspian Sea, and reaches China through Turkmenistan and Kazakhstan . . . the Middle Corridor will make a valuable contribution to the BRI. Turkey's relations with China reached the level of strategic cooperative relationship in 2010. We aim to further improve win-win relations by sharing a vision for the future – as embodied by the BRI."[46]

In order to institutionalize cooperation between the new Silk Road and Middle Corridor projects, on the sidelines of the 2015 G20 Antalya Summit, China and Turkey signed an MoU on the "Harmonization of the Silk Road Economic Belt and the 21st Century Maritime Silk Road with the Middle Corridor Initiative" as well as a "Railroad Cooperation Agreement between Turkey and China". Also, in 2016 just before the G20 Hangzhou Summit, both countries signed an MoU on the "Belt and Road" Initiative that included Turkey's "Middle Corridor" Project.[47]

Connectivity

Since Turkey has, on many occasions expressed interest in becoming a political and economic bridge between East and West, for China, this has meant to link the BRI with Ankara's Middle Corridor. China has given support to Turkey's infrastructural projects with loans provided by the AIIB and the Industrial Commercial Bank of China (ICBC), and with Chinese firms that are active in the construction of the projects. Turkey's unique position in the BRI makes the country a gateway to Europe and Africa for China's trade operations on the project's route. Therefore, Turkey would naturally become a logistics hub for trade on the three continents.

Turkey is a regional power located in Eurasia with an extremely important geopolitical location and thus plays a vital role in China's new Silk Road project. Firstly,

Turkey's geopolitical and geo-economic position is unique, making Turkey a natural candidate to be China's cooperative partner and the key bridge in building the BRI in Eurasia. Secondly, Turkey's economic strength is relatively strong. It has a close economic and cultural connection with the Caspian region in Central Asia and the Middle Eastern countries. It is also quite strong in regional investment and development, which makes it an unignorable participant in building the BRI. Thirdly, with its close economic connection with Europe, Turkey becomes the transit point between Europe and the outside world and the critical support of the realization of the long-term version of the BRI. Turkey is among the key channels of development for the future Silk Road extending to Europe and vital in fulfilling the prospect of the Silk Road from the Pacific Ocean to the Baltic Sea.[48]

Finally, in terms of geopolitical patterns, Turkey connects to parts of Europe, Asia, and Africa; south of Russia, west of the Caucasus, Central Asia, and Iran; and east of Europe. The Arab North Africa region is in its southern and southeastern flank. Turkey also controls the strait connecting the Black Sea and the Mediterranean Sea. Such a unique geographical advantage makes Turkey a bridge for the communication of Eastern and Western economies and cultures.[49]

The Middle Corridor represents Turkey's own version of a Silk Road initiative and includes the establishment of a region-wide railroad network. The corridor begins in Turkey and passes through the Caucasus region (Georgia, Azerbaijan, the Caspian Sea), then on to Central Asia, and then to China. Ankara aims to integrate the Middle Corridor into the BRI framework, and thereby to speed its domestic infrastructural developments. For instance, the completion of the Baku-Tbilisi-Kars railway line would realize the Turkey–Georgia–Azerbaijan–Turkmenistan-Afghanistan transit corridor (the Lapis Lazuli Corridor), help to modernize Turkey's existing railroads and develop links between the Silk Road and Turkish seaports and investments on the construction ports in Filyos, Çandarlı, and Mersin. Also part of the overall project is the construction of the Marmaray rail tunnel, the Edirne–Kars high-speed railway line, the Yavuz Sultan Selim Bridge (the third Bosphorus Bridge), the Eurasia Tunnel projects and the Three-Level Tube Tunnel Project, the Edirne–Kars High-Speed Rail Project, the Çanakkale Strait Bridge, the Gebze–Orhangazi-Izmir Motorway, and the Northern Marmara Motorway.[50]

The Baku–Tbilisi–Kars (BTK), also called 'The Iron Silk Road", is a central corridor railway project that opened in October 2017.[51] The BTK railway line is the most important milestone of the Middle Corridor and the biggest infrastructure project on the agenda of the BRI. The railway line will go through the capital city of Baku in Azerbaijan and the cities of Tbilisi and Ahilkelek in Georgia and on to the city of Kars in Ankara. The route will not only connect Azerbaijan to the Mediterranean Sea but will also link Turkey with Central Asia and China. With this railway and the Marmaray tunnel, Ankara plans to establish a continuous service along with the China–Kazakhstan–Azerbaijan–Turkey-Europe rail corridor.[52]

The total length of the railway is 838.6 km, and the total cost is 450 million dollars; 76 km of the railway will pass from Turkey, 259 km from Georgia, and 503 km from Azerbaijan. Previously, cargoes leaving China reached Europe within two months while now, thanks to this new railway line, they will be able to reach Europe within two weeks. The BTK line shortens the transportation route between Asia and Europe by approximately seven thousand kilometers. It carries one million passengers per year and has a load capacity of 6.5 million tons; it is projected to carry 3 million passengers and 17 million tons of cargo by 2034.[53] In addition, as a follow-up project to the BTK railway line, Ankara is interested in Chinese aid for building a high-speed internal railway connecting eastern and western Turkey (Kars–Edirne).[54]

China intends to construct a modern Kazakhstan to Baku railway, which will then merge with the existing BTK railway while rounding off and enhancing Middle Corridor connectivity. From there, China intends to build a railway linking the eastern Anatolian city of Kars to Edrine on the European side of the Bosporus. In this sense, a trans-Anatolian railway into continental Europe will help to complete this central leg of the Belt and Road, thus replicating one of the most important ancient trading routes whose new benefits to the world are substantial.[55] It will connect to the Middle Corridor, which seeks to link Turkey's culturally fraternal Central Asian partners to the Republic of Turkey.[56] The Middle Corridor via the BKR Rail is also a link through to the lesser-known Lapis Lazuli Corridor. This is the aim of the initiative (mostly Chinese-funded) to enhance regional economic cooperation and connectivity between Afghanistan, Turkmenistan, Azerbaijan, Georgia, and Turkey, as well as to expand economic and cultural links between Europe and Asia. In doing so, the initiative seeks to improve transport infrastructure and procedures (including for road, rail, and sea), increase exports, and expand the economic opportunities of the countries benefiting from this new transport corridor. China hopes that the link, effectively a regional spur from the Middle Corridor, will help keep Afghanistan quiet and promote peace via trade. Thus, the Lapis Lazuli Corridor has not just trade but also security significance for Beijing.

The Lapis Lazuli Corridor begins from Afghanistan's Aqina City in the northern Faryab province and Torghundi City in western Herat, both of which are situated close to the Afghani border with Turkmenistan. Crucially, both Aqina and Torghundi have rail connectivity through to Turkmenistan. From there, the routes continue west to the Caspian Sea Port of Turkmenbashi, in Turkmenistan. After transiting the Caspian, the route continues to Baku, capital of Azerbaijan, and then connects onward to Tbilisi, capital of Georgia, as well as the Georgian ports of Poti and Batumi. The corridor will connect to the cities of Kars in Turkey, the Middle Corridor, and onto Istanbul and the gates of Europe.[57]

Another vital trading corridor is the link between Ankara's Middle Corridor and the North–South Transportation Corridor, a 7,200-km interconnecting network of railways, roads, and shipping lanes designed to facilitate the flow of freight between India, Iran, Russia, Azerbaijan, as well as European and Central Asian states. This connects India and Iran to Europe (via Turkey) and extends northwards into Russia and their massive rail network. Although slightly more complex (shipping is involved both from India to Iran and then again across the Caspian to Russia), the route has been tested and found to be advantageous and economically viable. A western spur from this shoots off from Iran and connects with the Middle Corridor.[58]

In Turkey, China has made investments and built a transportation network and infrastructure construction that links the Middle Corridor with the new Silk Roads. In October 2015 a high-speed railway between Ankara and Istanbul (cutting the 533km journey between the two cities from a typical seven hours to three and a half) was launched, constructed by a Chinese–Turkish consortium (China National Machinery Import and Export Corporation joined with Turkish firms Cengiz Construction and Ibrahim Cecen Ictas Construction).[59] According to the *People's Daily*, Beijing also lent Turkey $750 million to partially finance the new link.[60]

The Marmaray rail tunnel is undoubtedly the most famous of all Turkey's transport initiatives. Marmaray is a railway project that connects the railway lines of Istanbul's European and Asian sides with a tube tunnel passing under the Bosphorus. The project, worth $3 billion, aims to become the primary rail solution for cargo between Europe and Asia.[61] When the Baku–Tbilisi–Kars railway project is combined with the Marmaray project, it will be possible to transport freight uninterruptedly from Europe to China by rail. With the Marmaray tunnel and the Third Bosphorus Bridge (the Yavuz Sultan Selim Bridge) being designed as part of the Iron Silk Road, Ankara will make a significant contribution to the Iron Silk Road by completing the middle line of the Beijing–London line.[62]

In November 2019, a westbound train from Xi'an, China, for the first time used Istanbul's $4 billion Marmaray sub-Bosporus railway tunnel to dispatch goods to central Europe. The train's voyage represents another of Beijing's attempts to shave time off its trans-Eurasian rail shipments; the train crossed two continents, ten countries, two seas, and 7,135 miles of railway in 12 days. The train started in Xi'an in central China, crossing Kazakhstan before being loaded on an Aktau train ferry to cross the Caspian Sea to Baku. From there, it proceeded to Turkey via the BTK railroad. Upon arriving in Istanbul, the train traveled northward to Kapikule, on Turkey's Bulgarian border, before continuing onward to Prague. The Marmaray passage underlines the growing potential of the Trans-Caspian Silk Road 'Middle Corridor' rail route – Turkey's vision for connecting China to Europe via Central Asia and the South Caucasus. It is also known as the 'Trans-Caspian International Transport Route' (TITR).[63]

In recent years, Turkey has been interested in creating links between the BRI and Turkish seaports and 16 international Ro-Ro lines in the Black Sea and the Mediterranean. There are also several ongoing significant port investments in Turkey. The Mersin Port (on the Eastern Mediterranean coast) will have an 11 million ton/year (TEU) capacity at an estimated cost of $3.8 billion. The Filyos Port (on the Western Black Sea coast) will have a 700,000 TEU capacity at the cost of $870 million. The Candarli Port at Izmir (on the Aegean coast) will have a 12 million TEU capacity, with the cost estimated at $1.24 billion. Turkey expects that the Candarli Port would play a crucial role in the development of the Middle Corridor.[64]

Since 2015, Chinese companies have also been investing in Turkish ports. In this context, Kumport, Çandarlı, and Mersin port were the most attractive ports for Chinese companies. In September 2015, a consortium of COSCO, China Merchants Holdings International, and China Investment Corporation, spent $920 million to buy a 65 percent stake in the Kumport terminal, which is part of Ambarli Port in Istanbul. Kumport is located on the northwestern coast of the Marmara Sea on Istanbul's European side. It can handle 1.84 million 20 TEU of cargo with six berths and has room for a 3.5 million TEU capacity.[65] However, it seems that China Merchants Holdings has made this investment to use Kumport as a gateway to the Turkish market rather than as a regional hub.

In the end, Turkey's location serves well for the facilitation of the connectivity of the BRI. China's investments in Turkey's infrastructure are important for the BRI because Beijing is trying to set up a logistics network in the eastern Mediterranean. However, Turkey is not a natural transit point for Silk Road traffic. There are many alternative transportation routes between China and Europe and powerful competitors (e.g., Russia and countries in Central Asia). Countries in the region have strategic plans and are expending enormous efforts to maximize their chances of success in linking to the BRI; for example, Russia's long-term efforts to double the train speed on the China–Europe route.

Thus, Ankara needs to mobilize all of its available resources to plan its path to success, upgrade the single-track rail network to increase the speed and capacity, and share information transparently to encourage private companies to start investing. If it succeeds, the Middle Corridor may become one of the leading transport corridors in Eurasia, which will strengthen Turkey's economic bonds with Europe, Central Asia, and China. Nevertheless, instability (e.g., disputes, wars, sanctions, and new political alliances) remains the biggest threat to facilitate connectivity in the region.[66]

Energy cooperation

As part of China's strategic partnership with Turkey, investment in energy infrastructure is considered one of the critical areas for cooperation to integrate the Middle Corridor into the BRI framework. The two countries have been cooperating extensively, and Chinese energy companies have increased their presence in Turkey's energy sector and invested in thermal power plants, and there are talks about building a third nuclear power plant in Turkey.

Moreover, Turkey is one of the essential nodes in the construction of the BRI and an important partner in China's energy investment strategy, being located at the junction of Europe and Asia, along the Silk Road, surrounded by the Black Sea and the Caspian Sea, and close to the world's largest energy consumption in Europe. Approximately 70 percent of the world's producible petroleum and natural gas reserves are situated in geographical regions that are close to Turkey. Its neighbor countries possess three-quarters of the world's petroleum and natural gas reserves and Turkey is participating in numerous significant projects as a natural "Energy Center" between the energy-rich Caspian, Central Asian, and Middle Eastern countries and the consumer markets in Europe.[67] Hence, the importance of Turkey as a corridor and energy transportation hub, located precisely in the central area between the supply and demand sides.[68]

Turkey also has a large number of coal reserves (3.2 percent of the total world reserves of lignite/sub-bituminous coal), ranking high among Middle Eastern countries besides Iran; it also has considerable reserves of metal minerals and oil and gas.[69] Mineral products and chemical products (e.g., salt, sulfur, earth, stone, plaster, lime, and cement) have been the leading products and account for 32 percent of Turkish exports to China in 2018.[70]

Turkey has actively promoted plans for an energy corridor by pipeline projects. According to the AIIB report of 2019, Turkey was highlighted as a priority country with rapidly growing pipeline projects.[71] Many oil and gas pipelines (e.g., the Iraq–Turkey pipeline and Baku–Tbilisi–Erzurum natural gas pipeline), which originate from the Caspian region, the Middle East and Russia to Europe, pass through Turkey. Turkey has been a vital country in the operation of Eurasian oil and gas resources and maintaining regional energy security.[72]

More importantly, the Turkish government has set ambitious infrastructure development plans to promote several infrastructure projects, including the renovation and transformation of the oil refinery, liquefied natural gas liquefaction plant, and energy storage facilities. According to the president of the Turkey Committee of the World

Energy Council, Turkey needs at least $70 billion in investment in the energy sector, including the construction of nuclear power plants and the transformation of existing energy systems.[73] Hence, there is an expectation that Chinese enterprises will increase their investment and expand cooperation with Turkey energy sector.

EMBA Electricity Production Co. Inc (a joint venture of Chinese Shanghai Electric Power Co., Avic-Intl Project Engineering Company, and two Turkish investors) is set to build a 1320-megawatt coal-fired thermal power plant in Yumurtalik, at the Iskenderun Bay area, district of Adana in Turkey. The project is expected to cost $1.7 billion and was announced as China's most significant direct investment in Turkey. The plant will use the latest technology in coal-fired power generation and will be stable, safe, efficient, and environmentally friendly.[74]

Additionally, China has invested $600 million in Turkey's renewable energy sector, and investments in this sector are expected to soar in the upcoming period. According to the state-run *Anadolu Agency*, the Chinese state company HT Solar Energy is considering investing $1 billion in Turkey's renewable energy industry. The Chinese company, which was not successful in the first Renewable Energy Resources Area Project (YEKA) tender that took place in 2017, wants to bid in the second YEKA tender with a Turkish company.[75]

Ankara and Beijing have been negotiating the construction of a third nuclear power plant in Turkey (possibly in Kirklareli), but the talks have yet to yield any firm results. In November 2014, Turkey's state-owned electricity generation company EUA , China's State Nuclear Power Technology Corporation Limited (SNPTC), and U.S.-based Westinghouse Electric Company, announced a multiparty agreement to enter exclusive negotiations to develop and construct Turkey's third nuclear power plant. In June 2016, Turkey and China signed an MoU for the development of nuclear technology. In June 2018, President Erdoğan said that the country would likely build its third nuclear power plant with China. In January 2019, the Energy Ministry announced that 32 students would be sent to Russia and China in a bid to provide a professional, skilled workforce for planned nuclear power plants in Turkey.[76]

According to Turkey's Energy and Natural Resources Minister Fatih Dönmez, in recent years Turkey and China made significant energy investments, with one of the major projects being a nuclear power plant that has seen the undertaking of detailed studies and feasibility reports for almost a year by China's National Nuclear Corporation. Another area of collaboration is in smart grid technology. The State Grid Corporation of China and Turkey's Electrical Installations and Engineering Services, which already have a cooperation agreement, reviewed this agreement, and updated the roadmap. Smart grids are necessary for increasing the operational efficiency of the electricity network while benefiting consumers who can use energy more efficiently.[77]

To sum up, Ankara is one of the critical nodes in the construction of Beijing's BRI and a key partner in the global Chinese energy investment strategy. The Turkey energy sector is desirable to Chinese energy companies' investment and can enhance the strategic partnership between the two sides. However, religious and cultural differences, Turkey's domestic economic problems (e.g., economic recovery, poor credit rating, and high inflation rate), political turmoil, and multiple other factors pose severe challenges to China's energy investment in Turkey.

Trade and investments

Part of China's strategic partnerships with Turkey includes efforts to ease as much as possible the barriers to free trade, investment, industrial cooperation, and technical and engineering services to facilitate the integration of the Middle Corridor into BRI. Both countries would have to undertake a series of measures, such as expanding free-trade zones, improving trade structures, seeking new potential areas for trade, and improving the trade balance, devising new initiatives for the promotion of conventional forms of trade.[78]

According to China Customs Statistics (export-import), China–Turkey bilateral trade decreased to $20.7 billion in 2019 (compared to $21.4 billion in 2018), still leaving China is one of Turkey's largest trade partners, after Germany and Russia.[79] The trade relationship is marked by a massive $14 billion imbalance in Beijing's favor, something that Ankara is seeking to address by expanding exports and attracting Chinese investment at a time that its economy is struggling. According to Turkish President Erdoğan, "Among our goals is to double our bilateral trade volume with China to $50 billion and, subsequently, $100 billion, on a more balanced and sustainable footing to serve the interests of both sides."[80]

Chinese investments in Turkey under the BRI framework in energy, logistics, infrastructure, manufacturing, and telecommunication has increased, albeit modestly. The number of Chinese companies operating in Turkey is increasing at a fast pace, and there are nearly 1,000 Chinese firms that have been operating in Turkey's logistics, electronics, energy, tourism, finance, and real estate sectors.[81] According to the *China Global Investment Tracker*, Beijing investments, and contracts in Ankara from 2013 to 2019 reached $10.1 billion.[82] With the entry of Bank of China (BOC) and ICBC, the flow of Chinese companies into Turkey has accelerated and also expanded into the e-commerce sector in the recent period.[83]

While Chinese companies expect to be more active in the Turkish market given the latter's key position in the new Silk Road initiative framework, Chinese firms have for some time been in a wait-and-see mode about Turkey, due to security and economy issues, such as terror attacks. The failed coup attempt and the weakening of the Turkish currency are also limiting Chinese investments in Turkey.[84] Moreover, Ankara's stance in support of the Uyghurs, the Turkic Muslim population of Xinjiang, is increasing tensions in relations between the two countries. As a consequence, the flow of foreign direct investment (FDI) from China to Turkey has slowed in recent years.

In 2018, Chinese FDI in Turkey exceeded $2 billion, a significant amount, and was expected to double by the end of 2019 and exceed $4 billion.[85] Yet, that does not fully reflect the potential that Turkey's economy has to offer to the BRI, with a sizeable market, attractive investment opportunities due to the low value of the lira, and favorable geographic location connecting European, Middle Eastern, and Eurasian markets.[86] Chinese FDI is concentrated in logistics, telecommunications, and manufacturing. Chinese companies have also opened representative trading offices in Turkey, especially for machinery sales. Besides, Ankara has concluded a deal with the China Development Bank to fund big scale projects, including railway projects.[87] According to the Chinese ambassador to Ankara, Deng Li, Beijing is looking to double its investments in Turkey, which is located in the middle corridor of the BRI project.[88]

Until now the single largest Chinese FDI in Turkey has been the purchase by a consortium of Chinese companies (Cosco Pacific and China Merchants Holdings) of 65 percent in Turkey's Kumport container terminal, near Istanbul, for $940 million, which is the country's third-largest seaport.[89] This investment is of vital importance not only for Turkey's shipping and trade capacity but also for the BRI as it allows the Chinese side to initiate a new regional service of container shipping that connects Northern European ports with those in the Mediterranean. The Industrial and Commercial Bank of China, BOC, and the telecommunication companies Huawei and ZTE have entered the market, but other Chinese corporate heavyweights are yet to explore Turkey.

Ankara sees China's FDI not only as a source of short-term finance that would help to rebuild its economy but especially as a major stakeholder in its long-term economic development. Turkey needs to attract foreign investment at the moment, but more importantly, the economy has to be placed on a sustainable long-term growth track to be more productive and less prone to crises. Hence, the Turkic Ministry of Trade has declared China to be one of the four priority markets for exporters along with Russia, India, and Mexico, and it has prepared a detailed road map for improving trade relations between the two countries.[90]

The China-led AIIB continues to look for new opportunities in Turkey, one of its largest investment markets and looks to invest in new projects in the country in the upcoming period. In 2018, the AIIB had invested around $1.4 billion in projects related to Turkey, and made loans and financing commitments of almost $7.5 billion as of the end of the year. The bank is expected to approve projects worth another $4 billion throughout this year. For example, the AIIB approved $600 million for the capacity expansion project of Lake Tuz underground natural gas storage facility, which will increase the reliability and security of Turkey's gas supply. The bank also invested $200 million for Turkey's Industrial Development Bank (TSKB) Sustainable Energy and Infrastructure On-lending Facility that will support long-term financing, primarily for renewable energy and energy efficiency projects.[91]

Moreover, in 2018 Turkey's national flag carrier, Turkish Airlines (THY), announced the formation of a logistics company in Hong Kong in partnership with China's ZTO Express and Hong Kong's PAL Air. The partners aimed to make the new joint venture one of the world's largest integrators and generate revenue of $2 billion within the first five years of its operation.[92]

Financial integration

Under China's strategic partnership with Turkey, the formation and promotion of financial integration between the two countries are considered one of the essential cooperation areas to facilitate the integration of the Middle Corridor into the BRI framework. Measures for the realization of financial integration between the two countries include: deepening financial cooperation and building a stable currency system, establishing an investment and financing system and a credit information system in Asia, expanding the scope and scale of bilateral currency swaps between the two countries, and developing the bond market in Asia. In addition, making joint efforts to establish the AIIB and having financial institutions with good credit rating issue RMB-denominated bonds in China, thereby encouraging qualified Chinese financial institutions and companies to issue bonds in both RMB and foreign currencies outside China and to use the funds thus collected in countries along the BRI.[93]

Turkey is one of the 50 founding members of the AIIB launched by China, a critical mechanism for funding BRI and other projects.[94] Ankara's registered capital is $2.6 billion, giving the country a 2.52 percent voting power and the 11th largest shareholder of the bank. Ankara is also the seventh-largest shareholder in its region and has a seat in the 12-member AIIB Board of Directors.[95] The AIIB's goals are to finance infrastructure on the new Silk Roads initiative route. According to Joachim von Amsberg, AIIB Vice President for policy and strategy, Turkey is a key market for the AIIB and offers huge potential for investing in energy and transport connectivity.[96]

In recent years, the banking sector has been one of the fast-evolving areas between Turkey and China. In the early 2000s, the Turkish banks Garanti and Isbank opened representative offices in China, while the ICBC, the largest bank in China (and the world), and the Bank of China did the same in Turkey after 2010. In May 2015, the ICBC bought a 75 percent stake in Tekstilbank, and consequently, became the first Chinese bank to take over the majority stake of a local bank operating in Turkey. Following the acquisition, the name of the bank was changed to ICBC Turkey.[97] In November 2016, the ICBC brokered an agreement between the Turkish and Chinese central banks to use Turkish lira and Chinese yuan instead of dollars and euros. As part of the currency swap agreement, which was signed to increase the trade volume between Turkey and China, the ICBC Turkey used a fund of TL 450 million.[98]

In December 2017, the Turkish Banking Regulation and Supervision Agency (BDDK) granted operational rights in Turkey to the Bank of China (BOC). The bank, the world's seventh-largest and the third-largest in China, will become the second Chinese lender to operate in Turkey.[99] Conversely, Turkish Akbank, Isbank (Turkey's largest bank), and Garanti Bank (the second-largest private bank in Turkey) have branches in China. However, they operate as representative offices and have yet to obtain the necessary permits to offer banking services.[100]

There has also been increasing financial cooperation, mostly in the form of Chinese infrastructure loans. In December 2017, Turkey's state lender Ziraat Bank signed a $600 million credit agreement with the China Development Bank, and Turkey's bank secured a $400 million loan agreement with the Export-Import Bank of China.[101] In June 2018, after Turkey was faced with currency depreciation, Chinese banks and financial institutions agreed to support Turkey to overcome the crisis. Ankara also secured a $1.2 billion loan in total to expand the Gas Storage Expansion Project in Tuz Gölü (Salt Lake) in Central Anatolia. The loans were secured from the World Bank ($600-million loan) and AIIB ($600-million loan) to increase the security of Turkish gas supplies.[102] In July 2018, ICBC agreed to provide a $3.6 billion loan package to increase the capacities of Silivri and Tuz Golu Natural Gas Storage Facilities, which will store 20 percent of Turkey's natural gas yearly.[103]

Moreover, the Turkey Wealth Fund (Varlık Fonu) tried unsuccessfully in October 2017 to borrow as much as $5 billion from ICBC. The Turkish fund holds several assets, including stakes in state lenders Turkiye Halk Bankasi AS and TC Ziraat Bankasi AS. It also owns flag-carrier THY, the country's biggest telephone operator Turk Telekomunikasyon AS, and national lottery company Milli Piyango.[104] In February 2019, the Wealth Fund hired Citigroup and ICBC to coordinate a $1.14 billion syndicated loan, making it the first time the fund took a foreign loan. The loan will have a two-year maturity with an option to extend for another year so that the Fund can inject cash into the companies it holds.[105]

Military ties

As part of China's strategic partnerships with Ankara, defense cooperation has become an increasingly significant part of the Middle Corridor–BRI integration. Traditionally, the U.S. and the West are the major defense partners with Turkey. Since the dawn of the Cold War, Ankara has been an anchor in the U.S. security system. The Truman Doctrine began seeking to shield Greece and Turkey from Soviet threats; Turkey joined NATO soon after to gain protection from the expansionist Soviet Union. For decades after, despite plenty of tensions, disagreements, and differing regional priorities, many in Washington considered Ankara a vital and necessary strategic partner, the keystone to NATO's southern flank, and a Western-friendly bridgehead in the Muslim world.[106]

Nevertheless, Turkey wants diversification in meeting its defense needs. The Beijing-Ankara security relations have focused primarily on a joint military exercise, military visits, counter-terrorism missions, and naval visits and weapons sales, particularly systems that other suppliers (e.g., the U.S. and the West) refused to sell or to share sensitive technology with Turkey.

In September–October 2010, Beijing–Ankara held a bilateral military exercise called the 'Anatolian Eagle,' in Turkey, the first such exercise that China conducted with a NATO member, albeit at a more modest scale compared with Turkey's cooperation in this field with NATO allies. This, coupled with the numerous high-level diplomatic and military visits between the two countries since 2009, has led to the establishment of a new strategic partnership between the two countries.[107] The military cooperation has continued to deepen between the two countries, and a few weeks after the joint exercise of the two air forces, the land forces worked on counter-terrorism missions on the Turkish land. This last drill was also unprecedented, as the Chinese army was operating in a NATO country for the first time for that purpose.[108]

Unlike the U.S. or the West, Beijing has demonstrated its willingness and eagerness to sell weapons and sensitive technology to strengthen the bilateral military and political cooperation with Ankara. In September 2013, the China Precision Machinery Import-Export Corporation (CPMIEC) agreed to deliver its FD-2000 air defense missile system at a relatively lower price in a joint production agreement with Turkey's government. U.S. and NATO opposition to the air and missile defense system sales came immediately due to the interoperability problems, making NATO systems in Turkey vulnerable to Chinese systems. Moreover, the CPMIEC was on the U.S. sanctions list on charges of proliferation activities with Iran.

As a result, after two years of negotiations, on November 2015, Ankara's defense ministry announced the cancellation of the agreement and said that Ankara intended to develop its own system from scratch. According to Turkish officials, the reason for the cancellation is that China refused to transfer the technology of the operating system which would allow Turkey to replicate it and develop its long-range air and missile defense system with domestic resources.[109]

Moreover, there were several naval visits between Ankara and Beijing. The Turkish frigate *Gemlik* made port calls in Shanghai and Hong Kong in 2011 for the celebration of the 40th anniversary of the establishment of diplomatic relations between both countries. In 2015, the Turkish frigate *Gediz* visited Hong Kong and Qingdao on a commemoration mission,[110] while Chinese warships visited in Istanbul three times (2012, 2015, and 2017) on a friendly mission.[111] These military visits and talks between Ankara-Beijing sent an important message regarding the strategic partnership and the desire to strengthen cooperation between the two countries in the defense and security sectors.

In July 2018, a Chinese military delegation headed by Maj. Gen. Licun Zhou, the political commissar for the Joint Warfare Institute of the PLA at National Defense University, visited the Turkish National Defense University. According to Turkish diplomatic sources speaking to *Al-Monitor*, the number of high-level meetings between the Chinese and Turkish militaries will increase in the coming months, and the discussions will cover boosting cooperation in professional military education, military training, the defense industry, terrorism, intelligence sharing, robotic systems, artificial intelligence and, cyberwarfare. There will also be some joint projects in which Turkish and Chinese engineers work together to boost defense cooperation. In May 2018, a large number of Chinese officers attended the Ephesus 2018 military exercise held in Izmir as observers.[112]

The delivery of the Russian-made S-400 missile defense system to Ankara, despite repeated and vociferous threats and warnings, led Washington to expel Turkey from the F-35 fighter jet program but could drive the country into China's arms. During the last visit to Beijing in July 2019, Turkish President Erdoğan called to strengthen cooperation with the PRC in all areas, including defense. "In the area of defense, Turkey and China proved their technological and manufacturing capabilities to the world by launching original projects in recent years. I am confident that our two nations can cooperate in this area as well."[113]

People-to-People Bond

Part of China's strategic partnerships with Turkey includes enabling the people of the two countries to bond along the Silk Road, vital to integrating the Middle Corridor into the BRI framework. The promotion of extensive cultural and academic exchanges aim to win public support for deepening bilateral and multilateral cooperation, as well as providing scholarships, holding annual cultural events, increasing cooperation in science and technology, and establishing joint laboratory or research centers and international technology transfer centers.[114]

As Turkish President Erdoğan said in a speech at the opening ceremony of the Belt and Road Forum for International Cooperation in Beijing on May 2017, "The promotion of comprehensive cultural cooperation in the fields of tourism, science, technology, and media along with the increase of student and personnel exchange programs will help achieve the goal."[115] Thus, linguistic, cultural, and tourism cooperation is an important aspect of the China–Turkey strategic partnership, and both nations have outlined their intention to expand the collaboration in these areas in the coming years. According to the *Hanban website*, the Chinese government established Confucius Institutes for providing Chinese language and culture teaching resources worldwide; by 2019, 550 Confucius Institutes and 1,172 Confucius Classrooms and 5,665 teaching sites had been established in 162 countries and regions, receiving about eleven million students.[116] In 54 countries involved in the BRI, there are 153 Confucius Institutes and 149 primary and high-school Confucius Classrooms.[117]

In the Middle East, there are eighteen Confucius institutes and three Confucius Classrooms, and four of these Confucius Institutes are in Turkey: the Middle East Technical University founded in 2006, at Bogazici University founded in 2008, at

Okan University founded in 2012, and at Yeditepe University founded in 2015.[118] According to *Hürriyet Daily News*, the Chinese language became the second most popular language in Turkey. In recent years, there is a great surge in the number of Turkish citizens wanting to learn Chinese, and the sale of books teaching Chinese has increased by 30 percent. In particular, there is a demand for learning Chinese in the Cappadocia region, which is a very popular area among the Chinese.[119]

The improving ties between Turkey and the PRC are also evident in the two countries' cultural ties as the rising number of students and interest in learning the Turkish language shows. Turkey presently is host to 1,965 Chinese nationals studying in the country's universities, while the number of Chinese universities offering Turkish classes doubled in two years. Istanbul University, one of the oldest universities in Turkey, hosts the largest number of Chinese students, with 338 Chinese citizens studying at the school. In the past two years, the number of universities offering Turkish language courses increased from only four to eight in China.[120]

The number of students has increased day by day in both countries, thanks to various scholarships and incentives. In May 2019, 37 Turkish university students, from more than ten universities and institutions, were awarded scholarships for their outstanding study of the Chinese language. In 2017, 36 Chinese students studying at Turkish universities were also granted scholarships set up by the Chinese consulate general.[121]

Relations with China also are tending to warm up in cultural terms. The years 2012 and 2013 were celebrated as the years of China and Turkey, and various events were held in these two countries. The program, named "Experience China in Turkey," included nine major events, such as the Chinese–Turkish political and economic forums, Chinese folk dance shows, Chinese movie and television weeks, and exchanges between journalists and writers.[122]

In January 2019, the 2019 Hurun Global Chinese New Year Series made its debut in Istanbul, bringing together about 200 Turkish industrialists and entrepreneurs to have a moment of joy and harmony with the Chinese. In Istanbul, awards were presented to three Turks in recognition of their contributions to China–Turkey relations. The lifetime achievement award going to Husnu Ozyegin, a billionaire businessman who founded Ozyegin University in Istanbul; the outstanding contribution award going to the Dorak tourism agency now in business for 20 years; and the future star award to Ugur Talayhan, general manager of the Swissotel the Bosphorus, which played host to the Chinese New Year event. These kinds of events make important contributions to the strengthening of the friendship between the two countries.[123]

In May 2019, dancers from Turkey joined their Chinese colleagues to take part in the Conference on Dialogue of Asian Civilizations (CDAC) that was hosted by the China Media Group (CMG). With the theme of "Celebration of Youth, Dream of Asia," the extravaganza showcased the distinctive charm of Asian civilizations and Chinese civilization through various art performances and high-tech stage effects. More than 30,000 performers from 47 countries took part in 15 performances at the celebration. The cast included famous performers from different countries, Asian youth leaders, and world-class artists.[124]

In September 2019, Ankara, the capital city, hosted events marking the Chinese Mid-Autumn festival with celebrations in several venues under a welcoming atmosphere and with traditional food. The festival came this year to the Turks who are interested in everything Chinese, especially food, culture and traditions, values that resonate strongly in their country too, connecting the two peoples. The Turkish attendants in the festival had the pleasure of seeing traditional Chinese folk art related to food, such as dough modeling, sugar painting, and music. According to the Cultural Counsellor of the Chinese Embassy in Turkey, Shi Ruilin, the cultural bonds between China and Turkey are growing stronger each year and underscored that the festival would contribute to the strengthening of bilateral cultural relations.[125]

In terms of the economy, Ankara's biggest problem is its over-reliance on the tertiary, or service, industries, among which tourism alone accounts for about 60 percent of its Gross Domestic Product (GDP). This has made the country vulnerable to turbulence in both foreign and domestic markets and the possible fluctuations in its relations with other countries.[126] More broadly, while Russians continue to represent one of the biggest single national groups to visit Turkey as tourists, Ankara and Beijing are working on expanding the number of Chinese tourists who last year increased their spending in Turkish businesses by 166 percent. In 2018, about 400,000 Chinese tourists visited Turkey, up more than 60 percent year-on-year. Turkish authorities have already begun work to make the country increasingly appealing to both Chinese visitors and investors.[127]

Turkish authorities are planning for the number of Chinese visitors to reach 500,000 by the end of 2019. After China declared 2018 "Turkey Tourism Year," the interest of Chinese tourists in Turkey has skyrocketed. Turkey's ambassador to Beijing, Abdülkadir Emin Önen, said that the year 2018 was a record year as 60 Turkey-oriented promotion activities in China were facilitated. In April 2019, Turkey opened a huge pavilion at the Beijing International Horticulture Exhibition, where architectural features and various dishes of the seven geographical regions of Turkey were introduced. Nearly two million Chinese visited the area in this period, making the Turkish pavilion the most popular section of the exhibition. The Turkish embassy also forged cooperation with authors, newspaper columnists, and influencers with over a million followers on social media. More than six Chinese delegations were sent to Turkey's top tourism cities, and they introduced Turkey on social media and shared the sites they visited in their articles.[128]

According to *Anadolu Agency*, the shopping activities of Chinese tourists in Turkey jumped by 85 percent year on year in the first seven months of 2019. Chinese visitors also accounted for 22 percent of tax-free shopping in Turkey in the same period, registering an increase of two percent. Chinese visitors have shown interest in luxury shopping, and the average spending of Chinese tourists in Turkey has exceeded $874.[129] Chinese Ambassador to Turkey, Deng Li, said Turkey is one of the most intriguing countries for Chinese tourists, pointing to the great potential of the tourism volume between China and Turkey. Beijing expects the number of Chinese tourists coming to Turkey to increase exponentially in the future.[130]

Summary

Turkey's Middle Corridor and China's BRI have converged on a joint economic development path and will provide new momentum for Ankara's rapid economic development. Although the strategic partnership relations of Turkey and China that were established in 2010 continue with the synergy between the BRI within the Middle Corridor, the project has heightened the question of whether the bilateral relations of

Turkey and China will go beyond strategic cooperation to develop into a comprehensive strategic partnership. While there are some positive developments in the strategic partnership framework, there are also some problematic issues that hinder an upgrading of the relationship into a comprehensive strategic partnership.

The issue of the Uyghur, the Muslim-Turkic ethnic minority in the Xinjiang Uyghur Autonomous Region of China, continues to be the most crucial obstacle to the relations of Turkey and China. Although some progress has been made toward a mutual understanding that would address both governments' concerns, it still has the potential to negatively affect China–Turkey relations, particularly in times of crisis in Xinjiang.[131]

The suspicions of debt-trap diplomacy regarding the BRI have the potential to affect China–Turkey cooperation. Ankara cited debt-trap diplomacy and the Uyghur issue as reasons not to attend the second BRI summit, having attended the first.[132] Turkey remains dissatisfied with the current level of economic engagement with China, as it has a significant trade deficit with China. According to China Customs Statistics (export-import) 2019, while the PRC's export value to Turkey is $17.3 billion, Beijing's import value from Ankara is just $3.4 billion.[133]

Despite the common will to integrate the Middle Corridor into the BRI framework, it is difficult to say that there is a road map for implementing the program. Turkey is demanding more Chinese investments in its transportation, energy, and mining infrastructure and the flow of Chinese financial assets to Turkey without offering lucrative tenders to Beijing. Meanwhile, China has not made its BRI vision clear to Ankara. Turkey's NATO membership and economic integration with the EU has made Beijing hesitant about establishing close relationships. China's bitter experiences with the Sinop nuclear power plant tender in 2013,[134] and the canceled $3.4 billion tenders to develop an air defense system in 2015, have also fed Beijing's hesitation to become involved in strategic projects in Turkey.[135]

Moreover, it seems that trends in global and regional politics such as the U.S.–Beijing trade war, the strained U.S.–Russia relationship, re-imposition of U.S. secondary sanctions on Iran, and the ongoing process to reach a final peace settlement in the Syria civil war, have made the prospect of further Sino–Turkish cooperation in general even more unclear. In the absence of concrete offers by Turkey for projects for Silk Road cooperation, China appears prepared to pursue a wait-and-see policy to avoid the political uncertainties associated with any Turkey-related initiative.[136] Hence, China–Turkey's bilateral relations have not yet developed into a comprehensive strategic partnership, and there are strong reasons to believe that it is unlikely that they will.

2 | Egypt

Egypt has had longstanding relations with China, ever since Cairo was the first Arab and African country to recognize the People's Republic of China (PRC). Full diplomatic relations were established in May 1956. In recent years, the two countries have also elevated their relationship to a comprehensive strategic partnership, providing the political underpinnings for what is now a growing new commercial relationship between the two countries. This chapter examines what lies behind the China–Egypt comprehensive strategic partnership and the synergy between the Belt and Road Initiative (BRI) and Egypt's Vision 2030 and Suez Canal Corridor Development Project (SCCDP) to understand the extent of economic engagement and bilateral relationship between the two nations. Cairo can play a particularly important role in the development of the Maritime Silk Road, with the Suez Canal functioning as the main transit point between the Indian Ocean and the Mediterranean Sea. That makes Egypt one of the few indispensable partners in the Middle East for the realization of the Belt and Road Project.

Chinese–Egyptian relations are one of the most important bilateral relations axes in the Middle East and North Africa region (MENA).[1] In recent years, China developed a comprehensive strategic partnership with Egypt, one of the most important regional powers, which aims to promote Beijing's aspirations to strengthen its influence and power in the Middle East, expand its commercial activity, and reinforce its strategic standing at the expense of the United States. The two countries are complementary in terms of natural resources, geographic location, industrial structures, and industrialization. As Chinese President Xi Jinping said during his state visit to Egypt, "China always treats and promotes its relationship with Egypt from a strategic and long-term perspective."[2]

The one trillion dollar BRI, put forward in October 2013 by Chinese President Xi Jinping, seeks to connect Beijing to the global market by linking Asia and Europe via a set of land and maritime trade routes. The concept took shape over several years and has now become a cornerstone of the PRC's diplomatic strategy and foreign policy. The BRI is structured in two different dimensions: The Silk Road Economic Belt (SREB) and the 21st Century Maritime Silk Road Initiative (MSRI), which are intended to link China to Europe via land (SREB) and sea (MSRI).

In the past six years, Egypt has emerged as a crucial component of the MSRI due to its unique geographical strategic position as the main transit point between the Indian Ocean and the Mediterranean Sea, serving the PRC's foreign trade, 90 percent of which is carried out through maritime routes.[3] Egypt also has many valuable features: a unique geographic location which makes it the meeting point of the Arab World, Africa, Asia, and Europe through the Mediterranean Sea and the Red Sea; and a unique civilization and culture, with a longstanding history and interaction throughout millennia with the ancient empires. Egypt is also considered a converging point of Islam and Christianity, boasting a relatively stable political and social order, and a full-fledged economic system. All these features help Egypt to have a global outreach, and contribute excellent value to the PRC's BRI, thus enabling Egypt to play a vital role in the world with China as a strategic partner.[4]

Commercially the MSRI is, above all, about aligning the connectivity of global shipping lanes and ports with Chinese capital. Thus, Egypt has emerged as a crucial component of China's MSRI projects due to the Suez Canal's geographically strategic location and its disproportionate influence in the Middle East and Africa affairs.[5] Egypt has the opportunity to serve as the 'hub' for the BRI as a portal for Africa, the Arab world (the Sunni axis), and the Middle East. Indeed, Egypt might wind up becoming the PRC's 'gateway to Europe,' and the Chinese have already designated it as one of the top five countries for mergers and acquisitions potential over the next five years.[6] As the Chinese Ambassador to Egypt, Song Aiguo, said, "Egypt is a very important country in the Chinese One Belt-One Road Initiative."[7]

Moreover, Egypt is a major regional power and a key ally of Washington, which holds a major role in achieving broader U.S. aims in the Middle East.[8] China considers Egypt a pivotal state in five circles: Arab states, African states, Islamic states, Mediterranean states, and developing states. Hence, this study examines the motivation behind China's measures to formalize a comprehensive strategic partnership with Egypt, and the synergy between the BRI and Egypt's Vision 2030 and SCCDP, to understand the extent of economic engagement and bilateral relationship between the two nations.

The chapter's main argument is that Beijing's measures to formalize a comprehensive strategic partnership framework with Cairo are based on shared or mutual complementary economic and political interests, especially to integrate Egypt's Vision 2030 and SCCDP within the BRI framework. Both sides are committed to linking the new Silk Road initiative and Egypt Vision 2030 together effectively and to seek out opportunities for developing new ways of win-win cooperation.

Egypt Vision 2030

Egypt's Vision 2030 represents a foothold on the way towards inclusive development. The Vision addresses the important and pressing issues facing Egypt today, such as corruption, poverty, environmental degradation, and the inadequacy of infrastructure in cities and regions. The program aims to place Egypt among the top 30 countries in the world by 2030 in terms of economic size (based on GDP), market competitiveness, human development, quality of life, and anti-corruption. As a whole, it starts from the three aspects of the economy, society, and environment, and seeks to achieve the following goals in each major area. Regarding economic development, Egypt will have become a market economy with a steady macro-economy by 2030; it can achieve sustainable growth, cope with the competition, diversity, and knowledge-based economy, and play an effective role in the world economy. It will have the ability to deal with changes in the world, increase the added value, provide job opportunities, and make real per capita GDP reach the level of medium and high-income countries.[9]

Concerning social development, the goal of Egypt by 2030 is to build a fair society with equal economic, social, and political rights, maximize social integration, motivate the driving force of social development, provide protection mechanisms for coping with life risks, and provide support and protection for marginalized communities and vulnerable groups. Concerning environmental development, by 2030, Egypt will have ensured environmental safety and will be supporting the rational use and investment of natural resources to ensure the rights and interests of the next generation; Egypt will be committed to the diversification of economic production, support competition, provide new job opportunities, eliminate poverty and realize social justice so that it can provide Egyptians with a clean, healthy, and safe living environment.[10]

Egypt and the Belt and Road Initiative

The PRC's comprehensive strategic partnership with Egypt includes seven areas for cooperation within the BRI. These areas are policy coordination, connectivity, trade and investments, energy cooperation, financial integration, military ties, and people-to-people bonds. However, each country views the BRI framework and reacts to it according to its perspective and the consequences for its national interests and international status. Therefore, there are very different attitudes between the two countries regarding how to realize the vision.[11]

Policy coordination

The PRC's comprehensive strategic partnership with Cairo is the highest level in Beijing's hierarchy of diplomatic relations, which aims at promoting political cooperation between the two countries, creating mechanisms for dialogue and consensus-building on global and regional issues, developing shared interests, deepening political trust, and reaching a new consensus on cooperation. These are all very important for integrating Egypt's Vision 2030 and SCCDP into the BRI framework.[12]

China attaches great importance to high-level exchanges and policy communication with the Egyptian government, and the two sides have maintained a close and cooperative relationship. The political and economic relations between China and Egypt have strengthened following six presidential visits between the two countries in recent years. President Abdel Fattah el-Sisi visited China five times in the past four years, while Chinese President Xi Jinping paid a historic visit to Egypt in early 2016. Both countries promoted their relations to the level of 'strategic partnership' in 1999 and more recently promoted the relations furthermore to a 'Comprehensive Strategic Partnership.'[13]

This happened during the first state visit of President of Egypt, Abdel Fattah el-Sisi to China in December 2014. This was a historic and significant visit, where he signed with Chinese President Xi Jinping, the Joint Declaration of promoting relations to the level of "Comprehensive Strategic Partnership", which includes cooperation in all fields, politically, economically, militarily, culturally, technologically, and in the international arena. During the visit, a large number of agreements and Memorandums of Understanding (MoUs) were signed, especially in the field of electricity, transport, and space technology, in addition to other fields, and both sides initiated a new mechanism, which has worked very efficiently to assign projects and follow their implementation.[14] The second visit of President of Egypt Abdel Fattah el-Sisi to China took place in September 2015 to attend celebrations marking the 70th anniversary of World War II V-Day, thereby consolidating the joint efforts of promoting relations and adding new elements to the ties between the two comprehensive strategic partners.[15]

In January 2016, the first official visit of President Xi Jinping to Egypt began a new chapter in the two countries' relations and opened a brand-new page in their foreign affairs. The historic visit by a Chinese leader to Egypt was a turning point and demonstrated the potential in the proposed commercial initiatives, as well as a blossoming in the economic ties between the two countries. Both leaders witnessed the signing of 21 agreements, MoUs, and contracts in many fields.[16] During the visit, Chinese President Xi also delivered a speech at the headquarters of the Arab League in Cairo, addressing the largest Arab nation, where he stressed the importance of relations between the two nations and expressed the PRC's support for the rightful causes of the Arab people, and foremost, the Palestinian question.[17]

The third visit of President Abdel Fattah el-Sisi to China was held at the invitation of the Chinese President to participate in the G20 Summit in September 2016, held at Hangzhou. Egypt was invited as the Summit's guest of honor since the G20 Summit host country usually invites one of the neighboring countries as a guest of honor. The fourth visit of Egyptian President el-Sisi to China was held when el-Sisi took part in the dialogue between emerging market economies and developing countries held in September 2017 in parallel with the BRICS Summit; Egypt was the only Arab country to participate in the Summit.[18]

In September 2018, Egyptian President Abdel-Fattah el-Sisi visited China for the Beijing Summit of the Forum on China–Africa Cooperation (FOCAC), his fifth visit to the country. Ahead of the FOCAC meetings, the Egyptian leader held talks with the Chinese President, and they agreed to jointly advance the China–Egypt comprehensive strategic partnership in the new era. Xi pointed out that China regarded Egypt as an important and long-term cooperative partner in the co-building of the Belt and Road Initiative, and was willing to closely synergize the Belt and Road Initiative and the development strategies of Egypt Vision 2030 and the SCCDP, thus promoting pragmatic cooperation between the two countries and strengthening their cooperation on counter-terrorism and security matters.

For his part, President Sisi said that Egypt placed a priority on the comprehensive strategic partnership with the PRC. As one of the earliest countries that supported the BRI, Egypt firmly believed that the initiative would create enormous opportunities for their bilateral cooperation as well as international and regional cooperation. As the incoming holder of the African Union rotating presidency, Egypt pledged to continue to promote cooperation between Africa and China.[19]

High-level exchanges between China and Egypt have been frequent, and mutual political trust has been further enhanced, as Chinese and Egyptian high-ranking diplomats have pointed out on several occasions. In September 2018, Chinese Premier Li Keqiang met Egyptian President el-Sisi ahead of the 2018 Beijing Summit of the FOCAC. According to the Chinese Premier, Beijing is willing to encourage its enterprises to invest in Egypt and to engage in cooperation in industrial capacity and processing trade via the Suez Canal industrial park for broader markets and mutual benefit. The Egyptian President welcomed the increase of investment by Chinese enterprises in Egypt, calling for efforts to make good use of Egypt's advantages in geographical location and the Suez Canal industrial park to jointly explore European, the Middle East, and African markets.[20]

In April 2017, Sun Chunlan, head of the United Front Work Department of the Communist Party of China (CPC) Central Committee, said, "China attaches great importance to developing friendly relations with Egypt and regards Egypt as an important partner in promoting the Belt and Road Initiative."[21] According to Egypt's former ambassador to Beijing, Mahmoud Allam, Egypt–China relations witnessed "strong momentum in building a strategic partnership". The exchange of visits between officials of the two countries during 2018 demonstrated the keenness of the political leadership in Egypt and China to communicate at all levels and discuss issues of common concern.[22]

In March 2019, the Egyptian Planning Minister, Hala al-Saeed, said in the conference held by the SCZone and the Organization for Economic Cooperation and Development, "Egypt's Suez Canal Economic Zone (SCZone) in function is fully integrated with China's BRI to reinforce the international trade movement." The SCZone is planned as an international logistics center, described by the minister as one of the most significant development projects in Egypt and the world.[23]

Chinese investments in MSRI projects depend on policy coordination, extensive financing capabilities, and institutions and economic forums that stand behind it, and Egypt could benefit by getting support and loans for carrying out developmental projects with better and easier conditions than through Western financial institutions. Thus, Egypt has made a point of joining the PRC's pet multilateral projects, from the Asian Infrastructure Investment Bank (AIIB), as a founding member, a critical mechanism for funding BRI and other projects, to participation in the Conference on Interaction and Confidence Building in Asia (CICA).[24]

Egypt has been an active player in the FOCAC, as well as the China–Arab States Expo.[25] The country is also an official member of the Silk Road Economic Belt Trade Union, which encompasses 92 Chinese and foreign associations.[26] In addition to enjoying guest-of-honor status at the G20 Summit in September 2016,[27] in September 2017, Egypt participated as a guest in the BRICS Summit hosted by China in Xiamen, Fujian province.[28] Egypt was also the guest of honor at the China–2017 Arab States Expo held in Ningxia, China.[29]

Connectivity

The facilitation of connectivity is one of the crucial ways to integrate Egypt's Vision 2030 and SCCDP into the BRI framework, utilizing Egypt's unique geographical strategic position and its Suez Canal vital waterway. Egypt must optimize its infrastructural connections and also adapt its technical systems to those of the other countries in the BRI framework. This would lead Beijing and Cairo to jointly develop international transport routes and create an infrastructural network that could gradually connect all the regions in Asia and also specific points in Asia, Africa, and Europe.[30]

The MSRI, the most ambitious Chinese integration project to date, is a massive scheme to connect wide swathes of East, Southeast, South, and West Asia through the building of enormous amounts of hard infrastructures, such as high-speed railways, highways and truck roads, air and seaports, utility stations and power grids, oil and Liquefied Natural Gas (LNG) pipelines and telecommunication networks. The MSRI will also entail the construction of large industrial parks and special economic zones (SEZs) coupled with manufacturing plants within these areas.[31] The MSRI is especially concerned with building and managing ports on its intended route. The Mediterranean Sea is the final stop and target of a consistent part of Chinese investments for the new Silk Road. The MSRI is paving the road for China's 'blue' (maritime) economy and could represent an important factor in developing a new form of political and economic dynamics among Mediterranean countries, especially in the Eastern Mediterranean. Turkey, Egypt, and Israel are all involved in BRI projects with different types of investments and different quantities.[32]

The MSRI is also designed to secure China's maritime energy supply chain across the Indian Ocean region and the South China Sea. The majority of Beijing's seaborne energy imports pass through these regions; thus, China attaches great importance to the security of the sea lanes of communication (SLOCs) and ensuring unimpeded access in these two areas.[33] Beijing's dependence on the import of foreign oil and gas is crucial for its energy security and continued economic growth. Thus it prioritizes securing reliable transport routes and diversifying transport routes to procure oil and LNG from the energy-rich Central Asia/Middle East through the construction of the land- and sea-based Silk Road.[34]

Accordingly, Beijing has vigorously pursued close diplomatic and economic interactions with numerous participating Middle East countries that view MSRI projects as a way to boost new partnerships and avenues for trade. Consequently, China and Middle East countries are constantly on the lookout for cooperative ventures to promote the realization of the MSRI projects and to create new economic opportunities and incentives for foreign investment.[35]

The MSRI places the Suez Canal as one of the key axes of facilitating connectivity, making Egypt an important strategic and economic center for the Arab region and the world at large, a trade hub between Beijing and the rest of the world; it serves Egypt's interests by increasing traffic revenues from the Suez Canal. The role of the Suez Canal is pivotal as it facilitates the trade movement between China to various countries across the world.[36] The Suez Canal is approximately 120 miles long and connects the Red Sea and the Gulf of Suez with the Mediterranean Sea. Cairo plays a vital role in international energy markets through its operation of the Suez Canal and the Suez–Mediterranean (SUMED) Pipeline. The Suez Canal is an important transit route for oil and liquefied LNG shipments traveling northbound from the Persian Gulf to Europe and North America and for shipments traveling southbound from North Africa and from countries along the Mediterranean Sea to Asia.[37]

Thus, the Suez Canal is attracting most of China's investments in Egypt through the renovation of the canal's many ports, such as Ismailia and Port Said. From the PRC's perspective, there was never any question over whether or not to include Egypt. It would be almost impossible to bypass the Suez Canal in the network of overland and maritime routes connecting China with the world, and Egypt lies at the intersection of many of the regions – the Middle East, Europe, and Africa – covered by the initiative. The decision to build a new Suez Canal and to develop the area to the west of the canal as both a service and logistics hub and a new manufacturing zone added to Egypt's relative advantages.[38]

Egypt is viewed as a central pillar of the Arab world, a regional heavyweight in the Middle East and North Africa (MENA), and a key plank of the Maritime Silk Road, thanks to its control of the Suez Canal. China and Egypt are promoting the MSRI as well as the Suez Canal economic corridor initiatives because the harbors at both ends of the Suez Canal have a great influence over the Middle East, Africa, and the entire planet in terms of geopolitics and global trade.[39] Egypt is also increasingly important for promoting the MSRI, since the Suez Canal with its Mediterranean Port Said, and its southern terminus at Port Tewfiq, serves China's foreign maritime trade with Europe.[40]

Ports

China's state-owned shipping companies have invested heavily in ports along the Suez Canal Corridor, from the Gulf of Suez to Port Said. The first significant Chinese investment in Egypt's port infrastructure was made in 2005 by Hutchison Port Holdings, which acquired a 50 percent share in a joint venture with Alexandria Port Authority to construct, operate, and manage two container terminals in the ports of Alexandria and El Dekheila on Egypt's northern Mediterranean coast.[41]

The Suez Canal Container Terminal (SCCT) in Port Said is the biggest transshipment terminal in this part of the Mediterranean. Here, COSCO invested $185.6 million in a joint venture to operate and manage the SCCT at Port Said's East Port, located in the western Sinai Peninsula at the northern end of the Canal.[42] The Chinese Harbor State Company (CHEC), a subsidiary of state-owned China Communications Construction Company, invested $219 million to construct a twelve-hundred-meter quay in Port Said's East Port and al-Arabiya port at the Suez Canal's southern end.[43]

In August 2018, CHEC started the main phase of the construction of a new terminal basin in Sokhna Port south of the Suez Canal northeast of Egypt. Sokhna Port is located within the SCZone, a main economic region in Egypt whose development is one of the country's mega projects to attract foreign investment for further economic growth. Dozens of Egyptian and Chinese workers, as well as scores of trucks, have been mobilized to start the new phase of the 'Basin 2' project that was expected to be completed by the last quarter of 2019.[44]

Economic and industrial zones

Beijing is also the largest foreign investor in two of Egypt's megaprojects: the first, the Suez Canal Corridor Project (SCCP), announced by Egypt in 2014 to build the area along the 190-kilometer canal into an international economic hub, integrating harbor, logistics, trade zones, and industrial parks.[45] China's MSRI can be well bonded with the SCCP, as well as with its second megaproject, the Suez Canal Economic Zone (SCZone), a world-class free zone and trade hub along the banks of the newly-expanded Suez Canal. Four hundred sixty-one square kilometers and four maritime ports and two development areas strategically located along one of the world's most traveled trading routes turn it into an international commercial hub (more than 13 percent of global trade passes through every year).[46]

Eighty-six Chinese companies have already invested over $1.1 billion there.[47] For instance, China's TEDA Corporation, one of the oldest industrial developers in the SCZone, has been developing an area of over 7.23 square km in Ain Sokhna district of Suez province, east of the Egyptian capital Cairo. It has completed its first phase, attracting some 68 enterprises, including Jushi, a fiberglass giant from China. The second phase in the industrial zone started in 2016.[48]

The Chinese Ambassador to Egypt, Song Aiguo, said Chinese companies are interested in building public facilities and industrial parks in the SCZone project, and the investments of Chinese companies in Egypt reached a total of $6.8 billion, most registered in the last five years.[49] In March 2017, China agreed to contribute $64 million to the Egyptian Earth Observation Satellite Program (EgyptSat), as part of a $7 billion Chinese grant to develop infrastructure along the SCZone connecting to Beijing's BRI. Beijing also provided a $23 million grant for an Egyptian satellite test, integration, and assembly facility.[50] In August 2018, Egypt and China signed mutual letters for the implementation of a satellite named EgyptSat-A. The Chinese grant hits $45 million for the remote-sensing Earth observation satellite built by the Russian RSC Energia.[51]

In May 2017, the Egyptian Minister of Investment and International Cooperation, Sahar Nasr, met with Jin Qi, chair of the Silk Road Fund, the largest investment fund in China with a capital of $40 billion to present the SCZone and several government priority transportation projects. The two sides also agreed to collaborate to finance infrastructure and construction projects through Chinese investments in entrepreneur incubators and training for young people in emerging projects.[52]

The *Daily News Egypt*, citing a senior Chinese official, reported that the Chinese government is set to pump in some $40 billion into big development projects in Egypt as part of its ambitious BRI through the Silk Road Fund.[53] In May 2017, at the Belt and Road Forum for International Cooperation (BRF) in Beijing, the two countries signed six MoUs. The agreements include investments by the China Development Bank and Export-Import Bank of China for a power transmission line in Egypt, a project to develop the El Sukhna Port, and a $500 million loan from the China Development Bank.[54]

In April 2018, the Government of Tianjin signed an MoU with the General Authority of the Economic Zone of the Suez Canal to develop the second phase of the Tianjin Economic-Technological Development Area (TEDA) industrial zone. According to the MoU, an area of six square kilometers will be developed to establish advanced industrial sectors within the geographical scope of the canal's economic zone. The company will immediately start to attract the target companies in the fields of textile, petrochemicals, and plastic industries, with a total of $5 billion, which will contribute to providing jobs and increase investment.[55]

While Egypt stands to benefit greatly from its involvement in MSRI, China is aware that once the Suez Canal is upgraded and under Chinese oversight, it will have considerable control, power, and potential to shape security and commercial dynamics in the region. Essentially, through MSRI, China aims to increase its global and regional influence by building new trade networks that facilitate connectivity and create investment opportunities that are anticipated to alter the global balance of economic power in the long term.[56]

Trade and investments

The PRC's comprehensive strategic partnership with Cairo is aimed at mitigating as much as possible the barriers to free trade, investment, industrial cooperation, and technical and engineering services to facilitate the integration of Egypt's Vision 2030 and SCCDP within the BRI framework. Both countries must take a series of additional measures – such as expanding free-trade zones, improving trade structures, seek new potential areas for trade to improve the trade balance, devise new initiatives for the promotion of conventional forms of trade.[57]

The economic relations between the two countries have witnessed steady development in terms of mutual trade and investment, which have expanded substantially in recent years in the light of the comprehensive strategic partnership and the BRI. The bilateral trade between China and Egypt has also seen significant growth in recent years. According to China Customs Statistics (export-import), China–Egypt trade volume has increased to $13.2 billion by 2019.[58]

According to the *China Global Investment Tracker*, Beijing's investments and construction in Egypt from 2013 to 2018 reached $19.9 billion. Most of the Chinese investments are in the energy sector ($10.4 billion) while the rest was invested in Egyptian transport, agriculture, logistics, and other sectors.[59] The number of Chinese companies operating in Egypt increased from 30 in 2014 to more than 1,459 Chinese companies now operating in various sectors, notably industry, information technology, and economic zones.[60]

Urban construction

In March 2015, the Egyptian government announced plans to build a new administrative capital adjacent to Cairo, in a massive new project whose first phase would cost $45 billion and take up to seven years to complete,[61] to be largely funded by Chinese state-owned developers. The new city, known for now as the New Administrative Capital, is eventually expected to cover about 700 square kilometers. The first phase, covering about 168 square km, will have ministries, residential neighborhoods, a diplomatic quarter, and a financial district. A large mosque and cathedral, as well as a hotel and conference center, have already been built. In early 2016, China Fortune Land Development Company (CFLD) and fellow state company China State Construction Engineering Corporation (CSCEC) signed preliminary agreements with Egyptian authorities to develop parts of the new capital city. CFLD retained its contract to provide $20 billion to build an upmarket residential district, an industrial zone, schools, a university, and recreational centers in the new capital, along with supporting infrastructure.[62]

According to a statement issued by the Egyptian investment and housing ministries, the final agreement could be reached by year-end, with construction beginning the following month.[63] However, the talks between Egypt and CFLD for a $20 billion development in the new administrative capital have fallen through over disagreements on how to share revenue from the project.[64] In September 2015, CSCEC signed an MoU to build the new parliament, twelve ministerial buildings, a national convention center, and an exhibition complex. However, in February 2017, it withdrew over a disagreement concerning contract terms.[65]

In June 2015, Egypt and China signed a framework agreement for the implementation of 15 projects worth $10 billion, to be funded by Chinese banks and built at least in part by Chinese companies. The projects aim to boost bilateral industrial and investment relations in electricity, petroleum, natural gas, railways, highways, ports, mining, construction materials, chemical and optical industries, textile, electrical appliances, and other fields. The projects include the establishment of three power plants, railways linking east Cairo with Tenth of Ramadan City (a new urban, highly industrialized community, part of Greater Cairo), a multi-purpose station in Alexandria port, and trains, glass and leather factories, as well as developing Alexandria-Abu Qir railways.[66] During President Xi's historic 2016 state visit to Egypt, the two countries signed 21 bilateral deals totaling $10 billion to strengthen cooperation in the fields of economic cooperation, funding electricity, energy projects, trade, civil aviation, science, technology, communications, and aerospace. The deals include a $2.7 billion package to build Egypt's new administrative capital, a $1 billion loan, and bilateral cooperation in infrastructure through the AIIB. The two countries are also planning together 15 projects in electricity, infrastructure, and transport with investments that could total $15 billion.[67]

Chinese companies view Egypt as a potentially profitable business environment and participate in various major projects industries such as electricity, petroleum, LNG, nuclear energy, railways, highways, and more, at a cost estimated at millions of dollars.[68] Moreover, according to Secretary-General of the Union of Arab Banks, Wessam Fattoh, in 2018 Chinese investments in Egypt reached $15 billion, and Chinese companies will invest $5 billion in Egypt's Suez Canal economic zone.[69]

In March 2018, the Egyptian government signed an MoU with China State Construction Engineering Co. on designing and constructing three closed gymnasiums in Sharm al-Sheikh, Hurghada and Luxor in preparation for hosting the 2021 World Men's Handball Championship. In May 2018, Egypt's New Urban Communities Authority (NUCA) signed an MoU with Chinese construction company CGCOC Group to establish the first industrial zone in the city of New Alamein. In September 2018, the Chairman of Egypt's Arab Organization for Industrialization (AOI), Abdel Moneim al-Taras, announced that he agreed with Chairman of China Railway 20 Bureau Group Corporation (CR20G) Deng Yong to establish an industrial facility to manufacture monorails and express trains.[70]

Transportation and railroads

Transportation is another area showing increased Chinese involvement. According to the Head of the Egyptian Transport Association (ETA), Mohammed Shehata, Beijing can be the main player in rebuilding the railway infrastructure and developing Egypt's railway system, since China is preferred over European countries, offering both expertise and finance for development projects, usually at a lower cost. China's participation in rebuilding Egypt's railway infrastructure will help boost links to Africa and Asia.[71] In terms of concrete endeavors, in April 2014 an MoU and a preliminary agreement were signed between Aviation Industry Corporation of China (AICC) and Egypt's Ministry of Transportation, to develop an 80 km electric railway from El-Salam City to Belbeis and Sharqeya in Greater Cairo. The Chinese company will finance the cost of this project through loan repayments due over 20 years, which is estimated at $800 million, and the railway will take three years to complete.[72]

In December 2014, the Egyptian government signed an initial agreement with CHEC to construct a high-speed train project line covering the 900-kilometer distance between Egypt's Mediterranean city of Alexandria and Aswan, close to the border with Sudan. The project will cost $10 billion, and the train's speed will reach 350 kilometers/hour, covering the distance between the two cities in 3 to 4 hours. Egypt will provide local materials, executive oversight, and 20 percent of the labor, which means that the majority of workers directly employed will be Chinese. Nevertheless, the parties have not yet reached an agreement.[73]

In January 2016, Egypt signed an MoU with China Railway Construction Corporation (CRCC) to construct Cairo's sixth metro line, a 30 km metro line from New Maadi in southern Cairo to Al-Khosous in Al Qalyubia. The line will have 24 stations and carry some 1.5 million passengers daily. This project will cost $3.5 billion, the financing of which remains under negotiation between the two parties.[74]

In July 2017, the Chinese company and Egypt's Ministry of Transportation reached an agreement on building the electric train project linking Salam City and the New Administrative Capital with an investment of $1.2 billion. The project's cost will be funded by $700 million from Exim Bank of China and $500 million from Egypt's state budget.[75] Egypt also signed an MoU with Bombardier to develop a plan for the new Cairo Metro Line 6, a project that could cost up to $4 billion.[76] This non-binding agreement may indicate difficulties in the negotiations with the CRCC or an attempt to pressure it for a better deal. In August 2017, the Egyptian Minister of Investment and International Cooperation signed an MoU with the China Exim Bank to finance national development projects and national investments over the next three years, in sectors including electricity, transportation, and ports.[77]

In May 2017, a contract for the modern agricultural greenhouse joint project, worth $400 million, was signed between China and Egypt to mark a new stage of agricultural cooperation between the two sides and a milestone in the development of Egypt's modern agriculture. According to China SINOMACH Heavy Industry Corporation (SINOMACH-HI), over the past two years, the company has been constructing 600 greenhouses that gradually turned 1,000 hectares of desert land into a green world of fresh fruits and vegetables in the Tenth of Ramadan City, some 65 kilometers northeast of Cairo.[78]

Until mid-2018, Chinese investments in Egypt totaled approximately $700 million, with more than 80 percent of these made in the last four years. According to data compiled by *fDi Intelligence*, a division of London's Financial Times, cumulative Chinese foreign direct investment in Egypt totaled $24.3bilion. This figure was skewed by a $20 billion investment announced but not yet realized by Shanghai-listed China Fortune Land Development in the planned new administrative capital in the desert east of Cairo. Moreover, CSCEC has been contracted to build 20 towers in the new city, including what is billed as the tallest tower in Africa. Chinese banks are expected to finance some 85 percent of $13 billion in costs cited in reports mentioning CSCEC. A Chinese company has also signed an MoU with the Egyptian government to build a rail link to the capital.[79]

Notwithstanding the investments outlined above, Beijing is heavily dependent on Egypt, which controls the Suez Canal, for its trade with the European continent. In 2018, the EU was China's second trading partner after the U.S. In terms of EU exports, China was the second-largest export partner, while in terms of EU imports China was the first largest export partner, accounting for around 15.4 percent of

Beijing's overall trade in goods (on average, about 1.5 billion per day).[80] China–EU trade in 2018 amounted to 605 billion euros. During this time, EU exports to China were 210 billion, and EU imports from China were 395 billion, with the EU's trade deficit with China standing at 185 billion.[81]

As seaborne trade constitutes the bulk of trade for both China and the EU, most of this trade has to pass through the Suez Canal, making the passage a strategic and central location for China's economy and the success of the Belt and Road Initiative framework. Any disruption in the navigation through Egypt waters would have a significant negative impact on China's implementation of the BRI, making China's stake in Egypt all the greater.

To be sure, China and Egypt are complementary in terms of natural resources, industrial structures, and industrialization, creating great potential for economic partnership. With both sides seeing clear benefits in expanding the relationship, China and Egypt are set to draw even closer together over the coming years. That increased cooperation and investment between the two countries is evident politically as well, but economic interests are the primary considerations in the burgeoning comprehensive strategic partnership.

Energy cooperation

As part of China's comprehensive strategic partnership with Cairo, investment in energy infrastructure is considered one of the critical cooperation areas to integrate Egypt's Vision 2030 and SCCDP into the BRI framework. Unlike China's other Middle Eastern partners, ties with Egypt are not motivated by oil imports, but by a more geographic calculation: the Suez Canal has long been China's primary shipping route for sending goods to Europe, China's largest market. Nevertheless, according to the *China Global Investment Tracker*, Beijing's investments in Egypt's energy sector from 2013 to 2018 reached $10.4 billion.[82]

The U.S. Energy Information Administration (EIA) defines world oil chokepoints as narrow channels along widely used global sea routes, some so narrow that restrictions are placed on the size of the vessel that can navigate through them. Chokepoints are a critical part of global energy security because of the high volume of petroleum and other liquids transported through their narrow straits.[83] The Suez Canal and the SuezMediterranean Pipeline (SUMED Pipeline) are strategic routes for Persian Gulf crude oil, petroleum products, and LNG shipments to Europe and North America. Located in Egypt, the Suez Canal connects the Red Sea with the Mediterranean Sea, and it is a critical chokepoint because of the large volumes of energy commodities that flow through it. The total oil flows through the Suez Canal, and the SUMED pipeline, accounted for about 9 percent of total seaborne traded petroleum (crude oil and refined petroleum products) in 2017; LNG flows through the Suez Canal and the SUMED pipeline accounted for about 8 percent of global LNG trade.[84]

The 200-mile long SUMED Pipeline transports crude oil through Egypt from the Red Sea to the Mediterranean Sea. The crude oil flows through two parallel pipelines that are 42 inches in diameter, with a total pipeline capacity of 2.34 million b/d. Oil flows north, starting at the Ain Sukhna terminal along the Red Sea coast to its endpoint at the Sidi Kerir terminal on the Mediterranean Sea. The SUMED Pipeline is the only alternate route to transport crude oil from the Red Sea to the Mediterranean Sea if ships cannot navigate through the Suez Canal. The closure of the Suez Canal and the SUMED Pipeline would require oil tankers to divert around the southern tip of Africa, the Cape of Good Hope, which would add approximately 2,700 miles to the transit, increase transit time, and increase the costs and shipping time.[85]

In August 2013, Sinopec agreed to pay $3.1 billion to buy a 33 percent stake in the Egyptian oil and gas business of U.S. firm Apache Corporation.[86] In 2015, the Egyptian Ministry of Petroleum with Star Oil & Gas (SOG) of China established an International Drilling Materials Manufacturing Company, which invested $30 million out of the planned investment of $250 million to establish a seamless pipe rolling mill to supply the entire MENA market, a joint venture that indicates its plan to use Egypt to branch into other markets in the region.[87]

In September 2018, CSCEC announced the construction of a $6.1 billion oil refining and petrochemical complex. The oil refinery and petrochemical plant, the larger of the two projects, are to be located in the Suez Canal Economic Zone, near the canal that symbolically divides Asia and Africa, two of the primary focuses for Belt and Road projects. The new Egyptian refining complex will have an annual capacity for 8 million tons of oil, and the facility is likely to mostly serve the Egyptian domestic market; imports currently supply about a third of the country's demand.[88]

Egypt is the third-largest dry LNG producer on the continent and the largest non-OPEC oil producer in Africa. As we know, the Suez Canal and Suez-Mediterranean Pipeline (SUMED) are strategic high-security global transit routes for oil shipped to Europe and the United States. Egypt's oil consumption outpaces oil production, and a core challenge remains to satisfy increasing local oil demand amid falling production. Estimates of Egypt's crude oil reserves declined from 4.5 billion barrels in 2010 to about 3.5 billion barrels in 2016 as a result of maturing oil fields and a lack of discoveries. Egypt's large-scale exploration activities have resulted in LNG findings rather than oil.

In 2015 an Italian company discovered the Zohr gas field that is considered one of the largest gas fields in the Mediterranean. The estimated area of the field is 100 square kilometers, and total gas estimates are 850 billion cubic meters, which could double Egypt's reserves of gas. Production of gas has been growing since Zohr started operations in 2017 with a total capacity of 350 million cubic feet daily. Zohr will increase LNG production to 2700 million cubic feet per day by the end of 2019.[89] The natural resources discovered in the Zohr offshore gas field are increasing Chinese opportunities to develop further energy partnerships in building offshore facilities within the MSRI platform and granting new chances for China in the energy sector.[90]

Energy cooperation also takes place between the two countries in the field of nuclear energy. In May 2015, the China National Nuclear Corporation (CNNC) and the Egyptian Nuclear Power Plant Authority (NPPA) signed an MoU for nuclear energy cooperation that could open a second overseas market for Chinese nuclear power technology.[91] The signing of the MoU marks a new phase in work to develop nuclear energy in Egypt and highlights the fact that China has become one of Egypt's official partners in its nuclear power projects. It appears that Egypt is promoting nuclear cooperation with Russia, too, with a plan to build a nuclear power plant at El-Dabaa.[92]

The two countries are also cooperating in the field of the electricity sector. China's investments in the Egyptian electricity sector are increasing continuously. Egypt and China are cooperating on a series of projects in production, distribution, transportation, and services of electricity. In September 2017, the two countries signed an investment agreement for a $1 billion project to boost the capacity of the local electricity grid as a part of the second phase of Egypt's electricity grid project.[93]

In September 2018, the two countries signed two deals that include the construction of a power plant in the Hamrawein region at the Red Sea coast. The plant will be built by China's Shanghai Electric and Dongfang Electric Cooperation and Egypt's Hassan Allam Construction, with investments worth $4.4 billion. The plant, the largest of its kind in the Middle East region, with a production capacity of 6,000 megawatts, will be constructed in six years. The other deal is to build a 600-meter-high pumping and storage station, which will rank fourth worldwide, in the Suez Canal Mountain of Ataka. Chinese Sinohydro Company will build the station in six years. It will have a production capacity of 2,400 megawatts with eight units and cost $2.6 billion.[94]

Additionally, Chinese companies seem set to have a presence in Egypt's solar energy market. In 2015, a Chinese solar energy company and photovoltaic (Yingli Solar), one of the world's largest solar panel manufacturers, signed an MoU with Egypt's Ministry of Electricity and Energy for the development of a solar energy plant. This agreement set a target of realizing 500MW of added photovoltaic (PV) capacity for local consumption in the following three years with the total PV installations to achieve 50GW by 2018.[95] In 2018, the Islamic Development Bank (IDB) will join forces with the AIIB to finance projects in Africa. China, the bank's largest stakeholder, will provide $210 million in debt financing for eleven solar PV projects in Egypt.[96]

In February 2019, the Chinese Yingli Solar Company agreed to collaborate with Misr Asset Management (MAM) to establish the solar station, with investments estimated at $80 million and agreed with Building Materials Industries Company (BMIC) to sell the generated electricity to its cement factory. The Asian Development Bank (ADB) approved financing of the station with $50 million. However, the final approval is yet to be issued to start implementing the project.[97]

Financial integration

Under the comprehensive strategic partnership, the formation and promotion of financial integration between the two countries are considered one of the essential cooperation areas to integrate Egypt's Vision 2030 and SCCDP into the BRI framework. There are several measures for the realization of financial integration between the two countries: including deepening financial cooperation and building a stable currency system, establishing an investment and financing system and a credit information system in Asia, expanding the scope and scale of bilateral currency swaps between the two countries, and developing the bond market in Asia.[98]

In December 2016, the Central Bank of Egypt (CBE) and the People's Bank of China signed a three-year bilateral currency swap agreement with a scale of RMB 18 billion ($2.62 billion), a move that would facilitate trade and improve foreign currency liquidity in cash-strapped Egypt.[99] In August 2018, the Governor of the CBE Tarek Amer announced in a press conference on the sidelines of the AACB meetings in Sharm El-Shiekh that Egypt and China were willing to renew their currency swap deal by the end of 2018. Amer also noted that the currency exchange agreement with China was to be renewed with $2.7 billion in December 2019, and this agreement states that trade between the two countries is to take place with their local currencies, not the US dollar.[100]

In the past year's financial institutions such as the China Development Bank, the Export-Import Bank of China, the AIIB, the Industrial and Commercial Bank of China, and the China Export & Credit Insurance Corporation, have provided loans and credits for Egypt in various means, and the contract amount exceeded $5 billion. China Development Bank issued a loan of $1.4 billion to financial institutions in Egypt, $900 million of which was issued to the central bank of Egypt, the first large-scale credit issued by the China Development Bank to an overseas central bank.[101]

In September 2018, the National Bank of Egypt (NBE) signed a loan agreement of $600 million with China Development Bank (CDB) in the Chinese capital of Beijing.[102] In January 2019, Egypt signed a $1.2 billion loan agreement with the Export-Import Bank of China (EximBank) to finance an electric railway project.[103] Chinese banks are set to finance New Egypt Capital's Tower District that is being developed by the CSCEC as part of Egypt's new administrative capital megaproject. The banks will finance about 85 percent ($3 billion) to cover the expenses of the tower district while Egypt's Housing Ministry will cover the rest of the costs. The tower district is planned to include 20 high-rise buildings and a 385-meter-tower, which is expected to be the tallest in Africa.[104]

In April 2017, Banque Misr, Egypt's oldest bank and the second-largest, officially opened its Guangzhou office in Guangdong province to help promote trade and financial activities between the two countries. The Banque Misr signed a series of co-operative agreements with major Chinese banks and financial organizations to provide financial solutions and financing activities to local and Egyptian small and middle enterprises in the future. Banque Misr chose Guangzhou for its first representative office in China as it has become one of the major commercial and port cities in the world.[105]

Military ties

Under China's comprehensive strategic partnership with Cairo, defense cooperation, including counter-terrorism, joint military drills, armed forces buildup, and defense industry, have become increasingly significant in integrating Egypt's Vision 2030 and SCCDP into the BRI framework. As Chinese State Councilor and Minister of National Defense Wei Fenghe said, Beijing attaches great importance to its military ties with Egypt and China's willingness to enhance strategic communication between the two militaries and exchanges, joint exercises, joint training, personnel training, and other areas.[106]

In December 2018, during the first international exhibition of military industries (EDEX 2018), the Egyptian Air Force signed an agreement to purchase drones, the Wing Loong II attack-reconnaissance UAVs, from China's National Aero-Technology Import and Export Corporation (CATIC). Before that, the Egyptian Ministry of Defense had shown a publicity video of the Wing Loong drone, taking off with missiles on its hard-points and knocking off a ground target. The video was telecast on Egyptian media on the occasion of the 45th Air Force Day and indicates that Egypt may already have the drones and may have signed up to buy more of them.[107]

In March 2019, President Abdel-Fattah el-Sisi held a meeting with visiting Chinese State Councilor and Minister of National Defense, Wei Fenghe, and expressed his hope that the two sides can further enhance defense cooperation and conduct more cooperation in the fields of counter-terrorism, joint military drills, armed forces buildup as well as the defense industry. For his part, the Chinese Minister of National Defense Wei Fenghe said: "We are willing to work together with the Egyptian armed forces to implement the important consensus between the two leaders and develop a higher level of relations between the two armies."[108]

People-to-People Bond

Under China's comprehensive strategic partnership with Cairo, enabling the people of the two countries to bond along the Silk Road is also vital to integrate Egypt's Vision 2030 and SCCDP into the BRI framework. By promoting extensive cultural and academic exchanges to win public support for deepening bilateral and multilateral cooperation, as well as providing scholarships, holding annual cultural events, increasing cooperation in science and technology, and establishing joint laboratory or research centers and international technology transfer centers.[109]

Linguistic, cultural, and tourism cooperation is another important aspect of China–Egypt's comprehensive strategic partnership, and both nations have outlined their intention to expand the collaboration in these areas in the coming years. According to the *Hanban website*, the Chinese government established Confucius institutes for providing Chinese language and culture teaching resources worldwide. In 2019, 550 Confucius Institutes and 1,172 Confucius Classrooms and 5,665 teaching sites were established in 162 countries and regions, receiving about eleven million students.[110] In 54 countries involved in the Belt and Road Initiative, there are 153 Confucius Institutes and 149 primary and high-school Confucius Classrooms.[111] In the Middle East, there are eighteen Confucius institutes and two of them are in Egypt (Cairo University and Suez Canal University) as well as three Confucius Classrooms (Ain-Shams University, Neil Thematic Channel, and South Valley University).[112]

In education, China's Renmin University and Egypt's Ain Shams University inaugurated the Belt and Road Cooperation Research Center in Cairo in January 2019. According to the President of Ain Shams University Abdel Wahab Ezzat, the establishment of the center came after one year of negotiations, and this is the second center of its kind after a similar one was established in Russia. The center aims to conduct economic, commercial, and technical studies for projects and cooperation between Egypt and China. The Ain Shams University is considered one of the largest and oldest Chinese language departments in the world, and thousands of Egyptians have graduated from the department and played key roles in promoting cultural exchanges between Egypt and China.[113]

Following an extensive meeting between Prime Minister Mostafa Madbouli and Chinese Vice-President in 2018, the two sides signed an MoU in the education sector that covers a Chinese grant to fund a remote learning project, which will be executed over three phases; in addition, 1,000 books are to be donated to the South Valley University and a Confucius Hall is to be built on its campus.[114] In April 2019, a Chinese company, NetDragon Websoft, developed smart classrooms to improve the education quality of Egypt students. The smart classrooms, referred to as "Pop-up Classrooms", were displayed at Fuzhou in southeast China's Fujian province. The Egyptian government is planning to build 265,000 Pop-up Classrooms across the country in the next three years. The cost of a Pop-up Classroom stands at around $29,726 and will reshape the imbalanced allocation of education resources.[115]

The Chinese Institute of Archaeology signed a cooperation agreement with the Egyptian Ministry of Antiquities in 2016, which is aimed to facilitate visits and exchange of knowledge between experts in both countries. Moreover, an MoU was signed between the Egyptian Museum and the Museum of Shanghai for the protection of cultural property, digital authentication and the exchange of scientific research studies, publications, and scholarships between both countries.[116] Under the Belt and Road, the Chinese archaeological team started excavation works in collaboration with Egyptian archeologists at Precinct of Montu, a part of Karnak temple in Luxor, the site of the ancient Egyptian city of Thebes.[117]

Cultural cooperation between Egypt and China was extended when the two countries marked the 60th anniversary of the establishment of diplomatic relations. China–Egypt Cultural Year was celebrated in 2016 by holding various cultural events in each other's country. The culture year included a total of 102 activities, with 63 hosted by China and 39 by Egypt, including music and dance shows, relic exhibitions, a photography contest, acrobatic performances, film screenings, tourism fairs, and literature forums to promote exchanges between the countries.[118] In November 2018, as part of cultural cooperation, Egyptian and Chinese media officials celebrated the broadcast of a dubbed Arabic version of Chinese popular TV series "Ode to Joy" on the Egyptian state TV channel.[119]

In June 2019, the Chinese Cultural Center in Cairo held the opening ceremony for a film festival to display popular Chinese movies to an Egyptian audience as part of the cultural exchange between China and Egypt. The China Film Festival was held in celebration of the 70th anniversary of the establishment of the People's Republic of China. The festival displayed six popular homegrown movies that promote Chinese culture among Egyptian audiences. The festival, one of several Chinese–Egyptian cultural activities, was held for the first time in Egypt.[120]

Chinese tourism in Egypt has been growing fast since a comprehensive strategic partnership was agreed between the two countries in 2014. China's outbound tourism market exports upwards of 150 million tourists annually and its spotlight have turned towards Egypt.[121] While the absolute numbers are still modest, the rate of growth is startling. In 2014, just 65,000 Chinese tourists visited Egypt, whereas nearly half a million Chinese tourists visited Egypt in 2018 compared with only 300,000 in 2017; the number of Chinese visitors was expected to exceed 500,000 in 2019.[122]

According to Egyptian Tourism Minister Rania al-Mashat, the Chinese market is one of the most promising markets for Egypt's tourism. The Chinese market has a special nature and unique social communication tools like Weibo and WeChat that can advertise Egyptian tourism. According to Egyptian statistics, China has become the fourth largest exporter of tourists to Egypt since the beginning of 2017, and Egypt falls behind only Vietnam in the pace of growth for incoming Chinese tourists.[123]

As one of the world's most ancient civilizations, Egypt has been working hard to uncover and preserve its archeological heritage across the country while organizing conferences abroad to promote its ancient heritage. According to the official statistics agency, Egypt netted $6.1 billion in tourism revenues in 2015, a drastic decline from $12.5 billion in 2010. Revenues from 2018 are expected to total $9 billion, up from $7.6 billion the previous year.[124] In the coming years, as ties between the two countries continue to grow stronger, there are expectations that more Chinese tourists will choose to visit Egypt. According to Egyptian Tourism Minister Rania el Mashat, "We attach importance to Chinese tourists, and Egypt has a comprehensive strategic partnership with China."[125]

Summary

An overall assessment of the PRC–Egypt's comprehensive strategic partnership clearly illustrates that the strong synergy between the BRI and Egypt's Vision 2030 and SCCDP has enormous potential for trading and economic opportunities for both countries. The 21st-Century Maritime Silk Road is designed to go from China's coast to Europe through the South China Sea and the Indian Ocean through the Red Sea and into the Mediterranean via the Suez Canal.[126] Egypt is positioned to play a critical role in China's expanding footprint in the Middle East, and it has been elevated to a springboard position in China's MSRI aspirations because of its unique strategic geographic location and special economic zones along the Suez Canal, and its prime position to act as a hub for Africa, the Middle East, and Europe. The Suez Canal lies at the heart of the Maritime Silk Road, which is a crucial component of Chinese President Xi Jinping's all-encompassing BRI, making Egypt one of the few genuinely indispensable partners in the Middle East for turning the new Silk Road into a reality.

3 | Israel

Since the establishment of diplomatic ties between the People's Republic of China (PRC) and Israel in 1992, relations between the two countries have warmed and developed rapidly in diverse areas, including diplomacy, trade, investment, construction, educational partnerships, scientific cooperation, and tourism. For Beijing, Israel is a global powerhouse in technology and innovation in areas such as cybersecurity, bio-agriculture, and green technology, which is at the heart of its attraction. Geopolitically, too, Israel's location is another potential node in the Belt and Road Initiative (BRI).[1] For Israel, China not only has a vast, rapidly expanding economy presenting infinite opportunities, but it also has little interest in the politics of the Middle East. Jerusalem seeks to expand its diplomatic, economic, and strategic ties with the world's fastest-growing major economy and diversify its export markets and investments from the US and Europe.[2]

Although China–Israel relations are developing smoothly and the two countries do not have historical issues or direct conflicts of interest, their relations are always affected by the third party, namely the United States, which is watching, not necessarily with jealousy but with grave concern mixed, at times, with anger. This is due to Israel's all-too-frequent disregard for Washington's unease as China makes inroads, figuratively and literally, deep into areas of America's vital interests in the Middle East. In this context, the China–U.S. trade war has changed the nature and meaning of Sino–Israeli economic ties and increased the tension between Israel and the U.S., as the latter attempts to limit the terms of Sino–Israeli engagement.[3]

Israel is not prepared to jeopardize its unquestionable collaboration with the U.S. because of China. Like other countries in the world, Jerusalem, a close – and small – ally of Washington, looks at the dynamics of world power to chart its course. Situated in the heart of the Middle East/North Africa region, it finds itself in a delicate position. While seeking to expand relations with Beijing and tap into the vast and growing Chinese market, Israel continues to view its relations with the U.S. as a core pillar of its national security. A zero-sum competition between Washington and Beijing, therefore, would complicate the Israeli position. Jerusalem is eager to engage China regarding its future role in the Middle East while hoping for continued and robust U.S. involvement in the region.

The Middle East is a key part of the PRC's BRI, and closer ties with Israel fit into Beijing's larger regional aspirations while helping to advance China's technology sector. Jerusalem has the potential to be one stop on the 21st Century Maritime Silk Road (MSRI) connecting the Indian Ocean and the Mediterranean Sea through the Gulf of Suez. In the context of the Silk Road Economic Belt (SREB), they intend to construct a high-speed railway line between Asia, the Red Sea, and Mediterranean ports (the Red–Med project). Though Israel seems to be a small and dispensable stop on the BRI routes, its significance should not be underestimated.[4]

Despite their immense differences in population and territorial size, a pattern of relations has evolved in which Beijing values Jerusalem as one of the global hubs of technological innovation, while Israel – as a small country – sees before it a vast Chinese market and an economic power which is willing to invest in its economy. This chapter examines the motivation behind Beijing's measures to formalize an innovative comprehensive partnership with Jerusalem, and the synergy between the BRI and investments in Israeli innovation and infrastructure projects, to understand the extent of economic engagement and bilateral relationship between the two nations.[5] The main argument presented is that China's measures to formalize an innovative comprehensive partnership with Israel are based on shared or mutually complementary economic interests, especially to integrate the BRI framework within Israel's aspiration for economic growth.

Israel and the Belt and Road Initiative

The PRC's innovative comprehensive partnership with Jerusalem includes five areas for cooperation within the BRI. These areas are policy coordination, connectivity, trade and investments, energy cooperation, and people-to-people bond. However, each country views the BRI framework and reacts to it according to its perspective and the consequences for its national interests and international status. Therefore, there are very different attitudes among the countries that are part of the BRI framework regarding how to realize the vision.[6]

Policy coordination

Under China's innovative comprehensive partnership with Israel, promoting political cooperation between the two countries, creating mechanisms for dialogue and consensus-building on global and regional issues, developing shared interests, deepening political trust, and reaching a new consensus on cooperation is important to integrate Israel's economic growth into the BRI framework.[7]

The two sides' top leaders have paid frequent visits to each other. This not only showed that both sides attached great importance to the two countries' relations but also reflects the smooth development of the bilateral relationship. During the period from 2012 to 2019, senior Chinese leaders made a total of five visits (at the level of foreign minister) to Israel. Only one visit was at the level of head of state: then-President Jiang Zemin's visit in April 2000. The most senior Chinese visit to Israel in recent years was by Vice-President Wang in October 2018, which could indicate a growing emphasis on engagement with Israel.[8] While from 2012 to 2019, senior Israeli leaders made four visits to China – one at the level of foreign minister (Liberman,

March 2012),[9] one at the level of head of state (President Peres, April 2014)[10]   and two at the level of head of government (Prime Minister Netanyahu, May 2013, March 2017).[11]

Prime Minister Benjamin Netanyahu's two official visits to China marked the growing Israeli interest in China and produced several economic agreements between the two countries. During the last visit, Chinese President Xi Jinping announced the establishment of an 'Innovative Comprehensive Partnership' with Israel (only Switzerland holds this status with China), which Prime Minister Netanyahu hailed as 'a tremendously important decision'.[12] This initiative was developed after Netanyahu's May 2013 visit to China, when the two governments created five task forces in the fields of "high technology, environmental protection, energy, agriculture, and financing".[13] The two sides would reportedly "put a priority on strengthening cooperation in the fields of scientific and technological innovation, water resources, agriculture, medical care, and public health, and clean energy."[14]

The designation of the relationship as an 'innovative comprehensive partnership' signaled China's main interest in Israel (economic and technological partner, not strategic). As Chinese Vice-Premier Liu Yandong said, Beijing-Jerusalem had agreed to upgrade bilateral relations, including by forming an innovative comprehensive partnership meant to bring the ties and the cooperation between the two countries to new heights.[15] At this stage, various joint mechanisms for cooperation began to appear (such as conferences, joint committees, fairs, etc.) in support of this designation. The launch of the BRI, in which Jerusalem is involved, and Israel's membership in the Asian Infrastructure Investment Bank (AIIB) since its inauguration (2015), also showcase Sino–Israeli relations and their prospects.[16]

In October 2018, Prime Minister Netanyahu and China's Vice-President Wang Qishan, a close confidant of President Xi, co-hosted a high-profile trade and innovation conference in Jerusalem.[17] According to Prime Minister Netanyahu, "This is the most important visit by a Chinese leader in the last 18 years. It's a sign of our growing friendship. The fact that the Vice-President of China came to Israel at my invitation for the Prime Minister's Innovation Conference is a tremendous compliment to Israel and a reflection of the growing ties between China and Israel."[18]

During his visit, Wang praised Israel, saying that "Israel leads the world in electronics, information technology, modern medicine, and agriculture. China is still striving to achieve modernization".[19] His statement illustrates what Beijing seeks most from its partnership with Israel: to learn from policies and practices that Jerusalem has put in place regarding innovation and entrepreneurship as the PRC attempts to shift its economy from one that is led by investment and export to one that is led by consumption and innovation.

The Chinese Vice-President's visit helped highlight the tightening of relations between the two countries, namely, that both sides would complete a free-trade agreement in 2020, and that the PRC plans to invest heavily in Israeli infrastructure, including new ports and a light rail system.[20] However, the following year witnessed growing criticism of China's involvement in Israel (inside and outside the country), particularly the involvement of Chinese engineering companies in many of Israel's upcoming infrastructure projects (a topic dealt with later in this chapter).

Although little attention has been paid to the role of Israel in the BRI framework, Chinese policymakers have their eyes on the country as an important node within the BRI architecture. During Netanyahu's third visit (March 2017) to China, President

Xi said that the two countries would "steadily advance major cooperative projects within the framework of jointly building the Silk Road Economic Belt and the 21st Century Maritime Silk Road". Prime Minister Netanyahu also mentioned the BRI in his remarks, saying, "The Israeli side is ready to actively participate in infrastructure and other cooperation under the framework of the Silk Road Economic Belt and the 21st Century Maritime Silk Road".[21]

In February 2019, the Chinese Ministry of Commerce said that Israel is an important partner in the Middle East and along the BRI.[22] In March 2019, Tzachi Hanegbi, Israeli Minister for Regional Cooperation, in an interview with *Xinhua*, said, "the potential of win-win cooperation between China and Israel is gigantic as engagement will become more effective in the future. The BRI is boosting the economy of many countries while hoping to see more and more Chinese companies get involved in the Israeli market. The future is about working together and this is the real idea behind the connectivity of the BRI. The Israeli minister is confident that more and more Israeli and Chinese companies will find common areas to work together. I am optimistic about the future."[23]

In December 2019, Zhao John, the Chinese special envoy to the Middle East, stated: "Given the fact that Israel–China relations and cooperation are strong, I am sure that under the 'One Belt One Road initiative', China–Israel cooperation will grow with potential. The Middle East is an important component of the Belt and Road Initiative, there is much that can be developed in the region in the field of infrastructure and connectivity, and China is ready and willing to talk about this development, and I sincerely expect to strive for it, even personally [. . .] and I have discussed it with Israeli Foreign Ministry Katz and we agree on many points."[24]

Connectivity

According to China's innovative comprehensive partnership with Jerusalem, the facilitation of connectivity is one of the crucial ways to integrate Israel's economic growth into the BRI framework.[25] Israel is situated between Europe and Asia, between the Middle East and Africa. As such, its strategic positioning for the PRC's BRI is obvious. Jerusalem has the potential to be a small but important stop on the MSRI, connecting the Indian Ocean and the Mediterranean Sea through the Gulf of Aqaba and the Suez Canal. Chinese construction companies have been increasingly involved in Israel's transportation, seaports, railways, and other infrastructure projects that can be combined with the SREB.[26]

Jerusalem sees its connection with the BRI as an opportunity to improve its economic growth and ties with China, and to open commercial opportunities for Israeli companies. The construction of the BRI economic corridor requires seaports, railways, logistic centers, warehouses, airports, and transport system hardware and software. Israeli companies could contribute to the BRI project construction by developing and integrating transportation and logistics technologies and related systems for trains, aircraft, and marine engineering, for example.[27] At the same time, however, Israel's role in the BRI is likely to be limited by its small geographic size and limited transportation connectivity with countries in its region, and lack of experience in very large-scale projects.

According to Prime Minister Netanyahu, there are two main ways to contribute to the success of the BRI framework: One is the mutual exchange of Israeli technology with Chinese business and advancing the free trade association, which would enable a two-way movement to proceed. Second is the construction of a transportation route that connects Asia, the Red Sea and Mediterranean ports (such as the construction of a railway line from Eilat to Ashdod).[28]

Beijing highlights the advantages of Israel as a hub for China's BRI framework. Jerusalem's well-endowed human capital, developed economy, high-tech base, stable society, and government business environment make the country a particularly valuable asset for Beijing's BRI framework. Moreover, not only is Israel at the nexus of China's far-flung trade routes, but its stability is the exception in the turbulent Middle East. The geostrategic significance of Israel within the BRI is also an important factor due to its location near the Arab states as a 'balancer' that can lend credibility to Chinese soft power in the Middle East. According to one Chinese government investment index, Israel is rated 22 out of 63 countries located along the MSRI, and the operational risk to Chinese investment in Israel is lower than average among countries along the route.[29]

Furthermore, Beijing launched the Asian Infrastructure Investment Bank (AIIB) in October 2014, and the deadline to join and apply as a founding member was March 31, 2015. On the last day, Israeli Prime Minister Netanyahu formally signed an application to join the AIIB (Jerusalem is one of the last seven countries that applied to join) and became one of the 57 founding member states. Joining the AIIB proved that Israel responded positively to China's BRI framework.[30] Though functioning independently of the BRI, the AIIB is a crucial financial source for the implementation of the Silk Road. Furthermore, the massive development of energy resources in the Eastern Mediterranean, new ports coming online on its Mediterranean shores, new trade routes between Israel and its Arab neighbors, a growing geo-economic alliance between Israel, Cyprus and Greece, and significant financial resources in Israeli investment intuitions, make it a highly attractive BRI market for China.[31]

In May 2015, Israel's Minister of Transportation Israeli Katz spoke highly of China's BRI during the signing ceremony of the 25-year franchise right for the Shanghai International Port Group (SIPG) at the new Haifa Bay Port. The Israeli Minister of Transportation said that Israel was at a stage of the rapid development of infrastructure construction; it was building the new airport, port, railway, and highway with an annual investment of about $40 billion. Thus, the cooperation in infrastructure between the two countries has huge potential and would benefit both sides.[32]

Aware of the above advantages, Chinese companies are increasingly active in the infrastructure sector in Israel. From 2014 to 2015, Chinese companies gained access to Israel's two major seaport construction project. The first is the Port Engineering Construction project of China Harbor Engineering Company (CHEC) in Ashdod, in southern Israel, in June 2014. The new port project is one of Israel's largest investment projects, with a total investment of $930 million, and is the largest port construction project contracted by Chinese enterprises in the overseas market. The main content of the port project includes the construction of 1200 meters of the port, 2800 meters of the breakwater, as well as the entrance road and warehouse, office, and other ancillary works. The new port project construction is expected to be completed in 2022. Once the port is completed, it is expected to have a container-handling capability of one million standard containers and will become the most important port in southern Israel.[33]

The second major construction project is the tender won by SIPG to build and operate a new terminal at the Haifa Port in March 2015 (a lease for 25 years). SIPG will invest NIS 1 billion ($ 252 million) in facilities and infrastructure before the launch of the new port, adding to its previous investment of NIS 3.96 billion, or over $2 billion by the time it is completed. The new Haifa Port construction is expected to be completed in 2020; after the completion, the pier length will be 1500 meters long. It is designed for an annual handling capacity of 1.86 million standard containers. It covers an area of 78 hectares in total; the frontier has a maximum depth of minus17.3 meters and can load and unload the world's largest container ships (19,000 standard container ships). It will be the largest seaport in Israel.[34] Another mega-Chinese infrastructure project in Israel is the construction of the 'Red Sea–Mediterranean high-speed railway' (Red–Med high-speed railway), which will facilitate connectivity between the Israeli ports of Eilat and Ashdod. To ensure reliable access for Chinese commercial shipping from the Red Sea to the Mediterranean Sea, Beijing has invested in building a regional network of sea infrastructure and rail lines aimed at connecting China with Europe via Asia and the Middle East.

The Red–Med railway, a 350-kilometer line, would include 63 bridges spanning a total of some 4.5 kilometers as well as five tunnels totaling 9.5 kilometers. The trains on the Red–Med railway line would travel at 250–300 km/h and are expected to accommodate both passengers and cargo. After the completion, the trip from Tel Aviv to Eilat will take only 2 hours. The project is expected to cost over $6.5 billion, but this figure could reach $13 billion. Operations are projected to begin five years from the start of construction.[35]

The Red–Med railway through Israel thus has regional geo-strategic and geo-economic significance. For Israel (and other countries in the world), this is land access through Eurasia, connecting the Mediterranean Sea and the Red Sea; it has even been referred to as the 'Suez Canal on land'.[36] It would provide a safe route, complementary to the Suez Canal, by which raw materials and energy vessels could be transported from Europe to China. It would also serve to move China's finished products back to Europe through the Gulf of Aden. Since the Red–Med line is not designed to compete with the Suez Canal for Far Eastern-European trade, the land-based trade corridor could strengthen relations between Egypt and Israel. The cargo rail line would facilitate transport between the industrial centers of the north and those of the south, which would be of economic and political benefit to both states. The rail project would increase economic cooperation and strengthen security coordination, thus helping to maintain regional peace and stability.[37]

Jerusalem hopes to finance the construction of this railway through international cooperation. Since the announcement of the Red–Med project, there have been ten countries, such as India and Spain that expressed interest in this cooperation project. However, so far, only China has truly entered into substantive negotiations with Israel. For Jerusalem, Beijing's involvement also means that Chinese banks and investment companies will invest in the project. The railway construction companies in China, which have mature experience and technology, will also be responsible for the project. Because the Red–Med project is of great significance, many ordinary Israelis have mixed feelings: they are greatly concerned about its repercussions for the local industry while harboring high expectations of China's participation.[38]

Nevertheless, it is not clear when the Red–Med railway will be constructed, and the project has yet to receive final approval or secure funding. Although the Israeli cabinet unanimously approved the project in 2012, the start date has not been set nor has the tender been announced. The legal process is complicated and there are negative reactions by Israeli environmental organizations who fear irreparable harm to the Negev's unique landscapes.[39] Israel and China, however, remain committed to the project, which was on the agenda during Netanyahu's 2017 visit to Beijing.[40]

Following massive Chinese investment in recent years in vital and often especially sensitive Israeli infrastructure projects, the ports in Haifa and Ashdod present a set of concerns. China has shown great interest in Israeli ports and has been involved in construction activities as well as in future operations management. Some observers in Israel have begun to note these potential effects on Israel's security interests, particularly the effect that Chinese involvement in local ports might have on the US military's willingness to operate in these areas, although it is not clear whether they differentiate between Chinese control over an entire port versus Chinese operations at a section of a port.[41] Haifa is a frequent port of call for the U.S. Sixth Fleet and serves as the base for Israel's submarines,[42] making some experts question the tradeoff between economic value and security risks raised by potential Chinese surveillance of the naval port. For example, in 2018 there were three port calls in Haifa, by the aircraft carrier *USS George H.W. Bush*, the amphibious assault ship USS *Iwo Jima*, and the guided-missile destroyer USS *Donald Cook*.[43] Admiral (Ret.) Gary Roughead, former chief of U.S. Naval Operations, said that the Chinese port operators could monitor U.S. ship movements and maintenance activity, and might have access to information systems, increasing the likelihood of threats to U.S. information and cybersecurity.[44]

The SIPG (and the Israeli companies involved) will operate only one terminal in the Haifa Port (New Bay Terminal) and not the entire port so that many of the concerns that have been raised have little to do with the reality on the ground.[45] Nonetheless, the U.S. government was quick to use the Haifa Port issue as an opportunity to pressure Israel into rethinking its overall relationship with China and to coax Israel into limiting the scope of its ties to China. However, the SIPG continues to work full steam ahead on the Haifa port (expected to become operational in 2021).

China's CHEC, a state-owned company developing Ashdod's new port, will operate near Israel's navy base, and to the national electricity company and the regional refineries, two other key infrastructure assets. Such proximity could lead to intelligence-gathering, and even sharing that intelligence with Israel's adversaries.[46] Moreover, developing Israeli ports gives Beijing not only an opportunity to compete more effectively with the U.S. navy in the MENA region but also potentially allows it to monitor and gather intelligence.[47] For instance, Chinese involvement in certain key infrastructures in Israel, like the light rail in Tel Aviv, which runs by the *Kirya*, the Israel Defense Forces headquarters in Tel Aviv, could have security implications for Israel, including in the U.S. military's willingness to operate in these areas.[48]

Beijing's national development has become increasingly dependent on maritime commerce to reach the global marketplace. Consequently, the PRC has sought to minimize the risk of shipping disruptions by reducing its dependence on any single route, through the development of a variety of sea and land transportation corridors. Hence, the Israeli national infrastructures can play a key role in the international networking launched by Beijing through the BRI. Israel's geographical location, as well as its technological capabilities and potential for infrastructure engagement, position it as an attraction for the MSRI and a critical constituent in promoting the BRI framework.[49]

Trade and investments

The PRC's innovative comprehensive partnership with Jerusalem is aimed at mitigating as much as possible the barriers to free trade, investment, industrial cooperation, and technical and engineering services to facilitate integrating Israel's economy into the BRI framework. Both countries must take a series of additional measures, such as expanding free-trade zones, improving trade structures, seeking new potential areas for trade and improving the trade balance, devising new initiatives for the promotion of conventional forms of trade, developing trans-border electronic trade and other advanced models of business. These measures, together with regularly sharing information in these areas, will help create a system for supporting trade in services to strengthen and expand conventional trade and increase customs cooperation.[50]

The economies of Beijing and Jerusalem are highly complementary. Commercial ties are developing rapidly, and trade volume has been increasing year by year. According to Chinese customs statistics, in 2019 bilateral trade between China and Israel maintained a steady growth; imports and exports amounted to $14.7 billion.[51] The Chinese Ambassador to Israel Zhan Yongxin said that the Sino–Israeli trade is only 0.3 percent of China's trade with the world, but there is still a lot of potential in the relations.[52]

China has become Israel's largest trading partner in Asia and the second-largest partner in the world, following the US (7.7 percent consumption of total Israeli exports).[53] For a long time, Jerusalem's exports to Beijing consisted of high-tech products, including electronics components (just over 50 percent of Israeli exports), with other leading categories including technological equipment, chemicals, minerals, and machinery, while China's exports to the Israeli market include popular and competitive raw materials, textile products, and consumer goods.[54]

In addition, Jerusalem and Beijing agreed to begin negotiations for a bilateral free trade agreement (they began negotiations in 2016 which may end in 2020, after seven rounds of official talks). Once this agreement is completed, it has the potential to double the total trade value between both countries, boost technological cooperation, and open the way for more Chinese investments in the next few years, if all goes as expected. While Beijing possesses enormous manufacturing and economic power, Jerusalem has know-how and quality in technology, research and development, agriculture, environmentally friendly construction, the environment, water, development of advanced medical equipment, and digitalized medical services. This makes the two economies highly complementary with much future potential.[55]

As a matter of principle, the PRC is keen on investing in fields that serve its national interest either domestically or internationally, and are connected to its innovation aspirations. Hence, Beijing sees Jerusalem as a particularly useful partner in achieving four broad goals. First, and most important, Israel could help China spur indigenous innovation and research and development (R&D) capabilities. Second, China looks to Israeli experience and technology in defense, security, cyber, and counterterrorism as a means of promoting its own needs in military and domestic security capabilities. Third, Beijing views Jerusalem as an important player in its overall Middle East policy and seeks to balance its close relations with Israel and other regional powers (e.g., Saudi Arabia, Turkey, Egypt, and Iran). In this context, this might manifest in Beijing's effort to make inroads with a key U.S. ally in the region with the intent of undermining the global Washington alliance and partner networks. Finally, the PRC sees Jerusalem as an important component of the BRI framework.[56]

According to the *China Global Investment Tracker*, China's investments and construction in Israel from 2013 to 2019 reached $10.6 billion. Most of the Chinese investments are in the sectors of entertainment ($4.4 billion), agriculture ($2.9 billion), and transport ($2.2 billion).[57] In 2017, with a pause in Chinese investments worldwide to regulate how they are supervised, Chinese investments totaled some $70 billion, as opposed to some $160 billion that left China in 2016. In 2018 Chinese investments totaled some $125 billion, as a result of restrictive government policies in reaction to significant capital outflows during 2015–2016.[58]

According to the *RAND* study, between 2007 and 2018 Chinese investment and construction activities in Israel rose dramatically. Ninety-two investments (both direct investments and investments through venture capital) and infrastructure projects involving 42 Chinese companies and 80 Israeli companies were targets for Chinese investment. The Chinese investment totaled $12.9 billion, while contracts for the construction and operation of infrastructure projects totaled more than $4 billion.[59] Beijing is expanding its economic interests and strategic position in the Israeli economy mainly by investing significant capital and resources in innovation, technology, venture capital, agriculture, infrastructure, and construction projects and acquiring influential positions in key Israeli industries.

Innovation

Scientific and technological innovation has played an instrumental role in shaping contemporary Beijing–Jerusalem relations. Despite a dearth of natural resources and a challenging geopolitical environment, Israel has become a technological and innovation powerhouse. China is interested in Israel's technology and innovation model, as it aims to transform its economic model from one based on manufacturing to one based on innovation and to a rise in the production value chain.[60] Chinese companies are searching for cutting-edge technology that can complement the country's strengths as a rising innovation nation, while Israeli companies are looking to Beijing for market expansion opportunities.

This kind of investment will continue to grow since many of the projects under the Belt and Road Initiative require investment in innovation on regional and global tracks.[61] As China's President, Xi Jinping, said in his meeting with Israel's Prime Minister Netanyahu in March 2017, "Israel is a world-renowned innovative country, and at the same time, China is also pushing forward innovation-driven development, so innovation has become the common focus of our two countries. It is also the priority for our cooperation."[62]

The establishment of the innovative comprehensive partnership in 2017 captures the role of innovation as a catalyst in encouraging investment and is the main purpose of the economic diplomacy between Jerusalem–Beijing.[63] The economic diplomacy has centered on innovation and has been highly instrumental in strengthening trade and investment between the two countries, despite the global economic slowdown. As the Chinese Ambassador to Israel, Zhan Yongxin, said: "Israel is well known as the Start-Up Nation, strong in creation and innovation, or going from 0 to 1. China, with its strong manufacturing capacity and huge market, is good at going from 1 to 100."[64]

In May 2019, the two countries established the China–Israel Innovation Hub located in the Taopu Smart City in Shanghai, which is home to research and development initiatives, drawing on a $145 million innovation fund to promote joint-cooperation and possibly technological breakthroughs. According to Wang Zhigang, China's Minister of Science and Technology, the hub is expected to bolster scientific and technological achievements, accumulate financial capital, and attract top talents while setting an example for global cooperation on innovation. The Israeli ambassador to China, Zvi Heifetz, said, "The establishment of the innovation hub will bring new development opportunities to Israel as the two sides complement each other in many aspects."[65]

In September 2019, China's first provincial-level innovation center was opened for trial operation in the city of Tel Aviv, to work as a bridge and platform to further enhance the innovation cooperation between Jerusalem–Beijing. The Israel Jiangsu Center, an innovation hub, is expected to help both Israeli startups and Chinese companies that are interested in joining with Israelis firms to cooperate in the innovation sector. The center, established via the China–Changzhou Israel Innovation Park located in east China's Jiangsu Province (the first Chinese province where Israel established the innovation cooperation agreement), a bi-national governmental initiative, is jointly operated by the Park and professional experts and personnel from Israel. It aims to promote the development of more China–Israel innovation cooperation projects and attracts capital, technology, and talents.[66]

In December 2019, the two nations launched the China–Israel Innovation Hub (Shanghai) in Putuo District. The opening of the innovation hub is a major step in Shanghai's implementation of a national strategy to promote Chinese and Israeli scientific and technological innovation. Twenty companies or institutions, 10 of them from Israel, will be based at the China–Israel Innovation Hub. Leading Israeli business incubators, such as Ehealth and Trendlines, which focus on medical and agrifood tech, will operate at the hub in the under-construction Taopu Smart City, serving Israeli high-tech and startup firms. Both incubators, among the 19 registered with the Israeli Innovation Authority, were attracted to the hub by the large market and strong production ability of China.[67]

Technology

Beijing values and recognizes Jerusalem as a global center of technology, and despite the vast differences in population and size, it sees it as a natural economic partner. According to a *RAND* study, between 2007 to 2018, 55 of the 92 Chinese investments were in Israeli technology companies and most of the Israeli venture capital companies to which Chinese entities have provided funding invest primarily in the technology or biomedical technology sectors.[68] As Israel's Prime Minister Netanyahu said during the second visit at an Israel–China innovation summit in Beijing, "We want to marry our technology with China's capacity."[69]

In this context, the Chinese see the Israeli economy in general, and its science and technology industry in particular, as especially useful. Beijing tries to benefit from Israel through investment to gain access to technology and learn from Israeli innovation practices. For about a decade, through the middle of the 2010s, Beijing's investments in Jerusalem were largely in agriculture and the food industry, although they were tilted toward the technology side of that industry. These included the acquisition of the Israeli agrochemical and crop protection company Adama (Machteshim-Agan) and Tnuva. These transactions helped improve Chinese productivity and gain a foothold in the bio-agriculture market.

Nevertheless, in the first decade of the 21st century, Beijing began to focus its investments in technology start-ups in Israel. According to the IVC Research Center report in February 2018, China is a relatively minor player in Israeli high-tech, and Chinese companies mainly invest for strategic purposes. The Chinese companies invest in innovative Israeli technology that they can utilize for their own specific needs. The IVC's data found that the actual number of Chinese companies investing in Israeli high-tech entities rose from 18 in 2013 to 34 in 2017 and that annual Chinese investment in start-ups from 2015 to 2017 was in the range of $500 million to $600 million, 12 percent (compared to 7.5 percent-9 percent in the previous three years) of all capital raised by Israeli start-ups during that period. Over the past five years, around $1.5 billion was invested in around 300 Israeli companies.[70]

Beijing has now become one of the financial sources of Israeli high-tech enterprises. Baidu, Qihoo 360, Lenovo, Ping An, and other famous companies of science and technology are investing in Israel's science and technology funds. In May 2013, China Fosun Pharmaceutical Company acquired 95 percent of the ALMA Lasers' equity for $220 million. Similarly, Israeli start-ups are working harder to penetrate the Chinese market.[71] In October 2017, Chinese e-commerce giant Alibaba announced that it was opening an R&D lab in Tel Aviv to cultivate IT talent in Israel and abroad.[72]

According to the IVC Research Center report, November 2018, Chinese investment activity in Israeli tech startups (the lion's share of Chinese investment is directed at software and life science companies) has increased steadily over the past two years, from an average of 15 investments per quarter to an average of 20 investments. In 2018, $325 million was invested, compared with $308 million in 2017, and $274 million in 2016. Chinese investors have participated in six out of the 17 (higher proportion than in previous years) largest funding deals in the Israeli venture market.[73]

Venture Capital

According to the Bloomberg Innovation Index 2019, Israel was ranked in fifth place overall, jumping five spots. In the World's Most Innovative Economies Israel was ranked first as the most innovative country in terms of research and development (R&D) capabilities in the world; ranked second as the most innovative country in terms of researcher concentration; ranked fourth in patent activity; and ranked fifth as the most high-tech density country.[74] Jerusalem has a very diverse high-tech industry, with entrepreneurship and innovative economy, built on cutting-edge innovations in fields ranging from healthcare, agricultural technology, and clean-tech to digital printing, communication, and computers.

Chinese entities have also been active in investing in Israeli venture capital firms (e.g., JVP, Pitango, OurCrowd, Catalyst, Canaan Partners, Viola Ventures, and Singulariteam). As a 'start-up nation', Israel has become a powerhouse of advanced technology, strong innovation, numerous start-ups, and high-tech. Many of these venture capital companies (Tnuva, ThetaRay, Kaymera, Toga Networks, HexaTier, Rainbow Medical, and Copyleaks) focus on investing in other Israeli companies innovating in areas of sensitive or potentially dual-use technology, such as cybersecurity, AI, and robotics.[75]

In May 2019, Beijing hosted over 100 high-tech companies and Israeli startups, and thousands of Chinese investors, at a business event in the Shandong Province. The international investment conference 'GoforIsrael' was held for the third time outside the borders of Israel. The conference showcased the best of Israeli innovation in fields such as advanced production technologies, IT, life sciences, water technologies, cleantech, agri-tech, energy, and more. Israeli entrepreneurs scheduled meetings with more than 1,000 investors in one-on-one meetings.[76]

Nevertheless, a close look at China's investments in Israel provides a complex picture: China's direct investments in Israel's high-tech industry are relatively small and sporadic. In 2018, over 90 percent of China's ($9.5 billion) direct investment into Israel was comprised of the acquisition of only three companies, of which only one is a high-tech company. The rest of its investments in technology are limited to a few hundred million U.S. dollars each year. Other Chinese investments in Israel are made through capital venture funds, providing investors with very limited access to know-how. Chinese investments in Israel constituted just 4 percent of Israel's foreign direct investments (FDI), compared to the U.S. which had a share totaling 35 percent. Considering the limited flow of Chinese FDI to Israel (in 2018 around $100 million out of the total $21.8 billion), the PRC is far from gaining a foothold in Israel's high-tech sector.[77]

Agriculture

The agriculture and technology sectors were the biggest targets of Chinese investment, at approximately $5.3 billion in agriculture and $5.7 billion in technology; together, these two sectors accounted for approximately 87 percent of total Chinese investment in Israel. Furthermore, the agriculture-related investment included a strong technology component in that it focused on agricultural technology. For agriculture, the investment figure is driven by the acquisition of Adama for $2.8 billion by ChemChina[78]

Moreover, the collaboration between the two countries in agriculture starts with bilateral agreements such as the 2015 joint action plan for increasing agricultural trade volume to $450 million by 2020 and then expands to the transfer of innovation technology from Beijing to Jerusalem (e.g., water technology).[79] For instance, the Israeli company IDE built the PRC's largest desalination plant in Tienjin, producing 200,000 cubic meters of freshwater daily.[80]

Key Industries

Beijing's growing acquisitions and investment in key Israeli industries are one of the main pillars of the relationship. Over the last decade, Chinese companies have acquired several key Israeli industries (Tnuva, Makhteshim-Agan [Adama], Shahal, Alma Lasers, and Ahava). The Chinese are operating in every possible manner to invest billions of dollars in the Israeli market, in areas such as renewable energy, water treatments, medical equipment, communications, and agriculture. Chinese investments in the Israeli market vary from direct investment to cooperative arrangements with Israeli venture capital firms or joint efforts to raise capital with other investors and joint enterprises. Many of the Chinese transactions aim to improve productivity, penetrate overseas markets, and improve technological capabilities or management skills.[81]

More importantly, over 1,000 Israeli companies are operating in China, and they can help in the development of the industrial sector in China by streamlining work procedures and improving performance.[82] Israeli companies will also be able to contribute to the realization of the BRI in areas where Israel has a relative advantage, such as agriculture, especially in arid zones, including water management, desalination and recycling, food production, and technological greenhouses.[83]

Infrastructure Projects

Chinese corporations have become some of the strongest players in Israel's transport, construction, and national infrastructure sectors; prior, U.S. and Western European companies were the prime movers. Chinese firms began to enter the Israeli economy via constructing roads, tunnels, ports, and train tracks; in the coming years, they will build and manage transport projects totaling tens of billions of dollars.[84]

Beijing became the dominant force in Israel's transport infrastructure in 2007 when the China Civil Engineering Construction Corporation (CCECC) was awarded the contract for digging the Carmel tunnel in Haifa,[85] and later joined a venture with Danya-Cebus to dig the tunnels on the Akko–Karmiel train line.[86] Moreover, two Chinese railway manufacturers, China North Railway (CNR) and China South Railway (CSR) are competing in the Israel Railways tenders for projects worth billions of dollars, for supplying electric locomotives and 90–120 railroad cars for the 'Red Line' light rail in the Tel Aviv metro.[87] In the end, China Railway Construction Co (CRRC) in Changchun was selected in November 2015 for a contract to supply 90 light railway carriages for the Red Line, plus a 16-year maintenance contract for both the carriages and infrastructure.[88] In December 2015, CNR won the tender for the supply of 120 cars for the Tel Aviv light rail transit system with a value of 216 million.[89]

According to *Globes*, five Chinese companies (CRCC, CRTG, China Harbor, CSCEC, and PCCC) will submit bids for construction and tunneling of the underground section of the Green Line (it will be 39 kilometers long, the longest of all the planned Tel Aviv light rail lines). The bids are likely to be around the NIS 1.5–NIS 2 billion mark out of the total estimated cost of NIS 15 billion for building the Green Line. The work was scheduled to begin at the start of 2020 and will include digging a 4.6-kilometer tunnel and building three underground stations. In contrast to previous tenders, the Chinese companies will bid separately and not as part of a consortium with Israeli construction companies.[90]

Meanwhile, all these investments in the Israeli transportation sector are just a prelude to the flagship venture, the 'Red–Med' rail project, which would connect Eilat on the Red Sea to the port of Ashdod on the Mediterranean. The implementation of the 'Red–Med' rail project will triple the profits of Chinese contractors and investors. For instance, a Chinese company will build the train line to Eilat, and other Chinese companies will provide the locomotives, train cars, and infrastructure at a cost of billions of dollars. Additionally, Chinese firms will be able to compete for the tender and probably will build a direct link to the new Ashdod port. If approved, this would give China a direct land bridge that would complement the Suez Canal, connecting the Red Sea to the Mediterranean Sea.[91]

More importantly, in the coming year's Chinese construction companies will increase their influence in the Israeli construction industry. In November 2016, five

Chinese construction giants won Israeli government tenders to build residential housing in Israel and to manage residential construction projects as the company responsible for all the engineering and performance aspects of the project.[92] In January 2017, after years of fruitless negotiations, Israel and China signed a final agreement for bringing thousands of Chinese professional construction workers to Israel. The agreement paves the way to bring 20,000 Chinese professional construction workers to Israel in the coming years.[93]

In July 2018, the Israeli Population and Immigration Authority approved the residence status of 2,200 long-employed Chinese workers, most of whom have been in Israel for over 12 years. During the first six months of the agreement, some 6,000 workers were expected to arrive in Israel. By March 2020, 3,500 workers of these had arrived, and another 700 were commissioned by contractors and are expected to arrive soon. Meanwhile, 1800 Chinese workers are still in China. The Israeli cabinet has approved extending the visas of 1,700 Chinese construction workers. The extension was motivated by coronavirus concerns about the arrival of new workers from China to replace them. As a result of the coronavirus outbreak, 1,000 Chinese workers who were to have come to Israel, starting on February 10, 2020, will be unable to come, and so it was suggested to extend the work period of the veteran construction workers by another period.[94]

Since the late 2000s, Chinese companies have been involved in building and operating major infrastructure projects in Israel. These ports, rail, and road projects fit in with the general concept of 'critical infrastructure', which could require special strategic consideration from Israeli policymakers. But although Israel's government prevents companies affiliated with foreign governments from bidding on tenders, this limitation does not exist when it comes to Chinese companies. This has enabled Chinese companies, including those with clear ties to the PRC government, to compete in and win tenders for construction and operation of major infrastructure projects, arguably without sufficient scrutiny. For instance, Israel's Commissioner of Capital Markets Dorit Salinger blocked all attempts by Chinese firms to acquire, in part or fully, Israeli insurance companies: Phoenix Holdings, Meitav-Dash, and Clal Insurance Enterprises.[95]

In January 2019, the Israeli government decided to prevent China and Turkey from competing in the tender process for a massive infrastructure project involving the establishment of a new international airport, due to concerns over Beijing's spying and tensions with Istanbul. Jerusalem decided that only NATO countries will be permitted to participate in the bidding process, as a means of excluding China from the competition. The tender is not for the completion of the project itself, but rather $40 million for the initial stages, with the possibility of future involvement when the plan is implemented.[96]

In September 2019, Israeli defense officials warned against letting Hutchison Water International, a subsidiary of Hong Kong-based holding company CK Hutchison Holding, to construct a major desalination facility planned for Nahal Sorek, near the Palmachim airbase and a nuclear research facility in the area. Hutchison Water is now in the final round of a government tender to build a major new desalination plant that had previously been flagged as a security concern due to its China-based ownership. When the new facility, Israel's sixth, is completed, it will provide some 200 million cubic meters of water per year or about one-fifth of household and municipal water consumed in Israel each year. Israel is under pressure from the Trump administration not to sign major infrastructure projects with China due to its contentious relations with Washington.[97]

Chinese construction and operation of major infrastructure projects, which involve the installation of and access to cameras, radio, fiber optics, and cellular networks, raise potential concerns for Israel and/or the U.S. The primary concern regarding investment relates to Chinese ownership of companies that might possess sensitive technology (dual-use) or data (Huawei entering the Israeli solar power market to sell inverters),[98] while concerns over construction center on the use of infrastructure projects to further Chinese foreign policy goals. The operation of infrastructure projects could present risks of surveillance, especially in the telecommunications sector, as could contracts to operate such major infrastructure as rail and ports. Therefore, Israel should establish a mechanism to regulate foreign investments in Israel, especially considering the rapidly growing investments from China.[99]

The PRC's expanding footprint in Israeli strategic assets has also been a source of increased friction with Washington. Israel's close bond with the United States is one of several factors that exert pressure on Sino–Israel relations, limiting the depth and scope of their relationship. Such pressures existed since before the establishment of official diplomatic ties in 1992, and many continue to influence the scope of relations up to the present day.[100] Following three years of deliberations and intense pressure from Washington over growing Chinese investments in Israeli companies, particularly in technology firms, Israel's security cabinet decided to set up a new mechanism to monitor foreign investments in the country.

The initiative to set up a new advisory panel on foreign investments in Israel – defined as investments, mergers, and acquisitions – has been in the works for over a year (writing in March 2020), to create a formal and organized process for vetting foreign investment. Israel joins many countries in the world, including the U.S., Canada, Britain, Germany, and Australia, which have launched a mechanism to monitor foreign investment in their country for national security reasons.[101] Although the Cabinet decision is framed as 'supervision over foreign investment,' the real goal is to create a mechanism for screening investments by Chinese firms and investment funds in Israeli strategic assets. The companies subject to vetting would be designated as critical to the economy or national security, including firms involved in infrastructure or with access to Israeli data, such as telecommunications companies, financial institutions, and arms makers.

According to the Cabinet decision, multiple government agencies will participate in the committee, including the Finance Ministry. The committee will include members from the National Security Council and Defense Ministry, as well as observers from the Foreign Affairs and Economy ministries and the National Economic Council. Regulators will consult with the committee voluntarily; business transactions that do not require government approval will not be brought before it. The committee's function is to help regulators to incorporate national security considerations in the process of approving foreign investments in the finance, communications, and infrastructure, transportation, and energy sectors – but not in the tech industry.[102] The Cabinet decided that the committee would be set up within 45 days, and regulators would be able to contact the committee starting in January 2020. The Cabinet is due to convene in six months to review the body's work and make adjustments if necessary. Due to the elections in Israel, the timetable for implementing these arrangements was changed.

The Trump administration wants Jerusalem to take action on regulating investments amid a bitter trade war with the PRC and anxiety over Beijing's aspiration to become a global high-tech leader. In April 2019, when U.S. President Donald Trump signed the document recognizing Israeli sovereignty of the Golan Heights, he demanded that Jerusalem cool ties with China. President Trump even warned that failure to do so could harm American military aid to Israel.[103] According to the *RAND* study, eleven companies of the 42 Chinese companies involved in investments and infrastructure projects in Israel raise potential concerns. These concerns include connections with the Chinese military or government; issues related to security, privacy, or censorship; business activities with Israel's adversaries, and the possible implications of Chinese development and operation of major infrastructure that might be important to Israel's security.[104]

Israel itself has sought to avoid taking sides in the conflict and to remain neutral. It took a long time for Israel to decide on the matter because it was trying to balance its interests, between not wanting to do anything that could harm its relationship with its most reliable ally and not wanting to do anything to harm its booming economic ties with China or place obstacles in attracting investment into Israel, something which is an essential engine of the country's economy.

Thus, the new committee will only play an advisory role on prospective foreign investments in Israeli companies, and government regulators do not have to consult with the committee or accept its recommendations. It is still unclear if the new committee's mandate will satisfy the Trump administration, which demanded stronger restrictions on Chinese investments, especially in the tech industry. Whether it will satisfy the Trump administration or will anger China and drive out Chinese investors entirely remains to be seen. It seems that the Cabinet decision was a compromise between national security and maintaining close relations with both the U.S. and China.[105]

Energy cooperation

As part of Beijing's innovative comprehensive partnership with Jerusalem, investment in energy infrastructure is considered one of the main areas of cooperation for integrating Israel's economic growth into the BRI framework. As far as gas reserves in the Eastern Mediterranean are concerned, Beijing's interest is currently theoretical but could become tangible in the future. In July 2012, Israeli Transport Minister Katz gave an interview to *The Global Times*, saying that gas in Israel could be a basis for Sino–Israeli discussions.[106] Israel's exports of gas to Beijing would have important strategic implications not because the sale in itself is problematic, but because relations with other gas-producing countries in the region and with the EU might be affected.[107]

In December 2015 it was reported that the Chinese investment group Fosun International sought to buy two small natural gas fields in the eastern Mediterranean from Israel's Delek Group.[108] In January 2016, both countries signed a document of understanding, expanding their cooperation in energy technology research and development, including the establishment of funds for renewable energy. The Israeli Minister of National Infrastructure, Energy, and Water Resources, Yuval Steinitz, invited Chinese companies (e.g., Sinopec Group, China Gezhouba Group Corporation (CGGC) and CMEC) to participate in tenders for oil and gas exploration in Israel's economic waters.[109]

In November 2019, the Chinese–Israeli company MRC Alon Tavor Power signed a 15-year natural gas supply agreement in Israel with Britain-based oil and gas producer Energean. The Alon Tavor power plant is the first privatized power plant in Israel as part of the process of the country's reforms in privatizing its power plants. The Chinese-Israeli MRC consortium acquired the Alon Tavor plant from Israel Electric Corporation in July 2019 for around $530 million. The consortium consists of China Harbor Engineering Company (CHEC) that holds 34.5 percent of shares, and two Israeli companies, Mivtach Shamir Holdings, and Rapac Energy. According to the long-term agreement, Energean will supply about 500 million cubic meters of natural gas per year for 15 years for the Alon Tavor gas-fired power plant located in northern Israel, with an accumulated natural gas value of more than 1 billion U.S. dollars. The natural gas supplying the Alon Tavor power plant will first be drilled from the Israeli offshore Karish gas field, owned and operated by Energean.[110]

People-to-People Bond

Under China's innovative comprehensive partnership with Jerusalem, enabling the people of the two countries to bond along the Silk Road is vital to integrate Israel's economic growth into the BRI framework. This is to be achieved by promoting extensive cultural and academic exchanges to win public support for deepening bilateral and multilateral cooperation, as well as providing scholarships, holding annual cultural events, increasing cooperation in science and technology, and establishing joint laboratory or research centers and international technology transfer centers.[111]

There are increasing investments and cooperation between the two countries in the scientific and academic fields. Cooperation between universities from Israel (Technion, University of Haifa, Tel Aviv University, Bar Ilan University, and the Ben-Gurion University of the Negev) and China in academic collaborations, research, and teaching has become stronger; this includes cooperation in desalination, water treatment, and reclamation projects, ecology, big data, biomedicine, and neurobiology. These activities will serve as a platform to encourage connections between Chinese and Israeli businesspeople and push further investments in the Israeli industry.[112]

In January 2015, the Israeli Council for Higher Education and the Chinese Ministry of Education agreed to establish the Beijing-Jerusalem 7+7 Research-based University Alliance to promote research and academic cooperation between research universities in Israel and China. This effort included the establishment of a $300 million XIN Center, a joint research center for Tel Aviv University and Beijing's Tsinghua University, which was designed to concentrate on cooperation in the area of nanotechnology; a joint laboratory building for the University of Haifa and East China Normal University on the campus of the latter, specializing in ecology, big data, biomedicine, and neurobiology; and a joint center for entrepreneurship and innovation for Ben-Gurion University of the Negev and Jilin University.[113]

The establishment of Israeli research institutions in China is a very recent phenomenon. Israel had four campuses or institutions in China, while China had none in Israel. In May 2014, Tel Aviv University partnered with Tsinghua University to establish the XIN Center, a joint center for innovative research and education to be funded by government and private enterprise.[114] In December 2015, the Technion-Israel Institute of Technology began construction on the Guangdong Technion-Israel Institute of Technology (GTIIT) in Shantou (the GTIIT began welcoming its first students in the summer of 2017), the first Israeli university in China and one of only two foreign universities allowed to establish an independent program in China.[115] In March and April 2016, Ben-Gurion University of the Negev also established a joint center for entrepreneurship and innovation with Jilin University, while the University of Haifa established a joint laboratory building on the campus of East China Normal University in Shanghai.[116]

Cultural exchanges between Beijing–Jerusalem have rich content and good foundations. In the media sphere, *The Times of Israel*, a major English-language newspaper in Israel, for a time produced a Chinese-language edition. *China Plus*, of China Radio International, China's state-owned international broadcaster, has a Hebrew channel among its channels in dozens of other languages. The 19th China Shanghai International Arts Festival held an Israel Culture Week in November 2017, to honor the 25th anniversary of the establishment of diplomatic relations between Beijing-Jerusalem.[117] In the PRC, there have been efforts by various organizations to promote China's positive role in saving Jewish refugees during the Holocaust. In August 2017, Shanghai Jiaotong University Publishing House announced that it would be establishing a "Jewish Refugees to China Database". The National Office for Philosophy and Social Sciences, under the National Social Science Fund of China, researched Jewish refugees to China and issued periodic work reports on research progress.[118]

Linguistic cooperation is another important aspect of Beijing-Jerusalem's innovative comprehensive partnership, and both nations have outlined their intention to expand the collaboration in these areas in the coming years. According to the *Hanban website*, the Chinese government established Confucius Institutes for providing Chinese language and culture teaching resources worldwide. In 2019, there were 550 Confucius Institutes and 1,172 Confucius Classrooms and 5,665 teaching sites established in 162 countries and regions, receiving about eleven million students.[119] In 54 countries involved in the Belt and Road Initiative, there are 153 Confucius Institutes and 149 primary and high school Confucius Classrooms.[120] In the Middle East, there are eighteen Confucius institutes and three Confucius Classrooms. There were two Confucius Institutes in Israel, one each at Tel Aviv University and the Hebrew University of Jerusalem.[121]

There is also constant growth in tourism in both directions with the introduction of more direct flights between the two countries annually. In recent years, several significant steps have been taken to attract Chinese tourists and businessmen to Israel. The two main barriers (a shortage of direct flights, especially of Chinese airlines, and a visa procedure that requires significant time and paperwork) underwent major changes following a concerted effort by the ministries of Foreign Affairs, Interior, and Tourism. In 2015, an agreement signed between Jerusalem and Beijing went into effect, providing a mutual visa exemption for holders of diplomatic passports and service passports; diplomatic and economic work with provincial government offices become easier and convenient, and Israel has become a more attractive destination. In 2016, the two countries signed a 10-year multiple-entry visa agreement, making Israel the third country, after the U.S. and Canada, to have such an arrangement with Beijing. This visa agreement allows Israeli and Chinese businesspeople and tourists to enter China or Israel multiple times with the same visa.[122]

In addition, steps were taken to streamline the procedure for obtaining a visa. The Israeli Ministry of Tourism has also promoted a fee exemption for visas for Chinese tourist groups. Regarding direct flights, which have created a travel bottleneck between the countries: over the past two years, with a joint push by all of the Israeli government ministries and missions in China, Hainan Airlines introduced direct flights from Beijing and Shanghai, and Cathay Pacific and Sichuan have direct flights from Hong Kong. In 2018, a direct route from Chengdu was opened, and a direct route from Guangzhou is expected to open, with more direct flights expected to be launched in 2020.[123] These steps have led to a surge in the number of Chinese entering Israel. From 2015 to 2018, the number of Chinese visiting Israel almost tripled from less than 50,000 to 139,000, and in 2019 the expectation is that the number will reach 150,000.[124]

Summary

Israel was the first country in the Middle East to recognize the PRC, but the last one to establish diplomatic relations with China. In the 21st century, Sino–Israeli relations have experienced complex and tortuous development. As a part of China's Belt and Road strategy, Israel is an important key state in the Middle East in its initiative; its innovative comprehensive partnership with Beijing has also kindled extraordinary attention. The relations between the two countries are broadening and deepening on multiple fronts. Although bilateral relations appear not to be especially close in some areas, they are booming in others. In the political and defense realm, for example, relations are cordial but not particularly warm, with each side having other, more preferred partners. In the economic field, however, the relations are much stronger, as noted by the increase in trade and investment between the two countries. Similarly, there is a lot of potential for growth in the realm of tourism, and, at least on the Israeli side, there is a high interest in fueling that growth.[125]

In the construction of the new Silk Road, Israel has an important geopolitical and geo-economic value. As a Middle East country, Jerusalem has a democratic system, a sound system for the rule of law, economic prosperity, social stability, advanced education, is a leading power in science and technology, and has a significant advantage in human capital. Israel can play an important strategic role as a strategic partner with China, and Beijing can utilize the BRI as an opportunity to further enhance economic and trade exchanges, cultural exchanges, and other aspects of cooperation with Israel.[126]

In October 2018, Prime Minister Netanyahu hailed the 'natural partnership' between the two countries as he hosted the Chinese Vice-President Wang Qishan at a meeting of the Israel–China Joint Committee on Innovation Cooperation in Jerusalem. Since then, a string of U.S. officials has taken issue with the relationship, including the National Security Adviser John Bolton and Secretary of State Mike Pompeo, who threatened to limit intelligence sharing with Israel unless the country falls into line.

The PRC and Israel, however, are hardly natural partners, although they share interests in technology and innovation cooperation. Jerusalem's longstanding partner and close ally, the U.S., has raised varying concerns over the growing Sino–Israeli relationship. Science and technology cooperation has always been a central part of Beijing–Jerusalem relations. That includes defense technology transfers, but also collaboration in purely civilian areas. Recently, China has also shown interest in emerging technologies being developed in Israel, such as artificial intelligence, nanotechnology, and autonomous vehicle technology.

As long as the defense relationship remains limited between the two countries, the main concerns about the Sino–Israeli relationship involve investment, related technology, and intellectual property issues, and construction projects. This is not only true for Jerusalem and its security or economic interests, but also for Washington, which is primarily concerned with the transfer of defense-related technology to Beijing and other technologies and capabilities that could strengthen the PRC's military edge.[127]

Thus, the only area in the Beijing–Jerusalem relationship that is limited is military technology. Since the beginning of the 21st century, Israeli high-tech transfers to China are limited because of the ambiguity of U.S. restrictions, not just regarding the export of military technology to China but also dual-use technologies in which Beijing is very much interested.[128] Although military relations were the forerunner to China–Israel relations in the late 1970s, they are also the cause of the worst crisis between the countries. Washington's sensitivity and U.S. export restrictions have limited Israel's defense and dual-use technology transfers to China. Consequently, Israel's ties with China are concentrated in non-military commercial, scientific, and academic fields.[129]

Washington has enough reasons to be sensitive and concerned about Sino–Israeli science and technology cooperation. First, Jerusalem's high-tech sector has strong connections with the defense establishment. Many high-tech companies are established by veterans of military technological units, others are financially supported by the Ministry of Defense, and a relatively large share of them are suppliers of the defense establishment. Even when Israeli high-tech products are categorized as civilians, many of them are still defense-oriented (dual-use). Second, while Israel strictly bans defense and dual-use exports to the PRC, the U.S. suspects that Israel's monitoring of FDI and the involvement of Chinese firms in infrastructure projects – another growing source of Washington concern – is relatively weak. Given Jerusalem's past defense relations with the PRC, it is plausible for Washington to harbors doubts as to whether Israel shares its concerns over China and incorporates these concerns adequately into its investment monitoring process. Finally, science and technology cooperation with Israel allows the PRC to get closer to an important U.S. partner, exposing Washington's failure to keep its allies and partners out of Beijing's reach. After Washington forced Israel in the early 2000s to cut off defense relations with Beijing, the latter kept its distance from Jerusalem for about a decade.[130]

Israel relies on Washington for security, economic ties, and geopolitical assistance, while the China–U.S. relationship has grown increasingly tense. However, the continuation of the trade war and its larger implications and indirect effects on Israel might create further friction in the Sino–Israeli relationship and the prospect of expanding it. There is fear that U.S. concerns over these developments will lead it to pressure Israel not only to slow down the exchange but to end it. In the past, under considerable pressure, Israel caved into Washington and canceled its deal with China to install the Phalcon advanced airborne radar system and upgrade the Harpy drone.[131]

The Chinese Special Envoy for the Middle East, Zhai Jun, accused the United States of trying to block China's economic development with Israel. "The US is not very happy about China's development and rapid growth and tries to make trouble. They are using bullying tactics to curb and contain the PRC's development and set obstacles to China–Israel cooperation. Beijing never set obstacles to the U.S.–Israel cooperation, so I don't think it makes any sense for the U.S. to question China–Israel cooperation."[132]

Jerusalem's advanced technology sector attracts Chinese investment, while its position along the BRI economic corridor further increases its attractiveness as a location for major Chinese-built infrastructure projects. There are enormous economic benefits to Israel in its commercial relations with Beijing. Chinese investment can help Jerusalem to diversify its sources of capital, and links with Chinese businessmen can help Israeli firms enter the rapidly growing Chinese market. Involving Chinese construction companies can prove a lower-cost and more efficient source of project development and completion than could be gained from either Israeli or other foreign firms working on those tasks.[133] However, Israel's longstanding relationship with the United States as ally and friend presents complex challenges to the development of the Sino–Israeli relationship, especially in the defense and dual-use sectors, and Jerusalem will have to navigate with diplomacy in order not to jeopardize its bi-lateral relations with either power.

4 | Syria

China's engagement with Syria is part of its continuous attempts to increase its presence in the Arab world and to expand its influence in the Middle East. Beijing-Damascus relations go back to ancient times; modern relations between the two nations, however, were not officially established until 1956, when Syria was the second Arab country after Egypt to establish diplomatic relations with China. Syria offers significant economic opportunities for Beijing that could play an influential role in the post-war reconstruction, and bring enormous benefit to China's Belt and Road Initiative (BRI). However, the extent of China's future involvement in Syria depends on various challenges and obstacles that could significantly influence Beijing's financial and entrepreneurial contributions in the coming years.[1]

Historically, Syria was a vital node in the centuries-old Silk Routes that fanned out from Beijing across Asia to Europe and Africa. Today, China sees the situation in Syria as an opportunity to benefit economically, expand its influence in the Middle East, and even boost its globe-spanning BRI infrastructure investment initiative. Syria's geographical location at the crossroads of East and West has a particular value for the Chinese New Silk Road, and Beijing is likely to leverage a role in Syria's reconstruction to advance its BRI. As such, Beijing could play an influential role in post-conflict reconstruction in Syria, which would have significant implications for the development projects, and consequently, for the future socio-economic shape and stability of the country.[2]

Throughout the eight-year Syrian civil war, Beijing's Syria policy has derived from its broader security and economic interests in the Middle East. China's two primary policy objectives are first, the conviction that Chinese economic and security interests are best served by a stable and friendly regime in Damascus capable of preventing the country from becoming a sanctuary or training ground for radical jihadists, and second, developing economic interests that are compatible with the BRI framework.[3] Since Chinese companies have experience in war-torn Middle Eastern nations, they are reportedly queuing up to win contracts for rebuilding entire towns and villages, roads, bridges, schools, hospitals, and communication networks in the reconstruction process of Syria.[4]

Syria lies at the crossroads of Southeast Asia, Southwest Asia, Europe, and Africa.

It has held an essential position on the Silk Road ever since ancient times when Chinese products such as silk and porcelain were sold to Western Asia via the route. The connection between the two nations dates back a thousand years ago, when Tadmor (Palmyra) presented a vital trade center between the East and the West.[5] Syria's central geographic location, namely its seaports in Tartus and Latakia, make the country strategically crucial to become major terminals for Chinese goods in the Mediterranean.[6]

In this context, it is essential to understand the new phase in the rebuilding and reconstruction of Syria, a process of deepening Beijing-Damascus relations, and the impact on the implementation of the BRI. This chapter examines developing China–Syria relations in the forthcoming post-war reconstruction of the country, and the synergy between the BRI and the rebuilding of Syria, to understand the extent of the bilateral engagement and the importance of integrating Damascus within the BRI.

The main argument presented is that Beijing's relations with Damascus in the post-war reconstruction are based on shared or mutually complementary economic interests. Syria's strategic geographic position in the Levant region and China's involvement in the Syria rebuilding process fit perfectly into its grand global vision of BRI economic integration. As Chinese President Xi Jinping said on June 2019, Beijing stands ready to participate in Syria's reconstruction within its own ability.[7]

Syria's Reconstruction

The widespread destruction in Syria since March 2011 has been disastrous for the economy, human life (over half a million lives lost, 5.6 million Syrians became refugees, and more than 6.1 million people were displaced internally),[8] and the country's critical infrastructure. The costs of repairing this damage are daunting to the international community. In August 2018, the UN Economic and Social Commission for Western Asia (ESCWA) estimated the cost of damage at more than $388 billion, and the cost of lost productivity to GDP at around $268 billion.[9] Most experts agree that the Syrian government cannot afford such a massive undertaking, and it will take at least a decade to repair the war damage.[10]

The nearly $400 billion price tag for rebuilding Syria after eight years of civil war is too big a sum for a single partner to undertake. Notwithstanding, the U.S. and Europe are not poised to play any role in the rebuilding process since the Syrian regime has rejected their interference in reconstruction, the oil-rich Gulf countries remain estranged, and its allies Russia and Iran both suffer from sanction-damaged economies.[11] Hence, China is in a privileged position as the potential stakeholder due to two factors: its political closeness to the Syrian regime – which the West and Gulf countries lack – and its vast resources – which Russia and Iran lack.[12] As Syria's ambassador to Beijing, Imad Moustapha, has said, "because China, Russia, and Iran have provided substantial support to Syria during the military conflict . . . [they] should play a major role in the reconstruction of Syria."[13]

China's proven capabilities in infrastructure, the scale of its economy, its available capital, and the infrastructure enterprises it leads worldwide, could meet the requirements for the enormous undertaking of reconstructing a devastated Syria. More broadly, the Syrian reconstruction projects, especially in the infrastructure field (e.g., roads, railroads, power plants, communications, and energy), dovetail perfectly with

China's grand global vision of the BRI framework, which focuses on the establishment of transport, trade, and communications infrastructure between Beijing and the global markets and sources of raw materials, especially in Europe and Africa, by land, sea, and air.[14]

Nevertheless, as mentioned, this wide-scale investment in Syria's post-war reconstruction is too large for any one state, even China, to meet on its own. China's infrastructure investment comes in multiple forms, all of which entail different risks. Beijing is likely to be a lender rather than a donor, and investment would likely go through Chinese public-private partnerships (PPP) and state-owned enterprises rather than being funneled through the Syrian regime and its state-linked businesses.[15] Beijing also typically funds infrastructure abroad through a model of investment loans, usually requiring Chinese companies to undertake the construction, but this model does not allow for wide-scale investments. The Chinese government is generally wary of risking its investments and interests abroad, and it is not eager to expose itself to further risks before Syria is stabilized and the fighting there has ceased. Thus, there is little reason to expect significant Chinese involvement in terms of wide-scale investments or infrastructure projects in Syria in the foreseeable future.[16]

At the July 2018 China–Arab States Cooperation Forum (CASCF), Chinese President Xi Jinping pledged more than $23 billion in lines of credit, loans, and humanitarian assistance to Arab countries, including $90 million in humanitarian aid to Yemen, Lebanon, Jordan, and Syria. Another $151 million was earmarked for aid projects, with the remaining funds designated for financial and economic cooperation. However, it is unclear how much of this money will go directly to Syria, and it is not unlikely that a significant portion of the aid and loan package will be invested in post-war reconstruction.[17]

In contrast, on the humanitarian plane, China's aid to Syria came down to pledging tens of millions of dollars – if and when this will be delivered, it is hard to know – which provides excellent evidence of China's playing a larger role in providing humanitarian aid through bilateral and multilateral channels. In January 2017, President Xi, in his keynote speech at the UN Office in Geneva, committed to providing $30 million in humanitarian assistance for refugees and displaced persons in Syria.[18] In February 2017, the Chinese Embassy and the Syrian Planning and International Cooperation Commission (ICC) signed two agreements whereby China will provide two batteries of humanitarian aid to the Syrian government worth $16 million.[19]

In November 2017, the Chinese Embassy in Damascus communicated that China had donated $1 million to the World Health Organization (WHO), the World Food Program (WFP), and the International Committee of the Red Cross (ICRC) respectively, to improve food security and health conditions in Syria, as well as to provide special assistance to internally displaced people and returnees.[20] In the same month, China delivered 1,000 tons of rice to Syria's northwestern city of Latakia as part of its food aid to the developing countries, as one component of China's effort to promote its BRI. China has also made direct donations in Syria. In the first half of 2017, the Chinese government signed three agreements with the Syrian government to provide humanitarian aid to Syria worth over $40 million.[21] In 2017, China also funded a $1.5 million World Food Program (WFP) initiative to feed newly-arrived Syrian refugees in Jordan. Part of the donation also went to the School Meals Program, benefiting some 12,500 Syrian children who received fresh-baked pastries, fruits, and vegetables daily.[22]

In August 2018, The Red Cross Society of China (RCSC) donated two bus-turned mobile medical clinics and two ambulances to Syria's Arab Red Crescent (SARC).[23] In October 2018, China donated 800 electrical power generator transformers with various capacities and 60 kilometer-long electric cables to Latakia, Syria's largest port.[24] In December 2018, China donated 1,000 tons of wheat worth $724,000 in humanitarian assistance for Syrian refugees in Lebanon.[25] In June 2019, China donated 100 buses to Syria to facilitate public transportation in the country.[26]

Syria and the Belt and Road Initiative

The People's Republic of China's (PRC) relations with Syria includes five major areas for cooperation within the BRI. These areas are policy coordination, connectivity, trade and investments, energy cooperation, and military ties. Because for each country the BRI has different implications and serves different interests, each country inevitably has a different perspective on how to realize the project. Beijing wants to play an influential role post-conflict, but the economic and security circumstances in the country moderate its enthusiasm to invest in Syria's reconstruction.

Policy coordination

As part of China's relations with Syria, important elements of integrating the reconstruction of Syria within the BRI framework are: promoting political cooperation between the countries, creating mechanisms for dialogue and consensus-building on global and regional issues, developing shared interests, deepening political trust and reaching a new consensus on cooperation.[27]

In June 2004, Syria President Bashar al-Assad visited Beijing, four years after he took office in 2000. This was the first visit by a Syrian head of state to China since the two countries established relations in 1956. At his meeting with then Chinese president Hu Jintao, the Syrian President described China as a close friend of Syria and welcomed Chinese companies to invest in the country.[28] In March 2016, the Syrian President interviewed with *Russia's Sputnik News Agency*, where he identified China as one of three primary actors that are expected to participate in the reconstruction process, along with Russia and Iran.[29]

In another interview with Hong Kong-based *Phoenix TV* on March 2017, President Assad said that China–Syria relations are 'on the rise' because Beijing was 'a real friend' that could be relied upon. The Syrian President also suggested that Beijing would play a role in Syria's rebuilding process. "China can be in every sector with no exception, because we have damage in every sector," noting that the residential sector, infrastructure, and industrial projects could use Chinese investment.[30]

For many years, Syrian officials at all levels have consistently sought to present China as a key player in post-war reconstruction and the BRI as playing a major role According to Syrian Presidential Political and Media Advisor Bouthaina Shaaban, "The Silk Road is not a silk road if it does not pass through Syria, Iraq, and Iran."[31] In September 2017, during the United Nations General Assembly, Chinese Foreign Minister Wang Yi met with Syrian Deputy Prime Minister and Foreign Minister Walid Muallem. At the meeting, the Chinese Foreign Minister said, "Syria is an important node in the ancient Silk Road, and the 'Belt and Road' construction can serve as an important opportunity for bilateral cooperation in the future. China welcomes Syria's active participation in the 'Belt and Road' construction and stands ready to carry out cooperation with Syria within this framework for the sake of common development."[32]

In November 2017, Chinese Foreign Minister Wang Yi met with Presidential Political and Media Advisor Bouthaina Shaaban, who visited China. Shaaban expressed Syria's support for the BRI which is not just an economic project, but a cultural, human, and intellectual project that serves all humankind. For his part, Chinese Foreign Minister Wang welcomed the participation of Syria and its support for the initiative and reiterated his statements about the historical friendship between the two countries and the fact that Syria is an important partner in this initiative.[33]

Moreover, Bouthaina Shaaban, who also attended the second Belt and Road Forum for International Cooperation held in April 2019 in Beijing, told Russia's *Sputnik News Agency*: "So we hope that Syria, which is historically a very important partner to the Silk Road, will participate also in rebuilding this new Belt and Road [initiative]. And we hope that Syria, Iraq, Iran will be able to build bridges because this is really our major problem in the Middle East, that we are prevented from connectivity with each other by force."[34]

At the regular press briefing in November 2017, Chinese foreign ministry spokesperson Geng Shuang explained Beijing's motive for actively engaging in the rebuilding process in Syria and other Middle East countries recently: "Too many people in the Middle East are suffering at the brutal hands of terrorists . . . We support countries in the region in exploring a development path suited to their national conditions and are ready to share governance experience and jointly build the Belt and Road and promote peace and stability through common development."[35]

Similarly, in February 2018, Chinese Ambassador to Syria Qi Qianjin told the *Xinhua News Agency*: "I think it's about time to focus all efforts on the development and reconstruction of Syria, and I think China will play a bigger role in this process by providing more aid to the Syrian people and the Syrian government."[36] In August 2018, the Chinese Embassy in Damascus released a letter written by Ambassador Qi Qianjin, which restated China's plan to use infrastructure investment and reconstruction deals to rejuvenate Syria and the region, including to develop railways and seaports to create greater economic interconnectivity. Increasing cooperation with Syria helps China's BRI ambitions in the region with its promises of financial injections into the Middle East.[37] In an interview with *TASS Russian News Agency* and the government-owned daily, *Rossiyskaya Gazeta*, on June 2019, Chinese President Xi Jinping said that China stands ready to participate in Syria's reconstruction, "within its own ability." This statement is a confirmation of the assessment that Beijing will assume a significant role in the Syria rebuilding process, including infrastructure.[38]

Energy cooperation

Chinese investment in energy infrastructure is considered one of the areas of cooperation critical to integrate Damascus into the BRI framework. Syria has traditionally been a low focus for Chinese investment compared to the oil and gas-producing countries in the region, like Iran or Iraq and the Arab Gulf states. However, the advent of the BRI means Syria has emerged from economic insignificance in Chinese eyes to become a location of increasing interest.

According to Energy Information Administration (EIA), Syria is the only relatively significant crude oil-producing country in the Eastern Mediterranean region. Although Syria produces relatively modest quantities of oil and gas, its location is strategic in terms of regional security and prospective energy transit routes. Regional integration in the energy sector is expected to increase as a result of ongoing plans for the expansion of the regional oil and gas pipeline networks connecting Syria with neighboring countries. However, Syria's energy sector is in turmoil because of the ongoing civil conflict that began in the spring of 2011, with oil and natural gas production declining dramatically since then.[39]

Before the current conflict, when Syria produced 383,000 barrels per day (b/d) of oil and 316 million cubic feet per day (Mmcf/d) of natural gas, Syria's oil and gas sector accounted for approximately one-fourth of government revenues.[40] China, before the war, had already invested tens of billions of dollars in Syria's oil and gas industry. Now Syria is no longer able to export oil, and as a result, government revenues from the energy sector have fallen significantly. Naturally, the priority for China, once the war is over, that is the Chinese oil companies would rebuild much of the destroyed oil infrastructure, which has been left unmaintained for years, but would also gain back their investment.

One of the most important Chinese companies eyeing re-entry into Syria is its China National Petroleum Company, the world's third-largest oil company. The state-owned giant owns stakes in two of Syria's state-owned oil companies: al-Furat and the Syrian Petroleum Company, with assets estimated at 21 billion barrels.[41] The stakes give China partial ownership of all oil revenue in eastern Syria. In November 2017, Syria's ambassador to Beijing said his country would be willing to provide China with oil in exchange for loans, and would even be prepared to make these transactions in yuan, following China's aspirations to incorporate its currency within the global exchange market.[42]

Before the war began in 2011, China Petroleum & Chemical Corporation (Sinopec) was a significant investor in northeastern and eastern Syria. In 2008, Sinopec made its first major venture into the country, through the acquisition of Canadian-based Tanganyika Oil (an estimated 21 billion barrels of oil). The deal also provided Sinopec with Tanganyika's access to one trillion cubic feet (tcf) of natural gas, and control of three oil fields, Sheikh Mansour, Oudeh, and Tishrin, all located in Syria's northeast.[43]

In 2011, as stated, Sinopec acquired a 20.3 percent stake in the al-Furat Petroleum Company, the leading Syrian government oil producer.[44] Nevertheless, Sinopec cannot return to work in Syria since the oil fields it was mandated to drill are all located in territory presently held by the Americans and their Kurdish allies in Syria's northeast. China will continue to leverage its oil relationship with the Syrian government to find a way to make an eventual agreement.[45]

Connectivity

The facilitation of connectivity is one of the crucial ways to integrate the rebuilding of Damascus within the BRI framework. The Levant is set to become a critical node in the BRI's China–Central Asia–West Asia economic corridor, as it offers an alternative route to the Mediterranean besides the Suez passage. Syria becomes a crucial junction within the 21st Century Maritime Silk Road Initiative (MSRI): possible development of its transport and port infrastructures, adequately connected and with the BRI, would allow China a further maritime outlet for its land trade and a formidable trade post in the Mediterranean.

Syria had never been a strategic priority or played an essential role in China's economy like other oil and gas-producing countries in the region until the emergence of the BRI, which has boosted China's interest in the development of Syrian and Lebanese ports. A further advantage is represented by the increased quantity of goods that China could deliver into the Mediterranean, by developing a secondary route to the Mediterranean and southern Europe, overcoming the bottleneck of the Suez Canal.[46]

The end of the Syrian Civil War also represents opportunities for Chinese companies to gain access to Syria's Mediterranean seaports (Latakia and Tartus). A statement from the Chinese embassy in Damascus affirmed the importance of the Tartus port, a connectivity goal that extends to the BRI framework.[47] Commercially the MSRI is, above all, about aligning the 'connectivity' of global shipping lanes and ports and with Chinese capital. The Syrian port of Latakia could also play a vital role in the MSRI economic corridor by reducing reliance on the Suez Canal and decreasing the cost of trade to European countries. However, Russia has a major military presence, with an airbase in Latakia and a naval base in Tartus that has already been leased to Russia for 49 years,[48] while Iran is moving to establish a permanent coastal foothold in Latakia.[49]

The nearby harbor of Tripoli in Lebanon has also been positioning itself as another prime location for the BRI framework.[50] Since 2012, China Harbor Engineering Company Ltd (CHEC) has been working to develop the Port of Tripoli – the only deep-water port in the area not under effective Russian control – so that it can accommodate larger vessels (and perhaps serve as an access point for Syrian reconstruction and trans-shipment hub).[51]

Tripoli is set to become a Special Economic Zone within the MSRI, with the Tripoli port planned to be a main transshipment hub for the eastern Mediterranean. The zone provides Chinese (and other regional businesses) with low tax options for consolidating and adding value to parts sourced elsewhere to then be exported to Syria.[52] This will also provide a more direct route for Chinese goods to Europe rather than relying on the Suez Canal. Ultimately China can develop these harbors as prime routes from Asia overland to not only Europe but to Turkey, North Africa, and through the Suez Canal, linking up with the String of Pearls in the Indian Ocean.[53]

In order to service this port, there are Chinese plans to reconstruct the Tripoli–Homs railway network.[54] China also plans to invest in a railway from the port city of Tripoli in Lebanon to the Lebanon–Syria border, which would provide Beijing with a means to transport materials from Tripoli into Syria. Without such a railway, the only other plausibly efficient entry points for Chinese goods into Syria are the Mediterranean ports of Latakia and Tartus. However, neither of the two major Mediterranean ports in Latakia and Tartus is deep enough to take large container ships.[55] Additionally, as part of the initiative's land route, China intends to build a railway through Iran and Turkey into northern Syria.[56]

In parallel, Syria also hopes to implement the agreement with Beijing which calls for the establishment of a special zone for Chinese companies seeking to do business in the country as part of the ambitious BRI framework. The special zone would be established in the coastal city of Latakia, complementing a similar project that the Chinese are working on in the port of Tripoli in Lebanon, just over the southern border.[57]

Trade and investments

Part of the PRC's relations with Syria includes attempting to mitigate barriers to free trade, investment, industrial cooperation, and technical and engineering services to facilitate the integration of Syria's rebuilding process within the BRI framework. Both countries must take steps in that direction, such as expanding free-trade zones, improving trade structures, seeking new potential areas for trade and improving the trade balance, devising new initiatives for the promotion of conventional forms of trade, developing trans-border electronic trade and other advanced models of business, creating a system for supporting trade in services to strengthen and expand conventional trade, increasing customs cooperation, and regularly sharing information in these areas.[58]

According to Imad Moustapha, Syria's ambassador to China, Damascus was keen for China to play a part in the country's reconstruction. Chinese businesses have been preparing to open representative offices across Syria, and have sent frequent delegations to the country, leading to numerous contracts being in the pipeline or having already been signed.[59] In July 2017, the PRC hosted the "First Trade Fair on Syrian Reconstruction Projects," and pledged $2 billion toward rebuilding the Syrian industry, centered on a plan to construct an industrial estate that could house up to 150 companies.[60]

At the 60th Annual Damascus International Trade Fair in September 2018, more than 200 Chinese, mostly state-owned, companies attended, all of which were involved in different fields. The fair is one of the oldest of its kind in the Middle East but was suspended from 2011 to 2016 as protests against the Assad regime grew into an armed rebellion and civil war. The re-established fair allows international companies to set up shop in a Damascus exhibition center, pitching deals either to Syria or to one another. They invest billions of dollars for stability, and once it is achieved, Chinese business will be ready to build off extensive groundwork. With little competition present, the PRC pledged to manufacture its own cars within Syria and provide mobile hospitals, including deals for the construction of steel and power plants,[61] and it reaffirmed its ambition to develop post-war Syria's infrastructure.[62]

For the PRC, the fair offered the opportunity for its companies to strike deals and joint ventures with an eye to long-term partnerships with Syria's key industries in the post-war period. Some of China's flagship involvements include Chinese tech giant Huawei committing in 2015 to rebuild Syria's telecommunications system by 2020, though this is still a work very much in progress.[63] Since the majority of the Chinese companies at the fair were state-owned enterprises, Chinese government-backed entities were likely looking to build working relationships, which could lead to a PPP reconstruction ecosystem in Syria. However, to date, none of those initiatives have materialized into major investments.[64] Chinese ambassador Feng Biao stated that fifty-eight Chinese companies planned to attend the sixty-first Damascus International Fair in September 2019.[65]

In 2017, Qin Yong, vice chairman of the China Arab Exchange Association (CAFA), made four trips to Syria. In April 2017, at the invitation of the Syrian government, Qin led a business delegation on a visit to Damascus and Homs and confirmed that several major Chinese companies had expressed interest in participating in infrastructure projects in Syria.[66] The CAFA, an organization founded by the State Council of the People's Republic to increase political, cultural, economic, and commercial partnerships between China and the Arab countries, also issued a list of planned reconstruction projects in Syria's infrastructure, electricity, building materials, agriculture, etc. Reportedly as many as 1,000 Chinese companies are involved, including some of the leading Chinese companies in harbor engineering, steel, hydropower, metallurgy, aircraft, and agriculture. According to the *Guangming Daily*, several business representatives in Syria have "expressed their willingness to shoulder the glorious mission of the BRI."[67]

According to China Customs Statistics (export-import), China–Syria trade volume decreased to $1.3 billion by 2019 (compared to nearly $2 billion in 2018).[68] The Chinese government has long expressed its interest in increasing the scale of its investments for the reconstruction of Syria. Yet according to the *China Global Investment Tracker*, Beijing's investments and contracts in Syria, which from 2005 to 2011 reached $4 billion, stood at zero between 2011 and 2019.[69]

Military ties

Security cooperation, including arms and equipment sales and training military forces, has become an increasing part of integrating Syrian reconstruction into the BRI. The Chinese Ambassador to Syria, Qi Qianjin told *Al-Watan* in August 2018 that the Chinese military would be willing to participate "in some way" in the campaign in Idlib or other parts of the country. The report also quoted the Chinese military attaché in Syria as saying that the Chinese military wishes to enhance its relations with the Syrian military.[70] However, Hua Chunying, the Chinese Ministry of Foreign Affairs spokesperson, has denied that China plans to be involved "in some way" in the Syrian conflict.[71]

In August 2016, People's Liberation Army Navy (PLAN) Rear Admiral Guan Youfei, who sits on China's Central Military Commission, met Lt. General Fahd Jassem al-Frejj, the Syrian defense minister, in Damascus. The Chinese Rear Admiral pledged that the PLA would be willing to continue exchanges and cooperation with the Syrian military, including providing training.[72] According to *The Global Times*, there are Chinese military advisors on the ground in Syria that train regime forces in the use of Chinese-bought weapons, including sniper rifles, rocket launchers, and machine guns.[73] Nevertheless, a close review of China's military activities in Syria reveals that they are mostly symbolic and rhetorical, while any active engagement is limited and of negligible impact. In the past eight years, China has continued to steer clear of direct military involvement in the conflict. Hence, Chinese military advisors are sent to Syria to deal only with soft issues: medicine and logistics.[74]

Similarly, in December 2015, China passed its first counter-terrorism law, which allows it to conduct joint counter-terrorism operations overseas.[75] In late 2017, reports in Arab-language media claimed that a Chinese Special Forces unit, the "Tiger of Dark Night" or "Night Tigers," was being deployed in the port city of Tartus to fight Uyghur jihadi forces in Syria.[76] However, the Chinese Special Envoy for Syria, Xie Xiaoyan, denied these rumors and said this is a false picture of the Chinese policy and that the Chinese military will not be deploying to Syria.[77]

In the end, the PRC has its security concerns in the Middle East, and its core concern regarding Damascus has been the return of radicals (primarily ethnic Uyghurs from China's western Xinjiang province) from Syria to the mainland. Unlike Russia, which has directly intervened in Syria by launching air-strikes, Beijing has tried to keep a safe distance from the conflict.[78] This allows China to hold high-level discussions about strengthening military ties with Syria while also retaining a level of deniability regarding its actual role. China has, meanwhile, expressed interest in increased arms and equipment sales, and training military forces would allow Beijing to participate in the conflict without actually being on the ground, still adhering to its domestic   principles of non-intervention and international norms.

Summary

The PRC's relations with Damascus in the post-war reconstruction are based on shared or mutual complementary economic interests and strategic geographic position in the Levant region; hence, China's involvement in Syria's rebuilding process fits perfectly with its grand global vision of BRI economic integration. The Levant is set to become a critical node in the BRI's China–Central Asia–West Asia economic corridor, as it offers an alternative route to the Mediterranean instead of the Suez passage. Syria's geographical location at the crossroads of East and West has a particular value for the Chinese MSRI, and Beijing is likely to leverage a role in Syria's reconstruction to advance its BRI.

Nevertheless, the aim to increase the PRC's access and to connect its economy with those of the Middle East, Central Asia, and eventually, Europe through massive infrastructure building could be seriously affected by the instability generated in the region's hotspots. Syrian instability presents a formidable obstacle to the BRI's strategic design, as it undermines connectivity, threatens infrastructure projects, and makes an economic corridor through the volatile Middle East to the markets of developed Europe less viable.

Syria's reconstruction process is likely to unfold for many years to come, possibly even decades. According to the International Monetary Fund (IMF) estimates, Syria's reconstruction will take more than 20 years. This means that even under the best of circumstances, Syria will need a very long period to regain even the (poor) status it had before the civil war.[79] Syria's severe security problems are compounded by legislative challenges and legal uncertainties; political instability; general lawlessness, nepotism, and corruption; and bureaucratic dysfunction, as well as a challenging business environment that only increased during the war years, creating impossible conditions for the reconstruction process. Given these conditions as well as the needs and priorities of the Assad regime, it seems reasonable to assume that Syria's post-war reconstruction, now and for the foreseeable future, does not allow any partner to make wide-scale investments.

Under such extreme circumstances, Chinese companies are unlikely to engage and invest their vast resources in Syria's reconstruction projects. Instead, Chinese firms can be expected to participate in Syria's reconstruction on a scale, at a tempo, and in a manner that limits their exposure to risk while enabling China to remain in good standing with the Syrian regime and thus advance the prospects of the BRI framework.[80] Thus, it seems that Syria's post-war reconstruction will take the form of expropriation and not development, and will consist mainly of discrete projects executed piecemeal rather than as part of a comprehensive national reconstruction process. In this setting, Chinese public-private partnerships could well find profitable economic opportunities in the Syria reconstruction process.

More important, an overview of Chinese interests and actions in Syria's post-war reconstruction reveals that there is a significant gap between the Syrian regime's expectations and Chinese companies' actual investments and operations. After Beijing was burned by the loss of its investments in Libya and by being forced to evacuate its citizens from the region's hotspots during the series of uprisings across the Middle East, it is not eager to expose itself to further risks before Syria is stabilized and the fighting there has ceased.

There is no doubt that the PRC has the necessary capabilities and the vast resources to play a part in Syria's reconstruction process, but its policy and conduct regarding Damascus raise serious doubt as to the likelihood of its investing these capabilities and resources at this time.[81] As Chinese president Xi stated, China would join the efforts to rebuild Syria "within its own ability," which most likely would also depend on how and when the reconstruction process will take place.[82] Hence, in the future, the PRC is likely to continue to keep a low profile and avoid investing significant economic resources in Syria.[83]

5 | Lebanon

The Republic of Lebanon is an often overlooked country in the Middle East, with complex political circumstances and opposition groups, situated in the middle of complex sectarian divisions (e.g., Sunni, Shi'a, Christian, and Druze).[1] The diverging interests of its domestic groups and its neighboring countries have embroiled Lebanon in prolonged conflicts that affect its economic development, infrastructure, and access to resources. Nevertheless, ever since the Middle East became increasingly important for the Chinese new Silk Road strategy, Beijing began to strengthen its ties with Lebanon. The country represents a strategic geographic position for the Belt and Road Initiative (BRI) as it is part of the Levant region and has direct access to the Mediterranean Sea.[2]

In recent years, relations between the People's Republic of China (PRC) and Lebanon have developed steadily, accompanied by practical cooperation in various fields. This cooperation is driven by the offer of Lebanon's strategic geographic positioning along the new Silk Road in exchange for China's aid in infrastructure development, which plays an essential role in economic and social development in Lebanon. Beirut is expected to play a significant role in the Syrian rebuilding process, as a gateway for reconstruction materials, expertise, and human resources. These prospects prompt Beijing to increasingly focus on making inroads in the region to advance its BRI framework.

Beijing and Beirut have made substantial progress in their bilateral cooperation in culture, education, press, arts, and military fields, which also enrich the friendly exchanges between the two nations. As Chinese Ambassador to Lebanon, Wang Kejian, said: "We are confident that a promising future is ahead of the ongoing cooperation between Lebanon and China. I would like to maintain China's continuous support for Lebanon's sovereignty, unity, and territorial integrity, as well as for the social and economic development process in Lebanon . . . the Chinese side is ready to work with the Lebanese side on deepening the ongoing bilateral cooperation based upon mutual benefit, and promoting the Chinese-Lebanese relations to a higher level."[3]

The BRI proposed by China in 2013, refers to the Silk Road Economic Belt (SREB) and the 21st Century Maritime Silk Road (MSRI). It aims to build a trade and infrastructure network connecting Asia with Europe and Africa, along with and beyond the ancient Silk Road trade routes. In return for cooperating in the BRI projects and increased Chinese investments, Middle East countries receive preferential financing in terms of grants, interest-free and concessional loans, and other forms of government funding. They also receive a full development package to stimulate their economic development plan.

Moreover, even if the Middle East countries do not directly derive economic benefits from the BRI projects beyond the initial investment capital, they can serve as catalysts for other projects to grow up around them (e.g., factories need local suppliers, workers, etc.). The idea behind these Chinese investments and projects is for them to become international hubs of transport, production, and commerce and bring in investments from various countries around the world.[4] In Lebanon, the Chinese are eying the Tripoli port that could be a central transshipment hub for the Eastern Mediterranean, since, before the civil war in Syria, Lebanon's ports were used to transship goods to Syria and even Iraq, and thus bypass the longer sea route through the Suez Canal and around the Arabian Peninsula.[5]

The central thesis of this chapter is that the PRC's relationship framework with Lebanon is based on shared or mutual complementary economic interests and its strategic geographic position in the Levant region, especially the integration of the Lebanon Economic Vision with the implementation of the BRI.

Lebanon Economic Vision

In January 2018, *McKinsey & Company* was appointed by the Lebanese Government to conduct a comprehensive study on the Lebanese economy and draft a National Economic Plan (NEP). In July 2018, *McKinsey* provided a report entitled "Lebanon Economic Vision" that gave a detailed description of the current state of the Lebanese economy, identified major areas and priority sectors to be tackled, and suggested action plans and systematic approaches to achieving a set of targets by each of the years 2025 and 2035. With a total of 160 initiatives, the report aims at addressing significant economic challenges faced by Lebanon. The Vision seeks to transform the country's economy into a productive, successful, and competitive one by 2025 and a high-income, diversified, knowledge-based, and sustainable one by 2035; this entails promoting its government into a fiscally-disciplined, credible, and accountable one by 2025 and securing a healthy macro-fiscal position for it by 2035. The initiatives were mainly focused on the sectors of agriculture (15 initiatives), industry (12 initiatives), tourism (22 initiatives), financial services (28 initiatives), and knowledge economy (28 initiatives).[6]

Lebanon and the Belt and Road Initiative

The PRC's relationship with Beirut includes five major areas for cooperation within the BRI. These areas are policy coordination, connectivity, trade and investments, military ties, and people-to-people bonding. Inevitably, each country views the BRI framework and reacts to it according to its unique perspective and the consequences for its own national interests and international status. Therefore, in realizing the shared vision, the two countries have very different attitudes.[7] Nonetheless, the Lebanon Economic Vision and China's BRI could converge on a joint economic development path, and their synergetic strategy will bring new opportunities for both sides. As a result, the realization of the BRI may provide new momentum for Lebanon's economic transformation.

Policy coordination

China's relationship with Lebanon is being translated into promoting political cooperation between countries, creating mechanisms for dialogue and consensus-building on global and regional issues, developing shared interests, deepening political trust, and reaching a new consensus on cooperation.[8]

The BRI framework offers new prospects regarding China's relationship with Lebanon. In November 2013, Chinese People's Political Consultative Conference (CPPCC) Vice-Chairman Luo Fuhe attended the reception marking the 70th Independence Day of Lebanon.[9] A working group from the International Department of the CPC Central Committee and a delegation from China's State Administration of Press, Publication, Radio, Film, and Television visited Lebanon successively. In addition, Lebanon's major political parties sent delegations or key members for training programs or workshops to China. The two countries maintain sound communication and cooperation on international and regional issues of mutual interest and coordinate their voting in the elections in multilateral institutions, including the United Nations.[10]

In May 2016, Chinese Foreign Minister Wang Yi said, during a meeting with his Lebanese counterpart, Joubran Bassil, at the 7th Ministerial Meeting of the China–Arab Cooperation Forum, that Beijing welcomes Beirut's participation in the BRI. For his part, Lebanese Foreign Minister Bassil said his country wants to play an active role in the BRI. He also expressed support for Beijing's position on the South China Sea and added that Lebanon would enhance its communications with China on international and regional affairs.[11]

In November 2016, President Xi Jinping sent a congratulatory message to newly-appointed President Michel Aoun of Lebanon. In his message, President Xi pointed out that the Chinese and Lebanese people enjoy profound friendship and "have achieved steady development in bilateral relations, constantly enhanced political mutual trust, continuously advanced cooperation in economy and trade, gradually intensified people-to-people and cultural exchanges and maintained sound communication and coordination in international and regional affairs. Attaching great importance to the development of China–Lebanon relations, I am willing to make joint efforts with President Michel Aoun to develop China–Lebanon friendship and mutually beneficial cooperation constantly and better benefit the two countries and the two peoples."[12]

In April 2017, the Arab Chambers of Commerce and the China Council to Promote International Trade (CCPIT) signed two Memorandums of Understanding (MoUs) to boost the BRI framework. The MoUs regulate the establishment of a Business Council of the Silk Road and Beirut becoming a key center for the Silk Road.[13] At the July 2018 China–Arab States Cooperation Forum (CASCF), Chinese President Xi Jinping pledged more than $23 billion in lines of credit, loans, and humanitarian assistance to Arab countries, including $90 million in humanitarian aid to Yemen, Lebanon, Jordan, and Syria. Another $151 million was earmarked for aid projects, with the remaining funds designated for financial and economic cooperation. However, it is unclear how much of this money will go directly to Beirut; a significant portion of the aid and loan package will be in the form of investments in infrastructure construction in Lebanon.[14]

The BRI represents the central aspect of the future bilateral relationship of China with Lebanon. In July 2018, State Councilor and Foreign Minister Wang Yi met in Beijing with Minister of Economy and Trade Raed Khoury of Lebanon, who was in China for the 8th Ministerial Meeting of the CASCF. The Chinese Foreign Minister stated that Beijing–Beirut relations have maintained sound and stable development for a long time. He added, "The PRC welcomes the active response of Lebanon to the joint construction of the Belt and Road and congratulates Beirut on becoming the 87th member state of the Asian Infrastructure Investment Bank (AIIB). Beijing supports the efforts of the Lebanese government in developing its economy and will continue to encourage Chinese enterprises with strength and good reputation to invest and establish a business in Lebanon and actively participate in the infrastructure construction in the country."[15]

Lebanese and Chinese officials emphasized the importance of boosting ties between the two countries in various areas under the framework of the BRI. In February 2019, Chinese Ambassador to Lebanon, Wang Kejian, during his meeting with Lebanese Prime Minister Saad Hariri said, China is willing to take Chinese-Lebanese relations to a new level by strengthening policy docking under the BRI framework in deepening pragmatic cooperation. For his part, Lebanese Prime Minister Saad Hariri said he expects to see more progress and achievements in cooperation with China on many levels.[16] Moreover, at the investment forum between China and Lebanon held in Beirut in March 2019, Chinese Ambassador to Lebanon Wang Kejian said that the Chinese government would enhance coordination in policy match-making, to back up the integration of Lebanon's development plan with China's BRI. Beijing will assist with the matching of enterprises of both sides and bolster Lebanon's efforts in safeguarding the country's sovereignty, security, and stability.[17]

In May 2019, the Chinese Ambassador to Lebanon, Wang Kejian, exchanged ideas with Lebanese lawmakers on ways to promote cooperation between Beijing-Beirut in various fields of economy, trade, infrastructure, construction, and culture. Ambassador Wang introduced the ideas behind BRI, the historical development of bilateral relations between China and Lebanon, and expressed his country's willingness to strengthen and support policies adopted by the Lebanese government while encouraging Chinese companies to come to Lebanon and explore mutually beneficial cooperation. Meanwhile, Lebanese lawmakers expressed a wish to see progress in the framework of cooperation between Beijing and Beirut under the BRI.[18]

Connectivity

The facilitation of connectivity is one of the crucial ways to integrate the Lebanon Economic Vision into the BRI framework. Beirut should attempt to optimize its infrastructural connections and adapt its technical systems to those of the other countries in the BRI framework. This would lead Beijing–Lebanon to jointly contribute to the development of international transport maritime and overland routes, and the creation of an infrastructural network that could gradually connect all the regions in Asia and also at specific points in Asia, Africa, and Europe.[19] Thus, Lebanon's government has ambitions to be an important part of the Belt and Road Initiative framework.[20]

Lebanon's strategic geographic position in the Levant region, with direct access to the Mediterranean Sea, makes it an interesting partner for infrastructures investments that could become a logistical hub for land and sea trade routes connecting the Mediterranean to Central Asia, a corridor Beijing needs to reduce transport times and to avoid having to transit the Suez Canal.[21] Commercially the MSRI is, above all, about aligning the connectivity of global shipping lanes and ports and with Chinese capital. Accordingly, Beirut and Tripoli ports can become central locations for the PRC's MSRI throughout the Mediterranean Sea. Toufic Dabbousi, head of the Chamber of Commerce, Industry, and Agriculture, emphasized the need to expand the Tripoli Port and Qlayaat Airport in a bid to take part in projects along with the BRI framework.[22]

Tripoli is located on the eastern shores of the Mediterranean, about 80 kilometers from the Lebanese capital Beirut, and about 30 kilometers from the Syrian-Lebanese border. The Port of Tripoli, a major port in Lebanon, could become a central destination for weekly shipments from China to the Eastern Mediterranean. Thanks to its geographic location, the port is positioned to act as a gateway into northern Lebanon, with transit access to Syria by sea or land, and transshipment to Iraq. Since 2012, the China Harbor Engineering Company has worked on rehabilitating Tripoli's port to be ready to receive large vessels.[23]

In November 2017, the Union of Lebanon's Tripoli Municipalities signed an agreement with China's Silk Road Chamber of International Commerce (SRCIC) to join the Chamber for an active role in the Belt and Road Initiative. According to Adnan Kassar, Chairman of the Economic Bodies of Lebanese–Chinese relations, the agreement was of particular importance to Tripoli and has the vast potential not only for Lebanon but for the whole region, by enabling enhanced trade with China. "We will not spare any effort in boosting Tripoli's standing and its openness on Chinese markets, and such an alliance will prepare it to become a special hub for cooperation with China within the Belt and Road initiative."[24] Tripoli Port has expanded its terminal to receive the largest types of vessels in addition to creating a terminal to receive Chinese cranes capable of lifting and transporting more than 700 containers a day. In October 2018, a container ship of China Ocean Shipping Company (COSCO) arrived at the Port of Tripoli, ending its journey as the first vessel to sail the company's new route from China to the Mediterranean. This route development will facilitate the expansion of commercial exchange with Lebanon through a direct route.[25]

While most shipping companies own/operate terminals and ports on foreign terrain as shipping-centric operations, Chinese state-owned shipping differs in that they open new ports and invest in adjoining free trade/special economic zones and other development initiatives so that host countries get the entire development package.[26] As Chinese Ambassador to Lebanon Wang Kejian said: "Chinese companies have visited northern Lebanon, and they are ready to take part in infrastructure projects including the expansion of Tripoli Port and Qlayaat Airport in addition to the construction of railways, roads, and bridges."[27]

Tripoli Port's geo-proximity with Syria can facilitate China's intentions to invest in the reconstruction of Syria. Tripoli is located less than 30 kilometers (18 miles) from the Syrian border and thus accessible to the Gulf and the Arab World. According to Tripoli Port manager, Ahmed Tamer, "China has not invested in our port yet [for] reconstruction of Syria. We are looking forward to doing that, but it has not been done yet." While Chinese firms took plum contracts in Tripoli's port, including a new $58 million quay plus the manufacturing and installing of six gantry cranes, no further investment has been forthcoming. A proposal to expand Tripoli Port by Qingdao Heavy Duty Machinery is under review by stakeholders in Lebanon's caretaker government.[28]

Beijing also could cooperate with Lebanon in developing Tripoli's Special Economic Zone (TSEZ) for the Syrian rebuilding process. The zone provides Chinese (and other regional businesses) with low tax options for consolidating and adding value to stock sourced elsewhere and then to be exported to Syria. The TSEZ lies on the shortest path out to Syrian-Turkish trade routes, a short distance to the Rene Mouawad Airport (RMA), and will shortly benefit from a planned railway network linking Tripoli to the Syrian border. In addition to granting the TSEZ a significant role in the reconstruction of Syria, these features allow it to become a platform for upstream and downstream oil and gas activities and offer easy access to the growing economies of the Gulf, Levant and North Africa.[29]

Beijing–Beirut can further contribute to the development of regional overland routes as part of the PRC's SREB framework by the creation of an infrastructural network that could gradually connect Asia, Africa, and Europe. Recently there were official talks between China and Lebanon to revive the latter's national rail network, connecting Beirut and Tripoli to Damascus.[30] Lebanon's railway, built by a French count in 1895 during the Ottoman rule, had extended 408 kilometers, connecting Beirut and Tripoli to Damascus and Haifa. However, Lebanon's civil war brought the operation to a halt, and the train stations were abandoned. While the war ended over two decades ago, governmental attention has been lacking and the station buildings and trains have fallen into ruin. Today, after decades of disregard, there are finally talks of resuscitating Lebanon's railway. The economic potential for such a development would help boost the Lebanese economy.

According to Eliana Ibrahim, president of the China–Arab Association for Promoting Cultural & Commercial Change, "We are ready to support Lebanon with our technical knowledge. But we are more interested in connecting Beirut to Tripoli, Tripoli to Aleppo, Aleppo to Damascus, and so on." The railway would initially be a substantial investment, and Chinese investors are primarily concerned with the return that this investment would generate. The potential railway would serve as a means of public transport and revenue from cargo.[31]

Trade and investments

Part of Beijing's relationship with Lebanon includes attempts to mitigate as much as possible the barriers to free trade, investment, industrial cooperation, and technical and engineering services, to facilitate the integration of Lebanon Economic Vision–BRI framework. Measures must be taken by both countries, such as expanding free-trade zones, improving trade structures, seeking new potential areas for trade and improving the trade balance, devising new initiatives for the promotion of conventional forms of trade, developing trans-border electronic trade and other advanced models of business, creating a system for supporting trade in services to strengthen and expand conventional trade, increasing customs cooperation, and regularly sharing information in these areas.[32]

Trade and economic partnerships between Beijing–Beirut have developed more extensively in recent years. Lebanon has been part of Beijing's increased attention to Arab countries regarding trade. The central interest of the bilateral relationship appears to be directly connected to commercial purposes, although relatively limited compared to China's economic foothold in other Middle Eastern countries. According to China Customs Statistics (export-import), Beijing–Beirut trade volume decreased to $1.7 billion by 2019 (compared to $2 billion in 2018), preserving China's status from 2011 as the principal trading partner of Lebanon.[33]

According to the country's ambitious capital investment program launched at the Conférence économique pour le développement, par les réformes et avec les entre-prises (CEDRE), an international development conference for Lebanon held in Paris in April 2018, Beirut needs $22.9 billion to revamp its dilapidated infrastructure. The international community, in particular the World Bank, pledged $11.6 billion to the capital investment plan. The Lebanon government has made increasing Foreign Direct Investment (FDI) a priority and sent positive signals to the investment commu-nity that Lebanon is open for investment inflows.[34] Yet despite Beirut's efforts to bring more Chinese investment, according to the *China Global Investment Tracker*, Beijing's investments and contracts in Lebanon from 2013 to 2019 stood at zero.[35]

In June 2018, the China-led Asian Infrastructure Investment Bank (AIIB) approved a new membership application from Lebanon, a critical mechanism for funding BRI and other projects, bringing AIIB's total approved membership to 87. According to the statement released on AIIB's official website, Lebanon will officially join the AIIB once it completes required internal processes and deposits the first capital installment with the bank.[36] In January 2018, Lebanon was chosen as the Middle East and North Africa regional headquarters for the China Council for the Promotion of International Trade. Lebanon was chosen due to its strategic location, free economy, and openness to investment.[37]

China has also given every possible assistance to support social and economic development in Lebanon. In March 2015, it also offered financial assistance worth 30 million yuan to help the Lebanese government face the implications of the Syrian refugee influx. Lebanon and China maintained intensified cooperation in human resource development, and more than 80 Lebanese cadres from different sectors trav-eled to China to partake in the exchange and training programs last year.[38] In January 2017, China offered $10 million in aid to the Syrian refugees in Lebanon.[39]

In December 2018, the Chinese government donated 1,000 tons of wheat worth 5 million yuan in humanitarian assistance for Syrian refugees in Lebanon.[40] In April 2019, the Chinese government offered a donation to the Lebanese government for the construction of a new conservatory in the country.[41] The SRCIC is open to granting $2 billion in loans with low-interest rates to Lebanon. The allocation is part of a $5 billion Silk Road International Development Fund that aims to finance deals introduced by SRCIC members.[42]

Lebanese and Chinese officials emphasized the importance of boosting ties between the two countries in various areas. In March 2019, during the China–Lebanon Investment Forum, which aimed at drawing a roadmap for the future of cooperation between Lebanon and China, Gao Yan, chairwoman of CCPIT, said that the Council was committed to increasing ties between the two countries in different areas, which will have a positive impact on the peoples of China and Lebanon. Beijing and Beirut need to increase mutual investments while inviting Lebanese companies to take part in exhibitions in China. Chinese companies need to invest in Lebanon's industrial zones, which will increase the country's exports while expanding Middle East markets.[43]

According to Adnan Kassar, Honorary Chairman of the General Union of Chambers of Commerce, Industry, and Agriculture in the Arab countries, Lebanon's new government welcomes more investment from China. The Lebanon government also welcomes Lebanese enterprises to participate in the Belt and Road construction.[44] According to Lebanon Telecommunication Minister, Mohamad Shoukeir, "There is no doubt that today there is a favorable environment for progress on this path, which is reinforced by the solid and historic friendship between the two countries and the strength of our economic relations, as China is the first trading partner for Lebanon." Accordingly, the Lebanese minister encouraged Chinese companies to invest in these projects, assuring them of Beirut's readiness to cooperate.[45]

In May 2019, Prime Minister Saad Hariri met with a delegation led by Wang Kejian, the Chinese Ambassador to Lebanon. Discussion surrounded investments in energy and included members from the China Energy Group. This indicates the willingness of the Chinese side, both at the level of government or companies, to cooperate with the Lebanese side in the field of economic development for the mutual benefit of both countries.[46] To sum up: there are a lot of desires and many statements of politicians and officials about commercial cooperation between the two countries, but to date few results to show for it.

People-to-People Bond

China's relationship with Beirut, enabling the people of the two countries to bond along the Silk Road, is also vital to integrating the Lebanon Economic Vision within the BRI framework. Extensive cultural and academic exchanges are being promoted to win public support for deepening bilateral and multilateral cooperation, as well as providing scholarships, holding yearly cultural events, increasing cooperation in science and technology, and establishing joint laboratory or research centers and international technology transfer centers.[47]

Thus, linguistic, cultural, and tourism cooperation is an important aspect of Beijing–Beirut relations and both nations have outlined their intention to expand this collaboration in the coming years. According to the *Hanban website*, the Chinese government established Confucius Institutes for providing Chinese language and culture teaching resources worldwide. In 2019, 550 Confucius Institutes and 1,172 Confucius Classrooms and 5,665 teaching sites were established in 162 countries and regions, admitting about eleven million students.[48] In 54 countries involved in the Belt and Road Initiative, there are 153 Confucius Institutes and 149 primary and high-school Confucius Classrooms.[49] In the Middle East, there are eighteen Confucius Institutes and three Confucius Classrooms, and one of them is in Lebanon. The Confucius Institute at Saint-Joseph University in Beirut, founded in 2006, has become an important platform for teaching the Chinese language and disseminating Chinese culture in Lebanon.[50]

The increasing trade ties between Beijing–Beirut have encouraged more Lebanese to be involved in Chinese culture and traditions. One way to gain increased awareness about Chinese culture is to learn Beijing's rich language, and young Lebanese students are developing an intellectual curiosity to learn Chinese. A growing number of university students also learn about the importance of Chinese culture, which adds value to their careers. According to Liu Li, former vice-director at Confucius Institute, some of the institute's students were employed by Chinese companies in Dubai while others have majored in translation, and they succeeded in finding jobs in the field. Most of the teenagers who are learning the language have parents who are doing business with Beijing and realize that knowing the Chinese language will allow them to have a successful future.[51]

In November 2018, Chinese Ambassador to Lebanon, Wang Kejian, visited Hassan Kassir High School in Beirut and donated school bags and stationery to Amal educational institutions at the beginning of the academic year. According to the ambassador, Beijing–Beirut have had friendly relations for a long time, and the two countries have continuously supported each other. The Chinese embassy has offered much help to Lebanese students through Lebanon's Ministry of Education and High Education.[52]

Lebanese University is the only educational establishment in Lebanon to offer a bachelor's degree in the Chinese language. Other universities, such as Saint Joseph University and the Holy Spirit University of Kaslik, offer elective courses to their students. At the end of 2018, the number of students registered at Confucius Institutes reached 302 for the two semesters, a number that has been increasing at the annual rate of 10 percent for the past five years. Ten students from all over Lebanon received scholarships to study at a university in China in partnership with the Confucius Institute, and every year, Beijing hosts a summer camp in the mainland. Last year, 19 students attended summer camps in China and spent ten days learning the Chinese language and culture, with another four days touring in Beijing.[53]

Cultural exchange is another aspect of the Beijing–Beirut relationship that has also strengthened. Lebanon is among the countries that may have the best model of cultural exchange with Beijing. Lebanon's Caracalla Dance Theater, one of the most famous theatres in the world, has played an important role in deepening the cultural links between Beijing–Beirut. Caracalla Dance Theater first explored the Chinese market in 2005, where it performed the dazzling drama "Two Thousand and One Nights". Since then, the international theatre performed at least five of its creations in China. In 2014, Caracalla Dance Theater signed a five-year cooperation agreement for cultural exchange with China's National Center for the Performing Arts (NCPA), the major platform for international arts exchange and an important base for the cultural and creative industry. In February 2016, the Caracalla Dance Theater performed "Two Thousand and One Nights" on stage at the NCPA (Nansha College Preparatory Academy), bringing the unique mysteries and exotic Arabian flavor to Beijing audiences. In March 2018, the theatre performed "Sailing the Silk Road" for the Chinese audience.[54]

In January 2019, the Chinese Embassy in Lebanon celebrated the Lunar New Year and the beginning of its spring season with a performance by Beijing's Chongqing Symphony Orchestra. The event saw the participation of Lebanese officials and ambassadors representing different countries. The Chinese Ambassador to Lebanon, Wang Kejian, expressed his happiness to celebrate the special occasion in the presence of Chinese expatriates in Lebanon and Lebanese friends.[55]

In October 2019, the Chinese Embassy in Lebanon marked the 70th anniversary of the founding of the PRC with three activities: the Chinese National Day at UNIFIL (United Nations Interim Force in Lebanon), a reception at the Phoenicia Hotel, and a Chinese cultural evening at Baabda Serail Seray (House of the Slave) archeological site. In a statement issued on this occasion, the Embassy said, "Lebanon is an important partner in building 'the Belt and the Road.' Beijing will continue to support Lebanon's sovereignty, independence, and territorial integrity, and uphold its efforts to maintain security and stability."[56]

In December 2005, Beijing–Beirut signed a tourism cooperation accord. This accord was set to promote investments in mutual tourism sectors and increase communication between tourist companies through the exchange of professional skills.[57] In September 2019, Lebanese Tourism Minister, Avedis Guidanian, said that Lebanon is making efforts to promote Chinese-Lebanese tourism ties. In an interview with *Xinhua*, he said: "One of the best-implemented achievements to date which will attract more Chinese tourists to Lebanon is their exemption from long procedures to receive a visa and from paying fees to enter our country. All they need to have is a roundtrip ticket and a hotel reservation." In 2018, the number of Chinese tourists in Lebanon reached 9,450. There was a 22 percent increase in the number of Chinese tourists in the first eight months of 2019 compared with the same period in 2018, so the expectation is that Chinese tourists will reach around 12,500 by the end of 2019.[58]

Military ties

As part of the PRC's relationship with Lebanon, security cooperation, including arms and equipment sales and training military forces, has become an increasing part of integrating the Lebanon Economic Vision within the BRI framework. As the Chinese Ambassador to Lebanon, Wang Kejian, said during his meeting with Lebanese Defense Minister Elias Bou Saab, Beijing would continue to support the Lebanese army and intends to approve donations for Lebanon's military institutions.[59]

Although China has only recently developed a military foothold in other Middle Eastern countries, it has a relatively long history of military engagement with Lebanon. For instance, China is the largest contributor of peacekeepers among the permanent members of the United Nations Security Council and also the second-largest financier for the fund. Since the 2006 Israel-Lebanon war, the Chinese government has sent 18 groups of peacekeeping forces to Lebanon to engage in mine clearance and explosive ordnance disposal, reconstruction, medical assistance, and border patrol. From 2006 to 2019, they defused over 12,000 mines without any casualties – highlighting China's desire to present itself as a peacekeeper in the region.[60]

Military cooperation continues and is expected to grow in the future. China provided military support to Lebanon in 2015 when its army was fighting against the Islamic State and al-Qaida-linked Nusra Front fighters on its northeastern border. Lebanon also inked a military grant agreement with China in 2016, whereby China prepared a multi-year military aid program for Lebanon.[61]

Summary

Chinese economic interests in Lebanon had been limited, but this changed with the BRI since Beirut can be a geostrategic partner and collaborate in China's infrastructure-based development strategy to develop their country's Economic Vision. However, the domestic situation still limits trade collaboration between the two countries. Hence, China will probably take advantage of limited infrastructure development in Lebanon through a prudent approach towards loans and support. Besides, the complexity of the Lebanese conflict, involving sectarian division and the collaboration of these sub-groups with a different power state, represents an essential challenge for the BRI framework. The fragility of Lebanon's domestic situation could be an incentive for Beijing to find other regional alternatives in the development of the BRI.

Although formally established in 1971, China's relationship with Lebanon, a country that has repeatedly suffered war and political assassinations, was minimal for many years. To understand Beijing's approach towards Lebanon, it is essential to consider the characteristics that shape the country. It is not a significant producer of natural resources, is located on the coast of the Mediterranean Sea, and is constituted of sectarian divisions. For many years Lebanon has been involved in conflicts that have affected its domestic stability and infrastructures. Its complex characteristics (mostly the political instability and the security situation) could raise challenges for Beijing's economic interests and developing the BRI. This creates a significant gap between the Lebanon government's expectations and China's investments and operations. Hence, in the future, Beijing is likely to continue to keep a low profile and avoid investing significant economic resources in Lebanon.

6 | Jordan

The Hashemite Kingdom of Jordan is distinguished by its strategic geographic position because it links the continents of Asia, Africa, and Europe, making it an ideal place for regional and global investments and an export gateway to the entire Levant region. As a steadfast island of stability in the Middle East that has weathered many conflicts, Jordan is becoming the regional hub for security, development, humanitarian, and reconstruction efforts occurring in neighboring countries.[1]

The Jordanian economy provides many opportunities for the industrial and logistics sectors in development zones and industrial estates across the Kingdom, especially because of the international and regional free trade agreements it is part of, and the economic, development, free, and industrial zones and business parks that have been established there. Jordan is a hub for the Levantine countries, which in contrast to the Gulf States, have relatively little oil. Though the Kingdom cannot satisfy Beijing's energy needs, it at least provides a market for Chinese goods, by giving access to more than 350 million consumers in the Arab world due to the free trade agreements it has with many countries and regional blocs.[2]

In recent years, Jordanian–Chinese relations have witnessed remarkable development as Beijing has provided economic support to the kingdom. In addition, official visits were exchanged between officials, and rapprochement was seen in political positions concerning many critical regional issues, including the Palestinian issue, the Syrian crisis, and others. The People's Republic of China (PRC) believes in the two-state solution, with Jerusalem as the capital of Palestine and the Hashemite Kingdom holding trusteeship of the Islamic and Christian holy sites in the holy city of Jerusalem, and supports the need for a political solution that preserves Syria's unity.[3]

The Belt and Road Initiative (BRI), proposed by China in 2013, refers to the Silk Road Economic Belt (SREB) and the 21st Century Maritime Silk Road (MSRI). It aims to build a trade and infrastructure network connecting Asia with Europe and Africa, along with and beyond the ancient Silk Road trade routes. In this regard, the Levant is also set to become a critical transit hub for Chinese energy and resource projects for the BRI framework and offers an alternative route to the Mediterranean as opposed to the Suez passage. China is eyeing Syria and Lebanon in the long term as the key region in the Levant to achieve this aim. However, due to the instability and high-risk environment prevailing there, Beijing is pivoting to Amman in the short-term, as the kingdom presents a more immediate low-risk environment and relative stability.[4]

Chinese Ambassador in Jordan, Pan Weifang, stressed at the Talal Abu-Ghazaleh Knowledge Forum in July 2017 the deep relations between China and Jordan and the strategic location of Jordan, especially with the availability of qualified human cadres and the safe and stable environment the country enjoys. Ambassador Pan expressed appreciation for the support and facilities provided by King Abdullah II to attract Chinese investments to Jordan, making the Kingdom a gateway to regional and global markets, and stated that the strategic relationship between Amman and Beijing is a model of what relations should be between countries.[5]

This chapter examines the motivation behind Beijing's measures to formalize a strategic partnership with Amman and the synergy between the Belt and Road Initiative and Jordan's Vision 2025 to understand the extent of economic engagement and bilateral relationship between the two nations. The main argument presented is that China's measures to formalize a strategic partnership framework with Jordan are based on shared or mutual complementary economic interests and Jordan's strategic geographic position in the Levant region, especially the shared interest in integrating Jordan's Vision 2025 within the BRI framework.

Jordan Vision 2025

The vision charts a path for the future and determines the integrated economic and social framework that will govern the economic and social policies based on providing opportunities for all. It is a long-term national vision and strategy rather than a detailed government action plan. Its basic principles include promoting the rule of law and equal opportunities, increasing participatory policy-making, achieving fiscal sustainability, and strengthening institutions. The most crucial goal that the vision seeks to achieve is improving the welfare of citizens and increasing essential services to create a balanced society, where opportunities are available to all, and the gap between governorates is bridged. The vision puts Jordanian citizens at the heart of the development process; success and failure are measured by the extent of the progress made at the level of individuals, and therefore the welfare of the community. It includes more than 400 policies or procedures that are to be implemented through a participatory approach shared by the government, business sector, and civil society.[6]

Jordan and the Belt and Road Initiative

The PRC's strategic partnership with Jordan includes five areas for cooperation within the Belt and Road Initiative. These areas are policy coordination, connectivity, trade and investments, energy cooperation, and people-to-people bonds. However, each country views the BRI framework and reacts to it according to its perspective and the consequences for its national interests and international status. Therefore, there are very different attitudes among the countries that are part of the BRI framework regarding how to realize the vision.[7]

Policy coordination

Under the PRC's strategic partnership with Amman, promoting political cooperation between the two countries, creating mechanisms for dialogue and consensus-building on global and regional issues, developing shared interests, deepening political trust, and reaching a new consensus on cooperation is important to integrate Jordan's Vision 2025 into the BRI framework.[8]

In September 2015, Chinese President Xi Jinping and Jordanian King Abdullah II Bin Al-Hussein signed a joint statement on the establishment of a strategic partnership between the two countries. The Chinese President said to King Abdullah that the decision to set up the strategic partnership was an important milestone for their relationship. According to the statement, both countries are to hold regular consultations on international and regional affairs of concern to both to reach greater understanding and enhance mutual trust. Beijing and Amman pledged to support each other on issues involving their core interests and boost reciprocal cooperation within the framework of the BRI.[9]

According to the Chinese President, the establishment of the strategic partnership will boost cooperation in various areas (trade, investment, industrial capacity, infrastructure, energy, finance, and law enforcement, among other sectors, and increase cultural, educational and military-to-military exchanges) and benefit the people of both countries. President Xi proposed that the two countries would increase exchanges between political parties, legislatures, and ordinary people of both sides, and share their experience of governance. For his part, King Abdullah said that Amman values the traditional friendship with Beijing and his country stood ready to boost cooperation with China in pursuit of common development and prosperity.[10]

Both countries are eager to increase political cooperation in several global and regional issues. Xie Yuan, vice president of the Chinese People's Association for Friendship with Foreign Countries (CPAFFC), said at a meeting with a Jordanian media delegation that visited China in April 2019: "We are always seeking to strengthen our ties with Jordan . . . there are exchange visits with friendly countries such as Jordan, and we are keen on increased cooperation", while a representative from the embassy pointed out that the "ties between China and Jordan are strategic and deep-rooted".[11]

Jordanian and Chinese officials emphasized the importance of boosting ties between the two countries under the framework of the Belt and Road Initiative. In May 2017 at the Belt and Road Forum for International Cooperation (BRF), Jordan Minister of Planning and International Cooperation, Imad Fakhoury, said that the Kingdom will be a major gateway to the efforts for regional reconstruction, and there will be several investment opportunities for mega-infrastructure projects in the context of the Jordan Vision 2025 and the Economic Stimulation Plan of 2018–2022.[12] In July 2017, Vice Chairman of the Standing Committee of China's National People's Congress (NPC), Qiangba Puncog, pledged to dovetail China's Belt and Road Initiative with "Jordan 2025" to better serve the development of the two countries.[13]

In November 2017, Jordan and China held talks regarding the signing of a memorandum of understanding (MoU) on cooperation, as part of China's BRI. According to the Chinese ambassador in Jordan, Pan Weifang, the signing of the MoU meant increased cooperation and projects between the two sides in various areas, since

Beijing was interested in boosting relations with Jordan, and relations were progressing on all fronts.[14]

In May 2018, Pan Weifang said that China would continue to enhance the Beijing-Amman strategic partnership, boost bilateral practical cooperation in all fields, and contribute to the Kingdom's social and economic development; he explained that China was willing to work with other developing countries, including Jordan, to build and share the Belt and Road Initiative.[15] In July 2018, the Jordanian Foreign Minister, Ayman Safadi, said in a meeting with Chinese Foreign Minister Wang Yi that Chinese investments could rely on the efficiency of qualified Jordanian human resources and exports from the Kingdom to large markets, through free trade agreements into which Amman had entered with major world economies. Jordan, in turn, expressed its support for the Chinese Belt and Road initiative, welcoming a bigger economic, political, and cultural Chinese role in the region.[16]

In April 2019, the Chinese deputy ambassador in Jordan, Zhang Haihao, repeated assurances of Beijing's interest in increased cooperation with Amman and support for development in the Kingdom. He stated that Sino–Jordanian relations were "outstanding and exemplary" in several fields, highlighting strong cooperation in political and economic arenas. Such progress indicates that the Belt and Road Initiative will benefit the Kingdom.[17]

Connectivity

According to China's strategic partnership with Amman, the facilitation of connectivity is one of the crucial ways to integrate Jordan Vision 2025 into the BRI framework. Jordan's strategic geographic position, connecting three continents and making it a focal point for the Belt and Road Initiative, requires it to optimize its infrastructural connections and adapt its technical systems to those of the other countries in the BRI framework. This would lead Beijing and Amman to work jointly to develop international transport routes and contribute to the creation of an infrastructural network that could gradually connect all the regions in Asia, and specific points in Asia, Africa, and Europe.[18] Jordan Minister of Planning and International Cooperation, Imad Fakhoury, confirmed that Amman was looking forward to benefiting from China's Belt and Road Initiative, which is expected to create promising opportunities.[19]

Given China's ambition to connect its investments in the Arab Gulf, Africa, and Eurasia, the Levant is becoming a critical transit hub for Chinese energy and resource projects within its Belt and Road Initiative. The Levant region could become a critical node in the MSRI by providing an alternative route to the Mediterranean Sea in contrast to the Suez Canal. Beijing considers Syria and Lebanon to be the major Levantine countries to achieve this aim in the long run. However, the current instability and high-risk environment of these countries position neighboring Jordan as the alternative focus for the immediate future. Accordingly, Chinese ties and large-scale investments in Amman have flourished in recent years. It is increasingly clear that Beijing hopes to prepare Amman to serve as the gateway – or lynchpin – for the BRI's expansion into the Levant region and a center for its reconstruction efforts in Syria.[20]

In addition, a Beijing-Amman alliance can contribute to the development of regional overland routes as part of the PRC's SREB framework by creating an infrastructural network that could gradually connect Asia, Africa, and Europe. The

Red–Med rail project, an alternative land avenue that China is developing to ensure guaranteed access to the Mediterranean, is planned to connect the Israeli Red Sea port city of Eilat to the Israeli port of Ashdod on the Mediterranean. However, the port of Eilat is not currently equipped to permit entry to container vessels of the size that travel on the Asia-Europe loops. This, in turn, means that Israel would have to invest billions of dollars in the Eilat port to prepare it to receive larger vessels (10,000-plus TEUs) – with no guarantee that the mega-ships will call at their port. Israel would also have to invest heavily in port infrastructure, including expanded railroad and highway capacity, to handle cargo from these ships. Such an extensive investment in the port, on top of the high costs of the rail project, makes little commercial sense.[21]

Israel has acknowledged that Amman could be involved in the Red–Med project, and there are plans to extend the line to Aqaba after the construction of the cargo rail line. Israel's use of the Aqaba Port facilities, which are among the largest and most modern in the Middle East, could create an alternative to overland transport, which is limited in terms of capacity and availability. Furthermore, involving Jordan in the project would strengthen bilateral relations and encourage Arab countries to use the Eilat port infrastructure.[22]

In September 2015, Sino–Jordanian negotiators signed several investment agreements worth over $7 billion. The agreements include a $2.8 billion investment to construct the Jordanian national railway network,[23] which is another step toward the development of a regional rail network that seeks to link Jordan to its Gulf neighbors. Closer integration between the transport markets of the Mediterranean will make transport connections faster, cheaper, and more efficient. The "North–South corridor," from the Syrian Border to the Port of Aqaba (509 km), is the main rail line of this proposed network, connecting the national capital of Amman, the surrounding logistics centers, and the nation's gateway Port of Aqaba. As the corridor is the backbone of the project, the links to the neighboring countries are foreseen for later stages. Through the project, the region will be connected to Turkey and Europe and the Gulf Cooperation Council countries.[24]

Additionally, the Jordan National Railway Project (JNRP) involves the development of three corridors. The central north–south spine of the network will be a 509-kilometer line connecting the Red Sea Port of Aqaba with Amman, the industrial city of Zarqa, and the Syrian border. The second line will branch off the north–south axis near Zarqa, following the route of Highway 10 for around 290 km to reach the Iraqi frontier near the Tarbil Border Crossing. The third section of the JNRP is a 90.5-kilometer link from a junction with the Zarqa-Tarbil line east of Amman to the Saudi border near Haditha, where it will meet the Saudi Norton-South Railway to Riyadh and the Persian Gulf.[25]

Such infrastructure plans are consistent with China's BRI framework, which seeks to develop an overland route from China to Europe via Central Asia. Nevertheless, with violence continuing in Iraq and Syria, the situation points to Jordan not only being a regional fulcrum of BRI but also being positioned as the staging point for Beijing's impending reconstruction efforts in Syria.[26]

Trade and investments

The PRC's strategic partnership with Amman is aimed at mitigating as much as possible the barriers to free trade, investment, industrial cooperation, and technical and engineering services to facilitate the integration of Jordan Vision 2025 within the BRI framework. Both countries must take a series of additional measures, such as expanding free-trade zones, improving trade structures, seeking new potential areas for trade and improving the trade balance, devising new initiatives for the promotion of conventional forms of trade, developing trans-border electronic trade and other advanced models of business, and regularly sharing information in these areas to create a system for supporting trade in services to strengthen and expand conventional trade and increase customs cooperation.[27]

According to China Customs Statistics (export-import), Beijing–Jordan trade volume had increased to $4 billion by 2019.[28] According to the *China Global Investment Tracker*, Beijing's investments and construction in Jordan from 2013 to 2019 reached $6.1 billion. Most of the Chinese investments are in the energy sector ($4.6 billion) while the rest was invested in Amman Chemicals and other companies and industries.[29] Beijing has become the second-largest commercial partner for the Kingdom, and the favorable business environment, security, and free trade agreements with the US, Canada, and Europe enable foreign companies like China to export to markets of more than one billion consumers.[30]

Sino–Jordanian strategic partnerships have proliferated since 2015, when the Kingdom joined, as a founding member, the newly-established Asian Infrastructure Investment Bank (AIIB), a critical mechanism for funding the BRI framework and other projects.[31] Beijing-Amman, on the sidelines of the 2015 China–Arab States Expo in Yinchuan, signed investment agreements across transportation, energy, and trade sectors worth more than $7 billion. The deals include a $1.7 billion project to build Jordan's first oil shale-fired power plant in the Attarat area, which will produce roughly 15 percent of Jordan's national energy needs; $2.8 billion investment to construct the national railway network and to build a 1,000-megawatt renewable energy power plant at a cost of nearly $1 billion.[32]

In April 2017, the Jordanian–Chinese Business Forum was jointly hosted by the China Council for the Promotion of International Trade (CCPIT) and the Jordan Chamber of Commerce. More than 100 entrepreneurs from China and Jordan participated in this forum, where intentions for cooperation were reached in engineering, trade, finance, and other sectors.[33] In November 2017, according to the Chinese Ambassador in Jordan, Pan Weifang, both countries were also holding negotiations over the tenets of the Belt and Road Initiative cooperation MoU, signaling that Amman could be close to formally joining the BRI.[34] In April 2018, Chinese officials also announced plans to build the Fujian Maritime Silk Road Commodity Center in partnership with the Jordan Ministry of Transportation and a joint Sino–Jordan university in Amman to strengthen Jordan's role in BRI.[35] In September 2018, Beijing signed an agreement with Amman to finance the expansion of the Al-Salt road. This project is the first of its kind among the projects financed through the assistance of the Chinese government. Usually, such projects require Chinese design and implementation. However, this project is to be implemented through qualified local companies in coordination with Chinese companies in Jordan.[36]

Chinese Ambassador Pan Weifang said in a press conference at the eighth ministerial meeting of the China–Arab States Cooperation Forum (CASCF) in July 2018, "Chinese investors are focusing on Jordan and have their eyes focused on the Kingdom for more investments because of the country's strategic location to key neighboring markets and due to the country's stability. Relations with Jordan are strong and strategic, and we want to develop cooperation further to cover various areas. The One Belt One Road project will help increase trade ties and cooperation with the entire Arab world, including Jordan."[37]

Minister of State for Investment Affairs, Muhannad Shehadeh, at the launching of the Jordanian–Chinese business forum in October 2018, noted that the partnership with China had seen several "success stories," such as the Attarat project aimed at producing electricity from oil shale in the Attarat Umm Ghadran region. The Jordanian Minister expressed his government's commitment to sustaining close coordination with the Chinese to establish new partnerships and enhance cooperation, especially in the fields of infrastructure, renewable energy, ICT (information and communications technology), innovation, and training. Officials at the Jordan Investment Commission (JIC), which co-organized the event with the JIC, acquainted the Chinese delegates with available investment opportunities in the Kingdom.[38]

In September 2019, on the sidelines of the Jordanian participation in the third China–Arab States Expo and fourth China–Arab States Business Summit, Jordan Industrial Estates Corporation (JIEC) and the Arab Businessmen Forum in China, signed an MoU to enhance cooperation between the two countries and promote Jordan's investment environment. The MoU was aimed at intensifying the Kingdom's promotional efforts with a focus on the Chinese market, along with exploring potential investment opportunities, mainly in industrial zones. The MoU also emphasized active public-private sector partnership intended to serve the Kingdom's investment environment, affirming that the forum would make every effort to support Jordan Industrial Estates Corporation's (JIEC) promotional efforts in the Chinese market. Under the agreement, the two sides are to hold a variety of forums and workshops on promoting investment opportunities available in Jordan's industrial zones affiliated with JIEC.[39]

The Middle East occupies some significant real estate, located in the middle of the BRI's land and maritime routes. Increased instability in the region could derail Beijing's plans for Eurasian connectivity and gives Chinese leaders reason to deepen their strategic stakes in the Middle East where economic interests have traditionally dominated the PRC's presence. In the July 2018 CASCF, Chinese President Xi Jinping pledged more than $23 billion in lines of credit, loans and aid to Arab states (e.g., Yemen, Lebanon, Jordan, and Syria), with money bookmarked for infrastructure and reconstruction projects, humanitarian aid, and efforts to support social stability in Arab countries.[40] Beijing also announced a $91 million aid package for Syria, Yemen, Jordan, and Lebanon, with $15 million to go to Jordan to assist with the plight of refugees in the Kingdom.[41]

China's assistance to the Kingdom is represented in three areas, including infrastructure projects, humanitarian assistance, and human resources development. According to the Chinese Ambassador in Jordan, Pan Weifang, more and more Jordanian officials are going to China to attend seminars and training programs, which have enhanced bilateral exchanges and cooperation. Over the past years, nearly 2,000 Jordanian officials and technicians have attended Beijing-aided training programs. In 2017 alone, 305 Jordanians attended such programs in China. Huawei plans to establish three academies, in cooperation with Jordanian universities, to train 3,000 students in the fields of IT and telecommunications.[42]

In recent years, Amman has accepted a large number of Syrian refugees, creating a new burden on its economy. Beijing has already provided humanitarian assistance of about $9.4 million to the refugees in the kingdom. Meanwhile, China has offered other means of economic aid, including improving its water and sewage services, and building shelters and roads.[43] In July 2018, the PRC helped Jordan to meet refugees' needs by providing 475 scholarships for vocational training students.[44] Beijing also funded a $1.5 million World Food Program initiative to feed newly arrived Syrian refugees in Jordan.[45] Chinese aid to the Kingdom has also assisted in the construction of Balqa Hospital, housing for the needy, and the expansion of the water supply network in Rusayfah.[46]

The preliminary results of Chinese investment in the Kingdom are hard to measure in the short term. However, expectations of increased domestic energy production and new markets for Jordanian goods in the mid-to-long-term are strong incentives for Amman to welcome Chinese companies. Furthermore, Amman is the second most-desired location for regional expansion – after Egypt – for Chinese companies based in Saudi Arabia and the United Arab Emirates. Jordan's strategic geographic position, as a means for bridging Chinese investments in the Arab Gulf and Africa, makes it a critical entry point to the Levant region. More specifically, China aims to firmly establish the Kingdom as a base for its reconstruction efforts in Syria.[47]

Energy cooperation

Investment in energy infrastructure is considered one of the critical areas of cooperation to integrate Jordan Vision 2025 into the BRI framework. As Chinese ambassador in Jordan, Pan Weifang, said, Amman's investment environment is attractive to Chinese investors from east and west. Beijing has invested in energy infrastructure including the pipeline between the Iraqi city of Basra and the Jordanian city of Aqaba, the oil shale project, the expansion of the Jordan Oil Refinery, and the renewable energy projects, amounting to tens of billions of dollars.[48]

According to the U.S. Energy Information Administration (EIA), Jordan, unlike its immediate neighbors, does not possess significant energy resources and consequently relies heavily on imports of crude oil, petroleum products, and natural gas to meet domestic energy demand. However, oil shale resources have the potential to increase Jordan's reserves significantly, and the Kingdom plans to build the first oil shale-fired electricity generation facility in the Middle East.[49]

The Kingdom's reliance on foreign energy imports comes at considerable risk to its energy security and the state budget. According to a report by the World Energy Council, total world oil shale resources are estimated at 6.5 trillion barrels. Oil shale technology has long remained under the radar, however, as the extraction process was neither cost-efficient nor environmentally friendly relative to its shale oil counterpart. While recent technological advances may be changing the environmental picture, the economic picture remains unclear, with costs running anywhere between $20 to $95 per barrel depending on a variety of factors such as the location of the shale, the technology employed, and the regulatory environment.[50]

Jordan's biggest oil-shale project, the first of its kind in the region, uses direct burning of oil shale to generate electricity at a capacity of 485 megawatts, or 15 percent of the Kingdom's generation capacity. In 2006, the Jordanian government-commissioned Estonian-owned Enefit to undertake a feasibility study of the El Lajjun and Attarat oil shale deposits in Central Jordan. This study resulted in a concession agreement covering 70 square kilometers of the Attarat. In 2009, Shell Oil also signed an oil shale concession with Jordan that is expected to yield 300,000 barrels per day by 2022.[51]

In March 2017, Attarat Power Co. (APCO), a Jordanian affiliate of Estonian-owned Enefit, reached a financial closure agreement for a planned $2.1 billion plant with the assistance of Chinese banks. This agreement will allow the company to start construction of a 470-megawatt plant, which is scheduled to begin generating electricity for local consumption in mid-2020.[52] The move comes after the power utility last year signed initial agreements with Bank of China and the Industrial and Commercial Bank of China for $1.6 billion in debt financing. Additionally, the state-run China Export & Credit Insurance, which acts as an underwriter, will also support debt financing. The project was initially agreed upon in 2014 but faced delays and discord over the price proposed to sell electricity from the plant and connect it to the national grid. The project, spurred at the outset by high gas and fuel prices, was hit as cheaper oil in recent years led to delays in securing finance.[53] China's $2.1 billion power plant construction contract will be crucial to converting the Kingdom's domestic oil shale resources into power for its burdened electricity grid. The project will be the first to commercially utilize Amman's abundant oil shale reserves, significantly reducing the country's reliance on imported oil and gas, and is expected to meet 10–15 percent of Jordan's annual power demand. When completed, the facility will be the world's second-largest oil shale-fired power facility. With estimated reserves of 90–100 billion barrels of oil in shale deposits, the government has set an ambitious target of supplying 14 percent of its energy needs from shale deposits by 2020.[54]

In January 2019, Chinese Ambassador to Jordan, Pan Weifang, said during a meeting with Jordanian Minister of Energy and Mineral Resources Hala Zawati, that Chinese companies are interested in investing energy and minerals projects in Jordan. Beijing was keen on increasing cooperation with Jordan and the Gulf states in the field of renewable energy, and the training courses conducted in China for Jordanian trainees are part of China's support to Amman to provide the kingdom with technical expertise in this sector.[55]

People-to-People Bond

Under China's strategic partnership with Amman, enabling the people of the two countries to bond along the Silk Road is also vital to integrate Jordan Vision 2025 into the BRI framework. The plan includes promoting extensive cultural and academic exchanges to win public support for deepening bilateral and multilateral cooperation, as well as providing scholarships, holding annual cultural events, increasing cooperation in science and technology, and establishing joint laboratory or research centers and international technology transfer centers.[56]

Linguistic, cultural, and tourism cooperation is another important aspect of the Beijing–Amman strategic partnership, and both nations have outlined their intention to expand the collaboration in these areas in the coming years. According to the *Hanban website*, the Chinese government established Confucius Institutes for providing Chinese language and culture teaching resources worldwide. In 2019, 550 Confucius Institutes and 1,172 Confucius Classrooms and 5,665 teaching sites were established in 162 countries and regions, receiving about eleven million students.[57] In 54 countries involved in the Belt and Road Initiative, there are 153 Confucius Institutes and 149 primary and high school Confucius Classrooms.[58]

In the Middle East, there are eighteen Confucius institutes and three Confucius classrooms, and two of them are in Jordan: the Amman TAG-Confucius Institute was founded in 2008 and the Confucius Institute at Philadelphia University in 2011. Both Confucius Institutes have become an important platform for teaching the Chinese language and disseminating Chinese culture in the Kingdom.[59] According to the Chinese deputy ambassador in Amman, Zhang Haihao, there is growing cooperation in the fields of culture and education between the two countries, and there are more than ten centers in Jordan that teach Mandarin.[60]

In January 2018, China and Jordan signed an agreement for launching a Chinese cultural center in Amman that will feature a wide range of activities promoting Chinese culture. Under the agreement, the Chinese cultural center will provide training courses on Chinese calligraphy, handicrafts, art, language, literature, books, movies, among other activities. According to the Chinese Ambassador to Jordan, Beijing funded a Chinese cultural center in Jordan capital to increase the cooperation between the two countries.[61]

Another important aspect of the Sino–Jordanian strategic partnership is the cultural exchange between the two countries. In October 2015, Talal Abu-Ghazaleh Organization (TAG-Org) signed a memorandum of understanding with the Chinese Chaning University (specializing in teaching languages) to establish a TAG center for teaching the Arabic language in China; it is expected to be the largest center of its kind in the country.[62] In October 2017, a Jordanian media delegation participated in the 4th China–Arab States Broadcasting and Television Cooperation Forum in Hangzhou, eastern China's Zhejiang Province, along with several Arab and Chinese officials. In remarks at the Forum, Jordan Radio Director Muhannad Safadi stressed the importance of such gatherings, since media is becoming influential and has a vital role in building concepts of individuals and communities.[63]

In 2018, a series of Chinese cultural shows were held in Jordan to celebrate the upcoming Chinese New Year. A cultural performance was held by the Chinese embassy in Amman in cooperation with Jordan's Ministry of Culture and the Greater Amman Municipality at the Royal Cultural Center. The shows include folk music, traditional dance, acrobatics, puppet dance, and the mysterious Sichuan opera "face-changing" performed by artists from Chengdu Tianfu Cultural Troupe.[64] In October 2019, the Chinese Embassy in Amman celebrated the 70th anniversary of the founding of the People's Republic of China in the presence of several political and academic figures at the Grand Hyatt Hotel in Amman City.[65]

Tourism is a major sector in the Sino–Jordanian strategic partnership. The Kingdom is an up-and-coming niche destination among well-traveled Chinese tourists who are looking for something new after having been to more mainstream Asian and European destinations. This development has taken place over the last two years when Jordan began to target the Chinese market; since then, Beijing has become one of Amman's most important source markets for tourism. According to the Chinese Ambassador to Jordan, the Kingdom is one of the most popular tourist destinations for Chinese people, and the number of Chinese tourists visiting Jordan is constantly increasing.[66]

In October 2019, Jordan's Interior Minister, Salameh Hammad, decided that the Chinese tourists would have the option to obtain visas from Jordanian diplomatic missions in their country or upon arrival to facilitate procedures for investors and help boost the tourism sector.[67] However, the Minister of Tourism, Majd Shwaikeh, said that the lack of direct flights between Jordan and China is one of the main challenges for the industry.[68] According to the government of Jordan, in 2016 the number of Chinese tourists to Jordan reached 37,000, an increase of 50 percent compared with 2015.[69]

Summary

The Hashemite Kingdom of Jordan stands to gain from the PRC's increased economic and infrastructure investment and political engagement in the Middle East. To date, China has become a source of investment, consultation, funding, and infrastructure projects for the Middle East and the most important trade partner in the Levant. There is a natural synergy between the two nations in their infrastructure-based development strategy. The Kingdom has a strategic geographic position in the Levant and resources (shale oil and chemicals) as well as an increasing need for development, while the PRC seeks to win an additional market share for its BRI framework, promote regional stability and peace through investments, and secure guaranteed access to energy resources in the Middle East. Nevertheless, despite the closer relationship between China and Jordan, even Chinese officials acknowledge that the Kingdom's most important bilateral relationship is with the United States.

In September 2015, a military cooperation agreement of $4.9 million was signed between the Jordan Armed Forces (JAF) and the Chinese army to procure Chinese-made military equipment.[70] However, Beijing is unlikely to replace the U.S. as Jordan's leading military supplier. The Kingdom is considered a key U.S. partner in the Middle East, especially with the ongoing instability in neighboring Syria and Iraq. Although a formal treaty has never linked them, both countries have cooperated on regional and international issues for decades. Washington has provided economic and military aid to Jordan since 1951 and 1957, respectively. Total bilateral U.S. aid to Jordan in 2017 amounted to approximately $20.4 billion. Approximately 2,795 U.S. military personnel are deployed in the Kingdom to support Defeat-ISIS operations, enhance Jordan's security, and promote regional stability. Currently, Amman is the third-largest recipient of annual U.S. foreign aid globally, after Afghanistan and Israel.[71]

As the growing strategic partnership appears to be mutually advantageous for both sides, China and Jordan are expected to boost their partnership in the coming years. The Sino–Jordanian strategic partnership may expand into fields including tourism, a railway project, renewable energy, culture, and education. For the Kingdom, strategic partnership with the Chinese offers them low-cost consumer products and much-needed foreign investments. Meanwhile, it opens a vast opportunity for Beijing to access a promising consumer market for its exports and worthwhile investments in the Levant.

7 | Yemen

The Republic of Yemen and the People's Republic of China (PRC) established diplomatic relations in 1956. The establishment of formal relations with Yemen was China's most significant diplomatic development in the Arabian Peninsula region at that time. Yemen was the first state in the Arabian Peninsula region, and the third country in the Arab world, to acknowledge the Beijing government as the legitimate representative of China. Furthermore, Yemen is a significant and strategically important state in the southern Arabian Peninsula bordering Saudi Arabia, Oman, the Red Sea, and the Gulf of Aden within the Arabian Sea. The geographical location of Yemen makes it an essential state for the PRC because it enables it an observation point over three regional trouble spots: the Arabian Gulf, the Red Sea, and the Horn of Africa. In this regard, Yemen can be considered as a geographical belt encompassing the southern part of the Gulf and the Arabian Peninsula, which controls the Bab al-Mandab Strait and the navigational routes in the Rea Sea and the Arabian Sea.[1]

Yemen enjoys a unique geographical strategic position at the intersection of the Belt and Road Initiative (BRI) that includes the Silk Road Economic Belt (SREB) and the 21st Century Maritime Silk Road (MSRI). The Strait of Bab al-Mandab is a strategic waterway and critical junction for world trade, located between Yemen, Djibouti, and Eritrea, where the Red Sea joins the Indian Ocean. Yemen can become the bridge between Asia and Africa, and between the Indian Ocean and the Mediterranean, and is thus a vital component of China's infrastructure-based development strategy.[2]

The historical ties between the PRC and Yemen go back 2,000 years when the ancient Silk Road connected trade between them and led to cultural interaction between the Arab and Chinese peoples. Yemen played a significant role in ancient history when it dominated the trade routes, called "the incense and gum routes," and many powerful nations from east and west set sail and drove their camel caravans in its direction, seeking trade and exchange of knowledge. The ancient Greeks and Romans called Yemen 'Arabia Felix' because it was perceived as a happy, or prosperous nation.[3]

The BRI scheme gives China and Yemen extra incentive to boost cooperation, as this will help to reduce risks and project costs and, in the long term, fully capture the mutual benefits of increased trade, investment and connectivity in the Middle East. As Chinese Ambassador to Yemen Kang Yong said in September 2019, Yemen was among the first countries to recognize the new political system in China. Mutual relations will develop between the two countries because the people of Yemen are seeking a brighter future as a result of this friendship.[4]

This chapter investigates aspects behind the China–Yemen relationship and examines the synergies between the BRI and Yemen's unique geographical strategic position and natural resources to understand the extent of economic engagement and bilateral relationship between the two nations. The main argument is that China's relationship with Yemen is based on shared or mutually complementary economic interests and unique geographical strategic position, especially Yemen's postwar reconstruction through the integration and implementation of the new Silk Road Initiative. A cessation of hostilities in Yemen would have significant economic benefits for Beijing, as it would give it access to Yemen's Bab al-Mandeb Strait, a critical chokepoint that facilitates its objective of expanding the BRI to Saudi Arabia and allow it to actively participate in the trade of seaborne oil across Yemen's maritime straits.

Yemen Civil War and the Postwar Reconstruction

The Yemen civil war, which began in 2014, is one of the more complex events to have emerged since the start of the Arab Spring. The current conflict has deep historical roots and reflects long-standing societal and political grievances within Yemen. As the Arab Spring swept through Egypt and Tunisia, Yemen's deep political divisions were further exacerbated by the involvement of competing for regional powers: Saudi Arabia and the United Arab Emirates backed Yemen's government while, to a lesser extent, Iran assisted the Houthis.[5]

Nearly a quarter of a million people have been killed directly by fighting and indirectly through a lack of access to food, health services, and infrastructure. According to Yemen's Minister of Planning and International Cooperation, Najib al-Auj, the war-torn country needs a baseline of $28 billion funds for reconstruction efforts over the next four years. In the long term, Yemen's reconstruction could run up a bill as high as $60 billion for the postwar restoration of institutions, stability, and security.[6]

The immediate interest at stake for Beijing in the Yemen civil war is the protection of its economic investments and the safety of Chinese personnel. According to statistics published by the Chinese Ministry of Commerce, Beijing has 14 enterprises and 460 personnel in Yemen. China's trade projects concentrate on oil extraction, telecommunication, construction, roads and bridges, and fishery.[7] While the scale of the investment is small, Beijing does strengthen its economic relations with Yemen through expanding investment. In response to the Yemen crisis, China has finished personnel evacuation and temporarily closed its embassy in Sana'a and the Consulate General in Aden; the date of return to normal operation remains unknown.[8]

Since the early days of the civil war, the PRC's policy toward the Yemeni conflict has been clear and consistent, driven primarily by its interest in maintaining close strategic relations with Saudi Arabia. In both bilateral and multilateral initiatives, China has steadily supported the internationally recognized government of Yemen, always stressing the importance of Yemen's national independence, sovereignty, and territorial integrity. Beijing has also regularly urged all parties to the conflict to reject the use of violence and resolve the conflict through political means through intra-Yemeni dialogue.[9]

As for the role of other states in the Yemeni conflict, Beijing generally encouraged regional countries to take the lead in addressing the crisis, and it suggested that the international community should not only support the Yemeni political dialogue but also provide development and humanitarian assistance to the country.[10] China also welcomed the Riyadh agreement signed between the Yemeni government and the Southern Transitional Council (STC), for the formation of a new government and integrating the armed forces.[11]

The PRC's growing economic ties in the Middle East give it a large stake and the influence to be more active in helping to mediate conflicts in the region. Unlike other major powers, Beijing has stayed out of regional rivalries and has forged ties with all sides. China also carries little of the historical or cultural baggage associated with other players in the region. As such, it is well-placed to serve as an honest broker in making dialogue possible.[12] Following unsuccessful rounds of UN negotiations, Beijing tried to bridge the trust deficit between the Houthis, the Yemeni government, and the UN. In December 2016, a high-level delegation of Yemen's Houthi rebel movement held a three-day visit to China and met with Foreign Ministry's Director-General Deng Li to discuss the ongoing conflict in Yemen.[13] Although Beijing's attempt to mediate was unsuccessful, Houthi leaders and representatives of the Yemeni government thanked Beijing for taking an objective and impartial stance on the Yemen issue and said they would be willing to maintain close communication with China.[14]

Beijing would also be interested in playing a role in reconstruction efforts in Yemen, and could be open to participating in, and possibly financing, postwar reconstruction in the region. This could be a logical extension of its BRI framework, in terms of infrastructure-based development strategy, and could help raise China's diplomatic and financial profile in an area that it regards as strategically important.[15] As a major trade partner, Beijing has an outsized economic presence in Yemen and can play a significant economic role in the country's postwar reconstruction through its BRI framework. As the Chinese ambassador to Yemen, Tian Qi, said, Beijing is "willing to actively participate in Yemen's future economic reconstruction process," as it promotes its Belt and Road Initiative in the region.[16] Nevertheless, the ongoing conflict in Yemen has exacted a disastrous toll on the country's people, economy, infrastructure, and institutions, as well as the ties that bind them. The effort to rebuild both the tangible and intangible aspects of Yemeni society will be complicated by not only the fragmentation among Yemen's political and military factions, but also by the multitude of foreign actors and interests that, directly and indirectly, have come to exert an influence over the conflict, or could do so in the future.[17]

Yemen and the Belt and Road Initiative

The PRC's relationship with Yemen includes four major areas for cooperation within the BRI. These areas are policy coordination, connectivity, trade and investments, and energy cooperation. However, each country views the BRI framework and reacts to it according to its perspective and the consequences for its own national interests and international status. Therefore, the two countries have very different attitudes regarding how to realize the new Silk Road vision.[18]

Policy coordination

China's relations with Yemen include promoting political cooperation between countries, creating mechanisms for dialogue and consensus-building on global and regional issues, developing shared interests, deepening political trust, and reaching a new consensus on cooperation.[19] Beijing and Yemen enjoy friendly relations and new political and economic developments; in 2013 the two countries also held a series of high-level exchanges.

In January 2013, Vice Foreign Minister Zhai Jun visited Yemen. In March 2013, Chinese Ambassador to the UK Liu Xiaoming attended and spoke at the fifth Friends of Yemen Ministerial Meeting in London on behalf of the Chinese government. In September 2013, Foreign Minister Wang Yi attended the sixth Friends of Yemen Ministerial Meeting held on the sidelines of the 68th Session of the UN General Assembly in New York. That same month, Yemeni Minister of Industry and Trade Saadaldeen Ali Salim Talib visited China and attended the China–Arab States Expo 2013 in Ningxia. Minister of Defense Muhammed Nasser Ahmed also visited China.[20]

In November 2013, at the invitation of Chinese President Xi Jinping, President Abdu-Rabbuh Mansour Hadi paid a state visit to China. President Xi told his counterpart that the peoples of China and Yemen enjoy a profound traditional friendship. He also said that bilateral cooperation had developed smoothly in all areas, and the two countries supported each other on issues concerning each other's core interests and major concerns. President Xi assured President Hadi that no matter how the international situation changes, both sides are always each other's reliable good friend, a good brother, and a good partner. China is willing to conduct friendly exchanges with the Yemeni government, its legislative bodies, and political parties, to exchange experiences in governing state affairs and political actions.[21]

During President Hadi's visit, the two countries signed the Agreement on Economic and Technical Cooperation Between the Government of the People's Republic of China and the Government of the Republic of Yemen and an Agreement on Enhancing Educational Cooperation Between Ministry of Education of the People's Republic of China and Ministry of Higher Education and Scientific Research and Ministry of Technical Education and Vocational Training of the Republic of Yemen.[22] However, Yemen was soon after mired in political unrest and armed conflict, which intensified in early 2015. Houthi rebels – a minority Shia group from the north of the country – drove out the U.S.-backed government and took over the capital, Sanaa.[23] The crisis quickly escalated into a multi-sided war, with neighboring Saudi Arabia leading a coalition of Gulf countries against the Houthi rebels.[24] As a result, the PRC suspended its embassy operations in Yemen.[25]

In recent years, Yemeni and Chinese officials emphasized the importance of boosting ties between the two countries in various areas under the framework of the Belt and Road Initiative. In July 2017, Chinese Ambassador to Yemen, Tian Qi, said, "China firmly supports a political solution to the crisis and hopes Yemen can restore peace and stability at the earliest date. China would like to join hands with Yemen to push forward the Belt and Road initiative to benefit the people of the region."[26]

In July 2018, Chinese Foreign Minister Wang Yi held talks with Yemen Foreign Minister Khaled Hussein Alyemany, who was in China for the 8th Ministerial Meeting of the China–Arab States Cooperation Forum (CASCF). Foreign Minister Wang said that Beijing and Yemen are traditionally friendly countries. Since the establishment of

China–Yemen diplomatic relations, bilateral relations have enjoyed forward-looking development. China is ready to work with the Arab states, including Yemen, to implement the outcomes of the 8th CASCF Ministerial Meeting and continually deepen China–Yemen cooperation in the joint construction of the Belt and Road Initiative. For his part, Foreign Minister Khaled reaffirmed their joint commitment to the initiatives and propositions put forward in the speech, including the joint construction of the BRI by the Arab states and China.[27]

In June 2019, Chinese Ambassador to Yemen Kang Yong, in a statement to the *Yemeni News Agency (Saba)*, stressed the importance of Yemen's role and participation in the BRI due to Yemen's significant geographical location and its natural resources. "The Chinese side eagerly hopes that Yemen can practically contribute to building the 'Belt and Road,' achieve peace, stability, and economic development. The ongoing war Yemen has been experiencing [. . .] prevented Yemen from practically contributing [. . .]. As a result, Yemen could not turn its potential natural resources into economic assets."[28]

In July 2019, a meeting took place between the Yemeni prime minister and Chinese Ambassador to Yemen Kang Yong in Riyadh. Yemeni Prime Minister, Maeen Abdulmalik, praised Yemeni–Chinese historical relations and China's firm support for the government of Yemen and Yemeni people in ending the coup, realizing security and stability, and regaining the state. For his part, the Chinese ambassador said that his country was closely following the work of the Yemeni government and its achievements on the ground in tangibly improving services, especially in Aden, and its support for all the Yemeni government's efforts to normalize the situation and overcome the effects of the war.[29]

Connectivity

Facilitation of connectivity is one of the essential ways to integrate Yemen's postwar reconstruction within China's BRI framework. Yemen should attempt to optimize its infrastructural connections and also adapt its technical systems to those of the other countries in the BRI. The Bab al-Mandeb Strait is a critical chokepoint since the strait forms a vital strategic link in the maritime trade route between the Mediterranean Sea and the Indian Ocean via the Red Sea and the Suez Canal. It can facilitate Yemen's objective of expanding the BRI framework to Saudi Arabia and allow China to actively participate in the trade of seaborne oil across Yemen's maritime straits.

The U.S. Energy Information Administration (EIA) defines world oil chokepoints as narrow channels along widely used global sea routes, some so narrow that restrictions are placed on the size of the vessel that can navigate through them. Chokepoints are a critical part of global energy security because of the high volume of petroleum and other liquids transported through these narrow straits. The Bab al-Mandeb Strait is a chokepoint between the Horn of Africa and the Middle East, and it is a strategic link between the Mediterranean Sea and the Indian Ocean. The strait is located between Yemen, Djibouti, and Eritrea, and it connects the Red Sea with the Gulf of Aden and the Arabian Sea.[30]

Geographically, the strait controls the southern access to the Red Sea and the Suez Canal, which links the Indian Ocean and the Mediterranean Sea. As a result, the Bab al-Mandeb Strait is a key chokepoint in the main maritime route connecting Asia and Europe, as well as an important passage in China's MSRI. Sailing between Asia and

Europe without transiting through the strait would entail circumnavigating either the whole of Africa via the Cape of Good Hope, or the whole of Eurasia via the Arctic Sea. The fact that both alternative routes would be extremely inconvenient makes the Strait of Bab al-Mandeb a true "maritime chokepoint."[31]

As a crucial hotspot for global trade, each year billions of dollars in maritime trade pass through the strait, with more than 8 percent of global trade passes through every year.[32] According to the EU's Maritime Security Centre – Horn of Africa (MSCHOA) estimates, between 12.5 percent and 20 percent of global trade passes through the strait every year.[33] The Strait of Bab al-Mandeb has become crucial for China's MSRI that relies on maritime shipping for its international trade relations. Commercially the MSRI is, above all, about aligning the 'connectivity' of global shipping lanes and ports and with Chinese capital. The large majority of China's total international trade, with estimates ranging from 60 percent to 90 percent, passes through the strait.[34]

In November 2013, Yemen Gulf of Aden Ports Corporation Captain/Sami Saeed Farea and China Harbor Engineering Company signed an agreement on the expansion and deepening of Aden Container Terminal. The project is being implemented at the cost of $507 million and includes the construction of an additional berth on the western side of the terminal with a thousand-meter length and a depth of 18 meters, as well as the deepening and expansion of the outer navigational channel. The agreement also allows for the deepening and expansion of the turning area and installation of giant container cranes, RTGs, and tractors for the first phase of the berth, to raise the capacity of handling up to a million and a half containers in the year, by adding 500,000 containers as well as other utilities such as a container storage yard, service facilities, administrative buildings and a central workshop for general maintenance. Completion of the project would make Aden and the other Yemeni ports key components of global trade and economic exchange. However, the project was not carried out because of the ensuing dangerous security situation.[35]

The Chinese intention was to connect the Aden Container Terminal to the BRI framework, on the land route to Oman and across the Hormuz Strait to Iran and Asia, and westward through a tunnel/bridge to Djibouti and Africa. Another connection to the BRI is through the main ports of Aden, Al-Hudaidah, and Mokha, where in addition to transshipment and logistics operations, new industrial parks could be built, benefiting from the proximity to international trade routes and the locally abundant human and natural resources.[36]

The tremendous developments taking place around Yemen, especially on the African continent, due to the BRI – such as the Djibouti–Addis Ababa railway, the Mombasa–Nairobi railway, the Lamu Port–South Sudan–Ethiopia Transport Corridor (LAPSSET), and many more projects – have the potential to transform the continent into one of the fastest-growing regions.[37] This is a great advantage for Yemen in its postwar reconstruction, which should consider the region as having great market potential, and also consider itself as a major logistics hub. Moreover, in east Yemen, the Chinese-led Asian Infrastructure Investment Bank (AIIB) has already financed feasibility studies and preliminary work on a pan-Omani railway network extending from the Hormuz Strait to the border with Yemen, and new ports and industrial parks on the long coast of the Arabian Sea.[38]

According to the United Nations Conference on Trade and Development (UNCTAD), around 80 percent of global trade by volume and over 70 percent of global trade by value are carried by sea and are handled by ports worldwide. The global seaborne trade expanded by 4 percent, the fastest growth in five years, and is projected to increase by 3.8 percent in the period 2018–2023. This trend is driven by booming infrastructure investments generated by China's BRI, digitalization, electronic commerce (e-commerce), India through its connectivity strategy and the Gulf monarchies with their projects for building container ports and other efforts to forge energy and trade alliances in the East.[39]

From the side of the Arabian Peninsula, the major challenges to maritime security in and around the Bab al-Mandeb chokepoint come from Yemen's Houthi rebels. Most of Yemen's western coastline along the Red Sea is still controlled by the Houthis, the Iran-backed Shiite insurgents in the north of the country. Since 2016, the Houthis' long-range missiles and remote-controlled boats filled with explosives have hit American, Saudi, and Emirati warships as well as Saudi oil tankers and merchant ships passing through the southern end of the Red Sea. Hence, the need to counter the rising maritime terrorism and to guarantee the security of the many container ports currently under construction or expansion. This means that freedom of navigation through the Bab al-Mandeb Strait will become an increasingly important issue for the Chinese national interest and the interests of the global community, providing scope for possible bilateral and/or multilateral cooperation, albeit in a context marked by strong competition.[40]

From the side of the Horn of Africa, a fragile region that has been plagued for decades by high levels of violence and instability within and across borders, the major challenges to maritime security in and around Bab al-Mandeb chokepoint come from terrorism, piracy, human trafficking, and smuggling operations.[41] In December 2008, the People's Liberation Army Navy (PLAN) launched its first anti-piracy missions in the Indian Ocean and Gulf of Aden.[42]

The Gulf of Aden, between the coasts of Yemen and Somalia, connects to the Red Sea through the Bab al-Mandab Strait and is an important waterway for shipping oil from the Persian Gulf to Europe and North America. About 20,000 ships, from more than 100 countries and regions, pass through the Gulf of Aden every year, with a freight volume that accounts for about one-fifth of the world's total sea cargo. All exports from Asia to the West must pass through the Gulf of Aden before entering the Suez Canal, with more than 1,000 merchant ships traveling from China to Europe every year via this route.[43]

In the last decade, because of its geographically strategic location and importance for global trade and shipping, the Gulf of Aden was the world's most frequented area for pirate attacks against merchant ships. According to Chinese sources, 20 percent of Chinese ships sailing through the Gulf of Aden faced pirate attacks of some kind.[44] To secure its merchant and fishing ships, the PLAN joined the missions of the European Operation Atalanta and its force – officially named the EU Naval Force (EU NAVFOR). China has also shown a willingness to cooperate internationally to obtain higher benefits.[45]

In August 2017, China inaugurated its first naval base outside China, in Djibouti, at a cost of $600 million and accommodating up to 10,000 soldiers. According to the Chinese government, the base is intended to help Beijing in its humanitarian and peacekeeping missions in Africa and Western Asia and to lead emergency relief, protection, and evacuation work of Chinese citizens living overseas; additional benefits are, of course, engagement in military cooperation, including joint maneuvers, and to combat piracy. The base will also be responsible for ensuring the security of international and strategic seaways near the Bab al-Mandeb Strait, to protect China's massive economic interests in Africa and the Middle East. It will serve as a transport route for raw materials from the Horn of Africa countries to China and electronic products from China to the Horn of Africa.

The Chinese naval base in Djibouti came after several years of increasing geostrategic and geo-economic interests in Africa and the Middle East. Beijing is seeking through its naval base to protect its growing economic and strategic interests in this part of the world. It is seeking to secure natural resources to support its economic growth, as is clear when one considers that half the oil imported by Beijing passes through the Bab al-Mandeb Strait, and most Chinese exports to Europe are channeled through the Gulf of Aden and the Suez Canal. The naval base in Djibouti will be mainly for commercial purposes, but it will also provide a military base that will boost the ability of the Chinese navy to project its power, and it will be upgradeable in the future.[46]

After Djibouti unilaterally terminated the contract with DP World, nationalized the container terminal, and granted the right to develop Doraleh Multipurpose Port (DMP) to China Merchants Port (CM) Port without first having offered the opportunity to DP World, CM Port began an expansion of the port facilities. When completed, they will provide Chinese-flagged vessels with priority handling and lower docking fees. The DP World subsequently filed suit against China Merchants to enforce its legal claims and the two global port operators are currently at the center of legal disputes over Doraleh Container Terminal.[47]

The establishment of the Chinese base in Djibouti marks a break with Beijing's traditional non-intervention policy in the Middle East and North Africa (MENA) region. It is a projection of Chinese power that expresses the country's growing interest in the MENA, especially in the BRI framework, which aims to establish land and sea routes linking China to Europe via Eurasia and the Middle East. The base was constructed as a result of China's MSRI strategy joining up with the "string of pearls" in the shape of a series of Chinese navy footholds linking the Indian Ocean, the Gulf region, and the Red Sea.[48]

Energy cooperation

In China's relationship with Yemen, investment in energy infrastructure is considered one of the critical areas of cooperation to integrate Yemen's postwar reconstruction through the BRI. Therefore, the new Silk Road can provide a new framework for more extensive Chinese investments in the Yemen energy industry. In terms of natural resources, Yemen boasts 1,200 miles of coastline, deep-water ports, and a geographic location along major shipping routes which represent economic assets that can be exploited, along with a limited but not insignificant supply of hydrocarbons, especially natural gas.[49]

According to EIA, Yemen is not a major hydrocarbon producer relative to several other countries in the Middle East, but the country has sufficient oil and natural gas resources for both domestic demand and exports. Nevertheless, Yemen's difficult security environment hinders the production and transport of those resources. Yemen's oil production declined after 2001 as a result of the country's maturing fields, and attacks on the country's oil infrastructure since 2011 have led to significant short-term disruptions. Attacks on Yemen's key oil infrastructure continue to curtail both domestic petroleum consumption and exports. Since 2009 the country has been a Liquefied Natural Gas (LNG) exporter, and the government aims to increase the use of natural gas in many sectors, including in electricity generation. This development could help the country stabilize its economy even without an extremely high oil export price. However, replacing oil export revenues with LNG export revenues does not reduce the country's dependence on its hydrocarbons sector.[50]

Most exports of petroleum and natural gas from the Persian Gulf that transit the Suez Canal or the SUMED Pipeline pass through both the Bab al-Mandeb and the Strait of Hormuz. Closure of the Bab al-Mandeb Strait could keep tankers originating in the Persian Gulf from transiting the Suez Canal or reaching the SUMED Pipeline, forcing them to divert around the southern tip of Africa, the Cape of Good Hope, which would add approximately 2,700 miles to the transit, increasing transit time and costs. Shipping around Africa would add 15 days of transit to Europe and 8–10 days to the United States.[51]

The Bab al-Mandeb Straits is one of the world's most strategic maritime transit points.[52] In 2018, an estimated 6.2 million barrels per day (b/d) of crude oil, condensate, and refined petroleum products flowed through the strait, an increase from 5.1 million b/d in 2014. The total petroleum flows through the chokepoint accounted for about 9 percent of total seaborne-traded petroleum in 2017.[53]

For Beijing, the unique geographical strategic position of Bab al-Mandab derives from its proximity to the Strait of Hormuz, which provides a vital link to the trade route between the Mediterranean and Asia. Most vessels carrying goods between Europe and Asia, as well as oil from the Middle East to China, pass through the strait before navigating Egypt's Suez Canal. In the context of Beijing's growing energy needs and the Middle East as a market to satisfy these needs, securing the Bab al-Mandab Strait is important for China.[54] However, only 3–4 percent of Beijing's oil and gas imports are estimated to pass through the Bab al-Mandab Strait, because oil and gas shipped from the Persian Gulf and the Gulf of Oman to China will not pass through this strait. Hence, the oil and gas passing through the strait will only be that coming from Beijing's suppliers in North Africa (e.g., Algeria) or the western part of Saudi Arabia.

In the past, the PRC had been active in the exploration of Yemen's oil reserves, nearly 3 billion barrels of oil and approximately 17 trillion cubic feet of gas. Unfortunately, current instability and violence in recent years make production and export a challenge. In early 2015, the security situation in Yemen was so complicated that a Chinese-owned oil company had to cease operations in the east Al Hajr field.[55] Nevertheless, according to *Saba News Agency*, during his meeting with the newly appointed Chinese ambassador to Yemen, Kang Yong, in October 2019, the Yemeni president said that he is looking forward to the return of Chinese investments to Yemen in terms of oil, gas, and energy.[56]

Trade and investments

As part of the PRC's relations with Yemen, the aim is to mitigate as much as possible the barriers to free trade, investment, industrial cooperation, and technical and engineering services to facilitate the integration of Yemen's postwar reconstruction through the Belt and Road Initiative framework. Both countries should take a series of measures, such as expanding free-trade zones, improving trade structures, seeking new potential areas for trade, and improving the trade balance, devising new initiatives for the promotion of conventional forms of trade.[57]

Yemen enjoys great human resources, as most of its population are children and youth under 30 years of age, making it a young society capable of progress and continuity into the future through comprehensive and long-term visions and economic plans. Yemen also has abundant natural resources and a diverse climate and topography, making it suitable for integrated agro-industrial development. Such a raised economic platform could allow Yemen and its people to take control of their economy, their resources, and their future.[58]

From a purely economic perspective, Sino–Yemeni relations are a secondary concern for Beijing. According to China Customs Statistics (export-import), Beijing–Yemen trade volume has increased to $3.8 billion by 2019 (compared to $2.5 billion in 2018).[59] Arguably due to Yemen's troubled political situation since the Arab Spring, the trade between the two countries has been highly irregular. As for trade, Chinese investment in Yemen has also been a small proportion of the PRC's regional investment. According to the China Global Investment Tracker, Beijing's investments and construction in Yemen from 2005 to 2013 reached $1.2 billion, while in 2014–2019, they stood at zero. Most of the Chinese investment in Yemen was in real estate ($730 million) while the rest ($470 million) was invested in the energy sector.[60]

The last Chinese investment in Yemen dates back to 2013 when the two countries signed a $507 million deal to build power plants and to expand two container ports in the southern cities of Aden through the BRI framework.[61] Since then, however, no further Chinese investments in Yemen have been recorded. Thus, it can be concluded that China does not have a particularly keen economic interest in Yemen, at least not from a purely economic perspective. Notwithstanding this circumstance, Beijing is heavily dependent on Yemen, which controls the Bab al-Mandab Strait, for its trade with the European continent. In 2018, the EU was China's second trading partner after the U.S. In terms of EU exports, China was the second-largest export partner, while in terms of EU imports, China was the first largest export partner, accounting for around 15.4 percent of Beijing's overall trade in goods (on average, about €1.5 billion per day).[62] China–EU trade in 2018 amounted to €605 billion. During this time, EU exports to China were €210 billion, and EU imports from China were €395 billion; the EU's trade deficit with China reaching €185 billion.[63]

As seaborne trade constitutes the bulk of trade for both the PRC and the EU, most of this trade has to pass through the Bab al-Mandab Strait, making the passage a central location for China's economy and the success of the BRI framework. Therefore, when looking at Yemen from its unique geographical strategic position, the PRC's interests in Yemen stability are significant. Any disruption in the navigation through Yemeni waters would have a significant negative impact on China's implementation of BRI.

Yemen's humanitarian crisis is now considered the worst in the world. The war in the impoverished Arab nation has resulted in widespread famine, illness, and death. According to the United Nations, 75 percent of Yemen's population, just over 22 million people, are in dire need of humanitarian assistance. More than two million Yemenis are internally displaced, almost 18 million food-insecure – about half of those are at risk of starvation – and approximately 16 million lack access to safe water, sanitation, and adequate healthcare. Over a million cases of cholera have been reported inside the country – the worst epidemic in modern history.[64]

The humanitarian crisis and the desire to maintain stability in Yemen have led China to provide humanitarian assistance. In July 2017, Beijing successfully delivered its first tranche of humanitarian aid to Yemen's southern port city of Aden. The Chinese government's assistance package consisted of $22.5 million in relief supplies aimed at ameliorating food shortages in Yemen.[65] Beijing also funds the UN's World Food Programme (WFPP) and the World Health Organization to help combat the cholera epidemic. The Chinese government contributed $5 million which will provide one month of much-needed food assistance to more than 930,000 people suffering from hunger in Yemen.[66]

In July 2018, at the CASCF (China–Arab States Cooperation Forum), China pledged $23 billion in loans and aid to Arab states, much of which is to support reconstruction and humanitarian efforts in countries like Syria, Yemen, and Jordan.[67] As Chinese Foreign Minister Wang Yi told his Yemeni counterpart at the 8th Ministerial Meeting of the CASCF, Beijing and Yemen are traditionally friendly countries. Since the establishment of China–Yemen diplomatic relations, the Chinese side is willing to continue to assist with the Yemeni side within China's capacity, especially to help Yemen ease the humanitarian crisis.[68]

In January 2019, in a speech at the CASCF in Beijing, Chinese President Xi Jinping pledged $105 million in humanitarian aid to Palestine, Yemen, Syria, and Jordan. The Chinese government will hand $90 million to Yemen, Syria, and Jordan, with another $15 million earmarked for Palestine. The forum seeks to enhance Chinese-Arab trade relations and has boosted bilateral trade volume. Since 2004, China and Arab countries have launched 15 mechanisms of cooperation as part of the CASCF.[69]

Summary

Yemen has emerged as a crucial component of China's MSRI projects due to its unique geographical strategic position and natural resources. As the main transit point between the Indian Ocean and the Mediterranean Sea, the country offers a vantage point on three troubled areas: the Arabian Gulf, the Red Sea, and the Horn of Africa. However, Yemen's complex characteristics (mostly the political instability and the security situation) could raise challenges for Beijing's economic interests and BRI development. Maintenance of security at the Arabian Peninsula's southernmost pinch point, not to mention the Strait of Hormuz, is a real concern for Beijing and other international actors who rely on the region's maritime trade.

The Bab al-Mandeb Strait will remain an essential strategic chokepoint for trade and the free flow of oil and gas and remains an essential node or chokepoint for China's Belt and Road Initiative framework. Chinese President Xi Jinping's massive infrastructure plan focuses on the establishment of transport, trade, and communications infrastructure between Beijing and the global markets and sources of raw materials, especially in Europe and Africa, by land, sea, and air.

Yemen's reconstruction process is likely to unfold for many years, at least, and even decades. There is no doubt that Beijing has the necessary capabilities and the vast resources for Yemen's reconstruction process, but its policy and conduct in the country raise serious doubts as to the likelihood of its investing these capabilities and resources there. As Chinese Foreign Minister Wang Yi stated, the Chinese side is willing to continue to assist with the Yemeni side within China's capacity, especially to help Yemen ease the humanitarian crisis. Given these conditions as well as the needs and priorities of the Yemen government, it seems reasonable to assume that the post-war reconstruction, now and for the foreseeable future, does not allow China or any partner to make wide-scale investments.

8 | Saudi Arabia

In the last few years, Saudi Arabia and China have built a new framework for their comprehensive strategic partnership based on shared or mutually complementary economic and commercial interests. This chapter examines the new horizons opened by the growing comprehensive strategic partnership between Riyadh and Beijing, to understand the extent of economic engagement and the level of the bilateral relationship between the two nations. The strategic synergy between the Belt and Road Initiative (BRI) and Saudi Vision 2030 has forged a joint economic development path that will bring new opportunities for both sides. Nevertheless, several challenges could complicate a broader bilateral partnership.

Since the establishment of diplomatic relations in 1990, the ties between the People's Republic of China (PRC) and Saudi Arabia have witnessed sustained and rapid development, characterized by enhanced mutual political trust, ties that were elevated to a comprehensive strategic partnership in 2016. This level of partnership means that Beijing has built a deep relationship with the Kingdom and maintains significant cooperation on economic, political, and security issues. As Chinese President Xi Jinping said to Saudi Arabia's crown prince, Mohammed bin Salman al-Saud (MBS), "China regards Saudi Arabia as a good friend and partner" and is ready to "open up a new horizon for bilateral friendship and strategic relationship." The relationship between two nations has "advanced in an all-around way, at multiple levels and in a wide variety of fields."[1]

The Kingdom of Saudi Arabia is situated close to the center of a Belt and Road megaproject that connects Asia, Africa, and Europe, and this strategic location means that Saudi's Vision 2030 could fuse perfectly with the BRI. Accordingly, Riyadh could serve as a natural and essential partner of China in building the BRI. This chapter examines the new horizon and the growing comprehensive strategic partnership between Riyadh and the PRC, and the synergy between the BRI and the Saudi Vision 2030 to understand the extent of economic engagement and bilateral relationship between the two nations. Chinese President Xi Jinping stated his view that the two countries should speed up the signing of an implementation plan on connecting the BRI with the Saudi Vision 2030.[2]

The main argument presented is that the PRC's comprehensive strategic partnership framework with Riyadh is based on shared or mutual complementary economic and commercial interests, especially with the integration and implementation of the BRI and Saudi Vision 2030. This development in relations is emerging at the same time that both countries find themselves the object of widespread international criticism, and both countries seek political allies and economic opportunities. The Saudi Vision 2030 and the PRC's Belt and Road vision have converged on a common economic development path, and their synergetic strategy will bring new opportunities for both sides.

Saudi Vision 2030

In 2016, Saudi authorities unveiled 'Vision 2030', aimed at making the Kingdom a global investment powerhouse and the heart of the Arab and Islamic world while also diversifying the country's economy, now heavily dependent on oil. The Saudi national strategy is designed to reduce its dependence on energy-related exports and increase its service sector in areas such as health care, education, recreation, and tourism.[3] The economic reform program relies on parallel reforms and procedures to be carried out, constituting three main axes: a Public Investments Fund Program, a Financial Balancing Program, and a National Transformation Program. This combined vision centralizes a vibrant society, diversifies the thriving economy, and develops an ambitious, effective government and responsible citizenry.[4]

Saudi Arabia and the Belt and Road Initiative

The PRC's comprehensive strategic partnerships with Riyadh include six major areas for cooperation within the BRI. These areas are policy coordination, connectivity, trade and investments, energy cooperation, military ties, and people-to-people bond. However, each country views the BRI framework according to its perspective and the consequences for its own national interests and international status. Therefore, the two countries have very different attitudes about how to realize the vision.

Policy coordination

As part of China's comprehensive strategic partnerships with Saudi Arabia, promoting political cooperation between countries, creating mechanisms for dialogue and consensus-building on global and regional issues, developing shared interests, deepening political trust, and reaching a new consensus on cooperation is important to integrate the Saudi Vision 2030 into the BRI framework.[5]

The Beijing–Riyadh comprehensive strategic partnership developed following frequent top-level exchanges and cooperation agreements to promote policy coordination, trade, and economic ties. The new round of interaction between the highest leaders of the two countries opened a new era of the comprehensive and rapid development of China–Saudi Arabia relations. In January 2016, President Xi Jinping made a historic visit to the Kingdom, and the two countries established a comprehensive strategic partnership and decided to establish a High-Level Joint Committee of China and Saudi Arabia to push bilateral relations into a new stage of rapid development.[6]

In August 2016, Saudi Deputy Prime Minister Crown Prince MBS visited China; he held the first meeting of the China–Saudi Arabia High-Level Joint Committee and attended the G20 Hangzhou Summit. During the visit, both parties signed bilateral cooperation agreements in politics, energy, finance, investment, real estate, water resource, quality testing, science and technologies, and cultural exchanges.[7] In March 2017, King Salman Bin Abdulaziz al-Saud paid a state visit to China, which further promoted the alignment of development strategies of the two countries and deepened the practical cooperation under the BRI framework.[8]

In August 2017, Chinese Vice Premier Zhang Gaoli visited Saudi Arabia and held the second meeting of the High-Level Joint Committee with Crown Prince MBS, which brought the practical cooperation in various fields to a new level. During the meeting, the two sides signed a list of critical projects for production capacity and investment cooperation, of which 30 projects were identified.[9] In February 2019, Crown Prince Muhammad Bin Salman visited China and held the third meeting of China–Saudi Arabia High-Level Joint Committee with Chinese Vice Premier Han Zheng. The two sides agreed to strengthen the synergy of the BRI and the Saudi Vision 2030 and enhance pragmatic cooperation on energy, infrastructure construction, and finance.[10] In this context, it is essential to understand the new horizon and the growing comprehensive strategic partnership between Riyadh and Beijing, and the impact on the implementation of the BRI, in light of the frequent top-level exchanges and the cooperation agreements signed. The considerable warming in relations between Riyadh and Beijing came at a time when both countries were under increasingly harsh global criticism and thus eager to find political support as well as business opportunities.

For Beijing, the West has been actively demanding that China stop its crackdown on the Muslim minority in Xinjiang. According to reports on Human Rights Practices for 2018, China had significantly intensified its campaign of the mass detention of members of Muslim minority groups in Xinjiang. They were reported to have arbitrarily detained from 800,000 to possibly more than two million Uighurs, ethnic Kazakhs, and other Muslims in camps to erase religious and ethnic identities.[11] In March 2019, the U.S. State Department said the sort of abuses in China had inflicted on its Muslim minorities had not been seen "since the 1930s", and U.S. Secretary of State Mike Pompeo said China was "in a league of its own when it comes to human rights violations."[12] In May 2019, the U.S. accused China of putting more than a million minority Muslims in "concentration camps".[13]

Riyadh received harsh global criticism over the killing of *Washington Post* journalist Jamal Khashoghghi in Saudi Arabia's Consulate General in Istanbul as well as for the country's human rights record,[14] and its role in the conflict in Yemen,[15] thus forcing the Kingdom to turn elsewhere for new partners and a friendly business environment to secure support for Saudi Vision 2030.[16] For instance, at the G20 summit in Argentina late November 2018, when most leaders shunned MBS in the wake of the Khashoggi murder, Chinese President Xi Jinping was one of the few leaders, along with Vladimir Putin, who publicly offered support to the Saudi prince.[17]

More importantly, the Saudi Arabia government seeks to diversify its economy, attract more foreign direct investments, and increase its global market presence for alternative sources of revenue in the wake of low oil prices. The BRI represents fresh business opportunities for the Kingdom. The key to this endeavor is establishing a comprehensive strategic partnership between Riyadh and Beijing, namely, to link up the two strategic conceptions: China's BRI and Saudi Arabia's Vision 2030. According to Chinese State Councilor and Foreign Minister Wang Yi, there should be a 'deeper synergy' between the Belt and Road megaproject, and the Saudi Vision 2030 development strategy. Beijing's backing of Saudi Arabia's blueprint for building a thriving economy by exploring cooperation in numerous fields may include infrastructure projects supporting the BRI and Vision 2030. Adel bin Ahmed al-Jubeir, Saudi Arabia's Foreign Minister, has stated that the country's economic diversification and industrial development roadmap was 'highly consistent' with the Asian powerhouse's BRI megaproject. Connecting the two projects would help Beijing and Riyadh strengthen cooperation in industries including energy, mining, economy and trade, investment, and tourism.[18]

Connectivity

The facilitation of connectivity is one of the important ways to integrate the Saudi Vision 2030 into the BRI framework. The PRC has always regarded Saudi Arabia as a priority in its Middle East foreign policy as well as an important cooperation partner in the BRI, for several reasons. First, given its core Islamic values, Saudi Arabia plays a vital role in politics, economy, religion, and security affairs in the Middle East and among Islamic countries.[19] Second, Beijing could utilize the Kingdom's unique location at the nexus of three continents, Asia, Africa, and Europe.[20] Third, the Kingdom has a large and scalable infrastructure that would ease the flow of goods and commodities efficiently among the three continents. Moreover, Saudi Vision 2030 also prioritizes connectivity and economic integration, which is at the heart of the BRI.[21]

Further, integrating Saudi Arabia into the BRI is a significant geopolitical and useful geographic space for the Chinese presence in the Persian Gulf. This is not only because it increases Riyadh's capabilities to respond to Chinese energy needs, but also because it promotes the opening of the MSRI to the Red Sea. The Saudi ports (e.g., Yanbu and Djeddah) improve the access of the Chinese civil fleet to the Red Sea, then to the Suez Canal, and thus to the Mediterranean markets of the Middle East, the Near East, the Maghreb, and Southern Europe.[22]

Additionally, the development of transportation networks is vital for the implementation of the BRI, and Saudi Arabia's transportation infrastructure supports sectors like petroleum, petrochemicals, mining, industry, and commerce. The Kingdom is now building various performance-enhancing systems like electronic systems, active customs procedures, and advanced information systems.[23] Finally, Saudi's Vision 2030 could fuse perfectly and contribute to the construction of the BRI. For example, in March 2017, Beijing–Riyadh signed a series of deals worth about $65 billion involving 35 cooperative projects, with a clear majority of these being directly linked with the Saudi Vision 2030.[24]

The Kingdom's participation in China–Pakistan Economic Corridor (CPEC) projects is timely as Beijing and Riyadh are moving closer and aligning their goals under BRI and Saudi Vision 2030. The CPEC, the flagship project of China's BRI, is a series of bilateral infrastructure projects designed to connect China's far west region of Xinjiang with Gwadar Port in Pakistan via a network of major highways and railways, higher-capacity ports, power stations, oil pipelines, and trading hubs. Located in the southwestern province of Balochistan, Gwadar is the crown jewel of China's $60 billion investment in its BRI projects in Pakistan.[25]

The Kingdom's support of BRI is significant, and the most practical example of the Saudi investment in Pakistan under CPEC is when Saudi Arabia's crown prince MBS signed eight MoUs worth about $20 billion. These included $10 billion in investments for a refinery and petrochemical complex at Gwadar in Pakistan, which lies at the heart of the China–Pakistan Economic Corridor, and the center of the Beijing–Islamabad BRI relationship.[26] Saudi Arabia's agreement to participate in CPEC projects is also a key example of its warming relations with China and hugely beneficial for the success of BRI.

As Chinese Foreign Ministry spokesman Lu Kang told a media briefing, "the CPEC is an important project under the Belt and Road Initiative. The BRI projects followed wide consultations and shared benefits. So such cooperation has always been open and transparent. If any other party would like to contribute positive factors to promote the inter-connectivity and prosperity of the region on the basis of consultation, I think this is a positive factor."[27]

It is important to understand that the Kingdom's participation in CPEC projects would provide China an open window of opportunity to gain access easily to Africa and Eurasia through Oman and Riyadh. China also desires to link with Central Asia via Afghanistan through CPEC. Furthermore, China's active presence in Gwadar and the Persian Gulf would make China a "two-ocean power" at the same time.[28]

Another major project of the Saudi Vision 2030 is the creation of the NEOM ["new future"] megacity in the north-west of the country that could integrate with China's BRI. The project will be built on 26,500 square kilometers of uninhabited land along the Red Sea coastline near Egypt and Jordan. Riyadh hopes it will pull in more than $500 billion of investment and contribute $100 billion to the Saudi Arabian economy by 2030. This large project (the largest of the 2030 Vision) is the most obvious example of the radical transformation that the Kingdom aims to achieve by transforming itself from an oil economy into a diversified industrial and touristic economy. Riyadh also plans to turn NEOM into a new economic zone that operates under separate traditional commercial rules from the rest of the Kingdom.[29]

Once completed in 2025, NEOM is expected to become the largest city entirely managed by artificial intelligence (AI). All transport will be autonomous, and power will come from renewable energies. Accordingly, Chinese companies will surely seek a role in building some of the infrastructures in the megacity, using AI cutting-edge technology focused on sustainable development. In his last visit to China, February 2019, Crown Prince MBS sought to attract Chinese investors for the innovative city project and to convince Chinese hi-tech leaders to develop projects in NEOM. The participation of Chinese companies is crucial for the development of NEOM. The new city of NEOM could serve as a laboratory for the latest innovations for Chinese high-tech companies and could be an integral part of the BRI.[30]

Energy cooperation

As part of the PRC's comprehensive strategic partnerships with Riyadh, investment in energy infrastructure is considered one of the important areas for cooperation to integrate Saudi Vision 2030 into the BRI framework. Therefore, the new Silk Road can provide a new framework for more extensive Chinese investments in the Kingdom energy industry. Although the Beijing–Riyadh partnership is growing significantly, especially under the BRI–Saudi Vision 2030 program, the relationship remains energy-economic partnership, based on energy products, and benefits both sides.

Beijing's dependence on crude oil imports from the Persian Gulf, a leading oil-producing region, has been increasing gradually since 1993 when it became a net importer of oil.[31] In 2019, the value of crude oil imported into China totaled $238.7 billion, expanding by 77.7 percent since 2015 but declining by –0.2 percent from 2018 to 2019. Forty-three countries supplied crude petroleum oil to China, but close to half (44.8 percent) of Chinese imported crude oil originates from just nine Middle Eastern nations, and six Persian Gulf states are among the top 15 crude oil suppliers to Beijing. In 2019, Saudi Arabia was ranked in the first place, exporting some $40.1 billion (16.8 percent) worth of oil to China.[32]

The Sino–Saudi energy partnership was solidified in 2009 when Beijing surpassed the U.S. as the top destination of Riyadh oil exports. Although Russia overtook Saudi Arabia as China's number-one supplier of oil in 2016, Beijing's reliance on Saudi oil will remain central to its energy security calculus.[33] According to the OPEC, Saudi Arabia possesses around 18 percent of the world's proven petroleum reserves and ranks as the second-largest crude oil producer and the largest exporter of petroleum. The oil and gas sector accounts for about 50 percent of Gross domestic product (GDP), and about 70 percent of export earnings.[34]

According to the Saudi Energy Ministry, at the end of 2017 Saudi Arabia's total oil reserves, including those in a zone shared with Kuwait, are up 0.8 percent to 268.5 billion barrels. The total gas reserves, including those in the shared zone, were revised up 5.6 percent to 325.1 trillion standard cubic feet. For almost 30 years, despite rising production, large swings in oil prices, and improved technology, the Kingdom had annually reported the same number for reserves, at around 261 billion barrels. The results indicate that Riyadh's reserves of oil and gas are bigger than reported.[35]

The growing ties between the two countries are fueled by the PRC's quest for the energy resources needed to feed its fast-growing economy and Riyadh's demand for cutting-edge technology, as the Saudi Arabia government tries to shift the Kingdom's economy away from relying too much on oil revenue. As Chinese Foreign Minister Wang Yi told his Saudi counterpart, China sees "enormous potential" in the Kingdom's economy and wants more high-tech cooperation.[36]

In the framework of the BRI, investment in energy infrastructure is considered one of the important cooperation areas between the countries involved. Therefore, this initiative can provide a new framework for more extensive Chinese investments in the Saudi Arabia energy industry. The Kingdom is the world's largest oil exporter, and China is the world's largest oil importer. Hence it is not surprising that the two countries are interested in deepening their cooperation with each other under the Belt and Road strategic outline and the Saudi Vision 2030 program. Saudi Arabia is now seeking to sustain its dominance in the Chinese energy market in the face of intensifying competition, mainly on the part of Iran and Russia. To this end, and to help stabilize the supply, Riyadh is operating in China through investments and the establishment of oil refineries and strategic stockpiling facilities for Saudi oil in China.

Development of refineries and petrochemical complexes

In January 2016, during President Xi Jinping's three-nation tour of the Middle East, China Petroleum and Chemical Corp (Sinopec), Asia's largest refiner, signed a strategic agreement with Saudi Aramco, to further explore business opportunities in Saudi's oil and gas industry. The deal came after construction began on the second phase of a major Red Sea oil refinery, a joint venture between Sinopec and Saudi Aramco, with the first phase becoming fully operational in April 2016. The venture, Yanbu Aramco Sinopec Refining Co (YASREF), estimated to cost nearly $10 billion, covers an area of about 5.2 million square meters. It will process 400,000 barrels of heavy crude oil per day. Aramco will hold a 62.5 percent stake in the plant, while Sinopec holds the rest.[37]

The YASREF refinery, established jointly by Sinopec and Saudi Aramco, is touted as the safest, most advanced, and efficient refinery. The project is highlighted as a good example of the energy partnership between China and Saudi Arabia and future bilateral cooperation within the BRI, due to its smooth operation, advanced technologies, and high efficiency. The joint venture has earned profits since it entered production in 2016. It has produced crude oil of 49.97 million tons, and fine gasoline and diesel oil of 39.98 million tons, which were sold to Europe and Asia.[38]

In February 2018, Saudi Aramco agreed to supply China's Huajin, a refinery and chemical complex controlled by Chinese defense conglomerate China North Industries Group Corp (NORINCO), 12 million barrels of crude oil under an annual deal for 2018. Although it is a fraction of Aramco's total supplies to China, the annual deal will help the Saudis boost its market share in the world's largest crude buyer in its race against Russia.[39]

In September 2018, Saudi Basic Industries Corp (SABIC) signed an MoU with China's Fujian provincial government to build a petrochemical complex, but SABIC did not give any details of the investment or a timeline. The Saudi company is already a partner with Chinese state oil and gas firm Sinopec Corp in an ethylene plant owned by Sinopec's Tianjin Petrochemical Corp. According to SABIC, the MoU is part of SABIC's strategy to diversify its operations, seek new investment opportunities, and strengthen its position in the Chinese market.[40]

In February 2019, during the visit of the Crown Prince MBS to Beijing, Saudi Aramco signed an agreement worth more than $10 billion for a refining and petrochemical complex in China. Saudi Aramco formed a joint venture with NORINCO Group and PanjinSincenon to develop a fully integrated refining and petrochemical complex in the city of Panjin in Northeast China's Liaoning province. The partners will create a new company, Huajin Aramco Petrochemical Co Ltd.; the Saudi producer will have a 35 percent interest, while China will hold the rest. The project will include a 300,000 barrel per day refinery with a 1.5 million metric tons per annum ethylene cracker and a 1.3 metric tons per annum PX unit. Saudi Aramco will supply up to 70 percent of the crude feedstock for the complex, which is expected to start operations in 2024. The investments could also help Saudi Arabia regain its place as the top oil exporter to China, a position Russia has held for the last three years.[41]

There are additional plans to set up fuel retail businesses, which will further integrate into the value chain. By the end of 2019, a three-party company is expected to be formed between Aramco, North Huajin, and the Liaoning Transportation Construction Investment Group Co. Ltd. to build a large-scale retail network over the next five years in Zhejiang province. Saudi Aramco also signed three MoUs aimed at expanding its downstream presence in Zhejiang province, one of the most developed regions in China. Aramco aims to acquire a 9 percent stake in Zhejiang Petrochemical's 800,000-bpd integrated refinery and petrochemical complex, located in the city of Zhoushan. Aramco's involvement in the project will come with a long-term crude supply agreement, and the ability to utilize Zhejiang Petrochemical's large crude oil storage facility to serve its customers in the Asian region.[42]

The demand stirred up by new Chinese refiners has been pushing Saudi Arabia back to be a top supplier to the world's largest oil buyer. This could increase China's oil imports from the Kingdom between 300,000 barrels per day (bpd) and 700,000 bpd. Saudi Aramco will sign five crude oil supply agreements that will take its 2019 contract totals with Chinese buyers to 1.67 million bpd. With the recent crude oil supply agreements and potential increase of refinery capacity, Saudi's market share in China could jump to nearly 17 percent next year if buyers requested full contractual volumes.[43]

Oil agreements and MoUs

In November 2016, Pan-Asia PET Resin (Guangzhou) Co – one of the biggest poly-ethylene terephthalate (PET) chip producers – signed an MoU with the National Industrial Clusters Development Program of Saudi Arabia to push forward preparation of the petrochemical and chemical fiber integrated production project. The project was initiated in response to China's BRI and is in line with Saudi Vision 2030.[44] In October 2018, Pan-Asia signed Investment Framework Agreement with Saudi Arabia's Energy Minister Khalid al-Falih, marking two key breakthroughs for its $3.2 billion petrochemical and chemical fiber integrated project in Saudi Arabia.[45]

In March 2017, during the visit of King Salman to China, the partners agreed to increase their cooperation in the oil sector, including Saudi oil exports to Beijing.[46] Saudi Basic Industries Corporation (SABIC) and Sinopec signed a strategic agreement to study opportunities for joint projects in both countries. The agreement supports the efforts of the two countries to integrate the Saudi Vision 2030 and China's BRI. Under the agreement, Riyadh and Chinese petrochemical companies are planning, for the first time, to study a joint venture with Chinese investment in the Kingdom. The agreement also seeks to explore opportunities for further investments in the existing joint venture Sinopec SABIC Tianjin Petrochemical Company (SSTPC) that will contribute to industrial development in the two countries, allowing them to target downstream key markets, such as automotive, electronics, lighting, and building and construction, packaging, and medical equipment.[47]

In June 2017, China's Development Research Center signed an MoU with Saudi Aramco to jointly collaborate on economic development, especially in the downstream energy sector. The focus of the collaboration will be on Saudi Aramco's downstream presence in China, including within oil refining, oil product marketing and retail, and oil storage. The research will also explore opportunities for Chinese companies to partner with Saudi Aramco or other Saudi Arabian entities on investment and partnerships.[48]

In addition, Saudi Arabia's state oil company, Saudi Aramco, is reckoned to be the world's most valuable company with an estimated value of $2 trillion.[49] Aramco plans to boost its refining capacity to between 8 million and 10 million barrels per day, from the current level of about 5 million bpd, and double its petrochemicals production by 2030. Alongside plans to add more value from each barrel of oil produced, the kingdom is undertaking an economic overhaul that includes the initial public offering (to take place by 2021) of Saudi Aramco on the local and a yet open international stock exchange.[50] In October 2017, Chinese state-owned oil companies PetroChina and Sinopec expressed interest in the direct purchase of 5 percent of Saudi Aramco. Chinese investment in Saudi Aramco could be entering a new era of energy strategic partnership with Riyadh and laying the groundwork for a profound economic shift in the Middle East and the world.[51]

In November 2019, Aramco officially kicked off its IPO, which could be the world's largest initial public offering, announcing it would likely begin listing shares of the offering on Riyadh's local exchange in December. Saudi Arabia is reportedly targeting a valuation between $1.5 trillion to $2 trillion for Aramco.[52] According to *Bloomberg's* report, China's state-owned entities (Beijing-based Silk Road Fund, state-owned oil producer Sinopec Corp and sovereign wealth fund China Investment Corp) are in talks about investing $5 billion to $10 billion in Saudi oil giant Aramco's planned initial public offering. The lineup of investors and the size of the investments will ultimately depend on the Chinese government.[53]

In December 2018, state-owned Power Construction Corporation of China (PowerChina) signed a contract for the construction of marine facilities for the mega-shipyard King Salman International Complex in Saudi Arabia. The project is located in eastern Saudi Arabia facing the Arabian Gulf and is an essential part of Saudi Vision 2030. The successful signing of the project is also an achievement for PowerChina in carrying out China's BRI. The contract, with a value of over three billion dollars, is the largest cash settlement project PowerChina has ever undertaken. The project will become the world's largest 'super shipyard' and is expected to build four offshore drilling platforms and more than 40 ships every year, including three large crude carriers (VLCC). After completion, it will provide engineering, manufacturing, and repair services for offshore rigs, commercial ships, and service vessels.[54]

In January 2019, Pan-Asia PET Resin set out plans to build plants producing 2.5 million metric tons/year (MMt/y) of purified terephthalic acid, 1 MMt/y of PET resin, and 200,000 metric tons/year each of polyester engineering plastics, thin-film, and polyester fiber. According to the Chinese company, the project is the first wholly foreign-owned petrochemical project in Saudi Arabia. The project is situated in the Jazan City for Primary and Downstream Industries (JCPDI), located at the junction of Europe, Asia, and Africa; the area enjoys transportation advantages from the Red Sea to the Suez Canal, allowing Pan-Asia to better serve the European, North African, and Central Asian markets.[55]

The project is considered a major foreign-funded project in the Kingdom as well as a key project to promote China–Saudi Arabia production capacity cooperation. The project, designed to cover the upstream and downstream of the PET industrial chain, will also help Riyadh reduce its reliance on imported products and optimize its economic structure. The construction of the first phase of the project was expected to start in the first quarter of 2019 and to come on stream in the third quarter of 2020.[56]

Renewable energy cooperation

According to a report by the International Renewable Energy Agency's Global Commission on the Geopolitics of Energy Transformation, Beijing's need to secure oil supplies and other natural resources to sustain its growth has led it to foster new and deeper ties with countries in Asia, Africa, and Latin America, as well as diversify its domestic energy supply with renewables. China has positioned itself as the world's renewable energy superpower. In aggregate, it is now the world's largest producer, exporter, and installer of solar panels, wind turbines, batteries, and electric vehicles, placing it at the forefront of the global energy transition. Thus, Saudi Arabia's growing reliance on Chinese-built renewable generation points to a wider shift in energy geopolitics.[57]

As part of Riyadh's ambitious Vision 2030, the Kingdom is seeking to position itself as a global trade hub. Saudi Arabia has established a special economic zone (SEZ) near Riyadh's flagship Airport (RUH). With the lure of tax incentives, the Integrated Logistics Bonded Zone (ILBZ) could serve as a hub for assembling solar (photovoltaic) components. Chinese solar firms have already sought to deepen their cooperation with their Saudi counterparts.[58] In May 2018, the Chinese solar panel manufacturer LONGI signed an MoU with the Kingdom's major commercial and industrial trading company, El Seif Group, to establish large-scale solar manufacturing infrastructure in Saudi Arabia. The partnership could also lead to further manufacturing opportunities in the Middle East region. Initially, the companies are understood to be undertaking various feasibility studies for collaboration in both the photovoltaic (PV) upstream and downstream sectors.[59]

Saudi Arabia is courting China for help with the next stage of the production of renewable energy, which is forecast to develop 41 gigawatts of solar capacity by 2032.[60] In February 2019, Saudi Arabia's Public Investment Fund (PIF) signed an MoU with China's National Energy Administration (NAE) on renewable energy cooperation. The MoU comes as part of the strengthening of cooperation between the two entities in the field of renewable energy and promoting Saudi Arabia's position as a leading center for the development of renewable energy projects. The MoU will contribute to enabling the PIF to support and develop manufacturing, power generation, and emerging technologies in the Kingdom's renewable energy sector over the next ten years.[61]

In January 2019, two Chinese solar giants unveiled Saudi manufacturing plans. The world's fourth-largest PV maker, Longi, is planning a $2 billion Saudi Arabia-based solar panel back sheet production plant in association with the South Korean firm OCI. Meanwhile, the world's largest thin-film PV manufacturer, Hong Kong-listed Hanergy, announced it would be investing more than $1 billion in a fabrication center to meet Saudi solar demand. The investment, which includes an unlikely partnership with local menswear manufacturer Ajlan & Bros, would see Saudi Arabia hosting the only large-scale thin-film manufacturing base in the Middle East. The announcements mean Beijing's interests are well-positioned to benefit from renewables growth in Saudi Arabia.[62]

In December 2018, Riyadh announced a 1.5-gigawatt solar procurement round that is expected to be dominated by Chinese companies alongside Middle Eastern renewable heavyweights, such as Acwa Power and Masdar. Beyond the current tender, with capacity split across seven projects, Saudi Arabia is aiming to install more than 27 gigawatts of renewables by 2024. Most of this capacity will be solar PV, a power source where Beijing reigns supreme. Seven of the top 10 PV module makers worldwide in 2018 were Chinese companies, including four of the top five and all of the top three. Admittedly, it will be some time before the value of Chinese renewable energy equipment sales in Saudi Arabia comes even close to the price the Asian giant pays for oil from Riyadh.[63]

In December 2019, State Grid Corporation of China (SGCC) won a $1.1 billion contract to install smart meters in Saudi Arabia. China Electric Power Equipment and Technology Company, a wholly-owned subsidiary of the state-owned enterprise, officially signed the contract with Saudi Electricity Company. The project involves the installation and commissioning of 10 million smart meters for consumers across the kingdom and the Chinese company said it was another important breakthrough for China's BRI in the region. The Chinese company will install five million smart meters in the western and southern areas of the kingdom, and a consortium formed by Mobily and Al Fanar Construction consortium will carry out the rest of the project. The project is expected to be completed by 2023. This is the first time that China's smart grid business had entered the global market, providing an opportunity to export the country's advanced electricity distribution and management systems.[64]

Nuclear energy

Although the Kingdom's nuclear program is in its infancy, Saudi Arabia declared in 2011 that it planned to spend over $80 billion to construct 16 reactors, and Chinese companies and others want to provide them. Nuclear power is essential to Saudi Arabia to help it meet its growing energy demand for both electricity generation and water desalination while reducing its reliance on depleting hydrocarbon resources. Nuclear energy would allow the Kingdom to increase its fossil fuel exports. About one-third of the kingdom's daily oil production is consumed domestically at subsidized prices; substituting nuclear energy domestically would free up this petroleum for export at market prices.[65]

Moreover, Saudi Arabia is also the largest producer of desalinated water in the world. According to government-owned Saudi Saline Water Conversion Corp (SWCC), the Kingdom raised its desalinated water production to five million cubic meters per day (m3/d) at the end of 2017. Ninety percent of its drinking water is desalinated, a process that burns approximately 15 percent of the 9.8 million barrels of oil it produces daily. Nuclear power could meet some of this demand.[66]

In January 2016, during the visit of Chinese President Xi Jinping to Saudi Arabia, the two countries signed an MoU on the construction of a high-temperature gas-cooled reactor (HTR). No details of the size of the high-temperature gas-cooled reactor or the project timeline building were disclosed. China Nuclear Engineering Corporation (CNEC) has been working with Tsinghua University since 2003 on the design, construction, and commercialization of HTR technology. The partners signed a new agreement in March 2014 aimed at furthering cooperation in both international and domestic marketing of the advanced reactor technology.[67]

In August 2017, Saudi Arabia and the PRC agreed to cooperate on nuclear energy projects to support the kingdom's nuclear energy program. CNNC signed an MoU with the Saudi Geological Survey (SGS) to promote further existing cooperation between the two sides to explore and assess uranium and thorium resources. The Saudi Technology Development and Investment Co (Taqnia) signed an MoU with CNEC to develop water desalination projects using gas-cooled nuclear reactors. Chinese nuclear companies could offer complete construction and operation packages with attractive financing options. Civil nuclear cooperation is officially a part of China's BRI, and combating climate change is central to China's pitch.[68]

China–Saudi Arabia's comprehensive strategic partnership is essential to help meet growing energy demand, especially under the Belt and Road strategic outline and the Saudi Vision 2030 program. The energy partnership between the two countries includes expanding cooperation in the fields of development of refineries/petrochemical complexes, renewable energies, and nuclear energy.

Trade and investments

Part of China's comprehensive strategic partnerships with Saudi Arabia includes efforts to ease as much as possible the barriers to free trade, investment, industrial cooperation, and technical and engineering services to facilitate the integration of Saudi Vision 2030 within the BRI framework. Both countries would have to undertake a series of measures, such as expanding free-trade zones, improving trade structures, seeking new potential areas for trade, and improving the trade balance, devising new initiatives for the promotion of conventional forms of trade.[69]

Over the past decade, Beijing–Riyadh economic relations have been transformed dramatically. Both countries have achieved fruitful results in trade and investments as they seek greater complementarity between the BRI and the Saudi Vision 2030. According to China Customs Statistics (export-import), the PRC's trade volume with Saudi Arabia grew sharply from $63.2 billion in 2018 to about $77.9 billion in 2019, and Riyadh has become China's most important trade partner in the Middle East.[70] The PRC is Saudi Arabia's largest trade partner, outstripping nearby European nations and a close ally to the U.S.

According to the *China Global Investment Tracker*, Beijing's investments and construction in Saudi Arabia from 2013 to 2019 reached $20.6 billion.[71] In 2018, according to Sultan Mofti, deputy governor for investment attraction and development at the Saudi Arabian General Investment Authority, 19 Chinese manufacturing companies obtained licenses in Saudi Arabia, 86 licenses in construction, six in information technologies, and eight in services.[72] In 2017, Beijing invested $88.79 million in Saudi Arabia, and the Kingdom invested $150 million in China.[73]

Furthermore, many Chinese companies are operating in the Kingdom market in the fields of infrastructure, construction, and communications, and employ tens of thousands of Chinese workers. By March 2017, around 160 Chinese organizations were operating in several sectors of the Saudi economy, and around 175 Chinese projects developed, notably in the telecommunication and construction sectors.[74] The two countries have collaborated on numerous projects in the health, transportation, and construction sectors. Saudi Arabia has become an increasingly important market for Chinese consumer goods, including electronics, textiles, and food, which accounted for most Saudi imports.[75]

Meanwhile, Beijing and Riyadh have identified the first batch of key projects on industrial capacity and investment cooperation worth $55 billion. The development of industrial clusters in Jizan is well underway, and groundbreaking was held recently on the $3.2 billion Guangzhou Pan-Asia PET petrochemical project, which was the first investment project in the clusters. Major energy and infrastructure projects, such as the Yanbu Refinery in Saudi Arabia, the Panjin Refinery in China's Liaoning Province, the Rabigh Power Station, and the Landbridge Railway, are being advanced steadily or are under close discussion. Cooperation on new and high technology has delivered successful outcomes. A Chinese satellite installed with an optical camera of

Saudi Arabia was launched last year, accomplishing the first lunar probe by an Arab country. Two Saudi Arabia-made satellites were successfully brought into orbit by China's Long March launch vehicle.[76]

The frequent high-level exchanges push forward and expand the two-way trade and investment between the two countries. In January 2016 Chinese President Xi Jinping visited Saudi Arabia, (about which few details were disclosed), and the two countries decided to establish a comprehensive strategic partnership.[77] In September 2016, Saudi Deputy Crown Prince MBS visited the G20 Summit held in Hangzhou, where the two countries signed 15 agreements and MoUs. The agreements range from energy development and oil storage to cooperation promises on housing development and water resource issues. In addition, Huawei, a leading global ICT solutions provider, received an investment license from Saudi Arabia.[78]

In March 2017, during Saudi King Salman's visit to Beijing, China and Saudi Arabia signed trade and investment packages worth $65 billion that included a wide range of areas on investment, space research, and more than 20 agreements on oil investment and energy. Among the agreements was an MoU between Saudi Aramco and China North Industries Group Corporation to build two refineries, one in the Chinese Fujian province, and one in Yanbu in Saudi Arabia.[79]

In August 2017, during Chinese Vice Premier Zhang Gaoli's visit to Saudi Arabia, both countries signed 60 various agreements and MoUs worth nearly $70 billion. The agreements and MoUs covered investment, trade, energy, postal service, communications, and media.[80] China and Saudi Arabia also announced the intention to establish and operate a $20 billion investment fund jointly.[81] In February 2019, China and Saudi Arabia signed 35 MoU economic cooperation agreements worth a total of $28 billion at a joint investment forum during a visit by Saudi Crown Prince MBS to Beijing. The agreements cover some key sectors, including energy and water, industry and manufacturing, petrochemicals, mining and minerals, housing, transport, logistics, and e-commerce.[82]

The agreements include an MoU between Saudi Arabia's Ministry of Energy, Industry & Mineral Resources, and Pan-Asia Resin in the petrochemicals sector with a total planned investment of $1.5 billion. An MoU between the Saudi Authority for Industrial Cities & Technology Zones (Modon) and Teda Investment Holding Company is for a total investment of $1 billion. An MoU between Jabal Omar Development Company and China State Construction Engineering Corporation in the infrastructure sector detailed a total planned investment of $533 million. An MoU between Sagia and Goldwind International Holdings for cooperation in establishing a wind-turbine manufacturing hub in the Kingdom set out a total investment of $18 million.[83]

In the end, the two sides reaffirmed their commitment to strengthen and expand two-way trade and investment in various fields under the BRI framework, and to align the Belt and Road initiative with Saudi's Vision 2030. As Saudi Arabia's Minister of Energy, Industry, and Mineral Resources, Khalid bin Abdulaziz Al-Falih, said in an interview with *Xinhua*, Saudi investment in China was "just starting".[84]

Military ties

As part of China's comprehensive strategic partnerships with Riyadh, defense cooperation has become an increasingly significant part of integrating Saudi Vision 2030 into the BRI framework. Traditionally, the U.S. was a major defense partner with the Kingdom, but Saudi Arabia wants diversification in meeting its defense needs. The Beijing–Riyadh security relations have focused primarily on weapons sales from China to Saudi Arabia, particularly systems that other suppliers (e.g., the U.S. and the West) refused to sell to the Kingdom, among other things, due to the restrictions of non-proliferation regimes and pressure from Israel.

Nevertheless, overall, Chinese security exports to Riyadh constitute merely a niche, since over the years the Kingdom acquired most weapons from the West (mainly from the U.S. and the UK), while imports from Beijing were only marginal in volume, though qualitative strategically. Riyadh's dependence on U.S. military equipment restricts its ability to purchase large quantities of Chinese arms.[85]

Nonetheless, the PRC is neither capable nor interested in supplanting Washington as the strategic security guarantor of Riyadh's safety and Persian Gulf regional stability, and shouldering the burden this entails. The scope of the U.S. military presence and its ability to project power, coupled with the quality of its weapons systems, the depth of its military and political relations, and its interoperability with allied militaries, are beyond the PRC's competitive capabilities, at least in the near and medium future.[86]

Historically, the security dimension in Beijing–Riyadh relations has been limited. The extent of the security relations is generally attributed to Riyadh's acquisition of 36 China's DF-3 (CSS-2 by NATO) nuclear-capable intermediate-range ballistic missiles (IRBMs) and nine launchers in the late 1980s,[87] and subsequently DF-5 (CSS-5) intercontinental ballistic missiles from Beijing. Riyadh is also reported to have procured the more advanced DF-21 missile system in 2007, allegedly with Washington's approval. Nevertheless, Saudi Arabia has demonstrated at least a passing interest in purchasing additional Chinese defense systems, including the jointly produced Chinese–Pakistani JF-17 fighter, but no such contract has been signed.[88]

Though Saudi Arabia is one of the biggest buyers of U.S. weapons, the country cannot buy ballistic missiles from the U.S. because of the 1987 Missile Technology Control Regime, an informal multi-country pact that seeks to limit the sale of rockets carrying weapons of mass destruction. According to U.S. intelligence, Saudi Arabia escalated its ballistic missile program with the help of China. This could be another step in the Saudi push forward in its attempt to obtain nuclear weapons and will impair the decade-long effort to limit the amassing of missiles in the Middle East.[89]

In the past several years the potential for Sino–Saudi military cooperation has increased, especially as Washington's appetite to play a role in the Middle East is diminishing while that of China is growing. The Kingdom has increased its interest in purchasing Chinese military technology, as Beijing is willing to sell arms to Riyadh without the geopolitical strings that frequently accompany U.S. arms sales. In particular, Saudi Arabia views China as a potentially important supplier of highly sophisticated missile and offensive weapons technologies. Both countries may enhance cooperation in the defense sector to satisfy each other's interests.[90]

In 2014, after Saudi Arabia became frustrated at restrictions on the export to the Kingdom of Western-origin UCAVs such as the GA-ASI Predator and Reaper, Saudi Crown Prince MBS met Chinese General Wang Guanzhong in China to reach a deal to supply Wing Loong IIs. The Wing Loong (Pterodactyl) series is produced by the Chengdu Aircraft Industry Group (CAIG) that had previously exported the Wing

Loong, a medium-altitude, long-endurance UAV, which can also be fitted with missiles to Saudi Arabia. According to the Chinese state news agency Xinhua, Saudi Arabia will acquire 300 Chinese Wing Loong IIs worth approximately $10 billion. Riyadh is the first Arab country to obtain this type of drone. However, the drone has not performed well in the Arabian Desert.[91]

In March 2017, during Saudi King Salman's visit to China, the two countries signed deals worth as much as $65 billion and a partnership agreement to construct a new facility to produce uncrewed aerial vehicles, in an agreement signed by China Aerospace Long-March International (ALIT) and manufacturers in Saudi Arabia. The new facility can operate as a hub for manufacturing and services for other CH-4 operators in the Middle East, including Egypt, Iraq, and Jordan. According to IHS Janes Defence Industry news, the King Abdulaziz City for Science and Technology signed a partnership with the state-owned China Aerospace Science and Technology Corporation (CASC) to establish a manufacturing plant in Saudi Arabia for the CH series of UCAVs. Riyadh already operates the turboprop-powered CH-4 UCAV series, but it was not made clear whether this new agreement covers only that type, or also the jet-powered CH-5.[92]

Another area of military cooperation between the two countries is in the field of observation satellites. In December 2018, two Saudi Arabian Earth observation satellites and ten small secondary payloads rode a Long March 2D rocket from the Jiuquan space base in China's northwestern Inner Mongolia region. The main payloads aboard the Long March 2D rocket were the SaudiSat 5A and 5B, two Earth-imaging satellites each weighing nearly a half-ton. The SaudiSat 5A and 5B satellites were built by the King Abdulaziz City for Science and Technology in Riyadh. The new spacecraft is the largest satellite manufactured in Saudi Arabia, capable of providing the country's government with high-resolution imagery of sites across the globe.[93]

In January 2016, President Xi Jinping's visit to Saudi Arabia yielded a commitment from both sides to increase bilateral security cooperation, especially in the counter-terrorism arena.[94] In November 2016 in Riyadh, Saudi King Salman met with Meng Jianzhu, a special envoy of Chinese President Xi Jinping to discuss a range of security issues.[95] Both sides announced a commitment to forging a five-year plan to increase bilateral security cooperation. This plan would include joint counter-terrorism exercises, and Chinese navy vessels have visited the Saudi port of Jeddah, cementing Saudi Arabia's status as a vital Chinese ally in the Middle East.

In October 2016, China and Saudi Arabia staged their first joint anti-terrorism exercise 'Exploration 2016' held over fifteen days in China's southwestern city of Chongqing. The exercise featured Special Forces units attached to the Royal Saudi Land Forces and their People's Liberation Army (PLA) counterparts. The exercises were designed to improve the respective capacities of both countries to conduct counterterrorism, hostage rescue, and other complex operations.[96]

In the end, the deepening security relations, the joint anti-terrorism exercises, and the acquisition of sensitive military technology are the expression of the Beijing–Riyadh comprehensive strategic partnership which has developed in recent years, reflecting Riyadh's desire to reduce its security dependence on Washington and to erode Iran's international and regional influence. More important, Washington's scathing criticisms of Saudi Arabia's sponsorship of terrorism and open calls for a re-evaluation of U.S. military assistance to Saudi Arabia could cause the latter to form a full-fledged defense partnership with Beijing in the years to come. However, in light of historical experience, Riyadh hopes mostly that expanded security links with China will give it fast access to sophisticated missile systems and convince Washington to outbid Beijing by exporting some of its most prized military assets to Saudi Arabia.

People-to-People Bond

Part of the PRC's comprehensive strategic partnerships with the Kingdom includes enabling the people of the two countries to bond along the Silk Road, vital to integrating the Saudi Vision 2030 within the BRI framework. The promotion of extensive cultural and academic exchanges aim to win public support for deepening bilateral and multilateral cooperation, as well as providing scholarships, holding annual cultural events, increasing cooperation in science and technology, and establishing joint laboratory or research centers and international technology transfer centers.[97]

Linguistic, cultural, and tourism cooperation is another important aspect of the Sino–Saudi comprehensive strategic partnership, and both nations have outlined their intention to expand the collaboration in these areas in the coming years. There have been dynamic cultural exchanges between the two countries. The exhibition of 'Roads to Arabia: Archaeological Treasures of Saudi Arabia', the "Exhibition of Chinese Cultural Relics" in the Kingdom, the joint archaeological excavation which unearthed relics indicating the maritime Silk Road at the port of Al-Serrian, and the performance by the Chinese symphony orchestra and musicians at the World Heritage Site of Al-Ula, are all vivid examples of exchanges and mutual learning between different civilizations.[98]

In September 2018 the exhibition 'Treasures of China' was held in the Kingdom. This exhibition marks the first major China cultural relic exhibition hosted by the National Museum in Riyadh. The display includes 264 items provided by 13 museums and cultural institutions, such as the Palace Museum, among which are 173 Chinese cultural relics. It will also showcase objects from China–Saudi Arabia joint archaeological excavations. Close to half the items are on display overseas for the first time. The exhibition consists of five sections in chronological order: 'Beginning of Civilization, Establishments of Etiquette', 'Unification, Consolidation and Development', 'Prosperities and Diversified Communication', 'Start-up of Business and Marine Trade', as well as 'Palace and Royal Art'. These cultural exchanges are important in illustrating how both nations see the future of bilateral relations.[99]

In February 2019, the Crown Prince MBS signed an agreement during his visit to China to include the Chinese language in curricula across the Kingdom. The Saudi plan is to include the Chinese language as a curriculum at all stages of education in schools and universities across the Kingdom. This will enhance the cultural diversity of students in the Kingdom and contribute to the achievement of the future national goals in the field of education in line with the Saudi Vision 2030. Introducing the Chinese language into the Saudi curricula is an important step toward opening new academic horizons for students at the various educational levels in the Kingdom. Learning the Chinese language will also serve as a bridge between the peoples of the two countries that will contribute to promoting trade and cultural ties.[100]

The proposal to include the Chinese language as a curriculum aims to strengthen friendship and cooperation between the two countries and to deepen the comprehensive strategic partnership at all levels. Currently, there are hundreds of Saudi students in Chinese universities (about 700 students have finished their studies and returned to Saudi Arabia), and the Kingdom has opened a branch of the King Abdul Aziz Public Library in Beijing to encourage exchanges between scholars, researchers, and students in both countries.[101] The country's cultural mission has signed 18 education and science cooperative agreements with 18 Chinese universities.[102]

According to the *Hanban website*, the Chinese government established Confucius institutes for providing Chinese language and culture teaching resources worldwide, in 2019, 550 Confucius Institutes and 1,172 Confucius Classrooms and 5,665 teaching sites established in 162 countries and regions, receiving about eleven million students.[103] In 54 countries involved in the BRI, there are 153 Confucius Institutes and 149 primary and high-school Confucius Classrooms.[104] In the Middle East, there are eighteen Confucius institutes and three Confucius Classrooms and one of them in Saudi Arabia. The Confucius Institute at the University of Jeddah was founded in 2019.[105]

In an interview with Chinese state news agency *Xinhua*, Saudi Arabia's Minister of Energy, Industry and Mineral Resources, Khalid bin Abdulaziz Al-Falih, said "Our culture is very compatible with the Chinese culture. We have sent hundreds of our students to study in China, and when they came back speaking Chinese, it makes thousands of Saudi people understand how great China is and how wonderful the Chinese people are. We need more of that; there will be great prosperity for both countries."[106]

In recent years, China's links with the GCC countries have strengthened due to the introduction of additional and direct airline routes, the strong growth of the Chinese economy and Chinese tourists' increasing disposable income. According to data from Colliers International published ahead of Arabian Travel Market (ATM) 2019, the number of Chinese tourists traveling to the GCC is expected to increase 81 percent from 1.6 million in 2018 to 2.9 million in 2022. The GCC countries currently attract just one percent of China's total outbound market, but positive trends are expected over the coming years for as many as 400 million. The Colliers data shows that Saudi Arabia will experience the highest proportionate increase in arrivals from China, with a projected compound annual growth rate (CAGR) of 33 percent between 2018 and 2022. Both Saudi Arabia and China's cultural and educational exchanges have been cited as one of the key elements driving this influx.[107]

According to China's Ambassador to Saudi Arabia, Li Huaxin, Saudi Arabia is set to be a major world tourist destination given its cultural, heritage, humanitarian, and civilization potential. He also affirmed that if tourist visas are introduced for foreign delegations in the Kingdom, the number of Chinese tourists will increase considerably. The Chinese Ambassador also stressed that Sino–Saudi relations have developed, especially in the area of culture, tourism, and archaeological exploration.[108] According to *Gulf News*, since the Kingdom launched its new visa program, the Chinese tourists are in the top number of visitors to the country.[109]

In summary, according to the World Travel & Tourism Council's (WTTC) annual review, the travel and tourism sector contributed 9 percent ($65.2 billion) of the economy of the Kingdom in 2018.[110] Since the Saudi Vision 2030 aims to increase the revenue generated from tourism to 18 percent in the next 14 years, the development of Saudi Arabia's tourism sector is a vital part of its economic transformation.[111] Thus, the growing number of Chinese tourists traveling to the Kingdom can contribute to achieving this goal. According to data from the China Tourism Academy (CTA), 140 million Chinese visited various tourist destinations, up 13.5 percent from the previous year's 129 million, and they spent more than $120 billion.[112]

Summary

In recent years, Saudi Arabia and China have expanded and transformed the nature of their relationship to a comprehensive strategic partnership. The significant warming in their relations comes at a time when both countries are under increasingly harsh global criticism and thus are eager to find political support as well as business opportunities. This creates a substantially increasing convergence of interests that are building a new horizon framework for cooperation, strengthening, and expanding the comprehensive strategic partnership between the countries.

Both countries have much to gain from the new horizon and the growing comprehensive strategic partnership. The PRC needs Saudi energy reserves and investments to secure oil supplies and other natural resources to sustain its growth, as well as to utilize the Kingdom's unique location at the nexus of three continents and its vital role in politics, economy, religion and security affairs in the Middle East and among Islamic countries. The Saudi Vision 2030 could fuse perfectly and contribute to the construction of the BRI. Saudi Arabia, on the other hand, can benefit from diversifying its relationships and expanding its diplomatic and economic ties with the world's fastest-growing major economy; Beijing can help it to diversify its economy, attract more foreign direct investments and increase its global market presence for alternate sources of revenue.

Nevertheless, there are several challenges to the growing comprehensive strategic partnership. First, Riyadh relies on Washington for security and geopolitical assistance, while China–U.S. relations have become increasingly tense. There is a growing concern in the U.S. about the implications of Chinese investments along the route of the New Silk Road that position Beijing in direct competition with Washington for economic influence in key countries around the world. In the short run at least, the Kingdom will continue to look to Washington for military and political support and the partnership with Beijing will remain primarily economic.

Second, China has a long-standing economic and defense partnership with Iran (the 'mortal enemy' of Saudi Arabia), particularly over the past decade and especially in the context of intensified Saudi-Iranian regional rivalry and the dispute over the Iranian nuclear program. In addition, there are disagreements over Bashar al-Assad's future in Syria and long-standing Chinese disdain for Saudi Arabia's sponsorship of Islamist networks as well as suspicions about China's intentions in Yemen's civil war given the diplomatic efforts to end the conflict. Third, the Kingdom's interests in Asia are not concentrated only on Beijing, but also Japan and India, which are viewed by Chinese as competitors in East Asia and Southeast Asia.

Moreover, the implementation of the BRI would be seriously affected by the instability generated by Riyadh and Tehran in hotspots such as Yemen, Iraq, Syria, and Qatar. Such regional instability presents a formidable obstacle to the BRI's strategic design, as it undermines connectivity, threatens infrastructure projects, and makes an economic corridor through the volatile Middle East to the markets of developed Europe less viable. Finally, Saudi Arabia has struggled to look beyond state-manipulated economies as part of large-scale reform efforts. Part of this trend has been an emphasis on privatizing historically state-owned enterprises while boosting foreign investment outside the oil and gas sectors. Initiatives exist to privatize state assets, but this process has proceeded slowly. In sum, all these factors could complicate the broader bilateral partnership.

9 | Iran

This chapter seeks to examine the new dynamic of the growing comprehensive strategic partnership between Iran and China to understand the impact and the extent of the re-imposition of U.S. secondary sanctions on Iran's engagement and integration in the implementation of the Belt and Road Initiative (BRI). Tehran has a special geographical and communication status in West Asia which makes it one of the important centerpieces of the new Silk Road trade route. However, Washington's decision to withdraw from the Irani nuclear agreement and to re-impose sanctions has created barriers in the new dynamic in Sino–Iranian trade and obstacles to integrating Iran into the realization of the BRI.

In recent years, the People's Republic of China (PRC) and the Islamic Republic of Iran established a comprehensive strategic partnership,[1] by complementing each other in various aspects such as trade, energy, and production capacity cooperation. The successful cooperation between the two nations arises from the historical ties tracing back to the ancient Silk Road as well as mutually complementary economic and political interests that facilitate these interactions. As Iranian Foreign Minister Mohammad Javad Zarif said, "Our relationship with China is very valuable to us. We consider the comprehensive strategic partnership between Iran and China as one of our most important relations."[2]

The $1 trillion BRI, put forward in October 2013 by Chinese President Xi Jinping, seeks to connect Beijing to the global market by linking Asia and Europe via a set of land and maritime trade routes. The concept took shape over several years and has now become a cornerstone of President Xi's foreign policy. The Islamic Republic was a significant gateway to the ancient Silk Roads, and thanks to its central position between the Arabian Peninsula, Central Asia, and South Asia, Iran continues to be an important crossroads in the new Silk Road.[3]

Given Iran's geographic and logistical location, engaging it within the BRI framework is essential to the realization of the new Silk Road trade route. Tehran's geopolitical position enables the PRC to exploit existing trade routes connecting Central Asian states with the Persian Gulf region and to create new transport corridors, with particular reference to the so-called Southern Corridor of the BRI, which is to cross Central Asia, Iran, Turkey, and the Balkans. Hence, the ultimate success of the Belt and Road Initiative depends to a large extent on Iranian participation and support, especially as far as geopolitical and logistical issues are concerned.[4] For this reason, the BRI framework provides Beijing and Tehran with an opportunity to strengthen and deepen their comprehensive strategic partnership.

In May 2018, President Trump announced that the United States was withdrawing from the Joint Comprehensive Plan of Action (JCPOA), setting in motion the re-imposition of secondary sanctions on Iran, which returned in full in November of that year.[5] Washington's decision to withdraw from the JCPOA and the re-imposition of sanctions created barriers in the new dynamic in Sino–Iranian trade and obstacles to integrate Iran as part of the realization of the BRI.

In this context, it is essential to understand the new dynamic and the growing comprehensive strategic partnership between the two countries and Washington's decision to withdraw from the nuclear agreement and to re-impose sanctions on the implementation of the new Silk Road. This chapter examines the new dynamic and the growing comprehensive strategic partnership between Iran and China to understand the impact and the extent of the re-imposition of U.S. secondary sanctions on Iran engagement and integration in the implementation of the BRI.

The main argument presented is that Beijing's comprehensive strategic partnership framework with Tehran is based on shared or mutually complementary economic and political interests, especially to integrate Iran within the BRI framework. Nonetheless, the re-imposition of U.S. secondary sanctions on Iran could hurt the new dynamic in Sino–Iranian comprehensive strategic partnership and have a long-term effect on China's ability to integrate Iran with the BRI and thereby significantly to impair the ability to realize the project. Officially, the PRC said it will maintain normal economic and trade exchanges with Tehran despite Trump's decision to withdraw from the nuclear agreement and re-impose sanctions on Iran. As Chinese President Xi Jinping declared, "No matter how the international and regional situation changes, China's resolve to develop a comprehensive strategic partnership with Iran will remain unchanged." However, according to data from the General Customs Administration of the People's Republic of China, the trade between the two countries has fallen dramatically in the two months following the re-imposition of U.S. secondary sanctions.[6]

Iran and the Belt and Road Initiative

The PRC comprehensive strategic partnership with the Islamic Republic includes seven areas for cooperation within the Belt and Road Initiative. These areas are policy coordination, connectivity, trade and investments, energy cooperation, financial integration, military ties, and people-to-people bond. However, each country views the BRI framework and reacts to it according to its own perspective and the consequences for its national interests and international status. Therefore, there are very different attitudes among the countries that are part of the BRI framework regarding how to realize the vision.[7]

Policy coordination

According to China's comprehensive strategic partnership with Iran, the highest level in Beijing's hierarchy of diplomatic relations, the aim to promote political cooperation between countries, to create mechanisms for dialogue and consensus-building on global and regional issues, to develop shared interests, deepen political trust, and reach a new consensus on cooperation are important to integrate Iran into the BRI framework.[8]

In January 2016, shortly after the JCPOA was implemented, President Xi Jinping made a successful visit to Iran during which the two heads of state agreed to establish a comprehensive strategic partnership. President Xi stressed the fact that both countries were natural partners as far as the implementation of the BRI was concerned. Furthermore, seventeen cooperation documents centered on the new Silk Road were signed in the areas of science, technology, communications, transportation, energy, and many other fields. The two sides also agreed to develop a roadmap for the strategic partnership during the next 25 years and to increase trade to $600 billion over the next ten years. Nevertheless, the programs discussed in these documents are yet to be fully operational.[9]

In February 2019, ahead of the visit to Beijing by Saudi Arabia's crown prince, Chinese President Xi Jinping welcomed a delegation that included Iran's Foreign Minister, Oil Minister, and Parliament Speaker and called for stronger cooperation to boost ties. President Xi spoke to the Iranian Parliament Speaker Ali Larijani of the enduring friendship between the two countries and said that the PRC's determination to develop its comprehensive strategic partnership with Iran will stay unchanged despite changes in the global and regional areas. The Chinese President called on both sides to deepen mutual trust and advance communication and coordination, increase cooperation on security and anti-terrorism, and improve cultural and people-to-people exchanges.[10]

Connectivity

According to the PRC's comprehensive strategic partnership with Iran, the facilitation of connectivity is one of the important ways to integrate Tehran into the BRI framework. It was recommended that the Islamic Republic optimize its infrastructural connections and also adapt its technical systems to those of the other countries in the BRI framework. This would lead Bejing and Tehran to jointly contribute to the development of international transport routes and the creation of an infrastructural network that could gradually connect all the regions in Asia and specific points in Asia, Africa, and Europe. Also, they agreed that there should be serious attempts to create low-carbon and green infrastructure.[11]

Iran has a special geographical and communication status in West Asia, in that it is connected to South and Central Asia, the Middle East and Europe through land and sea routes. In addition, access points at the Persian Gulf, the Gulf of Oman and the Caspian Sea combine to make Iran one of the important centerpieces of the Belt and Road. Therefore, the development of Iran's transport infrastructure is necessary for the realization of infrastructural connections in an important part of the BRI network to connect Asia, Europe, and Africa.[12]

According to the Iranian Minister of Transport Abbas Akhodi, his country is focusing on expanding its railway network so that it can better align with the PRC's Central Asian logistics strategy. The main goal for Iran's Department of Transportation would be to improve connections of the national rail network to neighboring railway networks. The Iranian development of international transport routes is seen as crucial to Chinese trade priorities, to expand commerce with Turkey, and widen access for its goods to Iranian ports near the Strait of Hormuz. Beijing hopes to see trains running between the western Chinese region of Kashgar and Istanbul as soon as 2020. Iranian railways figure to serve as key links in routes through both Central Asia and the Caucasus.[13]

In February 2016, the first noticeable event in the framework of the BRI took place when the first direct freight train from China arrived in Iran. The train, carrying 32 containers, arrived in Tehran after a 14-day, 10,399 kilometers (6,462 miles) journey from Yiwu city in east China. The cargo train's journey was 30 days shorter than the time usually taken by ships to sail from Shanghai to Iran's Bandar Abbas port. In September 2016, the second freight train service-connected Chinese city Yinchuan with Iran. According to Iran's Transport Minister, one freight train could now travel from China to Iran every month. These trains would eventually be bound for Europe, helping Tehran develop into a transit center between the two continents.[14]

Iran has a relatively good regular railway network, but the capability to link routes from Turkey through to Pakistan and India is of immense strategic importance to the framework of the BRI. The Iranian government plans are for three high-speed lines, from Tehran–Mashad near the border with Turkmenistan, Tehran–Tabriz, close to the borders with both Azerbaijan and Turkey and from Tehran to Isfahan.[15] China is the leading investor in Iranian transportation projects, especially railway development. The Tehran–Qom–Isfahan high-speed rail project and the electrification of Tehran–Mashhad Railway, at an estimated cost of about $4.2 billion, are the most important railway development projects in Iran, in both of which the PRC government and Chinese companies play important roles.[16]

The most important project agreed on by the two countries is the Tehran–Qom–Isfahan high-speed railway. State-owned China Railway Engineering Corp is building the Qom–Isfahan two-lane high-speed railway, with a length of 410 km, connecting Tehran to Qom and then to Isfahan in just 1.5 hours, with trains traveling at 300 km/h. Over the next two decades, approximately 12.5 million passengers will be carried by this railway each year. According to Iran's Minister of Roads and Urban Construction, Abbas Akhondi, the first phase of this project would be carried out at a cost of $22 billion. The Chinese contracting company would provide finance and carry out 40 percent of the construction.[17]

The second important project in the area of rail communications between the two countries is the electrification of the Tehran–Mashhad railway. According to the agreement, the task of reforming and constructing the current Tehran–Mashhad railway for trains to travel at speeds of 200 km/h, building an electric railway for trains to travel at speeds of 250 km/h and procuring 70 electric locomotives, was assigned to the consortium. The electrification of the Tehran–Mashhad line will reduce commute time between the two cities from 12 hours to about 6 hours, linking Tehran with Iran's second-largest city, Mashhad, in the east near its border with Turkmenistan and completing just under a third of the proposed BRI line required to link Tehran to western China.[18]

A consortium comprising Mapna Group Company, several Iranian companies, and the Chinese side is collaborating on this project. The total value of the contract stands at $1.7 billion; China's Exim Bank (the Export-Import Bank of China) will finance $1.5 billion of the project, and $200 million will be provided by Iran.[19] The development and speeding-up of this railway could be regarded as an important step in the implementation of a key part of the Silk Road's rail route because the track would enter Iran from the north-eastern part of the country and then continue to the north-west through Tehran and finally reach Turkey.[20] Chinese extensive engagement in Iran's railway projects suggests that Iran is seen as the southern route to Europe which effectively bypasses Russia.

Both these railway lines form a part of one of the six corridors in the new Silk Road. Six corridors have been defined along the route of the BRI framework. One of them is the China–Central Asia–Western Asia Corridor, a part of which passes through Iran, using the two aforementioned railway lines. This corridor enters Iran from Turkmenistan and follows two routes: an east-west route to Turkey and a north–south route to the Persian Gulf.[21] According to an article in *Foreign Affairs*, Beijing considers Central Asia its "exposed underbelly that needs to be closely integrated into China's economic and political sphere".[22]

Moreover, Iran's railway network can connect with the Baku–Tbilisi–Kars (BTK), a regional rail link project to directly connect Azerbaijan, Georgia, and Turkey, which became operational in October 2017. The BTK railway cargo across the Caspian Sea from Central Asia to Azerbaijan and is an essential step in reviving the historical Silk Road.[23] An Iranian rail link would provide a more contiguous and cost-effective route. Connecting with Iran's north–south rail links would provide a mostly vertical axis connecting China's central east–west corridor to the Middle East and the Arabian Sea.[24]

During 2012–2016, Chinese companies became the largest investors in and constructors of transport infrastructure in Iranian neighbor states, particularly those in Central Asia. Therefore, Iran's increasing need in the area of transport infrastructure and the growing capabilities of Chinese companies created more opportunities for sharing interests for the two countries. In November 2015, China Railway proposed a high-speed rail link that will carry both passengers and cargo between China and Iran. The most recently proposed route would begin in Urumqi, the capital of the PRC's western Xinjiang province, and end in Tehran some 3,200 km (2,000 miles) away, where it would eventually continue northwest through Turkey into Europe. Along the way, it would stop in Kazakhstan, Kyrgyzstan, Uzbekistan, and Turkmenistan. Beijing plans to build a rail line that would cut down the time needed to transport goods and increase the route's competitiveness against ocean freight alternatives. The trains themselves would run at speeds of up to 300 km/h for passenger trains and 120 km/h for freight trains.[25]

In May 2018, within two days after the U.S. announced its withdrawal from the nuclear agreement, China inaugurated a new railroad connecting Bayannur, in Inner Mongolia, to Tehran. The train, carrying 1,150 tonnes of sunflower seeds, traveling 8,352 kilometers through Kazakhstan and Turkmenistan, arrived in Tehran in 15 days. The new train route will shorten transportation time by at least 20 days compared with ocean shipping. The railroad was planned and its construction began several years before the U.S. announcement, but the timing of the inauguration was not coincidental; rather, it was meant to convey a message of partnership to Iran.[26]

Nevertheless, the U.S. withdrawal from the JCPOA and the re-imposition of the sanctions have increased the difficulties for Iran to participate in the realization of the new Silk Roads. More importantly, this will cause new, essential challenges for Tehran–Beijing cooperation to the development of international transport routes and the creation of an infrastructural network that could gradually connect all the regions in Asia and also specific points in Asia, Africa, and Europe. The BRI is a multilateral project, and its success will depend on its ability to attract as many countries as possible. Iran has been a major gateway to the ancient Silk Roads, and thanks to its central position between the Arabian Peninsula, Central Asia, and South Asia, it continues to be a critical crossroads. However, the re-imposition of the U.S. sanctions could slow down the construction of infrastructure through Iran, and divert foreign investors from this economic corridor linking Europe to China. According to the official statistics published by the Iranian Government, Tehran needs $14.5 billion investment per year over the next decade to improve its current transport infrastructure and to build new facilities.[27]

Trade and investments

The PRC's comprehensive strategic partnership with Iran is aimed at mitigating as much as possible the barriers to free trade, investment, industrial cooperation, and technical and engineering services in order to facilitate the integration of Iran within the BRI framework. Both countries must take a series of additional measures, such as expanding free-trade zones, improving trade structures, seeking new potential areas for trade and improving the trade balance, devising new initiatives for the promotion of conventional forms of trade, developing trans-border electronic trade and other advanced models of business, and regularly share information in these areas, to create a system for supporting trade in services to strengthen and expand conventional trade and increase customs cooperation.[28]

The trade and ties between China and Iran date back over 2,000 years to the ancient Silk Road caravan routes that brought the textile to Europe. China has traditionally been Iran's leading trading partner. During the past eight years, China has always been the most important economic partner of Iran, and approximately 30 percent of the total Iranian foreign trade has been done with Beijing.[29] During President Xi Jinping's visit to Tehran, the customs administrations of the two countries reached an agreement on customs information sharing. According to a joint plan of action in customs cooperation, Beijing would transport a proportion of its exported commodities to Iranian ports and then transport them further to Europe.[30]

According to the latest data released by the Chinese Customs Administration, the trade turnover between the two countries was $51 billion in 2014, 31 percent more compared to the preceding year. In 2015 the figure stood at $34 billion, indicating a 34 percent plunge. In 2016, the trade turnover between Iran and China stood at $31.2 billion, down 7.7 percent from 2015. In 2017, the trade turnover between the two countries stood at $37.18 billion.[31] According to China Customs Statistics (export-import), China's trade volume with Iran (China's fourth partner in the Middle East) dropped sharply from $35 billion in 2018 to $22.9 billion in 2019 (a direct result of U.S. sanctions).[32]

Beijing has also been one of the major foreign investors in the Islamic Republic over the past decade.[33] Its investments have taken place in various sectors from energy to transportation. China has invested in various energy projects in Iran including the South Pars Gas Field and the Abadan Refinery.[34] Beijing's investments totaled $48.6 billion in the 2005–2019 period. Of this $27 billion $11.83 billion was an investment in energy, $6.3 billion in transport, $2 billion in utilities and $5 billion in metals, and another $21.6 billion in construction contracts relating to energy, transportation, chemicals, and metals.[35] Meanwhile, based on the official statistics published by the Iranian government, over the next decade, Tehran needs to attract $500 billion in investment for various sectors of its economy, a large part of which must be provided from abroad.[36] China is one of the most critical countries Tehran hopes to make these investments, and the BRI can provide a framework for increased Chinese investments in Iran.

The Islamic Republic is an important emerging economy with rich energy resources and a market of 80 million people that is larger than the whole Central Asian market with its 66 million people. In the post-JCPOA era, the prospect of Iran's potential economic growth is encouraging, which, in turn, could lead to a considerable increase in its economic interactions with China.[37] Overall, the two states have set the ambitious goal of increasing bilateral trade tenfold, to $600 billion, by 2026. However, such a high increase in the bilateral trade turnover looks unrealistic, at least for the time being, and many obstacles need to be removed to achieve such an ambitious economic goal.[38]

Following the 2015 nuclear agreement, Tehran has received most of its foreign finance from Beijing. Based on an agreement between Iran's Central Bank and the CITIC Trust Group, the Group has provided Iran with a $10 billion credit line to finance medium- and long-term Iranian projects (e.g., energy and transport projects). This is the most extensive credit line extended to Iran in recent decades.[39] In addition to the credit line, the China Development Bank signed preliminary deals with Iran worth $15 billion for other infrastructure and production projects. Moreover, the PRC has also opened two credit lines worth $4.2 billion to build high-speed railway lines linking Tehran–Mashhad–Isfahan.[40] More broadly, following the U.S. withdrawal from the JCPOA, many major European companies have ceased their activities in Iran and ended their cooperation with the country.[41] This makes China the only major foreign investor in the country, and in the future, Tehran is expected to focus more on Beijing to attract foreign investment.

Nevertheless, Washington's decision to re-impose the economic sanctions could negatively impact Beijing's investments and trade with Tehran, although officially, Chinese Foreign Ministry spokesman Geng Shuang said that China would maintain "normal economic and trade exchanges" with Iran, despite Trump's decision to re-impose sanctions on Tehran.[42] However, given the potential risk of being targeted by the American sanctions, only those small- and medium-sized Chinese companies with no presence in the Western markets and fewer ties with the global financial system are expected to become active in this sphere.

According to trade data from the General Customs Administration of the People's Republic of China, the Beijing–Tehran trade fell dramatically in the two months following the re-imposition of U.S. secondary sanctions. Chinese exports to Iran, mainly crucial machinery and parts for Iran's manufacturing sector, fell from $1.2 billion in October 2018 to just $428 million in February 2019.[43] Exports had averaged $1.6 billion a month in the period from 2014 until the beginning of 2018. Imports from Iran, mainly crude oil, which had fallen to $1 billion in October, rose after November when the Trump administration granted China a waiver to permit continued oil purchases. The imports hit $1.3 billion in February, of which $866 million is attributed to oil imports.[44]

The trade data demonstrate a new negative dynamic in China–Iran trade under sanctions, and it is not yet conclusive as to whether these restrictions primarily reflect the decision to limit commerce to humanitarian trade. In the end, if the PRC remains unwilling or unable to sustain its investments and trade ties with Tehran in the face of U.S. sanctions, the consequences will prove significant to Iran's economic rehabilitation.

More importantly, in the post-JCPOA era, the prospects for Iran's contribution to the BRI have become further complicated. The re-imposition of sanctions on Iran has not only increased the risks of economic interactions with Iran, especially in the fields of investment and infrastructural projects but also posed severe challenges to the country's economic stability. Indeed, the Chinese government is still committed to the JCPOA and the continuation of regular trade ties with Iran. However, Chinese companies that have considerable benefits in the U.S. and are afraid of being punished by Washington are having increasing difficulties in cooperating with Iran to promote BRI-related projects. For instance, two major Chinese telecommunication companies, ZTE and Huawei, have faced severe penalties from the U.S. over their trade ties with Iran.[45] The U.S. sanctions have created new complexities in Iran–China interactions in general and their cooperation within the context of the BRI in particular.

Energy cooperation

According to the PRC's comprehensive strategic partnership with Tehran, investment in energy infrastructure is considered one of the important cooperation areas to integrate Iran into the BRI framework. Therefore, the new Silk Road can provide a new framework for more extensive Chinese investments in the Iranian energy industry. Beijing offers Tehran a market for its energy exports and investment in energy infrastructure; Iran enables China to diversify its energy sources, so as not to be overly reliant on, for instance, Saudi Arabia or Russia.

According to the Energy Information Administration (EIA), Iran contains some of the world's largest proven deposits of oil and natural gas. Tehran deposits contain an estimated 157 billion barrels of crude oil and a further 1,193 trillion cubic feet of natural gas deposits, making those the fourth and second-largest deposits in the world, respectively. The abundance of energy reserves, Iran's relatively proximate geographic location to China, and its geopolitical situation in the Middle East make Tehran an attractive country with which to develop a relationship for the PRC's energy security.[46] Hence, the Islamic Republic is one of the key countries involved in the BRI framework, with considerable potential to attract Chinese investment and technology for the development of its energy infrastructure.

Tehran is one of the world's most important oil producers, and Beijing is the largest energy consumer in the world, and hence, one of the most important options to attract global resources required for promoting Iran's energy infrastructure development. The PRC is the most important buyer of Tehran oil and receives about one-third of Iranian oil exports. China's enormous demand for energy resources has led to its long-standing commercial and political ties with Iran.[47]

Furthermore, the Islamic Republic's geographical status enables it to connect the energy infrastructure of West Asia countries involved in the BRI. Tehran is the only country in the Middle East with the potential to meet part of Beijing's oil and gas needs through both land and sea. Currently, all Iranian oil exports to China are conducted by sea, but Central Asia and Pakistan are two potential land routes that could connect Iran's energy resources to the Chinese market. Tehran has also already connected parts of its energy infrastructure to some of the other important Silk Road countries; namely, Turkmenistan, Turkey, and Pakistan. Development of the ties between Tehran and these countries in the form of separate trilateral cooperation initiatives with the participation and investment of Chinese companies could be regarded as another source of potential in this area.[48]

Since Beijing is predicted to become the world's largest energy consumer by 2030, it is wasting no time in availing itself of Iran's energy resources. The PRC's demand for oil imports is expected to grow from 6 million barrels per day to 13 million by 2035, and Iran, ranked fourth in the world with proven oil reserves and second with reserves of natural gas, is considered a reliable supplier.[49] Conversely, Tehran will need massive investments in its energy sector in the future and considers China an important source of investment. In the next five years, Iran needs to attract $134 billion investment in the upstream oil sector and an additional $52 billion in its petrochemical industry. The National Iranian Oil Company currently has 515 projects as well as 88 mega-projects and 2000 sub-projects on its agenda.[50]

In the JCPOA era, and, as a result of the lifting of most of the international sanctions against Iran, the situation had gradually improved for energy cooperation between the two countries. In the year since the finalization of the nuclear deal, there was an increase in the activities of Chinese oil and gas companies in Iran. In February 2017, the two countries signed a $3 billion contract to upgrade the Abadan oil refinery capacity, the largest refinery in Iran. Sinopec Company provided the initial $1.2 billion in finance for the first phase of the project. The deal called for improving the quality of oil byproducts by upgrading the refinery's production process and expected to be completed in four years.[51]

In December 2018, Sinopec offered a $3 billion deal to further develop the Yadavaran oil field in south-west Iran, replacing the British–Dutch oil giant, Royal Dutch Shell, which concluded that operations in Iran were too risky and to avoid repercussions in its U.S. market activities. The Yadavaran is one of the world's biggest undeveloped oilfields with reserves of 31 billion barrels of light and heavy crude oil. The deal would double production at the field to 180,000 barrels a day within six months. Sinopec believes that the offer would not violate a U.S. ban on signing new development deals with Iran, as its proposal for further development of Yadavaran is part of an existing contract to operate the field.[52]

In November 2016, China National Petroleum Corporation (CNPC) brought online the first phase of North Azadegan with 75,000 barrels per day (bpd) of output. The field on the border with Iraq is estimated to contain 5.7 billion barrels of crude reserves. In March 2017, former managing director of the National Iranian Oil Company (NIOC), Ali Kardor, said the second phase of North Azadegan was being considered for development under a new contract model, and CNPC was interested.[53]

In the post-JCPOA era, the most important Chinese investment in the Iranian energy sector was made, when a $4.879 billion contract was signed between the National Iranian Oil Company, and a consortium consisted of Total (a French multinational integrated oil and gas company), CNPC, and Iran's Petropars, for the development of phase 11 of South Pars Gas Field, the world's largest gas field. The project will have a production capacity of 400,000 bpd. The contract provisioned a 50.1 percent and a 30 percent share for Total and CNPC, respectively, with Petropars enjoying the remaining 19 percent.[54] However, shortly after the U.S. withdrawal from the JCPOA, Total announced its continuing in the project would depend on whether it could secure a sanctions waiver from Washington. As a result, the Iranian oil ministry announced that Total's share in the contract would be handed over to CNPC.[55]

President Trump's decision to withdraw from the JCPOA and to re-impose sanctions includes measures meant to punish any international company that does business with Iran's oil sector. The idea, according to Secretary of State Mike Pompeo, is to eventually reduce Iranian oil exports to zero. Just a few days before the re-imposition of secondary sanctions in November, the PRC was among eight countries that received a Significant Reduction Exemption (SRE) from the U.S. government which permitted the continued importation of Iranian oil, if the proceeds of Tehran's sales were exclusively used for the purchase of humanitarian goods, such as foodstuffs and medicine.[56]

The Chinese response to the new round of unilateral sanctions has been tepid and, to some extent, unsatisfactory. Beijing partially filled the vacuum left by European companies forced to abandon Iran, but suspended investments in the South Pars gas field and delayed many infrastructural projects. At the time the U.S. sanctions were re-imposed, China was buying 650,000 barrels a day of Iran's crude, or 6.3 percent of total Chinese imports, which would put their worth at $ 15 billion. According to data, China's crude oil imports from Iran are 27.9 percent lower in the period of January-March 2019 than in the same period a year ago.[57]

CNPC convinced the U.S. administration that it needed to continue investing in the North Azadegan and Masjid-i-Suleiman (MIS) oilfields to recoup the billions of dollars spent under buy-back contracts signed years ago. In December 2018, however, CNPC decided to suspend its investment in Iran's South Pars natural gas project in response to U.S. pressure and to minimize tensions amid trade negotiations between Beijing and Washington. South Pars is the world's largest gas field, and CNPC's investment freeze is a blow to Tehran's efforts to maintain financing for energy projects amid. Iran had 120 days to review CNPC's role in South Pars and decide whether to keep the Chinese firm as a dormant investor or cancel the deal, but so far, no decision has been made.[58]

According to *Reuters*, some 20 million barrels of Iranian oil sitting on China's shores in the northeast port of Dalian for the past six months now appears stranded as Washington hardens its stance on importing crude from Tehran. The Islamic Republic sent the oil to Dalian ahead of the reintroduction of U.S. sanctions last November 2018, as it looked for alternative storage for a backlog of crude at home. The oil is being held in bonded storage tanks at the port, which means it has yet to clear Chinese customs. Despite a six-month waiver to the start of May that allowed China to continue some Iranian imports, shipping data shows little of this oil has been moved because the uncertainty over the terms of the waiver and independent refiners have made China unable to secure payment or insurance channels, while state refiners struggled to find vessels. The future of the crude, worth well over $1 billion at current prices, has become unclear.[59]

Chinese officials have publicly stated that they have no intention of following Washington's demands to stop importing Iranian oil completely, but also agreed to refrain from increasing its oil purchases from Iran. Chinese oil companies (e.g., Sinopec) have made arrangements to keep Iranian oil flowing after U.S. sanctions come into force.[60] For example, they have switched to using Iranian tankers to deliver the oil, to sidestep sanctions and reduce their own risk.[61] Meanwhile, the re-imposition of U.S. sanctions helped the PRC to secure deep discounts on Iranian oil while selling Chinese goods to Tehran at inflated prices paid from the restricted Iranian oil funds sitting in escrow accounts at Chinese banks.[62]

The PRC was a signatory to the 2015 deal and expressed opposition to any unilateral sanctions against Iran. Nonetheless, the Chinese oil companies faced mounting pressure from Washington to comply with the new energy sanctions or face sanctions themselves if they had not obtained U.S. waivers by November 2018.[63] Chinese oil giants Sinopec and CNPC stopped loading Iranian oil in November 2018.[64] However, they resumed again after obtaining the U.S. waiver which allows them to buy 360,000 barrels per day for 180 days. In any case, this is only half of what the Chinese were importing at the time the sanctions were announced.[65]

In the previous sanctions period from 2008 to 2016, Chinese businesses and companies significantly expanded their commercial presence in Iran, stepping in as Western companies exited the market.[66] In the face of U.S. secondary sanctions, Iran's government had hopes that China would continue to purchase crude oil in high volumes and invest in energy development projects. However, the Bank of Kunlun, the state-owned bank at the key Chinese conduit for transactions with Iran, decided in October 2018 to suspend most financial transactions with Iran. Even before the sanctions came into effect, the Bank of Kunlun had stopped handling euro-dominated payments from Teheran. The bank, a subsidiary of the CNPC, is the main channel for money flows between the two countries; in 2012 it had faced U.S. sanctions for doing business with Iran and for transferring money to an Islamic Revolutionary Guard Corps (IRGC) linked group.[67]

Although the Bank of Kunlun resumed trade in January 2019, the bank announced a new policy that it would only service trade which was exempt from U.S. secondary sanctions. This means to trade in food, medicine, and consumer goods, for which China is not Iran's leading source of imports. The Bank of Kunlun's move is consistent with the terms of the oil waiver, which requires Iran's earnings to be paid into an escrow account and to be used exclusively for non-sanctioned bilateral trade.[68] Beijing will hold Iran's money, which can be used only to buy non-sanctioned goods inside China, another financial benefit for Chinese companies.

More important, while Europe has made extraordinary efforts to both assert its economic sovereignty and preserve the nuclear deal, even going so far as to establish a new state-owned trade financial intermediary, the PRC has taken no commensurate effort to shield its trade from the long arm of American law. To be sure, it remains a mystery how the new circumstances in the aftermath of the U.S. re-imposition of sanctions will impact China's role in Iran's petroleum sector. Nevertheless, it is possible that Chinese–Iranian oil trade could recover to a new steady-state in 2019, and that Beijing could designate a new bank to facilitate non-oil exports. However, when the waivers come up for renewal in early May 2019, the Trump administration could make such a waiver contingent on China continuing to downsize its non-oil trade with Iran.

After the waivers ended in May 2019, the Trump administration demanded that the five nations that used the waivers should halt all imports of Iranian oil. In July 2019, the administration imposed economic sanctions on the Chinese state-owned Zhuhai Zhenrong oil trading company and its chief executive, Li Youmin, for buying Iranian oil in violation of the American ban. Zhuhai Zhenrong and Sinopec are the two main

Chinese companies that import Iranian oil. This was the first time the administration has penalized a Chinese company and executive for defying recent U.S. sanctions on Iranian oil exports.[69]

However, since Iran is more important for China as an energy supplier than as an export market, China will likely sacrifice its exports to sustain oil imports.[70] Weeks after the U.S. imposed sanctions on Zhuhai Zhenrong, China was still importing oil from Iran. According to official customs data, China imported between 4.4 million and 11 million barrels of Iranian crude or 142,000 to 360,000 barrels per day (bpd). The upper end of that range would mean July 2019 imports still added up to close to half of their year-earlier level despite the sanctions. Senior Trump administration officials estimate that 50–70 percent of Iran's oil exports are still flowing to China, while roughly 30 percent go to Syria.[71]

In October 2019, U.S. officials were concerned that Chinese ships are turning off their automatic identification systems, used by vessels to transmit their location so that their movements to and from Iran remain hidden. The Trump administration has been making clear to carriers that they face punishment if they are caught violating sanctions with regard to transiting Iranian oil. COSCO shipping tanker has drawn U.S. attention after nearly a third of its fleet stopped transmitting locations via the automatic identification system. The U.S. then put sanctions on five Chinese individuals and two Chinese COSCO Shipping Corporation subsidiaries, accusing them of shipping Iranian crude oil. A few days later, 14 COSCO Shipping Tanker (Dalian) vessels stopped using their AIS, from September 30 to October 7.[72]

While European oil companies have explored ways to circumvent U.S. sanctions or seek waivers, the threat of sanctions is likely to scare away many foreign companies from doing business in Iran. This will leave a void that Chinese oil companies are likely to fill and gain a near-monopoly on the Iranian energy sector. This can also cause Tehran to become more amenable to Chinese global initiatives, such as the Belt and the Road Initiative. However, while these moves follow the common pattern of Chinese foreign policy, most notably Beijing's willingness to take more significant risks and conduct business in shunned nations, they have wider implications for its relations with the U.S. Eventually, in the midst of the trade war with Washington, Beijing seems to lack the political will to contrast the effects of U.S. sanctions by increasing the quantity and quality of its presence in the Iranian energy sector.[73]

Financial integration

Under China's comprehensive strategic partnership with Tehran, the formation and promotion of financial integration between the two countries are considered one of the essential cooperation areas to integrate Iran into the BRI framework. There are several measures for the realization of financial integration between the two countries: including deepening financial cooperation and building a stable currency system, establishing an investment and financing system and a credit information system in Asia, expanding the scope and scale of bilateral currency swaps between the two countries, and developing the bond market in Asia.[74]

Besides, China–Iran needs to make joint efforts with others to establish the Asian Infrastructure Investment Bank (AIIB), and to conduct negotiations with related parties to the Shanghai Cooperation Organization (SCO) financing institution, and financial institutions with good credit ratings. China–Iran needs also to issue RMB-denominated bonds in China, and encourage qualified Chinese financial institutions and companies to issue bonds in both RMB and foreign currencies outside China and to use the funds thus collected in countries along the BRI.

Sino–Iranian financial cooperation is still at the initial stage. In June 2015, Iran signed the documents with China to join the AIIB, which were ratified only in January 2017 after a long delay.[75] The AIIB was planned to play a key role in financing the Iranian projects related to the BRI and facilitate foreign investment in the country.[76] However, Iran is still an observer state in the SCO and, thus, is not able to contribute to the creation of its financial institution. Beijing's refusal to swiftly incorporate Iran in the SCO can be explained by its concerns that Iranian membership would give the SCO an unambiguously anti-Western character.[77]

The CITIC investment group, a Chinese state-owned investment firm, has provided a $10 billion credit line for Iranian banks to finance water, energy, and transport projects. In addition to the credit line, the China Development Bank signed preliminary deals with Iran worth $15 billion for other infrastructure and production projects. The credit line will use euros and yuan to help bypass U.S. sanctions that have continued despite the JCPOA. Since the lifting of sanctions at that time, the PRC opened two credit lines worth $4.2 billion to build high-speed railway lines linking Tehran with Mashhad and Isfahan.[78]

Another area of financial cooperation between the two countries is strengthening the internationalization of the RMB. Since 2012, Iran has accepted the Chinese currency for its crude oil exports to Beijing.[79] In the post-JCPOA era, this phenomenon could be amplified. Tehran may seek to diversify its currency reserves and reduce its reliance on U.S. dollars. In August 2018, Tehran replaced the U.S. dollar with China's yuan in its official currency rate reporting platform to reduce the country's vulnerability to U.S. economic sanctions as well as the depreciation of the rial.[80]

Military ties

Under China's comprehensive strategic partnership with Iran, defense cooperation, including arms and technology trade and joint military drills, has become an increasingly significant part of integrating Tehran into the BRI framework. As the Chinese Defense Minister Wei Fenghe said, in September 2018, relations between the armed forces of China and Iran are developing positively. Beijing is ready to strengthen the strategic communication with Tehran, expand the spheres of cooperation, achieve new fruitful results of cooperation between the two armies, and thereby contribute to the development of a comprehensive strategic partnership of the two states.[81]

Military relations between the two countries date back to the early 1980s, but they went through a period of reduced cooperation as a result of international nuclear sanctions on Tehran. In the 1980s and early 1990s, Beijing provided Iran with arms, tactical ballistic missiles and anti-ship cruise missiles in its fight against Iraq. China has facilitated Iran's military modernization, even being suspected of transferring technology and equipment to Tehran via North Korea. Both countries developed significant arms sector cooperation, with Beijing supplying Iran with advanced fighter aircraft, tanks, radars, cruise missiles, fast-attack patrol craft, and other weapons. The U.S. has sanctioned several Chinese entities for allegedly assisting Iran's missile, nuclear, and conventional weapons program.[82]

Chinese military cooperation with Tehran declined in the 2000s, coinciding with international concern over Iran's evolving nuclear program and the imposition of UN sanctions. Resolutions adopted in the United Nations Security Council (UNSC) – with Beijing's support – prohibited cooperation with Iran's nuclear and ballistic missile industries and were expanded in 2010 with a resolution imposing an embargo on exports of major conventional weapons to Iran. These included tanks, large-caliber artillery systems, combat aircraft, certain naval ships, and missiles with a maximum range of at least 25 kilometers.[83] From the 1979 Iranian Revolution until 2018, China exported arms worth $4.25 billion to Iran, becoming Tehran's No. 2 arms supplier. Though China recently stopped providing arms to Iran, the latter plans to revive that relationship if the UN's arms embargo on Iran expires in October 2020 as scheduled.[84]

In the post-JCPOA era, the PRC has once again poised to resumption its arms exports to Iran according to UN Security Council procedures. The JCPOA retained the UN arms and missiles embargoes for five and eight years respectively, although China could attempt to secure waivers as a permanent member of the Security Council.[85] In November 2016, Chinese Defense Minister Chang Wanquan concluded a three-day trip to Tehran, the latest in a series of high-ranking bilateral military exchanges over the past two years, and called the latest meetings a "turning point" in the strategic partnership. Both sides signed an agreement pledging closer military cooperation in several areas including military training and counterterrorism operations, and they pledged to hold joint military exercises in the near future.[86]

In September 2019, for the first time in 40 years, the Iranian armed forces chief of staff, Maj. Gen. Mohammad Bagheri, traveled to China for a three-day visit. During the visit, he held talks with senior military and political figures of China. The key objective of the visit was said to be the promotion of defense diplomacy between the two countries. Establishing a joint military commission, visiting industrial and scientific centers, and giving a speech at the PLA National Defence University were also on the agenda of the Iranian commander in China.[87]

According to the UN Security Council's approval, Beijing could provide Iran's navy with a wide range of naval equipment, including frigates, submarines, and missiles. For instance, China could transfer advanced cruise missiles or technical expertise that could enable Iran to improve its domestic production of anti-ship or land-attack cruise missiles.[88] The PRC could also enhance its cooperation with Tehran in areas such as unmanned aircraft systems, space, or counter-space systems, missile defense components, or electronic warfare capabilities. In October 2015, Iranian electronic defense firm SaIran signed an agreement with Chinese firms to begin using their BeiDou-2 satellite navigation system for military purposes. The system's military-grade signals are more accurate than commercially available GPS services, so they could significantly improve Iran's use of satellite navigation in its missiles, UAVs, and other hardware. In land warfare, Beijing could allow Tehran to examine, purchase, or even assemble modern Chinese tank designs or armored personnel carriers.[89]

The military ties between the two countries also include joint naval drills. In September 2014, Beijing conducted joint naval exercises with Tehran when two Chinese warships docked at Iran's Bandar Abbas port to take part in joint naval exercises in the Persian Gulf, and an Iranian admiral was given tours of a Chinese submarine and warships.[90] Since 2014, Chinese military cooperation with Iran has deepened, including a joint naval exercise in the Strait of Hormuz in June 2017. According to a Tehran news agency, Iran's navy conducted a joint exercise with a

Chinese fleet near the strategic Strait of Hormuz in the Persian Gulf. The drill included an Iranian warship as well as two Chinese warships, a logistics ship, and a Chinese helicopter.[91]

In September 2019, Iran, China, and Russia conducted, for the first time, a four-day joint naval drill in the Indian Ocean and the Gulf of Oman at a time of heightened tensions. The exercise covered 17,000 square kilometers and consisted of various tactical exercises, which included target practice and rescuing ships from assaults and fires. The objectives of this exercise are improving the security of international maritime trade, countering maritime piracy and terrorism, exchanging information regarding rescue operations, and operational and tactical experience. According to the Chinese Defense Ministry spokesman Wu Qian, the drill would "deepen exchange and cooperation between the navies of the three countries". It was noted that the Chinese navy's guided-missile destroyer *Xining* took part in the exercise.[92]

Beijing is one of Iran's main supplier of advanced weaponry, with some $316 million worth of weaponry exported to Tehran between 2007 and 2016. Some of the naval equipment China has sold includes tactical ballistic and anti-ship cruise missiles, advanced anti-ship mines, and Houdong fast-attack boats.[93] According to Commander of the Iranian Navy Rear Admiral Hossein Khanzadi, there are very good capacities for military cooperation between the navies of the two countries, and Iran wants to promote exchanges with the Chinese navy in various areas, including the development of military cooperation at sea, educational ties and joint technical activities.[94] As geopolitics evolve in the Middle East, Iran and China are becoming strategic partners, but their partnership in the area of security is expected to produce only limited development.

Another possible collaboration between the two countries can exist in the civil nuclear industry. After the nuclear deal, China saw Iran as a major market for cooperation on peaceful nuclear energy in the Middle East. Under the JCPOA, China is allowed to help Iran develop its civil nuclear program for peaceful purposes. Ever since the Iranian nuclear deal was secured, China vied to grab an opportunity for its own civil nuclear sectors in the Iranian nuclear energy market. China–Iran cooperation in the nuclear field on its peaceful use is likely to grow from strength to strength. China views the Iran civil nuclear industry as great scope for an investment opportunity.[95]

From the mid-1980s to the late 1990s, Beijing played a part in Iran's nuclear program. According to a *RAND* study, China has assisted in the development of Tehran's nuclear program by training Iranian nuclear engineers and providing various types of critical nuclear technology and machinery. It also assisted in uranium exploration and mining and helped Tehran master the uses of lasers for uranium enrichment. It is not clear whether Chinese aid was provided with the specific aim of helping Iran to develop a nuclear weapons capability, but the effect has been to assist Iran's acquisition of such capabilities.[96] By the time the controversy over Iran's undeclared facilities broke out in 2002, however, Beijing had distanced itself from the program.

In April 2017, after several rounds of talks over the past year, China National Nuclear Corporation (CNNC) and Iran had signed the first commercial contract for the reconstruction of Iran's Arak heavy water reactor. The core of the reactor was removed as part of an international agreement limiting Iran's nuclear program in return for the lifting of economic sanctions. The contract is mainly related to the design concept of the transformation of the Arak reactor and some preliminary design-related consulting services. Under the contract, the Chinese company was to complete the design concept for the renovation of the Arak reactor within the next eight months.[97] Nevertheless, if Washington refuses to extend or provide a new waiver and applies new sanctions, then Chinese cooperation with Iran on civil nuclear projects and the Arak heavy water reactor agreement will be in jeopardy. China's government and state-owned enterprises fear possible U.S. sanctions if they continue their cooperation with Iran, and therefore have reduced the speed of civil nuclear cooperation despite their commitment.[98]

People-to-People Bond

China's comprehensive strategic partnership with Iran, enabling the people of the two countries to bond along the Silk Road, is vital to integrate Tehran into the BRI framework. The promotion of extensive cultural and academic exchanges win public support for deepening bilateral and multilateral cooperation, as well as providing scholarships, holding annual cultural events, increasing cooperation in science and technology, and establishing joint laboratory or research centers and international technology transfer centers.[99]

Although the two countries have many common cultural and historical features, the number of people-to-people interactions between them is still minimal. One example is the Confucius Institute as the symbol of China's cultural interactions with other countries. In 2019, 550 Confucius Institutes and 1,172 Confucius Classrooms and 5,665 teaching sites established in 162 countries and regions, receiving about eleven million students.[100] More broadly, in 54 countries involved in the Belt and Road Initiative, there are 153 Confucius Institutes and 149 primary and high-school Confucius Classrooms, but although one of these branches has been established in the University of Tehran, it still does not offer any cultural or educational activities.[101]

Moreover, there are no reliable statistics on the number of fellowships granted by the Chinese Government to Iranian students or the exact number of Chinese students in Iran. Furthermore, the two countries still do not have any plans to hold regular celebrations for each other's cultural years. In the field of science and technology, during President Xi Jinping's visit to Tehran in early 2016, the two sides reached an MoU on establishing technology parks, but the plan is yet to be realized.[102] Both sides also signed several agreements in many areas such as cultural exchange and tourism.

In the tourism sector, the relationship between the two countries is still in its infancy. Iran with four seasons, four thousand years of civilization, and numerous historical and cultural monuments could be a unique destination for Chinese tourists. There are only seven flights per week between Iran and China. In 2017, of the 130 million Chinese tourists who traveled around the world, only 95, 000 chose Iran as their destination.[103] Tehran is aiming to increase the number of Chinese tourists to at least 2.5 million visitors, by improving its tourism infrastructures and services. This would include opening more Chinese restaurants, providing translation services, and facilitating visa applications. Meanwhile, the number of direct flights between China and Iran will also be increased.[104]

To this end, China's Belt and Road Initiative could afford both nations an opportunity to enhance the tourism industry. The new Silk Road could also be a tourism route linking Iranian and Chinese nations. According to data Wu Yi obtained from the airlines and the embassy, before 2015 the number of Chinese tourists to Iran was less than 50,000 every year. However, with the lifting of the sanctions on Iran in 2016, the number of Chinese tourists to Iran doubled, of which 60 to 70 percent were business tourists.[105] Thus, in this sphere also there is considerable potential for cooperation and interaction between the two countries, but in reality, there is still a long way to go. Although Iran has managed to become a safe destination for the Chinese since 2011, it has not caused it to be among China's top 20 destinations.[106]

Summary

Iran–PRC relations are wide-ranging and trace back to the ancient Silk Road. They were inextricably interwoven in the economic, political, and cultural spheres. China's interest in Iran goes beyond its energy resources. It has a keen interest in Iran's geostrategic location, bordering both the Caspian Sea and the Persian Gulf. The location enables China to carry out the realization of the new Silk Road trade route. Hence, the Islamic Republic is expected to be one of the main beneficiaries of China's BRI.

Beijing's energy dependence and Belt and Road Initiative have made Tehran an increasingly attractive partner. Beijing remains involved in building up Iran's infrastructure, including electricity, dams, cement plants, steel mills, shipbuilding, motorways, and airports. Defense cooperation, including arms and technology trade and joint military drills, has become an increasingly significant part of Iran's relationship with China in the Persian Gulf. Although China and Iran have established a formal comprehensive strategic partnership, the PRC's economic, political, and strategic interests are too complex and self-contradictory to permit a close alignment with Iran.

In the post-JCPOA era, Beijing seemed likely to remain Iran's top economic partner in the coming years. However, overestimating the Sino–Iranian partnership risks disappointment. The U.S. anti-Iranian policy and the sanctions that accompany it, and the geopolitical rivalry between Iran and Saudi Arabia, could prevent the emergence of a more solid partnership. For these reasons, the potential of Iran to fully integrate within the BRI framework is not high. Nevertheless, the new Silk Road trade route will be the key factor shaping Tehran–Beijing relations in the coming years. In the short to medium term, the Islamic Republic still finds in China an irreplaceable source of economic and political aid.

In September 2019, according to the *Petroleum Economist*, China will invest a $280 billion in Iran's oil, gas, and petrochemical sectors. This amount could be frontloaded into the first five-year period of the deal, with the understanding that more money would be available in every subsequent five-year period subject to the parties' agreement. There would be another $120 billion Chinese investment in upgrading Tehran's transport and manufacturing infrastructure, which similarly could be frontloaded into the first five-year period and added to each subsequent period. The updated agreement also includes benefits for Chinese companies operating in Iran. Chinese firms would be given first refusal to bid on any new, stalled, or uncompleted oil and gas field developments. They would also have the first refusal of opportunities to become involved with any petrochemical projects in the country, including the provision of technology, systems, process ingredients, and personnel.

Significantly, the updated agreement includes the provision of up to 5,000 Chinese security personnel on the ground in Iran to protect its assets. There would be additional personnel and material available to protect the last transit of oil, gas, and petrochemical supply from Iran to the PRC, where necessary, including through the Persian Gulf. Beijing would also be able to buy any oil, gas, and petrochemicals products at a minimum guaranteed discount of 12 percent to the six-month rolling low price of comparable benchmark products, plus another 6–8 percent of that metric for risk-adjusted compensation.

Under the terms of the new agreement, Beijing would be granted the right to delay payment for Iranian production for up to two years. The PRC would also be able to pay in soft currencies or renminbi, meaning no U.S. dollars will be involved in commodity transaction payments from China to Tehran. China's close involvement in the build-out of Iran's manufacturing infrastructure would be within the context of its BRI. The $400 billion deal comes in parallel with Iran's rejection of an offer of a $15 billion loan from Europe in return for the country's commitment to the nuclear deal – a signal that Tehran is not dependent on the West as long as there is a Chinese option.[107]

The $400 billion deal could mark a significant change in Chinese foreign policy and the principle of non-intervention. The updated agreement violates the American unilateral sanctions against the Islamic Republic. At a time when Washington is trying to squeeze Iran's exports out of the oil market, the deal would amount to an act of defiance of the U.S. According to Chinese FM spokesperson Geng Shuang, "I'm not aware of what you said and don't know where you got such information. What I can tell you is that China and Iran enjoy friendly relations, and our two countries conduct friendly and mutually beneficial cooperation in various fields within the framework of international law."[108]

However, China's envoy to Iran Chang Hua expounded on his country's policies towards Tehran at a press meeting in *Tasnim News Agencies*. According to China's ambassador to Iran, Beijing is willing to continue and expand the friendly ties with Iran within the framework of the BRI. Indeed, the U.S. sanctions have adversely affected the cooperation between Iran and China at present. Still, the two countries must have strategic patience and figure out together how to keep on collaboration between the two countries. As regards the roadmap for Tehran–Beijing ties in the next 25 years and speculations about China's plan for $400 billion in investment, the officials of the two countries have held several meetings and have achieved many agreements.[109]

The future Sino–Iranian comprehensive strategic partnership and their cooperation to the realization of the BRI will likely be influenced by two predominant factors. The first, Tehran's tense relations with the Gulf countries especially Iranian–Saudi competition and, more broadly, Sunni–Shi'i rivalry. The PRC's balancing act between Iran and Saudi Arabia will be much more difficult to sustain in the future. This situation would likely slow down BRI's progress, create tensions with the Gulf countries, and face Beijing with difficult choices about how to navigate Saudi-Iran competition.

The second factor is linked to tensions in the Iran–U.S. relations in a post-JCPOA era and the possibility of confrontation with Washington. The United States is likely to perceive the PRC's deepening engagement with Iran as a major challenge to its sanctions on Tehran and a factor enabling the Islamic Republic to feel more secure and, consequently, pursue a more expansionist policy in the Middle East. As a result, Tehran would likely reemerge as an important strategic issue in U.S.–Beijing relations, constraining China's freedom of action in West Asia and further increasing the strategic mistrust between the two global powers. Against this backdrop, Washington is likely to put pressure on Saudi Arabia and its other regional allies to limit their engagement with the PRC, creating obstacles to BRI's development and to China–Saudi relations.

10 | United Arab Emirates

The People's Republic of China (PRC) and the United Arab Emirates (UAE) relations are one of the most important bilateral axes in the Persian Gulf region. Over the past years, a new era of closer political and economic ties has begun to develop between the two countries. The ties range from broadening trade, through energy investments, building, and acquisition activities in infrastructure and logistics, financial services, military ties, and people-to-people bonds to realizing the Belt and Road Initiative (BRI). The mutually beneficial arrangement enables China to expand its Middle East footprint while providing opportunities for UAE to profit from partnerships.

The PRC enjoys highly fruitful cooperation with the UAE, of all the Middle East countries, and in July 2018 bilateral relations were elevated to a comprehensive strategic partnership, Beijing's highest level in its hierarchy of diplomatic relations. According to China–UAE comprehensive strategic partnership, they will strengthen their in-depth bilateral cooperation in various fields, and promote the continuous development of bilateral ties on higher levels, in broader areas and at greater depths.[1] Given China's rise as an economic and political power in the Middle East, the ties with the UAE are expected to become stronger and flourish in the years to come.

The BRI was put forward in October 2013 by Chinese President Xi Jinping. The $1 trillion projects seek to connect Beijing to the global market by linking Asia and Europe via a set of land and maritime trade routes. The concept took form over several years and has now become a cornerstone of President Xi's foreign policy. The UAE is in a unique strategic geographic location, as the gateway between East and West, and its natural resources make the country an ideal regional hub of trade, finance, energy, logistics, and a tourist destination as well as a commercial partner for leading Chinese enterprises to access some of the fastest-growing markets in Central, South, and Southeast Asia; Europe; the Middle East; Africa and beyond. More importantly, the Emirates can play a pivotal role in helping China realize its BRI.

This chapter examines what lies behind the China–UAE comprehensive strategic partnership and the synergy between the BRI and UAE Vision 2021 to understand the extent of economic engagement and bilateral relationship between the two nations. As Sheikh Mohammed bin Rashid Al Maktoum, ruler of Dubai, said in a tweet, "We have many areas of political and economic agreement and a solid base of projects in the energy, technology, and infrastructure sectors. More importantly, we have a strong political will to start a greater phase of cooperation and integration."[2]

The main argument to be presented is that the PRC's comprehensive strategic partnership framework with the UAE is based on shared or mutually complementary economic interests. The Emirates' strategic geographic location makes the country a marketplace of great potential and influence in the entire MENA region that is essential for the realization of the BRI. The mutually beneficial arrangement of China's investments and UAE's unique strategic geographic location on global trade routes enables China to expand its Middle East footprint while providing opportunities for the UAE to profit from the partnership and promote its Vision 2021.

UAE Vision 2021

In 2010, the Sheikh Mohammed bin Rashid Al Maktoum, Vice President and Prime Minister of the UAE and Ruler of Dubai, launched the 'UAE Vision 2021'. The Vision aims to make the UAE one of the best countries in the world by the year 2021 when the nation celebrates the Golden Jubilee of its formation as a federation. In order to translate the ruler's vision into reality, its pillars have been mapped into six national priorities, which represent the key focus sectors of government action in the coming years. First, united in responsibility, an ambitious and confident nation grounded in its heritage. Second, united in destiny, a strong union bonded by a common destiny. Third, united in knowledge, a competitive economy driven by knowledgeable and innovative Emiratis.

Fourth, united in prosperity, a nurturing and sustainable environment for quality living. Fifth, well-rounded lifestyles, the UAE will nurture a high quality of life built on world-class public infrastructure, government services, and a rich recreational environment. Final, a well-preserved natural environment: As a leader of the green revolution, the UAE is conscious of its responsibility to safeguard nature and mitigate the effects of climate change on its habitat and ecosystems to ensure that future generations inherit an environmentally sustainable world.[3]

UAE and the Belt and Road Initiative

The PRC's comprehensive strategic partnership with the Emirates includes seven major areas for cooperation within the BRI. These areas are policy coordination, connectivity, trade and investments, energy cooperation, financial integration, military ties, and people-to-people bond. However, each country views the BRI framework and reacts to it according to its perspective and the consequences for its own national interests and international status. Therefore, the two countries have very different attitudes regarding how to realize the vision.[4]

The UAE Vision 2021 and China's Belt and Road vision have converged on a common economic development path, and their synergetic strategy will bring new opportunities for both sides. As Chinese President Xi said in his visit in Abu Dhabi, the two countries need to translate the China–UAE comprehensive strategic partnership into concrete achievements, cement political mutual trust, continue to take care of each other's core interests and major concerns, and support each other's pursuit of the development path that suits themselves.[5]

Policy coordination

As part of China's comprehensive strategic partnership with UAE, promoting political cooperation between countries, creating mechanisms for dialogue and consensus-building on global and regional issues, developing shared interests, deepening political trust and reaching a new consensus on cooperation is important to integrate the UAE Vision 2021 into the BRI framework.[6]

In 1984, China and the UAE first established diplomatic ties, and in 2012, the Emirates was the first Gulf country to forge a strategic partnership with the PRC.[7] Over the past 34 years, UAE has enjoyed prosperous financial cooperation with China, and the bilateral economic and commerce relations between the two countries is expected to create further opportunities for cooperation. As Chinese ambassador to the UAE, Ni Jian, said, "UAE enjoys the most fruitful cooperation with China among all Middle East countries and the two nations are keen to take these ties to a new level. At present, the China–UAE's relationship is at its best. It is an exemplary model of mutual respect, friendship, and win-win cooperation."[8]

In July 2018 during his first, historic state visit to UAE, Chinese President Xi Jinping said that the establishment of a comprehensive strategic partnership would be conducive to deepening strategic mutual trust and raising the level of mutually beneficial cooperation. China and the UAE are natural partners for jointly building the BRI. China regards the UAE as a key pivot in implementing the BRI. The two sides need to create stronger links between their development strategies, strengthen communications on industrial policies and plan and manage well the flagship projects within the framework of the BRI, to boost the economic development of the Middle East region and the Gulf region.[9]

In April 2019, Sheikh Mohammed bin Rashid Al Maktoum, Vice President and Prime Minister of the UAE and Ruler of Dubai, met Chinese President Xi Jinping in Beijing. The meeting was held on the sidelines of the Second Belt and Road Conference for International Cooperation. According to Sheikh Mohammed, collaboration with China serves the future strategic vision of the UAE and supports the objectives of both countries to accelerate development. He stated that the partnership supports the development efforts of both countries and creates new growth opportunities. As noted in the media, the strong mutual will to expand collaboration provides a strong basis for the realization of our future joint strategic objectives.[10]

Chinese Ambassador to the UAE, Ni Jian, told the *Emirates News Agency, WAM*, that this year marks the 35th anniversary of the establishment of diplomatic relations between China and the UAE. "Our relationship is currently at its best period in history. Among all Middle East countries, the UAE has the deepest, broadest, and most fruitful cooperation with China. The upcoming visit by Sheikh Mohammed Bin Zayed is expected to consolidate and deepen our political and strategic mutual trust and elevate our political, military, commercial, cultural, people-to-people, and technological cooperation across the board. It will further substantiate the comprehensive strategic partnership to open a glorious new chapter of China–UAE friendship. Jointly building the Belt and Road is in line with the UAE's interests and brings opportunities and momentum to our development. As an important regional transport hub and financial and trade center, the UAE has a pivotal role to play to extend the PRC's cooperation with the Gulf and Middle East states and facilitate interconnectivity."[11]

In July 2019, President Xi Jinping met the Sheikh Mohammed bin Zayed Al Nahyan, crown prince of Abu Dhabi of the UAE, and called for joint efforts with the UAE to accelerate the high-quality building of the BRI. The Chinese President said the PRC and UAE should work toward increasing bilateral trade volume to $200 billion by 2030 and expand long-term and comprehensive strategic cooperation in the energy sector. The establishment of the bilateral global strategic partnership last year opened a new chapter for the joint progress of both countries, and deeper vital mutual trust and strategic cooperation is required. The PRC sees the UAE as an important strategic cooperative partner in the Middle East. According to the UAE crown prince, the Arab state will remain China's best strategic collaborative partner no matter how the global landscape changes, and it will continue to offer China strong support over issues that are related to its core interests and major concerns. The UAE is ready to expand investment and energy supplies to China and to step up cooperation in areas such as finance, aerospace, and people-to-people exchanges.[12]

Connectivity

Under China's comprehensive strategic partnership with Emirates, the facilitation of connectivity is one of the crucial ways to integrate the UAE Vision 2021 into the BRI framework. The UAE should attempt to optimize its infrastructural connections and also to adapt its technical systems to those of the other countries in the BRI framework. This would lead Beijing–UAE to jointly contribute to the development of international transport maritime and overland routes, and the creation of an infrastructural network that could gradually connect all the regions in Asia and also specific points in Asia, Africa, and Europe. In addition, there should be serious attempts to create low-carbon and green infrastructure.[13]

Generally, the Gulf countries, the UAE in particular, are essential for the PRC's BRI to create a network of manufacturing and logistics centers in Central Asia and Europe.[14] The Persian Gulf region occupies a key position in Beijing's BRI. Given that the Persian Gulf is at the crossroads of Europe, Africa, and Asia, Chinese state-owned shipping and logistics companies have already started ramping up infrastructure investments in Gulf ports.[15]

Given its unique geographic location, as the gateway between East and West, the UAE can play a pivotal role in helping realize the new Silk Road vision. The Emirates can provide many facilities in the land, air, and sea logistical support throughout the Middle East for the Chinese venture, which will link both sea and land to markets in Asia and Europe, thus taking bilateral and regional cooperation to new heights. China–UAE connectivity cooperation extends to many areas ranging from an industrial and trade zone, container terminals/ports, and logistics centers as part of the cooperation to realize the new Silk Road vision. As the third-largest re-export hub in the world after Singapore and Hong Kong, Dubai, with Jebel Ali Free Zone (JAFZA), the world's largest free zone, and Jebel Ali port for re-export, is the site of approximately 60 percent of China's pass-through trade.[16]

Accordingly, the Dubai International Financial Centre (DIFC) has signed an MoU with China Everbright Group to collaborate in BRI-related opportunities. Abu Dhabi Global Market (ADGM) approved the Industrial Capacity Co-operation Financial

Group Limited (ICCFG), the first Chinese state-owned financial services firm to be established in the financial center to provide strategic investment and financial support to Chinese enterprises as part of the BRI project. DP World also signed an agreement with the Zhejiang China Commodities City Group (ZCCCG) to jointly construct a new traders market at JAFZA in Dubai to provide further impetus to China's BRI.[17]

Trade zones

In July 2018, the UAE's state-owned DP World, which operates in 40 countries, announced an agreement with ZCCCG to jointly construct a new traders market at its flagship JAFZA. The new facility will cover three square kilometers at the Jebel Ali site, which is the Middle East's largest trade zone.[18] The new traders market in Dubai will host a vast range of goods from food and cosmetics to building materials and technology. However, DP World did not announce the value of the deal or provide a timeframe for its construction. The new traders market will be composed of clusters of traders from all over the world (divided by sector) and will enable Chinese manufacturers to benefit from Dubai's geostrategic location by enabling trade with other places in the GCC, the Middle East, and Indian Subcontinent.[19]

The ICCFG, which is owned by East China's Jiangsu provincial government, will be set up in the Abu-Dhabi's financial hub to offer lending facilities (investment and financial support) to Chinese enterprises operating in the Emirates' industrial zone. This will be the first Chinese financial services firm in the UAE bank free zone ADGM. According to Wang Bin, chairman of China Jiangsu International, about $2 billion of investment will be managed by this financial services platform to support the Chinese companies in the demonstration park.[20]

In September 2017, Dubai Multi Commodities Centre (DMCC), the biggest free trade zone in UAE, signed an MoU with Xi'an International Trade & Logistics Park in central China's Shaanxi Province at the Xi'an Dubai Free Trade Zone Economic Cooperation Conference. The purpose of the MoU is to open doors for investors in both nations and to expand into new markets as well as organizing joint trade missions and economic delegations.[21] In April 2018, Abu Dhabi Ports and the Jiangsu Provincial Overseas Cooperation and Investment Company Limited (JOCIC) announced that 15 Chinese companies had signed agreements to invest in Khalifa Port Free Trade Zone (KPFTZ), the largest free zone in the Middle East, totaling $1 billion in value. Under the terms of the investment cooperation agreement, China–UAE Industrial Capacity Cooperation (Jiangsu) Construction Management Co. would occupy and develop approximately 2.2sq km of the free trade zone for companies from the Chinese province of Jiangsu. The China–UAE Industrial Capacity Cooperation Industrial Park is part of the KPFTZ and is expandable to reach 12.2sq km.[22]

In July 2018, DMCC signed an MoU with China Council for the Promotion of International Trade (CCPIT) to strengthen the strong and longstanding economic ties between Dubai and China. The MoU highlights Dubai's geostrategic position as a global gateway and the ideal partner for leading Chinese companies to access some of the fastest-growing markets in Central, South and Southeast Asia, Europe, the Middle East, Africa, and beyond. The MoU with DMCC will promote significant commercial opportunities available to Chinese enterprises in Dubai.[23]

Logistic centers and container terminals

In June 2018, the Emirates Airline SkyCargo, Dubai's flagship carrier, signed an MoU with Cainiao Smart Logistics Network, the logistics arm of Alibaba, to jointly facilitate the delivery of cross-border parcels. Under the MoU, Cainiao and SkyCargo will work closely to manage e-commerce shipments in the Middle East and neighboring regions via Dubai, the biggest trade and logistics hub in the region. The SkyCargo's network spread, the frequent flights from China, and the state-of-the-art hub facilities as well as Dubai's geostrategic location, will contribute significantly to Cainiao's operations in the Middle East and beyond.[24]

In September 2016, COSCO Shipping won a 35-year concession with a five- year option to build and operate a new container terminal at Khalifa Industrial Zone Abu Dhabi (KIZAD). This investment is valued at $738 million and will double the container-handling capacity of Khalifa port. COSCO's Khalifa Port Container Terminal 2 (KPCT 2) will span approximately 70 hectares with three berths and will add 2.4 million TEUs (twenty-foot equivalent units) a year to Khalifa Port's existing capacity of 2.5 million TEUs once the first two phases of the development are completed. The first 800 meters of the quay and the corresponding yard was earmarked to be operational in the first half of 2018 with the additional 400 meters to come on stream in 2020. In July 2017, a consortium of five Chinese companies from Jiangsu province invested $300 million in building diverse industries in KIZAD. This investment is for a 50-year lease on a 2.2 sq. km. property in the KIZAD.[25]

Ports

The UAE is home to the world's busiest port outside of Asia and a key connection point for the PRC's Maritime Silk Road Initiative (MSRI), which is vital as investment flows from China through the Emirates to the rest of the world. UAE's position as a gateway to Africa, the Middle East, and Europe, with its financing capabilities and professional services, along with multi-national and local companies that are capable of running large infrastructure projects, makes this a huge opportunity for Chinese companies. The PRC seeks to integrate the UAE ports into China's MSRI to boost investment and create a new platform for multilateral economic cooperation as part of the comprehensive strategic partnership between both nations. The Middle East, in general, and the Emirates, in particular, play an essential and crucial part of China's MSRI. Chinese companies are increasingly seizing opportunities in the Gulf as Beijing seeks to expand overseas with their ambitious BRI.[26]

Chinese companies chose Khalifa Port, the flagship of Abu Dhabi Ports, as the next stop on China's 21st Century Maritime Silk Road. This investment in the Khalifa Free Trade Zone and Khalifa Port is all part of the MSRI execution, which seeks to establish an enhanced and interconnected network of Chinese-run ports and manu- facturing zones along the route from the east coast of China to Europe. The Chinese companies operating in the Emirates are different from other shipping companies foreign that operate in the UAE's ports since often they do not only come in and open a new port but also invest in an adjoining free trade/special economic zone and other development initiatives. Moreover, Chinese investments in the Emirates can serve as catalysts for other projects to grow up around them (i.e., factories need local suppliers, workers, etc.).

In July 2017, a consortium of five Chinese companies from Jiangsu province signed a $300 million deal with the UAE's Abu Dhabi Ports to develop a manufacturing operation in the free trade zone of Khalifa Port (KIZAD).[27] In December 2018, COSCO Shipping Ports (CSP), a subsidiary of China COSCO Shipping, and Abu Dhabi Ports inaugurated the CSP Abu Dhabi Container Terminal at Khalifa Port (the deep-water, semi-automated container terminal includes the largest container freight station in the Middle East, covering 275,000 meters), positioning Abu Dhabi as the regional hub for COSCO's global network of 36 ports and further connecting the Emirate to the major trade hubs along the BRI. The new terminal in Khalifa Port is the first international green-field subsidiary of CSP that invested $299 million in capital expenditure on construction and machinery at the terminal. CSP and Abu Dhabi Terminals (ADT) also signed an MoU to increase collaboration between the two facilities.[28]

Hence, Beijing's efforts to establish a comprehensive strategic partnership with the UAE must be seen within the wider context of its ambitious BRI, which focuses on connectivity and cooperation stretching from China across Eurasia. As President Xi Jinping said during his successful visit to the UAE, China and the UAE are natural partners for jointly building the new Silk Road. Beijing regards the UAE as a key pivot in implementing the BRI.[29]

Trade and investments

According to the PRC's comprehensive strategic partnership with the Emirates, the aim is to mitigate as much as possible the barriers to free trade, investment, industrial cooperation, and technical and engineering services to facilitate the integration of UAE Vision 2021 within the BRI framework. Both countries should take a series of measures, such as expanding free-trade zones, improving trade structures, seeking new potential areas for trade, and improving the trade balance, devising new initiatives for the promotion of conventional forms of trade.[30]

Both countries are working to increase the bilateral trade volume as a part of their comprehensive strategic partnership. According to China Customs Statistics (export-import), China's trade volume with UAE stood at $48.6 billion in 2019 (compared to $45.8 billion in 2018), and the Emirates has become China's second-largest trade partner in the Middle East.[31] According to the UAE International Investors Council, the annual trade volume between the PRC and the Emirates is forecast to grow to $70 billion by 2020 as the Asian country tops a list of targets for UAE investors.[32]

In April 2019, China signed $3.4 billion worth of new deals as part of China's BRI. The latest agreement is expected to boost an existing $53 billion worth of bilateral trade to $70 billion next year. As part of the new deals, the two countries launched several new investments including the development of a 60 million square feet station at the new Silk Road in Dubai for Expo 2020. The first agreement was signed with the Chinese company Yiwu, which will invest $2.4 billion in the project while the second agreement was signed with the China–Arab investment Fund, which will invest $1 billion to implement a 'vegetable basket' project in Dubai. These agreements will position Dubai well in the Belt and Road project where the emirate will be a major supply link to the global initiative and play an important role in international trade by further developing its logistics and shipping sectors.[33]

Beijing is the UAE's second-largest trading partner and largest source of imports in the Arab region. According to Ali Obaid Al Dhaheri, the UAE Ambassador to the

People's Republic of China, about 60 percent of the Chinese trade is re-exported through the UAE's ports to the MENA as well as the broader African continent. China deems the Emirates the first transit gateway to the MENA region due to its international stature and the facilities provided to investors in all fields,[34] with Dubai's Jebel Ali Free Zone being China's trade strategic gateway to the Middle East and Africa.[35]

The UAE's trade with the PRC accounted for nearly 30 percent of total Chinese exports to Arab countries and about 22 percent of total Arab-China trade, which amounted to $200 billion in 2018.[36] The Emirates has more than 4,000 registered Chinese companies operating in various sectors, including wholesale, financial, insurance, and real estate. There are more than 300 trade agencies, 817 Chinese investors, 5,000 trademarks, and 15 corporations, while between 200,000 and 300,000 Chinese residents are active on the Abu Dhabi and Dubai stock markets.[37] This figure places the UAE at the top of the list of Arab countries in terms of ties with China in addition to the fact that a significant proportion of Beijing's trade with the Arab world is passing through the country's ports as re-exports.

Exchange visits also strengthen a unique trade relationship, as manifested in Chinese President Xi Jinping's state visit to the UAE in July 2018, when the two countries signed 13 agreements and MoUs to strengthen strategic partnerships and bilateral cooperation across various sectors. The Agreements include approval for the Industrial Capacity Co-Operation Financial Group (ICCGC), the first Chinese state-owned financial services firm, to set up a financial center in Abu Dhabi Global Market, while the Abu Dhabi National Oil Company and the China National Petroleum Corporation (CNPC) agreed to explore joint business opportunities.[38]

The trade between China and the UAE is forecast to grow in the coming years. Beijing sees the Emirates as a gateway to access untapped consumer markets and lucrative investment opportunities in the Gulf region. As Chinese President Xi Jinping said, "The UAE is a friendly country and shares our dream, and so the Emirates has become a vital bridge between China and the Arab states."[39] In parallel, the UAE has been active in the PRC's economy, and hundreds of its companies are currently operating in China across various sectors including trade and industry, renewable energy, health, and financial services.[40] UAE enterprises and businesses have some 650 projects in China, such as UAE Stock Exchange and Dubai Pearl Project that are working hard to increase their foothold in China and to attract investors.[41]

In May 2019, Chinese manufacturing major East Hope Group said it is working with KIZAD on the feasibility of setting up development projects worth over $10 billion at Abu Dhabi's industrial hub. Under this agreement, both entities will look into a possible 15-year, three-phase plan to develop 7.6 sq km of land at KIZAD. In the first phase, East Hope would develop an alumina facility, while the second phase would include a red mud research center and recycling project. The final phase of the project would see large-scale upstream and downstream non-ferrous metal processing facilities, it stated. As part of the agreement, KIZAD would support East Hope Group across all areas as it investigates setting up in Abu Dhabi, including ensuring the best utility prices, acquiring the land, creating a masterplan, and handling the import of raw materials through Khalifa Port, and storage. The agreement also includes exploring options for the sustainable generation of energy and a sustainability program to preserve the environment, including a research center.[42]

Moreover, several major Chinese companies outside the financial sector have also begun to get access to untapped consumer markets and lucrative investment opportunities in the UAE. Between 2011 and 2017 about 35 mutual trade cooperation agreements were signed during 120 visits exchanged by officials from the two countries.[43] For example, Chinese companies, including Foton, Cherry, Dongfeng, and GAC Motors, entered the UAE's automobile sector. Chinese car sales are predicted to increase by 100 percent each year in the Emirates, and their market share is expected to reach double digits by 2020.[44] According to the *China Global Investment Tracker*, Beijing investments, and contracts in UAE from 2013 to 2019 reached $25.8 billion.[45]

In December 2017, Dubai Food Park (DFP) signed a $367 million investment agreement with Ningxia Forward Fund Management Company to build a China–UAE Food Industrial cluster in Dubai. The project will comprise six major components: meal processing, packaged food processing, cold chain storage, production of food packages, e-commerce and commodities exhibition, and bio-safety disposal of wastewater and wastes. The partnership marks a step forward to strengthen bilateral relations at various levels, particularly trade and economic relations between the UAE and PRC. The project is expected to consolidate China's stake in the Middle East food industry and further expand bilateral relations.[46]

In April 2019, on the sidelines of the Annual Investment Meeting (AIM) in Dubai, the Undersecretary for Foreign Trade of the UAE Ministry of Economy Abdulla Al Saleh said that the UAE is set to play a big role in China's BRI. Both countries have a strategic partnership to promote scientific research and renewable energy and water, and this cooperation is set to expand the mutual trade between the UAE and China.[47]

Financial integration

Under China's comprehensive strategic partnership with the Emirates, the formation and promotion of financial integration between the two countries are considered one of the essential cooperation areas to integrate UAE Vision 2021 into the BRI framework. There are several measures for the realization of financial integration between the two countries: including deepening financial cooperation and building a stable currency system, establishing an investment and financing system and a credit information system in Asia, expanding the scope and scale of bilateral currency swaps between the two countries, developing the bond market in Asia. In addition, making joint efforts to establish the Asian Infrastructure Investment Bank (AIIB), and financial institutions with good credit ratings to issue RMB-denominated bonds in China, thereby encouraging qualified Chinese financial institutions and companies to issue bonds in both RMB and foreign currencies outside China and to use the funds thus collected in countries along the BRI.[48]

In June 2015, the UAE signed the Articles of Agreement (AoA) for establishing the AIIB. The UAE joins 57 other nations that have already become founding members and now holds a 2.21 percent share. According to Sultan Ahmad Al Jaber, UAE Minister of State, establishing the AIIB articulates the vision of wise leadership and the importance they attach to supporting infrastructure development projects. This agreement is crucial in paving the way for accelerating economic development across Asia. In addition to enhancing the country's role within the global economy, the UAE's affiliation to the institution as a founding member will support the country's growing interests in Asia.[49]

Several Chinese banks have made their way into the UAE's banking sector. The Industrial and Commercial Bank of China (ICBC), China's largest lender, the China Construction Bank (CCB), the Agricultural Bank of China (ABC), and the Bank of China (BOC) have all established branches in the UAE to provide financial support to Chinese investments and local enterprises. Other banks, including China Development Bank, also plan to open branches in the UAE. The ABC established its Chinese Renminbi Clearing Center (RMB) for currency exchange in the UAE while the ICBC has become the largest bond issuer in Nasdaq Dubai.[50] At the same time, the UAE has been active and has established many branches and offices in China's banking sector. Union National Bank was the very first Emirati lender to enter China in 2007 and then set up an office in Shanghai; UNB was followed in 2012 by the National Bank of Abu Dhabi and Emirates NBD. The Dubai Gold and Commodities Exchange is the first foreign market to use the new yuan-based gold fix, the Shanghai Gold Benchmark Price, to develop derivative products.[51]

The importance of the UAE–China relationship has been further enhanced by the establishment of the Joint Investment Fund, a $10 billion strategic co-investment fund, which was launched in December 2015 to focus on diversified commercial investments in a range of growth sectors. The fund, which reflects the growing partnership between the two countries, will be administered and managed by the Abu Dhabi state fund, Mubadala, and a subsidiary of the China Development Bank. The goal behind the initiative, with both parties providing equal financing, is to build a balanced fund that incorporates diversified commercial investments and covers a spectrum of growing sectors.[52] In 2018, the fund finalized its plans for investment in 12 projects valued at $1.07 billion.[53]

Energy cooperatioe

In the PRC's comprehensive strategic partnership with the UAE, energy cooperation is considered one of the critical areas of cooperation to integrate UAE Vision 2021into the BRI framework. Therefore, the new Silk Road can provide a new framework for more extensive Chinese investments in the Emirates energy industry. The UAE's geostrategic location, strong ties, energy cooperation, and expressed support for the BRI make the Emirates an attractive place for energy security and a key pivot to Silk Road trade routes.

Beijing's dependence on crude oil imports from the Persian Gulf, a leading oil-producing region, has been increasing gradually since 1993 when it became a net importer of oil.[54] In 2019, the value of crude oil imported into China totaled $238.7 billion (expanding by 77.7 percent). Forty-three countries supplied crude petroleum oil to China, but close to half (44.8 percent) of Chinese imported crude oil originates from just nine Middle Eastern nations; six Persian Gulf states are among the top 15 crude oil suppliers to Beijing. In 2019, the UAE was ranked in 8th place (up 9.5 percent), exporting some $7.3 billion (3.1 percent) worth of oil to China. It is the fifth-largest oil supplier to China in the Persian Gulf.[55]

According to the EIA, the Emirates is among the world's ten largest oil producers and is a member of the OPEC and the Gas Exporting Countries Forum (GECF). The UAE holds the seventh-largest proved reserves of oil and natural gas in the world at 97.8 billion barrel, with most of the reserves located in Abu Dhabi (approximately 96 percent). The other six Emirates account for just 4 percent of the UAE's crude oil reserves, led by Dubai with approximately two billion barrels. The UAE holds approximately 6 percent of the world's proved oil reserves.[56] Given its geostrategic location between East and West, the UAE (particularly Dubai) has emerged as the strategic gateway to Energy trade in the Middle East, the major trade network connecting Asia with the Mediterranean and North Africa.[57]

Beijing's Middle East policy has in recent decades been driven mainly by energy and economic interests: besides the large quantities of oil China imports from the region,[58] Beijing now also sees as it an investment destination to expand its footprint across trade routes stretching through central Asia into the Middle East and Africa.[59] In line with this strategic priority, China aspires to implement the BRI, an ambitious plan to revive the ancient Silk Road trading routes with a global network of ports, roads, and railways.[60]

The UAE–China energy partnership, though not as extensive as the Qatari and Saudi Arabian partnerships so far, does not come as a surprise. The Emirates has emerged as a trusted partner of Chinese energy security after landmark agreements in 2017 and 2018 that awarded China National Petroleum Corporation (CNPC) shares in Abu Dhabi's 40-year onshore and offshore concessions, the first time that a Chinese oil company could acquire stakes in upstream cooperation in an oil-producing country in the Middle East. Under the agreements, PetroChina, which is majority-owned by CNPC, has been granted a 10 percent stake in the Umm Shaif and Nasr concession, and a 10 percent stake in the Lower Zakum concession. Both concessions will be operated by state-owned Abu Dhabi National Oil Company (ADNOC Offshore), which produces 4.5 percent of the world's total crude output, on behalf of all concession partners.[61]

In an agreement negotiated during the state visit of President Xi Jinping to Abu Dhabi and afterward confirmed by the UAE leadership, ADNOC awarded two contracts worth $1.6 billion to BGP Inc., a subsidiary of CNPC, to conduct one of the world's largest 3D onshore and offshore seismic surveys. The survey will search for oil and gas in onshore and offshore sites covering an area of 53,000 sq km. The state-run CNPC already has two concession rights contracts with ADNOC worth around $3 billion. Since ADNOC's plan to expand its refining and petrochemical operations attracted global investors, the company signed a wide-ranging agreement with CNPC to explore energy partnership opportunities in the UAE. CNPC will examine potential investments in downstream projects including an aromatics plant, a mixed feed cracker for petrochemical production, and a new refinery in the Emirates.[62] Moreover, China Petroleum Engineering and Construction Corporation (CPECC), which is affiliated with CNPC, has been involved in different other projects in the UAE, including building oil gathering stations, pipelines, power transmission lines, as well as sewage systems.[63]

In addition to supplying China with an important part of its energy security, the UAE can also contribute to China's aim to establish the largest petrochemical complex.[64] This is modeled after an MoU that ADNOC signed with Saudi Aramco to jointly develop and build an integrated refinery and petrochemicals complex on India's west coast, at a total cost of $44 billion. The project will be the single largest overseas investment in the Indian refining sector and joint partnership (50:50) between the consortium from India and Saudi Aramco and ADNOC.[65]

Solar energy

Solar energy investments was another component in the UAE–China energy partnership. UAE is a global leader in renewable solutions, environment conservation, and climate change mitigation, while Beijing is the driving force for a global surge in solar energy investments. According to the Global Trends in Renewable Energy Investment 2018 report, China saw some 53 gigawatts of solar capacity added (more than half the global total), and $86.5 billion invested, up 58 percent in 2017.[66] China–UAE has investments in the region's largest renewable energy projects that use concentrating solar power (CSP) and photovoltaic panels in Abu Dhabi and Dubai, with a total generation capacity of 1,800 megawatts.[67]

Moreover, China's Silk Road Fund will invest $3.9 billion in a concentrated solar power (CSP) project in Dubai, the first Middle East project financed by the fund. The CSP project will be the world's largest and most advanced solar thermal power plant and the second ACWA Power project in Dubai that the Silk Road Fund is investing in.[68] Beijing is also providing financing (Chinese banks are providing two-thirds of the $3. billion) and construction for the 2,400MW Hassyan Clean Coal project, the first Chinese power station in the Mideast, which is developing in partnership with China's Harbin Electric, Dubai Electricity and Water Authority (DEWA), and Saudi Arabia's ACWA Power (a developer, investor/operator of a portfolio of power generation and desalinated water production plants).[69]

Military ties

Under China's comprehensive strategic partnership with UAE, defense cooperation, including arms and technology trade and high-level exchange of visits, has become an increasingly significant part of integrating UAE Vision 2021 into the BRI framework. According to a UAE–China joint statement on strategic partnership in July 2018, the two countries are ready to enhance practical cooperation between the two armies. This aim is represented in high-level exchange visits and communication, joint weapons training, and the training of military personnel. The two sides are also keen on cooperating in the science, technology, and defense industry development of mutual interest through preparing a joint working plan. The two countries agree on enhancing cooperation and exchange of information on maritime security. The two sides also agree on rallying efforts on counter-terrorism issues, exchanging of expertise and information on combating terrorism, and strengthening individual training and capacity-building in that regard.[70]

In March 2019, Minister of National Defense Wei Fenghe said, China attaches great importance to the development of its relations with the UAE and regards the Middle Eastern country as a natural partner for joint construction of the Belt and Road Initiative proposed by China. In recent years, military ties between the two countries have witnessed rapid and in-depth development, demonstrated by frequent mutual visits by top military officials and the fruitful cooperation in related areas. China is willing to work with the UAE to promote bilateral military ties to a higher level and implement the important consensus reached by the leaders of the two countries.[71]

In February 2019, according to China's State Administration for Science, Technology, and Industry for National Defense (SASTIND), China Shipbuilding Industry Corporation (CSIC) established a representative office in Dubai. CSIC's new office will be used as a base to expand sales across the Gulf region and will be focused on pursuing both military and civilian business opportunities. The CSIC's presence in Dubai is in line with China's 'One Belt, One Road' initiative to deepen economic ties with countries in the Middle East.[72]

According to the *Stockholm International Peace Research Institute*, the Middle East is one of the world's biggest arms markets. Arms imports by countries in the Middle East increased by 61 percent between 2010–2014 and 2015–2019, because most states were directly involved in violent conflict, and accounted for 35 percent of total global arms imports over the past five years. Meanwhile, the PRC was the fifth-largest arms exporter in 2015–2019 and significantly increased the number of recipients of its major arms: from 40 in 2010–2014 to 53 in 2015–2019. Over the past 12 years, China has exported 16.2 billion units of ammunition mostly to countries in Asia, the Middle East, and Africa.[73]

China, according to the Royal United Services Institute, was a significant supplier of military drones to Middle East countries, especially those that are barred from importing them from the US. The UAE has had Chinese Wing Loong I drones since 2016 and started receiving its purchases of the upgraded and deadlier Wing Loong II in early 2018. The UAVs, intended for surveillance and reconnaissance, can carry a range of weapons including missiles and laser-guided bombs to blow up targets on land or in the air.[74]

People-to-People Bond

As part of China's comprehensive strategic partnership with Emirates, enabling the people of the two countries to bond along the Silk Road is vital to integrate the UAE Vision 2021 within the BRI framework. The promotion of extensive cultural and academic exchanges are aimed to win public support for deepening bilateral and multilateral cooperation, as well as providing scholarships, holding yearly cultural events, increasing cooperation in science and technology, and establishing joint laboratory or research centers and international technology transfer centers.[75]

Linguistic, cultural, and tourism cooperation is another important aspect of the China–UAE comprehensive strategic partnership, and both nations have outlined their intention to expand the collaboration in these areas in the coming years. China and the Emirates have come to recognize the importance of overcoming linguistic-cultural barriers; thus they are working in cooperation to increase the number of Emirati and Chinese professionals who are acquainted with each other's societal norms and customs, methods of performing business, and national and institutional interests.[76]

The two governments are pursuing this goal in a variety of ways, perhaps most importantly in the sphere of education. For some time, Chinese and Emirates universities have offered a wide range of Chinese and Arabic language courses, and also promoted Chinese cultural events, including an annual celebration of the Spring Festival. The academic cooperation between the two countries is part of the effort to promote cultural understanding between the nations.[77] In December 2015, China and the UAE signed an agreement for collaboration in scientific education, the granting of university scholarships, and the exchange of faculty members.[78]

In May 2019, China's Sun Yat-Sen University (one of China's elite research institutions), the UAE, and Gulf Medical University (GMU) signed an MoU for educational, training, research collaboration as well as joint research and academic and student exchanges to forge stronger ties between China and the Middle East. The collaboration includes several research, academic, staff, and student exchanges. The alliance will include the joint delivery of the Executive master's in healthcare management and Economics (EMHME), offered by GMU's College of Healthcare Management and Economics.[79]

Meanwhile, according to the *Hanban website*, the Chinese government established Confucius Institutes for providing Chinese language and culture teaching resources worldwide. In 2019, 550 Confucius Institutes and 1,172 Confucius Classrooms and 5,665 teaching sites were established in 162 countries and regions, receiving about eleven million students.[80] In 54 countries involved in the Belt and Road Initiative, there are 153 Confucius Institutes and 149 primary and high-school Confucius Classrooms.[81] In the Middle East, there are eighteen Confucius Institutes; two of them are in the UAE.[82]

The first Confucius institutes in the Persian Gulf region opened in 2011 at the University of Dubai and the second was officially inaugurated in 2012 at the Zayed University. Both institutes offer students the opportunity to learn the Chinese language as well as courses related to Chinese culture.[83] At the same time, the UAE became the first Arab country to establish an institution for Islamic studies in China.[84] Confucius Institutes in Abu Dhabi and Dubai, an ongoing initiative to teach Chinese in 200 UAE schools and frequent visits of Chinese artist groups to the UAE, have also enhanced cultural and educational relations. China's plan to open a Chinese Cultural Centre in the UAE is in progress.[85]

China's cooperation with the Emirates has increased the number of Chinese students learning the Arabic language, and at least 40 institutions (universities and schools) around the country now offer Arabic classes.[86] In the UAE, 20 Chinese teachers in eleven schools already started teaching the Chinese language, and the country is planning in 2019 to teach the Chinese language in 100 schools.[87] To strengthen their relationship, China and the Emirates have also initiated study abroad programs and educational exchanges,[88] including professors and administrative staff.[89]

The two governments also encouraged cultural diplomacy and dialogue, which will contribute to further deepening the comprehensive strategic partnership in the future. For instance, cultural activities such as the Chinese New Year celebrations 2018 were held in seven places in the Emirates and attracted an extraordinary number of Chinese tourists and locals.[90] In July 2018, the UAE–China Week – including Chinese Film Week and the Chinese Book Exhibition Week – was held for the first time, celebrated in both to highlight local heritage. The same venue also hosted daily events featuring traditional Chinese plays and musical performances along with showcasing traditional Emirati culture.[91] Noura Al Kaabi, Minister of Culture and Knowledge Development, said: "UAE–China Week facilitated cultural intermingling and has become a platform to allow thought leaders and artists to meet, exchange views, and learn about each other's cultures and traditions."[92] Furthermore, the Chinese president on his visit to the Emirates announced the opening of a Chinese cultural center in Abu Dhabi, and PRC support and participation for Expo 2020 in Dubai, which will be the first expo held in the Middle East.[93]

China's links with the GCC states have strengthened due to the introduction of additional and direct airline routes, the steady growth of the Chinese economy, and

Chinese tourists' increasing disposable income. According to data from Colliers International published ahead of Arabian Travel Market (ATM) 2019, the number of Chinese tourists traveling to the GCC is expected to increase 81 percent from 1.6 million in 2018 to 2.9 million in 2022, and the UAE will steadily increase their Chinese visitor arrivals with a growth of 13 percent. The GCC countries currently attract just one percent of China's total outbound market, but positive trends are expected over the coming years, to as many as 400 million tourists.[94]

According to the Chinese Ministry of Culture and Tourism, 149.72 million outbound trips were made by Chinese tourists in 2018, up 14.7 percent from the previous year.[95] The UAE is now the most favored first stop for Chinese tourists traveling to Arab destinations in the Middle East. In 2017, the number of Chinese tourist arrivals in the Emirates exceeded one million for the first time in history, and about 3.5 million Chinese tourists transited through the UAE. To facilitate and encourage the people-to-people exchange, Beijing granted visa-free status to citizens of the UAE in 2017, making it the first Middle Eastern state to enjoy such an arrangement in China.[96] According to the Chinese Ambassador to the UAE, Ni Jian, over 1.1 million Chinese tourists visited the UAE in 2018, thanks to the mutual visa-exemption arrangements between both nations.[97]

Dubai has become one of the favorite tourist destinations for Chinese tourists to the UAE (30 flights a week). According to the Dubai tourism office, the number of Chinese tourists to Dubai rose by 12 percent in 2018 over 2017. The number of visitors to Dubai in 2018 hit 15.95 million, up 0.8 percent than 2017, and China ranked the fourth year-on-year growth with 875,000 visitors.[98] In 2019, the number of foreign visitors to Dubai increased 5.1 percent to 16.7 million, and the number of Chinese visitors rose 15.5 percent to 989,000.[99] Chinese visitors China's expanding tourism relationship with the Emirates will help to strengthen the comprehensive strategic partnership between both nations.

Summary

The Emirates' strategic geographic location makes the country a marketplace of great potential and influence in the entire MENA region. The success and the rapid growth of China's ties with the Emirates stem from the UAE's pivot role as a regional re-export hub, with infrastructure, financial services, energy, transport, and communication, as well as a business-friendly environment. This provides a regional base of operations that gives Chinese companies a greater presence throughout the Arabian Peninsula and the Middle East – circumstances essential for the realization of the BRI. Both states have become important partners to each other, especially because the Emirates attempted to diversify its economy away from oil-reliance (UAE Vision 2021). The mutually beneficial arrangement of China's investments and the UAE's unique strategic geographic location on global trade routes enables China to expand its Middle East footprint while providing opportunities for UAE to profit from the partnership.

▌▌ Iraq

In April 2017, China made a policy decision to take an active role in the economic reconstruction of Iraq in the post-Islamic State era. Chinese Foreign Minister Wang Yi proposed that Iraq could become a component of the Belt and Road Initiative. This chapter examines the deepening China–Iraq strategic partnership and the synergy between the Belt and Road Initiative (BRI) within the rebuilding of Iraq to understand the extent of the bilateral engagement and Iraq's integration within the implementation process of the BRI. Beijing's strategic partnership framework with Baghdad is based on shared or mutually complementary economic interests, primarily a comprehensive strategic partnership on energy cooperation within the context of the BRI. However, in the post-Islamic State era, violence, terrorism, political instability, and social divisions are expected to continue to pose significant threats to Chinese investments in Iraq.

The relations between the PRC and Iraq have developed significantly in the past years, ever since the two countries established a strategic partnership in 2015. Upgrading their relationship to a strategic partnership has opened up a new chapter in China–Iraq friendship, which has brought new opportunities for mutually beneficial cooperation in various fields. As Chinese President Xi Jinping said in a meeting with Iraqi Prime Minister Haider al-Abadi, the new strategic partnership would provide "a solid foundation" for future advances in the relationship, and Chinese assistance in "energy, electricity, communication and infrastructure" projects in Iraq, tied to China's Belt and Road Initiative, will assist in Iraq's economic reconstruction.[1]

The One Belt, One Road Initiative, put forward in October 2013 by Chinese President Xi Jinping, is a $1 trillion project designed to connect Beijing to the global market by linking Asia and Europe via a set of land and maritime trade routes. The concept took form over several years and has now become a cornerstone of President Xi's foreign policy. Iraq stands at an ideal position, being neighbored by three participants in the BRI in the form of Turkey, Iran, and Saudi Arabia. The Iraqi government would stand to benefit more from engaging in bilateral projects with these countries to connect its infrastructure to theirs to gain access to the Belt and Road. Although Baghdad is not an official part of the BRI framework, it is surrounded by countries that are, and can, therefore, serve as a natural extension of the initiative.[2]

In this context, it is essential to understand the new phase in the rebuilding and reconstruction of Iraq, a process of deepening China–Iraq's strategic partnership, and the impact on the implementation of the BRI. This chapter examines developing China–Iraq strategic partnership, and the synergy between the BRI and the rebuilding process of Iraq, to understand the extent of the bilateral engagement and Iraq's integration within the implementation of the BRI.

The main argument presented is that Beijing's strategic partnership framework with Baghdad is based on shared or mutually complementary economic interests, and the main foundation of this comprehensive strategic partnership is energy cooperation within the context of the BRI. Chinese investment in the construction of power stations, cement factories, oilfields, and other projects, as part of their contribution to reconstruction in Iraq under the BRI framework, generates mutually beneficial cooperation and more economic benefits to the two nations.

Iraq and the Belt and Road Initiative

The PRC's strategic partnership with Iraq includes six major areas for cooperation within the Belt and Road Initiative. These areas are policy coordination, connectivity, trade and investments, energy cooperation, financial integration, and military ties. Nevertheless, each country views the Belt and Road Initiative framework and reacts to it according to its perspective and the consequences for its national interests and international status. Consequently, the two countries have very different attitudes about how to realize the vision. Despite the development of closer ties, the China–Iraq relationship remains largely centered on Iraqi oil and gas.

Policy coordination

As part of China's strategic partnership with Iraq, promoting political cooperation between countries, creating mechanisms for dialogue and consensus-building on global and regional issues, developing shared interests, deepening political trust and reaching a new consensus on cooperation are important elements of the potential to integrate the rebuilding of Iraq within the Belt and Road Initiative framework.[3]

In December 2015, during the visit of Iraqi Prime Minister Haider al-Abadi to China, the two countries decided to upgrade their relationship to a strategic partnership. According to Chinese President Xi Jinping, the new strategic partnership would provide "a solid foundation" for future advances in the relationship. The Chinese President also said that the PRC was ready to strengthen the integration of the two countries' development strategies within the framework of the Belt and Road Initiative and assist Iraq's reconstruction in energy, electricity, communication, and infrastructure. Beijing pledged to encourage and support Chinese companies to participate in the construction of large projects in Iraq.[4]

China and Iraq signed five agreements and MoUs on economic, technological, military, diplomatic, and oil and energy cooperation. The first MoU included participation in building the economic belt of the Silk Road and the Maritime Silk Road for the twenty-first century. The second MoU related to economic and technological cooperation between the two countries. The third was a framework agreement on cooperation in the field of energy. The fourth was in the field of military cooperation between the two countries, and the fifth was an agreement on the mutual visa exemption for diplomatic passports.[5]

In August 2018, using the occasion of the 60th anniversary of the establishment of diplomatic relations between China and Iraq, Chinese President Xi Jinping said he was willing to work with the Iraqi president to deepen the bilateral strategic partnership, adding that both countries would carry out mutually beneficial cooperation. In his congratulatory message, the Chinese president pointed out that, since the establishment of diplomatic relations 60 years ago, bilateral relations have maintained a good momentum of development, and cooperation in various fields has steadily advanced due to the joint efforts of both sides. The establishment of the strategic partnership in 2015 opened up a new chapter in China–Iraq friendship, which has brought new opportunities for bilateral ties. Beijing attaches great importance to the development of China–Iraq relations, adding that the two sides should synergize development strategies under the framework of jointly building the BRI, and carrying out mutually beneficial cooperation to bring more benefit to the two peoples.[6]

According to China's Ambassador to Iraq, Chen Weiqing, the Silk Road reduced the distance between the Chinese and Iraqi people, strengthened their friendship by starting friendly exchanges between the two cradles of past civilization and the joint development of the two countries in the present. In the post-Islamic State era, Iraq has entered into a new phase of building and reconstruction, and this provides new opportunities for further developing China–Iraq relations.[7]

In April 2019, a senior Chinese delegation led by Deputy Minister of Foreign Relations of the CPC Central Committee, Lee Joon, visited Iraq and expressed their country's readiness to contribute to the rebuilding of areas destroyed during the war with the Islamic State. According to a statement by the Iraqi Foreign Ministry, "Iraq attaches great importance to the strengthening of relations with the Republic of China and the expansion of . . . ties in all its political, economic and security forms." Iraq called for "increasing China's support for Iraq in the reconstruction of infrastructure through the expansion of investments between the two countries, as well as coordination in the area of security."[8]

China's new ambassador to Iraq, Zhang Tao, stated that Beijing is willing to work together with Baghdad to further deepen political mutual trust, strengthen pragmatic cooperation in various fields under the framework of the Belt and Road Initiative, and deepen China–Iraq strategic partnership. Iraqi President Barham Salih confirmed his country's willingness to extend relations with China and declared that he regards China as an important strategic partner and that Baghdad is willing to actively participate in the construction of the BRI to continuously further bilateral political, economic, and cultural cooperation.[9]

In September 2019, Iraqi Prime Minister, Adel Abdel Mahdi, announced during a state visit to Beijing that his country will sign on to China's BRI international infrastructure project. "Iraq has gone through war and civil strife and is grateful to China for its valuable support". According to Chinese President Xi Jinping, "China would like, from a new starting point together with Iraq, to push forward the China–Iraq strategic partnership". The two countries would collaborate on oil and infrastructure projects. Iraq is China's second-biggest oil supplier, while Beijing has become Baghdad's biggest trade partner over the last few years.[10]

Energy cooperation

As part of China's strategic partnership with Iraq, investment in energy infrastructure is considered one of the areas of cooperation critical to integrate Baghdad into the BRI framework. The central theme of the strategic partnership between the two nations is energy cooperation. Therefore, the new Silk Road can fuel a long-term and comprehensive strategic partnership on energy cooperation for more large-scale Chinese investment in the Iraqi energy industry. Beijing is considered the foremost trading partner of Baghdad, and Iraq, in turn, is the second-biggest oil supplier to China in West Asia, and the fourth biggest trading partner of China in the Middle East. Beijing imports about $20 billion worth of crude oil from Baghdad a year, while Iraqi imports from China now reach $7.9 billion annually.[11] In 2013, China became the world's largest net importer of total petroleum and other liquid fuels, and by 2017 had surpassed the US in annual gross crude oil imports by importing 8.4 million barrels per day (b/d) compared with 7.9 million b/d of US crude oil imports. In that year, an average of 56 percent of China's crude oil imports came from countries within the Organization of the Petroleum Exporting Countries (OPEC). New refinery capacity and strategic inventory stockpiling, combined with declining domestic production, were the significant factors contributing to its increase in imports.[12]

Beijing's dependence on crude oil imports from the Persian Gulf, a leading oil-producing region, has been increasing gradually since 1993 when it became a net importer of oil.[13] In 2019, the value of crude oil imported into China totaled $238.7 billion, expanding by 77.7 percent since 2015 but declining by –0.2 percent from 2018 to 2019. Forty-three countries supplied crude petroleum oil to China, but close to half (44.8 percent) of Chinese imported crude oil originates from just nine Middle Eastern nations, and six Persian Gulf states are among the top 15 crude oil suppliers to Beijing. In 2019 Baghdad was ranked in third place, exporting some $23.7 billion (9.9 percent) worth of oil to China.[14]

According to the U.S. Energy Information Administration (EIA), Iraq is the second-largest crude oil producer in OPEC, after Saudi Arabia. It holds the world's fifth-largest proved crude oil reserves, nearly 149 billion barrels (representing 18 percent of proved reserves in the Middle East and almost 9 percent of global reserves). Most of Iraq's major known fields – all of which are located onshore – are either producing or are in development. Iraq's crude oil production grew by an average of about 300,000 barrels per day (b/d) from 2013 through 2017 (including oil produced in the Iraqi Kurdistan Region), and it averaged 4.5 million b/d in the first half of 2018.[15] According to the International Monetary Fund (IMF), Iraq's economy is heavily dependent on crude oil export revenues. In 2017, crude oil export revenue accounted for an estimated 89 percent of Iraq's total government revenues.[16]

Energy security and infrastructure development are areas in which the two countries have great potential to cooperate within the context of the BRI. Baghdad is one of the world's most important oil producers, and Beijing is the largest energy consumer in the world. Under current conditions, and up to the foreseeable future, China is one of the most important options to attract global resources required for promoting Iraq's energy infrastructure development. They are linked together by their common interests in that their energy industries supplement and complement each other. On the one hand, China will look to direct investment in infrastructure assets associated with Baghdad's oil industry, which has emerged as an increasingly important export partner over the past decade. On the other, Beijing will aim to garner geopolitical influence by participating in broader reconstruction efforts in a country lying along a key artery of its BRI.[17]

In December 2015, China and Iraq pledged to establish a long-term, stable energy partnership. As part of the MoU, Beijing expressed its willingness to increase energy cooperation with Iraq, including oilfield projects and refinery construction in the country. Both countries agreed on a long-term and comprehensive strategic partnership on energy cooperation, especially in the oil and gas sector. More investment was to be channeled to the energy sector, and governments and enterprises were encouraged to cooperate in the areas of crude oil trade, oil-gas exploration and development, oilfield engineering service technology, construction of storage and transportation facilities, chemical refining engineering, and energy equipment. The two countries also reached a consensus on using China-made equipment to support oil-gas exploitation in Iraq.[18]

Oil

In the past decade, Chinese energy companies, such as CNPC, Sinopec, CNOOC, Sinochem, and Norinco, have become involved in investment and oil extraction in several major Iraqi oil fields, including al-Ahdab, ar-Rumaylah, al-Halfaya, and Misan. The close energy cooperation between Beijing and Baghdad brought about an increase in Iraqi oil exports to China from zero in 2007 to 270 million barrels annually by 2017, so that Iraq became China's second-largest oil supplier in West Asia, next only to Saudi Arabia.[19]

Today, the Chinese oil state-owned enterprises have a visible presence in the development of Iraq's major oil fields. The three major Chinese oil companies – China Nationa Petroleum Corporation (CNPC), China National Offshore Oil Corporation (CNOOC), and Sinopec – all operate in Iraq. CNPC and CNOOC operate in Iraq's south, and Sinopec operates in the Kurdistan Region, areas responsible for more than 90 percent of Iraq's oil production. However, because of the different types of contracts under which the Chinese oil operates, the high risks do not automatically generate high profits.[20] Other oil companies such as China Petroleum Pipeline Engineering Corporation (CPPE), a subsidiary of the CNPC, Zhenhua, and private-sector oil companies Geo-Jade Petroleum and United Energy Group Oil Corporation, were also involved in purchasing Iraqi oil and investing in its fields.

In December 2017, the Iraqi oil ministry signed a deal with China's state-run Zhenhua Oil, a subsidiary of China's defense conglomerate Norinco, to develop the southern portion of the East Baghdad oilfield, where investment needed to develop the oilfield could reach $3 billion. Iraq has made significant changes to the new service contract with the Chinese company that links global oil prices and the cost of development. The new contract will allow Zhenhua to receive a $3.50 fee for each barrel of crude produced from the oilfield and will serve as a model for all upcoming contracts with international companies. Baghdad plans to utilize 20 million cubic feet of gas produced as a by-product of oil production from the East Baghdad oilfield to supply a nearby power station.[21] Moreover, CNPC expressed that it was interested in developing the Majnoon Oil Field in southern Iraq. The field was under the management of Royal Dutch Shell, but the company had been looking for a way out, handing over its operations to Basra Oil Corporation.[22]

As of November 2018, stated-owned Zhenhua Oil was set to sign a letter of intent with Iraq's state oil marketer SOMO for the establishment of a joint venture, to be based in the northern Chinese port city of Tianjin. The joint venture, under negotiation for months, was intended to offer China another crude supply option as the country is under pressure to cut oil purchases from Iran after Washington re-imposed sanctions on Tehran.[23]

Iraq is OPEC's second-largest oil producer, after Saudi Arabia. Its refining capacity was curtailed when ISIS overran its largest oil processing plant in Baiji, north of Baghdad, in 2014. In April 2018, Baghdad signed a contract with two Chinese companies, PowerChina, and Norinco International, to build an oil refinery at the port of Fao on the Gulf, and is seeking investors to build three more.[24] The refinery in Fao will have a 300,000 barrel-per-day capacity and include a petrochemical plant. Two additional refineries, each with a 150,000-bpd capacity, are planned in Nasiriya, southern Iraq, and in the western Anbar province. The third, with a 100,000-bpd capacity, is planned in Qayara, near Mosul, the northern Iraqi city.[25]

Chinese oil companies are the biggest investors in Iraq's energy sector, especially in the modernization and development of its oil infrastructure.[26] According to China's state-run *Xinhua* news agency, three Chinese companies are set to begin developing oil fields in Iraq, seeking to ensure supplies as their country faces a growing demand for energy. Private-sector oil companies Geo-Jade Petroleum and United Energy Group, as well as state-owned China Zhenhua Oil, have won tenders for the development of oil fields in Iraq. Geo-Jade will develop the blocks of Naft Khana in the eastern province of Diyala and Huwieza in the southeastern province of Maysan. Hong Kong-listed United Energy signed an exploration and development contract to develop the al-Sindibad block in the southern province of Basra. Zhenhua Oil will develop an eastern Baghdad oil field, with production expected to start in 2019. It aims for 40,000 barrels a day within five years.[27] According to the head of the state-run Oil Marketing Co, Iraq aims to supply China with about 60 percent more crude. Baghdad is ready to ship about 1.45 MMbpd to Beijing in 2019. The director-general of SOMO said, on the sidelines of the China International Import Expo that this compares to current sales of 900,000 bbl to long-term buyers, among them state traders Chinaoil and Unipec. SOMO's push into China includes a deal to start an oil trading venture with Zhenhua Oil, which will be based in Tianjin. The venture tentatively plans annual sales of about 8 million metric tons or about 160,000 bpd to smaller, independent refiners known as teapots as well as large petrochemical plants.[28]

Moreover, the Iraqi oil ministry held an auction for international energy companies, with eleven blocks on offer near the borders with Iran and Kuwait and in offshore Gulf waters. In January 2019, Baghdad signed a contract with China's CNOOC to conduct a seismic survey for two oil exploration blocks. The offshore survey was to be the first in Iraq's territorial waters in the Gulf and the onshore block near the border with Iran. The oil ministry held an auction for international energy companies, with eleven blocks on offer near the borders with Iran and Kuwait and in offshore Gulf waters.[29]

Gas

According to the Oil & Gas Journal (OGJ), Iraq's proved natural gas reserves were the 12th largest in the world (nearly 135 trillion cubic feet (Tcf) at the end of 2017.

About three-quarters of Iraq's natural gas reserves are associated with oil, most of which lie in the supergiant fields in the south of the country. In 2017, Iraqi dry natural gas production was 357 billion cubic feet (Bcf), with an additional 18 Bcf reinjected during the year. Iraq also flared 629 Bcf of natural gas, ranking as the second-largest source country of flared gas in the world behind Russia.[30] Hence, Baghdad is one of the key countries involved in the BRI framework, with considerable potential to attract Chinese investment and technology for the development of its energy infrastructure

In February 2019, China's Petroleum Engineering and Construction Corporation (CPECC) and Iraq's Basra Gas Company (BGC) signed a contract for constructing a natural gas liquids (NGL) plant in Iraq's southern province of Basra. The BGC will increase the current gas production capacity by 40 percent in the Basra facility. The new project will also reduce gas flaring and increase dry gas supply and NGL export capabilities. The Basra NGL facility will be built in the Ar-Ratawi area in the west of Basra and is scheduled for completion at the end of 2020.[31]

Connectivity

As part of China's strategic partnership with Iraq, the facilitation of connectivity is one of the important ways to integrate the rebuilding of Iraq within the BRI framework. Baghdad must optimize its infrastructure reconstruction projects to connect them to its neighboring countries to gain access to the BRI framework. Iraq lies along a key route of the BRI, which seeks to foster growing East–West overland trade by promoting greater logistical connectivity. Beijing and Baghdad can thus jointly contribute to the development of international transport overland routes and the creation of an infrastructural network that could gradually connect all the regions in Asia and also specific points in Asia, Africa, and Europe.

The Belt and Road Initiative is important for Iraq because it is located on the Al-Hareer Road, a 12,000 km-long land and sea road that linked Asia, the Middle East, and Europe hundreds of years ago with commercial, cultural, religious, and philosophical links. This road enabled the exchange of goods and products, such as silk, perfumes, incense, and spices as well as the cultural and scientific exchanges.[32]

At present, Iraq has not been listed as an active participant in the Belt and Road Initiative.[33] However, given that Baghdad's southern (Saudi Arabia), northern (Turkey), and eastern (Iran) neighbors are all slated to be participants of the BRI, it is in an ideal position. The Iraqi Government would stand to benefit greatly by engaging in bilateral projects with these countries to connect its infrastructure to theirs to gain access to the Belt and Road without being an official part of the initiative. More broadly, since Iraq is surrounded by countries that are part of the BRI, it can, therefore, serve as a natural extension of the Silk Road, as well as serving as a support base for the pursuance of several Chinese interests in the region, such as Syrian reconstruction. Hence, there is great potential for regional synergy in which Iraq can play a bridging role.[34]

Financial integration

As part of China's strategic partnership with Iraq, the formation and promotion of financial integration between the two countries are considered one of the cooperation areas to integrate Iraq's rebuilding process within the BRI framework. There are several measures needed for the realization of financial integration between the two countries, including deepening financial cooperation and building a currency stability system, establishing an investment and financing system and a credit information system in Asia, expanding the scope and scale of bilateral currency swaps between the two countries, developing the bond market in Asia, making joint efforts to establish the Asian Infrastructure Investment Bank (AIIB) and financial institutions with good credit ratings to issue RMB-denominated bonds in China, and encouraging qualified Chinese financial institutions and companies to issue bonds in both RMB and foreign currencies outside China and to use the funds thus collected in countries along the BRI.[35]

The Sino–Iraqi economic cooperation is still in the initial stage, and Baghdad has the potential to become a new AIIB member. In March 2019, the Iraqi Ministry of Transportation, Abdullah Luaibi, discussed the possibility of speeding up procedures of Iraq's accession to the AIIB. According to a statement by the ministry's media office, the Transportation Minister held an extensive meeting to discuss "drawing a road map in cooperation with the Chinese side to activate the role of Iraq in the Belt and Road Initiative". The AIIB could play a key role in financing investment opportunities in Iraq's infrastructure related to the BRI and facilitate foreign investment in the country.[36]

In March 2019, Iraq and China were set to finalize a significant bilateral agreement that would give investors access to roughly $10 billion in credit for companies to invest, super-charging China's involvement in the Iraqi economy. The deal was designed to accelerate the pace and widen the breadth of Beijing's involvement in the Iraqi economy, including the energy sector, and provide money needed for reconstruction and infrastructure projects that cannot be funded by the Iraqi budget alone.[37]

Trade and investments

Part of the PRC's strategic partnership with Iraq includes attempting to mitigate as much as possible the barriers to free trade, investment, industrial cooperation, and technical and engineering services to facilitate the integration of the rebuilding process of Iraq's war-depleted country within the Belt and Road Initiative framework. Both countries must take steps in that direction, such as expanding free-trade zones, improving trade structures, seeking new potential areas for trade, and improving the trade balance, devising new initiatives for the promotion of conventional forms of trade.[38]

Although Beijing's rapidly increasing energy demand, especially for petroleum and other liquid fuels, has made Iraq an important business partner, the cooperation goes well beyond oil and gas. Chinese companies are also investing in rebuilding infrastructure and reconstruction projects under the framework of the BRI that will become a crucial theme of their bilateral relations and could create new opportunities for partnerships in promising sectors between the Chinese companies and Baghdad.

According to China Customs Statistics (export-import), China–Iraq trade volume increased to $33.2 billion by 2019 (compared to $30.3 billion in 2018), and Baghdad was China's third partner in the Middle East.[39] The volume of trade exchange between the two countries is increasing every year by 10 percent. Beijing is considered the biggest trading partner of Baghdad, and Iraq is the second-biggest oil supplier to China and the fourth biggest trading partner of China in the Middle East.[40]

Beijing plays a meaningful role in Iraq's reconstruction in all areas. The Chinese government attaches great importance to participating in reconstruction, and Chinese companies are paying serious attention to training and qualifying Iraqi cadres. A significant number of Chinese companies are investing in Iraq, given Iraq's geographical significance in BRI. Chinese investments in Iraq are concentrated in oil explorations and infrastructure such as power plants, cement factories, and water treatment stations. As Iraqi Ambassador to Beijing Ahmad Berwari has said, "Chinese companies in Iraq produce about 60 percent of the electricity in the Iraqi capital, Baghdad."[41]

Since China and Iraq upgraded bilateral ties to a strategic partnership, the cooperation has generally been expanding significantly in various fields. This is best reflected through the growth of bilateral trade between the two countries, which grew from $2.6 billion in 2008 to $33.2 billion in 2019. More than half of the electricity in Baghdad city, the capital of Iraq, is produced by Chinese companies. In February 2018, China and other international states pledged $30 billion, mostly in credit facilities and investment, for reconstruction efforts in Iraq.[42]

According to Wang Di, Chinese Ambassador to Kuwait and envoy to the Kuwait international conference for the reconstruction of Iraq, China will continue to provide assistance within its capacity to Iraq through bilateral ways and participate in the economic reconstruction of the war-torn country. In recent years, the practical cooperation between the two counties is steadily moving forward, and China is willing to further cooperate with Iraq in all areas under the framework of the Belt and Road Initiative.[43] The Chinese approach brings together Iraq's reconstruction process and its integration within the implementation of the BRI framework. As Chinese Foreign Minister Wang Yi said to his Iraqi counterpart Ibrahim al-Jaafari on the sidelines of the Ancient Civilization Forum, "China will continue its active participation in the economic reconstruction of Iraq and do everything it can to help the country," and he thanked Iraq for its support of the BRI.[44]

In February 2019, Chinese company Tianjin Electric Power Construction Co., Ltd. (TEPC) won the bidding for an 800MW combined cycle power plant project in Maysan, Iraq. The project involves building an 800MW 9F class gas-steam combined cycle unit, which is expected to be completed in 33 months. The project marked the first oversea project TEPC won in 2019 as well as another breakthrough TEPC made in exploring the Iraqi market.[45]

The governor of Iraq's northern province of Kirkuk called for Chinese investment and expertise in the reconstruction of towns and villages in the province that were destroyed in battles against the Islamic State. "We in Kirkuk need Chinese expertise and support in the light of official and legal frames. Chinese companies can cooperate with the Kirkuk's provincial Chamber of Commerce and the Investment Board. We in Kirkuk are facing a severe shortage of services, especially in the field of electricity and the municipality, and we have some 130 destroyed towns and villages." For his part, the Chinese Ambassador to Iraq Chen Weiqing confirmed his keenness to cooperate with the Kirkuk province in the field of transport, communications, electricity, industry, and agriculture.[46]

Military ties

As part of the PRC's strategic partnership with Iraq, security cooperation including arms and technology trade has become an increasing part of integrating Baghdad into the BRI framework. In December 2015, during a visit to China, Iraqi Prime Minister Haider al-Abadi signed five agreements and MoUs on economic, technological, military, diplomatic, and oil and energy cooperation with Chinese Premier Li Keqiang.[47] According to the Chinese President, "China is keen to expand its military and defense cooperation, training and building of the Iraqi military capabilities and the exchange of information and military industries, and we are ready to respond to support Iraq in these areas."[48]

In the past, the two countries have also engaged in military trade, though it has often paled compared to Iraq's other military trade partners. During Iran–Iraq War, Baghdad was a major recipient of Chinese tanks and armored vehicles, which China also sold to Iran during the same period.[49] Shortly after the agreement for Bilateral Military Cooperation 2015, the Iraqi Security Forces (ISF) revealed that it was now capable of conducting drone warfare after having purchased Chinese-made CH-4B armed unmanned aerial vehicles in 2014. The CH-4, built by Chinese Aerospace and Technology Corporation, is a medium-altitude, long-endurance UAV with a payload of 350 kg. The CH-4B that Iraq ordered from China can carry a payload of 761 pounds, compared to the CH-4A with its 254-pound payload. Weapons can include two AR-1/HJ-10 anti-tank guided missiles, Chinese equivalents of the Lockheed Martin AGM 114 Hellfire, and two FT-9 GPS-guided bombs.[50]

In February 2018, according to the Iraqi Ministry of Defense, the Chinese-made CH-4B drones executed most of their attack and reconnaissance missions in northwest Iraq. Since their entry into operational service, they performed no fewer than 260 airstrikes against Islamic State targets, with a success rate close to 100 percent. This development suggests there is a market in Iraq for Chinese arms and technology trade, specialized military equipment that is either too heavily regulated in the US markets or prohibitively expensive.[51]

According to the Iraqi news agency, the government of Iraq acquired the Chinese FD-2000 air defense system, the export version of the HQ-9, an anti-aircraft system that successfully shot down a ballistic missile in 2010. It has gained a reputation for being a cheap substitute for the American Patriot or Russian S-300. The HQ-9, manufactured by the China Precision Machinery Import-Export Corporation (CPMIEC), is ideal for defending bases and critical infrastructure from air attack. In sum, Baghdad is a perfect customer for Beijing's arms industry in genuine war-fighting products, including new tanks, APCs, missiles, and UAVs.[52]

Summary

China and Iraq enjoy a traditionally friendly relationship. Baghdad is considered China's important cooperative partner in West Asia. In recent years, the practical cooperation between the two counties has been steadily progressing, and Beijing is willing to further cooperate with Iraq in all areas under the framework of the BRI. Iraq certainly stands to benefit from the integration and participation in the Chinese Silk Road, especially from investments in reconstruction and infrastructure projects. Nevertheless, such benefits are not guaranteed but are highly conditional on the Iraqi Government both knowing what to expect from Beijing and taking a strong, consistent, and realistic negotiating position on the matter. In particular, Baghdad needs to be aware of Beijing's risk-averse behavior, its strategic, political, and diplomatic limitations, and its economic self-interest. Although oil is key to understanding China's upgraded involvement in the rebuilding process of Iraq, Beijing's relationship with Baghdad is much deeper and broader. China is embarking on a strategic approach to the Persian Gulf in the context of the Belt and Road Initiative, which has evolved into a top national strategy in China. The BRI strategy has become China's most important tactic for engaging with West Asia. This strategy encourages Chinese companies to go abroad in search of new markets or investment opportunities, in the context of China's BRI.

12 | Kuwait

In July 2018, the Kuwaiti emir made a state visit to China of great significance. Both countries agreed to establish a strategic partnership to create new opportunities for Kuwait, which aspires to diversify its economy and seek investment opportunities. This chapter examines various aspects behind the establishment of this partnership and explains the synergy between the Belt and Road Initiative (BRI) and the Kuwait Vision 2035 to understand the extent of economic engagement and bilateral relationship between the two nations. Beijing's strategic partnership framework with Kuwait is based on shared or mutual complementary economic and commercial interests, especially with the integration and implementation of the BRI and the Kuwait Vision 2035. However, despite a considerable increase in Chinese trade and investments in Kuwait, some significant internal obstacles and external challenges remain to the successful implementation of the synergy between the BRI and the Kuwait Vision 2035.

The past two decades have seen substantial changes in the global economy and geopolitical trends, with the rise of the PRC on the global and regional stage. These developments are creating new opportunities for the Middle East (West Asia) countries as they look to diversify their economies, increase trade, and seek investment opportunities in emerging markets; this includes schemes such as forging strategic partnerships with China to promote the BRI and to incorporate it into their national development plan. All of this reflects a growing tendency among the GCC states, which seek to benefit from the favorable business conditions in China, as well as China's expertise and experience in its rapid path to economic development.

Kuwait, a very small country with an area of about 18,000 square kilometers, is no exception to this burgeoning trend. This tiny emirate is nestled atop the strategic Arabian Peninsula located in the northwestern corner of the Persian Gulf, sharing 462 kilometers of land boundaries with Iraq and Saudi Arabia, and commanding a coastline of 499 kilometers.[1] Kuwait was one of the first Gulf countries to establish diplomatic relations with China, 47 years ago, on March 22, 1971.[2] Relations between China and Kuwait have been developing smoothly and growing steadily since the establishment of diplomatic relations. The two countries enjoy cordial and friendly bilateral relations, share identical or similar views on many major international and regional issues, and are constantly tendering sympathy and support to each other. They have also been working in coordination to broaden and deepen cooperation in the political, economic, and social fields.

The relative decline of U.S. hegemony and power in the Middle East and the emergence of a rapidly rising China, which seeks to assume significant roles in the region, were seen to have the potential to impact the stability of the balance of power.[3] With this in view, Kuwait has started to seek ways to invest in stronger ties with China, as well as with other powers, to strengthen its position in this increasingly vulnerable geopolitical balance of power. Kuwait, like the other GCC countries, is determined to preserve its strategic alliance with the United States but is also seeking to hedge itself against the threats that emanate from regional crises or power competition to guarantee its security in the future.[4]

The one trillion-dollar One Belt, One Road initiative, put forward in October 2013 by Chinese President Xi Jinping, seeks to connect Beijing to the global market by linking Asia and Europe via a set of land and maritime trade routes. The concept took form over several years and has now become a cornerstone of President Xi's foreign policy. The BRI has become a key theme of bilateral relations, and could also create opportunities for partnerships in the many promising emerging markets between China and the countries in the Persian Gulf region. Although the Gulf region is not directly along Belt and Road Initiative's trade routes, the Gulf countries have high economic and geopolitical stakes in Beijing's planned multicontinental trade corridor.

More importantly, the PRC's goal of securing oil and natural gas reserves from as many diverse sources as possible has brought it close to the Persian Gulf states, which are China's top energy suppliers.[5] A stable Gulf region is vital for Beijing's sustainable growth, and with the completion of the Gulf Pearl Chain, China can achieve effective management and control the flow of its energy needs. Consequently, it can open new markets and trade routes for the Gulf Countries, as the Silk Road would connect Gulf economies with the Southeast and East Asian economies to enhance economic integration and cooperation.[6]

This chapter investigates some of the aspects behind the establishment of the China–Kuwait strategic partnership and examines the synergies between the BRI and the Kuwait Vision 2035 to understand the extent of economic engagement and bilateral relationship between the two nations. Since Chinese President Xi Jinping first unveiled the Belt and Road Initiative in September 2013, Kuwait was among the first Arab countries to sign a cooperation agreement with China under the BRI framework, as well as one of the founding members of the China-initiated Asian Infrastructure Investment Bank (AIIB).[7]

The chapter's main argument is that the Beijing strategic partnership framework with Kuwait is based on shared or mutual complementary economic and commercial interests, especially with the integration and implementation of the BRI and the Kuwait Vision 2035. The strategic partnership between Kuwait and China contributes to the development of trade relations that have become diversified beyond the energy industry, and the two sides have economic interests that are increasingly complementary. The BRI complements Kuwait's Vision 2035 and could help the Kuwait government achieve its national development strategy.

Kuwait Vision 2035

The Kuwait Vision 2035 was launched in January 2017 by the government of Kuwait, and its name reflects the national plan for development also known as "New Kuwait" which is designed to make Kuwait a regional leader by 2035. This plan includes "initiatives that will transform our economy, create jobs, attract foreign direct investments and facilitate knowledge transfer in the fields of renewable energy, information technology, and the services sector", as the Minister of State for Cabinet Affairs stated in his opening remarks.[8]

The 'Kuwait Vision for 2035', a long-term national development plan, is a new grand economic plan aimed at transforming the country into a financial, cultural, and commercial hub in the northern Persian Gulf with tactics to extend its activities to Asia and Europe via 164 strategic development projects. It also aims to increase foreign direct investment by 300 percent. The vision of the Amir Sheikh Sabah Al-Ahmad Al-Jaber Al-Sabah is to transform Kuwait into a financial, commercial, and service hub at local and international levels, through megaprojects and leading economic roles by the private sector.[9]

Kuwait's economy is heavily dependent on petroleum export revenues, which account for 88 percent of the government's budget revenues, 85 percent of exports, and 40 percent of GDP.[10] As a result, the Kuwaiti government hopes to push ahead with reforms to diversify the national economy to reduce its dependence on oil revenues and to transform the country so that it will be able to provide financial and commercial services worldwide. By 2035 the Kuwaiti government will have made investments of more than $100 billion in key economic and social sectors including oil and gas, North Zone Development, electricity and water, urban development and housing, health, education, transport, and communications, tourism and media, and the environment.[11]

The past two decades have seen substantial changes in the global economy and geopolitical trends, with the rise of China on the global stage. These developments are creating new opportunities for the GCC countries as they look to diversify their economies, increase trade, and seek investment opportunities in emerging markets; this includes schemes such as forging strategic partnerships with China to promote the BRI and to incorporate it into their national development plan. This reflects a growing tendency among the GCC states, which seek to benefit from the favorable business conditions in China, as well as from Beijing's expertise and experience in its rapid path to economic development.[12] The Gulf countries have strongly embraced and, in turn, benefitted from, a network of cooperation lines in various investment and infrastructure projects and other economic fields with China.

Kuwait and the Belt and Road Initiative

The PRC's strategic partnership with Kuwait includes five major areas for cooperation within the BRI. These areas are policy coordination, connectivity, trade and investments, energy cooperation, and people-to-people bonds. However, each country views the BRI framework and reacts to it according to its perspective and the consequences for its own national interests and international status. Therefore, the two countries have very different attitudes regarding how to realize the vision.[13] The

Kuwait Vision 2035 and China's Belt and Road vision have converged on a common economic development path, and their synergetic strategy will bring new opportunities for both sides. As a result, the realization of the BRI will provide new momentum for Kuwait's economic transformation.

Connectivity

According to China's strategic partnership with Kuwait, the facilitation of connectivity is one of the important ways to integrate the Kuwait Vision 2035 into the BRI framework. Kuwait should attempt to optimize its infrastructural connections and also to adapt its technical systems to those of the other countries in the BRI framework. This would lead Beijing–Kuwait to jointly contribute to the development of international transport maritime and overland routes and the creation of an infrastructural network that could gradually connect all the regions in Asia and also specific points in Asia, Africa, and Europe. In addition, there should be serious attempts to create low-carbon and green infrastructure.[14]

As a small state situated on the Persian Gulf, Kuwait's geographic location has been a significant factor in the development of the strategic partnership with the PRC. Kuwait's natural harbors are easier to access than those of other GCC states, which has led the country to become part of a major trade route. Given its unique geographic location, as a solid gateway for China to increase its ties to the GCC states and the Arabian Gulf countries, Kuwait is poised to play a pivotal role in helping realize the Belt and Road vision. For instance, an overland trade route running through Kuwait and continuing through Saudi territory could provide a safer and shorter route to the Suez Canal and the Red Sea than one that passes through the Bab el-Mandeb Strait, which has been facing instability ever since the outbreak of the war in Yemen. This would also provide the opportunity to enhance Chinese interaction with both Saudi Arabia and Kuwait.[15]

Kuwait enjoys a distinguished geographical location that connects the Persian Gulf with both maritime and overland routes, and this explains why China is so eager to collaborate with it on the BRI trade network. Beijing also wants to work with Kuwait on infrastructure projects, including the construction of Al-Hareer (Silk City). As part of the PRC's effort to revive the old Silk Road trading route that once connected Europe to Asia, Chinese companies are interested in building up to five uninhabited islands in Kuwait's eastern coast and connecting them to the BRI.[16]

Five years after Chinese President Xi Jinping first unveiled the Belt and Road Initiative, in September 2013, the Persian Gulf region is now emerging as one of the project's most important partners. Chinese infrastructure and construction projects in the Persian Gulf, which were spearheaded under the framework of the BRI, were extended to include Oman and UAE.[17] In Kuwait, China signed an agreement to cooperate on the $86 billion Silk City project. The Silk City and the five islands will serve as a huge economic free zone that will link the Arabian Gulf to central Asia and Europe. Beijing is also holding talks to link Kuwait with a planned network of railways that will make the country a major commercial center and a base for a network of railways which starts from China and passes through Central Asia and Gulf states.[18]

The Silk City and the five northern islands (Failaka, Warba, Boubyan, Miskan, and Awha) project are set to accommodate 700,000 residents within a designated urban area of 250 square kilometers, with the first phase expected to be completed by

2023. The Sheikh Jaber Al Ahmad Al Sabah Causeway (a bridge that links Kuwait City to Silk City) is now one of the largest infrastructure ventures in Kuwait. Currently 73 percent complete, the route will eventually be 37.5 km in length, extending from the Al Doha region, west of Kuwait City, to Al Shuwaikh Port in the capital and Al Sabiyah in the northeast. One of the main developments will be the Mubarak Seaport with a capacity of 24 berths that will help to increase trade through the Red Sea to Europe. The port, when complete, will be Kuwait's largest commercial trading hub.[19]

The Silk City mega-project has been under development since 2014 when the Kuwaiti government approved its final master plan and signed a cooperation MoU with the PRC for its development as a major component of China's Belt and Road Initiative.[20] The head of the Silk City project, Faisal Al Medlej, signed the agreement with China's National Development and Reform Commission, a government-run economic management agency, at its headquarters in Beijing.[21]

The Silk City, a $100 billion project, is the cornerstone of the Kuwait 2035 Vision and will play an important role in the country's diversification efforts to transform the country into a commercial and cultural hub for the region. It will also include a 1,000-metre skyscraper, a wildlife sanctuary, a new airport, a duty-free shopping zone, and media and conference facilities.[22] According to the Kuwaiti Ambassador to China, Samih Hayat, "There is a mutual and substantial consensus between New Kuwait 2035 vision and the BRI to revive the Silk Road and establish a commercial center to serve the world."[23]

As part of the Silk City and five islands development projects, Kuwait signed an MoU with the Huawei Company in July 2018 to implement the smart cities strategy in the country. (A "smart city" is an urban area that uses different types of electronic data collection sensors to supply information to efficiently manage assets and resources. For example, the strategy includes developing apps, such as to manage urban flows and provide real-time responses). The Huawei–Kuwait government MoU was divided into four sections that are connected with the development of intelligent infrastructure networks, security, virtual systems, and the digital transformation of various industries and central management in Kuwait. In November 2018, the Kuwait National Fund for Small and Medium Enterprise Development (SMEs) signed an MoU with the Huawei company to encourage and develop small- and medium-sized enterprises and to enhance companies' advanced services in information technology and communications, as part of the Kuwait Vision 2035.[24]

However, there is some skepticism about the implementation of the Silk City and the five islands development projects. This is not unexpected, given the uncertainty surrounding the Persian Gulf where ambitious leaders' mega-project proposals can come unstuck due to financial or political hurdles. There is also uncertainty regarding how many of these MoUs that were signed between Kuwait and China will be implemented. According to the International Monetary Fund, reform and project delays are major risks to Kuwait's outlook, alongside lower oil prices and regional security challenges. Kuwait's history of stop-start reforms and tardy project development sustains concerns about the ability to push the Silk City and the five islands development projects through the bureaucracy and the legal changes necessary to ease business procedures and open up the economy.[25]

Policy coordination

According to China's strategic partnership with Kuwait, promoting political cooperation between countries, creating mechanisms for dialogue and consensus-building on global and regional issues, developing shared interests, deepening political trust, and reaching a new consensus on cooperation is important to integrate the Kuwait Vision 2035 into the BRI framework.[26]

In July 2018, during the state visit of Kuwaiti Emir Sheikh Sabah Al-Ahmad Al-Jaber Al-Sabah in China, both countries agreed to establish a strategic partnership between the two countries to inject new impetus into bilateral ties and open up new prospects in the new era. President Xi Jinping called the two countries "tried and true friends".[27] Under the strategic partnership framework, China and Kuwait will synergize the BRI with Kuwait Vision 2035 and work to promote the establishment of a China–GCC free trade area at an early date.[28]

China plans to set up free trade zones with members of the GCC, which are an essential part of the Belt and Road project. In that respect, as long as the Qatar–Gulf crisis prevails and diplomatic and economic ties remain strained, let alone fully cut off, the creation of free-trade zones seems impossible. Though Chinese investments will not be directly affected by the current GCC conflict, the growing instability in the region could still harm China's economic cooperation with the Gulf States and will undoubtedly impact Beijing's regional trade prospects.[29]

Energy cooperation

In the PRC's strategic partnership with Kuwait, investment in energy infrastructure is considered one of the critical areas of cooperation to integrate Kuwait into the Belt and Road Initiative framework. Therefore, the new Silk Road can provide a new framework for more extensive Chinese investments in the Kuwait energy industry. Beijing is Kuwait's largest source of imports, and Kuwait is China's fourth-largest crude oil supplier in the Arab world. They are linked together by their common interests in that their energy industries supplement and complement each other.

According to the U.S. Energy Information Administration (EIA), Kuwait was the world's tenth-largest producer of oil and other petroleum liquids in 2017 and the fifth-largest producer of crude oil among the OPEC members. Despite its relatively small geographic size (about 6,900 square miles), in terms of production, it trailed only behind Saudi Arabia, Iraq, Iran, and the UAE in the production of oil and other petroleum liquids in 2017.[30] Kuwait holds the world's sixth-largest oil reserves and is one of the top ten global producers and exporters of total petroleum liquids (about 102 billion barrels, 6 percent of world reserves), and has an estimated 63 trillion cubic feet (Tcf) of proved natural gas reserves.[31]

In 2013, China became the world's largest net importer of total petroleum and other liquid fuels, and by 2017 China had surpassed the U.S. in annual gross crude oil imports by importing 8.4 million barrels per day (b/d) compared with 7.9 million b/d of U.S. crude oil imports. In that year, an average of 56 percent of China's crude oil imports came from countries within OPEC. New refinery capacity and strategic inventory stockpiling, combined with declining domestic production, were the significant factors contributing to its increase in imports.[32]

The year 2017 also highlighted some changes in the global oil market. First, despite the increase in the production of this raw material in the United States, its stored reserves were decreasing rapidly on an annual basis. Second, a sharp increase in oil imports from the United States to China contributed to the fact that Beijing became the world's largest importer of oil. Third, forecasts indicate that before 2025, the Middle Kingdom will overtake the U.S. as the largest consumer and will be responsible for 18–20 percent of the world's oil consumption.[33] According to the International Energy Agency's (IEA) World Energy Outlook 2017, China will overtake the U.S. as the largest oil consumer around 2030, and its net imports are forecast to reach 13 million barrels per day (mb/d) in 2040 (its oil import dependence will rise to 80 percent).[34]

China's dependence on crude oil imports from the Persian Gulf, a leading oil-producing region, has been increasing gradually since 1993 when it became a net importer of oil.[35] In 2019, the value of crude oil imported into China totaled $238.7 billion, expanding by 77.7 percent since 2015 but declining by -0.2 percent from 2018 to 2019. Forty-three countries supplied crude petroleum oil to China, but close to half (44.8 percent) of Chinese imported crude oil originates from just nine Middle Eastern nations, and six Persian Gulf states are among the top 15 crude oil suppliers to China. Kuwait is ranked in eighth place, exporting some $10.8 billion (4.5 percent) worth of oil to China.[36]

The PRC is Kuwait's largest source of imports, and Kuwait is China's fourth-largest crude oil supplier in the Arab world.[37] Kuwait's crude oil wealth and Beijing's heavy dependence on crude oil are the underlying keys to the rapidly growing energy relationship between the two countries. They are linked together by their common interests in that their energy industries supplement and complement each other. The energy relationship between the two countries includes cooperation in building oil refineries and petrochemical plants, in oil supplies, oil field services, and exploration, and oil services and equipment in the oil drilling sector.

In 2011, Kuwait Petroleum Corporation and China Petroleum and Chemical Corporation Limited (Sinopec) signed a $9 billion deal to build an oil refinery and petrochemical plant, with the completion date scheduled by 2017, in the southern coastal city of Zhanjiang.[38] In August 2014, Kuwait concluded a new ten-year deal with China's Sinopec Corp to nearly double its supplies by offering to ship the crude oil and sell it on a more competitive cost-and-freight basis. Under the deal, Kuwait will increase the volume of its crude oil exports to China up to 500,000 bpd over the next three years.[39]

In recent years, China has become one of the biggest oil drilling contractors in Kuwait. Chinese enterprises have won contracts for 64 projects in Kuwait, covering such sectors as oil field services and exploration, infrastructure, and telecommunications, with a total value of $13.7 billion. New contracts reached $3.01 billion in the oil drilling sector that are becoming landmark projects in China–Kuwait cooperation. Kuwait has so far bought Chinese-made rig equipment worth more than $635 million. The Sinopec International Petroleum Service Corp (SIPSC) owns 53 drilling rigs, taking up more than 45 percent of the Kuwait market.[40]

In July 2018, the Chinese oil services and equipment company Kerui Petroleum won $100 million worth of contracts for two ultra-deep well drilling rigs from Kuwait AREC. The contract follows another ultra-deep well drilling rig contract valued at $50 million concluded earlier this year, from Kuwait National Drilling Company.[41] In October 2018, Kuwait signed an MoU with Chinese NOC Sinopec to build a new refinery in south China. The new refinery unit will be constructed in partnership with Chinese NOC Sinopec.

In July 2018, Kuwait Petroleum Corporation (KPC) signed on a cooperation agreement with China's ShanDong Refining and Chemical Group to market Kuwaiti crude oil. This Chinese company is one of the leading oil industry bases in the country and is known for hosting a large number of private and state-owned oil refineries. The deal aims to expand joint investment platforms in the oil and logistics industries.[42] In November 2018, PetroChina, Sinopec, China's Sinochem Group (one by one) signed a 2019 crude oil supply deal with Kuwait, with volumes unchanged from this year.[43]

Trade and investments

According to the PRC's strategic partnership with Kuwait, the aim is to mitigate as much as possible the barriers to free trade, investment, industrial cooperation, and technical and engineering services to facilitate the integration of Kuwait Vision 2035 within the BRI framework. Both countries should take a series of measures, such as expanding free-trade zones, improving trade structures, seeking new potential areas for trade, and improving the trade balance, devising new initiatives for the promotion of conventional forms of trade.[44]

Although Beijing's rapidly increasing energy demand, especially for petroleum and other liquid fuels, has made Kuwait an important business partner, the cooperation goes well beyond oil and gas. Chinese companies are also investing in building infrastructure and construction projects under the framework of the BRI that becomes a crucial theme of bilateral relations and could create new opportunities for partnerships in promising sectors between the Chinese companies and Kuwait.[45] More important, Kuwait's signature on the agreement to establish a strategic partnership in July 2018 with China was an essential step in implementing and fulfilling the economic Vision 2035 and subsequent projects.

China views Kuwait as a key partner for cooperation in the BRI, and maintenance of regional peace and stability in the Gulf region. During his seventh visit to China in July 2018, the Kuwaiti Emir Sheikh Sabah Al-Ahmad Al-Jaber Al-Sabah and Chinese President Xi Jinping agreed to promote the BRI and incorporate it with the Kuwait Vision 2035. They also agreed to work together to establish a free trade area between China and the GCC. The two leaders found a consensus between the Kuwait Vision 2035 and China's BRI to revive the old Silk Road for creating a vibrant trade region and to restore Kuwait to its leading role in the commercial and economic fields within the region.[46]

Since the establishment of diplomatic relations between the two countries, bilateral economic and trade exchanges have become more frequent, and bilateral trade volume has been on the increase. The relationship commerce between the two countries has expanded rapidly over the years, and today, China is one of Kuwait's key trade partners.[47] According to *China Customs Statistics (export-import)*, China's trade volume with Kuwait decreased from $18.3 billion in 2018 to about $17.2 billion in 2019.[48] There are currently more than 40 Chinese companies operating in Kuwait with about 80 projects in progress in the sectors of oil, infrastructure, communications, and banking.[49]

According to the Chinese ambassador to Kuwait, Wang Di, the collective value of construction projects involving Kuwait and China in 2017 has hit $8.2 billion, the most lucrative deal Beijing has ever forged with a Gulf country.[50] In July 2018, a Chinese firm signed a $709 million contract with the Kuwaiti government to build infrastructure and roads for a new 18,000-unit housing project in Kuwait's South Matlaa, located west of the capital. Chinese technology and smartphone giant Huawei will execute the second phase of a fiber optics project after signing a $72 million contract.[51] Since the Kuwaiti government needs foreign investment to diversify its economy, it has urged Chinese companies to increase their investments in the country.[52]

The high-level contacts and the bilateral visits reflect the state of economic relations between the two countries. During these visits, several bilateral economic, trade, oil, and gas agreements were signed to boost bilateral trade and mutual investment. For instance, during the state visit of the Kuwaiti ruler Sheikh Sabah Al-Ahmad Al-Jaber Al-Sabah several agreements and MoUs were signed, aimed at boosting bilateral ties. The two countries have thus sealed a cooperation protocol to boost defensive industry cooperation, an MoU to encourage investment and upgrade cooperation between the Kuwait Direct Investment Promotion Authority (KDIPA) and the China Council for the Promotion of International Trade (CCPIT), and a cooperation agreement between Kuwait Petroleum Corporation (KPC) and China Export and Credit Insurance Corporation (Sinosure).

Moreover, an MoU on developing smart applications for Kuwait's Al-Hareer (Silk City) and Boubyan Islnds projects was also signed between Kuwait's Communication and Information Technology Regulatory Authority (CITRA) and Huawei Technology. Kuwait and China also inked an MoU on e-commerce, aimed to boost cooperation through facilitating trade between the two countries and achieving sustainable development in the field.[53]

The signing on several wide agreements/MoUs represents a significant step forward in China's commercial relationship with Kuwait business community, and will only serve to strengthen the strong and longstanding economic and commerce ties between the two countries. Although it is unclear how many of these agreements/MoUs represent completely new projects and how many mark incremental progress in deals struck over the past two years between Kuwait and China, one thing is clear: the test of these declared agreements/MoUs will be in their implementation and the promotion of follow-up transactions.

People-to-People Bond

According to China's strategic partnership with Kuwait, enabling the people of the two countries to bond along the Silk Road is also vital to integrate the Kuwait Vision 2035 within the BRI framework. The promotion of extensive cultural and academic exchanges are aimed to win public support for deepening bilateral and multilateral cooperation, as well as providing scholarships, holding yearly cultural events, increasing cooperation in science and technology, and establishing joint laboratory or research centers and international technology transfer centers.[54] In recent years, tourism and cultural cooperation have become another important aspect of the China–Kuwait strategic partnership, and both nations have outlined their intention to expand collaboration in these areas in the coming years. As Chinese Ambassador to Kuwait Li Minggang said, "People-to-people exchanges is a key factor to consolidate the foundation of relations between the two countries and the two governments have been actively engaging in visa issues to facilitate personnel exchanges."[55]

China's links with the GCC states have strengthened due to the introduction of additional and direct airline routes, the steady growth of the Chinese economy, and Chinese tourists' increasing disposable income. According to data from *Colliers International* published ahead of Arabian Travel Market (ATM) 2019, the number of Chinese tourists traveling to the GCC is expected to increase 81 percent from 1.6 million in 2018 to 2.9 million in 2022, and Kuwait will steadily increase their Chinese visitor arrivals with a growth of 7 percent. The GCC countries currently attract just one percent of China's total outbound market, but positive trends are expected over the coming years, to as many as 400 million tourists.[56]

Cultural cooperation has become another important aspect of the China–Kuwait strategic partnership and both nations have outlined their intention to expand the collaboration in this area in the coming years. In March 2018, Kuwait opened a Chinese center in its capital, Kuwait City, to promote cultural exchanges and deepen economic and trade cooperation. According to the director of the Chinese Center, Yao Jian, tea art, traditional Chinese medicine, and Chinese food are famous in Kuwait and it is hoped that more Kuwaitis and people from neighboring countries will enjoy the rich and colorful Chinese culture in this center.[57]

Summary

The Persian Gulf is in a unique geopolitical position, as it connects three continents Asia, Africa, and Europe, giving it a vital strategic significance in the realization of the BRI. In the last five decades, Kuwait and China have developed dense and multifaceted relations. Trade and economic relations have been foundational in developing these ties, with energy playing an important role. Increasingly, commercial relations are becoming more diverse and formalized, with foreign direct investment, and infrastructure and construction projects featuring heavily. Since China announced the BRI in 2013, Kuwait has regarded it as an engine to enhance bilateral cooperation.

Economic relations between Gulf countries and China have rapidly expanded, and the region's strategic importance to Beijing's infrastructure and energy-driven Belt and Road vision is clear although the Gulf region is not classified as a key corridor in the BRI architecture. This suggests China's determination to avoid being sucked into the region's multiple conflicts, with Beijing preferring to take a non-interventionist position, allowing it to remain neutral in most inter-regional disputes and to take advantage of the strategic and economic opportunities available. China is also switching its focus on energy in the region, which accounts for half of its imported oil, to more investments in trade and infrastructure construction projects that have risen substantially

Nevertheless, despite the potential economic opportunities for Kuwait's Vision 2035 to collaborate in the China BRI, there are some internal obstacles and external challenges. First, regional turbulence and political rivalry among major powers add to the challenges and uncertainties of cooperation between China and Kuwait. Second, some economic risks and barriers include susceptibility to the U.S. and European influence, the high barrier of market access, bureaucratic corruption and royal monopoly, fierce competition with other countries, bottlenecks in project funding, and local labor and commercial disputes.

Third, although state-owned companies remain the dominant investors in BRI projects, mainly in energy and transport, the Chinese private sector is less enthusiastic about investing in Kuwait's vast trade and infrastructure strategy. Beijing is also becoming warier of throwing money at the BRI project as it comes under pressure from the trade war with the United States; the decline in its foreign exchange reserves have further complicated its efforts to finance the new Silk Road.[58] Finally, as the BRI proceeds, there is a possibility that extremist groups and criminals might hijack or attack Chinese citizens and assets, as has taken place elsewhere in the region.[59]

13 | Qatar

China–Qatar ties have strengthened considerably in recent years. The relationship between the two countries has seen steady and smooth bilateral development in the political, economic, and cultural fields, in trade, energy, and other areas, and has given active play to the complementarities between the two economies. This chapter examines the motivation behind Beijing's measures to formalize a strategic partnership with Qatar to understand the impact and the extent of the Qatar–Gulf crisis on Doha engagement and integration within the Belt and Road Initiative (BRI).

Since the establishment of diplomatic relations in 1988, the People's Republic of China (PRC) and Qatar have enjoyed friendly relations, marked by the opening of embassies, mutual visits and exchanges of high-ranking official visits, and signing agreements in the field of investment and energy co-operation aimed at strengthening commerce and trade relations.[1] In recent years, the bilateral relations between Beijing and Doha have witnessed a significant development to further bilateral cooperation in the political, economic, cultural, trade, energy, and other fields, and have given active play to the complementarities between both economies.[2]

The $1 trillion BRI, put forward in October 2013 by Chinese President Xi Jinping, seeks to connect Beijing to the global market by linking Asia and Europe via a set of land and maritime trade routes. The concept took shape over several years and has now become a cornerstone of President Xi's foreign policy. The preeminent position of Qatar in the Gulf and extensively in the Middle East has a key role to play in the realization of China's new Silk Road Initiative, especially with its economic and geographical components.

This chapter analyzes the motivation behind China's measures to formalize strategic partnerships to understand the impact and the extent of the Qatar–Gulf crisis on Doha engagement and integration in the implementation of the new Silk Road initiative. The main argument is that China's measures to formalize strategic partnerships with Qatar are based on shared or mutually complementary economic and strategic interests. Doha discovered that more in-depth Sino–Qatari cooperation can brighten the prospects for Qatar's National Vision 2030 and could help it to escape from diplomatic and economic isolation. At the same time, Beijing finds Qatar a critical partner to promote the Belt and Road project, especially with its economic and geographical components which play a vital role in the creation of China–GCC free-trade zones.

Qatar National Vision 2030

The Qatar National Vision 2030 (QNV2030) is a master vision and roadmap towards Doha becoming a forward-thinking society capable of sustainable development to provide a high standard of living for all citizens by the year 2030. By defining long-term outcomes for Doha, it provides a framework within which national strategies and implementation plans can be developed. It assists Qatari government-led strategies, policy, planning, and allocation of funds and resources towards a unified goal. It also provides private sector companies and, to an extent, individuals, with a shared direction and purpose. The QNV2030 foresees development in four interconnected fields: human development, social development, economic development, and environmental development.[3]

There is a point of convergence of interests that can be built upon to forge a basis for cooperation between the QNV2030 and development of the BRI by linking these two projects in a way to set up a unified development strategy to the advantage of both. Qatar Vision 2030 is pretty much in line with the concept of development upheld by the Belt and Road vision, primarily in terms of the pursuit of economic, human, social, cultural, and environmental development. As Chinese Foreign Minister Wang Yi said, Qatar should take part in the realization of China's Silk Road Initiative since the Belt and Road project shares common cooperative opportunities with the Qatar National Vision 2030.[4]

Qatar and the Belt and Road Initiative

PRC measures to formalize strategic partnerships with Qatar includes seven major areas for cooperation within the BRI. These areas are policy coordination, connectivity, trade and investments, energy cooperation, financial cooperation, military ties, people-to-people bond. However, each country views the BRI framework and reacts to it according to its perspective and the consequences for its own national interests and international status. Therefore, the two countries have very different attitudes regarding how to realize the vision. The QNV2030 and China's BRI have converged on a common economic development path, and their synergetic strategy will bring new opportunities for both sides. As a result, the realization of the BRI will provide new momentum for Doha's economic transformation.

Policy coordination

China's measures to formalize strategic partnerships with Qatar involve: promoting political cooperation between countries, creating mechanisms for dialogue and consensus-building on global and regional issues, developing shared interests, deepening political trust, and reaching a new consensus on cooperation. These are the important goals to integrate the QNV2030 into the BRI framework.[5]

In November 2014, the historic visit of the Emir of Qatar, Tamim bin Hamad Al-

Thani, to China was a crucial milestone in the course of building the strategic partnership framework. The visit opened a new era of cooperation between the two countries and produced a clear and complete understanding to upgrade their relationship, as well as recognizing Qatar's regional role as an economic and security partner. As Chinese President Xi Jinping said, "Qatar is an important country that plays a unique role in the Middle East and Gulf region, and is a major partner of China in the region."[6]

The deep relations and strong economic ties in a wide range of cooperation areas that extend from the ongoing export of Qatari gas to Beijing to joint infrastructure construction projects and Chinese investments in Doha, through constructive and positive exchanges in the domains of finance, tourism, and culture, have helped to build a solid foundation for cementing these relations and to formalize a comprehensive strategic partnership in the future. As the Ambassador of the State of Qatar to the People's Republic of China, Sultan bin Salmeen al-Mansouri, said, "There has been comprehensive development. We have witnessed that since 2014."[7]

In January 2019, the Qatari Amir Sheikh Tamim bin Hamad Al-Thani arrived for a two-day state visit in China, and both countries agreed to deepen the bilateral strategic partnership and create a strategic dialogue between the governments. The last visit drew a roadmap to boost strategic partnership between the two countries in the fields of politics, economics, investment, energy, technology, and security cooperation. The Chinese President also called the two sides to further synergize their development strategies and jointly build the BRI.[8]

Connectivity

As part of China's measures to formalize strategic partnerships with Qatar, the facilitation of connectivity is one of the important ways to integrate the QNV2030 into the BRI framework. Qatar, which has a preeminent position in the Gulf and extensively in the Middle East, has a key role to play in the realization of China's Silk Road Initiative, especially with its economic and geographical components.[9]

Qatar is also in a position to benefit substantially from the implementation of the Silk Road Initiative since deeper Sino–Qatari cooperation can brighten the prospects for its National Vision 2030. In April 2017, the Qatar Chamber and the China Council for the Promotion of International Trade (CCPIT) signed an agreement to promote cooperation ties between the two sides to maximize the benefit for Qatari and Chinese private sectors and create more partnerships. The two sides also signed an MoU for the Qatari Chamber of Commerce to join the Silk Road Chamber of International Commerce.[10] In November 2018, China and Qatar signed an MoU to identify global maritime investment opportunities; the document serves both QNV2030 and China's BRI.[11] Nevertheless, in the synchronization process between the implementation of the Belt and Road projects with its QNV2030, Doha is unquestionably competing with other GCC members to establish itself as a regional business hub that attracts Chinese and global trade, investment, and tourism. And several obstacles can prevent Qatar from achieving their goal. First, with the sudden diplomatic isolation from its direct neighbors and supposedly close GCC allies, and with land, sea, and air barriers in place, Doha cannot possibly hope to be of regional economic centrality.[12]

Second, Qatar is highly unlikely to develop into a leading Gulf business hub since it will not be able to rival the UAE, Saudi Arabia, or Oman as the major maritime trade route on Beijing's 21st Century Maritime Silk Road Initiative. The UAE currently enjoys hub status in West Asia due to its advanced infrastructure, business-friendly regulatory environment, diversified economy, vast international human resource pool, and level of touristic attraction. The Chinese have long realized this, which is why most of their exports to the GCC, wider West Asia, and even Africa and Europe go through the UAE, the third largest re-export hub in the world; approximately 60 percent of China's pass-through trade is via this hub.[13]

Finally, China plans to set up free trade zones with members of the GCC, which are an important part of the Belt and Road project. In that respect, as long as the Qatar–Gulf crisis prevails and diplomatic and economic ties remain strained, let alone fully cut off, the creation of free-trade zones seems impossible. Though Chinese investments will not be directly affected by the current conflict, the growing instability in the region could still harm China's economic cooperation with the Gulf States and will certainly impact Beijing's regional trade prospects.[14]

Trade and investments

As part of China's measures to formalize strategic partnerships with Qatar, they are attempting to mitigate as much as possible the barriers to free trade, investment, industrial cooperation, and technical and engineering services to facilitate the integration of QNV2030 within the BRI framework. Both countries should take a series of measures, such as expanding free-trade zones, improving trade structures, seeking new potential areas for trade and improving the trade balance, devising new initiatives for the promotion of conventional forms of trade.[15]

Qatar trade and investments with China are significant, especially in light of the ongoing blockade imposed on it by its neighbors. Qatar also needs to boost economic cooperation and trade exchange with various countries, including China, to diversify the national economy from reliance on oil and gas export in order to become a global financial and commercial hub. Likewise, Doha needs technologies and the experience of Chinese companies that have great potentials in management and production.[16] Thus, the Qatari government is trying to promote strategic partnerships with China to incorporate the BRI into its national development plan. As the Qatari Amir Sheikh Tamim bin Hamad Al-Thani said, "Qatar attaches importance to ties with China and vows to promote cooperation in the BRI, as well as areas such as trade, sports, and tourism."[17]

Although the Qatar–Gulf crisis has directly undermined and threatened Beijing's economic cooperation and trade exchange in numerous ways, the diplomatic row has also represented available investment opportunities for China to gain influence in the oil-rich Gulf and to support a rapid expansion of conventional energy trade and investments with Doha, particularly as regards natural gas, as well as to promote the BRI. China is Qatar's third-largest trading partner (accounting for 10.92 percent of the country's total trade volume) and the second-largest source of imports.[18]

The trade volume between the two countries has increased from less than $50 million in 1988 at the beginning of bilateral diplomatic relations to $10.6 billion in 2017.[19] According to China Customs Statistics (export-import), China's trade volume with Qatar decreased to $11.1 billion in 2019 (compared to $11.5 billion in 2018).[20] More than 14 fully owned Chinese companies are currently operating in Qatar, in addition to 181 joint Qatari-Chinese firms. According to Minister of Commerce and

Industry Ali bin Ahmed al Kuwari, China represents an attractive destination for Qatari investments in the fields of shipbuilding, manufacturing, petrochemicals, technology, hospitality, tourism, and financial services among other vital industries. Qatar also allows foreign investors 100 percent ownership across various sectors and industries.[21]

Beijing and Doha are also connected through a network of cooperation arrangements in various investment and infrastructure projects, and other areas. According to the *China Global Investment Tracker*, Beijing investments, and contracts in Qatar from 2013 to 2019 reached $3.9 billion.[22] Chinese enterprises have participated in the construction of several strategic projects in Doha, such as the Hamad port, the 2022 World Cup main stadium, and other infrastructure works across the country, while Qatari companies are entering the Chinese market. The private sector in both countries could play a bigger role in the future of economic relations, especially given abundant investment and business opportunities.[23]

The Hamad port is located between the municipalities of Al Wakrah and Mesaieed, 40 km south of Doha, 14 times the size of the existing Doha port. The new port is one of the largest ports in the Middle East and considered to be the world's largest port development project built on unused land. The new $7.4 billion port replaced the existing Doha port, partly built and operating by China Harbor Engineering Company (CHEC) that constructed the port basin, the quay walls, and the inner breakwaters.[24]

In January 2017, Qatar launched the first-ever regular direct service between Hamad Port and Shanghai, which helps reduce the sailing time and increases the handling volume of containers coming to Doha from the Far East, Southeast Asia, and Southeast India. The Hamad container port forms part of the QNV2030, which aims at converting Qatar into a developed country and promoting trade and investment by bringing in machines, boilers, and electrical equipment. These new trading lines are helping Qatar diversify its economy by boosting its manufacturing capacity and breaking its dependence on its neighbors.[25]

In November 2018, CHEC signed an MoU with Qterminals to create joint employment opportunities and investments between the two sides around the world. In the signing ceremony, the Ambassador of China to Qatar, Li Chen, said "Qatar and China have a strategic partnership that is conducive to cooperation in all fields, and ports are one of those important areas. We have well-experienced companies in many fields and are fully prepared to participate in the field of investment in ports or other fields related to infrastructure".[26]

Furthermore, China is extensively involved in the infrastructure and construction of the Lusail Stadium for the 2022 FIFA World Cup. The stadium is located on a one-square kilometer precinct plot along the Al Khor Expressway in the western edge of Lusail City, 20 km north of Qatar's capital Doha. The construction of the Lusail Football Stadium is one of the most important Chinese projects in Qatar. The iconic 80,000-seater stadium, which is currently under construction in cooperation with China Railway Construction Corporation Limited (CRCC), is expected to be the largest in the world and will be used for the opening and final matches of the 2022 FIFA World Cup to be held in Qatar.[27]

Huawei Technologies, a leading global provider of communications and information technology (ICT) infrastructure and smart devices, become one of the first fully-owned technology companies in Qatar. Over the past few years, the Chinese company has launched several major projects in Qatar, as the telecom giant is working on developing the fifth-generation technology, which is expected to provide better communication services between individuals, vehicles, homes, and appliances.[28] The Chinese, together with Qatar's leading communications operator (Ooredoo), launched a fifth-generation (5G) network through the 3.5 GHz Spectrum in Qatar, the first in the world to launch the service commercially.[29]

Khalifa bin Jassim Al-Thani is chairman of Qatar Chamber that organizes business interests and represents the Qatari private sector locally and globally as well as supports the country's economic actors and productivity. He reports that since 2015, Qatar Chamber has been hosting an annual "Made in China" expo, a platform that enables Chinese companies to display their products in Qatar. It also aims to build commercial alliances to enhance Qatar–China trade relations. Qatar Chamber also organized joint meetings between businesspeople from both sides, to explore opportunities to set up joint projects and build business alliances between Chinese and Qatar companies.[30]

Qatari companies are also engaged in the investment business in China under the state-run Qatar Investment Authority (QIA), one of the world's most aggressive investors with an investment value estimated at approximately $15 billion. These include joint investments with Chinese companies in the sectors of finance, e-commerce, and the Internet, including those with privately-owned companies such as Alibaba and Baidu.[31] In 2014, Qatar's sovereign wealth fund (QIA) signed an MoU with the Chinese state-owned China International Trust and Investment Corporation (CITIC) Group to set up a $10 billion fund to invest in China's property, infrastructure, and healthcare sectors.[32] In September 2018, according to Bloomberg, the Qatar Investment Authority was negotiating the potential purchase of a minority stake in Lufax (about $500 million to $1 billion), which is an arm of China's Ping Insurance (Group) Co.[33]

In January 2019, Qatar's National Airline acquired a 5 percent stake in China Southern Airlines, in a move to gain access to the fast-growing mainland Chinese, one of the world's largest aviation markets. The Sino–Qatari deal came as Doha seeks new partners and routes for the national airline due to the ongoing diplomatic dispute in the Gulf. Qatar Airways' stake in China Southern is valued at roughly $530 million based on current stock prices, and Chief Executive Akbar Al Baker said in a written statement that there is "massive potential for cooperation in the future".[34]

Financial cooperation

Under China's measures to formalize strategic partnerships with Qatar, the formation and promotion of financial integration between the two countries are considered one of the essential cooperation areas to integrate QNV2030 into the BRI framework. There are several measures for the realization of financial integration between the two countries: including deepening financial cooperation and building a stable currency system, establishing an investment and financing system and a credit information system in Asia, expanding the scope and scale of bilateral currency swaps between the two countries, developing the bond market in Asia. In addition, making joint efforts to establish the Asian Infrastructure Investment Bank (AIIB), and financial institutions with good credit ratings to issue RMB-denominated bonds in China, and encouraging qualified Chinese financial institutions and companies to issue bonds in both RMB and foreign currencies outside China and use the funds thus collected in BRI countries.[35]

Doha has engaged in all the financial mechanisms underpinning the foundation of the initiative and was among the first countries to join the AIIB. Qatar's Renminbi clearing center in its capital is one of the most important steps taken to promote the implementation of the Belt and Road project.[36] Qatar, which is one of the primary shareholders in the AIIB,[37] and one of the first countries in the region that joined; this will assist in their aim to synergize the implementation of the BRI projects with its National Vision 2030.[38]

In April 2015, China established a renminbi (RMB) clearing center in Qatar, the first of its kind in the Middle East and North Africa, with a capital of RMB 30 billion. The center offers local financial institutions access to the Chinese renminbi and foreign exchange markets. It also aims to help promote trade, encourage expanded investment in the Chinese currency, and to facilitate financial transactions between Beijing and Doha on the one hand and between China and Gulf Arab economies and the rest of southwestern Asia, on the other. Moreover, in the long run, the center could help Gulf oil-exporting countries reduce their dependence on the U.S. dollar, another step in China's goal of becoming a significant economic player in the region and beyond.

China's electing to establish a renminbi clearing center in Doha is not surprising since according to the Qatar central bank, the country is presently sitting on around $340 billion of reserves, some $40 billion-plus gold at the central bank, and $300 billion at the Qatar Investment Authority, the sovereign wealth fund.[39] More broadly, Beijing accounts for more than 15 percent of all goods exported to the Middle East, and Chinese companies and investors are becoming increasingly active in the region. Through currency swap agreements and the RMB clearing center, Beijing is ensuring that a growing share of that trade will be cleared in Chinese currency. The RMB center in Qatar, in providing access to RMB-based financial products and exchanges, is strengthening financial ties between Beijing and the Middle East and fostering the widespread use of the renminbi in the region, thus enabling China to do business with the region on its terms.[40]

Qatar has also benefited from the establishment of the clearing center since it will bolster its position as a regional and international financial hub. In bilateral terms, Beijing is the third-largest trading partner of Doha, which makes it quite reasonable for the latter to diversify part of its large pool of foreign reserves away from American dollars and to strengthen links that already exist with China. In regional terms, the clearing center in Qatar also makes new financial products in RMB currency accessible to Qatar and other Gulf investors. According to recent data by global payment system provider Swift, more countries in the Middle East are turning towards the yuan, while Qatar and the UAE are the most active in using the yuan for direct payments with China and Hong Kong.[41]

In addition, there is Sino–Qatari bilateral cooperation in the financial services sector, including the banking and insurance sectors and capital markets, as well as opening branches of Chinese banks in Qatar, such as the Industrial and Commercial Bank of China (ICBC), and the People's Bank of China (PBOC).[42] The ICBC has been appointed as the clearing bank for yuan deals in Qatar; this will increase the strong ties between the two countries and Doha's position as the regional center for renminbi clearing and settlement.

Qatar's investment in China's financial sector, banks, and real estate fields has increased and is considered to be effective investments of a developmental nature. For example, The State of Qatar is represented by QIA (its sovereign wealth fund) as a shareholder of the Agricultural Development Bank of China with a 13 percent holding. The bank is currently one of the most important Chinese banks at this time, and there are many investment opportunities for Qatari businessmen in various parts of China.[43]

Energy cooperation

As part of China's measures to formalize strategic partnerships with Qatar, investment in energy infrastructure is considered one of the important cooperation areas to integrate QNV2030 into the BRI framework. Therefore, the new Silk Road can provide a new framework for more extensive Chinese investments in the Qatar energy industry. Beijing offers Doha a market for its Liquefied Natural Gas (LNG) export; Qatar enables China to diversify its energy sources to natural gas, so as not to be overly reliant on, for instance, Saudi Arabia or Russia.

The central theme of China's measures to formalize a comprehensive strategic partnership between the two nations is the energy sector; Qatar is the second-largest exporter of LNG.[44] Here the strategic significance of Qatar to China's energy security will be shaped by Qatar's uninterrupted supply of natural gas to China's rising demand for energy. According to Minister of Commerce and Industry Ali bin Ahmed al Kuwari, Qatar is the second-largest supplier of liquefied natural gas to China, and Doha is also home to numerous Chinese companies in engineering, consulting, contracting, information technology, trade, and services sectors.[45]

According to EIA (U.S. Energy Information Administration), in 2018 China became the world's top importer of natural gas and second-largest buyer of LNG, accounting for over one-third of net growth, an increase of 12 billion cubic feet per day (Bcf/d).[46] Doha is already the second-largest supplier of LNG to Beijing, and the volume of LNG imports from Qatar is expected to rise substantially as the demand for energy is growing at a rapid pace in Beijing.[47]

According to EIA, like many of its neighbors, Qatar's economy is largely based on oil and gas production and processing. The Qatar National Bank (QNB) reported that earnings from the hydrocarbon sector accounted for nearly half of the country's total government revenues in 2014, a figure that has declined over the past four years. Qatar's recoverable reserves of oil and gas are reported to be 25 billion barrels (bbl) and 872 trillion standard ft3 (scf), respectively. This puts Qatar behind only Russia and Iran in terms of natural gas reserves, with the ninth-largest reserves in the Organization of the Petroleum Exporting Countries (OPEC), and the 13th largest in the world in terms of crude oil reserves.[48] Qatar's North Field and its geological extension of Iran's South Pars Field have the world's largest non-associated gas reserves. Most of Qatar's natural gas production comes from the North Field, which at current gas production rates is expected to last another century.[49]

The PRC plans to cover its growing needs to diversify energy sources and shift to clean and renewable energy makes Qatar the world's largest exporter of LNG, essential to energy-hungry China, which has stepped up efforts to combat air pollution. Beijing's increasing inclination to reduce dependence on traditional sources of energy and achieve green, sustainable economic development makes Doha's supply of natural gas that more vital. As the Ambassador of the State of Qatar to the People's Republic of China, Sultan bin Salmeen al-Mansouri said, "Qatar's [has shown] constant readiness to meet China's gas needs, even beyond what is agreed upon."[50]

According to SIA Energy forecasts, China's LNG imports may surge by 70 percent over the next three years to 65 million tonnes in 2020. In 2017, China imported a record of 38.1 million tonnes, 46 percent more than the previous year. Beijing's imports are bound to grow as the country has only secured 43 million tonnes per year of imports and is expected to need 65 million tonnes per year of imports by 2020, rising to 87 million tonnes per year by 2020. Given China's growing appetite for imported LNG and Qatar's plan to expand its LNG capacity to 100 million tonnes per year, these mutual interests create a natural framework for strategic partnerships in the liquefied natural gas industry.[51]

In September 2018, state-owned Qatargas, the world's largest liquefied natural gas producer with a production capacity of 77 million tonnes per year, agreed on a 22-year deal with PetroChina International, a wholly-owned subsidiary of PetroChina Company Limited, to supply China with some 3.4 million tonnes of LNG annually. The Qatari state-owned company will supply LNG from the Qatargas 2 project to receiving terminals across China. The deal allows flexibility in delivering LNG to Chinese terminals, including those in Dalian, Jiangsu, Tangsha, and Shenzhen, using the Qatargas fleet of 70 conventional, Q-Flex and Q-Max vessels.[52]

In October 2018, Qatar Petroleum (QP) and China's Oriental Energy (Singapore), a subsidiary of China's largest Liquefied Petroleum Gas (LPG) player Oriental Energy, signed a sale and purchase agreement to directly supply the PRC with 600,000 metric tons of LPG per year for five years.[53] The contract with QP underscores the urgency faced by China to lock in stable and diversified energy supply, considering the trade war with the US and the sanctions on Iran. This deal also aims to improve QP's energy partnership with China, which is now the world's largest growing LPG market. QP also has joint ventures with several Chinese counterparts, including   exploration, production, and refining projects in Qatar and China.[54] Eventually, Qatar   can remain a significant player in the China gas industry as long as natural gas continues to be an essential energy source for achieving ecologically-sound economic development.

In November 2019, QP has signed a ten-year agreement to supply 800,000 metric tonnes of Liquefied Petroleum Gas (LPG) annually to China's Wanhua Chemical Group (one of the world's largest producers of polyurethane and also one of the largest LPG importers and consumers across China). The deal will go into effect starting in January 2020 and last for ten years. According to Saad Sherida Al-Kaabi, Qatari energy minister, and QP's CEO, the deal reinforces the company's "international strategic partnerships". He explained that the LPG market in China was "steadily growing" and that it was continuing to be an "important destination for Qatari energy exports". He said, "We look forward to strengthening our position in the Chinese energy market."[55]

Beijing's dependence on crude oil imports from the Persian Gulf, a leading oil-producing region, has been increasing gradually since 1993 when it became a net importer of oil.[56] In 2019, the value of crude oil imported into China totaled $238.7 billion (20.2 percent of total crude oil imports). Forty-three countries supplied crude petroleum oil to China, but close to half (44.8 percent) of Chinese imported crude oil originates from just nine Middle Eastern nations, and six Persian Gulf states are among the top 15 crude oil suppliers to Beijing.[57] Qatar's oil output is about 2 percent of OPEC (accounts for around 44 percent of global oil production and 81.5 percent of the world's oil reserves), and a modest contribution to the oil market. Thus, since

Qatar is not among the top 15 crude oil suppliers to China and its oil industry is small in regional and international terms, the energy partnership between the countries takes place mainly in the gas industry.

Military ties

Under PRC measures to formalize strategic partnerships with Doha, defense cooperation has become an increasingly significant part of integrating QNV2030 into the BRI framework. Even though it remains modest, since 2014 it has been maintaining a good momentum of development in the fields of personal training and academic exchange, and the transfer of military technology as well as high-level leadership visits.[58]

China–Qatar's cooperation in security, anti-terrorism, and the military have also been strengthened in recent years. During the period of turmoil in GCC–Qatar relations, Beijing decided to upgrade its security partnership with Doha. Although China's security ties with Qatar remain significantly less than those with Saudi Arabia or UAE,[59] the timing of its expanded security partnership with Doha's can be explained by the shared or mutual complementary economic and strategic interests between the two countries.

The relative decline of U.S. hegemony and power in the Middle East and the emergence of a risen China that seeks significant roles in the region might affect the stability of the balance of power.[60] Within this context and the tension with its neighbors, Qatar has started to seek ways to invest in stronger military ties with China, as well as other powers, to strengthen its position in an increasingly vulnerable geopolitical balance of power. Although Doha is determined to preserve its strategic alliance with the U.S., it is also seeking to hedge itself against the economic and trade embargo that has isolated it by air, land, and sea from its neighbors.[61]

For Beijing, the strengthened security partnership with Qatar is motivated by economic considerations. China is a significant importer of Qatari liquefied natural gas, and through military technology exports, it can improve its balance of trade with Doha.[62] According to the *Stockholm International Peace Research Institute (SIPRI)*, Qatari arms imports have drastically increased by 282 percent from 2012 to 2016, and Qatar became the world's third-biggest importer, despite only having entered the top ten for the first time in 2015.[63]

Moreover, the PRC's strengthened security partnership with Qatar is also motivated by strategic considerations. China views Qatar as a highly useful partner in the Arab world and the GCC, and can thereby bolster its own bid to act as a mediator in the rapidly intensifying Middle East security crisis.[64] China wants to preserve the GCC's cohesion and is supportive of a peaceful resolution to the Gulf–Qatar standoff. Instability in the Persian Gulf is a worrisome prospect for China's Belt and Road vision that includes the promotion of trade across the Arabian Peninsula.[65]

The security ties and the transfer of military technology must be interpreted within the context of Beijing's grander objectives in the Middle East pertaining to the ambitious new Silk Road initiative. Qatar and the other Gulf countries play essential roles in the PRC's vision for a multicontinental trade corridor that positions China at the center of the 21st-century global economy.

For Qatar, the growing defense ties with China are motivated by strategic considerations. The closer security ties to China may enable Doha to strategically hedge against future tensions from its more extensive and more powerful neighbors that are encouraging the U.S. to limit ties to the tiny gas-rich nation,[66] including discussing the possibility (even if remote) of Washington relocating the U.S. military presence at Qatar's al-Udeid to another Arab state. Notwithstanding this ever-present threat, in January 2019 the U.S. and Qatar signed an MoU regarding the expansion and renovation of al-Udeid Air Base, which hosts the forward headquarters of the U.S. military's Central Command and some 10,000 American troops.[67]

And yet, Qatar's deeper security ties with Beijing will further diversify its alliances away from Washington and other Western countries which will give it greater leverage in its relationship with the Trump administration. China has offered and will continue to offer Doha an opportunity to counter-balance the geopolitical interests of its Western allies. In particular, China's non-interventionist approach to arms sales makes it an attractive security partner for Doha during a period of tensions and unprecedented economic isolation.[68] Qatar, like the other GCC states which have conducted foreign policies closely aligned to Washington, has embraced a "Look East" approach, taking stock of the global shift in economic prosperity from North America and Europe to the Far East.[69] Thus, the Chinese-Qatari security partnership is expected to continue to deepen, strengthened by a complex network of interdependence based on energy, investments, and political cooperation.

The most significant Chinese defense sales and military technology export to Qatar was the SY-400 short-range ballistic missile system, with a range of 400 kilometers. Beijing's sale of the SY-400 missile system to Doha underscores how the Chinese security partnership with Qatar has reached its strongest point and how it is now balancing two adversaries – the Saudi–UAE-led coalition – to its own geopolitical and strategic advantage.[70] The sale of the SY-400 system enables Doha to assert greater clout as its geographically larger neighbors continue their siege. Qatar unveiled the missiles and accompanying launch systems during its 2017 National Day parade, and the media in Saudi Arabia and UAE warned that the new missiles could potentially strike targets in their countries.[71]

People-to-People Bond

As part of the PRC's measures to formalize strategic partnerships with Qatar, enabling the people of the two countries to bond along the Silk Road is also vital to integrate the QNV2030 within the BRI framework. The promotion of cultural and academic exchanges are aimed to win public support for deepening bilateral and multilateral cooperation; these ventures provide scholarships; increase cooperation in science and technology; and establish joint laboratory or research centers, and international technology transfer centers.[72] As Chinese President said in a meeting with Qatari Emir Sheikh Tamim Bin Hamad Al-Thani, the two countries need to advance cooperation in such areas as tourism, culture, sports, and media, especially by supporting each other in hosting the 2022 Beijing Winter Olympic Games and the 2022 World Cup in Qatar.[73]

China's links with the GCC states have strengthened due to the introduction of additional and direct airline routes (Qatar Airways flights from seven destinations in mainland China), the steady growth of the Chinese economy, and Chinese tourists' increasing disposable income. According to data from Colliers International published ahead of Arabian Travel Market (ATM) 2019, the number of Chinese tourists traveling to the GCC is expected to increase 81 percent from 1.6 million in 2018 to 2.9 million in 2022. The GCC countries currently attract just one percent of China's total outbound market, but positive trends are expected over the coming years, to as many as 400 million tourists.[74]

In recent years tourism and cultural cooperation have become another important aspect of the China–Qatar strategic partnership, and both nations have outlined their intention to expand the collaboration in these areas in the coming years. Qatar has seen the potential and huge market in China, especially in the tourism industry. Thanks to the broad economic development of the PRC in recent years, the Chinese have been able to see their purchasing power increase considerably and can now aspire to new experiences. More and more Chinese are traveling abroad every year, and Qatar is becoming a particularly popular destination for them. In 2017, the number of Chinese tourists who visited Qatar reached nearly 45,000, a sharp increase of 26 percent compared to the previous year.[75] According to the Akbar Al Baker, Secretary-General of Qatar National Tourism Council (QNTC) and Group Chief Executive of Qatar Airways, the number of Chinese tourists to Qatar in 2018 has grown 38 percent from the previous year.[76]

Qatar's tourism agencies are making efforts to create a Chinese-friendly environment at hotels and other tourism facilities to make it more appealing to the unique taste and culture of Chinese tourists and travelers, including providing services in the Chinese language, accepting payment by China UnionPay cards, providing hot water kettles to make Chinese tea, and carrying the channels of CCTV, the predominant state television broadcaster in China.[77] Beijing is also a desirable tourist destination for the Qataris, who mainly head to Shanghai and southern Chinese cities to enjoy the various tourist attractions.[78]

As part of Doha's desire to attract the travel and leisure-loving Chinese to the Qatari tourism market, both countries reached an agreement on comprehensive visa exemption for the citizens of both countries.[79] Qatar Airways currently operates 45 weekly direct flights to seven cities in China, and the Qatar Tourism Authority has also set up representative offices in several Chinese cities along with an exclusive project to welcome Chinese people.[80]

Currently, approximately 6000 Chinese citizens are living and 10,000 working in Qatar (working in Qatar Airways, Oil and Gas, and some in construction companies).[81] As Chinese companies win tenders for development projects in Qatar, there is an increasing back-and-forth of Chinese workers, both professionals, and non-professionals. The two countries have also signed an agreement regulating the employment of Chinese workers in Qatar. This agreement is not surprising, due to the growing presence of Chinese workers taking part in the construction of facilities for the FIFA World Cup in 2022 and because of the development and extensive infrastructure construction plans in Qatar.[82] It is expected that more Chinese tourists and workers will be visiting Qatar shortly with recent developments in the bilateral ties between the two countries.

Meanwhile, the PRC's BRI, which cuts through the Middle East, has the potential to put the region on the map for adventurous Chinese travelers who are seeking new destinations off the beaten path. The Middle East is also becoming a hotspot for China's growing group of luxury travelers. Many have already gone to Asia, Europe, and America and are seeking more unique getaways that blend great hospitality, unique culture and experiences, shopping, and local cuisine.[83]

The cultural ties between China and Qatar include academic and educational cooperation, language teaching, and cultural activities. The academic and educational cooperation is perhaps the most visible element of China's cultural ties with Qatar. China has exerted various efforts to bolster its academic and language and culture. For instance, the Translation and Interpreting Studies (TII) of Hamad bin Khalifa University (HBKU) have signed an MoU with the Chinese Embassy in Qatar to collaborate in the areas of language teaching and cultural activities.[84] There are student and academic exchange programs between Qatar University and some Chinese universities (e.g., Peking University, and other universities in Shanghai).[85] In 2014, the Qatari government decided to grant $10 million to establish a Qatar Chair for Middle East Studies at Peking University.[86]

The most important Beijing–Doha cooperation in cultural exchanges was the great success of the celebration of the 2016 China–Qatar Year of Culture, when Chinese arts and silk exhibitions, open-air Chinese festivals, movie weeks, and educational programs were featured, among other activities. This cultural initiative aimed to connect the people of China and Doha through exploring the contemporary and traditional cultures of both countries, innovative cultural exchange activities, exhibitions, festivals, and educational programs.[87] In the same year, Qatar organized cultural activities and exhibitions in China, foremost, the Pearl Jewelry Exhibition held at Beijing National Museum, and the Al Thani Jewelry Exhibition held in the Forbidden City in Beijing, featuring a dazzling collection of royal pieces from around the world, spanning various periods.[88]

Summary

Qatar is a small emirate located on the Persian Gulf's northeast coast in the Middle East, sharing a land border with Saudi Arabia in the southeast and sea borders on the Persian Gulf with the UAE and Iran. The motivation behind China's measures to formalize a strategic partnership reflects multiple issues and aspirations. Not least from the Qatar side is to better position the country given, the Qatar–Gulf crisis on Doha engagement and integration in the implementation of the BRI.

China has skillfully used its sophisticated foreign policy to take advantage of strategic opportunities and unique situations in light of the Qatar–Gulf crisis. The Chinese-Qatari strategic partnership is expected to continue to deepen, strengthened by a complex network of interdependence. Economic relations between Gulf countries and China have rapidly expanded and the region's strategic importance to Beijing's infrastructure and energy-driven Belt and Road vision is clear, although the Gulf region is not classified as a key corridor in the BRI architecture. This suggests China's determination to avoid being sucked into the region's multiple conflicts, with Beijing preferring to take a non-intervention position, allowing it to remain neutral in most inter-regional disputes and to take advantage of the strategic and economic opportunities available. China is also switching its focus on energy in the region, which presently accounts for half of its imported oil, to more investments in trade and infrastructure construction projects that have increased substantially.

14 | Oman

This chapter examines the Sino–Oman strategic partnership, and the synergy between the Belt and Road Initiative and the Oman Vision 2020 to understand the extent of economic engagement and bilateral relationship between the two nations. From the Chinese perspective, Oman is an attractive addition to the implementation of the Belt and Road Initiative (BRI). The 21st Century Maritime Silk Road Initiative (MSRI), part of the wider BRI, primarily seeks to create a continuous link of Chinese-controlled ports and industrial facilities throughout Southeast Asia, Oceania, the Indian Ocean, and East Africa. Nevertheless, there are certain constraints and barriers in the Sino–Omani strategic partnership that could prevent or disrupt the engagement between the two countries.

On May 2018, the occasion of the 40th anniversary of diplomatic relations, both countries' leaders decided to establish the strategic partnership and active Omani participation in the Belt and Road Initiative. These relations have witnessed significant progress towards strengthening and deepening the fields of cooperation between the two countries.[1] From the Chinese perspective, Oman is attractive to the implementation of the Belt and Road Initiative. The MSRI, part of the wider Belt and Road Initiative, essentially seeks to create a continuous link of Chinese-controlled ports and industrial facilities throughout Southeast Asia, Oceania, the Indian Ocean, and East Africa. Oman forms a crucial potential link in this chain, given its strategic location between India and East Africa outside the volatile Strait of Hormuz.[2]

The past two decades have seen substantial changes in the global economy and geopolitical trends, with the PRC on the global and regional stage. These developments are creating new opportunities for the Middle East (West Asia) countries as they look to diversify their economies, increase trade, and seek investment opportunities in emerging markets; this includes schemes such as forging strategic partnerships with China to promote the BRI and to incorporate it into their national development plan. All of this reflects a growing tendency in Oman and other GCC states to seek benefits from the favorable business conditions in China, as well as China's expertise and experience in its rapid path to economic development.

The $1 trillion BRI, put forward in October 2013 by Chinese President Xi Jinping, seeks to connect Beijing to the global market by linking Asia and Europe via a set of land and maritime trade routes. The concept took form over several years and has now become a cornerstone of President Xi's foreign policy. The BRI has become a key theme of bilateral relations, and could also create opportunities for partnerships in the many promising emerging markets between China and the countries in the Persian Gulf region. Although the Gulf region is not directly along Belt and Road Initiative's trade routes, the Gulf countries have high economic and geopolitical stakes in Beijing's planned multicontinental trade corridor.

More important, the PRC's goal of securing oil and natural gas reserves from as many diverse sources as possible has brought it close to the Persian Gulf states, which are China's top energy suppliers.[3] A stable Gulf region is vital for Beijing's sustainable growth, and with the completion of the Gulf Pearl Chain, China can achieve effective management and control the flow of its energy needs. Consequently, it can open new markets and trade routes for the Gulf Countries, as the Silk Road would connect Gulf economies with the Southeast and East Asian economies to enhance economic integration and cooperation.[4]

This chapter examines the Sino–Oman strategic partnership, and the synergy between the BRI and the Oman Vision 2020 to understand the extent of economic engagement and bilateral relationship between the two nations. As Chinese President Xi Jinping said, at the jointly announced establishment of Sino–Oman's strategic partnership, Beijing is willing to establish a strategic partnership with Oman to elevate ties between the two countries, and this will lead to achievements in the Belt and Road cooperation and safeguard the common interests of both sides in international and regional affairs.[5]

The chapter's main argument is that Beijing's strategic partnership framework with Oman is based on shared or mutual complementary economic and commercial interests, especially Oman Vision 2020 integration within the implementation of the BRI. The Sino–Oman strategic partnership is contributing to the development of trade relations that have become diversified beyond the energy industry, and the two sides have economic interests that are increasingly complementary. The BRI complements Oman's Vision 2020 and could help Muscat to achieve its national development strategy.

Oman Vision 2020

The Oman Vision 2020, a plan for Oman's economic future up to the year 2020, was announced in 1995 and provided a roadmap for the achievement of the country's economic and social goals over the fifth five-year plan period (1996–2000). The first phase took place between 1970 and 1995, and Oman Vision 2020 is the second phase. The key objectives include: economic and financial stability; changing the role of government in the economy and broadening private sector participation; diversifying the economic base and sources of national income; globalizing the Omani economy; and upgrading skills of the Omani workforce and developing human resources.[6]

The primary aim of the vision for Oman's economy in the next quarter of a century is to, at least, maintain the current level of per capita income in real terms and to strive to double it by 2020. The vision also aims at providing suitable conditions for economic take-off. The government will strive to use the proceeds of oil and gas for sustainable economic diversification and will accept full responsibility for promoting basic health education training for Omani citizens, in addition to adopting policies that promote their standard of living. The following three main strategies also assist the vision for Oman's Economy: Human Resources Development, Economic Diversification, and Private sector Development.[7] Oman's Vision 2020, despite its limited achievements, is paving the way for further and bolder reforms to be attempted under Vision 2040.[8]

Oman and the Belt and Road Initiative

The PRC's strategic partnership with Oman includes six major areas for cooperation within the BRI. These areas are policy coordination, connectivity, trade and investments, energy cooperation, financial integration, and people-to-people bond. However, each country views the BRI framework and reacts to it according to its perspective and the consequences for its national interests and international status. Therefore, the two countries have very different attitudes regarding how to realize the vision.[9] The Oman Vision 2020 and China's Belt and Road vision have converged on a common economic development path, and their synergetic strategy will bring new opportunities for both sides. As a result, the realization of the BRI will provide new momentum for Oman's economic transformation.

Connectivity

As part of China's strategic partnership with Muscat, the facilitation of connectivity is one of the essential ways to integrate the Oman Vision 2020 into the BRI framework. Muscat should attempt to optimize its infrastructural connections and also to adapt its technical systems to those of the other countries in the initiative. This would lead Beijing–Oman to jointly contribute to the development of international transport maritime and overland routes, and the creation of an infrastructural network that could in time connect all the regions in Asia and also specific points in Asia, Africa, and Europe. In addition, there should be serious attempts to create low-carbon and green infrastructure.[10]

The Persian Gulf forms a unique geopolitical position, as it connects three continents: Europe, Asia, and Africa; this geographical position gives it a vital strategic significance and value to the materialization of China's BRI.[11] On this basis, Beijing seeks to strengthen the mutual interdependency with Muscat in various sectors such as energy, trade, and investments in construction and infrastructure projects, to leverage its economic capabilities to realize the successful implementation of the MSRI.

Oman is situated closer to East Africa, India, Iran, Pakistan, Yemen, and the greater Indian Ocean region than other GCC states; it will be of immense strategic value to China's efforts to revive ancient maritime trade routes. Oman's strategic location (on the axis of the Indian Ocean and Arabian Gulf) enables it to act as a regional hub between Asia and GCC states and boasts accessible trade routes and speedy transit times to the world's most attractive emerging markets.[12]

In this context, Oman's port, Duqm, the most significant economic project in the Middle East region and one of the largest in the world, with a $10.7 billion Chinese investment, constitutes a vital link in Beijing's Belt and Road Initiative. On Oman's central-eastern seaboard, the port town of Duqm hopes to become a critical Middle East logistics hub, connecting the Gulf to the world's busiest maritime trade route. Duqm's economic zone comprises several projects, including a multi-purpose harbor, a refinery that aims to process 230,000 barrels of crude oil per day, and the largest dry dock in the Middle East, which will have a capacity of 200 ships per year.[13]

Duqm is strategically located outside the Strait of Hormuz, the sole passageway into the Gulf for a third of all oil traded by sea. The strait is the doorway to the Persian Gulf, and with Iran frequently threatening to block sea traffic passing through it, the Omani port is geographically well-positioned to be an alternative hub for shipping. Duqm also offers primary port access to the main sea lanes between the Red Sea and the Gulf. The port could provide unhindered access to the Indian Ocean for gas, oil, and other bulk products arriving overland from the Gulf states. Moreover, the Duqm economic zone is expected to host the first refinery in the Middle East to process crude from another Middle Eastern country on a long-term contractual basis. Duqm is aiming to emerge as a regional transshipment hub, docking large boats from Asia to offload cargo that will be re-shipped to the Gulf and East Africa.[14]

Oman has also started to build a regional rail network linking Duqm to other ports, industrial areas, and free zones at Sohar and Salalah with their wider GCC coverage.[15] There is an accelerated infrastructural program to boost the supply of power and water to meet rising demands from growth and development. For example, natural gas supply to the industrial estates in Sohar and Salalah has helped to promote such industries as petrochemicals and bitumen refinery.[16]

The Omani government responded positively to the Chinese invitation to cooperate in the MSRI projects. China–Oman cooperation is a win-win model because the investment and trade fit into the fields of infrastructure construction, finance, and capacity so that China can provide strong support for Oman's economic restructuring. China's investments are essential for Oman to achieve the robust logistics and infrastructure links needed to promote the downstream diversification goals outlined in its Vision 2020 strategy to diversify its economy away from a reliance on oil and gas. Due to economic problems stemming from cheap oil, as well as the major challenge of youth unemployment, the Omanis welcome China's growing investment.

Furthermore, the related financial mechanism of BRI will provide much-needed financial support for the economic restructure and infrastructure construction of Oman.[17] As Yu Fulong, China's Ambassador to Oman said at the eighth ministerial meeting of China–Arab States Cooperation Forum (CASCF) held in Beijing in July 2018, "in the next five years, China will make outbound investments of $750 billion worldwide, and Oman is among the countries that will benefit from such investment. Arab countries, including Oman, should grasp these opportunities. Being strategically located, huge investments are ideal for Oman, which will come from both the Chinese government and the private sector. Oman has played an important role in the Belt and Road Initiative due to its strategic geographical location in the region."[18]

Policy coordination

As part of China's strategic partnership with Oman, promoting political cooperation between the two countries, creating mechanisms for dialogue and consensus-building on global and regional issues, developing shared interests, deepening political trust and reaching a new consensus on cooperation is important to integrate the Oman vision 2020 within the BRI framework. Beijing appreciates the sultanate's unique climate of stability and peaceful sectarian co-existence, making it a reliable regional key player in realizing the MSRI and expanding its maritime presence in the Indian Ocean and the Arabian Sea for economic, political, and security reasons.[19]

According to Yu Fulong, Ambassador of the People's Republic of China to the Sultanate, China considers Oman an important country in the region and acknowledges and appreciates its peaceful foreign policies and its unique and constructive role in maintaining the security and safety of the region. The Sultanate is an important station along the Belt and Road Initiative, and it enjoys geographical advantages, including the ease of maritime transport and its proximity to many promising markets. The two sides seek to combine the advantages of the Sultanate with the potential of Chinese companies to turn them into a driving force that benefits both countries.[20]

In May 2018, Beijing and Oman issued a joint statement on the establishment of a strategic partnership between the two nations. Both countries agreed that since the establishment of their diplomatic ties, political mutual trust and traditional friendship have continued to increase and cooperation in the areas of energy, economy, and trade, connectivity, and culture has yielded fruitful results. They also agreed to strengthen exchanges and consultations between leaders of both countries, maintain regular communication and coordination on bilateral relations as well as international and regional issues of common concern, continuously expand consensus, and consolidate and deepen mutual political trust.[21]

More impartment, according to the joint statement, Oman welcomes and supports the China-proposed BRI and is willing to participate actively in projects under this framework. It will continue to support and participate in the Belt and Road Forum for International Cooperation. Beijing appreciates Oman's active participation in the Belt and Road construction and welcomes Oman to become a partner under the initiative. The two countries are willing to strengthen policy communication further, enhance alignment of the BRI and Oman's "Ninth Five-Year Plan" and actively implement the cooperative documents on the Belt and Road construction. The two sides will synergize their development strategies and focus on cooperation in such areas as the exploitation of energy resources, chemical industry, manufacturing, and marine industries.[22] During the meeting between Chinese Foreign Minister Wang Yi and Omani Foreign Minister Yousef Bin Alawi Bin Abdullah, they signed an MoU on the joint construction of the BRI. Thanks to this agreement, Oman is committed to participating in the realization of the new Silk Road.[23]

In December 2018, Hatem al-Tai, a member of the State Council of Oman, said during the Omani-Chinese Business Forum in capital Muscat, "The Belt and Road Initiative not only helps China but also aims to help the world to achieve common benefits. Beijing and Oman signed a strategic partnership agreement early this year, and there are many projects to be achieved between the two countries as a result of the agreement. Omani-Chinese relations are witnessing progress and prosperity of civilization, economy, and culture."[24]

Energy cooperation

In China's strategic partnership with Muscat, investment in energy infrastructure is considered one of the critical areas of cooperation to integrate Oman Vision 2020 into the BRI framework. Therefore, the new Silk Road can provide a new framework for more extensive Chinese investments in the Omani energy industry. In 2017, China was Oman's largest export market, receiving 70 percent of Oman's crude oil exports. They are linked together by their common interests in that their energy industries supplement and complement each other.

Beijing's dependence on crude oil imports from the Persian Gulf, a leading oil-producing region, has been increasing gradually since 1993 when it became a net importer of oil.[25] In 2019, the value of crude oil imported into China totaled $238.7 billion, expanding by 77.7 percent since 2015 but declining by -0.2 percent from 2018 to 2019. Forty-three countries supplied crude petroleum oil to China, but close to half (44.8 percent) of Chinese imported crude oil originates from just nine Middle Eastern nations, and six Persian Gulf states are among the top 15 crude oil suppliers to Beijing. In 2019 Oman was ranked in sixth place, exporting some $16.4 billion (6.9 percent) worth of oil to China.[26]

According to the EIA (U.S. Energy Information Administration), Oman is the largest oil and natural gas producer in the Middle East that is not a member of OPEC. According to the *Oil & Gas Journal*, in 2018 Oman had 5.4 billion barrels of estimated proved oil reserves, ranking Oman as the seventh-largest proved oil reserve holder in the Middle East. In 2017, Oman held 23 trillion cubic feet (Tcf) of proved natural gas reserves.[27] Like many countries in the Middle East, Oman is highly dependent on its hydrocarbon sector. According to the Central Bank of Oman, in 2017 the hydro-carbon sector accounted for 30 percent of Oman's nominal GDP, an increase from 27 percent from last year, and natural gas accounted for 68 percent of Oman's domestic energy consumption.[28]

Beijing's growing reliance on oil imports from the Middle East is a crucial reason for its substantial investment in its twin trade and infrastructure initiatives (SREB and MSRI); these are likely to become linked through ports or pipeline developments, with growing naval access and support facilities to help protect China's energy security. This is also a powerful driver to China's blue-water naval development and power projection capacity through the Indian Ocean, and development of a whole set of strong diplomatic ties with the littoral Indian Ocean countries. Hence, the oil trade is significant and will become increasingly so in Sino–Omani relations.[29]

Since the early 1980s, Oman has been an essential source of imported energy and became the first Arab nation and member of the GCC to export oil directly to China.[30] Indeed, over the years, energy cooperation has been the primary axis around which the Sino–Oman partnership revolves.[31] According to the Oman Ministry Oil & Gas, China remained Oman's largest export market and procured 87.2 percent of the Sultanate's crude oil exports in 2018, thanks to the perceived compatibility between the quality of the Sultanate's crude oil and the needs of Chinese refineries.[32]

As the Ambassador Extraordinary and Plenipotentiary of the People's Republic of China to Oman, Yu Furlong, said: Oman is one of the principal oil suppliers to China because the quality of Oman's oil is very good, and most importantly because it suits the (needs of) Chinese refineries.[33] According to Fitch Solutions, a part of the Fitch Rating report, China is also important for Oman as it is the largest customer of Omani oil. In the first eleven months of 2018, Beijing took 82.8 percent of Oman's total crude exports, and this percentage has broadly increased over the past several years.[34]

According to the Sino–Oman joint statement on the establishment of strategic part-nership, the two countries will synergize their development strategies and focus on cooperation in such areas as the exploitation of energy resources, the chemical industry, manufacturing, and marine industries. The two sides believe that energy cooperation is an important pillar of pragmatic cooperation and support further coop-eration in such fields as crude oil trading, exploration and development of oil and gas resources, service engineering, refining, and the chemical industry. They agreed to strengthen cooperation in new energy and renewable energy.[35]

In December 2019, Chinese State Grid Corp, the largest utility company in the world and the country's leading power distributor, agreed to buy 49 percent of Oman Electricity Transmission. State Grid is among several Chinese power companies that have recently stepped up efforts to expand their business presence abroad. The Electricity Holding, which is also known as Nama Holding and owner of Oman Electricity Transmission, did not disclose the value of the transaction. Still, a statement posted by Electricity Holding on Twitter said the deal was worth around $1 billion. The agreement is the single most significant investment in Oman by a Chinese company. It is also the first major privatization by the Middle East's largest non-OPEC oil producer.[36]

China's numerous objectives in the Persian Gulf region, mainly securing access to energy supplies, drive Beijing's growing interest in Oman because as China moves forward with MSRI, the sultanate is uniquely positioned to facilitate Chinese compa-nies' ability to better access markets throughout the Middle East and beyond. As a strategically situated and leading natural gas producer, Oman will play an increasingly important role in the materialization of Beijing's MSRI.

Trade and investments

As part of the PRC's strategic partnership with Muscat, both sides will mitigate as much as possible the barriers to free trade, investment, industrial cooperation, and technical and engineering services to facilitate the integration of Oman Vision 2020 within the BRI framework. Both countries should take a series of measures, such as expanding free-trade zones, improving trade structures, seeking new potential areas for trade, and improving the trade balance, devising new initiatives for the promotion of conventional forms of trade.[37]

Although petroleum exports serve as the foundation of Sino–Omani relation-ships, recent Chinese bilateral trade and massive investments in construction and infrastructure projects will certainly help grow relations further. According to China Customs Statistics (export-import), China's trade volume with Oman grew to about $22.5 billion in 2019 (compared to $21.4 billion in 2018).[38] According to the Sino–Oman joint statement on the establishment of a strategic partnership, the two countries agreed to make full use of the mechanism of China–Oman Joint Committee of Economics and Trade, expand mutually beneficial cooperation in infrastructure construction, industrial parks, railways, ports, power stations, and logistics, and promote the all-round development of bilateral economic and trade relations.[39]

As Yu Fulong, China's Ambassador to Oman said at the eighth ministerial meeting of the CASCF held in Beijing in July 2018, Oman is an attractive country to foreign investment as it is characterized by a stable political situation and legal system. In addi-tion to having natural resources, Oman is currently implementing the Ninth Five-Year Plan and National Program for Economic Diversification, which is an ambitious program launched for foreign investors to invest in Oman. "The country has taken many measures to facilitate the work of foreign companies within the sultanate, with a sophisticated investment law indicating that the volume of investments between Oman and China will increase in the coming years. The Omani and Chinese sides will form a joint working group to discuss ways of developing investment between the two countries. Chinese investment in the Sultanate will not be limited to Duqm but will also include Muscat, Salalah, Sohar, and other areas."[40]

In recent years, China has boosted its investment activity in the sultanate, most prominently in Duqm where numerous Chinese firms are funding a $10 billion China–Oman Industrial City.[41] Over the past years, China has become the key to Oman's efforts to transform Duqm, a fishing settlement about 550 km south of Omani capital Muscat, into an industrial center aimed to diversify its economy beyond oil and gas. The Duqm Industrial Park is the most important foreign cooperation project in Al Duqm Special Economic Zone.[42] Such investments could be the key to Oman as it looks to diversify its economy away from reliance on oil and gas. According to Li Lingbing, Ambassador of the People's Republic of China to the Sultanate, the volume of Chinese investments in the Sultanate was over $6 billion in 2018.[43]

Within the framework of Beijing's BRI, Chinese firms are planning investments as well as already investing in the construction of large industrial parks and special economic zones along with the tendrils of the MSRI across Asia, the Middle East, and Africa. Duqm, a remote and underutilized Omani port situated 550 km south of the capital, Muscat, is one of Beijing's more ambitious projects, transforming it into a vital nerve center of Sino–Omani global trade and manufacturing.[44] Oman Wanfang, a consortium of six private Chinese firms, the main developer of China–Oman Industrial Park at Duqm Special Economic Zone (SEZ), intends to invest $10.7 billion in building an industrial city there. The Chinese consortium has promised to develop at least 30 percent of the Oman Industrial Park in Duqm within five to seven years, and ten Chinese firms signed land lease agreements for building various projects, totaling an investment of $3.06 billion.[45]

There will be some 35 SEZ projects implemented in China–Oman industrial park: twelve projects in the field of heavy industries including the production of commercial concrete, building materials and related industries, production of glazed glass, methanol, and other chemicals. In the light industrial zone, there will be twelve projects, including the production of 1 GW of solar power units, production of oil and gas tools, as well as products for pipelines and drilling.[46] For Oman, the SEZ project's success is essential for its quest to diversify its economy beyond its traditional hydrocarbon sector and is in line with Vision 2020.[47]

If the SEZ projects materialize, which is by no means certain, given the multi-year timeframe and the many pressures on Chinese companies, it will be equivalent to over half of Oman's current stock of foreign direct investment. Duqm is marketing its location as a major attraction, lying on the Arabian Sea between the Gulf of Oman and the Gulf of Aden; the location of the port and SEZ combo at Duqm fits into the development and realization of China's MSRI.[48]

According to Yu Fulong, Ambassador of the People's Republic of China to the Sultanate, the Industrial Park at Duqm Special Economic Zone has received much attention from the business community and the governments of the two countries. The construction work in the project is underway, as the general design of the first phase of the project is currently under approval by the concerned authorities in the

Sultanate. The industrial city will play a major role in supporting trade cooperation between the two countries by taking advantage of the potentials of Chinese companies in industry and capital on one side, and the Sultanate's potentials on the other side, in terms of the strategic position and the proximity to promising markets and policies to facilitate and attract investments to the Duqm region, which contribute to the acceleration of the growth of non-Omani oil sectors and the diversification of the economic structure and the national income of the Sultanate.[49]

Financial integration

Under China's strategic partnership with Muscat, the formation and promotion of financial integration between the two countries are considered one of the essential cooperation areas to facilitate the integration of Oman Vision 2020 within the Belt and Road Initiative framework. There are several measures for the realization of financial integration between the two countries: including deepening financial cooperation and building a stable currency system, establishing an investment and financing system and a credit information system in Asia, expanding the scope and scale of bilateral currency swaps between the two countries, and developing the bond market in Asia. In addition, making joint efforts to establish the Asian Infrastructure Investment Bank (AIIB), and financial institutions with good credit ratings to issue RMB-denominated bonds in China, and encouraging qualified Chinese financial institutions and companies to issue bonds in both RMB and foreign currencies outside China and to use the funds thus collected in countries along the BRI.[50]

As part of the joint statement on the establishment of a strategic partnership in May 2018, the two countries are willing to promote financial cooperation. They support discussion on the possibility of developing monetary cooperation and playing the role of their own currency in bilateral trade and investment. They encourage financial institutions of the two sides to provide financial support for bilateral trade and investment cooperation.[51]

The Sino–Omani financial cooperation is still at an initial stage. In October 2014, Oman, represented by the State General Reserve Fund (SGRF), signed an MoU with 21 other Asian countries in preparation for the establishment of the Asian Infrastructure Investment Bank. According to Abdulsalam Al Murshidi, Executive President of SGRF, the Sultanate will have an opportunity to benefit from the facilities which the bank will provide for financing the ambitious infrastructural projects in the country. Furthermore, there will be job opportunities for qualified Omani candidates in the banking sector to work in AIIB.[52]

In March 2019, a delegation from the board of directors of AIIB visited Oman to meet with key officials from both the public and private sectors. The AIIB visit's agenda focuses on Oman's Vision 2040, a flagship program adopted by the sultanate. The visit aims to bring together infrastructure experts and support effective and project-driven networking, with a focus on utilizing innovative financing to address critical infrastructure needs. The program also includes field visits to Duqm port to familiarize themselves with the project and future development plans. During the visit, AIIB learned how to further support the Omani government to achieve its priorities for economic development.[53]

Besides, in August 2017, the Omani government has raised $3.55 billion through a loan from a group of Chinese financial institutions with a five-year maturity. The transaction – the largest ever for a regional borrower in the Chinese market – was increased from an initial target of $2 billion because of the keen interest received.[54]

People-to-People Bond

As part of China's strategic partnership with Muscat, enabling the people of the two countries to bond along the Silk Road is also vital to integrate the Oman Vision 2020 within the BRI framework. The promotion of cultural and academic exchanges helps win public support for deepening bilateral and multilateral cooperation; the means include providing scholarships, holding yearly cultural events, increasing cooperation in science and technology, and establishing joint laboratory or research centers and international technology transfer centers.[55]

In recent years, tourism and cultural cooperation have become another important aspect of China–Oman strategic partnership, and both nations have outlined their intention to expand the collaboration in these areas in the coming years. According to the Sino–Oman joint statement on the establishment of a strategic partnership, the two countries will carry out cultural exchanges in various forms to increase understanding and friendship between the two peoples. Beijing will provide more opportunities for Oman students to study in China and support Chinese language teaching in Oman. Both parties are willing to actively study the establishment of a Chinese cultural center in Oman.[56]

Cultural cooperation has become an important aspect of the Sino–Oman strategic partnership and both nations have outlined their intention to expand the collaboration in this area in the coming years. For instance, China–Oman Duqm Industrial Park, a project under the Belt and Road Initiative, which plays a critical role in boosting Chinese-Omani cooperation, has been sponsoring Omani students' studying trips to China. In cooperation with the Omani government, the park selects high-school graduates every year and sends them to study in China. The park plans to help train 1,000 students for Oman in the next eight to ten years. In June 2018, the first batch of 39 students returned to Oman after completing vocational training. They will finish their internships and then work for the industrial park.[57] In September 2018, Omani Minister of Information, Abdul Munim bin Mansour Al Hasani, visited China to participate in a cultural media event held in Beijing on the occasion of the 40th anniversary of the establishment of diplomatic relations between the two countries, in addition to the unveiling the plaque of the Sohar Vessel Memorial in the famous Chinese city of Guangzhou. The Omani-Sino Media and Cultural Festival includes many media, cultural, artistic, and musical events, which last for several days, and it reflects the importance of these relations at present and in the future.[58]

In addition, China's links with the GCC states have strengthened due to the introduction of additional and direct airline routes, the steady growth of the Chinese economy, and Chinese tourists' increasing disposable income. According to data from Colliers International published ahead of Arabian Travel Market (ATM) 2019, the number of Chinese tourists traveling to the GCC is expected to increase 81 percent from 1.6 million in 2018 to 2.9 million in 2022, and Oman will steadily increase their Chinese visitor arrivals with a growth of 12 percent. The GCC countries currently attract just one percent of China's total outbound market, but positive trends are expected over the coming years.[59]

According to Li Lingbing, ambassador of China to the Sultanate, at second Oman–China Tourism Forum, 22 major Chinese tourism companies participated. This is a positive sign for the promotion of the Sultanate in China to be carried out by these companies which have a presence in all parts of their country. The ambassador was confident that the number of Chinese tourists visiting Oman would increase in the coming years as the Ministry of Tourism of the Sultanate was taking a keen interest in promotional efforts in this huge market. Meanwhile, the number of Chinese tourists who visited the Sultanate has reached 20,476 in the first quarter of 2019. In 2018, the number of Chinese tourists who visited the Sultanate was 44,580, which was a huge jump from 19,470 of 2017. In the first half of 2019, the number of Chinese tourists arriving in Oman increased by 42 percent to around 64000.[60]

Summary

The Sultanate of Oman is a strategic partner (in terms of geopolitics, commerce, energy security, and non-traditional security) of China in the Persian Gulf, the Arab world, the Middle East, and the Indian Ocean. Beijing's strategic partnership framework with Oman is based on shared or mutual complementary economic and commercial interests, especially Oman Vision 2020 integration within the implementation of the BRI. The Sino–Oman strategic partnership contributes to the development of trade relations that have become diversified beyond the energy industry, and the two sides have economic interests that are increasingly complementary. The BRI complements Oman's Vision 2020 and could help Muscat to achieve its national development strategy.

Li Lingbing, Ambassador of China to the Sultanate has reaffirmed the Sultanate's important role in the BRI. Oman enjoys an important geographical location and excellent ports, such as Duqm, Salalah, and Sohar that have a natural advantage in participating in building the BRI.[61] More broadly, Oman can offer its geographical location (situated strategically at the juncture of the overland and seaborne routes), its important influence in international energy markets, and its record as a politically stable country. Unlike other Gulf Arab states, Oman, which follows the more moderate form of Ibadi Islam, has been spared sectarian unrest, radical Islamist terrorism, and unstable post-revolution transitions.[62]

However, there are certain constraints and barriers in the Sino–Omani relationship that could prevent or disrupt the engagement between the two countries. First, Oman is seeking to benefit from its geographical location to become a vital maritime global trade route but is forced to compete with other GCC countries that are also keen on capitalizing on their logistic hubs to play a more pivotal role in global trade via the region.

Second, geopolitical turmoil in the Persian Gulf in recent years may affect the investment security of Chinese companies. Oman is located between two regional powers: Saudi Arabia and Iran. Muscat, together with Tehran, shares the exit of the Strait of Hormuz, which is one of the world's major oil chokepoints. This strategic location involves more geopolitical risks to Oman (e.g., Iran has frequent conflicts with Saudi Arabia; the Trump government's tough policy against Iran). There are risks of a sudden outbreak of war in the entire Gulf region, which may influence Oman and hinder normal economic development and production in the region.[63]

Furthermore, India is likewise determined to take advantage of Omani trade networks to gain access to more markets in African and Middle Eastern markets and continues to compete for geopolitical influence across the Indian Ocean.[64] Oman and India have a tradition of close diplomatic, cultural, and economic ties that include extensive cooperation in the military and defense spheres. Oman's tendency to play on both sides of the line to protect its economic arrangements and to keep its options open is a fact that China will not ignore.

More important, Oman plays an important role in helping the U.S. realize its wide-ranging stability goals for the Persian Gulf region. Oman's longstanding partnership with the United States is critical to its mutual national security objectives, which include countering terrorism, increasing economic diversification and development opportunities, and halting Iran's pursuit of nuclear weapons. Oman has been a strategic ally of the U.S. since 1980 when it became the first of the Persian Gulf states to sign a formal accord permitting the U.S. military to use its facilities. Oman has hosted U.S. forces during every U.S. military operation in and around the Gulf since then and is a partner in U.S. efforts to counter regional terrorism and related threats.[65]

During the Obama administration, Oman played a critical role in securing U.S interests in the Middle East; the sultanate was a fruitful broker of Washington's diplomacy in areas where traditional lines of communication were unavailable. Most importantly, Oman's role in facilitating the Iran nuclear negotiations, starting secretly in 2013 and completed in 2015, vindicated the level of trust that the Obama government placed in its ally.[66] However, the Trump administration watered down the relationship due to accusations that Oman has been complicit in arms smuggling from Iran to Houthi rebels in Yemen.

There are no indications to suggest that Oman is contemplating either a shift in its traditionally pro-U.S. foreign policy orientation or replacing its Washington ally with China. Nevertheless, strained relations with the Trump administration on the one hand, and China's intention to invest billions of dollars in the Duqm industrial complex, and to construct storage facilities, refineries, and other transportation infrastructure to connect another link in the BRI, on the other hand, might change this picture. The Trump administration would be wise to repair its fraying relations with Oman, which is a valuable player in the complex Middle East; it would be a mistake to sideline such a critical strategic partnership and strengthen China's presence and influence in the region.

15 | Bahrain

Recent years have witnessed the expansion of Beijing's economic ties with Manama, because of Bahrain's fast-evolving startup ecosystem and the country's willingness to play a vital role in China's flagship One Belt, One Road Initiative. This chapter examines the various aspects that underlie the friendly cooperative relations between China and Bahrain and the synergies between the Belt and Road Initiative and Bahrain's Economic Vision 2030. An overview is presented of the shared or mutual complementary economic and commercial interests that power the relationship, as a result of the integration and implementation of the Belt and Road Initiative and Bahrain's Economic Vision 2030. Under these conditions, it can be expected that the growth of positive relations between China and Bahrain will continue over the next few years.

In 2019, the PRC and Bahrain celebrated the 30th anniversary of the establishment of their diplomatic ties. Ever since the establishment of diplomatic ties on April 15, 1989, bilateral relations have maintained a favorable momentum of development. While many have documented China's ties with the Gulf Cooperation Council (GCC) countries, Beijing's relations with the Kingdom of Bahrain remain undocumented. Although China's relations with Bahrain have been kept out of the limelight, they have developed well beyond diplomatic and political affairs.[1]

The $1 trillion One Belt, One Road Initiative (BRI), put forward in October 2013 by Chinese President Xi Jinping, seeks to connect Beijing to the global market by linking Asia and Europe via a set of land and maritime trade routes. The concept took form over several years and has now become a cornerstone of President Xi's foreign policy. The BRI has become a key theme of bilateral relations, and could also create opportunities for partnerships in the many promising emerging markets between China and countries in the Persian Gulf region. Although the Gulf region is not directly along the BRI's trade routes, the Gulf countries have high economic and geopolitical stakes in Beijing's planned multicontinental trade corridor. This is due to the strategic location of Bahrain as the gateway to the Arabian Gulf, and the fact that it is one of the key countries along the new Silk Road route, enabling it to serve as a transportation hub for the region.

Bahrain, known as 'the Pearl of the Gulf', is an important port on the ancient Maritime Silk Road. The kingdom is also one of the most open and dynamic countries within the top-ranking business environment in the Middle East. Its open and liberal lifestyle, unique market access, world-class regulatory environment, and highly competitive taxation system combined with the lowest operating costs in the region, high quality of life, and a technologically literate population makes the Kingdom the ideal location from which Chinese companies can access this $1.5 trillion GCC market.[2]

Since Bahrain is ideally positioned to play a vital role in China's Belt and Road Initiative, it is important to examine some of the aspects behind the friendly cooperative relations between China and Bahrain, and the synergies between the Belt and Road Initiative and the Bahrain's Economic Vision 2030 in order to understand the extent of economic engagement and bilateral relationship between the two nations. As the Chinese ambassador to Bahrain, An Wa'er, pointed out, Manama is a member of the Arab League and GCC and an important partner to Beijing; it has played an important role as a bridge between China and other countries in the GCC.[3] The central thesis of this chapter is that China's friendly cooperative relations framework with Bahrain is based on shared or mutual complementary economic and commercial interests, especially with the integration and implementation of the Belt and Road Initiative and Bahrain's Economic Vision 2030.

Bahrain's Economic Vision 2030

In 2008 the kingdom developed a national roadmap for government strategy (called the Economic Vision 2030) for the country's future, which was based on the three guiding principles of sustainability, fairness, and competitiveness. The country's national plan is aimed at growing and diversifying the economy by enhancing private sector growth and government investment in infrastructure, affordable housing, and human resources. Bahrain wants to attract foreign investment in five sectors: logistics, light manufacturing, financial services, digital technology, and tourism. The Economic Development Board (EDC) has led a program of coordinated economic and institutional reform intended to transform Bahrain from a regional pioneer to a global contender. The ultimate aim of the plan is to ensure that every Bahraini household has at least twice as much disposable income, in real terms, by 2030.[4]

In the past, oil has been the main force behind economic growth in Bahrain, accounting for over 70 percent of GDP and 80 percent of government revenue. While the hydrocarbon sector remains the dominant industry in Bahrain, continuing efforts to boost trade growth and industrial diversification bode well for the economy in the medium- to long-term. Non-oil industrial development is still at an early stage, but the country's strong logistics profile and supportive industrial policies may provide a base for stronger manufacturing growth and less reliance on oil revenues.[5]

According to the World Bank's "Doing Business 2019" report, Bahrain ranked 62th out of 190 countries on ease of doing business and fifth in the paying taxes category.[6] In the Global Competitiveness Report 2019, Bahrain ranked 45th out of 141 economies, mainly due to its strong institutions, growing and stable infrastructure, market efficiencies, and business sophistication.[7] According to official data from the World Bank and projections from Trading Economics, the kingdom's GDP was $37.75 billion in 2018, increasing to $39.3 billion in 2019.[8] According to International Monetary Fund (IMF), Bahrain's economy is expected to grow around 1.8 percent in 2019, the same pace as last year.[9]

The BRI has become a key theme of bilateral relations, and could also create opportunities for partnerships in the many promising emerging markets between China and countries in the Persian Gulf region. Although the Gulf region is not directly along BRI's trade routes, the Gulf countries have high economic and geopolitical stakes in Beijing's planned multicontinental trade corridor. More important, the PRC's pursuit of securing oil and natural gas reserves from as many diverse sources as possible has brought it close to the Persian Gulf states, which are China's top energy suppliers.[10] A stable Gulf region is vital for Beijing's sustainable growth, and with the completion of the Gulf Pearl Chain, China can achieve effective management and control the flow of its energy needs. This will open new markets and trade routes for the Gulf Countries, as the Silk Road would connect Gulf economies with the Southeast and East Asian economies which will enhance economic integration and cooperation.[11]

The past two decades have seen substantial changes in the global economy and geopolitical trends, with the rise of China on the global stage. These developments are creating new opportunities for the GCC countries as they look to diversify their economies, increase trade, and seek investment opportunities in emerging markets; this includes schemes such as forging strategic partnerships with China to promote the Belt and Road Initiative and to incorporate it into their national development plan. This reflects a growing tendency among the GCC states which seek to benefit from the favorable business conditions in China, as well as Beijing's expertise and experience in its rapid path to economic development.[12]

The Gulf countries have strongly embraced and benefitted from a network of cooperation lines in various investment and infrastructure projects and other fields with China. Hence, they have much to gain from the realization of the Belt and Road vision as the project aims to enhance the PRC's diplomatic and economic relations with countries that maintain a positive view of Beijing's global economic and political ascendancy, and can provide the energy resources that it needs to fuel its economy.[13]

Bahrain and the Belt and Road Initiative

The PRC's friendly cooperative relations with Bahrain include four major areas for cooperation within the Belt and Road Initiative. These areas are policy coordination, connectivity, trade and investments, tourism and cultural ties. Inevitably, each country views the Belt and Road Initiative framework and reacts to it according to its own perspective and the consequences for its own national interests and international status. Therefore, in realizing the shared vision, the two countries have very different attitudes.[14] Nonetheless, Bahrain's Economic Vision 2030 and China's Belt and Road vision have converged on a common economic development path, and their synergetic strategy will bring new opportunities for both sides. As a result, the realization of the Belt and Road Initiative will provide new momentum for Bahrain's economic transformation.

Policy coordination

China's friendly cooperative relations with Bahrain are being translated into promoting political cooperation between countries, creating mechanisms for dialogue and consensus-building on global and regional issues, developing shared interests, deepening political trust, and reaching a new consensus on cooperation. These are all important in order to integrate the Bahrain's Economic Vision 2030 into the Belt and Road Initiative framework.[15]

Bilateral relations have gathered momentum since the King of Bahrain Sheikh Hamad bin Isa Al-khalifa visited China in 2013 when he strengthened the ties between both sides and opened new channels of cooperation at several levels. Major agreements were signed in the areas of education, health, culture, and investment which boosted relations and bilateral cooperation.[16] Chinese President Xi Jinping said in talks with King Hamad that Bahrain is an important cooperative partner of China in the Middle East and Gulf region, and "the two countries should be jointly committed to building friendly cooperative relations of long-term stability."[17]

The friendly cooperative relations (友好 合作 关系) framework between the two nations has further strengthened over the past couple of years because of Bahrain's fast-evolving startup ecosystem and the country's willingness to play a vital role in China's flagship Belt and Road Initiative. According to Chinese Ambassador to Bahrain, Qi Zhenhong, China and Bahrain have become friendly partners of mutual understanding and trust, a cooperative partner of the win–win result and a respectable partner of learning from each other and deriving mutual benefit. He added that a further strengthening of the friendly cooperative relations between China and Bahrain will not only bring benefits to the two peoples, but also promote the strategic cooperation between China and GCC countries, and safeguard regional peace, stability, and prosperity.[18]

Connectivity

The facilitation of connectivity is one of the important ways to integrate the Bahrain's Economic Vision 2030 into the Belt and Road Initiative framework. Bahrain should attempt to optimize its infrastructural connections and also to adapt its technical systems to those of the other countries in the Belt and Road Initiative framework. This would lead Beijing–Manama to jointly contribute to the development of international transport maritime and overland routes and the creation of an infrastructural network that could gradually connect all the regions in Asia and also at specific points in Asia, Africa, and Europe. In addition, there should be serious attempts to create low-carbon and green infrastructure.

In the past, Bahrain traded pearls, dates, and copper, while it imported silk and musk from China. Now in the 21st century, Beijing has a reinvigorated interest in the kingdom and the broader GCC because of its Belt and Road Initiative. Bahrain was a trading outpost along the old Silk Road connecting the Gulf to the world for thousands of years, and traces of the history of this long trading relationship between Bahrain and China can be found at many of the archaeological sites around the kingdom.[19]

The kingdom's location in the heart of the Arabian Gulf makes accessibility and entry into any Middle East market (whether by land, sea, or air) fast and economically feasible. Bahrain's geographic location is a key strategic asset, enabling it to serve as a transportation hub for the region. The Khalifa Bin Salman Port (KBSP), the premier transshipment hub for the Northern Gulf, has enhanced the country's role as a primary supplier of goods to Saudi Arabia, the region's largest market. KBSP's strategic location in the middle of the Arabian Gulf, together with its deep-water berths and approach channel which enable it to accept the largest oceangoing container vessels, and its direct overland links to the mainland (Saudi Arabia and Qatar), position the port as a major regional distribution center.[20]

The kingdom is also linked to Saudi Arabia, the Gulf's largest economy, via the 25-kilometer King Fahd Causeway, which is being expanded to handle increased traffic. From 2014, a 45km causeway has linked Bahrain to Qatar, which has the world's third-largest natural gas reserves. The link will complete a single trans-Gulf highway, connecting the entire $1.1 trillion Gulf Market, with Bahrain at its center. By 2030, this causeway will also carry a freight railway, thus increasing its capacity. Additionally, Bahrain International Airport is undergoing an extensive expansion and modernization program, which is expected to further improve the country's status as a tourist destination and a center for logistics by 2020.[21] Hence, Bahrain can be considered a great regional transportation hub and a good place for fulfillment centers for Chinese companies that operate along the Silk Road.

There is a convergence of interests that can be built upon to forge a basis for cooperation and integration between the Bahrain Economic Vision 2030 and development of the Belt and Road Initiative by linking these two projects in a way to set up a unified development strategy to the best objectives of both countries. As the Ambassador of China to Bahrain, Qi Zhenhong, said, "I do believe under this big picture, the comprehensive cooperation between China and Bahrain is bound to face great and historical opportunity, especially with the integration and implementation of the Belt and Road Initiative and Bahrain's Economic Vision 2030."[22]

Moreover, according to Bahrain Minister for Transportation and Telecommunications Kamal bin Ahmed Mohammed, the BRI could become a great opportunity for the Gulf nations. The Gulf region, which is the central location of the Belt and Road Initiative, is a prime market for China and vice versa. "We think that China always will look for a new market for their services, they are manufacturing goods, every day they are increasing their production and we can be the market for these goods. We also have a lot of projects [going on] and . . . there will be a need for Chinese goods and products. There is a great opportunity for the GCC countries; the infrastructure already exists, already we have the routes and the [trade] corridor available, a politically stable region, a resilient financial sector, and there are many areas in which both regions, China and the GCC, can benefit from each other."[23]

In July 2018, the foreign ministers of Bahrain and China signed a Memorandum of Understanding (MoU) to advance the construction of the Belt and Road project jointly. "The two sides would continue to firmly support each other on issues concerning each other's core interests and promote pragmatic cooperation across the board under the Belt and Road framework. According to Bahrain Foreign Minister, Shaikh Khalid bin Ahmed Al Khalifa, the kingdom highly applauds and supports the Belt and Road Initiative and stands ready to strengthen all-round cooperation with China and boost bilateral ties."[24] In the end, Bahrain's central location in the Gulf and its transportation links to the rest of the Middle East, with rapid access by road, sea, and air, make it a unique partner in the implementation of the Belt and Road Initiative. Potentially, Bahrain could serve as a regional hub for the growing GCC trade flows and the economic expansion in the Middle East.

Trade and investments

Part of Beijing's friendly cooperative relations with Manama include attempts to miti-gate as much as possible the barriers to free trade, investment, industrial cooperation, and technical and engineering services, so as to facilitate the integration of Bahrain's Economic Vision 2030 within the Belt and Road Initiative framework. Measures must be taken by both countries, such as expanding free-trade zones, improving trade struc-tures, seeking new potential areas for trade and improving the trade balance, devising new initiatives for the promotion of conventional forms of trade, developing trans-border electronic trade and other advanced models of business, creating a system for supporting trade in services to strengthen and expand conventional trade, increasing customs cooperation, and regularly sharing information in these areas.[25]

Economic relations have gathered momentum since King Hamad's visit to China in 2013. Since then, the two sides have launched a large number of commerce and trade investments. For example, foreign investments in Bahrain have increased from $142 million in 2015 to $810 million in the first three quarters of 2018.[26] The kingdom has already attracted some big Chinese names to invest in the country, including Huawei Technologies, CPIC Abahsain Fiberglass, China Machinery Engineering Corporation, and China International Marine Containers Company (CIMC). For example, in 2009, Huawei moved its headquarters to Bahrain, and it is now creating and accelerating Bahrain's 5G mobile networks ecosystem.[27]

According to China Customs Statistics (export-import), China–Bahrain trade vol-ume increased to $1.6 billion by 2019 (compared to $ 1.3 billion in 2018).[28] Although the kingdom has fewer natural resources to offer compared to other Gulf states, the country offers Beijing a way to access untapped consumer markets for its exports, as well as lucrative investment opportunities. Leading Chinese companies such as Huawei have established operations in Bahrain, since Bahrain offers a favorable busi-ness environment in the Gulf, with attractive policies for foreign direct investment. Currently, about 600 Chinese companies are registered in Bahrain, and the total investment has increased from $50 million to $400 million.[29] According to the 2019 Index of Economic Freedom, Bahrain's economic freedom ranked 54 among the 178 countries in the world and ranked 5th among 14 countries in the Middle East and North Africa region, and its overall score is above the regional and world averages.[30]

In addition, the kingdom is one of the largest financial service centers in the Middle East, with more than 400 well-regulated financial services companies and many finan-cial institutions that have regional headquarters in the country. Investors have a great number of opportunities in Bahrain's mature and sizeable business system and its global, transparent mechanism and strong regulatory system also provide strong support.[31] In 2010, the Bahrain-China Joint Investment Forum (BCJIF) was formed to facilitate the growth of economic links between the two countries, and 18 Chinese commercial agencies, including the Bank of China, opened operations in Bahrain.[32]

Moreover, China is playing an increasingly significant role in several of Bahrain's major construction and infrastructure projects. In January 2014, Chinese construction companies signed an agreement with the Bahraini government to help build 40,000 new residential units across the country.[33] In February 2014, Bahrain announced its plan to open a vast, China-themed mall similar to that of Dragon Mart in Dubai, which it calls it 'Dragon City'; this is a 115,000 square meter mega-mall with more than 780 shops, which raise the profile of Chinese goods in the GCC.[34]

Chinese companies are actively developing business in the kingdom covering all fields of cooperation, including information and communication, high-end manufacturing, environment protection, and project contracting. Some 3,000–4,000 Chinese nationals are living and working in Bahrain. Most of them are tenants of Dragon City or staff of Huawei. CPIC Abahsain Fiberglass is planning to invest 500 million to extend to four production lines that are estimated to be complete in 2020. China Machinery Engineering Corporation (CMEC) is negotiating with the Ministry of Housing over guaranteed financing clauses for a social housing project. Once the agreement is reached, the amount of investment in the first phase will be a rather huge $550 million. [35]

The vigorous development of logistics in Bahrain and the central position of the Gulf allows Chinese companies to quickly and easily connect with other markets and attract more opportunities. The kingdom boasts a unique location, good transport links, large numbers of professional workers, rich natural resources, a highly-developed financial industry, and beautiful scenery. To better develop and utilize its advantages and increase its competitiveness in the Middle East, Bahrain is focusing on the development of its manufacturing, finance and high-tech industries, providing lower investment costs, and a free business environment for companies.[36] For example, in September 2019, Bahrain Tourism and Exhibitions Authority (BTEA), together with Hilal Conference and Exhibitions (HCE), will host the region's largest Chinese trade expo in the kingdom. More than 60 companies from China will showcase their latest offerings at the China Heavy Machinery and Industry Exhibition to be held in Bahrain.[37]

One of the important areas that has been gaining momentum in the trade relations between the two countries is e-commerce. Chinese tech companies are recognizing that Bahrain is a great regional hub for e-commerce. The Kingdom has been receiving more attention from Chinese e-commerce companies because like many other Middle Eastern economies, it is focusing on building a digital economy to reduce overreliance on revenues from energy.[38]

In September 2018, Bahrain-listed Investcorp agreed to invest $250 million, its first investment in China, in a Hong Kong-listed tech fund. Investcorp will partner with China Everbright Limited, a sovereign-backed cross-border asset manager publicly listed on the Hong Kong Stock Exchange, to invest up to $150 million in the second round of the China Everbright Limited New Economy Fund. The company has also agreed to an additional co-investment right of up to $100 million. In the first round, the fund received an aggregate commitment of $313 million from other investors that have been deployed into Chinese technology companies working in a wide variety of segments, including e-commerce, smart retail, and artificial intelligence. The fund's portfolio comprises investments in several high-profile companies in greater China, including one of the largest unlisted mobile e-commerce platforms in the world, one of the largest online-to-offline consumer services companies, and a popular long-form online video platform.[39]

In November 2018, a high-level business delegation from Bahrain led by the Capital Governor Sheikh Hisham Bin Abdulrahman Al Khalifa and organized by the Bahrain Economic Development Board visited China's leading commercial centers in cities such as Beijing, Shenzhen, Hebei, Hangzhou, Zhejiang, and elsewhere. Such high-level visits across China emphasized the continuing interest of the Kingdom in fostering deeper economic ties with Beijing; and the spirit of collaboration is growing over the years. These visits also highlight the mutual desire to expand cooperation between the two nations at all levels, from financial services to Information and Communication Technology (ICT), tourism, manufacturing, transportation and logistics services.[40] The agreements and MoUs that were signed represent an important step towards stronger economic ties between China and Bahrain.

In Shenzhen, the Bahrain business delegation signed eight landmark agreements in the areas of technology and transportation which include: An MoU between the EDB and the artificial intelligence (AI) firm, Intellifusion Technologies to advance AI dynamic portrait recognition that can benefit China, Bahrain, and the Middle East. EDB partnered with Shenzhen FinTech company, IAPPPAY, to establish a full mobile payment gateway in Bahrain and explore opportunities in cryptocurrency, and the potential for the establishment of a Mobile Internet Incubator in the Kingdom. This will accelerate regional digital economic development, the promotion of investment opportunities in Bahrain to leading industrial players in China, as well as the establishment of a FinTech ecosystem between MENA (the Middle East and North Africa region) and China. An MoU was also signed between EDB and Shenzhen Outbound Alliance, aimed at strengthening economic cooperation, information exchange, and establishing a regular communication channel for business information, and investment opportunities.

An MoU was signed between EDB and Softbank China Capital – Wonder News aiming to encourage Softbank China Capital and their investment portfolio companies to establish a presence in Bahrain and use the Kingdom as a regional hub to cover the Middle East. EDB and 4PX signed an MoU exploring the possibility of 4PX initiating and establishing funds together with Bahraini companies in order to invest in entrepreneurship in China and Bahrain. EDB and Shenzhen Cool-hi Network Culture Technology partnered to promote the development of E-sports between the Middle East and China including hosting E-sports events and exploring investment opportunities in E-sports downstream supply chain between MENA and China. The Bahrain Chamber of Commerce and Industry (BCCI) signed an MoU with the China Council for the Promotion of International Trade Shenzhen Branch (CCPITSZ) to harness and enhance collaborative initiatives to promote trade and investments between the two countries. EDB and CCPITSZ signed an MoU to harness and enhance collaborative initiatives between Bahrain and Shenzhen, strengthening information exchange and cooperation in economic and business activities.[41]

In Hebei, the delegation from Bahrain signed three strategic business partnerships with Hebei Business Forum, an essential region of China's economy, to explore opportunities to drive growth together. Hubei province ranks 2nd among the six provinces in central China and 8th among all provinces in China. Being the largest comprehensive transportation hub in central China, Hubei possesses strong regional advantages, including having excellent scientific and educational institutions, being rich in natural resources, having good transport and communication infrastructures and strong industrial bases. Hubei is focused on the development of advanced and emerging manufacturing industries and the promotion of smarter networking and digitization of the manufacturing industry. Privately-owned businesses are encouraged to engage with advanced electronic technology and to build "household brands." In 2016, Hebei established its Free Trade Zone to ensure orderly industry migration toward the central regions, and this has led to the establishment of a group of industrial bases for strategic emerging and high-tech industries.[42]

The Bahrain–Hebei Business Forum witnessed the signing of several MoUs: An MoU between the EDB and Hebei Provincial Department of Commerce to strengthen information exchange, establish a regular investment information exchange, and strengthen cooperation in economic and trade activities; an MoU between the EDB and CNBM International Corporation to explore opportunities for CNBM International to expand its presence in Bahrain, mobilize Chinese building material manufacturers, and promote high-level visits between the two parties; an MOU between the EDB and Baoding Hanyang Technology to explore the possibility of establishing a Middle East management office in Bahrain, assess Bahrain's demand for 3D printing and the possibility of Hanyang partnering with local companies to develop the MENA market, and explore opportunities to construct a platform that can facilitate exchanges in 3D printing.[43]

In Hangzhou, Bahrain and China signed several agreements to expand co-operation in the sectors of e-commerce, logistics, transportation, financial services, and tourism as the two countries deepen economic ties. Among major agreements signed during the delegation's visit to Hangzhou, Capital Governorate signed a pact on Friendly Cooperation with Hangzhou to enhance cooperation in the areas of logistics, transportation, financial services, tourism, and training.[44]

In Zhejiang, EDB and the Department of Commerce of Zhejiang Province signed a deal to strengthen information exchange, establish a channel for regular investment information exchange and strengthen cooperation in economic and trade activities. EDB also reached an agreement with Chinese e-commerce retailer JollyChic to explore the potential of using Bahrain as its Middle East hub. Bahrain Chamber of Commerce and Industry (BCCI) signed an agreement with the Zhejiang International Investment Promotion Centre to establish cooperation between Bahraini and Zhejiang companies and develop the private sector in both countries.[45]

Tourism and Cultural Ties

China's friendly cooperative relations with Bahrain, enabling the people of the two countries to bond along the Silk Road, are also vital to integrate the Bahrain's Economic Vision 2030 within the Belt and Road Initiative framework. Extensive cultural and academic exchanges are being promoted in order to win public support for deepening bilateral and multilateral cooperation, as well as providing scholarships; holding yearly cultural events; increasing cooperation in science and technology; and establishing joint laboratory or research centers and international technology transfer centers.[46]

In recent years, China's links with the GCC states have strengthened due to the introduction of additional and direct airline routes, following the strong growth of the Chinese economy and Chinese tourists' increasing disposable income. According to data from Colliers International published ahead of Arabian Travel Market (ATM) 2019, the number of Chinese tourists traveling to the GCC is expected to increase 81 percent, from 1.6 million in 2018 to 2.9 million in 2022. The GCC countries currently attract just one percent of China's total outbound market, but positive trends are expected over the coming years.[47]

Bahrain already has a large tourism industry (12 million visitors per year),[48] due to its vibrant history, rich culture, and diverse population, and attracts a large number of tourists, particularly from other GCC states. In October 2018, China and Bahrain signed a mutual visa exemption policy for diplomatic and special passport holders. The agreement allows diplomatic and special passport holders to stay for a 90-day duration from their date of entry. Such a move reflects the desire by both the countries to consolidate their ties at various levels and shows their efforts towards the development of political, economic and trade cooperation.[49]

The Chinese tourist arrivals in Bahrain as total arrivals to the GCC grew from 2012 (0.3 percent) to 2016 (0.4 percent), and the annual growth forecasted for Chinese tourist arrivals to the Kingdom is 7 percent. Given the desire of the Bahraini government to implement its Economic Vision 2030, this trend is expected to continue as more and more Chinese travelers are seeking to explore newer, unexplored cities, and cultures. The opening of new leisure attractions and business opportunities in the Kingdom, and falling visa barriers for Chinese travelers to Bahrain, will contribute to this trend.[50]

Bahrain has a long history, splendid culture, and rich tourism resources, which it is vigorously promoting to attract Chinese tourists who can experience Arab history and culture, Islam, and the charm of the Formula 1 Grand Prix and various international conferences and exhibitions. With a stable society and hospitable people, Bahrain is an oasis of harmonious coexistence between different religions and civilizations. In March 2018, Bahrain Tourism and Exhibition Authority set up a representative office in Beijing, and actively cooperates with the Ministry of Culture and Tourism of China, major travel agencies and airlines, to launch direct flights to China via Bahrain's Gulf Air.[51] These measures will undoubtedly further facilitate personnel exchanges and promote tourism cooperation between the two countries.

Cultural cooperation has become another important aspect of the China–Bahrain friendly cooperative relations, and both nations have outlined their intention to expand the collaboration in this area in the coming years. In mid-2013, a Chinese painting and calligraphy exhibition, hosted by the China International Culture Communication Center, was held in Bahrain, featuring over 70 works from more than 30 renowned contemporary Chinese artists. The Kingdom has also participated in China at the Arabic Arts Festival in 2014, an important event to improve understanding between Chinese and Arab people.[52] In 2018, Bahrain also participated in the Fourth Arabic Arts Festival in Chengdu that shows the latest achievements of cultural exchanges and cooperation between the two states under the framework of the BRI Initiative.[53]

In 2019, 550 Confucius Institutes and 1,172 Confucius Classrooms and 5,665 teaching sites were established in 162 countries and regions, receiving in total about eleven million students.[54] In 54 countries involved in the Belt and Road Initiative, there are 153 Confucius Institutes and 149 primary and high-school Confucius Classrooms.[55] In the Middle East, there are eighteen Confucius Institutes and three Confucius Classrooms, and one of them is in Bahrain.[56] In April 2014, China established the Confucius Institute at the University of Bahrain in collaboration with Shanghai University, which is dedicated to promoting the Chinese language and culture in Bahrain and furthering the understanding of contemporary China.[57]

In education, the Chinese Government Scholarship Program (Bahrain) offers annually five full scholarships for Bahraini students who wish to study abroad in China. The program was founded by China's Ministry of Education and aims to increase mutual understanding between the two nations.[58] According to the Chinese embassy in Bahrain, throughout the past decade a few dozen Bahraini students have studied at different universities across China. Going forward, a strong focus on tourism, culture, and education is set to strengthen the bonds of the friendly cooperative relations between China and Bahrain.[59]

Summary

As the Persian Gulf region becomes increasingly essential for Beijing's Belt and Road Initiative, the Chinese are expected to strengthen their friendly cooperative relations with the Bahraini government in the coming years. Although the kingdom has fewer natural resources compared to other Gulf states, the country offers China a way to access untapped consumer markets for its exports, as well as lucrative investment opportunities. Bahrain also could potentially serve as a regional hub for economic expansion in the Middle East and a logistics center for the growing GCC trade flows.

This chapter emphasizes the role of Bahrain in China's Belt and Road Initiative and the synergies with Bahrain's Economic Vision 2030, as well as the increasing mutual interdependency and economic interests in China's friendly cooperative relations with the Kingdom in major areas: policy coordination, connectivity, trade and investments, tourism and cultural ties. Bahrain's Economic Vision 2030 and China's Belt and Road Initiative have converged on a joint economic development path, and their strategic synergy will bring brand new opportunities for both sides. As a result, the realization of the Belt and Road Initiative will provide a new momentum for Bahrain's economic transformation.

Conclusions

The Middle East's geographical and strategic uniqueness has made every great power in history seek to advance its interests in the region. However, the region constitutes the most significant single reserve of oil in the world, which has made it a regular source of foreign interference in the post-World War II era. Due to its geopolitical importance, any inter-and intra-state conflict in the region has the potential not only for destabilizing the region as a whole or upsetting the regional balance of power but also affecting global stability. For these reasons, the Middle East has been a major center of world affairs and economically, politically, and culturally sensitive areas.

The Middle East is also situated at the heart of Beijing's BRI, one of the most ambitious infrastructure projects in modern history that has the potential to reconfigure and optimize global trade routes. The initiative aims to deepen and expand links between Asia, the Middle East, Europe, and Africa by recreating the ancient Silk Road trade routes through both land and sea. Hence, the Middle East has critical importance for the successful implementation of the new Silk Road strategy, especially to the MSRI, as much of the various straits, sea routes, and many hubs and offshoots run through the region. The Middle East is also offering substantial potential markets for Chinese exports, a key source of petroleum products for Beijing's energy security, and a growing destination for Chinese investment.

Although the Middle East is not considered the primary geopolitical sphere of influence for China (a distinction reserved for the East and South China Seas), the region has become of greater importance to China than ever before. Indeed, Beijing seems to perceive the Middle East as an extension of China's periphery and a zone of fragility. China seeks to develop its relationships with Middle Eastern states for the need to secure its energy imports, to secure its exports via routes that pass through the Middle East and, in the longer term, to increase its regional influence and displace the US in the region.

The central theme of Beijing's measures to formalize strategic partnerships with the Middle East countries is the strategic geographical position in the context of the BRI framework, and it is critically important for its energy security. Energy cooperation has long been at the heart of China–Middle Eastern state partnerships. While Western countries had been the primary export market for Middle East energy products, East Asian states have recently become the largest importers of the region oil and natural gas, a trend that is set to continue as the shale revolution and the push for greater diversification and development of alternative energy sources grow in the West. More importantly, energy is also one of the crucial pillars of the new Silk Road strategy, and huge China-led investments will be devoted to it within and across BRI countries.

This book has emphasized the significance of China's strategic partnerships diplomacy with the Middle Eastern countries in its BRI framework, as well as setting out the increasing mutual interdependency between both sides in various sectors such as energy, construction, and infrastructure building, political ties, trade and investments, financial integration, people-to-people bond, and defense ties. A stable Middle East is vital for China's sustainable growth, and with the completion of the Gulf Pearl Chain, it can achieve effective management and control the flow of its energy needs. This will open new markets and trade routes for the Middle Eastern states, as the BRI will connect regional economies with the Southeast and East Asian economies, thus enhancing economic integration and co-operation.

China's relationship with the Middle Eastern countries is based on a two-dimensional approach: the new Silk Road strategy and partnership diplomacy between them. Beijing's levels of interdependence with these states have increased dramatically in recent years, spanning a wide range of interests. China has been mostly successful in employing strategic partnerships, a prominent instrument in its limited diplomatic toolkit, in guaranteeing integration between the national development plan (e.g., Oman, Qatar, Saudi Arabia, Jordan, Kuwait, UAE, Bahrain, Egypt), economic reconstruction plan (e.g., Iraq, Yemen, Syria, Lebanon, and Iran) or economic growth (e.g., Israel and Turkey) and the Belt and Road vision.

China's partnership diplomacy has provided a platform for deepening and expanding the cooperation between China and the Middle Eastern countries under the framework of the BRI. Since 2013 Beijing has established a comprehensive strategic partnership or strategic partnership with ten of the fifteen states in the Middle East. There is a clear and direct connection between China's emerging strategic partnerships with the Middle Eastern countries and the new Silk Road strategy. Therefore, the key to understanding Beijing's upgraded involvement in the region must be in the context of the new Silk Road strategy. The BRI is an essential guide to China–Middle Eastern countries' strategic partnership diplomacy since the region holds a unique position in China's new foreign policy framework.

In promoting the new Silk Road strategy in the Middle East, China faces a dilemma of dealing with an oil-rich and strategically located region that is also politically complicated and unstable. The China–Middle East relationship has diversified beyond energy, and the two sides have economic interests that are increasingly complementary. Trade, investment, infrastructure, and construction projects are all areas where commercial relations have strengthened in recent years. Successful implementation of the Silk Road construction in the region depends in no small extent on Middle East countries' participation and support, and could be an excellent example of regional facilities connectivity along the Belt and Road and has the potential to increase motivation for preparing for a successful implementation of the BRI in the broader Asia region.

Notes

Preface

1   Chia-yi Lee, "China's Energy Diplomacy: Does Chinese Foreign Policy Favor Oil-Producing Countries?." *Foreign Policy Analysis*, 15 (4), 2019, 570–588; Jenkins Rhys, "Journal of Latin American Studies: China on the Ground in Latin America: Challenges for the Chinese and Impacts on the Region; The China Triangle: Latin America's China Boom and the Fate of the Washington Consensus; The Political Economy of China–Latin America Relations in the New Millennium: Brave New World; China's Strategic Partnerships in Latin America: Case Studies of China's Oil Diplomacy in Argentina, Brazil, Mexico, and Venezuela, 1991–2015," *Journal of Latin American Studies*, 51(1), 2019, 187–191; Evgeny Grachikov, "Chinese Partnership Strategy: Practice and its Conceptualisation(1993–2018)." *Mirovaia ekonomika i mezhdunarodnye otnosheniia*, 63 (3), 2019, 83–93; Zhongqi Pan and Anna Michalski, "Contending logics of strategic partnership in international politics," Asia Europe Journal, 17 (3), 2019, 265–280; Churen Sun and Yaying Liu, "Can China's Diplomatic Partnership Strategy Benefit Outward Foreign Direct Investment?," *China & World Economy*, 27 (5), 2019, 108–134; Quan Li, Min Ye, "China's emerging partnership network: what, who, where, when and why," *International Trade, Politics and Development*, 3 (2), 2019, 66–81.
2   Nicholas Lyall, "China in the Middle East: Past, Present, and Future," *The Diplomat*, February 16, 2019, https://thediplomat.com/2019/02/china-in-the-middle-east-past-present-and-future/.
3   Quan Li, Min Ye, "China's emerging partnership network: what, who, where, when and why," *International Trade, Politics and Development*, 3 (2), 2019, 66–81.

Introduction

1   Andrew Scobell and Alireza Nader, *China in the Middle East: The Wary Dragon*. Santa Monica, Calif.: RAND Corporation, 2016.
2   "Western Asia and North Africa," *Ministry of Foreign Affairs, the People's Republic of China*, 2019, https://www.fmprc.gov.cn/mfa_eng/gjhdq_665435/2797_665439/.
3   Nicholas Lyall, "China in the Middle East: Past, Present, and Future," *The Diplomat*, February 16, 2019, https://thediplomat.com/2019/02/china-in-the-middle-east-past-present-and-future/.
4   Christopher Layne, "The US–Chinese power shift and the end of the Pax Americana," *International Affairs*, 94 (1), 2018, 89–111.
5   Imad K. Harb, "Self-preservation and Strategic Hedging in the Gulf Cooperation Council," *Policy brief*, no. 23, June 26, 2018,

http://ams.hi.is/wp-content/uploads/ 2018/06/Self-Preservation-and-Strategic-Hedging-in-the-GCC-2.pdf.

6   Anchi Hoh, "China's Belt and Road Initiative in Central Asia and the Middle East," *Digest of Middle East Studies*, 28 (2), 2019, 241–276.

7   Lisa Watanabe, "The Middle East and China's Belt and Road Initiative," *CSS Analyses in Security Policy no. 254*, December 2019, https://css.ethz.ch/content/dam/ethz/special-interest/gess/cis/center-for-securities-studies/pdfs/CSSAnalyse254-EN.pdf.

8   "Full text: Vision for Maritime Cooperation under the Belt and Road Initiative," *Xinhua*, Jun 20, 2017, http://news.xinhuanet.com/english/2017-06/20/c_ 136380414.htm.

9   Peter Cai, *Understanding China's Belt and Road Initiative*. Sydney: Lowy Institute for International Policy, 2017.

10   Jeffrey S. Payne, "The G.C.C. and China's One Belt, One Road: Risk or Opportunity?," *Middle East Institute*, August 11, 2016, https://www.mei.edu/publications/gcc-and-chinas-one-belt-one-road-risk-or-opportunity.

11   Frank Umbach, China's Belt and Road Initiative and the Mediterranean Region: The Energy Dimension," *Mediterranean Dialogue Series 14*, June 8, 2018, https://www.kas.de/einzeltitel/-/content/china-s-belt-and-road-initiative-and-the-mediterranean-region-the-energy-dimension1.

12   "Greening the Belt and Road Initiative," *WWF's recommendations for the finance sector – in conjunction with HSBC*," January 1, 2018, file:///C:/Users/moti/Downloads/greening-the-belt-and-road-initiative.pdf.

13   Sumedh Anil Lokhande, "China's One Belt One Road Initiative and the Gulf Pearl Chain," *China Daily*, June 5, 2017, http://www.chinadaily.com.cn/opinion/2017beltandroad/2017-06/05/content_29618549.htm.

14   Anchi Hoh, "China's Belt and Road Initiative in Central Asia and the Middle East," *Digest of Middle East Studies*, 28 (2), 2019, 241–276.

15   Jane Perlez and Yufan Huang, "Behind China's $1 Trillion Plan to Shake Up the Economic Order," *The New York Times*, May 13, 2017, https://www.nytimes.com/2017/05/13/business/china-railway-one-belt-one-road-1-trillion-plan.html?mcubz=3.

16   Hichem Karoui, "Walking together on the new Silk Road," *China Daily*, July 23, 2018, http://www.chinadaily.com.cn/a/201807/25/WS5b58444fa31031a351e901ca.html?bsh_bid=2255047682.

17   Jean-Marc F. Blanchard and Colin Flint, "The Geopolitics of China's Maritime Silk Road Initiative," *Geopolitics*, 22 (2), 2017, 223–225.

18   Sumedh Anil Lokhande, "China's One Belt One Road Initiative and the Gulf Pearl Chain," *China Daily*, June 5, 2017, http://www.chinadaily.com.cn/opinion/2017beltandroad/2017-06/05/content_29618549.htm.

19   "China's Involvement in Global Infrastructure – 2019 Research Report with a Focus on the Belt & Road Initiative (BRI) – ResearchAndMarkets.com," *Business Wire*, November 12, 2019, https://www.businesswire.com/news/home/20191112005797/en/Chinas-Involvement-Global-Infrastructure—2019-Research.

20   "Greening the Belt and Road Initiative," *WWF's recommendations for the finance sector – in conjunction with HSBC*," January 1, 2018, file:///C:/Users/moti/Downloads/greening-the-belt-and-road-initiative.pdf.

21   Janne Suokas, "Chinese private firms cut back Belt and Road investment: report," *GB Times*, November 16, 2018, https://gbtimes.com/chinese-private-firms-cut-back-belt-and-road-investment-report.

22   "Annual trade between China, B&R countries reaches 1.3 trln USD," *Xinhua*, January 24, 2019, http://www.xinhuanet.com/english/2019-01/24/c_137771613.htm.

23 "The BRI progress, contributions and prospects," *China Daily*, April 23, 2019, https://global.chinadaily.com.cn/a/201904/23/WS5cbe5761a3104842260b7a41.html.

24 Zhan Yoncxin, "The Belt & Road Initiative: From vision to fruition," *The Jerusalem Post*, May 2, 2019, https://www.jpost.com/Opinion/The-Belt-and-Road-Initiative-588564.

25 Andrew Scobell "Why the Middle East matters to China," In A. Ehteshami and N. Horesh (eds), *China's Presence in the Middle East: The Implications of the One Belt, One Road Initiative* (pp. 9–23). New York: Routledge, 2018.

26 "China issues white paper on peaceful development," *Ministry of Foreign Affairs, the People's Republic of China*, September 7, 2011, http://www.fmprc.gov.cn/mfa_eng/topics_665678/whitepaper_665742/t856325.shtml.

27 Joseph Yu-Shek Cheng, "China's Relations with the Gulf Cooperation Council States: Multilevel Diplomacy in a Divided Arab World," *The China Review*, 16 (1), 2016, 35–64.

28 Wu Sike,"The Strategic Docking between China and Middle East Countries under the 'Belt and Road' Framework," *Journal of Middle Eastern and Islamic Studies (in Asia)*, 9 (4), 2015, 1–13.

29 Chris Zambelis, "China and the Quiet Kingdom: An Assessment of China–Oman Relations," *China Brief*, XV (22), 2015, 11–15.

30 Daniel Workman, "Top 15 Crude Oil Suppliers to China," *World's Top Exports*, March 31, 2020, http://www.worldstopexports.com/top-15-crude-oil-suppliers-to-china/.

31 Andrew Scobell and Alireza Nader, *China in the Middle East: The Wary Dragon*. Santa Monica, Calif.: RAND Corporation, 2016.

32 Shannon Tiezzi, "Why China Won't Lead in the Middle East," *The Diplomat*, July 28, 2014, https://thediplomat.com/2014/07/why-china-wont-lead-in-the-middle-east/.

33 Mordechai Chaziza, "China's Counter-Terrorism Policy in the Middle East," In: Clarke M. (ed.), *Terrorism and Counter-Terrorism in China: Domestic and Foreign Policy Dimensions* (pp. 141–156). New York: Oxford University Press, 2018.

34 Liu Li and Wang Zesheng, "Belt and Road Initiative in the Gulf Region: Progress and Challenges," *China Institute of International Studies*, September 11, 2017, http://www.ciis.org.cn/english/2017-11/09/content_40063037.htm.

35 Gordon Houlden and Noureddin M. Zaamout, *A New Great Power Engages with the Middle East: China's Middle East Balancing Approach*. China Institute and University of Alberta, January 2019, https://cloudfront.ualberta.ca/-/media/china/media-gallery/research/occasional-papers/mena.pdf.

36 "China unveils action plan on Belt and Road Initiative," *China Daily*, March 28, 2015, http://www.chinadaily.com.cn/business/2015-03/28/content_19938124.htm.

37 "Vision and actions on jointly building Silk Road Economic Belt and 21st Century Maritime Silk Road," *Chinese National Development and Reform Commission (NDRC)* March 28, 2015, http://en.ndrc.gov.cn/newsrelease/201503/t20150330_669367.html.

38 Wu Sike, "Constructing 'One Belt and One Road' to Enhancing China and GCC Cooperation," *Arab World Studies*, 2, 2015, 4–13.

39 Cui Shoujun, "Sino–Gulf Relations: From Energy to Strategic Partners," *JPC*, 2015, https://www.jewishpolicycenter.org/2015/08/31/china-gulf-relations/.

40 John Calabrese, "China and the Persian Gulf: Energy and Security," *Middle East Journal*, 52 (3), 1998, 351–366; Steve Yetiv and Chunlong Lu, "China, Global Energy, and the Middle East," *Middle East Journal*, 61 (2), 2007, 199–218.

41 Chen Aizhu, "China's 2019 annual crude imports set record for 17th year," *Reuters*, January 14, 2020, https://www.reuters.com/article/us-china-economy-trade-crude/chinas-2019-annual-crude-imports-set-record-for-17th-year-idUSKBN1ZD0CI.

42 Sumedh Anil Lokhande, "China's One Belt One Road Initiative and the Gulf Pearl Chain," *China Daily*, June 5, 2017, http://www.chinadaily.com.cn/opinion/2017 beltandroad/2017-06/05/content_29618549.htm.

43 Liu Li and Wang Zesheng, "Belt and Road Initiative in the Gulf Region: Progress and Challenges," *China Institute of International Studies*, September 11, 2017, http://www.ciis.org.cn/english/2017-11/09/content_40063037.htm.

44 Ivan Lidarev, "China and the Saudi–Iran conflict," *Observer Research Foundation*, December 20, 2017, https://www.orfonline.org/expert-speak/china-and-saudi-iran-conflict/.

45 Jonathan Fulton, "The G.C.C. Countries and China's Belt and Road Initiative (BRI): Curbing Their Enthusiasm?," *Middle East Institute*, October 17, 2017, https://www.mei.edu/publications/gcc-countries-and-chinas-belt-and-road-initiative-bri-curbing-their-enthusiasm.

46 Wu Sike, "Constructing 'One Belt and One Road' to Enhancing China and GCC Cooperation," *Arab World Studies*, 2, 2015, 4–13.

47 Feng Zhongping and Huang Jing, "China's Strategic Partnership Diplomacy: Engaging with a Changing World," *European Strategic Partnerships Observatory, ESPO Working Paper No. 8*, June 27, 2014, file:///C:/Users/moti/Downloads/SSRN-id2459948.pdf.

48 Georg Struver, "China's partnership diplomacy: International alignment based on interests of ideology," *The Chinese Journal of International Politics*, 10(1), (2017), 31–65.

49 Su Hao, "Zhongguo Waijiao De 'Huoban Guanxi' Kuangjia" ["The 'Partnership' Framework in China's Foreign Policy"], *Shijie Jishi* [World Knowledge], Vol. 5, 2000.

50 "Quick guide to China's diplomatic levels," *South China Morning Post*, January 20, 2016, https://www.scmp.com/news/china/diplomacy-defence/article/1903455/quick-guide-chinas-diplomatic-levels.

51 Avery Goldstein, *Rising to the Challenge: China's Grand Strategy and International Security*. Stanford: Stanford University Press, 2005.

52 Brock, F. Tessman, "System structure and state strategy: Adding hedging to the Menu," *Security Studies* 21(2), 2012, 192–231; Evelyn Goh, *Meeting the China Challenge: The United States in Southeast Asian Regional Security Strategies*. Washington: East-West Center, 2005.

53 Jonathan Fulton, "Friends with Benefits: China's Partnership Diplomacy in the Gulf," *POMEPS Studies 34: Shifting Global Politics and the Middle East*, March 2019, https://pomeps.org/wp-content/uploads/2019/03/POMEPS_Studies_34_Web.pdf.

54 "Speech by H.E. Wen Jiabao, Premier of the State Council of the People's Republic of China, at China-EU Investment and Trade Forum," *Chinese Ministry of Foreign Affairs*, May 6, 2004, http://www.chinamission.be/eng/zt/t101949.htm.

55 Avery Goldstein, *Rising to the Challenge: China's Grand Strategy and International Security*. Stanford: Stanford University Press, 2005.

56 Degang Sun, "China's approach to the Middle East: Development before Democracy," in Camille Lons (ed.), *China's Great Game in the Middle East* (pp. 17–24). European Council on Foreign Relations, October 2019, file:///C:/Users/moti/Downloads/ChinasGreatGameintheMiddleEast.pdf.

57 "China, UAE issue joint statement on establishing a strategic partnership," *Global Times*, January 18, 2012, http://www.globaltimes.cn/content/692650.shtml.

58 "China, UAE agree to lift ties to a comprehensive strategic partnership," *Xinhua*, July 21, http://www.xinhuanet.com/english/2018-07/21/c_137338423.htm

59 Jonathan D. Fulton, "China's challenge to US dominance in the Middle East," in Camille Lons (ed.), *China's Great Game in the Middle East* (pp. 10–17). European

Council on Foreign Relations, October 2019, file:///C:/Users/moti/Downloads/ChinasGreatGameintheMiddleEast.pdf.

60 Mordechai Chaziza, "Comprehensive Strategic Partnership: A New Stage in China–Egypt Relations," *Middle East Review of International Affairs*, 20 (3), 2016, 41–50.

61 "China Customs Statistics: Imports and exports by country/region," *The Hong Kong Trade Development Council (HKTDC)*, May 27, 2019, http://china-trade-research.hktdc.com/business-news/article/Facts-and-Figures/China-Customs-Statistics/ff/en/1/1X39VTVQ/1X09N9NM.htm.

62 Jonathan Fulton, "China Is Becoming a Major Player in the Middle East," *BRINK*, September 19, 2019, https://www.brinknews.com/china-is-becoming-a-major-player-in-the-middle-east/.

63 "Chinese Investments & Contracts in the Middle Eastern states (2013–2019)," *China Global Investment Tracker*, 2020, https://www.aei.org/china-global-investment-tracker/.

64 Afshin Molavi, "China's Global Investments Are Declining Everywhere Except for One Region," *Foreign Policy*, May 16, 2019, https://foreignpolicy.com/2019/05/16/chinas-global-investments-are-declining-everywhere-except-for-one-region/.

65 Daniel Workman, "Top 15 Crude Oil Suppliers to China," *World's Top Exports*, March 31, 2020, http://www.worldstopexports.com/top-15-crude-oil-suppliers-to-china/.

66 Jonathan Fulton, "Friends with Benefits: China's Partnership Diplomacy in the Gulf," *POMEPS Studies 34: Shifting Global Politics and the Middle East*, March 2019, https://pomeps.org/wp-content/uploads/2019/03/POMEPS_Studies_34_Web.pdf.

67 Jonathan D. Fulton, "China's challenge to US dominance in the Middle East," in Camille Lons (ed.), *China's Great Game in the Middle East* (pp. 10–17). European Council on Foreign Relations October 2019, file:///C:/Users/moti/Downloads/ChinasGreatGameintheMiddleEast.pdf.

68 Cui Shoujun, "Sino–Gulf Relations: From Energy to Strategic Partners," *JPC*, 2015, https://www.jewishpolicycenter.org/2015/08/31/china-gulf-relations/.

69 Georg Struver, "China's partnership diplomacy: International alignment based on interests of ideology," *The Chinese Journal of International Politics*, 10 (1), 2017, 31–65.

70 Feng Zhongping and Huang Jing, "China's Strategic Partnership Diplomacy: Engaging with a Changing World," *European Strategic Partnerships Observatory, ESPO Working Paper No. 8*, June 27, 2014, Available at http://dx.doi.org/10.2139/ssrn.2459948.

71 Jonathan Fulton, "China's approach to the Gulf dispute," *Asia Dialogue*, 2018, http://theasiadialogue.com/2018/05/03/chinas-approach-to-the-gulf-dispute/.

72 Jonathan Fulton, "Friends with Benefits: China's Partnership Diplomacy in the Gulf," *POMEPS Studies 34: Shifting Global Politics and the Middle East*, March 2019, https://pomeps.org/wp-content/uploads/2019/03/POMEPS_Studies_34_Web.pdf.

73 Jon B. Alterman, "China's Middle East Model," *Center for Strategic and International Studies (CSIS)*, May 23, 2019, https://www.csis.org/analysis/chinas-middle-east-model.

74 Sarah Zheng, "China's President Xi Jinping wraps up UAE visit with series of deals to boost presence in Middle East," *South China Morning Post*, July 21, 2018, https://www.scmp.com/news/china/diplomacy-defence/article/2156291/chinas-president-xi-jinping-wraps-uea-visit-series.

75 Sharon Li and Colin Ingram, *Maritime Law and Policy in China*. London: Routledge-Cavendish, 2013.

76 Mahmoud Ahmed Mohamed Mohamed Soliman and Jun Zhao, "The Multiple Roles of Egypt in China's 'Belt and Road' Initiative," *Asian Journal of Middle Eastern and Islamic Studies*, 13 (3), 2019, 428–444.

77 Mohsen Shariatinia and Hamidreza Azizi, "Iran–China Cooperation in the Silk Road

Economic Belt: From Strategic Understanding to Operational Understanding," *China & World Economy*, 25 (5), 2017, 46–61.

78 James M. Dorsey, *China, and the Middle East: Venturing into the Maelstrom*. Cham, Switzerland: Palgrave Macmillan, 2019; Andrew Scobell, and Alireza Nader, *China in the Middle East: The Wary Dragon*. Santa Monica, Calif.: RAND, 2016; Guang Yang, *China-Middle East Relations*. UK: Paths International Ltd, 2013; Jon Alterman and John Garver, *The Vital Triangle: China, the United States, and the Middle East*. Washington: Center for Strategic and International Studies, 2008; Jacqueline Armijo, "China and the Gulf: The Social and Cultural Implications of Their Rapidly Developing Economic Ties," In T. Niblock and M. Malik (eds.), *Asia–Gulf Economic Relations in the 21st Century: The Local to Global Transformation* (pp.141–156). Berlin: Gerlach Press, 2013; Marc Lanteinge, *Chinese Foreign Policy: An Introduction*. London: Routledge, 2013; Yitzhak Shichor, *The Middle East in China's Foreign Policy: 1949– 1977*. Cambridge: Cambridge University Press, 1979; Jon B. Alterman, "China's Soft Power in the Middle East," in C. Mcgiffert (ed.), *Chinese Soft Power and Its Implications for the United States* (pp. 63–76). Washington, D.C.: Center for Strategic and International Studies, 2009.

79 Mohamed Bin Huwaidin, *China's Relations with Arabia and the Gulf, 1949–1999*. London: Routledge, 2011; Wu Bingbing. "Strategy and Politics in the Gulf as Seen from China," In B. Wakefield and S. L. Levenstein (eds.), *China and the Persian Gulf: Implications for the United States* (pp.10–26).Washington: Woodrow Wilson International Center for Scholars, 2011; Joseph Y. S. Cheng, "China's Relations with the Gulf Cooperation Council States: Multilevel Diplomacy in a Divided Arab World," *China Review*, 16 (1), 35–64; Feng Chaoling, "Embracing Interdependence: The Dynamics of China and the Middle East," *Policy Briefing*. Doha, Brookings Doha Center, 2015.

80 James Reardon-Anderson, *The Red Star and the Crescent: China and the Middle East*. London: Hurst Publishers, 2018; Muhamad S. Olimat, *China and the Middle East since World War II: A Bilateral Approach*. Lanham: Lexington Books, 2014; Tim Niblock and Yang Guang, *Security Dynamics of East Asia in the Gulf Region*. Berlin: Gerlach Press, 2014; Enrico Fardella, "China's Debate on the Middle East and North Africa: A Critical Review," *Mediterranean Quarterly*, 26, (1), 2015, 5–25; Mo Chen, "Exploring Economic Relations between China and the GCC States," *Journal of Middle Eastern and Islamic Studies (in Asia)*, 5 (4), 2011, 88–105; Niu Xinchun and Haibing Xing, "China's Interest in and Influence Over the Middle East," *Contemporary International Relations*, 24, (1), 2014, 37–58; Sarah Kaiser-Cross and Yufeng Mao, "China's Strategy in the Middle East and the Arab World," in J. Eisenman and E. Heginbotham (eds.), *China Steps Out: Beijing's Major Power Engagement with the Developing World* (pp. 170–192). New York: Routledge, 2018.

81 Jonathan Fulton and Li-Chen Sim, *External Powers and the Gulf Monarchies*. London, Oxon; New York, NY: Routledge, 2019; Steven A. Yetiv, *Challenged Hegemony: The United States, China, and Russia in the Persian Gulf*. Stanford, California: Stanford University Press, 2018; Sun Degang and Yahia H. Zoubir, "China's Economic Diplomacy Towards the Arab Countries: Challenges Ahead?," *Journal of Contemporary China*, 24 (95), 2015, 903–21; Mathieu Duchâtel, Oliver Bräuner, and Zhou Hang, "Protecting China's Overseas Interests: The Slow Shift Away from Non-Interference," *Policy Paper No. 41*, Stockholm, Sweden: Stockholm International Peace Research Institute, 2014; Mordechai Chaziza, "Six Years After the Arab Spring: China Foreign Policy in the Middle East-North Africa," in C. Çakmak and A. O. Özçelik (eds.), *The World Community and Arab Spring* (pp.185–204). Cham.: Palgrave Macmillan, 2019.

82 Jonathan Fulton and Li-Chen Sim. *External Powers and the Gulf Monarchies*. London, Oxon; New York, NY: Routledge, 2019; Steven A. Yetiv, *Challenged Hegemony: The United States, China, and Russia in the Persian Gulf*. Stanford, California: Stanford University Press, 2018; Jonathan Fulton, "China's Presence in the Middle East: The Implications of the One Belt, One Road Initiative/The Red Star and the Crescent: China and the Middle East," *The Middle East Journal*, 72 (2), 2018, 341–343; Zhongmin Liu, "Historical evolution of relationship between China and the Gulf Region." *Journal of Middle Eastern and Islamic Studies (in Asia)* 10(1), 2016, 1–25.

83 Michael Hudson and Mimi Kirk, *Gulf Politics and Economics in a Changing World*. Washington D.C.: Middle East Institute, 2014; Qian Xuming, "The Belt and Road Initiatives and China–GCC Relations," *International Relations and Diplomacy*, 5(11), 2017, 687–693; Mohammed N. Jalal, The China–Arab States Cooperation Forum: Achievements, Challenges and Prospects," *Journal of Middle Eastern and Islamic Studies (in Asia)*, 8 (2), 2014, 1–21.

84 Anoushiravan Ehteshami, and Niv Horesh, *China's Presence in the Middle East: The Implications of the One Belt, One Road Initiative*. London; New York: Routledge, Taylor & Francis Group, 2018; Jonathan Fulton, *China's Relations with the Gulf Monarchies*. Abingdon, Oxon; New York, NY: Routledge, 2019; Yitzhak Shichor, "Vision, provision and supervision: The politics of China's OBOR and AIIB and their implications for the Middle East', in A. Ehteshami and N. Horesh (eds.), *China's Presence in the Middle East: Implications for One Belt, One Road Initiative* (pp. 38–53). London: Routledge, 2017; Theresa Fallon, "The New Silk Road: Xi Jinping's Grand Strategy for Eurasia," *American Foreign Policy Interests*, 37 (3), 2015, 140–147; Peter Ferdinand, "Westward ho-the China dream and 'one belt, one road': Chinese foreign policy under Xi Jinping," *International Affairs*, 92 (4), 2016, 941–957; Tom Miller, *China's Asian Dream*. London: Zed Books, 2017; Qian, Xuewen, "The New Silk Road in West Asia under 'the Belt and Road' Initiative," *Journal of Middle Eastern and Islamic Studies (in Asia)*, 10 (1), 2016, 26–55; Henelito A. Sevilla Jr., "China's New Silk Route Initiative: Political and Economic Implications for the Middle East and Southeast Asia," *Journal of Middle Eastern and Islamic Studies (in Asia)*, 11 (1), 83–106; Mordechai Chaziza, *China and the Persian Gulf: The New Silk Road Strategy and Emerging Partnerships*. Brighton, Chicago, Toronto: Sussex Academic Press, 2020.

1 Turkey

1 Zhiqiang Zou, "Sino Turkish Strategic Economic Relationship in New Era," *Alternatives: Turkish Journal of International Relations*, 14 (3), 2015, 13–25.

2 Miodrag Soric, "China's 'New Silk Road' goes straight through the Caucasus," *Deutsche Welle*, December 26, 2017, https://www.dw.com/en/chinas-new-silk-road-goes-straight-through-the-caucasus/a-41930469.

3 "China, Turkey to establish strategic cooperative relationship," *People's Daily Online*, October 8, 2010, http://en.people.cn/90001/90776/90883/7160072.html.

4 Kübra Merve Topgül, "Turkey–China Relations within the Scope of Belt and Road Project," *Bosphorus Center for Asian Studies (BAAM)*, August 26, 2019, http://en.bogaziciasya.com/turkey-china-relations-within-the-scope-of-belt-and-road-project/#_ftn44.

5 Liu Jianna, "Turkey looks to improve ties with China," *China Daily*, July 2, 2019, http://www.chinadaily.com.cn/a/201907/02/WS5d1a9d0ba3103dbf1432b513.html.

6 Kübra Merve Topgül, "Turkey-China Relations within the Scope of Belt and Road Project," *Bosphorus Center for Asian Studies (BAAM)*, August 26, 2019, http://en.bogazi-

ciasya.com/turkey-china-relations-within-the-scope-of-belt-and-road-project/#_ftn44.

7 Zhiqiang Zou, "Sino Turkish Strategic Economic Relationship in New Era," *Alternatives: Turkish Journal of International Relations*, 14 (3), 2015, 13–25.

8 Lintao Yu, "How the Belt and Road Initiative will help Turkey become the ultimate Eurasian playmaker," *Beijing Review*, May 13, 2017, http://scolakoglu.blogspot.com/2017/05/how-belt-and-road-initiative-will-help.html.

9 Selçuk Çolakoğlu, "Turkey's Perspective on Enhancing Connectivity in Eurasia: Searching for Compatibility between Turkey's Middle Corridor and Korea's Eurasia Initiative," In Jung-Taik Hyun (ed.), *Studies in Comprehensive Regional Strategies Collected Papers* (pp. 543–634). Sejong: KIEP Publishing, 2016.

10 Serkan Demirta , "Turkey to continue cooperation with China despite Uighur row: FM," *Hürriyet Daily News*, February 27 2019, http://www.hurriyetdailynews.com/turkey-to-continue-cooperation-with-china-despite-uighur-row-fm-141523.

11 "Turkey's president praises ties with China," *Hürriyet Daily News*, July 2, 2019, http://www.hurriyetdailynews.com/turkeys-president-praises-ties-with-china-144612.

12 "Vision and Actions on Jointly Building Silk Road Economic Belt and 21st-Century Maritime Silk Road," *National Development and Reform Commission, Ministry of Foreign Affairs, and Ministry of Commerce of the People's Republic of China*, March 28, 2015, http://en.ndrc.gov.cn/newsrelease/201503/t20150330_669367.html.

13 "China, Turkey to establish strategic cooperative relationship," *China Daily*, October 8, 2010, http://www.chinadaily.com.cn/china/2010-10/08/content_11386689.htm.

14 "Vice President Xi Jinping's Speech at the China–Turkey Economic and Trade Cooperation Forum (Full Text)," *Embassy of the People's Republic of China in the United States*, February 22, 2012, http://www.china-embassy.org/eng/zgyw/t908616.htm.

15 "Turkish PM Erdoğan set for landmark China visit," *Hürriyet Daily News*, April 7, 2012, http://www.hurriyetdailynews.com/turkish-pm-erdogan-set-for-landmark-china-visit-17863.

16 "Erdogan's visit sign of aligned Turkish–Chinese interests: experts," *People's Daily Online*, July 3, 2019, http://en.people.cn/n3/2019/0703/c90000-9594066.html.

17 Zou Luxiao, "President Xi Jinping Meets Turkish President Ahead of G20 Summit," *People's Daily Online*, November 15, 2015, http://en.people.cn/n/2015/1115/c90000-8976633.html.

18 "Xi Jinping Meets with President Recep Tayyip Erdogan of Turkey," *Ministry of Foreign Affairs, the People's Republic of China*, September 3, 2016, https://www.fmprc.gov.cn/mfa_eng/zxxx_662805/t1395029.shtml.

19 "Turkey plays key role in Belt and Road Initiative: Erdogan," *Xinhua*, May 13, 2017, http://www.xinhuanet.com//english/2017-05/13/c_136278110.htm.

20 "Xi calls on China, Turkey to share development opportunities," *China Daily*, December 1, 2018, http://www.chinadaily.com.cn/a/201812/01/WS5c01c568a310eff30328c26a.html.

21 "Xi, Erdogan agree to enhance China-Turkey cooperation," *Xinhua*, July 27, 2018, http://www.xinhuanet.com/english/2018-07/27/c_137350545.htm.

22 "Turkey's president praises ties with China," *Hürriyet Daily News*, July 2, 2019, http://www.hurriyetdailynews.com/turkeys-president-praises-ties-with-china-144612.

23 "Speech by H.E. Mevlüt Çavu oğlu, Minister of Foreign Affairs of the Republic of Turkey at the Opening Session of the Eighth Annual Ambassadors Conference, 11 January 2016, Ankara," *Ministry of Foreign Affairs of the Republic of Turkey*, January 11, 2016, http://www.mfa.gov.tr/speech-by-h_e_-mevl%C3%BCt-%C3%A7avu%C5%9Fo%C4%9Flu_-minister-of-foreign-affairs-of-the-republic-of-turkey-at-the-opening-

session-of-the-eighth-annual-ambassadors-conference_-11-january-2016_-ankara.en.mfa.

24 "Turkey promises to eliminate anti-China media reports," *Reuters*, August 3, 2017, https://www.reuters.com/article/us-china-turkey/turkey-promises-to-eliminate-anti-china-media-reports-idUSKBN1AJ1BV.

25 "Visit of Foreign Minister Mevlüt Çavuşoğlu to Thailand to attend the Turkey–ASEAN Meeting, 26–30 July 2019," *Ministry of Foreign Affairs of the Republic of Turkey*, July 26, 2019, http://www.mfa.gov.tr/sayin-bakanimizin-turkiye-asean-toplantisina-katilmak-uzere-tayland-i-ziyareti.en.mfa.

26 "Foreign Minister Mevlüt Çavuşoğlu visited People's Republic of China, 14–15 June 2018," *Ministry of Foreign Affairs of the Republic of Turkey*, June 14, 2018, http://www.mfa.gov.tr/disisleri-bakani-mevlut-cavusoglu-nun-cin-ziyareti-14-06-18_en.en.mfa.

27 Ali Ünal, "Belt and Road project to boost Turkish economy, new envoy to China says," *Daily Sabah*, November 19, 2017, https://www.dailysabah.com/economy/2017/11/20/belt-and-road-project-to-boost-turkish-economy-new-envoy-to-china-says-1511345526.

28 "Turkey assigned dialogue partner for SCO," *Anadolu Agency*, June 7, 2012, https://www.aa.com.tr/en/world/turkey-assigned-dialogue-partner-for-sco/363233.

29 "Fed up with EU, Erdogan says Turkey could join Shanghai bloc," *Reuters*, November 20, 2016, https://www.reuters.com/article/us-turkey-europe-erdogan-idUSKBN13F0CY.

30 "China ready to discuss Turkey's membership into Shanghai pact, says ambassador," *Daily Sabah*, May 12, 2017, https://www.dailysabah.com/diplomacy/2017/05/12/china-ready-to-discuss-turkeys-membership-into-shanghai-pact-says-ambassador.

31 Carlotta Gall, "Now, Erdogan Faces Turkey's Troubled Economy. And He's Part of the Trouble," *The New York Times*, June 25, 2018, https://www.nytimes.com/2018/06/25/world/europe/erdogan-turkey-election-economy.html.

32 "Turkey-EU international trade in goods statistics," *Eurostat Statistics Explained*, July 2, 2019, https://ec.europa.eu/eurostat/statistics-explained/index.php/Turkey-EU_international_trade_in_goods_statistics.

33 Daniel Workman, "Turkey's Top 10 Exports," *World's Top Exports*, July 15, 2019, http://www.worldstopexports.com/turkeys-top-10-exports.

34 Altay Atlı, "Making Sense of Turkey's Rapprochement with China," *The German Marshall Fund of the United States (GMF)*, November 26, 2018, file:///C:/Users/moti/Downloads/On%20Turkey%20-%20Making%20Sense%20of%20Turkey's%20Rapprochement%20With%20China.pdf.

35 Turkey's president praises ties with China," *Hürriyet Daily News*, July 2, 2019, http://www.hurriyetdailynews.com/turkeys-president-praises-ties-with-china-144612.

36 Altay Atlı, "Making Sense of Turkey's Rapprochement with China," *The German Marshall Fund of the United States (GMF)*, November 26, 2018, https://www.academia.edu/38232854/Making_Sense_of_Turkey_s_Rapprochement_with_China.

37 Kübra Merve Topgül, "Turkey-China Relations within the Scope of Belt and Road Project," *Bosphorus Center for Asian Studies (BAAM)*, August 26, 2019, http://en.bogaziciasya.com/turkey-china-relations-within-the-scope-of-belt-and-road-project/#_ftn44.

38 "Erdogan's visit sign of aligned Turkish-Chinese interests: experts," *People's Daily Online*, July 3, 2019, http://en.people.cn/n3/2019/0703/c90000-9594066.html.

39 Zou Luxiao, "President Xi Jinping Meets Turkish President Ahead of G20 Summit," *People's Daily Online*, November 15, 2015, http://en.people.cn/n/2015/1115/c90000-8976633.html.

40 "Xi Jinping Meets with President Recep Tayyip Erdogan of Turkey," *Ministry of Foreign Affairs, the People's Republic of China*, September 3, 2016, https://www.fmprc.gov.cn/mfa_eng/zxxx_662805/t1395029.shtml.

41 "Turkey plays key role in Belt and Road Initiative: Erdogan," *Xinhua*, May 13, 2017, http://www.xinhuanet.com//english/2017-05/13/c_136278110.htm.

42 "Xi, Erdogan agree to enhance China-Turkey cooperation," *Xinhua*, July 27, 2018, http://www.xinhuanet.com/english/2018-07/27/c_137350545.htm.

43 "Xi calls on China, Turkey to share development opportunities," *China Daily*, December 1, 2018, http://www.chinadaily.com.cn/a/201812/01/WS5c01c568a310eff30328c26a.html.

44 "Turkey's president praises ties with China," *Hürriyet Daily News*, July 2, 2019, http://www.hurriyetdailynews.com/turkeys-president-praises-ties-with-china-144612.

45 "Interview: Turkish president vows to boost strategic cooperative relationship with China," *Xinhua*, July 1, 2019, http://www.xinhuanet.com/english/2019-07/01/c_138189969.htm?from=singlemessage.

46 Recep Tayyip Erdogan, "Turkey, China share a vision for future," *Global Times*, July 1, 2019, http://www.globaltimes.cn/content/1156357.shtml.

47 Mehmet Söylemez, "Turkey and China: An Account of a Bilateral Relations Evolution," *Asia Centre*, December 2017, https://centreasia.hypotheses.org/files/2018/06/22-Soleymez-ChineTurquie_De%CC%81c2017.pdf.

48 Zhiqiang, Zou, "Sino–Turkish Strategic Economic Relationship in New Era", *Alternatives: Turkish Journal of International Relations*, 14 (3), 2015, pp. 13–25.

49 Tao, ZAN, " 'Turkey Dream' and the China-Turkish Cooperation under 'One Belt and One Road' Initiative," *Journal of Middle Eastern and Islamic Studies (in Asia)*, 10 (3), 2018, pp. 50–72.

50 Kübra Merve Topgül, "Turkey–China Relations within the Scope of Belt and Road Project," *Bosphorus Center for Asian Studies (BAAM)*, August 26, 2019, http://en.bogaziciasya.com/turkey-china-relations-within-the-scope-of-belt-and-road-project/#_ftn44.

51 "Baku–Tbilisi–Kars Railway Line Officially Launched," *RFE/RL's Azerbaijani Service*, October 30, 2017, https://www.rferl.org/a/baku-tbilisi-kars-railway-line-officially-launched-azerbaijan-georgia-turkey/28824764.html.

52 Onur F. Uysal, "The Iron Silk Road: How will Turkey be Involved?," *Caucasus International*, 2016 http://www.elibrary.az/docs/JURNAL/jrn2016_540.pdf.

53 Nurettin Akçay, "Turkey-China Relations within the Concept of the New Silk Road Project" *Aralık*, 1 (3), 2017, 73–96.

54 Altay Atli, "Turkey to Get Railroads from China, not Missiles," *Asia Times*, November 19, 2015, https://www.asiatimes.com/2015/11/article/turkey-to-get-railroads-from-china-not-missiles/.

55 Adam Garrie, "Erdoğan's China Visit Offers Historic Opportunities For Turkey And China as Well as Asia And Europe as a Whole," *Eurasia Future*, February 7, 2019, https://eurasiafuture.com/2019/07/02/erdogans-china-visit-offers-historic-opportunities-for-turkey-and-china-as-well-as-asia-and-europe-as-a-whole/.

56 Andrew Korybko, "Turkey's 'Middle Corridor' looking to integrate with China's BRI," *CGTN*, July 1, 2019, https://news.cgtn.com/news/2019-07-01/Turkey-s-Middle-Corridor-looking-to-integrate-with-China-s-BRI-HY61SsTa2k/index.html.

57 "China Funded Lapis-Lazuli Transport Corridor Unites Caucasus and Central Asia,"

Silk Road Briefing, December 5, 2017, https://www.silkroadbriefing.com/news/2017/12/05/china-funded-lapis-lazuli-transport-corridor-unites-caucasus-central-asia/#more-1053.

58   Chris Devonshire-Ellis, "Turkey's Pivotal Role in China's Belt and Road Initiative with Europe, Central Asia, and the Middle East," *Silk Road Briefing*, June 19, 2018, https://www.silkroadbriefing.com/news/2018/06/19/turkeys-pivotal-role-chinas-belt-road-initiative-europe-central-asia-middle-east/.

59   "The First China-built High-speed Rail in Turkey," *CCTV*, October 6, 2015, https://america.cgtn.com/2015/10/03/the-first-china-built-high-speed-rail-in-turkey.

60   Amy Qin, "China Exports High-Speed Rail Technology to Turkey," *Sinosphere*, July 28, 2014, https://sinosphere.blogs.nytimes.com/2014/07/28/china-exports-high-speed-rail-technology-to-turkey/?_php=true&_type=blogs&_r=0.

61   Onur F. Uysal, "The Iron Silk Road: How will Turkey be Involved?," *Caucasus International*, 2016 http://www.elibrary.az/docs/JURNAL/jrn2016_540.pdf.

62   Nurettin AKÇAY, Turkey-China Relations within the Concept of the New Silk Road Project," *Aralık*, 1 (3), 2017, 73–96.

63   John C. K. Daly, "Chinese Use of Marmaray Subsea Tunnel Another First for Belt and Road Initiative," *Eurasia Daily Monitor*, 16 (166), December 2, 2019, https://jamestown.org/program/chinese-use-of-marmaray-subsea-tunnel-another-first-for-belt-and-road-initiative/.

64   Altay Atlı, "Turkey Seeking its Place in the Maritime Silk Road," *Asia Times*, February26, 2017, http://www.atimes.com/turkey-seeking-place-maritime-silk-road/.

65   "Chinese consortium acquires 65 pct stake in Turkish port terminal," *Hürriyet Daily News*, September 17, 2015, http://www.hurriyetdailynews.com/chinese-consortium-acquires-65-pct-stake-in-turkish-port-terminal-88636.

66   Onur F. Uysal, "The Iron Silk Road: How will Turkey be Involved?," *Caucasus International*, 2016 http://www.elibrary.az/docs/JURNAL/jrn2016_540.pdf.

67   "Petroleum," *Republic of Turkey Ministry of Energy and Natural Resources*, 2019, https://www.enerji.gov.tr/en-US/Pages/Petroleum.

68   Tuncay Babali, "Turkey at the Energy Crossroads: Turkey, Present and Past," *Middle East Quarterly*, 16 (2), 2009, pp. 25–33.

69   "Coal," *Republic of Turkey Ministry of Energy and Natural Resources*, 2019, https://www.enerji.gov.tr/en-US/Pages/Coal.

70   "Turkey Exports to China," *Trading Economics*, 2019, https://tradingeconomics.com/turkey/exports/china.

71   "Asian Infrastructure Investment Bank invested $1.4B in Turkey-related projects in 2018," *Daily Sabah*, January 29, 2019, https://www.dailysabah.com/economy/2019/01/29/asian-infrastructure-investment-bank-invested-14b-in-turkey-related-projects-in-2018.

72   Zhiqiang Zou, "Sino Turkish Strategic Economic Relationship in New Era," *Alternatives: Turkish Journal of International Relations*, 14 (3), 2015, 13–25.

73   Yiling Huang, "Research on Chinese Energy Investment in Turkey under the Silk Road Strategy," *Earth and Environmental Science*, 94 (1), 2017, 12–45.

74   "Thermal power plant worth $1.7B to be established in Adana," *Daily Sabah*, October 26, 2017, https://www.dailysabah.com/energy/2017/10/27/thermal-power-plant-worth-17b-to-be-established-in-adana.

75   "Chinese company plans to invest $1 billion in Turkey's green energy market," *Hürriyet Daily News*, April 5 2018, http://www.hurriyetdailynews.com/chinese-company-plans-to-invest-1-billion-in-turkeys-green-energy-market-129862.

76   "Ankara boosts energy cooperation with Beijing," *Daily Sabah*, July 9, 2019,

https://www.dailysabah.com/energy/2019/07/09/ankara-boosts-energy-cooperation-with-beijing.

77 Zeynep Beyza Karabay, "Turkey boosts energy cooperation with China," *Anadolu Agency*, July 8, 2019, https://www.aa.com.tr/en/energy/electricity/turkey-boosts-energy-cooperation-with-china/26006.

78 "Vision and Actions on Jointly Building Silk Road Economic Belt and 21st-Century Maritime Silk Road," *National Development and Reform Commission, Ministry of Foreign Affairs, and Ministry of Commerce of the People's Republic of China*, March 28, 2015, http://en.ndrc.gov.cn/newsrelease/201503/t20150330_669367.html.

79 "China Customs Statistics: Imports and exports by country/region," *The Hong Kong Trade Development Council (HKTDC)*, January 24, 2020, http://china-trade-research.hktdc.com/business-news/article/Facts-and-Figures/China-Customs-Statistics/ff/en/1/1X39VTVQ/1X09N9NM.htm.

80 Recep Tayyip Erdogan, "Turkey, China share a vision for future," *Global Times*, July 1, 2019, http://www.globaltimes.cn/content/1156357.shtml.

81 "Chinese companies in Turkey exceeds 1000," *Hürriyet Daily News*. August 16, 2018, http://www.hurriyetdailynews.com/chinese-companies-in-turkey-exceeds-1-000-135875.

82 "Chinese Investments & Contracts in Turkey (2013–2019)," *China Global Investment Tracker*, 2020, https://www.aei.org/china-global-investment-tracker/.

83 "Chinese companies in Turkey exceeds 1000," *Hürriyet Daily News*. August 16, 2018, http://www.hurriyetdailynews.com/chinese-companies-in-turkey-exceeds-1-000-135875.

84 Altay Atlı, "Making Sense of Turkey's Rapprochement with China," *The German Marshall Fund of the United States (GMF)*, November 26, 2018, https://www.academia.edu/38232854/Making_Sense_of_Turkey_s_Rapprochement_with_China.

85 Metin Gurcan, "Turkey-China economic cooperation on rise," *Al-Monitor*, October 23, 2019, https://www.al-monitor.com/pulse/originals/2019/10/turkey-united-states-turkish-chinese-ties-rapidly-grow.html.

86 "Turkey sees a sudden spike in Chinese investments through 'Belt and Road Initiative'," *Daily Sabah*, June 30, 2018, https://www.dailysabah.com/economy/2018/06/30/turkey-sees-a-sudden-spike-in-chinese-investments-through-belt-and-road-initiative.

87 Mehmet Söylemez, "Turkey and China: An Account of a Bilateral Relations Evolution," *Asia Centre*, December 2017, https://centreasia.hypotheses.org/files/2018/06/22-Soleymez-ChineTurquie_De%CC%81c2017.pdf.

88 "China aims to double investments in Turkey to $6 billion by 2021," *Daily Sabah*, March 29, 2019, https://www.dailysabah.com/economy/2019/03/28/china-aims-to-double-investments-in-turkey-to-6-billion-by-2021.

89 Summer Zhen, "Chinese consortium to invest in Turkey's No 3 container terminal," *South China Morning Post*, 11 May, 2016, https://www.scmp.com/business/companies/article/1858962/chinese-consortium-invest-turkeys-no-3-container-terminal.

90 Altay Atlı, " Making Sense of Turkey's Rapprochement with China," *The German Marshall Fund of the United States (GMF)*, November 26, 2018, https://www.academia.edu/38232854/Making_Sense_of_Turkey_s_Rapprochement_with_China.

91 "Asian Infrastructure Investment Bank invested $1.4B in Turkey-related projects in 2018," *Daily Sabah*, January 29, 2019, https://www.dailysabah.com/economy/2019/01/29/asian-infrastructure-investment-bank-invested-14b-in-turkey-related-projects-in-2018.

92 Adam Garrie, "Erdoğan's China Visit Offers Historic Opportunities For Turkey And China as Well as Asia And Europe as a Whole," *Eurasia Future*, February 7, 2019, https://eurasiafuture.com/2019/07/02/erdogans-china-visit-offers-historic-opportunities-for-turkey-and-china-as-well-as-asia-and-europe-as-a-whole/.

93 "Vision and Actions on Jointly Building Silk Road Economic Belt and 21st-Century Maritime Silk Road," *National Development and Reform Commission, Ministry of Foreign Affairs, and Ministry of Commerce of the People's Republic of China,* March 28, 2015, http://en.ndrc.gov.cn/newsrelease/201503/t20150330_669367.html.

94 "Turkey Joins AIIB as Founding Member," *China Daily,* April 11, 2015, http://www.chinadaily.com.cn/business/2015-04/11/content_20410311.htm.

95 Ali Murat TA KENT, "Turkey became the 11th largest partner of the new Asian Infrastructure Investment Bank," *AV M Center for Eurasian Studies,* January 21, 2016, file:///C:/Users/moti/Downloads/TURKEY%20BECAME%20THE%2011th%20LARGEST%20PARTNER%20OF%20THE%20NEW%20ASIAN%20INFRA-STRUCTURE%20INVESTMENT%20BANK.pdf.

96 Kıvanç Dündar, "Turkey is key market for Asian investment bank AIIB: Official," *Hürriyet Daily News,* April 6, 2019, http://www.hurriyetdailynews.com/turkey-is-key-market-for-asian-investment-bank-aiib-official-142464.

97 "ICBC becomes the first Chinese bank in Turkey," *Daily Sabah,* May 25, 2015, https://www.dailysabah.com/finance/2015/05/25/icbc-becomes-the-first-chinese-bank-in-turkey.

98 "Turkey, China realize first currency swap transaction in a move to use national currency in foreign trade," *Daily Sabah,* December 8, 2016, https://www.dailysabah.com/economy/2016/12/09/turkey-china-realize-first-currency-swap-transaction-in-a-move-to-use-national-currency-in-foreign-trade.

99 "Turkish regulator approves license for Bank of China to operate in Turkey," *Hürriyet Daily News,* December 1, 2017, http://www.hurriyetdailynews.com/turkish-regulator-approves-license-for-bank-of-china-to-operate-in-turkey-123399.

100 Emre Erşen and Seçkin Köstem, *Turkey's Pivot to Eurasia Geopolitics and Foreign Policy in a Changing World Order.* New York: Routledge, 2019.

101 "Turkey's bank secures $400 million loan from China," *Hürriyet Daily News,* December 21, 2017, http://www.hurriyetdailynews.com/turkeys-isbank-secures-400-million-loan-from-china-124532.

102 "Turkey secures $1.2 billion financing to expand gas storage facility," *Hürriyet Daily News,* June 27, 2018, http://www.hurriyetdailynews.com/turkey-secures-1-2-billion-financing-to-expand-gas-storage-facility-133875.

103 "Chinese bank to lend $3.6 billion to Turkey: Albayrak," *Hürriyet Daily News,* July 27, 2018, http://www.hurriyetdailynews.com/chinese-bank-to-lend-3-6-billion-to-turkey-albayrak-135083.

104 Kerim Karakaya and Ercan Ersoy, "Turkey Wealth Fund Shows Signs of Life as It Seeks Foreign Loan," *Bloomberg,* October 20, 2017, https://www.bloomberg.com/news/articles/2017-10-20/turkey-wealth-fund-said-to-be-seeking-loan-from-a-foreign-bank.

105 "Turkey's wealth fund hires banks for first foreign loan," *Hürriyet Daily News,* February 7, 2019, http://www.hurriyetdailynews.com/turkeys-wealth-fund-hires-banks-for-first-foreign-loan-141082.

106 Keith Johnson and Robbie Gramer, "Who Lost Turkey? The blame for Ankara's antagonistic stance to Washington lies with both sides, a product of decades of misunderstandings," *Foreign Policy,* July 19, 2019, https://foreignpolicy.com/2019/07/19/who-lost-turkey-middle-east-s-400-missile-deal-russia-syria-iraq-kurdish-united-states-nato-alliance-partners-allies-adversaries/.

107 Karen Kaya, "Turkey and China: Unlikely Strategic Partners," *Foreign Military Studies Office* (Fort Leavenworth, Kansas), August 2013, file:///C:/Users/moti/Downloads/2013-08-21%20Turkey%20and%20China-Unlikely%20Strategic%20Partners%20(Kaya)%20(1).pdf.

108 Chris Zambelis, "Sino-Turkish Strategic Partnership: Implications of Anatolian Eagle 2010," *China Brief*, 11(1) January 14, 2011, http://jamestown.org/%20single/?%20tx_ttnews%5Btt_news%5D=37369.

109 Mordechai Chaziza, "Sino-Turkish 'Solid Strategic Partnership': China's Dream or a Reality?," *China Report*, 52 (4), 2016, 265–283.

110 Mehmet Söylemez, "Turkey and China: An Account of a Bilateral Relations Evolution," *Asia Centre*, December 2017, https://centreasia.hypotheses.org/files/2018/06/22-Soleymez-ChineTurquie_De%CC%81c2017.pdf.

111 "Chinese Warships Visited Istanbul," *Bosphorus Naval News*, July 25, 2017, https://turkishnavy.net/tag/china/.

112 Metin Gurcan, "Following deals with Russia, Turkey now expands military cooperation with China," *Al-Monitor*, August 3, 2018, https://www.al-monitor.com/pulse/originals/2018/08/turkey-china-intensifying-defense-security-partnership.html.

113 Recep Tayyip Erdogan, "Turkey, China share a vision for future," *Global Times*, July 1, 2019, http://www.globaltimes.cn/content/1156357.shtml.

114 "Vision and Actions on Jointly Building Silk Road Economic Belt and 21st-Century Maritime Silk Road," *National Development and Reform Commission, Ministry of Foreign Affairs, and Ministry of Commerce of the People's Republic of China*, March 28, 2015, http://en.ndrc.gov.cn/newsrelease/201503/t20150330_669367.html.

115 "A New Era will be Heralded in Our Region Based on Stability and Prosperity," *Presidency of the Republic of Turkey*, May 14, 2017, https://www.tccb.gov.tr/en/news/542/75199/a-new-era-will-be-heralded-in-our-region-based-on-stability-and-prosperity.

116 "8 more countries set up Confucius institutes or classrooms in 2019," *Xinhua*, December 11, 2019, http://www.xinhuanet.com/english/2019-12/11/c_138623776.htm.

117 Huang Zhiling, "10 new Confucius Institutes lift global total to 548, boosting ties," *China Daily*, December 5, 2018, http://global.chinadaily.com.cn/a/201812/05/WS5c07239da310eff30328f182.html.

118 "Confucius Institute/Classroom," *Confucius Institute Headquarters (Hanban)*, 2020, http://english.hanban.org/node_10971.htm.

119 "Chinese as second language growing in popularity in Turkey," *Hürriyet Daily News*, June 17 2019, http://www.hurriyetdailynews.com/chinese-as-second-language-growing-in-popularity-in-turkey-144255.

120 "More Chinese students in Turkey, rising interest in China for Turkish," *Daily Sabah*, October 5, 2018, https://www.dailysabah.com/education/2018/10/06/more-chinese-students-in-turkey-rising-interest-in-china-for-turkish.

121 "Turkish students granted scholarships for studying Chinese language," *Xinhua*, May 10, 2019, http://www.xinhuanet.com/english/2019-05/10/c_138049112.htm.

122 "Turkey to hold Chinese culture events," *People's Daily Online*, September 29, 2010, http://en.people.cn/90001/90776/90883/7153675.html.

123 "Hurun Chinese New Year event hosted in Istanbul," *Xinhua*, January 29, 2019, http://www.xinhuanet.com/english/2019-01/30/c_137785116.htm.

124 Hong Yaobin and Wu Yan, "All the highlights from the Asian Culture Carnival," *CGTN*, May 16, 2019, https://news.cgtn.com/news/3d3d674d78417a4e34457a6333566d54/index.html.

125 Leisure Pursuit, "Turks Marveled by Chinese Culture at Mid-Autumn Festival Celebrations," *Belt & Road News*, September 14, 2019, https://www.beltandroad.news/2019/09/14/turks-marveled-by-chinese-culture-at-mid-autumn-festival-celebrations/.

126 Liu Jianna, "Turkey looks to improve ties with China," *China Daily*, July 2, 2019, http://www.chinadaily.com.cn/a/201907/02/WS5d1a9d0ba3103dbf1432b513.html.

127 Adam Garrie, "Erdoğan's China Visit Offers Historic Opportunities For Turkey And China as Well as Asia And Europe as a Whole," *Eurasia Future*, February 7, 2019, https://eurasiafuture.com/2019/07/02/erdogans-china-visit-offers-historic-opportunities-for-turkey-and-china-as-well-as-asia-and-europe-as-a-whole/.

128 "Turkey looks to welcome over half a million Chinese tourists this year," *Daily Sabah*, June 3, 2019, https://www.dailysabah.com/tourism/2019/06/03/turkey-looks-to-welcome-over-half-a-million-chinese-tourists-this-year.

129 "Chinese tourists' shopping in Turkey surges 85 pct in first 7 months," *Xinhua*, August 22, 2019, http://www.xinhuanet.com/english/2019-08/22/c_138327294.htm.

130 "Number of visitors to Turkey from China to increase Exponentially," *Belt & Road News*, April 2, 2019, https://www.beltandroad.news/2019/04/02/number-of-visitors-to-turkey-from-china-to-increase-exponentially/.

131 Altay Atlı, "Making Sense of Turkey's Rapprochement with China," *The German Marshall Fund of the United States (GMF)*, November 26, 2018, https://www.academia.edu/38232854/Making_Sense_of_Turkey_s_Rapprochement_with_China.

132 Lily Kuo, "Belt and Road forum: China's 'project of the century' hits tough times," *The Guardian*, April 25, 2019, https://www.theguardian.com/world/2019/apr/25/belt-and-road-forum-chinas-project-of-the-century-hits-tough-times.

133 "China Customs Statistics: Imports and exports by country/region," *The Hong Kong Trade Development Council (HKTDC)*, January 24, 2020, http://china-trade-research.hktdc.com/business-news/article/Facts-and-Figures/China-Customs-Statistics/ff/en/1/1X39VTVQ/1X09N9NM.htm.

134 Selçuk Çolakoğlu, "Silk Road Project and Opportunities to Improve China-Turkey Relations, *The Journal of Turkish Weekly*, December 30, 2014, http://www.asianpacificcenter.org/silk-road-and-china-turkey.html.

135 "Turkey confirms cancellation of $3.4 billion missile defence project awarded to China," *Reuters*, November 18, 2015, https://www.reuters.com/article/us-turkey-china-missile/turkey-confirms-cancellation-of-3-4-billion-missile-defence-project-awarded-to-china-idUSKCN0T61OV20151118.

136 Selçuk Çolakoğlu, "China's Belt and Road Initiative and Turkey's Middle Corridor: A Question of Compatibility," *Middle East Institute*, January 29, 2019, https://www.mei.edu/publications/chinas-belt-and-road-initiative-and-turkeys-middle-corridor-question-compatibility.

2 Egypt

1 Wan Michelle, Lui Maomin, and Yang Guang, *China–Middle East Relations: Review and Analysis*. UK: Paths International Ltd, 2012.

2 "Chinese president hails friendship, cooperation with Egypt," *China Daily*, January 20, 2016, http://www.chinadaily.com.cn/world/2016xivisitmiddleeast/2016-01/20/content_23172191.htm.

3 Sharon Li and Colin Ingram, *Maritime Law and Policy in China*. London: Routledge-Cavendish, 2013.

4 Mahmoud Ahmed Mohamed Mohamed Soliman and Jun Zhao, "The Multiple Roles of Egypt in China's 'Belt and Road' Initiative," *Asian Journal of Middle Eastern and Islamic Studies*, 13 (3), 2019, 428–444.

5 Mordechai Chaziza, China's Relationship with Egypt and Oman: A Strategic Framework for the Implementation of China's Maritime Silk Road Implementation. In Michael Clarke, Matthew Sussex and Nick Bisley (eds.) *The Belt and Road Initiative and the Future of Regional Order in the Indo-Pacific* (pp. 141–157). London: Lexington Books.

6 Deborah Lehr and Yasser Elnaggar, "Greening the belt and road: opportunities for Egypt," *Middle East Institute*, January 23, 2018, https://www.mei.edu/publications/greening-belt-and-road-opportunities-egypt.

7 Mohammed El-Said, "Egypt is an important country in China's One Belt One Road Initiative," *Daily News Egypt*, March 14, 2018, https://ww.dailynewssegypt.com 2018/03/14/egypt-important-country-chinas-one-belt-one-road-initiative/.

8 Chris Zambelis, "A New Egypt Looks to China for Balance and Leverage," *China Brief*, XII (18), (2012, 8–11).

9 Chen Juan, "Strategic Synergy between Egypt 'Vision 2030' and China's 'Belt and Road' Initiative," *Outlines of Global Transformations: Politics, Economics, Law*, 11 (5), 2018, 219–235.

10 "Sustainable Development Strategy (SDS): Egypt Vision 2030," 2016, https://www.greengrowthknowledge.org/sites/default/files/downloads/policy-database/Egypt%20Vision%202030%20%28English%29.pdf.

11 Min Ye, "China and competing for cooperation in Asia-Pacific: TPP, RCEP, and the New Silk Road," *Asian Security*, 11(3), 2015, 206–224.

12 "Vision and Actions on Jointly Building Silk Road Economic Belt and 21st-Century Maritime Silk Road," *National Development and Reform Commission, Ministry of Foreign Affairs, and Ministry of Commerce of the People's Republic of China*, March 28, 2015, http://en.ndrc.gov.cn/newsrelease/201503/t20150330_669367.html.

13 Mordechai Chaziza, "Comprehensive Strategic Partnership: A New Stage in China–Egypt Relations," *Middle East Review of International Affairs*, 20 (3), 2016, 41–50.

14 "El-Sisi arrives in China for investment talks," *Ahram Online*, 22 December 2014, http://english.ahram.org.eg/NewsContentP/1/118574/Egypt/ElSisi-arrives-in-China-for-investment-talks.aspx.

15 "Xi meets Egypt President Sisi," *People's Daily Online*, September 2, 2015, http://en.people.cn/n/2015/0902/c90883-8945054.html.

16 Lin Noueihed and Ali Abdelaty, "China's Xi visits Egypt, offers financial, political support," *Reuters*, 21 January 2016, http://www.reuters.com/article/us-egypt-china-idUSKCN0UZ05I.

17 "President Xi's Speech at Arab League Headquarters: Full Text," *China Daily*, January 22, 2016, http://www.chinadaily.com.cn/world/2016xivisitmiddleeast/2016-01/22/content_23191229.htm.

18 "Sisi visits China and Vietnam," *Egypt State Information Service (SIS)*, August 29, 2017, http://www.sis.gov.eg/Story/117390/Sisi-visits-China-and-Vietnam.

19 "China, Egypt to advance comprehensive strategic partnership," *Xinhua*, September 1, 2018, http://www.xinhuanet.com/english/2018-09/01/c_137437048.htm.

20 "Chinese premier meets Egyptian president," *People's Daily Online*, September 3, 2018, http://en.people.cn/n3/2018/0903/c90000-9496609.html.

21 "China, Egypt seeks to promote Belt and Road Initiative," *Xinhua*, April 13, 2017, http://www.xinhuanet.com//english/2017-04/13/c_136206645.htm.

22 Ahmed Shafiq and Abdel Meguid Kamal, "Yearender: China–Egypt relations see a strong push in 2018," *Xinhua*, December 28, 2018,

https://www.egypttoday.com/Article/3/62708/Egypt-China-relations-witness-remarkable-boost-in-2018.

23 "Egypt's Suez Canal economic zone integrates with China's BRI: minister," *Xinhua*, March 20, 2019, http://www.xinhuanet.com/english/2019-03/20/c_137908213.htm.

24 "Egypt adds a name to join China-backed AIIB investment bank," *Reuters*, March 30, 2015, http://uk.reuters.com/article/asia-aiib-denmark/egypt-adds-name-to-join-china-backed-aiib-investment-bank-idUKL3N0WW4FI20150330.

25 Muhamad S. Olimat, *China and North Africa since World War II: A Bilateral Approach*. London: Lexington Books, 2014.

26 "Egypt officially joins China's Silk Road Economic Belt union," *Daily News Egypt*, June 27, 2015, https://dailynewsegypt.com/2015/06/27/egypt-officially-joins-chinas-silk-road-economic-belt-union/.

27 "Interview: Egypt eyes further Chinese investments in national development projects: minister," *Ministry of Foreign Affairs: the People's Republic of China*, September 9, 2016, http://www.focac.org/eng/zfgx/t1396130.htm.

28 "Sisi visits China and Vietnam," *Egypt State Information Service (SIS)*, August 29, 2017, http://www.sis.gov.eg/Story/117390/Sisi-visits-China-and-Vietnam.

29 "China–Arab Expo to enhance bilateral all-round cooperation: senior AL official," *Xinhua*, September 3, 2017, http://www.xinhuanet.com//english/2017-09/03/c_136580240.htm.

30 "Vision and Actions on Jointly Building Silk Road Economic Belt and 21st-Century Maritime Silk Road," *National Development and Reform Commission, Ministry of Foreign Affairs, and Ministry of Commerce of the People's Republic of China*, March 28, 2015, http://en.ndrc.gov.cn/newsrelease/201503/t20150330_669367.html.

31 Jean-Marc F. Blanchard and Colin Flint, "The Geopolitics of China's Maritime Silk Road Initiative," *Geopolitics*, 22 (2), 2017, 223–225.

32 "Belt and Road Initiative (BRI): Reshaping the Political Scenario of the Eastern Mediterranean?," *Mediterranean Affairs*, November 7, 2018, http://mediterranean affairs.com/belt-road-initiative-bri-mediterranean/.

33 Christopher Len, "China's 21st Century Maritime Silk Road Initiative, Energy Security and SLOC Access," *Maritime Affairs: Journal of the National Maritime Foundation of India*, 11(1), 2015, 1–18.

34 Tai Hwan Lee, "One Belt, One Road strategy and Korean-Chinese cooperation," *The Newsletter*, No. 74, 2016, https://iias.asia/sites/default/files/IIAS_NL74_16-1.pdf.

35 Sumedh Anil Lokhande, "China's One Belt One Road Initiative and the Gulf Pearl chain," *China Daily*, June 5, 2017, http://www.chinadaily.com.cn/opinion/2017beltan-droad/2017-06/05/content_29618549.htm.

36 "Egypt to Become the Region's Digital Hub: El-Sisi Says at 'Belt and Road' Summit," *Egyptian Streets*, April 28, 2019, https://egyptianstreets.com/2019/04/28/egypt-to-lead-the-regions-digital-economy-el-sisi-says-during-his-speech-at-belt-and-road-summit/.

37 "Egypt," *Energy Information Administration (EIA)*, May 24, 2018, https://www.eia.gov/beta/international/analysis.php?iso=EGY.

38 Mohamed Fayez Farahat "Egypt's astute move towards China's Belt and Road Initiative," *Ahram Online*, May 2, 2019, http://english.ahram.org.eg/News/330982.aspx.

39 "China to establish 50 factories near Suez canal," *CNTV*, August 7, 2015, http://en.people.cn/business/n/2015/0807/c90778-8933176.html.

40 Sharon Li and Colin Ingram, *Maritime Law and Policy in China*. London: Routledge-Cavendish, 2013.

41 Oded Eran, "China Has Laid Anchor in Israel's Ports," *Strategic Assessment*, 19 (1), 2016, 51–59.

42 Emma Scott, "China–Egypt Trade and Investment Ties: Seeking a Better Balance," *Centre for Chinese Studies*, June 2015, file:///C:/Users/moti/Downloads/scott_trade_2015.pdf.

43 Emma Scott, "China's Silk Road Strategy: A Foothold in the Suez, but Looking to Israel," *China Brief*, 14 (19), 2014, 4–10.

44 "China Harbour builds new terminal south of Egypt's Suez Canal," *Xinhua*, August 28, 2018, http://www.xinhuanet.com/english/2018-08/29/c_137428464.htm.

45 Ahmed Farouk Ghoneim, "Egypt's Suez Canal Corridor Project," *Middle East Institute*, August 19, 2014, https://www.lexology.com/library/detail.aspx?g=66240360-91e2-46ff-81b9-5ac777345d26; "China now biggest investor in Suez," *China Daily*, March 23, 2017, http://www.chinadaily.com.cn/business/2017-03/23/content_28648386.htm.

46 Al-Masry Al-Youm, "SCZone head: 13% of world trade passes through Suez Canal," *Egypt Independent*, June 23, 2019, https://egyptindependent.com/sczone-head-13-of-world-trade-passes-through-suez-canal/.

47 "China now the biggest investor in Suez," *China Daily*, March 23, 2017, http://www.chinadaily.com.cn/business/2017-03/23/content_28648386.htm.

48 Hong Zhao, "Egypt announces new Chinese investments in textile," *China Daily*, April 5, 2017, http://www.chinadaily.com.cn/business/2017-04/05/content_28803966.htm.

49 "Chinese firms eye investing in New Admin Capital: Ambassador," *Egypt Today*, August 29, 2017, https://www.egypttoday.com/Article/3/20062/Chinese-firms-eye-investing-in-New-Admin-Capital-Ambassador.

50 "China Grants Egypt $US 71 Million for Satellite Project, Vocational Training Centre," *Egyptian Streets*, March 22, 2017, https://egyptianstreets.com/2017/03/22/china-grants-egypt-us-71-for-satellite-project-vocational-training-centre/.

51 "Egypt, China ink $45 mln deal to establish 'Egypt Sat-2'," *Ahram Online*, August 13, 2018, http://english.ahram.org.eg/NewsContent/3/12/309566/Business/Economy/Egypt,-China-ink–mln-deal-to-establish-Egypt-Sat-.aspx.

52 "Agreement with the head of Silk Road Fund to enhance investments to activate joint Egyptian Chinese projects," *Daily News Egypt*, May 15, 2017, https://www.menafn.com/qn_news_story_s.aspx?storyid=1095480921&title=Agreement-with-head-of-Silk-Road-Fund-to-enhance-investments-to-activate-joint-Egyptian-Chinese-projects&src=RSS.

53 "China to invest $40bn in Egypt development projects," *Trade Arabia*, May 16, 2017, http://www.tradearabia.com/news/CONS_325023.html.

54 "Full text: List of deliverables of Belt and Road forum," *Xinhua*, May 15, 2017, http://www.xinhuanet.com/english/2017-05/15/c_136286376.htm.

55 Al-Masry Al-Youm, "China to invest US$5 billion in Egypt's Suez Canal Economic Zone," *Egypt Independent*, April 28, 2019, https://ww.egyptindependent.com/author/al-masry-al-youm/.

56 Mandira Bagwandeen, "The African Link in China's OBOR Initiative," *Center for Chinese Studies*, May 15, 2017, http://daofeiconsults.com/wpcontent/uploads/2015/05/CCS_Commentary_Africa_OBOR_15MAY2017.pdf.

57 "Vision and Actions on Jointly Building Silk Road Economic Belt and 21st-Century Maritime Silk Road," *National Development and Reform Commission, Ministry of Foreign*

Affairs, and Ministry of Commerce of the People's Republic of China, March 28, 2015, http://en.ndrc.gov.cn/newsrelease/201503/t20150330_669367.html.

58 "China Customs Statistics: Imports and exports by country/region," *The Hong Kong Trade Development Council (HKTDC)*, January 24, 2020, http://china-trade-research.hktdc.com/business-news/article/Facts-and-Figures/China-Customs-Statistics/ff/en/1/1X39VTVQ/1X09N9NM.htm.

59 "Chinese Investments & Contracts in Egypt (2013–2018)," *China Global Investment Tracker*, 2019, https://www.aei.org/china-global-investment-tracker/.

60 Hisham Abu Bakr Metwally, "BRI Chinese Investment Grabs Egypt's Attention," *China Focus*, September 19, 2018, http://www.cnfocus.com/bri-chinese-investment-grabs-egypt-s-attention/.

61 "Egypt plans new capital adjacent to Cairo," *Al Jazeera*, March 14, 2015, http://www.aljazeera.com/news/2015/03/egypt-plans-capital-adjacent-cairo-150314014400946.html.

62 Kieron Monks, "Egypt is getting a new capital – courtesy of China," *CNN*, October 10, 2016, http://edition.cnn.com/style/article/egypt-new-capital/index.html.

63 Ahmed Kamel, "Chinese project to build new Egyptian capital revived," *Nikkei Asian Review*, May 26, 2017, https://asia.nikkei.com/Business/Companies/Chinese-project-to-build-new-Egyptian-capital-revived.

64 "China's US$20 billion projects to develop a new capital for Egypt falls through amid discord over how to share revenue," *South China Morning Post*, December 17, 2018, https://www.scmp.com/magazines/post-magazine/travel/article/3016088/seven-silk-road-destinations-china-italy-towns-grew.

65 Neil Ford, "Egypt: New capital city project hit by Chinese withdrawal," *African Business Magazine*, February 23, 2017, http://africanbusinessmagazine.com/region/north-africa/egypt-new-capital-city-project-hit-chinese-withdrawal/.

66 "Egypt enters into the initial deal for 15 projects worth $10 bln with China – minister," *Reuters*, June 16, 2015, http://www.reuters.com/article/egypt-investment-china-idUSL5N0Z14NG20150615.

67 Lin Noueihed and Ali Abdelaty, "China's Xi visits Egypt, offers financial, political support," *Reuters*, January 21, 2016, https://www.reuters.com/article/us-egypt-china/chinas-xi-visits-egypt-offers-financial-political-support-idUSKCN0UZ05I.

68 Hou Liqiang, "Chinese companies boost operations in Egypt," *China Daily*, February 15, 2016, http://www.chinadaily.com.cn/business/2016-02/15/content_23481956.htm.

69 "Chinese investments in Egypt hit $15B," *Egypt Today*, November 14, 2018, https://www.egypttoday.com/Article/3/60437/Chinese-investments-in-Egypt-hit-15B; Al-Masry Al-Youm, "China to invest US$5 billion in Egypt's Suez Canal Economic Zone," *Egypt Independent*, April 28, 2019, https://ww.egyptindependent.com/china-to-invest-us5-billion-in-egypts-suez-canal-economic-zone/.

70 "Egypt-China relations witness a remarkable boost in 2018," *Egypt Today*, December 28, 2018, https://www.egypttoday.com/Article/3/62708/Egypt-China-relations-witness-remarkable-boost-in-2018.

71 "China key to modernizing Egypt's railway infrastructure: Official," *China Daily*, August 18, 2017, http://www.chinadaily.com.cn/business/2017-08/14/content_30575962.htm.

72 "Ministry of Transportation signs $800m MOU with China for the railway project," *Daily News Egypt*, April 5, 2014, http://www.dailynewsegypt.com/2014/04/05/ministry-transportation-signs-800m-mou-china-railway-project/.

73 "Egypt's high-speed train project in progress: Minister," *The Cairo Post*, March 14, 2015, http://thecairopost.youm7.com/news/141695/business/egypts-high-speed-train-project-in-progress-minister.

74 "Egypt to Sign MOU With Chinese Company to Construct Sixth Metro Line," *All Africa*, January 11, 2016, http://allafrica.com/stories/201601041476.html.

75 "Egypt, China to establish electric train project worth $1.2B," *Egypt Today*, July 24, 2017, https://www.egypttoday.com/Article/3/13432/Egypt-China-to-establish-electric-train-project-worth-1-2B.

76 Alicja Siekierska, "Bombardier signs agreement with Egypt to develop a proposal for new Cairo metro line," *Financial Post*, July 12, 2017, http://business.financialpost.com/transportation/bombardier-signs-agreement-with-egypt-to-develop-proposal-for-new-cairo-metro-line.

77 "Investment Ministry signs MoU with China Exim Bank to support development projects," *Daily News*, August 29, 2017, https://dailynewsegypt.com/2017/08/29/investment-ministry-signs-mou-china-exim-bank-support-development-projects/.

78 Zhao Jiasong and Mahmoud Fouly, "Interview: China's greenhouse technologies turn Egypt's desert green: Chinese project manager," *Xinhua*, April 10, 2019, http://www.xinhuanet.com/english/2019-04/10/c_137966152.htm.

79 Heba Saleh, "Egypt sees Chinese investment, and tourists as a 'win-win' boost," *Financial Times*, October 30, 2018, https://www.ft.com/content/e490d960-7613-11e8-8cc4-59b7a8ef7d3d.

80 "European Union, trade in goods with China," *European Commission Directorate-General for Trade*, 2019, https://webgate.ec.europa.eu/isdb_results/factsheets/country/details_china_en.pdf.

81 "EU-China trade in goods: 185 billion deficit in 2018," *Eurostat*, April 9, 2019, https://ec.europa.eu/eurostat/web/products-eurostat-news/-/EDN-20190409-1.

82 "Chinese Investments & Contracts in Egypt (2013–2018)," *China Global Investment Tracker*, 2019, https://www.aei.org/china-global-investment-tracker/.

83 "World Oil Transit Chokepoints," *Energy Information Administration (EIA)*, July 25, 2017, https://www.eia.gov/beta/international/regions-topics.php?RegionTopicID=WOTC.

84 "The Suez Canal and SUMED Pipeline are critical chokepoints for oil and natural gas trade," *Energy Information Administration (EIA)*, July 23, 2019, https://www.eia.gov/todayinenergy/detail.php?id=40152.

85 "World Oil Transit Chokepoints," *Energy Information Administration (EIA)*, July 25, 2017, https://www.eia.gov/beta/international/regions-topics.php?RegionTopicID=WOTC.

86 "China's Sinopec signs $3.1bn Egypt oil deal with Apache," *BBC*, August 30, 2013, https://www.bbc.com/news/business-23894284.

87 Emma Scott, "China–Egypt Trade and Investment Ties: Seeking a Better Balance," *Centre for Chinese Studies*, June 2015, file:///C:/Users/moti/Downloads/scott_trade_2015.pdf.

88 Yang Ge, "Egypt Emerges as China's Africa Bulwark with $9.6 Billion in Deals," *Caixin Global*, September 6, 2018, https://www.caixinglobal.com/2018-09-06/egypt-emerges-as-chinas-africa-bulwark-with-96-billion-in-deals-101323291.html.

89 "Zohr: Massive new natural gas discoveries in the Mediterranean will meet and exceed Egypt's national demand for years," *Brussels Research Group (BRG)*, February 3, 2019, https://brusselsresearchgroup.org/index.php/2019/02/03/zohr-massive-new-natural-gas-discoveries-in-the-mediterranean-will-meet-and-exceed-egypts-national-demand-for-years/.

90 "Belt and Road Initiative (BRI): Reshaping the Political Scenario of the Eastern Mediterranean?," *Mediterranean Affairs*, November 7, 2018, http://mediterranean affairs.com/belt-road-initiative-bri-mediterranean/.

91 "China, Egypt agree to nuclear cooperation," *World Nuclear News*, May 28, 2015, http://world-nuclear-news.org/Articles/China,-Egypt-agree-to-nuclear-cooperation.

92 "Egypt, Russia Co-Sign Agreement to Build Dabaa Nuclear Plant," *Asharq Al-Awsat*, December 12, 2017, https://aawsat.com/english/home/article/1110841/egypt-russia-co-sign-agreement-build-dabaa-nuclear-plant.

93 "Egypt, China Sign Energy Contract," *Egypt oil-gas*, September 5, 2017, https://egyptoil-gas.com/news/egypt-china-sign-energy-contract/.

94 Marwa Yahya, "Interview: Chinese investments in Egypt's electricity sector in continuous increase: official," *Xinhua*, September 8, 2019, http://www.xinhuanet.com/english/2018-09/08/c_137452789.htm.

95 "Yingli will build 500MW solar PV project in Egypt," *OFweek*, February 10, 2015, http://en.ofweek.com/news/Yingli-will-build-500MW-solar-PV-project-in-Egypt-25326.

96 Tom Kenning, "Asian Bank providing US$210 million for 490MW of Egyptian solar," *PVTECH*, September 5, 2017, https://www.pv-tech.org/news/aiib-providing-us210-million-for-470mw-of-egyptian-solar.

97 Mohamed Farag, "Egyptian–Chinese alliance offers to sell solar power to BMIC," *Daily News Egypt*, February 27, 2019, https://www.zawya.com/mena/en/business/story/EgyptianChinese_alliance_offers_to_sell_solar_power_to_BMIC-SNG_138936031/.

98 "Vision and Actions on Jointly Building Silk Road Economic Belt and 21st-Century Maritime Silk Road," *National Development and Reform Commission, Ministry of Foreign Affairs, and Ministry of Commerce of the People's Republic of China*, March 28, 2015, http://en.ndrc.gov.cn/newsrelease/201503/t20150330_669367.html.

99 Al-Masry Al-Youm, "Will the Chinese yuan truly relieve Egypt's need for US dollar?," *Egypt Independent*, December 14, 2016, https://ww.egyptindependent.com/will-chinese-yuan-truly-relieve-egypt-s-need-us-dollar/.

100 Loay Wael, "Egypt, China to renew currency swap deal: CBE governor to AACB," *Ahram Online*, August 8, 2018, http://english.ahram.org.eg/NewsContent/3/12/309321/Business/Economy/Egypt,-China-to-renew-currency-swap-deal-CBE-gover.aspx.

101 Chen Juan, "Strategic Synergy between Egypt "Vision 2030" and China's "Belt and Road" Initiative," *Outlines of Global Transformations: Politics, Economics, Law*, 11 (5), 2018, 219–235.

102 "Egypt–China relations witness a remarkable boost in 2018," *Egypt Today*, December 28, 2018, https://www.egypttoday.com/Article/3/62708/Egypt-China-relations-witness-remarkable-boost-in-2018.

103 "Egypt borrows $1.2bn from China to fund electric train project," *Middle East Monitor*, January 16, 2019, https://www.middleeastmonitor.com/20190116-egypt-borrows-1-2bn-from-china-to-fund-electric-train-project/.

104 "Chinese firm finalizes the deal for building huge business district in Egypt's new capital," *Xinhua*, October 12, 2017, http://www.xinhuanet.com//english/2017-10/12/c_136672905.htm.

105 Zheng Caixiong, "Egypt's oldest bank sets up base in Chinese port city," *Xinhua*, April 20, 2017, http://www.chinadaily.com.cn/business/2017-04/20/content_29014780.htm.

106 "China to Boost Military Cooperation with Egypt," *Global Business Press*, December 2, 2018, https://gbp.com.sg/china-to-boost-military-cooperation-with-egypt/.

107 "Edex 2018 Concludes with Several Arms Contracts," *Egypt Defense Expo*, December 7, 2018,
https://www.egyptdefenceexpo.com/news/edex-2018-concludes-with-several-arms-contracts.

108 "Egypt: Defence cooperation with China and support for Belt and Road Initiative," *DefencePoint*, March 23, 2019, https://defence-point.com/2019/03/27/egypt-defence-cooperation-with-china-and-support-for-belt-and-road-initiative/.

109 "Vision and Actions on Jointly Building Silk Road Economic Belt and 21st-Century Maritime Silk Road," *National Development and Reform Commission, Ministry of Foreign Affairs, and Ministry of Commerce of the People's Republic of China*, March 28, 2015, http://en.ndrc.gov.cn/newsrelease/201503/t20150330_669367.html.

110 "8 more countries set up Confucius institutes or classrooms in 2019," *Xinhua*, December 11, 2019, http://www.xinhuanet.com/english/2019-12/11/c_138623776.htm.

111 Huang Zhiling, "10 new Confucius Institutes lift the global total to 548, boosting ties," *China Daily*, December 5, 2018,
http://global.chinadaily.com.cn/a/201812/05/WS5c07239da310eff30328f182.html.

112 "Confucius Institute/Classroom," *Confucius Institute Headquarters (Hanban)*, 2020, http://english.hanban.org/node_10971.htm.

113 "Spotlight: Belt and Road Cooperation Research Center Inaugurated in Cairo," *Xinhua*, January 14, 2019, http://www.xinhuanet.com/english/2019-01/14/c_137741043.htm.

114 "Egypt and China . . . Partnership for Development," *Egypt State Information Service (SIS)*, October 28, 2018, http://www.sis.gov.eg/Story/135872/Egypt-and-China%E2%80%A6Partnership-for-Development?lang=en-us.

115 "China-developed smart classrooms to improve the education quality of Egypt," *People's Daily Online*, April 29, 2019, http://en.people.cn/n3/2019/0429/c90000-9573828.html.

116 Lu Wen'ao and Wei Xi, "Egypt seek bilateral benefits with China in Belt, Road initiative," *Global Times*, May 10, 2017, http://www.globaltimes.cn/content/1046292.shtml.

117 "China, Egypt enhance Archaeological Cooperation under Belt & Road," *Belt & Road News*, April 15, 2019, https://www.beltandroad.news/2019/04/15/china-egypt-enhance-archaeological-cooperation-under-belt-road/.

118 "China–Egypt Cultural Year 2016," *China Culture*, April 11, 2016, http://en.china culture.org/2016-04/11/content_751353.htm.

119 "Egypt's state TV to play Chinese soap opera as part of cultural cooperation," *Xinhua*, November 19, 2018, http://www.xinhuanet.com/english/2018-11/19/c_137615966.htm.

120 "Chinese film fest draws fans in Egypt," *China Daily*, July 11, 2019, http://www.chinadaily.com.cn/a/201907/11/WS5d26768ea3105895c2e7cd2f.html.

121 "Interview: Egypt works on attracting more Chinese tourists: tourism minister," *Xinhua*, May 12, 2018, http://www.xinhuanet.com/english/2018-05/12/c_137173071.htm.

122 "Egypt sees surging number of Chinese tourists: Cultural counselor," *Egypt Today*, June 14, 2019, http://www.egypttoday.com/Article/9/71576/Egypt-sees-surging-number-of-Chinese-tourists-Cultural-counselor.

123 "China promising market for Egypt's tourism: minister," *Xinhua*, April 4, 2018, http://www.xinhuanet.com/english/2019-04/04/c_137950684.htm.

124 "Egypt sees surging number of Chinese tourists," *Asia Times*, June 13, 2019, https://www.asiatimes.com/2019/06/article/egypt-sees-growing-number-of-chinese-tourists/.

125 "Egypt's tourism recovering, eyeing more Chinese visitors: minister," *Egypt Today*, February 11, 2019, https://www.egypttoday.com/Article/9/64504/Egypt-s-tourism-recovering-eyeing-more-Chinese-visitors-minister.

126 "Vision And Actions On Jointly Building Silk Road Economic Belt And 21st-Century Maritime Silk Ro," *National Development and Reform Commission, Ministry of Foreign Affairs, and Ministry of Commerce of the People's Republic of China, with State Council authorization*, March, 30. 2015, https://eng.yidaiyilu.gov.cn/qwyw/qwfb/1084.htm.

3 Israel

1   Zhiqun Zhu, "China–Israel Relations: Past, Present and Prospect," *East Asian Policy*, 11(4), 2019, 37–45.

2   Shira Efron, Howard J. Shatz, Arthur Chan, Emily Haskel, Lyle J. Morris and Andrew Scobell, *The Evolving Israel–China Relationship*. RAND Corporation, Santa Monica, Calif., 2019.

3   Ori Sela and Brandon Friedman, "Sino–Israeli Relations: Challenges amid Growing Ties," in Enrico Fardella and Andrea Ghiselli (eds.), *China MED Report 2019: China's New Role in the Wider Mediterranean Region* (The ChinaMed Project, 2019), pp. 45–49.

4   Galia Lavi, Jingjie He, and Oded Eran, "China and Israel: On the Same Belt and Road?," *Strategic Assessment*, 18 (3), 2015, pp. 81–91.

5   The Chinese system, which places significant emphasis on defining relations with core countries in its foreign relations, thus serves as a kind of working guideline for the professional echelons to assign priority to cooperating with Israel on innovation. The upgrade in relations between the countries was made possible, in part, by the strengthened connection and dialogue between governmental bodies and figures, complementary interests in access to Israeli civilian technologies in return for access to the Chinese market, strengthened academic and research connections, and promoting the movement of people between the two countries by opening direct flight routes and easing the visa approval process.

6   Min Ye, "China and competing for cooperation in Asia-Pacific: TPP, RCEP, and the New Silk Road," *Asian Security*, 11(3), 2015, 206–224.

7   "Vision and Actions on Jointly Building Silk Road Economic Belt and 21st-Century Maritime Silk Road," *National Development and Reform Commission, Ministry of Foreign Affairs, and Ministry of Commerce of the People's Republic of China*, March 28, 2015, http://en.ndrc.gov.cn/newsrelease/201503/t20150330_669367.html.

8   John Gee, "President Jiang Zemin's visit in Israel," *Washington Report on Middle East Affairs*, June 2000, https://www.wrmea.org/000-june/hinese-president-jiang-zemin-in-israel.html.

9   "FM Liberman meets with Chinese Vice President and Foreign Minister," *Israel Minister of Foreign Affairs*, March 16, 2012, https://mfa.gov.il/MFA/PressRoom/2012/Pages/FM-Liberman-meets-with-Chinese-Vice-President-and-Foreign-Minister-16-Mar-2012.aspx.

10 "President Peres on state visit to China," *Israel Minister of Foreign Affairs*, April 9, 2014, https://mfa.gov.il/MFA/PressRoom/2014/Pages/President-Peres-on-state-visit-to-China-8-April-2014.aspx.

11 "PM Netanyahu meets with Chinese President Xi Jinping," *Israel Minister of Foreign Affairs*, May 9, 2013, https://mfa.gov.il/MFA/PressRoom/2013/Pages/PM-Netanyahu-meets-Chinese-President-Xi-Jinping-9-May-2013.aspx; "PM Netanyahu pays official visit to China," *Israel Minister of Foreign Affairs*, March 19, 2017,

https://mfa.gov.il/MFA/PressRoom/2017/Pages/PM-Netanyahu-pays-official-visit-to-China-.aspx.

12   Mordechai Chaziza, "Israel–China Relations Enter a New Stage: Limited Strategic Hedging," *Contemporary Review of the Middle East*, 5 (1), 2018, 30–45.

13   Gao Yanping, "China–Israel Relations Are Bound to Blossom," *The Jerusalem Post*, April 3, 2014, https://www.jpost.com/Opinion/Op-Ed-Contributors/China-Israel-relations-are-bound-to-blossomHE-GAO-YANPING-347495.

14   "Xi Jinping Meets with Prime Minister Benjamin Netanyahu of Israel," *Ministry of Foreign Affairs, the People's Republic of China*, March 21, 2017, https://www.fmprc.gov.cn/mfa_eng//zxxx_662805/t1448057.shtml.

15   Raphael Ahren, "In Beijing, Netanyahu looks to 'marry Israel's technology with China's capacity," *The Times of Israel*, March 21, 2017, https://www.timesofisrael.com/in-beijing-netanyahu-looks-to-marry-israels-technology-with-chinas-capacity.

16   Xiao Xian, "The "Belt and Road Initiative" and China–Israeli Relations," *Journal of Middle Eastern and Islamic Studies (in Asia)*, 10 (3), 2016, 1–23.

17   Mordechai Chaziza, "Chinese VP Visits Israel Innovation Conference," *BESA Center Perspectives Paper* No. 996, November 5, 2018, https://besacenter.org/perspectives-papers/china-wang-qishan-israel/.

18   Raphael Ahren, "PM lauds 'growing friendship' between Israel, China as he hosts vice president," *The Times of Israel*, October 23, 2018, https://www.timesofisrael.com/pm-lauds-growing-friendship-between-israel-china-as-he-hosts-vice-president/.

19   Lilach Baumer, "Chinese Vice President Wang Qishan Lands in Israel for Official Visit," *CTECH*, October 22, 2018, https://www.calcalistech.com/ctech/articles/0,7340,L-3748151,00.html.

20   Michael Bachner and Toi Staff, Foreign Ministry said to warn of clash with US unless China investments curbed," *The Times of Israel*, August 6, 2019, https://www.timesofisrael.com/foreign-ministry-said-to-warn-of-clash-with-us-unless-china-investments-curbed/.

21   "Xi Jinping Meets with Israeli Prime Minister Netanyahu," *Ministry of Foreign Affairs, the People's Republic of China*, March 21, 2017, https://www.fmprc.gov.cn/mfa_eng//zxxx_662805/t1448057.shtml

22   "China and Israel Have the Fifth Round of Negotiations on Free Trade Area," *China FTA Network*, February 4, 2019, http://fta.mofcom.gov.cn/enarticle/enrelease/201902/39840_1.html.

23   "Win-win cooperation between Israel, China has huge potential: Israeli minister," *Xinhua*, March 21, 2019, http://www.xinhuanet.com/english/2019-03/17/c_137902485.htm.

24   Erez Linn, "Relations between China and Israel are very well," *Israel Hayom*, December 10, 2019, https://www.israelhayom.com/2019/12/10/relations-between-china-and-israel-are-going-on-very-well/.

25   "Vision and Actions on Jointly Building Silk Road Economic Belt and 21st-Century Maritime Silk Road," *National Development and Reform Commission, Ministry of Foreign Affairs, and Ministry of Commerce of the People's Republic of China*, March 28, 2015, http://en.ndrc.gov.cn/newsrelease/201503/t20150330_669367.html.

26   Dubi Ben-Gedalyahu, "China to be Israel's Biggest Infrastructure Partner," *Globes*, May 10, 2015, https://en.globes.co.il/en/article-china-becoming-israels-biggest-infrastructure-partner-1001031690; Niv Elis, "Private Ashdod Port Building Ahead of Schedule, Says Ports Company," *The Jerusalem Post*, April 12, 2016, https://www.jpost.com/Business-and-Innovation/Private-Ashdod-port-building-ahead-of-schedule-says-ports-company-451039.

27 Galia Lavi, Jingjie He, and Oded Eran, "China and Israel: On the Same Belt and Road?," *Strategic Assessment*, 18 (3), 2015, pp. 81–91.

28 Raphael Ahren and Yifeng Zhou, "Netanyahu to Times of Israel Chinese: I hope Beijing's 'superb' relations with Israel will affect its UN votes," *The Times of Israel*, March 23, 2017, https://www.timesofisrael.com/netanyahu-to-tois-chinese-site-i-hope-beijings-superb-relations-with-israel-will-affect-its-un-votes/.

29 Shira Efron, Howard J. Shatz, Arthur Chan, Emily Haskel, Lyle J. Morris and Andrew Scobell, *The Evolving Israel–China Relationship*. RAND Corporation, Santa Monica, Calif., 2019.

30 Xiao Xian, "The "Belt and Road Initiative" and China–Israeli Relations," *Journal of Middle Eastern and Islamic Studies (in Asia)*, 10 (3), 2016, 1–23.

31 Mercy A. Kuo, "China and Israel in the Belt and Road Initiative," *The Diplomat*, September 19, 2018, https://thediplomat.com/2018/09/china-and-israel-in-the-belt-and-road-initiative/.

32 Xiao Xian, "The "Belt and Road Initiative" and China–Israeli Relations," *Journal of Middle Eastern and Islamic Studies (in Asia)*, 10 (3), 2016, 1–23.

33 David Shamah, "China firm to build new Ashdod 'union buster' port," *The Times of Israel*, September 23, 2014, https://www.timesofisrael.com/china-firm-to-build-new-ashdod-union-buster-port/.

34 Ofer Petersburg, "Chinese company wins bid to run new Haifa port," *Ynet*, March 24, 2015, https://www.ynetnews.com/articles/0,7340,L-4640513,00.html.

35 Mordechai Chaziza, "The Red–Med Railway: New Opportunities for China, Israel, and the Middle East," *BESA Center Perspectives Paper*, December 11, 2016, https://besacenter.org/perspectives-papers/385-chaziza-the-red-med-railway-new-opportunities-for-china-israel-and-the-middle-east/.

36 Xiao Xian, "The 'Belt and Road Initiative' and China–Israeli Relations," *Journal of Middle Eastern and Islamic Studies (in Asia)*, 10 (3), 2016, 1–23.

37 Mordechai Chaziza, "The Red–Med Railway: New Opportunities for China, Israel, and the Middle East," *BESA Center Perspectives Paper*, December 11, 2016, https://besacenter.org/perspectives-papers/385-chaziza-the-red-med-railway-new-opportunities-for-china-israel-and-the-middle-east/.

38 Xiao Xian, "The 'Belt and Road Initiative' and China–Israeli Relations," *Journal of Middle Eastern and Islamic Studies (in Asia)*, 10 (3), 2016, 1–23.

39 "Eilat Railway," *The Society for the Protection of Nature in Israel* (SPNI), 2019, https://natureisrael.org/EilatRailway.

40 Raphael Ahren and Yifeng Zhou, "Netanyahu to Times of Israel Chinese: I hope Beijing's 'superb' relations with Israel will affect its UN votes," *The Times of Israel*, March 23, 2017, https://www.timesofisrael.com/netanyahu-to-tois-chinese-site-i-hope-beijings-superb-relations-with-israel-will-affect-its-un-votes/.

41 Amos Harel, "Israel Is Giving China the Keys to Its Largest Port – and the U.S. Navy May Abandon Israel," *Haaretz*, September 17, 2018, https://www.haaretz.com/us-news/.premium-israel-is-giving-china-the-keys-to-its-largest-port-and-the-u-s-navy-may-abandon-israel-1.6470527.

42 Justin Jalil, "Israel Navy Welcomes New Submarine in Haifa," *Times of Israel*, September 23, 2014, https://www.timesofisrael.com/israel-navy-welcomes-new-submarine-in-haifa/.

43 "Chinese Port Operator at Haifa Will Mean Questions for U.S. Navy," *The Maritime Executive*, September 14, 2018, https://www.maritime-executive.com/article/chinese-port-operator-at-haifa-will-mean-questions-for-u-s-navy.

44 Shira Efron, Howard J. Shatz, Arthur Chan, Emily Haskel, Lyle J. Morris and Andrew

Scobell, *The Evolving Israel–China Relationship*. RAND Corporation, Santa Monica, Calif., 2019.

45 Assaf Orion and Galia Lavi, eds., *Israel–China Relations: Opportunities and Challenges* (Tel Aviv: The Institute for National Security Studies, 2019), https://css.ethz.ch/content/dam/ethz/special-interest/gess/cis/center-for-securities-studies/resources/docs/INSS_Memo194_e-1.pdf.

46 Shira Efron, Howard J. Shatz, Arthur Chan, Emily Haskel, Lyle J. Morris and Andrew Scobell, *The Evolving Israel–China Relationship*. RAND Corporation, Santa Monica, Calif, 2019.

47 Eytan Halon, "Israel-China, Experts Downplay Impact of Haifa Port Decision," *The Jerusalem Post*, June 18, 2019, https://www.jpost.com/Israel-News/Israel-China-experts-downplay-impact-of-Haifa-Port-decision-576988.

48 Mercy A. Kuo, "Israel Balancing US-China Relations: Geostrategic Context," *The Diplomat*, April 16, 2019, https://thediplomat.com/2019/04/israel-balancing-us-china-relations-geostrategic-context/.

49 Mordechai Chaziza, "Israel-China Relations Enter a New Stage: Limited Strategic Hedging," *Contemporary Review of the Middle East*, 5 (1), 2018, 30–45.

50 "Vision and Actions on Jointly Building Silk Road Economic Belt and 21st-Century Maritime Silk Road," *National Development and Reform Commission, Ministry of Foreign Affairs, and Ministry of Commerce of the People's Republic of China*, March 28, 2015, http://en.ndrc.gov.cn/newsrelease/201503/t20150330_669367.html.

51 "China Customs Statistics: Imports and exports by country/region," *The Hong Kong Trade Development Council (HKTDC)*, January 24, 2020, http://china-trade-research.hktdc.com/business-news/article/Facts-and-Figures/China-Customs-Statistics/ff/en/1/1X39VTVQ/1X09N9NM.htm.

52 "Ambassador Zhan Yongxin Gives a Live Interview to Ynet," *Embassy of the People's Republic of China in the State of Israel*, August 22, 2019, http://il.china-embassy.org/eng/gdxw/t1691080.htm.

53 Daniel Workman, "Israel's Top Trading Partners," *World's Top Exports*, March 1, 2019, http://www.worldstopexports.com/israels-top-trading-partners/. Trade metrics that inspire global thinking.

54 Xiao Xian, "The "Belt and Road Initiative" and China–Israeli Relations," *Journal of Middle Eastern and Islamic Studies (in Asia)*, 10 (3), 2016, 1–23.

55 Mordechai Chaziza, "Israel-China Relations Enter a New Stage: Limited Strategic Hedging," *Contemporary Review of the Middle East*, 5 (1), 2018, 30–45.

56 Shira Efron, Howard J. Shatz, Arthur Chan, Emily Haskel, Lyle J. Morris and Andrew Scobell, *The Evolving Israel–China Relationship*. RAND Corporation, Santa Monica, Calif., 2019.

57 "Chinese Investments & Contracts in Israel (2013–2019)," *China Global Investment Tracker*, 2019, https://www.aei.org/china-global-investment-tracker/.

58 "World Investment Report 2018," *UNCTAD*, 2018, https://unctad.org/en/PublicationsLibrary/wir2018_en.pdf.

59 Shira Efron, Howard J. Shatz, Arthur Chan, Emily Haskel, Lyle J. Morris and Andrew Scobell, *The Evolving Israel–China Relationship*. RAND Corporation, Santa Monica, Calif., 2019.

60 Mercy A. Kuo, "Israel–China Relations: Innovation, Infrastructure, Investment," *The Diplomat*, July 17, 2018, https://thediplomat.com/2018/07/israel-china-relations-innovation-infrastructure-investment/.

61 Hadas Peled, "Connectivity as an Engine for Innovation – the Israeli Perspective on BRI," *China Daily*, June 12, 2017, https://www.chinadaily.com.cn/opinion/2017beltandroad/2017-06/12/content_29717111.htm.

62 An Baijie, "Xi: Innovation is 'Common Focus'," *China Daily*, March 22, 2017, https://www.chinadaily.com.cn/china/2017-03/22/content_28633164.htm.

63 Yan Qiong, "President Xi, Israeli PM Netanyahu vow 'innovative comprehensive partnership'," *CGTN*, March 21, 2017, https://news.cgtn.com/news/ 3d41544d79457a4d/share_p.html.

64 Yongxin Zhang, "China's New Era of Development is Win-Win with Israel," *The Jerusalem Post*, October 26, 2017, https://www.jpost.com/Opinion/Chinas-new-era-of-development-is-win-win-with-Israel-508572.

65 Cao Chen, "China–Israel Innovation Hub launched in Shanghai," *China Daily*, May 27, 2019, http://www.chinadaily.com.cn/a/201905/27/ WS5ceba0dea3104842260be074.html.

66 Chen Wenxian, "Spotlight: Israel Jiangsu Center opens to further enhance China-Israel innovation cooperation," *Xinhua*, September 19, 2019, http://www.xinhuanet.com/ english/2019-09/19/c_138405278.htm.

67 Yang Jian, "China–Israel Innovation Hub marks a milestone in scientific research," *SHINE*, December 6, 2019, https://www.shine.cn/news/ metro/2001260633/.

68 Shira Efron, Howard J. Shatz, Arthur Chan, Emily Haskel, Lyle J. Morris and Andrew Scobell, *The Evolving Israel–China Relationship*. RAND Corporation, Santa Monica, Calif, 2019.

69 Raphael Ahren, "In Beijing, Netanyahu looks to 'marry Israel's technology with China's capacity'," *The Times of Israel*, March 21, 2017, https://www.timesofisrael.com/in-beijing-netanyahu-looks-to-marry-israels-technology-with-chinas-capacity/.

70 "IVC: China minor player in Israeli high-tech," *Globes*, February 22, 2018, https://en.globes.co.il/en/article-ivc-china-minor-player-in-israeli-high-tech-1001224974.

71 Xiao Xian, "The 'Belt and Road Initiative' and China–Israeli Relations," *Journal of Middle Eastern and Islamic Studies (in Asia)*, 10 (3), 2016, 1–23.

72 "Alibaba to Open Israel R&D Center," *Globes*, October 11, 2017, https://en.globes.co.il/en/article-alibaba-to-open-israel-rd-center-1001207672.

73 "Chinese Investment in Israeli Tech Is Growing, Report Says," *CTECH*, November 12, 2018, https://www.calcalistech.com/ctech/articles/0,7340,L-3749619,00.html.

74 Michelle Jamrisko, Lee J, Miller and Wei Lu, "These Are the World's Most Innovative Countries," Bloomberg, January 22, 2019, https://www.bloomberg.com/news/articles/2019-01-22/germany-nearly-catches-korea-as-innovation-champ-u-s-rebounds.

75 Shira Efron, Howard J. Shatz, Arthur Chan, Emily Haskel, Lyle J. Morris and Andrew Scobell, *The Evolving Israel–China Relationship*. RAND Corporation, Santa Monica, Calif., 2019.

76 "Third China–Israel Investment Conference GoforIsrael to be held in Shandong Province," *Israel Defense*, May 2, 2019, https://www.israeldefense.co.il/en/node/38373.

77 Yoram Evron, "Why is the United States concerned about Israel–China technology cooperation?," *East Asia Forum*, November 15, 2019, https://www.eastasiaforum.org/2019/11/15/why-is-the-united-states-concerned-about-israel-china-technology-cooperation/.

78 Yoram Gabison, "IDB Selling Remaining 40% Stake in Adama to ChemChina for $1.4 Billion," *Haaretz*, July 18, 2016, https://www.haaretz.com/israel-news/business/.premium-idb-selling-remaining-40-in-adama-to-chemchina-1.5411505.

79 Sharon Udasin, "Israel-China Sign Joint Agricultural Action Plan to Strengthen Cooperation," *The Jerusalem Post*, November 16, 2015, https://www.jpost.com/ Business-and-Innovation/Environment/Israel-China-sign-joint-agricultural-action-plan-to-strengthen-cooperation-433203.

80 Matthew Kalman, "Israeli Water Technology Meets China's Needs," *CCTV*, October 23, 2013, http://matthewkalman.blogspot.com/2013/10/.

81 Mordechai Chaziza, "Israel-China Relations Enter a New Stage: Limited Strategic Hedging," *Contemporary Review of the Middle East*, 5 (1), 2018, 30–45.

82 Arthur Herma, Israel and China Take a Leap Forward-but to Where?," *Hudson Institute*, November 5, 2018, https://www.hudson.org/research/14663-israel-and-china-take-a-leap-forward-but-to-where.

83 Galia Lavi, Jingjie He, and Oded Eran, " China and Israel: On the Same Belt and Road?," *Strategic Assessment*, 18 (3), 2015, pp. 81–91.

84 Mordechai Chaziza, "Israel–China Relations Enter a New Stage: Limited Strategic Hedging," *Contemporary Review of the Middle East*, 5 (1), 2018, 30–45.

85 Avi Bar-Eli, "Chinese miners claim NIS 50m more for Carmel tunnels," *Haaretz*, December 21, 2010, http://www.haaretz.com/israel-news/business/chineseminers-claim-nis-50m-more-for-carmel-tunnels-1.331738.

86 Amiram Barket, "Akko-Karmiel train tunnels completed," *Globes*, April 23, 2014, http://www.globes.co.il/en/article-akko-karmiel-train-tunnelscompleted-1000933415.

87 Hedy Cohen, "China CNR disqualified from Israel Railways tender," *Globes*, July 15, 2015, http://www.globes.co.il/en/article-china-cnr-disqualified-from-israelrailways-tender-1001053190.

88 Dubi Ben-Gedalyahu, "First TA light rail trains roll off production line," *Globes*, April 18, 2019, https://en.globes.co.il/en/article-first-ta-light-rail-trains-roll-off-production-line-1001282881.

89 "The tender for the supply of cars for the Tel Aviv Light-Rail Transit system was won by Chinese company," *Port2Port*, December 6, 2015, http://www.port2port.com/article/Land-Transport/Train/The-tender-for-the-supply-of-cars-for-the-Tel-Aviv-Light-Rail-Transit-system-was-won-by-Chinese-company/.

90 Daniel Schmil, "5 Chinese companies to bid for TA light rail tunnels," *Globes*, May 20, 2019, https://en.globes.co.il/en/article-5-chinese-cos-to-bid-for-ta-light-rail-tunnels-1001286355.

91 Dubi Ben-Gedalyahu, "China to be Israel's biggest infrastructure partner," *Globes*, May 10, 2015, http://www.globes.co.il/en/article-china-becoming-israelsbiggest-infra-structure-partner-1001031690.

92 Alfi E. Shauly, "Gov't selects 6 foreign building companys to work in Israel," *Globes*, October 26, 2016, http://www.globes.co.il/en/article-govt-selects-6-foreignbuilding-cos-to-work-in-israel-1001157605.

93 Ori Chudy, "Israel signs to take 20,000 Chinese building workers," *Globes*, January 4, 2017, https://en.globes.co.il/en/article-agreement-signed-to-bring-20000-chinese-building-workers-to-israel-1001170312.

94 Guy Lieberman, "Israel extends visas of 1,700 Chinese building workers," *Globes*, February 10, 2020, https://en.globes.co.il/en/article-israel-extends-visas-of-1700-chinese-building-workers-1001317957.

95 Raheli Bindman, Diana Bahur-Nir and Lilach Baumer, "Why Israel Stopped All Attempts by Chinese Companies to Buy Local Insurers," *CTECH*, August 14, 2018, https://www.calcalistech.com/ctech/articles/0,7340,L-3744295,00.html.

96 Toi Staff, "Israel said to bar China, Turkey from bidding for $40 million airport tender, *The Times of Israel*, January 25, 2019, https://www.timesofisrael.com/israel-said-to-bar-china-turkey-from-bidding-for-airport-tender/.

97 Toi Staff, "Company advances in tender for plant despite security concerns over China ties," September 6, 2019,

https://www.timesofisrael.com/company-advances-in-tender-for-plant-despite-security-concerns-over-china-ties/.

98 Sue Surkes and Shoshanna Solomon, "Huawei enters Israel's solar power market, hours after quitting US," *The Time of Israel*, June 26, 2019, https://www.timesofisrael.com/huawei-enters-israels-solar-power-market-hours-after-quitting-us/.

99 Omri Milman, "Israel's National Security Council Pushing for Local Committee on Foreign Investments," *CTECH*, March 3, 2019, https://www.calcalistech.com/ctech/articles/0,7340,L-3757449,00.html

100 Dale Aluf, "Changing world, shifting relations: Israel's ties with China," *SIGNAL Perspectives*, September 9, 2019, http://en.sino-israel.org/publications/signal-perspectives/changing-world-shifting-relations-israels-ties-with-china/.

101 Noa Landau, "Israel to Form Committee to Monitor Chinese Investments Following U.S. Pressure," *HAARETZ*, October 30, 2019, https://www.haaretz.com/israel-news/.premium-israel-to-form-committee-to-monitor-chinese-investments-following-u-s-pressure-1.8058754.

102 "Under pressure from US, Israel forms panel to examine foreign investments," *The Times of Israel*, 30 October 2019, https://www.timesofisrael.com/under-pressure-from-us-israel-forms-panel-to-examine-foreign-investments/.

103 Noa Landau, "Israel to Form Committee to Monitor Chinese Investments Following U.S. Pressure," *Haaretz*, October 30, 2019, https://www.haaretz.com/israel-news/.premium-israel-to-form-committee-to-monitor-chinese-investments-following-u-s-pressure-1.8058754.

104 Shira Efron, Howard J. Shatz, Arthur Chan, Emily Haskel, Lyle J. Morris, Andrew Scobell, *The Evolving Israel-China Relationship*. RAND Corporation, Santa Monica, Calif, 2019.

105 Mordechai Chaziza, "Israel Agrees to Monitor Foreign Investment," *BESA Center Perspectives Paper* No. 1,340, November 11, 2019, https://besacenter.org/perspectives-papers/israel-monitor-foreign-investment/.

106 Cong Mu, "China Set to Build Strategic Railway in Israel, Gas Export Deal May Follow," *Global Times*, July 5, 2012, http://www.globaltimes.cn/content/719100.shtml.

107 Oded Eran, "Will Israel Sell its Natural Gas to China?," *INSS Insight*, December 16, 2012, https://www.inss.org.il/publication/will-israel-sell-its-natural-gas-to-china/.

108 Reuters website, "China's Fosun Looks to Buy Israel Gas Fields from Delek-Israeli Source," *Reuters*, December 1 2015, https://af.reuters.com/article/energyOilNews/idAFL8N13Q23O20151201.

109 Hedy Cohen, "Energy Minister Yuval Steinitz has Invited Chinese Energy Companies to Bid for Israeli Oil and Gas Exploration Licenses," *Globes*, January 5, 2016, https://en.globes.co.il/en/article-israel-china-sign-energy-cooperation-agreement-1001093283.

110 "Chinese–Israeli consortium inks 15-year gas supply deal with UK-based firm," *Xinhua*, November 24, 2019, http://www.xinhuanet.com/english/2019-11/24/c_138578602.htm.

111 "Vision and Actions on Jointly Building Silk Road Economic Belt and 21st-Century Maritime Silk Road," *National Development and Reform Commission, Ministry of Foreign Affairs, and Ministry of Commerce of the People's Republic of China*, March 28, 2015, http://en.ndrc.gov.cn/newsrelease/201503/t20150330_669367.html.

112 Lidar Grave-Lazi, "Looking to China for higher education," *The Jerusalem Post*, May 11, 2016, https://www.jpost.com/Israel-News/Politics-And-Diplomacy/Looking-to-China-for-higher-education-453772.

113 Shira Efron, Howard J. Shatz, Arthur Chan, Emily Haskel, Lyle J. Morris and Andrew Scobell, *The Evolving Israel–China Relationship*. RAND Corporation, Santa Monica, Calif., 2019.

114 Tova Cohen, "Tel Aviv, Tsinghua Universities Set Up $300 mln Research Center," *Reuters*, May 19, 2014, https://www.reuters.com/article/us-israel-china-research/tel-aviv-tsinghua-universities-set-up-300-mln-research-center-idUSKBN0DZ18N2014 0519.

115 "Launch of First Israeli University in China," *Technion-Israel Institute of Technology*, December 16, 2015, https://www.technion.ac.il/en/launch-of-first-israeli-university-in-china-five-thousand-in-attendance-for-groundbreaking-of-guangdong-technion-is rael-institute-of-technology/.

116 David Shamah, "Haifa, Ben-Gurion Universities to Open R&D Centers in China," *Times of Israel*, April 6, 2016, https://www.timesofisrael.com/haifa-ben-gurion-univer-sities-to-open-rd-centers-in-china/.

117 Qi Xijia, "Israel Culture Week," *Global Times*, November 2, 2017, http://www.global-times.cn/content/1073258.shtml.

118 Shira Efron, Howard J. Shatz, Arthur Chan, Emily Haskel, Lyle J. Morris and Andrew Scobell, *The Evolving Israel-China Relationship*. RAND Corporation, Santa Monica, Calif., 2019.

119 "8 more countries set up Confucius institutes or classrooms in 2019," *Xinhua*, December 11, 2019, http://www.xinhuanet.com/english/2019-12/11/ c_ 138623776.htm.

120 Huang Zhiling, "10 new Confucius Institutes lift the global total to 548, boosting ties," *China Daily*, December 5, 2018, http://global.chinadaily.com.cn/a/201812/05/ WS5c07239da310eff30328f182.html.

121 "Confucius Institute/Classroom," *Confucius Institute Headquarters (Hanban)*, 2020, http://english.hanban.org/node_10971.htm.

122 Raphael Ahren, "Israel and China to sign 10-year multiple entry visa deal," *The Times of Israel*, March 27, 2016, https://www.timesofisrael.com/israel-and-china-to-sign-10-year-multiple-entry-visa-deal/.

123 Hagai Shagrir, "Israel–China Relations: Innovative Comprehensive Partnership," in Assaf Orion and Galia Lavi (eds.), *Israel–China Relations: Opportunities and Challenges*. Tel Aviv: Institute for National Security Studies, 2019.

124 Zhan Yongxin, "New energy in the friendship between China and Israel," *The Jerusalem Post*, November 17, 2019, https://www.jpost.com/Opinion/New-energy-in-the-friendship-between-China-and-Israel-608047.

125 Yoram Evron, "Why is the United States concerned about Israel-China technology cooperation?," *East Asia Forum*, November 15, 2019, https://www.eastasiaforum.org/ 2019/11/15/why-is-the-united-states-concerned-about-israel-china-technology-coop-eration/.

126 Xiao Xian, "The "Belt and Road Initiative" and China–Israeli Relations," *Journal of Middle Eastern and Islamic Studies (in Asia)*, 10 (3), 2016, 1–23.

127 Shira Efron, Howard J. Shatz, Arthur Chan, Emily Haskel, Lyle J. Morris and Andrew Scobell, *The Evolving Israel–China Relationship*. RAND Corporation, Santa Monica, Calif, 2019.

128 Yitzhak Shichor, "On probation: The open-ended future of Sino–Israeli relations," *Middle East Institute*, September 5, 2014, https://www.mei.edu/publications/probation-open-ended-future-sino-israeli-relations.

129 Mordechai Chaziza, "Israe–China Relations Enter a New Stage: Limited Strategic Hedging," *Contemporary Review of the Middle East*, 5 (1), 2018, pp. 30–45.

130 Yoram Evron, "Why is the United States concerned about Israel–China technology cooperation?," *East Asia Forum*, November 15, 2019, https://www.eastasiaforum.org/2019/11/15/why-is-the-united-states-concerned-about-israel-china-technology-cooperation/.

131 Yitzhak Shichor, "The U.S. Factor in Israel's Military Relation with China," *China Brief*, 5 (12), May 24, 2005, https://jamestown.org/program/the-u-s-factor-in-israels-military-relations-with-china/.

132 Lahav Harkov, "Chinese envoy rails against US 'bullying' Israel over investments," *The Jerusalem Post*, December 9, 2019, https://www.jpost.com/Israel-News/Chinese-envoy-rails-against-US-bullying-Israel-over-investments-610402.

133 Shira Efron, Howard J. Shatz, Arthur Chan, Emily Haskel, Lyle J. Morris and Andrew Scobell, *The Evolving Israel–China Relationship*. RAND Corporation, Santa Monica, Calif., 2019.

4 Syria

1 Isaac Kfir, "What's China up to in the Arab world? Taking advantage of the Syrian conflict," *Policy Forum*, August 7, 2019, https://www.policyforum.net/whats-china-up-to-in-the-arab-world/.

2 James M. Dorsey, "How China Gets Sucked Into the Middle East," *The Globalist-Rethinking Globalization*, May 3, 2018, https://www.theglobalist.com/middle-east-china-russia-syria-oil/.

3 John Calabrese, "China and Syria: In War and Reconstruction," *Middle East Institute*, July 9, 2019, https://www.mei.edu/publications/china-and-syria-war-and-reconstruction.

4 Tom O'connor, China may be the Biggest Winner of all if Assad takes over Syria," *Newsweek*, January 19, 2018, https://www.newsweek.com/china-did-not-fight-syria-won-war-754644.

5 "The Belt and Road: A New Page of Cooperation Between China and Syria," *The Syrian Observer*, May 13, 2019, https://syrianobserver.com/EN/news/50356/the-belt-and-road-a-new-page-of-cooperation-between-china-and-syria.html.

6 Mohamad Zreik,"China's Involvement in the Syria Crisis and the Implications of its Natural Stance in the War" *Journal of Political Science*, 2019, 21 (1), 56–65.

7 "Xi expounds China's position on Syrian conflict, Venezuelan crisis, Iran's nuclear issue," *Xinhua*, June 5, 2019, http://www.xinhuanet.com/english/2019-06/05/c_138116801.htm.

8 "UN High Commissioner for Refugees (UNHCR)," September 26, 2019, https://data2.unhcr.org/en/situations/syria.

9 "Experts discuss post-conflict reconstruction policies after political agreement in Syria," *UN Economic and Social Commission for Western Asia*, August 7, 2018, https://www.unescwa.org/news/syrian-experts-discuss-post-conflict-reconstruction-policies-after-political-agreement-syria.

10 Jospeh Daher, The Paradox of Syria's Reconstruction," *Carnegie Middle East Center*, September 4, 2019, https://carnegie-mec.org/2019/09/04/paradox-of-syria-s-reconstruction-pub-79773.

11 Angus McDowall, "Long reach of U.S. sanctions hits Syria reconstruction," *Reuters*, September 2, 2018, https://www.reuters.com/article/us-mideast-crisis-syria-sanctions/long-reach-of-u-s-sanctions-hits-syria-reconstruction-idUSKCN1LI06Z.

12 Chloe Cornish and Archie Zhang, "Lebanese port eyes China as it sells itself as hub for Syria," *Financial Times*, January 3, 2019, https://www.ft.com/content/386b3fd2-01db-11e9-99df-6183d3002ee1.

13 Laura Zhou, "Syria courts China for rebuilding push after fall of Islamic State's strong-holds," *South China Morning Post*, November 25, 2017, https://www.scmp.com/news/china/diplomacy-defence/article/2121552/syria-courts-china-rebuilding-push-after-fall-islamic.

14 Galia Lavi and Assaf Orion, "Will China Reconstruct Syria? Not So Fast," *INSS Insight No. 1187*, July 14, 2019, https://www.inss.org.il/publication/will-china-reconstruct-syria-not-so-fast/.

15 Paul McLoughlin, "Syria Weekly: Will China fund post-war reconstruction?," *The New Arab*, June 21, 2019, https://www.alaraby.co.uk/english/indepth/2019/6/21/syria-weekly-will-china-fund-post-war-reconstruction-.

16 Galia Lavi and Assaf Orion, "Will China Reconstruct Syria? Not So Fast," *INSS Insight No. 1187*, July 14, 2019, https://www.inss.org.il/publication/will-china-reconstruct-syria-not-so-fast/.

17 "Highlights of Xi's speech at China-Arab forum," *China Daily*, July 10, 2018, http://www.chinadaily.com.cn/a/201807/10/WS5b441634a3103349141e1cb7.html.

18 "Full Text of Xi Jinping keynote speech at the United Nations Office in Geneva," *CGTN*, January 18, 2017, https://america.cgtn.com/2017/01/18/full-text-of-xi-jinping-keynote-speech-at-the-united-nations-office-in-geneva.

19 "China to donate humanitarian aid to Syria worth $16m," *State Council of the People's Republic of China*, February 6, 2017, http://english.gov.cn/news/international_exchanges/2017/02/06/content_281475560.

20 Haifa Said, "China's humanitarian contribution to Syria adds to its int'l profile," *China.org*, January 18, 2018, http://www.china.org.cn/opinion/2018-01/18/content_50239714.htm.

21 "China delivers 1,000 tons of rice to Syria in food aid," *China Daily*, November 21, 2017 http://www.chinadaily.com.cn/world/2017-11/21/content_34803942.htm.

22 "WFP, China conclude food aid programme for Syrian refugees," *Jordan Times*, March 14, 2018, http://www.jordantimes.com/news/local/wfp-china-conclude-food-aid-programme-syrian-refugees.

23 "China's Red Cross donates mobile clinics, ambulances to Syria," *Xinhua*, August 17, 2018, http://www.xinhuanet.com/english/2018-08/17/c_137396336.htm.

24 "China donates electrical transformers to Syria for reconstruction process," *Xinhua*, October 11, 2018, http://www.xinhuanet.com/english/2018-10/11/c_137523945.htm.

25 "China donates 1,000 tons of wheat in humanitarian aid to Syrian refugees in Lebanon," *Xinhua*, December 21, 2018, http://www.xinhuanet.com/english/2018-12/21/c_137690264.htm.

26 "China donates 100 buses to support public transportation in Syria," *Xinhua*, June 20, 2019, http://www.xinhuanet.com/english/2019-06/20/c_138159276.htm.

27 "Vision and Actions on Jointly Building Silk Road Economic Belt and 21st-Century Maritime Silk Road," *National Development and Reform Commission, Ministry of Foreign Affairs, and Ministry of Commerce of the People's Republic of China*, March 28, 2015, http://en.ndrc.gov.cn/newsrelease/201503/t20150330_669367.html.

28 "Syria President Al-Assad visits China," *China Daily*, June 22, 2004, http://www.chinadaily.com.cn/english/doc/2004-06/22/content_341612.htm.

29 Laura Zhou, "Syria courts China for rebuilding push after fall of Islamic State's strong-holds," *South China Morning Post*, November 25, 2017, https://www.scmp.com/news/china/diplomacy-defence/article/2121552/syria-courts-china-rebuilding-push-after-fall-islamic.

30 "President al-Assad to Chinese Phoenix TV: Any foreign troops coming to Syria

without permission are invaders – video," *Syrian Arab News Agency (SANA)*, March11, 2017, https://sana.sy/en/?p=101799.

31   "Shaaban: China's invitation to Syria to participate in Belt and Road Forum defies US sanctions," *Syrian Arab News Agency (SANA)*, April 26, 2019, https://sana.sy/en/?p=164263.

32   "Wang Yi Meets with Deputy Prime Minister and Foreign Minister Walid Muallem of Syria," *Ministry of Foreign Affairs, the People's Republic of China*, September 23, 2017, https://www.fmprc.gov.cn/mfa_eng/zxxx_662805/t1496960.shtml.

33   "Chinese FM: Fighting terrorism, dialogue, and reconstruction form pillars of ending crisis in Syria," *Syrian Arab News Agency (SANA)*, November 24, 2017, https://sana.sy/en/?p=119197.

34   Sumaira Hussain, "Syria Eager To Become Belt And Road Initiative Participant – Presidential Adviser," *UrduPoint Network*, May 1, 2019, https://www.urdupoint.com/en/world/syria-eager-to-become-belt-and-road-initiativ-610541.html.

35   "Foreign Ministry Spokesperson Geng Shuang's Regular Press Conference on November 29, 2017," *Permanent Mission of the People's Republic of China to the UN*, November 29, 2017, http://www.china-un.org/eng/fyrth/t1515157.htm.

36   "China to play bigger role in Syria's reconstruction, development process: ambassador," *Xinhua*, February 12, 2018, http://www.xinhuanet.com/english/2018-02/12/c_136967861.htm.

37   Logan Pauley, "China stakes out a role for itself in post-war Syria," *Asia Times*, October 3, 2018, https://www.stimson.org/content/china-stakes-out-role-itself-post-war-syria-0.

38   "Xi expounds China's position on Syrian conflict, Venezuelan crisis, Iran's nuclear issue," *Xinhua*, June 5, 2019, http://www.xinhuanet.com/english/2019-06/05/c_138116801.htm.

39   "Syria," *Energy Information Administration (EIA)*, August 2011, https://www.eia.gov/beta/international/analysis_includes/countries_long/Syria/archive/pdf/syria_2011.pdf.

40   "EIA: Country Information on Syria," *Energy Information Administration (EIA)*, June 24, 2015, https://www.eia.gov/beta/international/analysis.php?iso=SYR.

41   Gideon Elazar, "Moving Westward: The Chinese Rebuilding of Syria," *BESA Center Perspectives Paper No. 673*, December 5, 2017, https://besacenter.org/perspectives-papers/moving-westward-chinese-rebuilding-syria/.

42   Galia Lavi and Assaf Orion, "Will China Reconstruct Syria? Not So Fast," *INSS Insight No. 1187*, July 14, 2019, https://www.inss.org.il/publication/will-china-reconstruct-syria-not-so-fast/.

43   "Tanganyika Oil to Sinopec for C$2 Billion," *Dealbook*, September 25, 2008, https://dealbook.nytimes.com/2008/09/25/tanganyika-oil-to-sinopec-for-c2-billion/?mtrref=thediplomat.com&gwh=9FC857C498695B2F2D6BF70141F2DC9C&gwt=pay&assetType=REGIWALL.

44   "Syria," *Energy Information Administration (EIA)*, August 2011, https://www.eia.gov/beta/international/analysis_includes/countries_long/Syria/archive/pdf/syria_2011.pdf.

45   George Marshall Lerner, "Why China Can't Ignore Syria's Rebel Factions," *The Diplomat*, February 14, 2017, https://thediplomat.com/2017/02/why-china-cant-ignore-syrias-rebel-factions/.

46   "BRI, the Chinese bid for Syria's Reconstruction," *Mediterranean Affairs*, December 5, 2018, http://mediterraneanaffairs.com/bri-china-syria-reconstruction/#_ftn2.

47   Shirley Tay, "As the US withdraws from Syria, China may boost its influence in the country," *CNBC*, April 4, 2019,

https://www.cnbc.com/2019/04/05/as-us-withdraws-from-syria-china-may-boost-influence-in-the-country.html.

48   "Syrian regime okays lease of Tartus port to Russia for 49 years," *The New Arab & Agencies*, June 13, 2019, https://www.alaraby.co.uk/english/news/2019/6/12/syrian-regime-okays-russian-lease-of-tartus-port.

49   Seth J. Frantzman, "Iranian IRGC in Syria's Latakia?," *Jerusalem Post*, May 21, 2019, https://www.jpost.com/Middle-East/Iran-News/Iranian-IRGC-in-Syrias-Latakia-Report-590253.

50   Chloe Cornish and Archie Zhang, "Lebanese port eyes China as it sells itself as hub for Syria," *Financial Times*, January 3, 2019, https://www.ft.com/content/386b3fd2-01db-11e9-99df-6183d3002ee1.

51   "Lebanon's Tripoli port becomes central destination for weekly shipments from China to Eastern Mediterranean: director," *Hellenic News*, December 27, 2018, https://www.hellenicshippingnews.com/lebanons-tripoli-port-becomes-central-destination-for-weekly-shipments-from-china-to-eastern-mediterranean-director/.

52   Chris Devonshire-Ellis, "China's Belt & Road Initiative In The Middle East," *Silk Road Briefing*, June 21, 2019, https://www.silkroadbriefing.com/news/2019/06/21/chinas-belt-road-initiative-middle-east/.

53   Kevin Brown, "Is China Exploiting Trump's Syria Withdrawal?," *RealClearDefense (RCD)*, April 11, 2019, https://www.realcleardefense.com/articles/2019/04/11/is_china_exploiting_trumps_syria_withdrawal_114325.html.

54   Philip Issa, "Lebanon prepares for Syria's post-war construction windfall," *Associated Press*, August 17, 2017, http://www.apnewsarchive.com/2017/Lebanon-seeks-jump-aboard-wagon-of-Syria-s-reconstruction-boom-once-peacearrives/id-b3491b276c84 46e3acf8e445890d3ba.

55   Finbar Anderson, "China looks to invest in north Lebanon," *The Daily Star Lebanon*, July 12, 2018, https://www.dailystar.com.lb/News/Lebanon-News/2018/Jul-12/456223-china-looks-to-invest-in-north-lebanon.ashx.

56   Sam Brennan, "China's Middle Eastern intervention: Sino-Syrian cooperation," *Foreign Brief*, June, 2, 2017, https://www.foreignbrief.com/asia-pacific/china/chmiddle-eastern-intervention-sino-syrian-cooperation/.

57   Sami Moubayed, "In Beijing, Assad's envoy seeks construction cash," *Asia Times*, June 19, 2019, https://www.asiatimes.com/2019/06/article/in-beijing-assads-envoy-seeks-construction-cash/.

58   "Vision and Actions on Jointly Building Silk Road Economic Belt and 21st-Century Maritime Silk Road," *National Development and Reform Commission, Ministry of Foreign Affairs, and Ministry of Commerce of the People's Republic of China*, March 28, 2015, http://en.ndrc.gov.cn/newsrelease/201503/t20150330_669367.html.

59   Laura Zhou, "Syria courts China for rebuilding push after fall of Islamic State's st007strong-holds," *South China Morning Post*, November 25, 2017, https://www.scmp.com/news/china/diplomacy-defence/article/2121552/syria-courts-china-rebuilding-push-after-fall-islamic.

60   "Syria, China discuss investment opportunities in Syrian industrial sector," *Syrian Arab News Agency Syrian Arab News Agency (SANA)*, April 16, 2017, https://sana.sy/en/?p=104437.

61   Logan Pauley, "China stakes out a role for itself in post-war Syria," *Asia Times*, October 3, 2018, https://www.stimson.org/content/china-stakes-out-role-itself-post-war-syria-0.

62   "China in postwar Syria," *Belt & Road News*, March 13, 2019, https://www.beltandroad.news/2019/03/13/china-in-postwar-syria/.

63 Shane Harris, "China Looks at Syria, Sees $$$," *The Daily Beast,* 27 October 2015, https://www.thedailybeast.com/china-looks-at-syria-sees-dollardollardollar.

64 Logan Pauley, "China stakes out a role for itself in post-war Syria," *Asia Times,* October 3, 2018, https://www.stimson.org/content/china-stakes-out-role-itself-post-war-syria-0.

65 Mazen Eyon, "Chinese Ambassador: US Threats Will Not Deter Chinese Companies From Participating in Damascus International Fair," *Syrian Arab News Agency (SANA),* August 27, 2019, https://www.sana.sy/en/?p=172120.

66 Harvey Morris, "China extends helping hands to rebuild Syria," *China Daily,* February 10, 2018,
http://www.chinadaily.com.cn/a/201802/10/WS5a7e4f48a3106e7dcc13bee2.html.

67 "China Prepared To Jump Right into Reconstruction of Syria," *The international Schiller institute,* July 29, 2018, https://schillerinstitute.com/blog/2018/07/31/china-prepared-to-jump-right-into-reconstruction-of-syria/.

68 "China Customs Statistics: Imports and exports by country/region," *The Hong Kong Trade Development Council (HKTDC),* January 24, 2020, http://china-trade-research.hktdc.com/business-news/article/Facts-and-Figures/China-Customs-Statistics/ff/en/1/1X39VTVQ/1X09N9NM.htm.

69 "Chinese Investments & Contracts in Syria (2011–2019)," *China Global Investment Tracker,* 2019, https://www.aei.org/china-global-investment-tracker/.

70 "Chinese Ambassador To Syria: We Are Willing To Participate 'In Some Way' In The Battle For Idlib Alongside The Assad Army," *The Middle East Media Research Institute (MEMRI),* August 1, 2018, https://www.memri.org/reports/chinese-ambassador-syria-we-are-willing-participate-some-way-battle-idlib-alongside-assad.

71 "Foreign Ministry Spokesperson Hua Chunying's Regular Press Conference on August 29, 2018," *Ministry of Foreign Affairs, the People's Republic of China,* August 29, 2018,
https://www.fmprc.gov.cn/mfa_eng/xwfw_665399/s2510_665401/t1589364.shtml.

72 Christopher Bodeen, "Chinese admiral visits Syria in show of support," *AP News,* August 18, 2016, https://apnews.com/ca3252c672b445b0a8318ec9d44a6b4d.

73 Yang Sheng, "China boosts Syria support," *Global Times,* August 18, 2016, http://www.globaltimes.cn/content/1001150.shtml.

74 Galia Lavi and Assaf Orion, "Will China Reconstruct Syria? Not So Fast," *INSS Insight No. 1187,* July 14, 2019, https://www.inss.org.il/publication/will-china-reconstruct-syria-not-so-fast/.

75 Phoenix Kwong, "China passes landmark law to battle terrorism at home and overseas," *South China Morning Post,* December 27, 2015, https://www.scmp.com/magazines/style/news-trends/article/3032954/how-bruce-lee-fan-zhang-weili-found-inspiration-her.

76 "Chinese Night Tigers Special Forces Arrive in Syria," *Syria News,* December 16, 2017, https://www.syrianews.cc/chinese-night-tigers-special-forces-arrive-syria/.

77 Leith Aboufadel, "Chinese military will not deploy to Syria for Idlib offensive – envoy," *Al-Masdar News,* August 20, 2018, https://www.almasdarnews.com/article/chinese-military-will-not-deploy-to-syria-for-idlib-offensive-envoy/.

78 Laura Zhou, "China's role in Syria's endless civil war," *South China Morning Post,* April 7, 2017, https://www.scmp.com/news/china/diplomacy-defence/article/2085779/backgrounder-chinas-role-syrias-endless-civil-war.

79 Jeanne Gobat and Kristina Kostial, "Syria's Conflict Economy," *IMF Working Paper,* WP/16/123, June 2016, https://www.imf.org/external/pubs/ft/wp/2016/wp16123.pdf.

80 John Calabrese, "China and Syria: In War and Reconstruction," *Middle East Institute,* July 9, 2019,

https://www.mei.edu/publications/china-and-syria-war-and-reconstruction.

81   Galia Lavi and Assaf Orion, "Will China Reconstruct Syria? Not So Fast," *INSS Insight No. 1187*, July 14, 2019, https://www.inss.org.il/publication/will-china-reconstruct-syria-not-so-fast/.

82   "Xi expounds China's position on Syrian conflict, Venezuelan crisis, Iran's nuclear issue," *Xinhua*, June 5, 2019, http://www.xinhuanet.com/english/2019-06/05/c_138116801.htm.

83   Andrea Ghiselli and Mohammed Al-Sudairi, "Syria's 'China Dream': Between the Narratives and Realities," *The King Faisal Center for Research and Islamic Studies (KFCRIS)*, September 15, 2019, http://www.kfcris.com/pdf/5d3b55b0e7feb358b59ee9976da485dc5d808e942f04b.pdf.

5 Lebanon

1   Ben Simpfendorfer, *The New Silk Road; How a Rising Arab World Is Turning Away from the West and Rediscovering China*. London: Palgrave Macmillan, 2009.

2   David Perez-Des Rosiers, "A Comparative Analysis of China's Relations with Lebanon and Syria," *Sociology of Islam*, 7 (2–3), 2019, 189–210.

3   "Chinese Ambassador renews China support for Lebanon's sovereignty," *National News Agency (NNA)*, October 1, 2018, http://nna-leb.gov.lb/en/show-news/95686/Chinese-Ambassador-renews-China-support-for-Lebanon-39-sovereignty.

4   Christina Lin, "The Belt and Road and China's Long-term Visions in the Middle East," *ISPSW Strategy Series: Focus on Defense and International Security*, No. 512, October 2017, https://css.ethz.ch/content/dam/ethz/special-interest/gess/cis/center-for-securities-studies/resources/docs/ISPSW-512%20Lin.pdf.

5   Philip Issa, "Lebanon prepares for Syria's post-war construction windfall," *Associated Press*, August 17, 2017, http://www.apnewsarchive.com/2017/Lebanon-seeks-jump-aboard-wagon-of-Syria-s-reconstruction-boom-once-peacearrives/id-b3491b276c8446e3acf8e445890d3bac.

6   "Lebanon Economic Vision," *Friedrich Ebert Stiftung (FES)*, May 16, 2019, https://www.fes-lebanon.org/fileadmin/user_upload/documents/Mckinsey_Plan/Lebanon_Economic_Vision_-_Assessment_and_Recommendations.pdf.

7   Min Ye, "China and competing cooperation in Asia-Pacific: TPP, RCEP, and the New Silk Road," *Asian Security*, 11 (3), 2015, 206–224.

8   "Vision and Actions on Jointly Building Silk Road Economic Belt and 21st-Century Maritime Silk Road," *National Development and Reform Commission, Ministry of Foreign Affairs, and Ministry of Commerce of the People's Republic of China*, March 28, 2015, http://en.ndrc.gov.cn/newsrelease/201503/t20150330_669367.html.

9   "Vice Chairman of the National Committee of the Chinese People's Political Consultative Conference (CPPCC) Luo Fuhe Attends the Reception of the 70th National Day of Lebanon," *Embassy of the People's Republic of China in the Kingdom of Denmark*, November 22, 2013, https://www.mfa.gov.cn/ce/cedk/eng/zgxw/t1104056.htm.

10   "China and Lebanon," *Ministry of Foreign Affairs, the People's Republic of China*, 2013, https://www.fmprc.gov.cn/mfa_eng/wjb_663304/zzjg_663340/xybfs_663590/gjlb_663594/2843_663676/.

11   "China welcomes Lebanon's participation in Belt and Road Initiative," *Xinhua Finance Agency*, May 12, 2016, http://en.xfafinance.com/html/BR/Analysis/2016/222368.shtml.

12 "Xi Jinping Sends Congratulatory Message to Newly-appointed President Michel Aoun of Lebanon," *Embassy of the People's Republic of China in the Hellenic Republic*, November 4, 2016, http://zm.chineseembassy.org/eng/zgxw/t1413671.htm.

13 "Lebanon, China to boost Belt and Road Initiative," *Xinhua*, April 22, 2017, http://www.xinhuanet.com/english/2017-04/22/c_136227260.htm.

14 "Highlights of Xi's speech at China–Arab forum," *China Daily*, July 10, 2018, http://www.chinadaily.com.cn/a/201807/10/WS5b441634a3103349141e1cb7.html.

15 "Wang Yi meets top Arab states diplomats in Beijing," *CGTN*, July 10, 2018, http://www.chinaembassy-fi.org/eng/zxxx/t1576559.htm.

16 "China willing to boost ties with Lebanon: Envoy," *Xinhua*, February 19, 2019, http://www.xinhuanet.com/english/2019-02/19/c_137832119.htm.

17 "Lebanon welcomes Investment from China," *Belt & Road News*, April 10, 2019, https://www.beltandroad.news/2019/04/10/lebanon-welcomes-investment-from-china/.

18 "China to cooperate more with Lebanon in economic areas," *Xinhua*, May 30, 2019, http://www.xinhuanet.com/english/2019-05/31/c_138103757.htm.

19 "Vision and Actions on Jointly Building Silk Road Economic Belt and 21st-Century Maritime Silk Road," *National Development and Reform Commission, Ministry of Foreign Affairs, and Ministry of Commerce of the People's Republic of China*, March 28, 2015, http://en.ndrc.gov.cn/newsrelease/201503/t20150330_669367.html.

20 "Lebanon, China to boost Belt and Road Initiative," *Xinhua*, April 22, 2017, http://www.xinhuanet.com/english/2017-04/22/c_136227260.htm.

21 "China drops anchor in Mediterranean ports," *MERICS*, May 5, 2016, https://www.merics.org/en/blog/china-drops-anchor-mediterranean-ports.

22 "China interested in Lebanon's infrastructure projects: envoy," *Global Times*, March 3, 2019, http://www.globaltimes.cn/content/1140663.shtml.

23 "New shipping line opens between China, Lebanon's Tripoli port," *Xinhua*, October 9, 2018, http://www.xinhuanet.com/english/2018-10/09/c_137521492.htm.

24 "Lebanon's Tripoli keen for active role in Belt and Road initiative," *China Daily*, November 27, 2017, http://www.chinadaily.com.cn/business/2017-11/27/content_35056335.htm.

25 "New shipping line opens between China, Lebanon's Tripoli port," *Xinhua*, October 9, 2018, http://www.xinhuanet.com/english/2018-10/09/c_137521492.htm.

26 Christina Lin, "The Belt and Road and China's Long-term Visions in the Middle East," *ISPSW Strategy Series: Focus on Defense and International Security*, No. 512, October 2017, https://css.ethz.ch/content/dam/ethz/special-interest/gess/cis/center-for-securities-studies/resources/docs/ISPSW-512%20Lin.pdf.

27 "China interested in Lebanon's infrastructure projects: envoy," *Global Times*, March 3, 2019, http://www.globaltimes.cn/content/1140663.shtml.

28 Chloe Cornish and Archie Zhang, "Lebanese port eyes China as it sells itself as hub for Syria," *Financial Times*, January 3, 2019, https://www.ft.com/content/386b3fd2-01db-11e9-99df-6183d3002ee1.

29 *Tripoli Special Economic Zone*, 2019, https://tsez.gov.lb/tsez.

30 "Lebanon needs to build a Railway Network," *Belt & Road News*, July 11, 2019, https://www.beltandroad.news/2019/07/11/lebanon-needs-to-build-a-railway-network/.

31 Olivia Azadegan and Sebastian Shehadi, "China makes tracks to invest in Lebanese railway," *FDi Magazine*, June 5, 2019, https://www.fdiintelligence.com/Locations/Middle-East-Africa/Lebanon/China-makes-tracks-to-invest-in-Lebanese-railway.

32 "Vision and Actions on Jointly Building Silk Road Economic Belt and 21st-Century Maritime Silk Road," *National Development and Reform Commission, Ministry of Foreign Affairs, and Ministry of Commerce of the People's Republic of China*, March 28, 2015, http://en.ndrc.gov.cn/newsrelease/201503/t20150330_669367.html.

33 "China Customs Statistics: Imports and exports by country/region," *The Hong Kong Trade Development Council (HKTDC)*, January 24, 2020, http://china-trade-research.hktdc.com/business-news/article/Facts-and-Figures/China-Customs-Statistics/ff/en/1/1X39VTVQ/1X09N9NM.htm.

34 Olivia Azadegan and Sebastian Shehadi, "China makes tracks to invest in Lebanese railway," *FDi Magazine*, June 5, 2019, https://www.fdiintelligence.com/Locations/Middle-East-Africa/Lebanon/China-makes-tracks-to-invest-in-Lebanese-railway.

35 "Chinese Investments & Contracts in Lebanon (2013–2019)," *China Global Investment Tracker*, 2020, https://www.aei.org/china-global-investment-tracker/.

36 "AIIB Approves Lebanon Membership," *Asian Infrastructure Investment Bank (AIIB)*, June 26, 2018, https://www.aiib.org/en/news-events/news/2018/20180626_003.html.

37 "Chinese trade agency selects Beirut for MENA headquarters," *The Daily Star*, January 16, 2018, https://www.dailystar.com.lb/Business/Local/2018/Jan-16/433923-chinese-trade-agency-selects-beirut-for-mena-headquarters.ashx.

38 "Jiang Jiang – China's Ambassador to Lebanon," *The Monthly Magazine*, March 5 2015, https://monthlymagazine.com/article-desc_1656_.

39 "China offers aid to Syrian refugees in Lebanon," *Xinhua*, January 14, 2017, http://www.xinhuanet.com//english/2017-01/14/c_135981160.htm.

40 "China donates 1,000 tons of wheat in humanitarian aid to Syrian refugees in Lebanon," *Xinhua*, December 21, 2018, http://www.xinhuanet.com/english/2018-12/21/c_137690264.htm.

41 "China offers donation to help Lebanon build new conservatory," *Xinhua*, April 11, 2019, http://www.xinhuanet.com/english/2019-04/11/c_137969385.htm.

42 Yassmine Alieh, "$2 billion available from China Silk Road," *Business News*, April 6, 2017, http://www.businessnews.com.lb/cms/Story/StoryDetails/5997/$2-billion-available-from-China-Silk-Road.

43 "China launches new initiatives to boost ties with Lebanon," *Xinhua*, March 30, 2019, http://www.xinhuanet.com/english/2019-03/30/c_137936691_4.htm.

44 "Lebanon welcomes Investment from China," *Belt & Road News*, April 10, 2019, https://www.beltandroad.news/2019/04/10/lebanon-welcomes-investment-from-china/.

45 "Shoukeir represents Hariri at the China-Lebanon Investment Forum," *National News Agency*, March 30, 2019, https://www.mtv.com.lb/en/news/local/912981/shoukeir_represents_hariri_at_the_china-lebanon_investment_forum.

46 "Chinese delegation discusses plans to revive Lebanon's railway," *The Daily Star*, May 24, 2019, https://www.dailystar.com.lb/News/Lebanon-News/2019/May-24/483941-chinese-delegation-discusses-plans-to-revive-lebanons-railway.ashx.

47 "Vision and Actions on Jointly Building Silk Road Economic Belt and 21st-Century Maritime Silk Road," *National Development and Reform Commission, Ministry of Foreign Affairs, and Ministry of Commerce of the People's Republic of China*, March 28, 2015, http://en.ndrc.gov.cn/newsrelease/201503/t20150330_669367.html.

48 "8 more countries set up Confucius institutes or classrooms in 2019," *Xinhua*, December 11, 2019, http://www.xinhuanet.com/english/2019-12/11/c_138623776.htm.

49 Huang Zhiling, "10 new Confucius Institutes lift global total to 548, boosting ties,"

China Daily, December 5, 2018, http://global.chinadaily.com.cn/a/201812/05/WS5c07239da310eff30328f182.html.

50 "Confucius Institute/Classroom," *Confucius Institute Headquarters (Hanban)*, 2020, http://english.hanban.org/node_10971.htm.

51 "Learning Chinese increasingly popular in Lebanon amid growing trade ties," *China Daily*, March 16, 2019, http://www.chinadaily.com.cn/a/201903/16/WS5c8c4f6ba3106c65c34eef3f.html.

52 "China donates school bags to educational institutions in Lebanon," *CGTN*, November 10, 2018,
https://news.cgtn.com/news/3d3d774e784d444e30457a6333566d54/index.html.

53 "Learning Chinese increasingly popular in Lebanon amid growing trade ties," *China Daily*, March 16, 2019, http://www.chinadaily.com.cn/a/201903/16/WS5c8c4f6ba3106c65c34eef3f.html.

54 "Lebanese Caracalla Dance Theater enhances Cultural Links with China," *Belt & Road News*, September 24, 2019, https://www.beltandroad.news/2019/09/24/lebanese-caracalla-dance-theater-enhances-lebanons-cultural-links-with-china/.

55 "China celebrates Lunar New Year in Lebanon," *Xinhua*, January 24, 2019, http://www.xinhuanet.com/english/2019-01/24/c_137769214.htm.

56 "Chinese Embassy celebrates founding day: Lebanon important partner in building belt, road," *National News Agency (NNA)*, October 1, 2019,
http://nna-leb.gov.lb/en/show-news/108128/Chinese-Embassy-celebrates-founding-day-Lebanon-important-partner-in-building-belt-road.

57 "China, Lebanon sign tourism cooperation accord," *Xinhua*, December 10, 2005, http://english.sina.com/life/1/2005/1210/57451.html.

58 "Lebanon takes steps to promote Chinese–Lebanese tourism ties to new height: minister," *China Daily*, September 12, 2009, http://www.chinadaily.com.cn/a/201909/12/WS5d799653a310cf3e3556b1ee.html.

59 "China vows to continue support for Lebanon's military," *Xinhua*, March 5, 2019, http://www.xinhuanet.com/english/2019-03/05/c_137868900.htm.

60 Wang Kejian, "Keeping the peace in South Lebanon," *China Daily*, September 30, 2019, http://www.chinadaily.com.cn/global/2019-09/30/content_37513297.htm.

61 "China vows to continue support for Lebanon's military," *Xinhua*, March 5, 2019, http://www.xinhuanet.com/english/2019-03/05/c_137868900.htm.

6 Jordan

1 Jesse Marks and Salvatore Borgognone, "Can Jordan Harmonize Chinese and American Interests in the Levant?," *The Diplomat*, May 4, 2018,
https://thediplomat.com/2018/05/can-jordan-harmonize-chinese-and-american-interests-in-the-levant/.

2 "Jordan participates in China's Belt and Road Forum," *The Jordan Times*, May 16, 2017,
http://www.jordantimes.com/news/local/jordan-participates-china%E2%80%99s-belt-and-road-forum.

3 "Friendship ties deepen between Jordan and China," *Al-Anbat News*, October 6, 2018, http://www.alanbatnews.net/post.php?id=206542.

4 Nicholas Lyall, "Can China Remake Its Image in the Middle East?," *The Diplomat*, March 4, 2019, https://thediplomat.com/2019/03/can-china-remake-its-image-in-the-middle-east/.

5 "Ambassador of China Highlights "Jordan's Role as a Host for Chinese Investments"

at Talal Abu-Ghazaleh Knowledge Forum," *Talal Abu-Ghazaleh Organization (TAG-Org)*, July 27, 2017,
http://tagconfucius.com/article/view/Ambassador-of-China-Highlights-%E2%80%98Jordan's-Role-as-a-Host-for-Chinese-Investments%E2%80%99.

6   "Jordan Vison 2025," *Ministry of Planning and International Cooperation*, 2015, http://inform.gov.jo/en-us/by-date/report-details/articleid/247/jordan-2025.

7   Min Ye, "China and competing for cooperation in Asia-Pacific: TPP, RCEP, and the New Silk Road," *Asian Security*, 11(3), 2015, 206–224.

8   "Vision and Actions on Jointly Building Silk Road Economic Belt and 21st-Century Maritime Silk Road," *National Development and Reform Commission, Ministry of Foreign Affairs, and Ministry of Commerce of the People's Republic of China*, March 28, 2015, http://en.ndrc.gov.cn/newsrelease/201503/t20150330_669367.html.

9   "Jordan, China sign strategic partnership agreement," *The Jordan Times*, September 10, 2015, https://www.jordantimes.com/news/local/jordan-china-sign-strategic-partnership-agreement.

10 "China, Jordan announce strategic partnership," *China Daily*, September 9, 2015, http://www.chinadaily.com.cn/china/2015-09/09/content_21835445.htm.

11 Mohammad Ghazal, "China keen on increasing ties, partnerships with Jordan-association," *The Jordan Times*, April 15, 2019, http://www.jordantimes.com/news/local/china-keen-increasing-ties-partnerships-jordan-%E2%80%94-association.

12 "Jordan participates in China's Belt and Road Forum," *The Jordan Times*, May 16, 2017, http://www.jordantimes.com/news/local/jordan-participates-china%E2%80%99s-belt-and-road-forum.

13 "Senior Chinese official highlights Belt and Road construction in Middle East tour," *Xinhua*, July 18, 2017, http://www.xinhuanet.com/english/2017-07/18/c_136453148.htm.

14 Mohammad Ghazal, "China's One Belt, One Road initiative to benefit Jordan-ambassador," *The Jordan Times*, November 13, 2017, https://www.jordantimes.com/news/local/china%E2%80%99s-one-belt-one-road-initiative-benefit-jordan-%E2%80%94-ambassador.

15 "China's B&R Initiative brings promising opportunities to Jordan: minister," *Xinhua*, May 17, 2018, http://www.xinhuanet.com/english/2018-05/17/c_137184315.htm.

16 "Jordan welcomes a bigger Chinese role in Middle East," *The Jordan Times*, July 11, 2018,
http://www.jordantimes.com/news/local/jordan-welcomes-bigger-chinese-role-middle-east.

17 Mohammad Ghazal, "Jordanian-Sino relations 'exemplary'-deputy ambassador," *The Jordan Times*, April 27, 2019, http://www.jordantimes.com/news/local/jordanian-sino-relations %E2%80%98exemplary%E2%80%99-%E2%80%94-deputy-ambassador.

18 "Vision and Actions on Jointly Building Silk Road Economic Belt and 21st-Century Maritime Silk Road," *National Development and Reform Commission, Ministry of Foreign Affairs, and Ministry of Commerce of the People's Republic of China*, March 28, 2015, http://en.ndrc.gov.cn/newsrelease/201503/t20150330_669367.html.

19 "Jordan participates in China's Belt and Road Forum," *The Jordan Times*, May 16, 2017,
http://www.jordantimes.com/news/local/jordan-participates-china%E2%80%99s-belt-and-road-forum.

20 Jesse Marks and Salvatore Borgognone, "Can Jordan Harmonize Chinese and American Interests in the Levant?," *The Diplomat*, May 4, 2018,

https://thediplomat.com/2018/05/can-jordan-harmonize-chinese-and-american-interests-in-the-levant/.

21 Mordechai Chaziza, "Israel–China Relations Enter a New Stage: Limited Strategic Hedging," *Contemporary Review of the Middle East*, 5 (1), 2018, 30–45.

22 Mordechai Chaziza, "The Red–Med Railway: New Opportunities for China, Israel, and the Middle East," *BESA Center Perspectives Paper* No. 385, December 11, 2016, file:///H:/my%20articals/Red-Med-Canal-China-BRI.pdf.

23 Omar Obeidat, "Jordan, China sign agreements worth $7b, including national railway deal," *The Jordan Times*, September 11, 2015, http://www.jordantimes.com/news/local/jordan-china-sign-agreements-worth-7b-including-national-railway-deal.

24 Itay Greenspan, "Jordanian National Railway Project as part of a Regional Railway Network," *Environment And Climate In The Middle East*, January 29, 2013, http://mideastenvironment.apps01.yorku.ca/2013/01/jordanian-national-railway-project-as-part-of-a-regional-railway-network/.

25 Keith Barrow, "Jordan: a future hub for the Middle East network?," *International Railway Journal*, February 4, 2013, https://www.railjournal.com/in_depth/jordan-a-future-hub-for-the-middle-east-network.

26 Nicholas Lyall, "Can China Remake Its Image in the Middle East?," *The Diplomat*, March 4, 2019, https://thediplomat.com/2019/03/can-china-remake-its-image-in-the-middle-east/.

27 "Vision and Actions on Jointly Building Silk Road Economic Belt and 21st-Century Maritime Silk Road," *National Development and Reform Commission, Ministry of Foreign Affairs, and Ministry of Commerce of the People's Republic of China*, March 28, 2015, http://en.ndrc.gov.cn/newsrelease/201503/t20150330_669367.html.

28 "China Customs Statistics: Imports and exports by country/region," *The Hong Kong Trade Development Council (HKTDC)*, October 28, 2019, http://china-trade-research.hktdc.com/business-news/article/Facts-and-Figures/China-Customs-Statistics/ff/en/1/1X39VTVQ/1X09N9NM.htm.

29 "Chinese Investments & Contracts in Jordan (2013–2019)," *China Global Investment Tracker*, 2019, https://www.aei.org/china-global-investment-tracker/.

30 "Jordan-China ties moving 'on right path' – PM," *The Jordan Times*, July 19, 2019, http://www.jordantimes.com/news/local/jordan-china-ties-moving-%E2%80%98-right-path%E2%80%99-%E2%80%94-pm.

31 Jesse Marks and Salvatore Borgognone, "Can Jordan Harmonize Chinese and American Interests in the Levant?," *The Diplomat*, May 4, 2018, https://thediplomat.com/2018/05/can-jordan-harmonize-chinese-and-american-interests-in-the-levant/.

32 Omar Obeidat, "Jordan, China sign agreements worth $7b, including national railway deal," *The Jordan Times*, September 11, 2015, http://www.jordantimes.com/news/local/jordan-china-sign-agreements-worth-7b-including-national-Railway-deal.

33 "Jordanian–Chinese Business Forum held in Amman," *China Council for the Promotion of International Trade (CCPIT)*, April 27, 2017, http://en.ccpit.org/info/info_4028811758d70820015bad3ba3d50084.html.

34 Mohammad Ghazal, "China's One Belt, One Road initiative to benefit Jordan-ambassador," *The Jordan Times*, November 13, 2017, https://www.jordantimes.com/news/local/china%E2%80%99s-one-belt-one-road-initiative-benefit-jordan-%E2%80%94-ambassador.

35 Jesse Marks and Salvatore Borgognone, "Can Jordan Harmonize Chinese and American Interests in the Levant?," *The Diplomat*, May 4, 2018,

https://thediplomat.com/2018/05/can-jordan-harmonize-chinese-and-american-interests-in-the-levant/.

36 "Jordan-China: $31.5 million for Salt-Aredah road expansion," *Roya News*, September 30, 2018, https://en.royanews.tv/news/15307/Jordan-China:%20$31.5%20million%20for%20Salt-Aredah%20road%20expansion.

37 "China to Increase Investments in Jordan," *Al-Bawaba*, July 10, 2018, https://www.albawaba.com/business/china-increase-investments-jordan-1157266.

38 "Jordan-China business forum opened with call for more Chinese investments," *The Jordan Times*, October 23, 2018, http://www.jordantimes.com/news/local/jordan-china-business-forum-opened-call-more-chinese-investments.

39 "JIEC, China ink deal to enhance cooperation," *Jordan Industrial Estates Corporation (JIEC)*, September 10, 2019, https://www.jiec.com/en/news/77/.

40 "Highlights of Xi's speech at China-Arab forum," *China Daily*, July 10, 2018, http://www.chinadaily.com.cn/a/201807/10/WS5b441634a3103349141e1cb7.html.

41 "Jordan welcomes a bigger Chinese role in Middle East," *The Jordan Times*, July 11, 2018, http://www.jordantimes.com/news/local/jordan-welcomes-bigger-chinese-role-middle-east.

42 "Chinese embassy organises meeting to discuss investments, ties," *The Jordan Times*, April 15, 2019, http://www.jordantimes.com/news/local/chinese-embassy-organises-meeting-discuss-investments-ties.

43 "China's B&R Initiative brings promising opportunities to Jordan: minister," *Xinhua*, May 17, 2018, http://www.xinhuanet.com/english/2018-05/17/c_137184315.htm.

44 "Jordan welcomes a bigger Chinese role in Middle East," *The Jordan Times*, July 11, 2018, http://www.jordantimes.com/news/local/jordan-welcomes-bigger-chinese-role-middle-east.

45 "WFP, China conclude food aid programme for Syrian refugees," *The Jordan Times*, March 14, 2018, http://www.jordantimes.com/news/local/wfp-china-conclude-food-aid-programme-syrian-refugees.

46 Nicholas Lyall, "Can China Remake Its Image in the Middle East?," *The Diplomat*, March 4, 2019, https://thediplomat.com/2019/03/can-china-remake-its-image-in-the-middle-east/.

47 Jesse Marks and Salvatore Borgognone, "Can Jordan Harmonize Chinese and American Interests in the Levant?," *The Diplomat*, May 4, 2018, https://thediplomat.com/2018/05/can-jordan-harmonize-chinese-and-american-interests-in-the-levant/.

48 "Ambassador of China Highlights "Jordan's Role as a Host for Chinese Investments" at Talal Abu-Ghazaleh Knowledge Forum," *Talal Abu-Ghazaleh Organization (TAG-Org)*, July 27, 2017, http://tagconfucius.com/article/view/Ambassador-of-China-Highlights-%E2%80%98Jordan's-Role-as-a-Host-for-Chinese-Investments%E2%80%99.

49 "Jorden," *Energy Information Administration (EIA)*, March 2014, https://www.eia.gov/beta/international/analysis.php?iso=JOR.

50 Hans-Wilhelm Schiffer, "The World Energy Resources," *The World Energy Council*, 2016, https://www.worldenergy.org/assets/images/imported/2016/10/World-Energy-Resources-Full-report-2016.10.03.pdf.

51 Greg Everett, "Jordan's pivot to China," *Asia & the Pacific Policy Society*, January 28, 2016, https://www.policyforum.net/jordans-pivot-to-china/.

52 Tsvetana Paraskova, "Jordan Secures Funding To Build $2.1B Oil Shale Plant," *Oil*

price, March 16, 2017, https://oilprice.com/Latest-Energy-News/World-News/Jordan-Secures-Funding-To-Build-21B-Oil-Shale-Plant.html.

53   Suleiman Al-Khalidi, "Jordan moves ahead with $2.1 bln oil shale power plant," *Reuters*, March 16, 2017, https://www.reuters.com/article/jordan-energy-power-idUSL5N1GT4IF.

54   "Jordan power shortage: Kingdom turns to renewables, nuclear and oil-shale," *Power Technology*, August 1, 2018, https://www.power-technology.com/comment/jordan-power-shortage-kingdom-turns-renewables-nuclear-oil-shale/.

55   "Chinese companies interested in energy projects in Jordan: Chinese ambassador," *China Daily*, January 25, 2019,
http://www.chinadaily.com.cn/a/201901/25/WS5c4aa525a3106c65c34e68fe.html.

56   "Vision and Actions on Jointly Building Silk Road Economic Belt and 21st-Century Maritime Silk Road," *National Development and Reform Commission, Ministry of Foreign Affairs, and Ministry of Commerce of the People's Republic of China*, March 28, 2015, http://en.ndrc.gov.cn/newsrelease/201503/t20150330_669367.html.

57   "8 more countries set up Confucius institutes or classrooms in 2019," *Xinhua*, December 11, 2019,
http://www.xinhuanet.com/english/2019-12/11/c_138623776.htm.

58   Huang Zhiling, "10 new Confucius Institutes lift the global total to 548, boosting ties," *China Daily*, December 5, 2018, http://global.chinadaily.com.cn/a/201812/05/WS5c07239da310eff30328f182.html.

59   "Confucius Institute/Classroom," *Confucius Institute Headquarters (Hanban)*, 2020, http://english.hanban.org/node_10971.htm.

60   Mohammad Ghazal, "Jordanian-Sino relations 'exemplary'-deputy ambassador," *The Jordan Times*, April 28, 2019, http://www.jordantimes.com/news/local/jordanian-sino-relations-%E2%80%98exemplary%E2%80%99-%E2%80%94-deputy-ambassador.

61   "Chinese cultural centre to open in Amman soon," *The Jordan Times*, January 8, 2018, http://www.jordantimes.com/news/local/chinese-cultural-centre-open-amman-soon.

62   "Talal Abu-Ghazaleh Center for Arabic Language in China in collaboration with Chinese Chaning University Sign MoU," *Talal Abu-Ghazaleh electronic Encyclopedia (Tagepedia)*, October 25, 2015,
http://register.tagepedia.org/article/25556/Talal%20Abu-Ghazaleh%20Center%20for%20Arabic%20Language%20in%20China%20in%20collaboration%20with%20Chinese%20Chaning%20University%20Sign%20MoU.

63   "Jordan participates in China–Arab States Broadcasting Forum," *Petra*, October 17, 2019,
http://petra.gov.jo/Include/InnerPage.jsp?ID=19581&lang=en&name=en_news.

64   "Chinese cultural performance for Chinese New Year held in Jordan," *China Daily*, February 6, 2018,
http://www.chinadaily.com.cn/a/201802/06/WS5a78fa16a3106e7dcc13af51.html.

65   "The Chinese Embassy in Amman celebrates the 70th anniversary of the founding of the Republic of China," *Nayrouz Agency*, October 16, 2019, http://nayrouz.com/The-Chinese-Embassy-in-Amman-celebrates-the-70th-anniversary-of-the-founding-of-the-Republic-of-China.

66   "Ambassador of China Highlights "Jordan's Role as a Host for Chinese Investments" at Talal Abu-Ghazaleh Knowledge Forum," *Talal Abu-Ghazaleh Organization (TAG-Org)*, July 27, 2017, http://tagconfucius.com/article/view/Ambassador-of-China-Highlights-%E2%80%98Jordan's-Role-as-a-Host-for-Chinese-Investments%E2%80%99.

67   "Jordan to issue visas on arrival for Chinese, Indian nationals," *Xinhua*, October 25, 2019, http://www.xinhuanet.com/english/2019-10/25/c_138502616.htm.

68 "Jordan tourist numbers up 10% in July," *Brazil – Arab News Agency (ANBA)*, August 6, 2019, https://anba.com.br/en/jordan-tourist-numbers-up-10-in-july/.

69 "Jordan to issue visas on arrival for Chinese, Indian nationals," *Xinhua*, October 25, 2019, http://www.xinhuanet.com/english/2019-10/25/c_138502616.htm.

70 "Jordan, China sign military cooperation deal," *The Jordan Times*, September 10, 2015, http://www.jordantimes.com/news/local/jordan-china-sign-military-cooperation-deal.

71 Jeremy M. Sharp, "Jordan: Background and U.S. Relations," *Congressional Research Service*, April 9, 2019, https://fas.org/sgp/crs/mideast/RL33546.pdf.

7 Yemen

1 Yahya Yahya Yahya Al Awd, Muhammad Fuad Bin Othman and Norafidah Binti Ismail, "Yemen-China Relations: History and Development in Bilateral Relations," *The Social Sciences*, 12 (10), 2017 1775–1794.

2 World Oil Transit Chokepoints," *Energy Information Administration (EIA)*, July 25, 2017,

    https://www.eia.gov/beta/international/regions-topics.php?RegionTopicID=WOTC.

3 Hussein Askary, "Operation Felix: The Miracle of Yemen's Reconstruction and Connection to the New Silk Road," *Executive Intelligence Review*, 45 (26), June 29, 2018,

    https://larouchepub.com/eiw/public/2018/eirv45n26-20180629/20-29_4526.pdf.

4 "China renews support to Yemen's president," *Al-Sahwah*, September 15, 21019, https://alsahwa-yemen.net/en/p-33134.

5 I-wei Jennifer Chang, "China and Yemen's Forgotten War," *Peace Brief*, January 16, 2018, https://www.usip.org/publications/2018/01/china-and-yemens-forgotten-war.

6 Abdulhadi Habtor, "Yemeni Minister: $28 Billion Needed for Short-Term Reconstruction Plans," *Asharq Al-Awsat*, May 10, 2019, https://aawsat.com/english/home/article/1716141/yemeni-minister-28-billion-needed-short-term-reconstruction-plans.

7 Mordechai Chaziza, "China's Middle East foreign policy and the Yemen Crisis: Challenges and Implications," *Middle East Review of International Affairs*, 19 (2), 2015, 1–9.

8 "Foreign Ministry Spokesperson Hua Chunying's Announcement of the Temporary Closure of the Chinese Diplomatic and Consular Missions in Yemen", *Ministry of Foreign Affairs, the People's Republic of China*, April 6, 2015, http://ye.china-embassy.org/eng/fyrth/t1252339.htm.

9 "China calls for political solution to Yemen crisis," *Xinhua*, June 18, 2017, http://www.xinhuanet.com/english/2019-06/18/c_138151410.htm.

10 "China urges regional countries to create conditions for Yemen to ease tensions: envoy," *Xinhua*, October 18, 2019, http://www.xinhuanet.com/english/2019-10/18/c_138480322.htm.

11 "China hails Riyadh Agreement, hopes for Yemen peace, independence," *Global Times*, November 7, 2019, http://www.globaltimes.cn/content/1169348.shtml.

12 Mordechai Chaziza, "China's Mediation Efforts in the Middle East and North Africa: Constructive Conflict Management," *Strategic Analysis*, 42 (1), 2018, 29–41.

13 Robert Cusack, "Houthis go to China: Yemen's rebel delegation discuss peace-deal," *The New Arab*, December 1, 2016,

    https://www.alaraby.co.uk/english/news/2016/12/1/houthis-go-to-china-yemens-rebel-delegation-discuss-peace-deal.

14 I-wei Jennifer Chang, "China and Yemen's Forgotten War," *Peace Brief*, January 16, 2018, https://www.usip.org/publications/2018/01/china-and-yemens-forgotten-war.

15 Sebastian Hornschild, "China in the Middle East: Not Just about Oil," *European Union Institute for Security Studies Alert*, 31, July 2016, https://www.iss.europa.eu/sites/default/files/EUISSFiles/Alert_31_China_MENA.pdf.

16 I-wei Jennifer Chang, "China and Yemen's Forgotten War," *Peace Brief*, January 16, 2018, https://www.usip.org/publications/2018/01/china-and-yemens-forgotten-war.

17 Kristin Smith Diwan, Hussein Ibish, Peter Salisbury, Stephen A. Seche, Omar H. Rahman, Karen E. Young, "The Geoeconomics of Reconstruction in Yemen," *The Arab Gulf States Institute in Washington (AGSIW)*, November 16, 2018, https://agsiw.org/wp-content/uploads/2018/11/Yemen_UAESF_ONLINE.pdf.

18 Min Ye, "China and competing cooperation in Asia-Pacific: TPP, RCEP, and the New Silk Road," *Asian Security*, 11 (3), 2015, 206–224.

19 "Vision and Actions on Jointly Building Silk Road Economic Belt and 21st-Century Maritime Silk Road," *National Development and Reform Commission, Ministry of Foreign Affairs, and Ministry of Commerce of the People's Republic of China*, March 28, 2015, http://en.ndrc.gov.cn/newsrelease/201503/t20150330_669367.html.

20 "China and Yemen," *Ministry of Foreign Affairs, the People's Republic of China*, 2013, https://www.fmprc.gov.cn/mfa_eng/wjb_663304/zzjg_663340/xybfs_663590/gjlb_66 3594/2908_663816/.

21 "Ambassador to Yemen Chang Hua Gives Exclusive Interview to Yemeni Al-Thawra," *Ministry of Foreign Affairs, the People's Republic of China*, December 11, 2013, https://www.fmprc.gov.cn/mfa_eng/wjb_663304/zwjg_665342/zwbd_665378/t11093 59.shtml.

22 "China and Yemen," *Ministry of Foreign Affairs, the People's Republic of China*, 2013, https://www.fmprc.gov.cn/mfa_eng/wjb_663304/zzjg_663340/xybfs_663590/gjlb_66 3594/2908_663816/.

23 Jethro Mullen, "Yemen conflict: What's going on? What happens next?," *CNN*, April 23, 2015, https://edition.cnn.com/2015/04/23/middleeast/yemen-conflict-explainer-photos/index.html.

24 Judith Vonberg and Nima Elbagir, "All sides in Yemen conflict could be guilty of war crimes, says UN," *CNN*, August 28, 2018, https://edition.cnn.com/2018/08/28/middleeast/un-yemen-report-intl/index.html.

25 "Foreign Ministry Spokesperson Hua Chunying's Announcement of the Temporary Closure of the Chinese Diplomatic and Consular Missions in Yemen," *Ministry of Foreign Affairs, the People's Republic of China*, April 6, 2015, http://ye.china-embassy.org/eng/fyrth/t1252339.htm.

26 "China Contributes US$5 Million To Support WFP Fight Against Famine In Yemen," *World Food Programme*, July 17, 2017, https://www.wfp.org/news/china-contributes-us5-million-support-wfp-fight-against-famine-yemen.

27 "Wang Yi Holds Talks with Foreign Minister Khaled Hussein Alyemany of Yemen," *Ministry of Foreign Affairs, the People's Republic of China*, July 11, 2018, https://www.fmprc.gov.cn/mfa_eng/wjb_663304/wjbz_663308/activities_663312/t15 76876.shtml.

28 "Importance of Yemen's Contribution to Belt & Road asserts Ambassador," *Belt & Road News*, June 8, 2019, https://www.beltandroad.news/2019/06/08/importance-of-yemens-contribution-to-belt-road-asserts-ambassador/.

29 "Saudi-Yemen, China discuss bigger role in the region," *MENAFN – Saudi Press Agency*, July 21, 2019, https://menafn.com/1098784632/Saudi-Yemen-China-discuss-bigger-role-in-the-region.

30 World Oil Transit Chokepoints," *Energy Information Administration (EIA)*, July 25, 2017,

https://www.eia.gov/beta/international/regions-topics.php?RegionTopicID=WOTC.

31   Jean-Paul Rodrigue, Claude Comtois, and Brian Slack, *The Geography of Transport Systems*. New York: Routledge, 2013.

32   "Suez Canal: China's Trade Flows Via The Suez," *HSBC*, 2019, https://www.business.hsbc.ae/en-gb/ae/article/suez-canal-chinas-trade-flows-via-the-suez.

33   "EU NAVFOR Somalia day-to-day interface with seafarers," *The Maritime Security Centre-Horn of Africa (MSCHOA)*, 2019, https://eunavfor.eu/mschoa/.

34   Christopher D. Yung, Ross Rustici, Scott Devary and Jenny Lin, *"Not an Idea We Have to Shun": Chinese Overseas Basing Requirements in the 21st Century*. National Defense University, Institute for National Strategic Studies: National Defense University Press, 2014; Andrew S. Erickson and Austin M. Strange, *Six Years at Sea . . . and Counting: Gulf of Aden Anti-piracy and China's Maritime Commons Presence*. Washington D.C.: Brookings Institution Press, 2015.

35   "Yemen and China Enter Aden Port Development Agreement," *World Maritime News*, November 15, 2013, https://worldmaritimenews.com/archives/97733/yemen-and-china-enter-aden-port-development-agreement/.

36   Hussein Askary, "Operation Felix: The Miracle of Yemen's Reconstruction and Connection to the New Silk Road," *Executive Intelligence Review*, 45 (26), June 29, 2018,
https://larouchepub.com/eiw/public/2018/eirv45n26-20180629/20-29_4526.pdf.

37   David Styan, "China's Maritime Silk Road and Small States: Lessons the Case of Djibouti," *Journal of Contemporary China* 29 (122), 2020, 191–206.

38   "Asian Infrastructure Investment Bank to fund $301m for Duqm port, railway project," *Times of Oman*, December 10, 2016, https://timesofoman.com/article/98185/Business/Asian-Infrastructure-Investment-Bank-to-fund-301m-for-Duqm-port-railway-project.

39   "The Review of Maritime Transport 2018," *United Nations Conference on Trade and Development (UNCTAD)*, October 3, 2018, https://unctad.org/en/PublicationsLibrary/rmt2018_en.pdf.

40   Eleonora Ardemagni, "The Geostrategy of Straits: Hormuz and Bab al-Mandeb," *About Energy*, 2018, https://www.aboutenergy.com/en_IT/topics/geostrategy-straits.shtml#.

41   John Calabrese, "The Bab el-Mandeb Strait: Regional and great power rivalries on the shores of the Red Sea," *Middle East Institute*, January 29, 2020, https://www.mei.edu/publications/bab-el-mandeb-strait-regional-and-great-power-rivalries-shores-red-sea.

42   Andrew S. Erickson and Austin M. Strange, *Six Years at Sea . . . and Counting: Gulf of Aden Anti-piracy and China's Maritime Commons Presence*. Washington D.C.: Brookings Institution Press, 2015.

43   World Oil Transit Chokepoints," *Energy Information Administration (EIA)*, July 25, 2017,
https://www.eia.gov/beta/international/regions-topics.php?RegionTopicID=WOTC.

44   Simone Dossi, "The EU, China, and nontraditional security: Prospects for cooperation in the Mediterranean region," *Mediterranean Quarterly*, 26 (1), 2015, 77–96.

45   Julia Gurol and Parisa Shahmohammadi, "Projecting Power Westwards: China's Maritime Strategy in the Arabian Sea and its Potential Ramifications for the Region," *Center for Applied Research in Partnership with the Orient (CARPO)*, November 11, 2019, https://carpo-bonn.org/wp-content/uploads/2019/11/carpo_study_07.pdf.

46   Mordechai Chaziza, "China's Military Base in Djibouti," *Mideast Security and Policy Studies*, 153, The Begin-Sadat Center for Strategic Studies Bar-Ilan University, 2018,

https://besacenter.org/wp-content/uploads/2018/08/153-Chaziza-Chinas-Military-Base-in-Djibouti-web.pdf.

47 John Calabrese, "The Bab el-Mandeb Strait: Regional and great power rivalries on the shores of the Red Sea," *Middle East Institute*, January 29, 2020, https://www.mei.edu/publications/bab-el-mandeb-strait-regional-and-great-power-rivalries-shores-red-sea.

48 "Bab Al-Mandeb Strait: Sino-American duel in the Red Sea," *Belt & Road News*, January 4, 2019, https://www.beltandroad.news/2019/01/04/bab-al-mandeb-strait-sino-american-duel-in-the-red-sea/.

49 "The Forgotten War: The Ongoing Disaster in Yemen," *The Soufan Center*, June 2018, http://thesoufancenter.org/wp-content/uploads/2018/05/Report-The-Forgotten-War-The-Ongoing-Disaster-in-Yemen-The-Soufan-Center.pdf.

50 "Yemen," *Energy Information Administration (EIA)*, April 23, 2019, https://www.eia.gov/beta/international/analysis.php?iso=YEM.

51 Geoffrey F. Gresh, "A Vital Maritime Pinch Point: China, the Bab al-Mandeb, and the Middle East," *Asian Journal of Middle Eastern and Islamic Studies*, 11(1), 2017, 37–46.

52 Geoffrey F. Gresh, "A Vital Maritime Pinch Point: China, the Bab al-Mandeb, and the Middle East," *Asian Journal of Middle Eastern and Islamic Studies*, 11(1), 2017, 37–46.

53 Justine Barden, "The Bab el-Mandeb Strait is a strategic route for oil and natural gas shipments," *Energy Information Administration (EIA)*, August 27, 2019, https://www.eia.gov/todayinenergy/detail.php?id=41073.

54 Julia Gurol, "Rivals or Partners? Interdependencies Between the EU and China in the Middle East," *Center for Applied Research in Partnership with the Orient (CARPO)*, October 2018, https://carpo-bonn.org/en/portfolio/carpo-study-05-rivals-or-partners/.

55 Geoffrey F. Gresh, "A Vital Maritime Pinch Point: China, the Bab al-Mandeb, and the Middle East," *Asian Journal of Middle Eastern and Islamic Studies*, 11(1), 2017, 37–46.

56 "Yemeni president looking forward to the return of Chinese oil, gas and energy investments," *Arab News*, October 19, 2018, https://carpo-bonn.org/wp content/uploads/2018/10/carpo_study_05_2018_Gurol.pdf.

57 "Vision and Actions on Jointly Building Silk Road Economic Belt and 21st-Century Maritime Silk Road," *National Development and Reform Commission, Ministry of Foreign Affairs, and Ministry of Commerce of the People's Republic of China*, March 28, 2015, http://en.ndrc.gov.cn/newsrelease/201503/t20150330_669367.html.

58 Hussein Askary, "Operation Felix: The Miracle of Yemen's Reconstruction and Connection to the New Silk Road," *Executive Intelligence Review*, 45 (26), June 29, 2018, https://larouchepub.com/eiw/public/2018/eirv45n26-20180629/20-29_4526.pdf.

59 "China Customs Statistics: Imports and exports by country/region," *The Hong Kong Trade Development Council (HKTDC)*, January 24, 2020, http://china-trade-research.hktdc.com/business-news/article/Facts-and-Figures/China-Customs-Statistics/ff/en/1/1X39VTVQ/1X09N9NM.htm.

60 "Chinese Investments & Contracts in Yemen (2013–2019)," *China Global Investment Tracker*, 2020, https://www.aei.org/china-global-investment-tracker/.

61 "China to build power plants in Yemen, expand ports," *Reuters*, November 16, 2013, https://www.reuters.com/article/us-yemen-china-power/china-to-build-power-plants-in-yemen-expand-ports-idUSBRE9AF05A20131116.

62 "European Union, trade in goods with China," *European Commission Directorate-General for Trade*, 2019, https://webgate.ec.europa.eu/isdb_results/factsheets/country/details_china_en.pdf.

63 "EU–China trade in goods: 185 billion deficit in 2018," *Eurostat*, April 9, 2019,

https://ec.europa.eu/eurostat/web/products-eurostat-news/-/EDN-20190409-1.

64 "The Forgotten War: The Ongoing Disaster in Yemen," *The Soufan Center*, June 2018, http://thesoufancenter.org/wp-content/uploads/2018/05/Report-The-Forgotten-War-The-Ongoing-Disaster-in-Yemen-The-Soufan-Center.pdf.

65 "First Batch of China's Emergency Humanitarian Aid Arrives in Yemen," *Xinhua*, July 14, 2017, http://news.xinhuanet.com/english/2017-07/14/c_136442006.htm.

66 "China Contributes US$5 Million To Support WFP Fight Against Famine In Yemen," *World Food Programme (WFP)*, July 17, 2017, https://www.wfp.org/news/china-contributes-us5-million-support-wfp-fight-against-famine-yemen.

67 Laura Zhou, "China pledges US$23 billion in loans and aid to Arab states as it boosts ties in Middle East," *South China Morning Post*, July 10, 2018, https://www.scmp.com/news/china/diplomacy-defence/article/2154642/china-pledges-us23-million-loans-and-aid-arab-states-it.

68 "Wang Yi Holds Talks with Foreign Minister Khaled Hussein Alyemany of Yemen," *Ministry of Foreign Affairs, the People's Republic of China*, July 11, 2018, https://www.fmprc.gov.cn/mfa_eng/wjb_663304/wjbz_663308/activities_663312/t1576876.shtml.

69 "China offers $105m to Arab countries, political support to Palestine," *Middle East Eye*, January 29, 2019, https://www.middleeasteye.net/news/china-offers-105m-arab-countries-political-support-palestine.

8 Saudi Arabia

1 Xu Wei, "Xi hails Saudi Arabia as good friend," *China Daily*, February 23, 2019, http://www.chinadaily.com.cn/a/201902/23/WS5c7044c2a3106c65c34eaef5.html.

2 "Chinese president meets Saudi crown prince," *China Daily*, February 22, 2019, http://www.chinadaily.com.cn/a/201902/22/WS5c6ff654a3106c65c34eaebd.html.

3 "Our Vision: Saudi Arabia the heart of the Arab and Islamic worlds, the investment powerhouse, and the hub connecting three continents," *Kingdom of Saudi Arabia*, March, 2019, https://vision2030.gov.sa/sites/default/files/report/Saudi_Vision2030_EN_2017.pdf.

4 Mohamed Negm, "The Suez Canal axes, Neom and the Silk Road initiative an alliance between Egypt, Saudi and China for a century's project in formation," *The Middle East Observer*, March 13, 2018, http://www.meobserver.org/?p=16092.

5 "Vision and Actions on Jointly Building Silk Road Economic Belt and 21st-Century Maritime Silk Road," *National Development and Reform Commission, Ministry of Foreign Affairs, and Ministry of Commerce of the People's Republic of China*, March 28, 2015, http://en.ndrc.gov.cn/newsrelease/201503/t20150330_669367.html.

6 "Xi begins Middle East tour with elevation of Sino–Saudi ties," *China Daily*, January 20, 2016, http://www.chinadaily.com.cn/world/2016xivisitmiddleeast/2016-01/20/content_23162646.htm.

7 "China, Saudi Arabia ink cooperation deals," *The State Council: The People's Republic of China*, August 30, 2016, http://english.gov.cn/state_council/vice_premiers/2016/08/30/content_281475429522366.htm.

8 "China, Saudi Arabia agree to boost all-round strategic partnership," *China Daily*, March 16, 2017, http://www.chinadaily.com.cn/china/2017-03/16/content_28585346.htm.

9 "Crown Prince meets with Chinese Vice Premier," *Saudi Gazette*, August 25, 2017, http://saudigazette.com.sa/article/515872.

10 "China, Saudi Arabia agree to expand cooperation," *Xinhua*, February 22, 2019, http://www.xinhuanet.com/english/2019-02/22/c_137842899.htm.

11 "Country Reports on Human Rights Practices for 2018: China," *United States Department of State*, 2018, https://www.state.gov/documents/organization/289281.pdf.

12 Lesley Wroughton and David Brunnstrom, "U.S. says China's treatment of Muslim minority worst abuses 'since the 1930s'," *Reuters*, March 13, 2019, https://www.reuters.com/article/us-usa-rights/pompeo-says-china-in-a-league-of-its-own-in-human-rights-violations-idUSKBN1QU23W?feedType=RSS&feedName=worldNews.

13 Phil Stewart, "China putting minority Muslims in 'concentration camps,' U.S. says," *Reuters*, May 4, 2019, https://www.reuters.com/article/us-usa-china-concentrationcamps/china-putting-minority-muslims-in-concentration-camps-us-says-idUSKCN1S925K.

14 Esther Felden, Nina Raddy, Kyra Levine, "Saudi women refugees in Germany: Still living in fear," *Deutsche Welle*, February 19, 2019, https://www.dw.com/en/saudi-women-refugees-in-germany-still-living-in-fear/a-47576575.

15 Declan Walsh and Tyler Hicks, "The Tragedy of Saudi Arabia's War," *The New York Times*, October 26, 2018, https://www.nytimes.com/interactive/2018/10/26/world/middleeast/saudi-arabia-war-yemen.html.

16 Zahraa Alkhalisi, "Saudi Arabia seeks Asia's support for its economic makeover," *CNN Business*, February 19, 2019, https://edition.cnn.com/2019/02/19/business/mbs-asia-tour-business/index.html.

17 Helene Fouquet, Jonathan Gilbert and Alex Morales, "Saudi Prince Finds Both Friends and Disapproval at G-20 Summit," *Bloomberg*, December 3, 2018, https://www.bloomberg.com/news/articles/2018-12-01/saudi-prince-finds-both-friends-and-disapproval-at-g-20-summit.

18 Oscar Rousseau, "China wants Saudi as key Belt and Road partner," *Arabian Industry*, July 11, 2018, https://www.arabianindustry.com/construction/news/2018/jul/11/china-wants-saudi-as-key-belt-and-road-partner-5952245/#.W0YMp2LblFQ.twitter.

19 Turki Al Faisal bin Abdul Aziz Al Saud, "Saudi Arabia's Foreign Policy," *The Middle East Policy Council*, XX (4), October 22, 2013, https://www.mepc.org/saudi-arabias-foreign-policy.

20 P. R. Kumaraswamy and Md. Muddassir Quamar, *India's Saudi Policy: Bridging the Gulf*. Singapore: Palgrave Macmillan, 2019.

21 "Saudi Energy Minister Labels 'One Belt, One Road' Initiative as Historic," *Asharq Al-Awsat*, May 15, 2017, https://eng-archive.aawsat.com/asharq-al-awsat-english/business/saudi-energy-minister-labels-one-belt-one-road-initiative-historic.

22 Jean-Michel Valantin, "Saudi Arabia and the Chinese New Silk Road," *The Red (Team) Analysis Society: Strategic Foresight & Warning, Risk Management, Horizon Scanning*, May 15, 2017, https://www.redanalysis.org/2017/05/15/saudi-arabia-and-the-chinese-new-silk-road/.

23 "Saudi Energy Minister Labels 'One Belt, One Road' Initiative as Historic," *Asharq Al-Awsat*, May 15, 2017, https://eng-archive.aawsat.com/asharq-al-awsat-english/business/saudi-energy-minister-labels-one-belt-one-road-initiative-historic.

24 "China, Saudi Arabia sign agreements worth $65bn," *China Radio International*, March 16, 2017, https://gbtimes.com/china-vows-to-deepen-support-for-saudi-arabia.

25 "Saudi Arabia To Build $10 Billion Oil Refinery In Pakistan's Gwadar," *RFE/RL*, January 12, 2019, https://www.rferl.org/a/saudi-arabia-to-build-10-billion-oil-refinery-in-pakistan-s-gwadar/29706488.html.

26 Zamir Ahmed Awan, "New era in Sino–Saudi relations," *China Daily*, February 25, 2019, http://www.chinadaily.com.cn/a/201902/25/WS5c734f98a3106c65c34eb2e8.html.

27 "China's Guarded Response To Pak Bringing Saudi In Trade Corridor Work", *NDTV*, October 08, 2018, https://www.ndtv.com/world-news/chinas-guarded-response-to-pak-bringing-saudi-arabia-in-trade-corridor-work-1928715.

28 Asif Amin, "Why Saudi Arabia's interest in CPEC, BRI is good news," *China Daily*, October 12, 2018, http://www.chinadaily.com.cn/a/201810/12/WS5bc047a4a310eff3032820f6.html.

29 "A Shenzhen for Arabia," *Week in China*, November 3, 2017, https://www.week-inchina.com/2017/11/a-shenzhen-for-arabia/.

30 "NEOM and the BRI," *OBOReurope*, February 28, 2019, https://www.oboreurope.com/en/neom-and-the-bri/.

31 John Calabrese, "China and the Persian Gulf: Energy and Security," *Middle East Journal*, 52 (3), 1998, 351–366; Steve Yetiv and Chunlong Lu, "China, Global Energy, and the Middle East", *Middle East Journal*, 61 (2), 2007, 199–218.

32 Daniel Workman, "Top 15 Crude Oil Suppliers to China," *World's Top Exports*, April 26, 2020, http://www.worldstopexports.com/top-15-crude-oil-suppliers-to-china/.

33 Chris Zambelis, "China and Saudi Arabia Solidify Strategic Partnership Amid Looming Risks," *China Brief*, 17 (3), March 2, 2017, https://jamestown.org/program/china-saudi-arabia-solidify-strategic-partnership-amid-looming-risks/.

34 "Saudi Arabia facts and figures," *Organization of the Petroleum Exporting Countries*, September 23, 2018, https://www.opec.org/opec_web/en/about_us/169.htm.

35 Rania El Gamal, "UPDATE 3-Saudi Arabia announces rise in oil reserves after external audit," *Reuters*, January 9, 2019, https://www.reuters.com/article/saudi-oil-reserves/update-3-saudi-arabia-announces-rise-in-oil-reserves-after-external-audit-id USL8N1Z93WO.

36 "China see' "enormous potential' in Saudi economy as crown prince visits," *Reuters*, February 22, 2019, https://www.reuters.com/article/asia-saudi-china/china-sees-enormous-potential-in-saudi-economy-as-crown-prince-visits-idUSL3N20H05S.

37 Lyu Chang and Xing Zhigang, "Sinopec, Saudi Aramco sign strategic agreement," *China Daily* January 21, 2016, http://www.chinadaily.com.cn/world/2016xivisitmiddleeast/2016-01/21/content_23174517.htm.

38 "Yanbu's joint venture refinery shines as example for beneficial China–Saudi energy cooperation," *Xinhua*, July 9, 2018, http://www.xinhuanet.com/english/2018-07/09/c_137312287.htm.

39 "Saudi to supply 12 million barrels crude to China's Huajin in 2018 deal," *Reuters*, February 26, 2018, https://www.reuters.com/article/us-saudi-china-crude-huajin/saudi-to-supply-12-million-barrels-crude-to-chinas-huajin-in-2018-deal-idUSKCN1GA0VR.

40 "Saudi's SABIC signs MOU to build petrochemical complex in China," *Reuters*, September 11, 2018, https://www.reuters.com/article/us-sabic-china/saudis-sabic-signs-mou-to-build-petrochemical-complex-in-china-idUSKCN1LR0L8.

41 "China and Saudi Arabia sign 35 cooperation deals worth $28 bln in Beijing," *China Global Television Network (CGTN)*, 24 February 2019, https://news.cgtn.com/news/3d3d414f306b444f32457a6333566d54/index.html.

42 "Saudi Aramco agrees to $10 billion joint venture deal in China," *ARAB NEWS*, February 22, 2019, http://www.arabnews.com/node/1456321/business-economy.

43 Florence Tan, Chen Aizhu and Rania El-Gamal, "Saudi Arabia nabs new China oil demand, challenges Russia's top spot," *The Globe and Mail*, November 28, 2018, https://www.theglobeandmail.com/business/article-saudi-arabia-nabs-new-china-oil-demand-challenges-russias-top-spot/.

44 "Pan-Asia PET Resin (Guangzhou, China) Plans to Invest $3.8 Billion to Build a Polyester Manufacturing Complex at Jazan, Saudi Arabi," *Bloomberg*, July 10, 2017, https://www.bloomberg.com/research/stocks/private/snapshot.asp?privcapid=30395182.

45 Natasha Alperowicz, "Chinese firm to invest in huge polyester complex in Saudi Arabia," *Borderless*, June 27, 2017, https://www.borderless.net/chinese-firm-to-invest-in-huge-polyester-complex-in-saudi-arabia/.

46 "Beijing, Saudi Arabia agree to more oil cooperation, exports to China," *Reuters*, March 18, 2017, https://www.reuters.com/article/us-china-saudi/beijing-saudi-arabia-agree-to-more-oil-cooperation-exports-to-china-idUSKBN16P055.

47 Hisham Al-Joher, "SABIC and SINOPEC Support Saudi Vision 2030 and China's One Belt, One Road Initiative by Singing a Strategic Cooperation Agreement," *SABIC*, March 16, 2017, https://www.sabic.com/en/news/6098-sabic-and-sinopec-support-saudi-vision-2030-and-china-s-one-belt-one-road-initiative-by-signing-a-strategic-co operation-agreement.

48 "Saudi-China Tie Up Furthers 'One Belt One Road'," *Port Technology*, June 5, 2017, https://www.porttechnology.org/news/saudis_joins_up_on_one_belt_one_road.

49 "Saudi Arabia 2018," *The Oil & Gas Year Saudi Arabia 2018*, 2019, https://www.theoilandgasyear.com/market/saudi-arabia/.

50 Dania Saadi, "Saudi Arabia announces rise in oil and gas reserves after independent audit," *The National*, January 9, 2019, https://www.thenational.ae/business/energy/saudi-arabia-announces-rise-in-oil-and-gas-reserves-after-independent-audit-1.811247.

51 Rania El Gamal, Alex Lawler, "Exclusive: China offers to buy 5 percent of Saudi Aramco directly- sources," *Reuters*, October 16, 2017, https://www.reuters.com/article/us-saudi-aramco-ipo-china-exclusive/exclusive-china-offers-to-buy-5-percent-of-saudi-aramco-directly-sources-idUSKBN1CL1YJ.

52 Carmen Reinicke, "Saudi Arabia officially kicked off Saudi Aramco's IPO, which could be the largest in the world," *Markets Insider*, November 3, 2019, https://markets.businessinsider.com/news/stocks/saudi-arabi-aramco-ipo-largest-2019-11-1028653492?utm_source=markets&utm_medium=ingest.

53 "China considers up to $10 billion investment in Aramco IPO: Bloomberg," *Reuters*, November 6, 2019, https://www.reuters.com/article/us-saudi-aramco-ipo/china-considers-up-to-10-billion-investment-in-aramco-ipo-bloomberg-idUSKBN1XG2B6.

54 " PowerChina signs marine facilities construction contract in Saudi Arabia," *State-owned Assets Supervision and Administration Commission of the State Council*, December 4, 2018, http://en.sasac.gov.cn/2018/12/04/c_685.htm.

55 "Chinese group launches $1bn Saudi industrial project," *Trade Arabia*, January 31, 2019, http://www.tradearabia.com/news/OGN_350428.html.

56 "Massive Chinese project in Saudi Arabia makes big breakthroughs," *China Daily*, January 9, 2019, http://www.chinadaily.com.cn/regional/2019-01/10/content_37425087.htm.

57 Global Commission on the Geopolitics of Energy Transformation, "A New World the Geopolitics of the Energy Transformation," *International Renewable Energy Agency (IREA)*, 2019, http://www.geopoliticsofrenewables.org/assets/geopolitics/Reports/wp-content/uploads/2019/01/Global_commission_renewable_energy_2019.pdf.

58 Juergen Braunstein and Oliver McPherson-Smith, "The US–China Trade War and its Implications for Saudi Arabia," *Global Policy*, February 12, 2019, https://www.globalpolicyjournal.com/blog/12/02/2019/us-china-trade-war-and-its-implications-saudi-arabia.

59 Mark Osborne, "LONGi set for agreement to develop major solar manufacturing hub in Saudi Arabia," *PV-Tech*, May 25, 2018, https://www.pv-tech.org/news/longi-signs-agreement-to-develop-major-solar-manufacturing-hub-in-saudi-ara.

60 "Hanergy to set up the region's first thin-film solar power industrial park in Middle East," *EIN Newsdesk*, 2019, https://www.einnews.com/pr_news/475415644/hanergy-to-set-up-the-region-s-first-thin-film-solar-power-industrial-park-in-middle-east.

61 "Saudi Arabia's PIF signs MoU with China's NAE on renewable energy," *ARAB NEWS*, February 22, 2019, http://www.arabnews.com/node/1456326/business-economy.

62 Jason Deign, "Saudi Arabia Looks to China for Solar as Power Politics Shift," *Greentech Media*, February 5, 2019, https://www.greentechmedia.com/articles/read/saudi-looks-to-china-for-solar-as-power-politics-shift#gs.26fdtx.

63 "Shift in Power Politics, Saudi Arabia Courting China for Help in Solar," *Times of Saudia*, February 5, 2019, https://www.timesofsaudia.com/saudi-arabia/shift-in-power-politics-saudi-arabia-courting-china-for-help-in-solar/.

64 "Chinese state grid company signs US$1.1bn smart meter contract with Saudi Arabia," *South China Morning Post*, December 21, 2019, https://www.scmp.com/news/china/diplomacy/article/3043099/chinese-state-grid-company-signs-us11bn-smart-meter-contract.

65 Chen Kane, "Why proposals to sell nuclear reactors to Saudi Arabia raise red flags," *The Conversation*, February 23, 2019, https://theconversation.com/why-proposals-to-sell-nuclear-reactors-to-saudi-arabia-raise-red-flags-112276.

66 "Saudi Arabia, Largest Producer of Desalinated Water, to Build 9 More Plants," *Al-bawaba*, January 22, 2018, https://www.albawaba.com/business/saudi-arabia-desalination-plants-red-sea-coast-1077706.

67 "China, Saudi Arabia agree to build HTR," *World Nuclear News*, January 20, 2016, http://www.world-nuclear-news.org/NN-China-Saudi-Arabia-agree-to-build-HTR-2001164.html.

68 "Saudi Arabia signs cooperation deals with China on nuclear energy," *Reuters*, August 25, 2017, https://www.reuters.com/article/saudi-china-nuclear/saudi-arabia-signs-cooperation-deals-with-china-on-nuclear-energy-idUSL8N1LB1CE.

69 "Vision and Actions on Jointly Building Silk Road Economic Belt and 21st-Century Maritime Silk Road," *National Development and Reform Commission, Ministry of Foreign Affairs, and Ministry of Commerce of the People's Republic of China*, March 28, 2015, http://en.ndrc.gov.cn/newsrelease/201503/t20150330_669367.html.

70 "China Customs Statistics: Imports and exports by country/region," *The Hong Kong Trade Development Council (HKTDC)*, January 24, 2020, http://china-trade-research.hktdc.com/business-news/article/Facts-and-Figures/China-Customs-Statistics/ff/en/1/1X39VTVQ/1X09N9NM.htm.

71 "Chinese Investments & Contracts in Saudi Arabia (2013–2018)," *China Global Investment Tracker*, 2020, https://www.aei.org/china-global-investment-tracker/.

72 "China, Saudi Arabia sign multiple deals," *Global Times*, February 22, 2019, http://www.globaltimes.cn/content/1139770.shtml.

73 Ibrahim Al-Othaimin, "Win-win cooperation usher in new type of international ties," *Saudi Gazette*, May 4, 2018, http://saudigazette.com.sa/article/534190.

74 Lindsay Hughes, "China in the Middle East: The Saudi Factor," *Future Directions International*, October 2, 2018, http://www.futuredirections.org.au/publication/china-in-the-middle-east-the-saudi-factor/.

75 Joseph A. Kéchichian, "Saudi Arabia and China: The Security Dimension," *Middle*

East Institute, February 9, 2016, https://www.mei.edu/publications/saudi-arabia-and-china-security-dimension.

76   "State Councilor and Foreign Minister Wang Yi gave an interview to Asharq Al-Awsat," *Embassy of the People's Republic of China in the Kingdom of Saudi Arabia*, February 22, 2019, http://www.chinaembassy.org.sa/eng/zsgx/t1640239.htm.

77   "Xi Jinping Holds Talks with King Salman bin Abdulaziz Al Saud of Saudi Arabia: Two Heads of State Jointly Announce Establishment of China–Saudi Arabia Comprehensive Strategic Partnership," *Ministry of Foreign Affairs, the People's Republic of China*, January 20, 2016, https://www.fmprc.gov.cn/mfa_eng/topics_665678/xjpdstajyljxgsfw/t1333527.shtml.

78   Wang Jin, "China and Saudi Arabia: A New Alliance?," *The Diplomat*, September 2, 2016, https://thediplomat.com/2016/09/china-and-saudi-arabia-a-new-alliance/.

79   Catherine Wong, "China, Saudi Arabia sign US$65 billion in deals as King Salman starts Beijing visit," *South China Morning Post*, March 16, 2017, https://www.scmp.com/news/china/policies-politics/article/2079528/china-saudi-arabia-sign-us65-billion-deals-king-salman.

80   "China–Saudi Arabia cooperation to enter more fruitful era, broad consensus reached on key projects," *Xinhua*, August 25, 2017, http://www.xinhuanet.com//english/2017-08/25/c_136554724.htm.

81   Andrew Torchia, "Saudi Arabia, China plan joint $20 billion investment fund," *Reuters*, August 24, 2017, https://www.reuters.com/article/us-saudi-china-funds/saudi-arabia-china-plan-joint-20-billion-investment-fund-idUSKCN1B40KO.

82   "Saudi Arabia, China sign $28 billion worth of economic accords," *Arab News*, February 22, 2019, http://www.arabnews.com/node/1456366/business-economy.

83   "Saudi Arabia and China sign agreements worth $28 billion," *Offshore Technology*, February 27, 2019, https://www.offshore-technology.com/comment/saudi-arabia-and-china-sign-agreements-worth-28-billion/.

84   "Interview: Saudi crown prince's visit to China expected to bring ties to new high: minister," *Xinhua*, February 21, 2019, http://www.xinhuanet.com/english/2019-02/21/c_137837773.htm.

85   Ahmed Al-Quiasy, "Saudi–Chinese Rapprochement and Its Effect on Saudi–American Relations," *The Washington Institute*, February 2, 2018, https://www.washingtoninstitute.org/fikraforum/view/saudi-chinese-rapprochement-and-its-effect-on-saudi-american-relations.

86   Yoel Guzansky and Assaf Orion, "Slowly but Surely: Growing Relations between Saudi Arabia and China," *INSS Insight No. 891*, January 29, 2017, https://www.inss.org.il/publication/slowly-surely-growing-relations-saudi-arabia-china/.

87   Thomas Woodrow, "The Sino–Saudi Connection," *China Brief*, 2 (21), October 24, 2002, https://jamestown.org/program/the-sino-saudi-connection/.

88   Muhammad Saleh Zaafir, "Saudi Arabia planning procurement of JF-17 Thunder, Mashshaks, says Saudi air chief," *The News*, November 7, 2016, https://www.thenews.com.pk/print/163018-Saudi-Arabia-planning-procurement-of-JF-17-Thunder-Mashshaks-says-Saudi-air-chief.

89   Phil Mattingly, Zachary Cohen and Jeremy Herb, "Exclusive: US intel shows Saudi Arabia escalated its missile program with help from China," *CNN*, June 5, 2019, https://edition.cnn.com/2019/06/05/politics/us-intelligence-saudi-arabia-ballistic-missile-china/index.html.

90   Zamir Ahmed Awan, "New era in Sino–Saudi relations," *China Daily*, February 25, 2019,

http://www.chinadaily.com.cn/a/201902/25/WS5c734f98a3106c65c34eb2e8.html.

91 Chen Chuanren and Chris Pocock, "Saudi Arabia Buying and Building Chinese Armed Drones," *AIN online*, April 12, 2017, https://www.ainonline.com/aviation-news/defense/2017-04-12/saudi-arabia-buying-and-building-chinese-armed-drones.

92 "Saudi Arabia imports UAV production line from China: reports," *People's Daily Online*, March 27, 2017, http://www.ecns.cn/military/2017/03-27/250906.shtml.

93 Stephen Clark, "China launches satellites for Saudi Arabia," *Spaceflight Now*, December 7, 2018, https://spaceflightnow.com/2018/12/07/china-launches-satellites-for-saudi-arabia/.

94 "Xi Jinping Holds Talks with King Salman bin Abdulaziz Al Saud of Saudi Arabia," *Embassy of the People's Republic of China in the Kingdom of Saudi Arabia*, January 19, 2016, http://sa.china-embassy.org/eng/zt/2/t1335502.htm.

95 "King receives special envoy of Chinese president," *Saudi Gazette*, November 7, 2016, http://saudigazette.com.sa/article/166742/King-receives-special-envoy-of-Chinese-president.

96 Chris Zambelis, "China and Saudi Arabia Solidify Strategic Partnership Amid Looming Risks," *China Brief*, 17(3), March 2, 2017, https://jamestown.org/program/china-saudi-arabia-solidify-strategic-partnership-amid-looming-risks/.

97 "Vision and Actions on Jointly Building Silk Road Economic Belt and 21st-Century Maritime Silk Road," *National Development and Reform Commission, Ministry of Foreign Affairs, and Ministry of Commerce of the People's Republic of China*, March 28, 2015, http://en.ndrc.gov.cn/newsrelease/201503/t20150330_669367.html.

98 "State Councilor and Foreign Minister Wang Yi gave an interview to Asharq Al-Awsat," *Embassy of the People's Republic of China in the Kingdom of Saudi Arabia*, February 22, 2019, http://www.chinaembassy.org.sa/eng/zsgx/t1640239.htm.

99 "China to host its first major cultural relic exhibition in Saudi Arabia," *China Daily*, August 23, 2018, http://www.chinadaily.com.cn/a/201808/23/WS5b7e24dda310add14f387556_4.html.

100 "Saudi Arabia plans to include Chinese language in education curriculum," *Saudi Gazette*, February 22, 2019, http://saudigazette.com.sa/article/559758/SAUDI-ARABIA/Saudi-Arabia-plans-to-include-Chinese-language-in-education-curriculum.

101 "China, Arab states agree to enhance cooperation under new strategic partnership," *Arab News*, July 10, 2018, http://www.arabnews.com/node/1336746/saudi-arabia.

102 Yang Feiyue, "Program helps young Saudis study abroad," *China Daily*, January 21, 2016, http://www.chinadaily.com.cn/world/2016xivisitmiddleeast/2016-01/21/content_ 23177839.htm.

103 "8 more countries set up Confucius institutes or classrooms in 2019," *Xinhua*, December 11, 2019, http://www.xinhuanet.com/english/2019-12/11/c_138623776.htm.

104 Huang Zhiling, "10 new Confucius Institutes lift global total to 548, boosting ties," *China Daily*, December 5, 2018, http://global.chinadaily.com.cn/a/201812/05/WS5c07239da310eff30328f182.html.

105 "Confucius Institute/Classroom," *Confucius Institute Headquarters (Hanban)*, 2020, http://english.hanban.org/node_10971.htm.

106 "Interview: Saudi crown prince's visit to China expected to bring ties to new high: minister," *Xinhua*, February 21, 2019, https://edition.cnn.com/2019/02/21/asia/saudi-arabia-china-mohammed-bin-salman-intl/index.html.

107 Sam Bridge, "Gulf forecast to see 81% rise in Chinese tourists by 2022," *Arabian Business*, December 19, 2018, https://www.arabianbusiness.com/travel-hospitality/409972-gulf-forecast-to-see-81-rise-in-chinese-tourists-by-2022.

108 "Chinese envoy sees KSA as a major tourist destination," *Arab News*, July 10, 2018, http://www.arabnews.com/node/1336756/saudi-arabia.

109 Matthias Ang, "Chinese tourists top number of visitors to Saudi Arabia in wake of visa launch," *Mothership*, October 10, 2019, https://mothership.sg/2019/10/chinese-tourists-saudi-arabia/.

110 Travel & Tourism crucial to Saudi Arabia's economy," *World Travel & Tourism Council*, March 25, 2019, https://www.wttc.org/about/media-centre/press-releases/press-releases/2019/travel-and-tourism-crucial-to-saudi-arabias-economy/ .

111 Staff writer, "Saudi Arabia aims to attract 1.5m tourists by 2020," *Arabian Business*, June 5, 2016, https://www.arabianbusiness.com/saudi-arabia-aims-attract-1-5m-tourists-by-2020-634057.html.

112 "Chinese tourists travel more, spend more in 2018," *CGTN*, January 11, 2019, https://news.cgtn.com/news/3d3d774d3051544f31457a6333566d54/share_p.html.

9 Iran

1 "China, Iran Upgrade Ties to Carry Forward Millennia-Old Friendship," *Xinhua*, January 24, 2016, http://news.xinhuanet.com/english/china/2016-01/24/c_135039635.htm.

2 "Ahead of Saudi visit, China seeks 'deeper trust' with Iran," *Reuters*, February 19, 2019, https://www.reuters.com/article/us-china-iran/ahead-of-saudi-visit-china-seeks-deeper-trust-with-iran-idUSKCN1Q80PY.

3 Alex Vatanka, "China Courts Iran: Why One Belt, One Road Will Run Through Tehran," *Foreign Affairs*, November 1, 2017, https://www.foreignaffairs.com/articles/china/2017-11-01/china-courts-iran.

4 Mohsen Shariatinia and Hamidreza Azizi, "Iran-China Cooperation in the Silk Road Economic Belt: From Strategic Understanding to Operational Understanding," *China & World Economy*, 25 (5), 2017, 46–61.

5 "Remarks by President Trump on the Joint Comprehensive Plan of Action," *The White House*, May 8, 2018, https://www.whitehouse.gov/briefings-statements/remarks-president-trump-joint-comprehensive-plan-action/.

6 "When the Sun Sets in the East: New Dynamics in China–Iran Trade Under Sanctions," *Bourse & Bazaar*, January 2, 2019, https://static1.squarespace.com/static/54db7b69e4b00a5e4b11038c/t/5c4ad5ffc74c505f6368f1a8/1548408321766/B%26B_Special_Report_China_Iran_Trade_v2.pdf.

7 Min Ye, "China and competing cooperation in Asia–Pacific: TPP, RCEP, and the New Silk Road," *Asian Security*, 11(3), 2015, 206–224.

8 "Vision and Actions on Jointly Building Silk Road Economic Belt and 21st-Century Maritime Silk Road," *National Development and Reform Commission, Ministry of Foreign Affairs, and Ministry of Commerce of the People's Republic of China*, March 28, 2015, http://en.ndrc.gov.cn/newsrelease/201503/t20150330_669367.html.

9 "President Xi meets Iran's Supreme Leader Khamenei," *Ministry of Foreign Affairs, the People's Republic of China*, January 25, 2016, https://www.fmprc. gov.cn/mfa_eng/sp/t1334695.shtml.

10 "China's desire for close Iran ties unchanged, Xi says ahead of Saudi prince's visit," *Reuters*, February 20, 2019, https://www.reuters.com/article/us-china-iran/chinas-desire-for-close-iran-ties-unchanged-xi-says-ahead-of-saudi-princes-visit-idUSKCN1QA065.

11 "Vision and Actions on Jointly Building Silk Road Economic Belt and 21st-Century Maritime Silk Road," *National Development and Reform Commission, Ministry of Foreign*

Affairs, and Ministry of Commerce of the People's Republic of China, March 28, 2015, http://en.ndrc.gov.cn/newsrelease/201503/t20150330_669367.html.

12 Mohsen Shariatinia and Hamidreza Azizi, "Iran–China Cooperation in the Silk Road Economic Belt: From Strategic Understanding to Operational Understanding," *China & World Economy,* 25 (5), 2017, 46–61.

13 Tristan Kenderdine, "China Eyes Iran As Important Belt And Road Hub," *Eurasia Review,* September 9, 2017, https://www.eurasiareview.com/09092017-china-eyes-iran-as-important-belt-and-road-hub/.

14 "First freight train from China arrives in Iran in 'Silk Road' boost: media," *Reuters,* February 16, 2016, https://www.reuters.com/article/us-china-iran-railway-idUSKCN0VP0W8.

15 "China's OBOR Developments with Iran & the Arab States," *Silk Road Briefing,* March 29, 2017, https://www.silkroadbriefing.com/news/2017/03/29/chinas-obor-developments-with-iran-the-arab-states/.

16 "1.7 Trillion Dollar Deal Signed with China for Electrification of Tehran–Mashhad Railway," *Tasnim News Agency,* July 25, 2017, https://www.tasnimnews.com/fa/news/1396/05/03/1474373.

17 "China Finances Tehran–Isfahan High-Speed Railroad," *Financial Tribune,* July 21, 2017, https://financialtribune.com/articles/economy-domestic-economy/68698/china-finances-tehran-isfahan-high-speed-railroad.

18 Warren Reinsch, "Iran Ready to Join China's Belt and Road Initiative," *The Trumpet,* February 26, 2019, https://www.thetrumpet.com/18674-iran-ready-to-join-chinas-belt-and-road-initiative.

19 "Tehran–Mashhad railway electrification project to start within 45 days," *Tehran Times,* May 4, 2018, https://www.tehrantimes.com/news/423220/Tehran-Mashhad-railway-electrification-project-to-start-within.

20 Manoj JoshiI, "China and Iran: JCPOA and beyond," *ORF,* February18, 2019, https://www.orfonline.org/expert-speak/china-and-iran-jcpoa-and-beyond-48244/.

21 Ben Derudder, Xingjian Liu and Charles Kunaka, "Connectivity Along Overland Corridors of the Belt and Road Initiative," *The World Bank,* October 2018, http://documents.worldbank.org/curated/en/264651538637972468/pdf/130490-MTI-Discussion-Paper-6-Final.pdf.

22 Alex Vatanka, "China Courts Iran: Why One Belt, One Road Will Run Through Tehran". *Foreign Affairs,* November 1, 2017, https://www.foreignaffairs.com/articles/china/2017-11-01/china-courts-iran.

23 Israfil Abdullayev, "Reviving an Ancient Route? The Role of the Baku–Tbilisi–Kars Railway," *Modern Diplomacy,* December 1, 2017, http://www.ris.org.in/aagc/sites/default/files/Modren%20Diplomacy-01-12-2017-Reviving%20an%20Ancient%20Route%20The%20Role%20of%20the%20Baku%20%E2%80%93%200Tbilisi%20%E2%80%93%20Kars%20Railway.pdf.

24 Micha'el Tanchum, "Facing sanctions, Iran pioneers framework for cooperation with Russia, China and India: Analysis," *Hurriyet Daily News,* November 9, 2018, http://www.hurriyetdailynews.com/facing-sanctions-iran-pioneers-framework-for-cooperation-with-russia-china-and-india-138703.

25 Zheng Yanpeng, "New rail route proposed from Urumqi to Iran," *China Daily,* November 21, 2015, http://www.chinadaily.com.cn/china/2015-11/21/content_22506412.htm.

26 "New freight train links Inner Mongolia and Iran," *Xinhua,* May 10, 2018, http://www.xinhuanet.com/english/2018-05/10/c_137170361.htm.

27 Mohsen Shariatinia and Hamidreza Azizi, "Iran–China Cooperation in the Silk Road

Economic Belt: From Strategic Understanding to Operational Understanding," *China & World Economy*, 25 (5), 2017, 46–61.

28 "Vision and Actions on Jointly Building Silk Road Economic Belt and 21st-Century Maritime Silk Road," *National Development and Reform Commission, Ministry of Foreign Affairs, and Ministry of Commerce of the People's Republic of China*, March 28, 2015, http://en.ndrc.gov.cn/newsrelease/201503/t20150330_669367.html.

29 "Iran's Trade Partners in Three Seasons of the Year," *Donya-e Eghtesad*, April 17, 2017, http://www.donyae-eqtesad.com/fa/tiny/news-3342172.

30 Mohsen Shariatinia and Hamidreza Azizi, "Iran–China Cooperation in the Silk Road Economic Belt: From Strategic Understanding to Operational Understanding," *China & World Economy*, 25 (5), 2017, 46–61.

31 "Iran–China trade increases by 19pct," *AzerNews*, February 8, 2018, https://www.azernews.az/region/126825.html.

32 "China Customs Statistics: Imports and exports by country/region," *The Hong Kong Trade Development Council (HKTDC)*, January 24, 2020, http://china-trade-research.hktdc.com/business-news/article/Facts-and-Figures/China-Customs-Statistics/ff/en/1/1X39VTVQ/1X09N9NM.htm.

33 Ahmad Jamali, "8 Trillion Dollars of Foreign Investment were Attracted in 2017," *Tasnim News Agency*, 14 December 2017, https://www.tasnimnews.com/fa/news/1396/09/23/1601258.

34 "Biggest post-JCPOA Investors in Abadan Refinery," *Iranian Petro-Energy Information Network (SHANA)*, January 21, 2017, http://www.shana.ir/fa/newsagency/275727.

35 Manoj JoshiI, "China and Iran: JCPOA and beyond," *ORF*, February18, 2019, https://www.orfonline.org/expert-speak/china-and-iran-jcpoa-and-beyond-48244/.

36 Iran economy's recovery needs at least $500B in mid-term', *Azer News*, January 28, 2016, https://www.azernews.az/region/92174.html.

37 Mohsen Shariatinia and Hamidreza Azizi, "Iran–China Cooperation in the Silk Road Economic Belt: From Strategic Understanding to Operational Understanding," *China & World Economy*, 25 (5), 2017, 46–61.

38 "China, Iran Agree to Expand Trade to $600 Billion in a Decade," *Bloomberg*, January 23, 2016, www.bloomberg.com/news/articles/2016-01-23/china-iran-agree-to-expand-trade-to-600-billion-in-a-decade.

39 "Iran, China Sign $10 Billion Finance Deal," *Financial Tribune*, September 14, 2017, https://financialtribune.com/articles/economy-business-and-markets/72363/iran-china-sign-10-billion-finance-deal.

40 "China gives billions to Iran," *News24*, September 16, 2017, https://www.news24.com/World/News/china-gives-billions-to-iran-20170916.

41 Ellen R. Wald, "10 Companies Leaving Iran As Trump's Sanctions Close In," *Forbes*, June 6, 2019, https://www.forbes.com/sites/ellenrwald/2018/06/06/10-companies-leaving-iran-as-trumps-sanctions-close-in/#542a960ac90f.

42 "EU, Russia, China rally behind Iran after Trump's move," *PressTV*, May 9, 2018, https://www.presstv.com/DetailFr/2018/05/09/561113/France-Iran-JCPOA.

43 "When the Sun Sets in the East: New Dynamics in China–Iran Trade Under Sanctions," *Bourse & Bazaar*, January 2, 2019, https://static1.squarespace.com/static/54db7b69e4b00a5e4b11038c/t/5c4ad5ffc74c505f6368f1a8/1548408321766/B%26B_Special_Report_China_Iran_Trade_v2.pdf.

44 Esfandyar Batmanghelidj, "Why China Isn't Standing By Iran," *Bloomberg*, March 27, 2019, https://www.bloomberg.com/opinion/articles/2019-03-27/spooked-by-u-s-sanctions-china-isn-t-standing-by-iran.

45 Raymond Zhong, "Chinese Tech Giant on Brink of Collapse in New U.S. Cold War," *The New York Times*, May 9, 2018, https://www.nytimes.com/2018/05/09/technology/zte-china-us-trade-war.html.

46 Lindsay Hughes," China in the Middle East: The Iran Factor," *Future Directions International*, October 25, 2018, http://www.futuredirections.org.au/publication/china-in-the-middle-east-the-iran-factor/.

47 Zhao Hong, "China's Dilemma on Iran: Between Energy Security and a Responsible Rising Power," *Journal of Contemporary China*, 23 (87), 2014, 408–424.

48 Mohsen Shariatinia and Hamidreza Azizi, "Iran–China Cooperation in the Silk Road Economic Belt: From Strategic Understanding to Operational Understanding," *China & World Economy*, 25 (5), 2017, 46–61.

49 Debalina Ghoshal, "China Pivots to the Middle East and Iran," *Yale Global*, July 7, 2016, https://yaleglobal.yale.edu/content/china-pivots-middle-east-and-iran.

50 "Iran's Oil Industry Needs 445 Trillion Dollars of Investment," *Iranian Petro-Energy Information Network (SHANA)*, February 2, 2017, http://www.shana.ir/fa/newsagency/125796.

51 "China extends $1.3b for renovating Abadan refinery," *Iran Daily*, January 11, 2017, http://www.iran-daily.com/News/175552.html.

52 Benoit Faucon, "China Offers Iran $3 Billion Oil-Field Deal as Europe Halts Iranian Crude Purchases," *The Wall Street Journal*, January 17, 2019, https://www.wsj.com/articles/china-offers-iran-3-billion-oil-field-deal-as-europe-halts-iranian-crude-purchases-11547743480.

53 "China steady on Iran oilfields, to ditch South Pars project: Report," *PressTV*, December 12, 2018, https://www.presstv.com/Detail/2018/12/12/582717/Iran-gas-China-CNPC-US-sanctions-oil-North-Azadegan.

54 "Iran: Total and NIOC sign contract for the development of phase 11 of the giant South Pars gas field," *Total*, July 3, 2017, https://www.total.com/en/media/news/press-releases/iran-total-and-nioc-sign-contract-development-phase-11-giant-south-pars-gas-field.

55 "China's CNPC replaces Total in Iran's South Pars project: Iranian oil minister," *PressTV*, November 26, 2018 https://www.presstv.com/DetailFr/2018/11/26/581160/Iran-China-CNPC-South-Pars.

56 "When the Sun Sets in the East: New Dynamics in China–Iran Trade Under Sanctions," *Bourse & Bazaar*, January 2, 2019, https://static1.squarespace.com/static/54db7b69e4b00a5e4b11038c/t/5c4ad5ffc74c505f6368f1a8/1548408321766/B%26B_Special_Report_China_Iran_Trade_v2.pdf.

57 "China defends Iran business ties after Trump threat," *Reuters*, August 8, 2018, https://in.reuters.com/article/us-iran-nuclear-china/china-says-its-business-ties-with-iran-are-transparent-lawful-idINKBN1KT0TU.

58 Chen Aizhu, "CNPC suspends investment in Iran's South Pars after U.S. pressure: sources," *Reuters*, December 12, 2018, https://www.reuters.com/article/us-china-iran-gas-sanctions/cnpc-suspends-investment-in-irans-south-pars-after-u-s-pressure-sources-idUSKBN1OB0RU.

59 Chen Aizhu and Florence Tan, "Boxed in: $1 billion of Iranian crude sits at China's Dalian port," *Reuters*, April 30, 2019, https://www.reuters.com/article/us-china-iran-oil-sanctions/boxed-in-1-billion-of-iranian-crude-sits-at-chinas-dalian-port-idUSKCN1S60HS.

60 Tsvetana Paraskova, "China's Sinopec Looks To Make Special Arrangement For Iranian Oil Imports," *Oil Price*, October 31, 2018, https://oilprice.com/Latest-Energy-News/World-News/Chinas-Sinopec-Looks-To-Make-Special-Arrangement-For-Iranian-Oil-Imports.html.

61 Florence Tan, "Iran oil exports set to drop in August ahead of U.S. sanctions: data," *Reuters*, August 28, 2018, https://www.reuters.com/article/us-iran-crude/iran-oil-exports-set-to-drop-in-august-ahead-of-u-s-sanctions-data-idUSKCN1LD12M.

62 Josh Rogin, "China is reaping the rewards of undermining Trump's Iran strategy," *The Washington Post*, November 5, 2018, https://www.washingtonpost.com/news/josh-rogin/wp/2018/11/05/china-is-reaping-the-rewards-of-undermining-trumps-iran-strategy/?noredirect=on&utm_term=.c2e44eb8e843.

63 Chen Aizhu and Shu Zhang, "Exclusive: As U.S. sanctions loom, China's Bank of Kunlun to stop receiving Iran payments-sources," *Reuters*, October 23, 2018, https://www.reuters.com/article/us-china-iran-banking-kunlun-exclusive/exclusive-as-u-s-sanctions-loom-chinas-bank-of-kunlun-to-stop-receiving-iran-payments-sources-idUSKCN1MX1KA.

64 Chen Aizhu, "Exclusive: Sinopec, CNPC to skip Iran oil bookings for November as U.S. sanctions near," *Reuters*, October 24, 2018, https://www.reuters.com/article/us-china-iran-oil-exclusive/exclusive-sinopec-cnpc-to-skip-iran-oil-bookings-for-november-as-us-sanctions-near-idUSKCN1MY1C9.

65 Chen Aizhu and Florence Tan, "China's Iran oil imports to rebound in December as buyers use U.S. waivers," *Reuters*, December 7, 2018, https://af.reuters.com/article/commoditiesNews/idAFL4N1YA32E.

66 Jacopo Scita, "China–Iran: a Complex, Seesaw Relationship," *Italian Institute for International Political Studies (ISPI)*, February 8, 2019, https://www.ispionline.it/sites/default/files/pubblicazioni/commentary_scita_08.02.2018.pdf.

67 Chen Aizhu and Shu Zhang, "Exclusive: As U.S. sanctions loom, China's Bank of Kunlun to stop receiving Iran payments-sources," *Reuters*, October 23, 2018, https://www.reuters.com/article/us-china-iran-banking-kunlun-exclusive/exclusive-as-u-s-sanctions-loom-chinas-bank-of-kunlun-to-stop-receiving-iran-payments-sources-idUSKCN1MX1KA.

68 "Policy Change at China's Bank of Kunlun Cuts Iran Sanctions Lifeline," *Bourse & Bazaar*, January 2, 2019, https://www.bourseandbazaar.com/articles/2019/1/2/policy-change-at-chinas-bank-of-kunlun-cuts-sanctions-lifeline-for-iranian-industry.

69 Edward Wong, "U.S. Punishes Chinese Company Over Iranian Oil," *The New York Times*, July 22, 2019, https://www.nytimes.com/2019/07/22/world/asia/sanctions-china-iran-oil.html.

70 Esfandyar Batmanghelidj, "Why China Isn't Standing By Iran," *Bloomberg*, March 27, 2019, https://www.bloomberg.com/opinion/articles/2019-03-27/spooked-by-u-s-sanctions-china-isn-t-standing-by-iran.

71 "China continued Iran oil imports in July in teeth of U.S. sanctions: analysts," *Reuters*, August 8, 2019, https://www.reuters.com/article/us-china-iran-oil/china-continued-iran-oil-imports-in-july-in-teeth-of-u-s-sanctions-analysts-idUSKCN1UY11S.

72 "US 'concerned' over untrackable China ships carrying Iran oil," Al-Jazeera, 16 Oct. 2019, https://www.aljazeera.com/amp/news/2019/10/concerned-untrackable-china-ships-carrying-iran-oil-191016081016944.html

73 Jacopo Scita, "China–Iran: A Complex, Seesaw Relationship," *Italian Institute for International Political Studies (ISPI)*, February 8, 2019, https://www.ispionline.it/sites/default/files/pubblicazioni/commentary_scita_08.02.2018.pdf.

74 "Vision and Actions on Jointly Building Silk Road Economic Belt and 21st-Century Maritime Silk Road," *National Development and Reform Commission, Ministry of Foreign Affairs, and Ministry of Commerce of the People's Republic of China*, March 28, 2015, http://en.ndrc.gov.cn/newsrelease/201503/t20150330_669367.html.

75 "China says Iran joins AIIB as founder member," *Reuters*, April 8, 2015,

https://www.reuters.com/article/us-asia-aiib-iran/china-says-iran-joins-aiib-as-founder-member-idUSKBN0MZ08720150408.

76 "Iran AIIB Membership Unlocks Investment Potentials," *Financial Tribune*, February 12, 2017, https://financialtribune.com/articles/economy-business-and-markets/59465/iran-aiib-membership-unlocks-investment-potentials.

77 "China-led bloc keeps Iran at arm's length despite Russian backing," *Reuters*, June 23, 2016, https://www.reuters.com/article/us-uzbekistan-sco-idUSKCN0Z9213.

78 "China gives billions to Iran," *News24*, September 16, 2017, https://www.news24.com/World/News/china-gives-billions-to-iran-20170916.

79 "Iran accepts renminbi for crude oil," *Financial Times*, May 7, 2012, https://www.ft.com/content/63132838-732d-11e1-9014-00144feab49a.

80 "Tehran dumps the dollar for the yuan as reference currency," *Asia News*, August 23, 2018, http://www.asianews.it/news-en/Tehran-dumps-the-dollar-for-the-yuan-as-reference-currency-44731.html.

81 Anna Ahronheim,"Iran to Increase Naval Ties with China," *The Jerusalem Post*, April 23, 2019, https://www.jpost.com/Israel-News/Iran-to-increase-naval-ties-with-China-587680.

82 Joel Wuthnow, "China–Iran Military Relations at a Crossroads," *China Brief*, 15 (3), https://jamestown.org/program/china-iran-military-relations-at-a-crossroads/#.ViD-Kn6rTV0.

83 "UN Register of Conventional Arms," *United Nations Office for Disarmament Affairs* www.un.org/disarmament/convarms/Register/.

84 Mohsen Shariatinia, "Tehran welcomes China's presence in Middle East," *Al-Monitor*, November 14, 2019, https://www.al-monitor.com/pulse/originals/2019/11/iran-welcome-china-presence-middle-east.html#ixzz65Qdrny93b.

85 Lindsay Hughes," China in the Middle East: The Iran Factor," *Future Directions International*, October 25, 2018, http://www.futuredirections.org.au/publication/china-in-the-middle-east-the-iran-factor/.

86 Farzin Nadimi, "Iran and China Are Strengthening Their Military Ties," *The Washington Institute*, November 22, 2016, https://www.washingtoninstitute.org/policy-analysis/view/iran-and-china-are-strengthening-their-military-ties.

87 "Maj. Gen. Bagheri arrives in China," *Mehr News Agency*, September 11, 2019, https://en.mehrnews.com/news/149899/Maj-Gen-Bagheri-arrives-in-China.

88 Dennis M. Gormley, Andrew S. Erickson, and Jingdong Yuan, *A Low-Visibility Force Multiplier: Assessing China's Cruise Missile Ambitions*. Washington, DC: NDU Press, 2014.

89 Farzin Nadimi, "Iran and China Are Strengthening Their Military Ties," *The Washington Institute*, November 22, 2016, https://www.washingtoninstitute.org/policy-analysis/view/iran-and-china-are-strengthening-their-military-ties.

90 Thomas Erdbrink and Chris Buckley, "China and Iran to Conduct Joint Naval Exercises in the Persian Gulf," *The New York Times*, September 21, 2014, https://www.nytimes.com/2014/09/22/world/middleeast/china-and-iran-to-conduct-joint-naval-exercises-in-the-persian-gulf.html.

91 "Iran and China conduct naval drill in Gulf," *Reuters*, June 18, 2017, https://www.reuters.com/article/us-iran-china-military-drill/iran-and-china-conduct-naval-drill-in-gulf-idUSBKN1990EF.

92 "China, Russia and Iran begin joint naval drills," *Al-Jazeera*, December 27, 2019, https://www.aljazeera.com/news/2019/12/china-russia-iran-joint-naval-drills-191227183505159.html.

93 Anna Ahronheim,"Iran to Increase Naval Ties with China," *The Jerusalem Post*, April

23, 2019, https://www.jpost.com/Israel-News/Iran-to-increase-naval-ties-with-China-587680.

94 "Navy Commander Eyes Closer Iran-China Military Cooperation," *Tasnim News Agency*, April, 21, 2019, https://www.tasnimnews.com/en/news/2019/04/21/1994044/navy-commander-eyes-closer-iran-china-military-cooperation.

95 Debalina Ghoshal, "China's Nuclear Opportunities in Iran," *The Globalist*, May 30, 2016, https://www.theglobalist.com/china-nuclear-opportunities-in-iran/.

96 Scott Harold and Alireza Nader, *China and Iran Economic, Political, and Military Relations*. Santa Monica, CA; Arlington, VA; Pittsburgh, PA: RAND Corporation, 2012, https://www.rand.org/content/dam/rand/pubs/occasional_papers/2012/RAND_OP351.pdf.

97 "China, Iran sign first contract for Arak redesign," *World Nuclear News*, 24 April 2017, http://www.world-nuclear-news.org/Articles/China,-Iran-sign-first-contract-for-Arak-redesign.

98 Lee Jeong-ho, "China scales back Iran nuclear cooperation 'due to fears of US sanctions'," *South China Morning Post*, January 31, 2019, https://www.scmp.com/news/china/diplomacy/article/2184512/china-scales-back-iran-nuclear-cooperation-due-fears-us.

99 "Vision and Actions on Jointly Building Silk Road Economic Belt and 21st-Century Maritime Silk Road," *National Development and Reform Commission, Ministry of Foreign Affairs, and Ministry of Commerce of the People's Republic of China*, March 28, 2015, http://en.ndrc.gov.cn/newsrelease/201503/t20150330_669367.html.

100 "8 more countries set up Confucius institutes or classrooms in 2019," *Xinhua*, December 11, 2019, http://www.xinhuanet.com/english/2019-12/11/c_138623776.htm.

101 Huang Zhiling, "10 new Confucius Institutes lift global total to 548, boosting ties," *China Daily*, December 5, 2018, http://www.chinadaily.com.cn/a/201812/05/WS5c07239da310eff30328f182.html.

102 Mohsen Shariatinia and Hamidreza Azizi, "Iran–China Cooperation in the Silk Road Economic Belt: From Strategic Understanding to Operational Understanding," *China & World Economy*, 25 (5), 2017, 46–61.

103 Behzad Abdollahpour, "Iran a unique destination for Chinese tourists," *China Daily*, November 22, 2018, http://www.chinadaily.com.cn/a/201811/22/WS5bf62932a310eff30328a698.html.

104 "Iran seeks to attract more Chinese tourists in the future," *China Outbound Tourism Research Institute (COTRI)*, February 15, 2016, https://china-outbound.com/2016/02/15/iran-seeks-to-attract-more-chinese-tourists-in-the-future/.

105 Hu Yuwei and Qu Xiangyu "Chinese enterprises trying to survive in Iran despite policy shifts, US bluffs," *Global Time*, January 10, 2019, http://www.globaltimes.cn/content/1135325.shtml.

106 "Iran Vying to Be Among China's Top 20 Destinations," *Financial Tribune*, January 23, 2018, https://financialtribune.com/articles/travel/80618/iran-vying-to-be-among-chinas-top-20-destinations.

107 Simon Watkins, "China and Iran flesh out strategic partnership," *Petroleum Economist*, September 3, 2019, https://www.petroleum-economist.com/articles/politics-economics/middle-east/2019/china-and-iran-flesh-out-strategic-partnership.

108 Mordechai Chaziza, "Roadmap for a Chinese-Iranian Strategic Partnership," *BESA Center Perspectives Paper* No. 1303, October 2, 2019, https://besacenter.org/wp-content/uploads/2019/09/1303-China-Iran-Strategic-Partnership-Chaziza-final.pdf.

109 "Envoy Urges Strategic Patience to Shield China–Iran Ties from US Sanctions,"

Tasnim News Agency, September 13, 2019, https://www.tasnimnews.com/en/news/2019/09/13/2095259/envoy-urges-strategic-patience-to-shield-china-iran-ties-from-us-sanctions.

10 UAE

1 "China, UAE agree to lift ties to comprehensive strategic partnership," *Xinhua,* July 21, 2018, http://www.xinhuanet.com/english/2018-07/21/c_137338423.htm.

2 Stanley Carvalho, "Xi's visit to UAE highlights China's rising interest in Middle East," *Reuters,* July 20, 2018, https://ca.reuters.com/article/topNews/idCAKBN1KA26K-OCATP.

3 "UAE vision," *United Arab Emirates: Ministry of Cabinet Affairs,* 2019, https://uaecabinet.ae/en/uae-vision.

4 Min Ye, "China and competing cooperation in Asia–Pacific: TPP, RCEP, and the New Silk Road," *Asian Security,* 11 (3), 2015, 206–224.

5 "China, UAE agree to lift ties to comprehensive strategic partnership," *Xinhua,* July 21, 2018, http://www.xinhuanet.com/english/2018-07/21/c_137338423.htm.

6 "Vision and Actions on Jointly Building Silk Road Economic Belt and 21st-Century Maritime Silk Road," *National Development and Reform Commission, Ministry of Foreign Affairs, and Ministry of Commerce of the People's Republic of China,* March 28, 2015, http://en.ndrc.gov.cn/newsrelease/201503/t20150330_669367.html.

7 Wei Min, "The Interests and Trends of Chinese Enterprises' Investment in the United Arab Emirates," *International Center for Risk Assessment,* May 4, 2016, http://icra.ae/article/the-interests-and-trends-of-chinese-enterprises-investment-in-the-study-by-ms-wei-min/.

8 Samir Salama, "UAE and China poised to take ties to next level, envoy says," *Gulf News,* July 13, 2018, https://gulfnews.com/uae/government/uae-and-china-poised-to-take-ties-to-next-level-envoy-says-1.2250794.

9 "China, UAE agree to lift ties to comprehensive strategic partnership," *Xinhua,* July 20, 2018, http://www.xinhuanet.com/english/2018-07/21/c_137338423.htm.

10 Sam Bridge, "UAE, China eye closer ties to drive $70bn trade in 2020," *Arabian Business,* April 27, 2019, https://www.arabianbusiness.com/politics-economics/418601-uae-china-eyes-deeper-ties-to-drive-70bn-trade-in-2020.

11 "China–UAE relationship at its best in history: Chinese envoy," *Gulf New,* July 19, 2019, https://gulfnews.com/uae/china-uae-relationship-at-its-best-in-history-chinese-envoy-1.1563545215820.

12 Xu Wei, "UAE hailed as strategic partner," *China Daily,* July 23, 2019, http://www.chinadaily.com.cn/a/201907/23/WS5d35721aa310d83056400587.html.

13 "Vision and Actions on Jointly Building Silk Road Economic Belt and 21st-Century Maritime Silk Road," *National Development and Reform Commission, Ministry of Foreign Affairs, and Ministry of Commerce of the People's Republic of China,* March 28, 2015, http://en.ndrc.gov.cn/newsrelease/201503/t20150330_669367.html.

14 Sarah Zheng, "China's President Xi Jinping wraps up UAE visit with series of deals to boost presence in Middle East," *South China Morning Post,* July 21, 2018, https://www.scmp.com/news/china/diplomacy-defence/article/2156291/chinas-president-xi-jinping-wraps-uea-visit-series.

15 Mordechai Chaziza, "The Significant Role of Oman in China's Maritime Silk Road Initiative," *Contemporary Review of the Middle East,* 6 (1), 2018, 1–14.

16 Jonathan Fulton, *China's Relations with the Gulf Monarchies.* New York: Routledge, 2019.

17 Fareed Rahman, "UAE set to play a big role in China's Silk Road project," *Gulf News*, July 21, 2018, https://gulfnews.com/business/markets/uae-set-to-play-a-big-role-in-chinas-silk-road-project-1.2254909.

18 "DP World, Zhejiang China Group sign deal for a new traders market," *Gulf News*, July 19, 2018, https://gulfnews.com/business/dp-world-zhejiang-china-group-sign-deal-for-a-new-traders-market-1.2254073.

19 Aarti Nagraj, "Dubai's DP World, Chinese group to open new Traders Market at JAFZA," *Gulf Business*, July 19, 2018, https://gulfbusiness.com/dubais-dp-world-chinese-group-open-new-traders-market-jafza/.

20 "China to set up financial firm in UAE's Abu Dhabi," *Xinhua*, July 20, 2018, http://www.xinhuanet.com/english/2018-07/21/c_137338432.htm.

21 "UAE's biggest industry zone signs agreement with China to boost trade," *Xinhua*, September 19, 2017,
http://www.xinhuanet.com/english/2017-09/19/c_136621829.htm.

22 "Chinese firms plan $1bn investment in Abu Dhabi free zone," *Arabian Business*, April 20, 2018, https://www.arabianbusiness.com/banking-finance/394657-wkd-chinese-firms-plan-1bn-investment-in-abu-dhabi-free-zone.

23 "UAE free zone inks deal to promote trade ties with China," *Xinhua*, July 11, 2018, http://www.xinhuanet.com/english/2018-07/11/c_137317118.htm.

24 "UAE's Emirates SkyCargo, China's Alibaba join hands over cross-border logistics," *Xinhua*, June 13, 2018,
http://www.xinhuanet.com/english/2018-06/14/c_137251849.htm.

25 Jonathan Fulton, *China's Relations with the Gulf Monarchies*. New York: Routledge, 2019.

26 Michael Fahy, "UAE on China's Silk Road map," *The National*, March 13, 2017, https://www.thenational.ae/business/uae-on-china-s-silk-road-map-1.638069.

27 Stanley Carvalho, "Chinese firms to invest $300 million in Abu Dhabi," *Reuters*, July 31, 2017, https://www.reuters.com/article/us-emirates-china-investment-idUSKBN1AG0UH?il=0.

28 Dania Saadi, "Khalifa Port to double container volumes in 2019, official says," *The National*, December 10, 2018, https://www.thenational.ae/business/economy/khalifa-port-to-double-container-volumes-in-2019-official-says-1.801010.

29 "China, UAE agree to lift ties to comprehensive strategic partnership," *Xinhua*, July 20, 2018, http://www.xinhuanet.com/english/2018-07/21/c_137338423.htm.

30 "Vision and Actions on Jointly Building Silk Road Economic Belt and 21st-Century Maritime Silk Road," *National Development and Reform Commission, Ministry of Foreign Affairs, and Ministry of Commerce of the People's Republic of China*, March 28, 2015, http://en.ndrc.gov.cn/newsrelease/201503/t20150330_669367.html.

31 "China Customs Statistics: Imports and exports by country/region," *The Hong Kong Trade Development Council (HKTDC)*, January 24, 2020, http://china-trade-research.hktdc.com/business-news/article/Facts-and-Figures/China-Customs-Statistics/ff/en/1/1X39VTVQ/1X09N9NM.htm.

32 Sam Bridge, "UAE–China trade forecast to hit $70bn by 2020 as ties grow," *Arabian Business*, 19 July, 2018, https://www.arabianbusiness.com/politics-economics/401134-china-uae-forecast-to-hit-70bn-by-2020-as-ties-grow.

33 "Mohammad Bin Rashid announces $3.4 billion UAE–China investment deals," *Gulf News*, April 26, 2019, https://gulfnews.com/uae/mohammad-bin-rashid-announces-34-billion-uae-china-investment-deals-1.1556286724883.

34 "Strategic shift in relations between the UAE, China, US$50 billion trade between two countries: UAE Ambassador to Beijing," *United Arab Emirates, Ministry of Foreign Affairs & International Cooperation*, July 15, 2018,

https://www.mofa.gov.ae/EN/MediaCenter/News/Pages/15-07-2018-UAE-China.aspx#sthash.6H1L36Ly.dpuf.

35 Jonathan Fulton, *China's Relations with the Gulf Monarchies*. New York: Routledge, 2019.

36 Mohammad Al Asoomi, "The UAE can assume a strategic role in China's ambitions," *Gulf News*, July 11, 2018, https://gulfnews.com/business/analysis/the-uae-can-assume-a-strategic-role-in-chinas-ambitions-1.2249814.

37 Khaled bin Dhai, "UAE and China, how comprehensive strategic relations are built," *China Daily*, July 20, 2018, http://www.chinadaily.com.cn/a/201807/20/WS5b51a9f0a310796df4df7be5.html.

38 Zhi Linfei, Tang Peipei, Su Xiaopo, "Xinhua Headlines: Xi's UAE visit showcases achievements, promises more Sino-Arab cooperation," *Xinhua*, July 21, 2018, http://www.xinhuanet.com/english/2018-07/21/c_137339974.htm.

39 Khaled bin Dhai, "UAE and China, how comprehensive strategic relations are built," *China Daily*, July 20, 2018, http://www.chinadaily.com.cn/a/201807/20/WS5b51a9f0a310796df4df7be5.html.

40 Sam Bridge, "UAE–China trade forecast to hit $70bn by 2020 as ties grow," *Arabian Business*, 19 July, 2018, https://www.arabianbusiness.com/politics-economics/401134-china-uae-forecast-to-hit-70bn-by-2020-as-ties-grow.

41 Muhammad Zulfikar Rakhmat, "The UAE and China's Thriving Partnership," *Gulf State Analytics*, June 2015, https://gallery.mailchimp.com/02451f1ec2ddbb874bf5daee0/files/June_GSA_ report.pdf.

42 Simeon Kerr and Lucy Hornby, "Chinese group eyes $10bn industrial investment in UAE," *Financial Times*, May 24, 2019, https://www.ft.com/content/1c93d350-7e2c-11e9-81d2-f785092ab560.

43 Khaled bin Dhai, "UAE and China, how comprehensive strategic relations are built," *China Daily*, July 20, 2018, http://www.chinadaily.com.cn/a/201807/20/WS5b51a9f0a310796df4df7be5.html.

44 Muhammad Zulfikar Rakhmat, "The UAE and China's Thriving Partnership," *Gulf State Analytics*, June 2015, https://gallery.mailchimp.com/02451f1ec2ddbb874bf5daee0/files/June_GSA _report.pdf.

45 "Chinese Investments & Contracts in UAE (2013–2019)," *China Global Investment Tracker*, 2020, https://www.aei.org/china-global-investment-tracker/.

46 "UAE–China sign major deal to boost Dubai's role as regional food hub," *Arabian Business*, September 10, 2017, https://www.arabianbusiness.com/uaepolitics-economics/378202-dubai-food-park-signs-367m-deal-to-create-china-uae-food-industrial-cluster.

47 "UAE to play big role in China's BRI: official," *Xinhua*, April 10, 2019, http://www.xinhuanet.com/english/2019-04/10/c_137966125.htm.

48 "Vision and Actions on Jointly Building Silk Road Economic Belt and 21st-Century Maritime Silk Road," *National Development and Reform Commission, Ministry of Foreign Affairs, and Ministry of Commerce of the People's Republic of China*, March 28, 2015, http://en.ndrc.gov.cn/newsrelease/201503/t20150330_669367.html.

49 "UAE becomes founding member of AIIB," *Gulf News*, June 29, 2015, https://gulfnews.com/business/banking/uae-becomes-founding-member-of-aiib-1.1542695.

50 "Spotlight: Fruitful China–UAE financial cooperation opens up possibilities for Gulf region," *Xinhua*, July 19, 2018, http://www.xinhuanet.com/english/2018-07/19/c_137336032.htm.

51 Muhammad Zulfikar Rakhmat, "The UAE and China's Thriving Partnership," *Gulf State Analytics*, June 2015,

https://gallery.mailchimp.com/02451f1ec2ddbb874bf5daee0/files/June_
GSA_report.pdf.

52 "UAE, China to set up $10bn joint strategic investment fund," *Arabian Business*, December 14, 2015, https://www.arabianbusiness.com/uae-china-set-up-10bn-joint-strategic-investment-fund-615348.html?utm_source=Jarvis&utm_medium=arabianb usiness.com&utm_campaign=recommended.

53 Xi Jinping, "China and the UAE are both proud to have enterprising and creative people who never give up on their dreams," *The National*, July 17, 2018, https://www.thenational.ae/opinion/comment/china-and-the-uae-are-both-proud-to-have-enterprising-and-creative-people-who-never-give-up-on-their-dreams-1.751254.

54 John Calabrese, "China and the Persian Gulf: Energy and Security," *Middle East Journal*, 52 (3), 1998, 351–366; Steve Yetiv and Chunlong Lu, "China, Global Energy, and the Middle East", *Middle East Journal*, 61, (2), 2007, 199-218.

55 Daniel Workman, "Top 15 Crude Oil Suppliers to China," *World's Top Exports*, March 31, 2020, http://www.worldstopexports.com/top-15-crude-oil-suppliers-to-china/.

56 "United Arab Emirates," *U.S. Energy Information Administration (EIA)*, March 21, 2017, https://www.eia.gov/beta/international/analysis.php?iso=ARE.

57 B. Rajesh Kumar, "The UAE's Strategic Trade Partnership with Asia: A Focus on Dubai," *Middle East* Institute, August 19, 2013, https://www.mei.edu/publications/uaes-strategic-trade-partnership-asia-focus-dubai.

58 Andrew Scobell and Alireza Nader, *China in the Middle East: The Wary Dragon*. Santa Monica: RAND Corporation, 2016.

59 Lin, H. "'Yidai yilu' zou ru mitu" ("'One Belt, One Road' going astray"). http://forum.hkej.com/print/130698.

60 Yiping Huang, "Understanding China's Belt & Road Initiative: Motivation, framework and assessment," *China Economic Review*, 40, 2016, 314–321.

61 Xu He, "China, UAE ties span a wide range," *China Daily*, July, 19, 2018, http://www.chinadaily.com.cn/a/201807/19/WS5b4dcbc6a310796df4df6fd4.html.

62 Deena Kamel and Jennifer Gnana, "Adnoc and CNPC agree to explore partnership opportunities as emirate plans downstream expansion," *The National*, July 20, 2018, https://www.thenational.ae/business/energy/adnoc-and-cnpc-agree-to-explore-part-nership-opportunities-as-emirate-plans-downstream-expansion-1.752415.

63 "China, UAE oil firms sign $330m worth oilfield development project," *China Daily*, May 18, 2015, http://europe.chinadaily.com.cn/business/2015-05/18/content _20745576.htm.

64 Mohammad Al Asoomi, "The UAE can assume a strategic role in China's ambitions," *Gulf News*, July 11, 2018, https://gulfnews.com/business/analysis/the-uae-can-assume-a-strategic-role-in-chinas-ambitions-1.2249814.

65 "Saudi ARAMCO and ADNOC sign MoU for participating in the Ratnagiri Refinery project in Maharashtra," *Press Information Bureau Government of India Ministry of Petroleum & Natural Gas*, June, 25, 2018, http://pib.nic.in/newsite/PrintRelease.aspx?relid=180158.

66 "Global Trends in Renewable Energy Investment 2018," *Frankfurt School of Finance & Management gGmbH*, 2018, http://www.iberglobal.com/files/2018/renewable_trends.pdf.

67 Thani bin Ahmed Al Zeyoudi, "UAE and China: Towards a brighter and more sustainable future," *Arabian Business*, July 19, 2018, https://www.arabianbusiness.com/politics-economics/401068-uae-china-towards-brighter-more-sustainable-future.

68 "China's Silk Road Fund is investing in Dubai solar project, Acwa says," *The National*, June 16, 2018, https://www.thenational.ae/business/energy/china-s-silk-road-fund-is-investing-in-dubai-solar-project-acwa-says-1.740613.

69 "Feature: Hassyan Clean Coal project symbol of UAE–China green partnership," *Xinhua*, July 9, 2018,
http://www.xinhuanet.com/english/2018-07/10/c_137313050.htm.

70 "Full text: UAE–China joint statement on strategic partnership," *Gulf News*, July 21, 2018, https://gulfnews.com/uae/government/full-text-uae-china-joint-statement-on-strategic-partnership-1.2254614.

71 "Abu Dhabi crown prince says committed to advancing UAE–China relations," *Xinhua*, March 22, http://www.xinhuanet.com/english/2019-03/22/c_137915785.htm.

72 "China's CSIC expands presence in UAE," *Jane's Defence Weekly*, February 21, 2019, https://www.janes.com/article/86729/china-s-csic-expands-presence-in-uae.

73 "USA and France dramatically increase major arms exports; Saudi Arabia is largest arms importer, says SIPRI," *Stockholm International Peace Research Institute (SIPRI)*, March 9, 2020, https://www.sipri.org/media/press-release/2020/usa-and-france-dramatically-increase-major-arms-exports-saudi-arabia-largest-arms-importer-says.

74 Natasha Turak, "Pentagon is scrambling as China 'sells the hell out of' armed drones to US allies," *CNBC*, February 21, 2019, https://www.cnbc.com/2019/02/21/pentagon-is-scrambling-as-china-sells-the-hell-out-of-armed-drones-to-americas-allies.html.

75 "Vision and Actions on Jointly Building Silk Road Economic Belt and 21st-Century Maritime Silk Road," *National Development and Reform Commission, Ministry of Foreign Affairs, and Ministry of Commerce of the People's Republic of China*, March 28, 2015, http://en.ndrc.gov.cn/newsrelease/201503/t20150330_669367.html.

76 Muhammad Zulfikar Rakhmat, "China and the UAE: New Cultural Horizons," *Middle East Institute*, March 19, 2015, https://www.mei.edu/publications/china-and-uae-new-cultural-horizons#_ftn5.

77 "UAEU a founding member of the Asian Universities Alliance (AUA) at the official launch in Beijing," *United Arab Emirates University*, May 8, 2017, https://www.uaeu.ac.ae/en/news/2017/may/aua.shtml.

78 "Agreements strengthen China–UAE ties," *The National*, December 14, 2015, https://www.thenational.ae/uae/agreements-strengthen-china-uae-ties-1.99839.

79 "China & UAE: Gulf Medical University & Sun Yat-Sen University Ink Alliance," *TrialSite News*, May 14, 2019, https://www.trialsitenews.com/china-uae-gulf-medical-university-sun-yat-sen-university-ink-alliance/.

80 "8 more countries set up Confucius institutes or classrooms in 2019," *Xinhua*, December 11, 2019,
http://www.xinhuanet.com/english/2019-12/11/c_138623776.htm.

81 Huang Zhiling, "10 new Confucius Institutes lift global total to 548, boosting ties," *China Daily*, December 5, 2018,
http://global.chinadaily.com.cn/a/201812/05/WS5c07239da310eff30328f182.html.

82 "Confucius Institute/Classroom," Hanban, 2018,
http://english.hanban.org/node_10971.htm.

83 Muhammad Zulfikar Rakhmat, "China and the UAE: New Cultural Horizons," *Middle East Institute*, March 19, 2015, https://www.mei.edu/publications/china-and-uae-new-cultural-horizons#_ftn5.

84 Daniel Bardsley, "China Honours Sheikh Zayed," *The National*, March 29, 2012, http://www.thenational.ae/news/uae-news/education/china-honours-sheikh-zayed.

85   "China–UAE relationship at its best in history: Chinese envoy," *Gulf New*, July 19, 2019, https://gulfnews.com/uae/china-uae-relationship-at-its-best-in-history-chinese-envoy-1.1563545215820.

86   Abdul Hannan Tago, "Over 40 Universities in China Teach Arabic," *Arab News*, February 23, 2014, http://www.arabnews.com/news/529946; Daniel Bardsley, "Arabic Studies Centre to Reopen in Beijing," *The National*, December 26, 2010, http://www.thenational.ae/news/world/south-asia/arabic-studies-centre-to-reopen-in-beijing.

87   Binsal Abdul Kader, "Over 1m Chinese tourists to visit UAE this year," *Gulf News*, September 18, 2018, https://gulfnews.com/world/asia/over-1m-chinese-tourists-to-visit-uae-this-year-1.2279920.

88   "Press Release: Chinese Delegation Visits Al Mushrif School," *Middle East business intelligence (MEED)*, March 8, 2012, http://www.meed.com/chinese-delegation-visits-al-mushrif-school/3128934.article.

89   "Chinese, UAE Universities Ink Deal to Boost Cooperation, Exchanges," *Global Times*, November 19, 2009, http://www.globaltimes.cn/content/486432.shtml.

90   Shreeja Ravindranathan, "7 places to celebrate Chinese New Year in the UAE," *Friday Magazine*, February 14, 2018, https://fridaymagazine.ae/life-culture/to-do/7-places-to-celebrate-chinese-new-year-in-the-uae-1.2173525.

91   Sami Zaatari, "UAE–China Week kicks off in Abu Dhabi," *Gulf News*, July 17, 2018, https://gulfnews.com/entertainment/arts-culture/uae-china-week-kicks-off-in-abu-dhabi-1.2253125.

92   "UAE–China Week to be held annually," *The National*, July 28, 2018, https://www.thenational.ae/uae/government/uae-china-week-to-be-held-annually-1.754727.

93   Xi Jinping, "China and the UAE are both proud to have enterprising and creative people who never give up on their dreams," *The National*, July 17, 2018, https://www.thenational.ae/opinion/comment/china-and-the-uae-are-both-proud-to-have-enterprising-and-creative-people-who-never-give-up-on-their-dreams-1.751254.

94   Sam, Bridge, "Gulf forecast to see 81% rise in Chinese tourists by 2022," *Arabian Business*, December 19, 2018, https://www.arabianbusiness.com/travel-hospitality/409972-gulf-forecast-to-see-81-rise-in-chinese-tourists-by-2022.

95   "Chinese tourists make nearly 150 mln outbound trips in 2018," *Xinhua*, February 13, 2019, http://www.xinhuanet.com/english/2019-02/13/c_137818975.htm.

96   Xi Jinping, "China and the UAE are both proud to have enterprising and creative people who never give up on their dreams," *The National*, July 17, 2018, https://www.thenational.ae/opinion/comment/china-and-the-uae-are-both-proud-to-have-enterprising-and-creative-people-who-never-give-up-on-their-dreams-1.751254.

97   "China–UAE relationship at its best in history: Chinese envoy," *Gulf New*, July 19, 2019, https://gulfnews.com/uae/china-uae-relationship-at-its-best-in-history-chinese-envoy-1.1563545215820.

98   "Chinese tourists to Dubai up 12% in 2018: Report," *China Daily*, February 25, 2019, http://www.chinadaily.com.cn/a/201902/25/WS5c7359a4a3106c65c34eb38b.html.

99   Alexander Cornwell, "Dubai registers 16.7 million tourists in 2019, Chinese visitors rise," *Reuters*, January 21, 2020, https://www.reuters.com/article/us-emirates-dubai-tourism/dubai-registers-16-7-million-tourists-in-2019-chinese-visitors-rise-idUSKB N1ZK2L5.

11 Iraq

1   Li Xiaokun, "China and Iraq agree to build strategic partnership," *China Daily*, December 23, 2015, https://thediplomat.com/2015/12/china-and-iraq-announce-strategic-partnership/.

2   "China's Belt and Road Initiative: An Opportunity for Iraq," *Al-Bayan Centre for Planning and Studies Series of Publications*, 2018, http://www.bayancenter.org/en/wp-content/uploads/2018/04/867563522.pdf.

3   "Vision and Actions on Jointly Building Silk Road Economic Belt and 21st-Century Maritime Silk Road," *National Development and Reform Commission, Ministry of Foreign Affairs, and Ministry of Commerce of the People's Republic of China*, March 28, 2015, http://en.ndrc.gov.cn/newsrelease/201503/t20150330_669367.html.

4   "China, Iraq establish strategic partnership," *Xinhua*, December 22, 2015, http://www.china.org.cn/world/2015-12/22/content_37376947.htm.

5   "Iraq and China sign five agreements and memoranda of understanding on economic, technological, military, diplomatic, and oil and energy cooperation," *Prime Minister's Media Office*, December 22, 2015, http://www.pmo.iq/pme/press2015en/22-12-20154en.htm.

6   "China, Iraq to deepen strategic partnership," *CGTN*, August 25, 2018, https://news.cgtn.com/news/3d3d774d7a4d7a4e79457a6333566d54/share_p.html.

7   "Spotlight: Iraq, China celebrate Silk Road initiative on 60th anniversary of bilateral ties," *Xinhua*, December 13, 2018, http://www.xinhuanet.com/english/2018-12/14/c_137672426.htm.

8   "China to contribute to the rebuilding of Iraq," *Kurdistan 24*, April 16, 2019, http://www.kurdistan24.net/en/news/2375d17c-7405-4f66-821b-e88d5fbd549e.

9   "Chinese ambassador presents credentials to Iraqi president," *Xinhua*, April 9, 2019, http://www.xinhuanet.com/english/2019-04/09/c_137960936.htm.

10 Tobias Hoonhout, "Iraq Set to Join China's Belt and Road Project amid Violent Anti-Government Unrest," *National Review*, October 4, 2019, https://www.nationalreview.com/news/iraq-set-to-join-chinas-belt-and-road-project-amid-violent-anti-government-unrest/.

11 "China–Iraq trade exceeds 30 bln USD in 2018 amid increasing cooperation: Chinese ambassador," *Xinhua*, May 6, 2019, http://www.xinhuanet.com/english/2019-05/06/c_138036250.htm.

12 Tim Daiss, "China's Growing Oil Demand Has Created A Geopolitical Dilemma," *Oil Price*, May 2, 2018, https://oilprice.com/Energy/Crude-Oil/Chinas-Growing-Oil-Demand-Has-Created-A-Geopolitical-Dilemma.html.

13 John Calabrese, "China and the Persian Gulf: Energy and Security," *Middle East Journal* 52 (3), (1998), pp. 351–366; Steve Yetiv and Chunlong Lu, "China, Global Energy, and the Middle East", *Middle East Journal* 61, (2) (2007), pp. 199–218.

14 Daniel Workman, "Top 15 Crude Oil Suppliers to China," *World's Top Exports*, April 26, 2020, http://www.worldstopexports.com/top-15-crude-oil-suppliers-to-china/.

15 "Country Analysis Executive Summary: Iraq," *U.S. Energy Information Administration (EIA)*, January 7, 2019, https://www.eia.gov/beta/international/analysis_includes/countries_long/Iraq/iraq_exe.pdf.

16 Ben Lando, "Iraq oil exports steady in June though federal revenues fall," *Iraq Oil Report*, July 2, 2018, https://www.iraqoilreport.com/news/iraqi-oil-exports-steady-in-june-though-federal-revenues-fall-31164/.

17 Richard Wachman, "China pushes for bigger role in Iraqi reconstruction," *Arab News*, March 3, 2018, http://www.arabnews.com/node/1257811/business-economy.

18 "China, Iraq ink economic, military agreements during Abadi visit," *The Brics Post*, December 23, 2015, https://www.thebricspost.com/china-iraq-ink-economic-military-agreements-during-abadi-visit/.

19 Wang Jin, "Opinion: China–Iraq Ties in the New Era," *CGTN*, August 26, 2018, https://news.cgtn.com/news/3d3d414e31557a4e79457a6333566d54/share_p.html.

20 Wei Li, "An Analysis of Current Political Situation and Oil and Gas Investment Prospect in Iraq" [in Chinese] *Sino–Global Energy*, no. 3 (March 2016): 10; Eberling, G. George, *China's Bilateral Relations With Its Principal Oil Suppliers*. Lanham: Lexington, 2017.

21 "Iraq Signs Deal with China's Zhenhua Oil as Exxon Mobil Agreement Stalls," *Asharq Al-Awsat*, 26 December, 2017, https://aawsat.com/english/home/article/1124441/iraq-signs-deal-china%E2%80%99s-zhenhua-oil-exxon-mobil-agreement-stalls.

22 "China's CNPC interested in Iraq's Majnoon oilfield -oil officials," *Reuters*, December 27, 2017, https://www.reuters.com/article/us-iraq-oil-majnoon/chinas-cnpc-interested-in-iraqs-majnoon-oilfield-oil-officials-idUSKBN1DR186.

23 Chen Aizhu and Rania El Gamal, "China's Zhenhua Oil to sign oil deals with Iraq, Saudi at Shanghai expo-sources," *Reuters*, November 3, 2018, https://uk.reuters.com/article/uk-china-iraq-zhenhua/chinas-zhenhua-oil-to-sign-oil-deals-with-iraq-saudi-at-shanghai-expo-sources-idUKKCN1N806Z.

24 "Iraq signs contract with PowerChina, Norinco to build Fao oil refinery," *Reuters*, April 29, 2018, https://www.reuters.com/article/iraq-oil-refining-china/iraq-signs-contract-with-powerchina-norinco-to-build-fao-oil-refinery-idUSL8N1S60M3.

25 "Iraq to build oil refinery in Fao with Chinese firms, plans three others," *Reuters*, January 29, 2018, https://www.reuters.com/article/us-iraq-oil-refining/iraq-to-build-oil-refinery-in-fao-with-chinese-firms-plans-three-others-idUSKBN1FI0I0.

26 Richard Wachman, "China pushes for bigger role in Iraqi reconstruction," *Arab News*, March 3, 2018, http://www.arabnews.com/node/1257811/business-economy.

27 Shunsuke Tabeta, "China looks to Iraq to secure oil supply," *Nikkei Asian Review*, June 15, 2018, https://asia.nikkei.com/Business/Companies/China-looks-to-Iraq-to-secure-oil-supply.

28 "Iraq to Boost China Oil Sales by 60% as OPEC Giant Eyes Asia," *Bloomberg News*, November 6, 2018, https://www.bloomberg.com/news/articles/2018-11-06/iraq-to-boost-china-oil-sales-by-60-as-opec-giant-eyes-asia.

29 "UPDATE 1-Iraq signs deal with China's CNOOC for seismic surveys of two oil blocks," *Reuters*, January 31, 2019, https://www.reuters.com/article/iraq-oil-exploration/update-1-iraq-signs-deal-with-chinas-cnooc-for-seismic-surveys-of-two-oil-blocks-idUSL5N1ZV48N.

30 "Country Analysis Executive Summary: Iraq," *U.S. Energy Information Administration (EIA)*, January 7, 2019, https://www.eia.gov/beta/international/analysis_includes/countries_long/Iraq/iraq_exe.pdf.

31 "Chinese oil, gas contractor inks deal to construct gas plant in Iraq," *Xinhua*, February 27, 2019, http://www.xinhuanet.com/english/2019-02/27/c_137855433.htm.

32 Shatha Khalil, "Al-Hareer Road . . . An economic belt linking Iraq with China," *Rawabet Center for Research and Strategic Studies*, December 14, 2017, https://rawabet-center.com/en/?p=4650.

33 "Interview: Iraq to reap from BRI through active participation: analyst," *Xinhua*, January 29, 2019, http://www.xinhuanet.com/english/2019-01/29/c_137782280.htm.

34 "China's Belt and Road Initiative: An Opportunity for Iraq," *Al-Bayan Centre for Planning and Studies Series of Publications*, 2018, http://www.bayancenter.org/en/wp-content/uploads/2018/04/867563522.pdf.

35   "Vision and Actions on Jointly Building Silk Road Economic Belt and 21st-Century Maritime Silk Road," *National Development and Reform Commission, Ministry of Foreign Affairs, and Ministry of Commerce of the People's Republic of China*, March 28, 2015, http://en.ndrc.gov.cn/newsrelease/201503/t20150330_669367.html.

36   "Iraq discusses possibility of joining Asian Infrastructure Investment Bank," *Xinhua*, March 4, 2019, http://www.xinhuanet.com/english/2019-03/04/c_137866422.htm.

37   Ben Van Heuvelen and Samya Kullab, "Iraq and China to sign massive financing deal," *Iraq Oil Report*, March 13, 2019, https://www.iraqoilreport.com/news/iraq-and-china-to-sign-massive-financing-deal-38041/.

38   "Vision and Actions on Jointly Building Silk Road Economic Belt and 21st-Century Maritime Silk Road," *National Development and Reform Commission, Ministry of Foreign Affairs, and Ministry of Commerce of the People's Republic of China*, March 28, 2015, http://en.ndrc.gov.cn/newsrelease/201503/t20150330_669367.html.

39   "China Customs Statistics: Imports and exports by country/region," *The Hong Kong Trade Development Council (HKTDC)*, January 24, 2020, http://china-trade-research.hktdc.com/business-news/article/Facts-and-Figures/China-Customs-Statistics/ff/en/1/1X39VTVQ/1X09N9NM.htm.

40   "China–Iraq trade exceeds 30 bln USD in 2018 amid increasing cooperation: Chinese ambassador," *Xinhua*, May 6, 2019, http://www.xinhuanet.com/english/2019-05/06/c_138036250.htm.

41   "China, Iraq to deepen strategic partnership," *CGTN*, August 25, 2018, https://news.cgtn.com/news/3d3d774d7a4d7a4e79457a6333566d54/share_p.html.

42   Maher Chmaytelli and Ahmed Hagagy, "Allies promise Iraq $30 billion, falling short of Baghdad's appeal," *Reuters*, February 14, 2018, https://www.reuters.com/article/us-mideast-crisis-iraq-reconstruction-ku/allies-promise-iraq-30-billion-falling-short-of-baghdads-appeal-idUSKCN1FY0TX.

43   "China to actively participate in reconstruction of Iraq: ambassador," *Xinhua*, February 14, 2018, http://www.xinhuanet.com/english/2018-02/15/c_136976540.htm.

44   "China vows active role in Iraqi post-war reconstruction," *Xinhua*, April 24, 2017, http://www.xinhuanet.com//english/2017-04/24/c_136232659.htm.

45   "Chinese company wins bidding for power station construction in Iraq," *Xinhua Silk Road Information Service*, February 21, 2019, https://en.imsilkroad.com/p/131156.html.

46   "Iraqi governor calls for Chinese investment, expertise for reconstruction," *Xinhua*, January 27, 2109, http://www.xinhuanet.com/english/2019-01/28/c_137779710.htm.f

47   "Iraq + China MOU Establishes Long Term Oil & Gas Partnership," *Oil and Gas360*, December 23, 2015, https://www.oilandgas360.com/iraq-china-mou-establishes-long-term-oil-gas-partnership/.

48   "China, Iraq ink economic, military agreements during Abadi visit," *The Brics Post*, December 23, 2015, https://www.thebricspost.com/china-iraq-ink-economic-military-agreements-during-abadi-visit/.

49   Richard A. Bitzinge, "Arms to Go: Chinese Arms Sales to the Third World," *International Security*, 17 (2), 1992, pp. 84–111.

50   Arnaud Delalande, "Iraq's Chinese-Made Killer Drones Are Actually Pretty Good," *War is Boring*, February 21, 2018, https://warisboring.com/iraqs-chinese-made-killer-drones-are-actually-pretty-good/.

51   Adam Rawnsley, "Meet China's Killer Drones," *Foreign Policy Magazine*, January 14, 2016, https://foreignpolicy.com/2016/01/14/meet-chinas-killer-drones/.

52   "Are China And Iraq Working On A Huge Arms Deal?," *21st Century Asian Arms Race*, January 1, 2017, https://21stcenturyasianarmsrace.com/2017/01/01/are-china-and-iraq-working-on-a-huge-arms-deal/.

12 Kuwait

1 Khizar Niazi, "Kuwait Looks towards the East: Relations with China," *The Middle East Institute Policy Brief*, 26, September 2009, https://www.files.ethz.ch/isn/106361/No_26_Kuwait_looks_towards_the_east.pdf.

2 "China Focus: China, Kuwait agree to establish strategic partnership," *Xinhua*, July 9, 2018, http://www.xinhuanet.com/english/2018-07/10/c_137312795.htm.

3 Christopher Layne, "The US-Chinese power shift and the end of the Pax Americana," *International Affairs*, 94 (1), 2018, 89–111.

4 Imad K. Harb, "Self-preservation and Strategic Hedging in the Gulf Cooperation Council," *Policy Brief*, 23, June 26, 2018, http://ams.hi.is/wp-content/uploads/2018/06/Self-Preservation-and-Strategic-Hedging-in-the-GCC-2.pdf.

5 Giorgio Cafiero and Daniel Wagner, "What the Gulf States Think of 'One Belt, One Road'," *The Diplomat*, May 24, 2017, https://thediplomat.com/2017/05/what-the-gulf-states-think-of-one-belt-one-road/.

6 Sumedh Lokhande, "China's One Belt One Road Initiative and the Gulf Pearl Chain", *China Daily*, June 5, 2017, http://www.chinadaily.com.cn/opinion/2017beltandroad/2017-06/05/content_29618549.htm.

7 Robert Anderson, "China and the GCC: Rebuilding the Silk Road," *Gulf Business*, December15, 2018 https://gulfbusiness.com/china-gcc-rebuilding-silk-road/.

8 "Kuwait National Development Plan," *New Kuwait*, January 30, 2017, http://www.newkuwait.gov.kw/image/NewKuwait_CampaignLaunchEvent.pdf.

9 "Govt launches ambitious 'New Kuwait' 2035 strategy," *Kuwait Times*, January 31, 2017, https://news.kuwaittimes.net/website/govt-launches-ambitious-new-kuwait-2035-strategy/.

10 Jasim Ali, "Revival of mega projects heralds positives for Kuwait," *Gulf News*, July 14, 2018, https://gulfnews.com/business/analysis/revival-of-mega-projects-heralds-posi-tives-for-kuwait-1.2251117.

11 Faten Omar, "Kuwait woos foreign investments, details progress on Vision 2035," *Kuwait Times*, March 20, 2018, https://news.kuwaittimes.net/website/kuwait-woos-foreign-investments-details-progress-on-vision-2035/.

12 "Changing times calls for new GCC relations with China, Russia," *Oxford Business Group*, 2019, https://oxfordbusinessgroup.com/analysis/east-meets-middle-east-changing-times-calls-new-relations-china-and-russia.

13 Min Ye, "China and competing cooperation in Asia–Pacific: TPP, RCEP, and the New Silk Road," *Asian Security*, 11 (3), 2015, 206–224.

14 "Vision and Actions on Jointly Building Silk Road Economic Belt and 21st-Century Maritime Silk Road," *National Development and Reform Commission, Ministry of Foreign Affairs, and Ministry of Commerce of the People's Republic of China*, March 28, 2015, http://en.ndrc.gov.cn/newsrelease/201503/t20150330_669367.html.

15 Samah Ibrahim, "Kuwait as a Gateway for Chinese Influence in the Arabian Gulf," *Future Directions International*, August 29, 2018, http://www.futuredirections.org.au/publication/kuwait-as-a-gateway-for-chinese-influence-in-the-arabian-gulf/.

16 Weida Li, "China and Kuwait agree to establish strategic partnership," *GB Times*, July 10, 2018, https://gbtimes.com/china-and-kuwait-agree-to-establish-strategic-partnership.

17 Mordechai Chaziza, "The Significant Role of Oman in China's Maritime Silk Road Initiative," *Contemporary Review of the Middle East*, 6 (1), 2018, 1–14.

18 Robert Anderson, "China and the GCC: Rebuilding the Silk Road," *Gulf Business*, December15, 2018 https://gulfbusiness.com/china-gcc-rebuilding-silk-road/.

19 "Island projects to attract international investments," *Times Kuwait*, October 30, 2018, http://www.timeskuwait.com/Times_Island-projects-to-attract-international-investments.

20 Habib Toumi, "Kuwait, China sign 10 cooperation accords," *Gulf News*, June 4, 2014, https://gulfnews.com/world/gulf/kuwait/kuwait-china-sign-10-cooperation-accords-1.1342938.

21 "Kuwait, China sign MoU on finding mechanism for Silk City, 5 islands," *Kuwait News Agency (KUMA)*, November 18, 2018, https://www.kuna.net.kw/ ArticleDetails.aspx?id=2760010&language=en.

22 Sam Bridge, "Kuwait, China ink deal to move forward with Silk City project," *Arabian Business*, November 24, 2018, https://www.arabianbusiness.com/politics-economics/408347-kuwait-china-ink-deal-to-move-forward-with-silk-city-project.

23 Naser Al Wasmi, "Kuwait and China push forward on Silk City development plan," *The National*, November 18, 2018, https://www.thenational.ae/world/gcc/kuwait-and-china-push-forward-on-silk-city-development-plan-1.793180.

24 "Kuwait, Huawei sign MoU to implement smart cities strategy," *Kuwait News Agency (KUMA)*, July 18, 2018, https://www.kuna.net.kw/ArticleDetails.aspx?id=2736348&language=en.

25 "Kuwait is spending its way to a new direction," *Financial Times*, September 10, 2018, https://www.ft.com/content/b8e6079e-4e32-11e8-ac41-759eee1efb74.

26 "Vision and Actions on Jointly Building Silk Road Economic Belt and 21st-Century Maritime Silk Road," *National Development and Reform Commission, Ministry of Foreign Affairs, and Ministry of Commerce of the People's Republic of China*, March 28, 2015, http://en.ndrc.gov.cn/newsrelease/201503/t20150330_669367.html.

27 "China Focus: China, Kuwait agree to establish strategic partnership," *Xinhua*, July 9, 2018, http://www.xinhuanet.com/english/2018-07/10/c_137312795.htm.

28 "China, Kuwait agree to establish strategic partnership," *Xinhua*, July 9, 2018, http://www.xinhuanet.com/english/2018-07/10/c_137312795.htm.

29 Philip Gater-Smith, "Qatar Crisis Impacts China's Ambitious Foreign Policy," International Institute for Middle-East and Balkan studies, June 13, 2017, http://www.ifimes.org/en/9426.

30 "What countries are the top producers and consumers of oil?," *U.S. Energy Information Administration (EIA)*, December 3, 2018, https://www.eia.gov/tools/faqs/faq.php?id=709&t=6.

31 "Kuwait," *U.S. Energy Information Administration (EIA)*, November 2, 2016 https://www.eia.gov/beta/international/country.php?iso=KWT.

32 Tim Daiss, "China's Growing Oil Demand Has Created A Geopolitical Dilemma," *Oil Price*, May 2, 2018, https://oilprice.com/Energy/Crude-Oil/Chinas-Growing-Oil-Demand-Has-Created-A-Geopolitical-Dilemma.html.

33 "Is the Chinese oil consumption growing faster than the US oil production?," *Newropeans Magazine*, March 23, 2018, http://www.newropeans-magazine.org/en/2018/03/27/is-the-chinese-oil-consumption-growing-faster-than-the-us-oil-production/.

34 "World Energy Outlook 2017," *International Energy Agency's (IEA)*, 14 November 2017, https://www.iea.org/weo2017/#section-1-5.

35 John Calabrese, "China and the Persian Gulf: Energy and Security," *Middle East*

Journal, 52 (3), 1998, 351–366; Steve Yetiv and Chunlong Lu, "China, Global Energy, and the Middle East", *Middle East Journal*, 61 (2), 2007, 199–218.

36 Daniel Workman, "Top 15 Crude Oil Suppliers to China," *World's Top Exports*, April 26, 2020, http://www.worldstopexports.com/top-15-crude-oil-suppliers-to-china/.

37 "Interview: Development of win-win Kuwait-China ties contributes to better well-being, common progress: Kuwaiti emir," *Xinhua*, July 7, 2018, http://www.xinhuanet.com/english/2018-07/08/c_137309006.htm.

38 Muhamad S. Olimat, *China and the Gulf Cooperation Council Countries: Strategic Partnership in a Changing World*. Maryland: Lexington Books, 2016.

39 "Kuwait to boost oil exports to China to 500,000 bpd in three years," *Gulf News*, August 23, 2014, https://gulfnews.com/business/energy/kuwait-to-boost-oil-exports-to-china-to-500000-bpd-in-three-years–1.1375610.

40 "China becomes one of the biggest oil drilling contractors in Kuwait: report," *Global Times*, July 16, 2017, http://www.globaltimes.cn/content/1056580.shtml.

41 "Kerui wins drilling rigs contract from Kuwait AREC," *Pipeline Oil and Gas News*, July 19, 2018,
https://www.pipelineoilandgasnews.com/regionalinternational-news/regional-news/2018/july/kerui-wins-drilling-rigs-contract-from-kuwait-arec/?utm_source=web&utm_medium=&utm_term=&utm_content=&utm_campaign=.

42 Asma Alsharif, "Kuwait signs agreement with Sinopec to build Chinese refinery," *Reuters*, October 25, 2018, https://www.reuters.com/article/kuwait-sinopec-corp/kuwait-signs-agreement-with-sinopec-to-build-chinese-refinery-idUSC6N1JG02J.

43 "PetroChina agrees 2019 annual crude supply deals with Saudi Aramco, Kuwait," *Reuters*, November 7, 2018, https://af.reuters.com/article/commoditiesNews/idAFB9N1X603U; "China's Sinopec signs 2019 annual crude oil supply deal with Kuwait," *Reuters*, November 8, 2018,
https://af.reuters.com/article/commoditiesNews/idAFB9N1XG001;
"China's Sinochem raises 2019 term oil supply from Saudi Aramco, Kuwait," *Today*, November 9, 2018, https://www.todayonline.com/world/chinas-sinochem-raises-2019-term-oil-supply-saudi-aramco-kuwait.

44 "Vision and Actions on Jointly Building Silk Road Economic Belt and 21st-Century Maritime Silk Road," *National Development and Reform Commission, Ministry of Foreign Affairs, and Ministry of Commerce of the People's Republic of China*, March 28, 2015, http://en.ndrc.gov.cn/newsrelease/201503/t20150330_669367.html.

45 "Government releases New Kuwait 2035 strategic plan," *The Economist Intelligence Unit*, February 3, 2017, http://country.eiu.com/article.aspx?articleid=1675084151.

46 "Xi Jinping Holds Talks with Kuwaiti Emir Sheikh Sabah Al-Ahmad Al-Jaber Al-Sabah," *Ministry of Foreign Affairs, the People's Republic of China*, July 9, 2018, https://www.fmprc.gov.cn/mfa_eng/wjb_663304/zzjg_663340/xybfs_663590/xwlb_663592/t1575565.shtml.

47 "China continues to be Kuwait's top trade partner," *Kuwait News Agency (KUMA)*, September 4, 2017,
https://www.kuna.net.kw/ArticleDetails.aspx?id=2631683&language=en.

48 "China Customs Statistics: Imports and exports by country/region," *The Hong Kong Trade Development Council (HKTDC)*, January 24, 2020, http://china-trade-research.hktdc.com/business-news/article/Facts-and-Figures/China-Customs-Statistics/ff/en/1/1X39VTVQ/1X09N9NM.htm.

49 "Interview: Development of win-win Kuwait-China ties contributes to better well-being, common progress: Kuwaiti emir," *Xinhua*, July 7, 2018, http://www.xinhuanet.com/english/2018-07/08/c_137309006.htm.

50 "Kuwaiti-Sino construction deals surge to $8.2bln in '17," *Kuwait News Agency (KUNA)*, November 27, 2017,
https://www.kuna.net.kw/ArticleDetails.aspx?id=2662355&language=en.

51 "Kuwaiti, Chinese officials discuss expanding strategic cooperation," *Xinhua*, July 12, 2018, http://www.xinhuanet.com/english/2017-07/13/c_136439230.htm.

52 "Kuwait calls for increased investment from China," *Xinhua*, March 20, 2018, http://www.xinhuanet.com/english/2018-03/21/c_137053484.htm.

53 Jaber Ali, "Kuwait, China ink several agreements, MoUs to boost ties," *Middle East Confidential*, July 9, 2018, https://me-confidential.com/19899-kuwait-china-ink-several-agreements-mous-to-boost-ties.html.

54 "Vision and Actions on Jointly Building Silk Road Economic Belt and 21st-Century Maritime Silk Road," *National Development and Reform Commission, Ministry of Foreign Affairs, and Ministry of Commerce of the People's Republic of China*, March 28, 2015, http://en.ndrc.gov.cn/newsrelease/201503/t20150330_669367.html.

55 "Interview: China–Kuwait cooperation enters fast tracks under BRI: Chinese envoy," *Xinhua*, April 24, 2019,
http://www.xinhuanet.com/english/2019-04/25/c_138006314.htm.

56 Sam, Bridge, "Gulf forecast to see 81% rise in Chinese tourists by 2022," *Arabian Business*, December 19, 2018, https://www.arabianbusiness.com/travel-hospitality/409972-gulf-forecast-to-see-81-rise-in-chinese-tourists-by-2022.

57 "Kuwait launches Chinese center for cultural exchanges", *Xinhua*, March 4, 2018.
http://www.xinhuanet.com/english/2018-03/04/c_137014119.htm.

58 Laura Zhou, "Chinese private investment in belt and road projects may be losing steam," *South China Morning Post*, 15 November, 2018,
https://www.scmp.com/news/china/diplomacy/article/2173467/chinese-private-investment-belt-and-road-projects-may-be-losing.

59 ZHU Weilie, "Middle East Terrorism, Global Governance and China's Anti-terror Policy," *Journal of Middle Eastern and Islamic Studies (in Asia)*, 5, (2), 2011, 1–16.

13 Qatar

1 "China now Qatar's third-largest trading partner, says top MCI official," *Gulf-Times*, November 7, 2018, https://www.gulf-times.com/story/612174/China-now-Qatar-s-third-largest-trading-partner-sa.

2 Santhosh V. Perumal, "Qatar seen playing a key role in China's Belt and Road plan," *Gulf-Times*, November 26, 2018, https://www.gulf-times.com/story/614255/Qatar-seen-playing-a-key-role-in-China-s-Belt-and-.

3 "Qatar National Vision 2030," *General Secretariat For Development Planning*, July 2008, https://www.gco.gov.qa/wp-content/uploads/2016/09/GCO-QNV-English.pdf.

4 "Chinese FM: Qatar a key partner to promote 'Belt and Road' initiative," *CCTV.com*, December 5, 2016,
http://english.cctv.com/2016/05/12/VIDENMyddtTBNQUM9zStLhAV160512.shtml.

5 "Vision and Actions on Jointly Building Silk Road Economic Belt and 21st-Century Maritime Silk Road," *National Development and Reform Commission, Ministry of Foreign Affairs, and Ministry of Commerce of the People's Republic of China*, March 28, 2015, http://en.ndrc.gov.cn/newsrelease/201503/t20150330_669367.html.

6 "China, Qatar announce strategic partnership," *China Daily*, November 11, 2014, http://www.chinadaily.com.cn/world/2014-11/04/content_18863364.htm.

7 Haifa Said and Du Chao, "Qatar and China: Developing a Comprehensive Strategic

Partnership," *China Today*, November 8, 2018, http://www.chinatoday.com.cn/ctenglish/2018/ii/201808/t20180811_800138032.html.

8   "China, Qatar agree to deepen strategic partnership," *Ministry of Foreign Affairs, the People's Republic of China*, January 31, 2019, https://www.fmprc.gov.cn/mfa_eng/zxxx_662805/t1634698.shtml.

9   "Chinese FM: Qatar a key partner to promote 'Belt and Road' initiative," *CCTV.com*, December 5, 2016, http://english.cctv.com/2016/05/12/VIDENMyddtTBNQUM9zStLhAV160512.shtml.

10 "Qatar Chamber Sign Agreements with China's Trade Promotion Council," *Qatar Chamber*, April 3, 2017, https://qatarchamber.com/qatar-chamber-sign-agreements-with-chinas-trade-promotion-council/.

11 "China Signs Port Investment MoU with Qatar," *Port Technology*, November 9, 2018, https://www.porttechnology.org/news/china_signs_port_investment_mou_with_qatar.

12 Anne Barnard and David D. Kirkpatrick, "5 Arab Nations Move to Isolate Qatar, Putting the U.S. in a Bind," *The New York Times*, June 5, 2017, https://www.nytimes.com/2017/06/05/world/middleeast/qatar-saudi-arabia-egypt-bahrain-united-arab-emirates.html.

13 Jonathan Fulton, *China's Relations with the Gulf Monarchies*. New York: Routledge, 2019.

14 Philip Gater-Smith, "Qatar Crisis Impacts China's Ambitious Foreign Policy," *International Policy Digest*, June 13, 2017, https://intpolicydigest.org/2017/06/13/qatar-crisis-impacts-china-s-ambitious-foreign-policy/.

15 "Vision and Actions on Jointly Building Silk Road Economic Belt and 21st-Century Maritime Silk Road," *National Development and Reform Commission, Ministry of Foreign Affairs, and Ministry of Commerce of the People's Republic of China*, March 28, 2015, http://en.ndrc.gov.cn/newsrelease/201503/t20150330_669367.html.

16 "Spotlight: Qatari emir's visit to China shows positive signals," *Xinhua*, February 3, 2019, http://www.xinhuanet.com/english/2019-02/03/c_137797580.htm.

17 "China's top legislator meets Qatari emir," *Xinhua*, January 31, 2019, http://www.xinhuanet.com/english/2019-01/31/c_137790222.htm.

18 "China now Qatar's third-largest trading partner, says top MCI official," *Gulf-Times*, November 7, 2018, https://www.gulf-times.com/story/612174/China-now-Qatar-s-third-largest-trading-partner-sa.

19 "China is Qatar's key trading partner; trade volume at QR38.6bn," *The Peninsula*, November 8, 2018, https://thepeninsulaqatar.com/article/08/11/2018/China-is-Qatar%E2%80%99s-key-trading-partner-trade-volume-at-QR38.6bn.

20 "China Customs Statistics: Imports and exports by country/region," *The Hong Kong Trade Development Council (HKTDC)*, January 24, 2020, http://china-trade-research.hktdc.com/business-news/article/Facts-and-Figures/China-Customs-Statistics/ff/en/1/1X39VTVQ/1X09N9NM.htm.

21 "Qatar-China trade jumps 27% to $13.5 bn in 2018, says Kuwari," *Qatar Tribune*, February 1, 2019, http://www.qatar-tribune.com/news-details/id/153980.

22 "Chinese Investments & Contracts in Qatar (2013–2019)," *China Global Investment Tracker*, 2020, https://www.aei.org/china-global-investment-tracker/.

23 Santhosh V. Perumal, "Qatar seen playing a key role in China's Belt and Road plan," *Gulf-Times*, November 26, 2018, https://www.gulf-times.com/story/614255/Qatar-seen-playing-a-key-role-in-China-s-Belt-and-.

24 "China Harbour and Engineering wins Doha port deal," *Construction Week Online* 15 March, 2011, https://www.constructionweekonline.com/article-11395-china-harbour-and-engineering-wins-doha-port-deal.

25 "Direct Service between Hamad Port and Shanghai launched," *Gulf-Times*, January 28 2017, https://www2.gulf-times.com/story/530771/Direct-Service-between-Hamad-Port-and-Shanghai-lau.

26 "Hamad Port development Phase II to start by early 2019," *The Peninsula*, November 9, 2018, https://www.thepeninsulaqatar.com/article/09/11/2018/Hamad-Port-development-Phase-II-to-start-by-early-2019.

27 "China Railway to build iconic Lusail Stadium for Qatar's World Cup," *Global Construction Review*, November 29, 2016, http://www.globalconstructionreview.com/news/china-railway-build-iconic-lus7ail-stadi7um-qa7ar/.

28 "China's Huawei becomes one of first fully-owned tech firms in Qatar," *Xinhua*, September 19, 2018,
http://www.xinhuanet.com/english/2018-09/19/c_137479605.htm.

29 "With world's first 5G, Qatar leads in communication tech," *Qatar-Tribune*, July 2, 2018, http://www.qatar-tribune.com/news-details/id/130696.

30 "Interview: China Int'l Import Expo boosts Qatar-China cooperation under Belt and Road Initiative," *Xinhua*, November 3, http://www.xinhuanet.com/english/2018-11/03/c_137579551.htm.

31 Haifa Said and Du Chao, "Qatar and China: Developing a Comprehensive Strategic Partnership," *China Today*, November 8, 2018, http://www.chinatoday.com.cn/ctenglish/2018/ii/201808/t20180811_800138032.html.

32 "Qatar sets up US$10bn fund to invest in China," *The Economist Intelligence Unit*, November 7, 2014,
http://country.eiu.com/article.aspx?articleid=182473202&Country=Qatar&topic=Economy&subtopic=Fore_11.

33 Dinesh Nair and Manuel Baigorri, "Qatar Fund Is Near Investment in China's Top Online Lender," *Bloomberg*, September 18, 2018, https://www.bloomberg.com/news/articles/2018-09-17/qatar-fund-said-to-near-investment-in-china-s-top-online-lender.

34 Li Wenfang and Zhu Wenqian, "Qatar Airways buys stake in China Southern," *China Daily*, September 5, 2019,
http://global.chinadaily.com.cn/a/201901/05/WS5c2fee84a31068606745efe2.html.

35 "Vision and Actions on Jointly Building Silk Road Economic Belt and 21st-Century Maritime Silk Road," *National Development and Reform Commission, Ministry of Foreign Affairs, and Ministry of Commerce of the People's Republic of China*, March 28, 2015, http://en.ndrc.gov.cn/newsrelease/201503/t20150330_669367.html.

36 "Chinese FM: Qatar a key partner to promote 'Belt and Road' initiative," *CCTV.com*, December 5, 2016,
http://english.cctv.com/2016/05/12/VIDENMyddtTBNQUM9zStLhAV160512.shtml.

37 Cary Huang, "57 nations approved as founder members of China-led AIIB," *South China Morning Post*, April 27, 2015, https://www.scmp.com/news/china/diplomacy-defence/article/1766970/57-nations-approved-founder-members-china-led-aiib.

38 "China, Qatar agree to deepen strategic partnership," *Xinhua*, January 31, 2019, http://www.xinhuanet.com/english/2019-01/31/c_137790332.htm.

39 Andrew Torchia and Tom Finn, "Qatar's $300 billion conundrum: how liquid are its reserves?," *Reuters*, July 19, 2017, https://www.reuters.com/article/us-gulf-qatar-reserves/qatars-300-billion-conundrum-how-liquid-are-its-reserves-idUSKBN1A415X.

40 Muhammad Zulfikar Rakhmat, "China, Qatar, and RMB Internationalization," *The Diplomat*, June 6, 2015, https://thediplomat.com/2015/06/china-qatar-and-rmb-internationalization/.

41 Esther Teo, "More Middle East countries using the yuan," *The Straits Times*, February 5, 2016, https://www.straitstimes.com/asia/east-asia/more-middle-east-countries-using-the-yuan.

42 Haifa Said and Du Chao, "Qatar and China: Developing a Comprehensive Strategic Partnership," *China Today*, November 8, 2018, http://www.chinatoday.com.cn/cteng-lish/2018/ii/201808/t20180811_800138032.html.

43 "Qatar-China ties promise economic partnerships and advanced stages of integration," *Gulf Times* January 30, 2019, https://www.gulf-times.com/story/620770/Qatar-China-ties-promise-economic-partnerships-and.

44 Jessica Jaganathan, "Australia grabs world's biggest LNG exporter crown from Qatar in November," *Reuters*, December 10, 2018, https://www.reuters.com/article/us-australia-qatar-lng/australia-grabs-worlds-biggest-lng-exporter-crown-from-qatar-in-nov-idUSKBN1O907N.

45 "Qatar-China trade jumps 27% to $13.5 bn in 2018, says Kuwari," *Qatar Tribune*, February 1, 2019, http://www.qatar-tribune.com/news-details/id/153980.

46 "Natural Gas Weekly Update," *U.S. Energy Information Administration (EIA)*, December 5, 2018, https://www.eia.gov/naturalgas/weekly/archivenew_ngwu/2018/12_06/.

47 Satyendra Pathak, "Qatar-China trade volume jumps 50% on LNG exports," *Qatar Tribune*, November 19, 2017, http://www.qatar-tribune.com/news-details/id/96747.

48 "Qatar," *U.S. Energy Information Administration (EIA)*, October 20, 2015, https://www.eia.gov/beta/international/analysis.php?iso=QAT#note.

49 Hassan E. Alfadala and Mahmoud M. El-Halwagi, "Qatar's Chemical Industry: Monetizing Natural Gas," *AIChE*, February 2017, https://www.aiche.org/resources/publications/cep/2017/february/qatars-chemical-industry-monetizing-natural-gas.

50 Haifa Said and Du Chao, "Qatar and China: Developing a Comprehensive Strategic Partnership," *China Today*, November 8, 2018, http://www.chinatoday.com.cn/cteng-lish/2018/ii/201808/t20180811_800138032.html.

51 Zheng Xin, "US LNG exports to China are declining," *China Daily*, August 22, 2018, http://www.chinadaily.com.cn/a/201808/22/WS5b7cc6fea310add14f3871b2_2.html.

52 Andrew Torchia, "Qatargas agrees on 22-year LNG supply deal with China," *Reuters*, September10, 2018, https://www.reuters.com/article/us-usa-china-trade-analysis/trump-wont-soften-hard-line-on-china-to-make-trade-deal-advisers-idUSKCN1PH02I.

53 Rania El Gamal, "Qatar Petroleum signs five-year LPG supply deal with China," *Reuters*, October 16, 2018, https://in.reuters.com/article/qatar-petroleum-china/qatar-petroleum-signs-five-year-lpg-supply-deal-with-china-idINKCN1MQ0NI.

54 Anas Iqtait, "China's rising interests in Qatar," *The Interpreter*, June 8, 2018, https://www.lowyinstitute.org/the-interpreter/china-s-rising-interests-qatar.

55 "Qatar signs agreement to supply gas to China," *The Middle East Monitor*, November 13, 2019, https://www.middleeastmonitor.com/20191113-qatar-signs-agreement-to-supply-gas-to-china/.

56 John Calabrese, "China and the Persian Gulf: Energy and Security," *Middle East Journal*, 52 (3), 1998, 351–366; Steve Yetiv and Chunlong Lu, "China, Global Energy, and the Middle East", *Middle East Journal*, 61(2), 2007, 199–218.

57 Daniel Workman, "Top 15 Crude Oil Suppliers to China," *World's Top Exports*, March 31, 2020, http://www.worldstopexports.com/top-15-crude-oil-suppliers-to-china/.

58 Brahim Saidy, "Qatar and Rising China: An Evolving Partnership," *China Report*, 53, 4 (2017): 447–466.

59 Samuel Ramani, "China's Growing Security Relationship with Qatar," *The Diplomat*,

November 16, 2017, https://thediplomat.com/2017/11/chinas-growing-security-relationship-with-qatar/.

60 Christopher Layne, "The US–Chinese power shift and the end of the Pax Americana," *International Affairs*, 94 (1), 2018, 89–111.

61 Imad K. Harb, "Self-preservation and Strategic Hedging in the Gulf Cooperation Council," *Policy brief*, no. 23, June 26, 2018, http://ams.hi.is/wp-content/uploads/2018/06/Self-Preservation-and-Strategic-Hedging-in-the-GCC-2.pdf.

62 Samuel Ramani, "China's Growing Security Relationship with Qatar," *The Diplomat*, November 16, 2017, https://thediplomat.com/2017/11/chinas-growing-security-relationship-with-qatar/.

63 Camilla Hodgson, Qatar has boosted spending by 282% to become the world's 3rd biggest weapons importer," *Business Insider*, August 10, 2017, https://www.businessinsider.com/qatar-becomes-worlds-third-biggest-weapons-importer-in-t wo-years-2017-8.

64 Julia Hollingsworth, "Why Qatar matters to China, in spite of Gulf isolation," *South China Morning Post*, June 12, 2017, https://www.scmp.com/news/china/diplomacy-defence/article/2097206/why-qatar-matters-china-spite-gulf-isolation.

65 Giorgio Cafiero and Daniel Wagner, "What the Gulf States Think of 'One Belt, One Road'," *The Diplomat*, May 24, 2017, https://thediplomat.com/2017/05/what-the-gulf-states-think-of-one-belt-one-road/.

66 Anas Iqtait, "China's rising interests in Qatar," *The Interpreter*, June 8, 2018, https://www.lowyinstitute.org/the-interpreter/china-s-rising-interests-qatar.

67 Matthew Lee, "Pompeo signs off on al-Udeid Air Base expansion, but says Qatar diplomatic crisis 'has dragged on too long'," *Military Times*, January 13, 2019, https://www.militarytimes.com/flashpoints/2019/01/13/pompeo-signs-off-on-al-udeid-air-base-expansion-but-says-qatar-diplomatic-crisis-has-dragged-on-too-long/.

68 Theodore Karasik and Giorgio Cafiero, "Why China Sold Qatar The SY-400 Ballistic Missile System," *Lobe Log* December 21, 2017, https://lobelog.com/why-china-sold-qatar-the-sy-400-ballistic-missile-system/.

69 Giorgio Cafiero and Muhammad Zulfikar Rakhmat, "China Eyes Qatar in its Quest to Build a New Silk Road," *The National Interest*, June 2, 2016, https://nationalinterest.org/blog/the-buzz/china-eyes-qatar-its-quest-build-new-silk-road-16437?nopaging=1.

70 Theodore Karasik and Giorgio Cafiero, "Why China Sold Qatar The SY-400 Ballistic Missile System," *Lobe Log* December 21, 2017, https://lobelog.com/why-china-sold-qatar-the-sy-400-ballistic-missile-system/.

71 "Qatar Displays Chinese Missile," *Arms Control Association*, March 1, 2018, https://www.armscontrol.org/act/2018-03/news-briefs/qatar-displays-chinese-missile.

72 "Vision and Actions on Jointly Building Silk Road Economic Belt and 21st-Century Maritime Silk Road," *National Development and Reform Commission, Ministry of Foreign Affairs, and Ministry of Commerce of the People's Republic of China*, March 28, 2015, http://en.ndrc.gov.cn/newsrelease/201503/t20150330_669367.html.

73 "China, Qatar agree to deepen strategic partnership," *Ministry of Foreign Affairs, the People's Republic of China*, January 31, 2019, https://www.fmprc.gov.cn/mfa_eng/zxxx_662805/t1634698.shtml.

74 Sam, Bridge, "Gulf forecast to see 81% rise in Chinese tourists by 2022," *Arabian Business*, December 19, 2018, https://www.arabianbusiness.com/travel-hospitality/409972-gulf-forecast-to-see-81-rise-in-chinese-tourists-by-2022.

75 "45,000 Chinese tourists visited Qatar in '17: Envoy," *The Peninsula*, July 3, 2018,

https://www.thepeninsulaqatar.com/article/03/07/2018/45,000-Chinese-tourists-visited-Qatar-in-%E2%80%9917-Envoy.

76 "Qatar sees 38% growth in Chinese arrivals," *The Peninsula*, May 3, 2019, https://www.thepeninsulaqatar.com/article/03/03/2019/Qatar-sees-38-growth-in-Chinese-arrivals.

77 "Qatar's tourism industry takes measures to attract more Chinese tourists," *China Daily*, April 13, 2018, http://www.chinadaily.com.cn/a/201804/13/WS5ad05bffa3105cdcf651827b.html.

78 Haifa Said and Du Chao, "Qatar and China: Developing a Comprehensive Strategic Partnership," *China Today*, November 8, 2018, http://www.chinatoday.com.cn/ctenglish/2018/ii/201808/t20180811_800138032.html.

79 "China–Qatar visa exemption agreement to take effect later this month," *Xinhua*, December 12, 2018, http://www.xinhuanet.com/english/2018-12/12/c_137669098.htm.

80 Ailyn Agonia, "Chinese Embassy marks 30th anniversary of Qatar-China diplomatic ties in style," *Qatar Tribune*, July 6, 2018, http://www.qatar-tribune.com/news-details/id/131203.

81 Jure Snoj, "Population of Qatar by nationality-2017 report," *Priya DSouza Communications*, February 7, 2017, http://priyadsouza.com/population-of-qatar-by-nationality-in-2017/.

82 Muhammad Zulfikar Rakhmat, "China–Qatar Relations: Media, Culture, Education, and People," *HuffPost*, May 18, 2017, https://www.huffingtonpost.com/muhammad-zulfikar-rakhmat/chinaqatar-relations-medi_b_10006408.html.

83 "Luxury Chinese Travel to the Middle East Hots Up; Chinese Travellers Seek New Silk Road Adventure," *The Luxury Conversation*, February 17, 2018, http://luxuryconversation.com/chinese-travellers-seek-new-silk-road-adventure-as-luxury-chinese-travel-to-the-middle-east-hots-up/.

84 "Memorandum of Understanding Signed by Translation and Interpreting Institute and the Chinese Embassy in Qatar," *Qatar Foundation*, February 22, 2015, https://www.qf.org.qa/news/tii-mou-chinese-embassy.

85 Wang Yue, "Delegation from Qatar University visits PKU," *Peking University*, November 24, 2014, http://newsen.pku.edu.cn/News_Events/News/Global/11776.htm.

86 "Qatar, China agree on 'strategic partnership'," *Gulf Times*, November 04 2014, https://www.gulf-times.com/story/414942/Qatar-China-agree-on-strategic-partnership.

87 Lesley Walker, "Qatar-China Year of Culture to kick off with exhibits, festival in 2016," *Doha News*, December 30, 2015, https://dohanews.co/qatar-china-year-culture-kick-off-exhibits-festival-2016/.

88 Haifa Said and Du Chao, "Qatar and China: Developing a Comprehensive Strategic Partnership," *China Today*, November 8, 2018, http://www.chinatoday.com.cn/ctenglish/2018/ii/201808/t20180811_800138032.html.

14 Oman

1 "Oman and China strategic partners," *Times of Oman*, September 8, 2018, https://timesofoman.com/article/140883.

2 Mordechai Chaziza, China's Relationship with Egypt and Oman: A Strategic Framework for the Implementation of China's Maritime Silk Road Implementation. In Michael Clarke, Matthew Sussex and Nick Bisley (eds.) *The Belt and Road Initiative*

and the Future of Regional Order in the Indo-Pacific (pp. 141–157). London: Lexington Books.

3 Giorgio Cafiero and Daniel Wagner, "What the Gulf States Think of 'One Belt, One Road'," *The Diplomat*, May 24, 2017, https://thediplomat.com/2017/05/what-the-gulf-states-think-of-one-belt-one-road/.

4 Sumedh A. Lokhande, "China's One Belt One Road Initiative and the Gulf Pearl Chain," *China Daily*, June 5, 2017, http://www.chinadaily.com.cn/opinion/2017 beltandroad/2017-06/05/content_29618549.htm.

5 "China, Oman announce establishment of strategic partnership," *CGTN*, May 25, 2018, https://news.cgtn.com/news/3d3d414f35676a4e77457a6333566d54/share_p.html.

6 "Oman 9th Five-Year Development Plan and the Strategic Economic Sectors (2016–2020)," *The Supreme Council of Planning in the Sultanate of Oman*, July 7, 2017, http://obfaoman.com/wp-content/uploads/2017/09/2.-Oman-Uk-comm-July17-V1-1.pdf.

7 Alfred Strolla and Phaninder Peri, "Oman 20/20 Vision," *A Middle East Point of View*, 2013, https://www2.deloitte.com/content/dam/Deloitte/xe/Documents/About-Deloitte/mepovdocuments/mepov12/dtme_mepov12_Oman2020vision.pdf.

8 Amar Diwakar, "Vision 2040: Oman's ambitious strategy towards a post-oil economy," *Al-Araby*, April 16, 2019, https://www.alaraby.co.uk/english/indepth/2019/4/16/vision-2040-omans-ambitious-strategy-towards-a-post-oil-economy.

9 Min Ye, "China and competing cooperation in Asia-Pacific: TPP, RCEP, and the New Silk Road," *Asian Security*, 11 (3), 2015, 206–224.

10 "Vision and Actions on Jointly Building Silk Road Economic Belt and 21st-Century Maritime Silk Road," *National Development and Reform Commission, Ministry of Foreign Affairs, and Ministry of Commerce of the People's Republic of China*, March 28, 2015, http://en.ndrc.gov.cn/newsrelease/201503/t20150330_669367.html.

11 Sumedh A. Lokhande, "China's One Belt One Road Initiative and the Gulf Pearl Chain," *China Daily*, June 5, 2017, http://www.chinadaily.com.cn/opinion/2017beltan-droad/2017-06/05/content_29618549.htm.

12 Giorgio Cafiero and Daniel Wagner, "What the Gulf States Think of 'One Belt, One Road'," *The Diplomat*, May 24, 2017, https://thediplomat.com/2017/05/what-the-gulf-states-think-of-one-belt-one-road/.

13 "Oman is a Key Regional Partner in the Belt and Road Initiative," *The Sirius Report*, June 7, 2018, https://www.thesiriusreport.com/geopolitics/oman-china-bri/.

14 "Oman's Duqm, a New Port City for the Middle East?," *Belt & Road News*, February 11, 2019, https://www.beltandroad.news/2019/02/11/omans-duqm-a-new-port-city-for-the-middle-east/.

15 Jonathan Schanzer and Nicole Salter, "Oman in the Middle: Muscat's Balancing Act Between Iran and America," *The Foundation for Defense of Democracies (FDD)*, May 9, 2019, https://www.fdd.org/analysis/2019/05/09/oman-in-the-middle/.

16 Alfred Strolla and Phaninder Peri, "Oman: 20/20 Vision," *World Finance Review*, May 2016, https://islamicmarkets.com/publications/oman-vision-2020.

17 Han Guo and Zhou Zhou, "China's Strategic Vision: Five Years on and Looking Ahead," *ICAS BULLETIN: Institute for China–America Studies*, November 1, 2017, https://chinaus-icas.org/bulletin/chinas-strategic-vision-five-years-on-and-looking-ahead/.

18 "Oman Stands to benefit from China-Arab Belt and Road Initiative: HE FULONG," *Muscat Daily*, July 16, 2018, https://muscatdaily.com/Archive/Oman/Oman-stands-to-benefit-from-China-Arab-Belt-and-Road-initiative-H-E-Fulong-5a0p.

19   "Vision and Actions on Jointly Building Silk Road Economic Belt and 21st-Century Maritime Silk Road," *National Development and Reform Commission, Ministry of Foreign Affairs, and Ministry of Commerce of the People's Republic of China,* March 28, 2015, http://en.ndrc.gov.cn/newsrelease/201503/t20150330_669367.html.

20   "Oman among top four Arab trading partners of China," *Times of Oman,* March 11, 2018, https://timesofoman.com/article/129848.

21   "China, Oman announce establishment of strategic partnership," *CGTN,* May 25, 2018, https://news.cgtn.com/news/3d3d414f35676a4e77457a6333566d54/share_p.html.

22   "China, Oman issue joint statement on establishment of strategic partnership," *Xinhua,* May 26, 2018, http://www.xinhuanet.com/english/2018-05/26/c_137206872.htm.

23   "China and Oman Sign the Memorandum of Understanding on Jointly Building the 'Belt and Road'," *Permanent Mission of the People's Republic of China to the UN,* May 15, 2018, http://www.china-un.org/eng/zgyw/t1560128.htm.

24   "Belt and Road Initiative aims to achieve mutual benefits for all: Omani officials," *Xinhua,* December 4, 2018, http://www.xinhuanet.com/english/2018-12/05/c_137650958.htm.

25   John Calabrese, "China and the Persian Gulf: Energy and Security," *Middle East Journal,* 52 (3), 1998, 351–366; Steve Yetiv and Chunlong Lu, "China, Global Energy, and the Middle East," *Middle East Journal,* 61 (2), 2007, 199–218.

26   Daniel Workman, "Top 15 Crude Oil Suppliers to China," *World's Top Exports,* April 26, 2020, http://www.worldstopexports.com/top-15-crude-oil-suppliers-to-china/.

27   "Oman-Overview," *US Energy Information Administration (EIA),* January 7, 2019, https://www.eia.gov/beta/international/analysis.php?iso=OMN.

28   "Annual Report 2017," *Central Bank of Oman,* June 2018, https://cbo.gov.om/sites/assets/Documents/English/Publications/AnnualReports/AnnualReport2017eng.pdf.

29   Mordechai Chaziza, "The Significant Role of Oman in China's Maritime Silk Road Initiative," *Contemporary Review of the Middle East,* 6 (1), 2018, 1–14.

30   Mahmoud Ghafouri, "China's Policy in the Persian Gulf," *Middle East Policy Council,* 16 (2), 2009, 80–92.

31   "Exploring the China and Oman Relationship," *The Diplomat,* May 10, 2014, https://thediplomat.com/2014/05/exploring-the-china-and-oman-relationship/.

32   "China remains largest buyer of Oman's crude in December: report," *Xinhua,* January 16, 2019, http://www.chinadaily.com.cn/a/201901/16/WS5c3ec328a3106c65c34e4cc7.html.

33   "China remains biggest importer of Omani oil," *Times of Oman,* July 15, 2018, https://timesofoman.com/article/138149.

34   "Oman–China Trade ties to deepen Further," *Muscat Daily,* January 13, 2019, https://muscatdaily.com/Archive/Business/Oman-China-trade-ties-to-deepen-further-5cpn.

35   "China, Oman issue joint statement on establishment of strategic partnership," *Xinhua,* May 26, 2018, http://www.xinhuanet.com/english/2018-05/26/c_137206872.htm.

36   Dave Yin, "China's State Grid Acquires 49% Stake in Oman Power Network," *Caixin Global,* December 17, 2019, https://www.caixinglobal.com/2019-12-17/chinas-state-grid-acquires-49-stake-in-oman-power-network-101494784.html.

37   "Vision and Actions on Jointly Building Silk Road Economic Belt and 21st-Century Maritime Silk Road," *National Development and Reform Commission, Ministry of Foreign Affairs, and Ministry of Commerce of the People's Republic of China,* March 28, 2015, http://en.ndrc.gov.cn/newsrelease/201503/t20150330_669367.html.

38 "China Customs Statistics: Imports and exports by country/region," *The Hong Kong Trade Development Council (HKTDC)*, January 24, 2020, http://china-trade-research.hktdc.com/business-news/article/Facts-and-Figures/China-Customs-Statistics/ff/en/1/1X39VTVQ/1X09N9NM.htm.

39 "China, Oman issue joint statement on establishment of strategic partnership," *Xinhua*, May 26, 2018, http://www.xinhuanet.com/english/2018-05/26/c_137206872.htm.

40 "Oman Stands to benefit from China–Arab Belt and Road Initiative: HE FULONG," *Muscat Daily*, July 16, 2018, https://muscatdaily.com/Archive/Oman/Oman-stands-to-benefit-from-China-Arab-Belt-and-Road-initiative-H-E-Fulong-5a0p.

41 Oman–China Trade ties to Deepen Further," *Muscat Daily*, January 13, 2019, https://muscatdaily.com/Archive/Business/Oman-China-trade-ties-to-deepen-further-5cpn.

42 "Oman–China trade topped $19bn in 2018," *Times of Oman*, April 27, 2019, https://timesofoman.com/article/1204030 https://timesofoman.com/article/1204030.

43 "Oman important partner in building Belt and Road: Chinese envoy," *Times of Oman*, April 30, 2019, https://timesofoman.com/article/1219648.

44 Wade Shepard, "Why China is Building A New City Out in the Desert of Oman," *Forbes*, September 8, 2017, https://www.forbes.com/sites/wadeshepard/2017/09/08/why-china-is-building-a-new-city-out-in-the-desert-of-oman/#6d3249316b2f.

45 James Kynge, Chris Campbell, Amy Kazmin & Farhan Bokhari, "How China rules the waves. *Financial Times*, January 12, 2017, https://ig.ft.com/sites/china-ports/.

46 "Oman Wanfang plans 25 new projects in Duqm," *Times of Oman*, August 12, 2017, http://timesofoman.com/article/114777/Business/Oman-Wanfang-plans-25-new-projects-at-Duqm.

47 "Oman's 2020 vision," *Arabian Business*, March 10, 2010, http://www.arabianbusiness.com/oman-s-2020-vision-89986.html.

48 Nawied Jabarkhyl, "Oman counts on Chinese billions to build desert boomtown," *Reuters*, September 5, 2017, https://www.reuters.com/article/us-oman-china-investment/oman-counts-on-chinese-billions-to-build-desert-boomtown-idUSKCN1BG1WJ.

49 "Oman among top four Arab trading partners of China," *Times of Oman*, March 11, 2018, https://timesofoman.com/article/129848.

50 "Vision and Actions on Jointly Building Silk Road Economic Belt and 21st-Century Maritime Silk Road," *National Development and Reform Commission, Ministry of Foreign Affairs, and Ministry of Commerce of the People's Republic of China*, March 28, 2015, http://en.ndrc.gov.cn/newsrelease/201503/t20150330_669367.html.

51 "China, Oman issue joint statement on establishment of strategic partnership," *Xinhua*, May 26, 2018, http://www.xinhuanet.com/english/2018-05/26/c_137206872.htm.

52 "Oman signs pact as founding member of Asian Infrastructure Investment Bank," *Times of Oman*, October 26, 2014, https://timesofoman.com/article/42316.

53 "Oman hosts AIIB delegation," *Muscat Daily*, March 4, 2019, https://muscatdaily.com/Archive/Business/Oman-hosts-AIIB-delegation-5dbs.

54 "UPDATE 1-Oman signs $3.55 billion loan with Chinese banks," *Reuters*, August 3, 2017, https://www.reuters.com/article/oman-loan/update-1-oman-signs-3-55-billion-loan-with-chinese-banks-idUSL5N1KP2XX.

55 "Vision and Actions on Jointly Building Silk Road Economic Belt and 21st-Century Maritime Silk Road," *National Development and Reform Commission, Ministry of Foreign Affairs, and Ministry of Commerce of the People's Republic of China*, March 28, 2015, http://en.ndrc.gov.cn/newsrelease/201503/t20150330_669367.html.

56 "China, Oman issue joint statement on establishment of strategic partnership," *Xinhua*, May 26, 2018, http://www.xinhuanet.com/english/2018-05/26/c_137206872.htm.

57 Liu Xi and Yang Yuanyong, "Spotlight: China, Oman establish industrial park to boost bilateral cooperation," *Xinhua*, December 19, 2018, http://www.xinhuanet.com/english/2018-12/19/c_137683272.htm.

58 "Oman and China strategic partners," *Times of Oman*, September 8, 2018, https://timesofoman.com/article/140883.

59 Sam Bridge, "Gulf forecast to see 81% rise in Chinese tourists by 2022," *Arabian Business*, December 19, 2018, https://www.arabianbusiness.com/travel-hospitality/409972-gulf-forecast-to-see-81-rise-in-chinese-tourists-by-2022.

60 "Oman–China trade topped $19bn in 2018," *Times of Oman*, April 27, 2019, https://timesofoman.com/article/1204030 https://timesofoman.com/article/1204030.

61 "Oman important partner in building Belt and Road: Chinese envoy," *Times of Oman*, April 30, 2019, https://timesofoman.com/article/1219648.

62 Marc M. Valeri, *Simmering Unrest and Succession Challenges in Oman*. Washington, DC: Carnegie Endowment for International Peace, 2015.

63 Zhibin Han and Xiaoqian Chen, "Historical Exchanges and Future Cooperation between China and Oman Under the 'Belt & Road' Initiative," *International Relations and Diplomacy*, 6 (1), 2018, 1–15.

64 Neeta Lal, "India, China Jockey for Influence in Oman," *Asia Sentinel*, February 21, 2018, https://www.asiasentinel.com/politics/india-china-jockey-influence-oman/.

65 Kenneth Katzman, "Oman: Reform, Security, and U.S. Policy," *Congressional Research Service*, March 8, 2018, https://fas.org/sgp/crs/mideast/RS21534.pdf.

66 Richard J. Schmierer, "The Sultanate of Oman and the Iran Nuclear Deal," *Middle East Policy*, 22 (4), 2015, 113–120.

15 Bahrain

1 Muhammad Zulfikar Rakhmat, "China and Bahrain: Undocumented Growing Relations," *Fair Observer*, May 22, 2014, https://www.fairobserver.com/region/middle_east_north_africa/china-and-bahrain-undocumented-growing-relations-66107/.

2 "Bahrain Strengthens Economic Ties with China, Signs 8 Landmark MoUs," *Asharq Al-Awsat*, November 19, 2018, https://aawsat.com/english/home/article/1469476/bahrain-strengthens-economic-ties-china-signs-8-landmark-mous.

3 "Bahrain has played an important role in consolidating relations between China and the rest of the Gulf States," *VAAJU.COM*, July 9, 2018, https://vaaju.com/lebanon/bahrain-has-played-an-important-role-in-consolidating-relations-between-china-and-the-rest-of-the-gulf-states/.

4 "The Economic Vision 2030," *Kingdom of Bahrain*, September 11, 2017, https://www.bahrain.bh/wps/portal/!ut/p/a1/jdDfE4FAEAfwv8VDr-3qqHg7TSlTwyByLybmHKY6k8ifLzz5Efbtdj7f2d0DBhGwLD7vRFzsZBYntzfTl-4Q9aZmagOchg7S4aTl-rZLcGxUYPEECLEroBsjY9bRdBP_y6MWWE2vVYEgQKRmb-xPHQuxT_7M1xT9OX_CM5gDe2HvV9zBtzUfoH6PATCRyNX9Txc0WxFTAMv5huc8V0951d4WxeHYVVDBsixVIaVIuLqWqYKfIlt5LCB6lnBIwzC6ePt2cvYpbTSuTGJy6Q!!/dl5/d5/L2dBISEvZ0FBIS9nQSEh/.

5 "Bahrain: Market Profile," *The Hong Kong Trade Development Council (HKTDC)*, February 8, 2019, file:///C:/Users/moti/Downloads/hktdc_1X0K7WJT_en.pdf.

6 "Doing Business 2019: Training of Reform," *The World Bank* Group, October 31, 2018, https://www.doingbusiness.org/content/dam/doingBusiness/media/Annual-Reports/English/DB2019-report_web-version.pdf.

7   Klaus Schwab "The Global Competitiveness Report 2019," *World Economic Forum,* October 8, 2019, http://www3.weforum.org/docs/WEF_TheGlobalCompetitivenessReport2019.pdf.

8   "Bahrain GDP," *Trading Economics,* 2020, https://tradingeconomics.com/bahrain/gdp.

9   "IMF expects Bahrain economy to grow 1.8 pct in 2019," *Reuters,* March 6, 2019, https://www.reuters.com/article/bahrain-economy-imf/imf-expects-bahrain-economy-to-grow-18-pct-in-2019-idUSL5N20T1S4.

10   Giorgio Cafiero and Daniel Wagner, "What the Gulf States Think of 'One Belt, One Road'," *The Diplomat,* May 24, 2017, https://thediplomat.com/2017/05/what-the-gulf-states-think-of-one-belt-one-road/.

11   Sumedh Anil Lokhande, "China's One Belt One Road Initiative and the Gulf Pearl Chain," China Daily, June 5, 2017, http://www.chinadaily.com.cn/interface/flip-board/158870/2017-06-05/cd_29618549.html.

12   "Changing times calls for new GCC relations with China, Russia," *Oxford Business Group,* 2019, https://oxfordbusinessgroup.com/analysis/east-meets-middle-east-changing-times-calls-new-relations-china-and-russia.

13   Giorgio Cafiero and Daniel Wagner, "What the Gulf States Think of 'One Belt, One Road'," *The Diplomat,* May 24, 2017, https://thediplomat.com/2017/05/what-the-gulf-states-think-of-one-belt-one-road/.

14   Min Ye, "China and competing cooperation in Asia-Pacific: TPP, RCEP, and the New Silk Road," *Asian Security,* 11 (3), 2015, 206–224.

15   "Vision and Actions on Jointly Building Silk Road Economic Belt and 21st-Century Maritime Silk Road," *National Development and Reform Commission, Ministry of Foreign Affairs, and Ministry of Commerce of the People's Republic of China,* March 28, 2015, http://en.ndrc.gov.cn/newsrelease/201503/t20150330_669367.html.

16   Habib Toumi, "King Hamad's visit to boost Bahrain–China relations," *Gulf News,* September 13, 2013, https://gulfnews.com/world/gulf/bahrain/king-hamads-visit-to-boost-bahrain-china-relations-1.1230640

17   "Xi Jinping Holds Talks with King of Bahrain Sheikh Hamad bin Isa Al-khalifa Stressing to Build China–Bahrain Friendly Cooperative Relations of Long-term Stability," *Ministry of Foreign Affairs, the People's Republic of China,* September 9, 2013, https://www.fmprc.gov.cn/mfa_eng/wjb_663304/zzjg_663340/xybfs_663590/gjlb_663594/2803_663606/2805_663610/t1078070.shtml.

18   Qi Zhenhong, "Join Hands To Push China–Bahrain Relations," Embassy of the People's Republic of China in the Kingdom of Bahrain, May, 9, 2018, http://bh.china-embassy.org/eng/xwdt/t1558049.htm

19   Ola Aboukhsaiwan, "China in Bahrain: building shared interests," *Wamda,* February 22, 2017, https://www.wamda.com/2017/02/china-bahrain-building-shared-interests-entrepreneurship.

20   Khalifa Bin Salman Port," *Ministry of Transportation and Telecommunications Kingdom of Bahrain,* 2019, http://www.transportation.gov.bh/content/khalifa-bin-salman-port.

21   "Investing in Bahrain," *The Bahrain Economic Development Board,* 2019, https://www.bahrainbay.com/wp-content/uploads/2016/08/Investing-In-Bahrain-Brochure-09-CS3.pdf.

22   "Ambassador Qi Zhenhong's Speech on the 2016 Chinese National Day Reception," *Embassy of the People's Republic of China in the Kingdom of Bahrain,* September 21, 2016, http://bh.china-embassy.org/eng/zbgx/t1399255.htm.

23   "China's 'One Belt, One Road' is a 'win-win' for GCC – Bahrain Minister," *Gulf Insider,* May 13, 2018, https://www.gulf-insider.com/chinas-one-belt-one-road-win-win-gulf-countries-bahrain-minister/.

24 "China, Bahrain ink MOU to promote Belt and Road Initiative," *Xinhua*, July 10, 2018, http://www.xinhuanet.com/english/2018-07/10/c_137312832.htm.

25 "Vision and Actions on Jointly Building Silk Road Economic Belt and 21st-Century Maritime Silk Road," *National Development and Reform Commission, Ministry of Foreign Affairs, and Ministry of Commerce of the People's Republic of China*, March 28, 2015, http://en.ndrc.gov.cn/newsrelease/201503/t20150330_669367.html.

26 "Bahrain Delegation to visit China to fortify economic and trade ties between the two nations," *EDS Bahrain*, November 11, 2018, https://bahrainedb.com/latest-news/bahrain-delegation-to-visit-china-to-fortify-economic-and-trade-ties-between-the-two-nations/.

27 "Huawei to accelerate 5G ecosystem in Bahrain," *Technical Review Middle East*, August 12, 2018. http://www.technicalreviewmiddleeast.com/it/communication/huawei-to-accelerate-5g-ecosystem-in-bahrain.

28 "China Customs Statistics: Imports and exports by country/region," *The Hong Kong Trade Development Council (HKTDC)*, January 24, 2020, http://china-trade-research.hktdc.com/business-news/article/Facts-and-Figures/China-Customs-Statistics/ff/en/1/1X39VTVQ/1X09N9NM.htm.

29 Han Lu, "Bahraini business environment gives it edge," *China Daily*, May 30, 2018, http://www.chinadaily.com.cn/cndy/2018-05/30/content_36295733.htm.

30 "The 2019 Index of Economic Freedom: Bahrain," *The Heritage Foundation*, 2019, https://www.heritage.org/index/country/bahrain.

31 Han Lu, "Bahraini business environment gives it edge," *China Daily*, May 30, 2018, http://www.chinadaily.com.cn/cndy/2018-05/30/content_36295733.htm.

32 Ahmed Al-Masri and Kevin Curran, *Smart technologies and innovation for a sustainable future: proceedings of the 1st American University in the Emirates International Research Conference – Dubai, UAE 2017*. Cham, Switzerland: Springer, 2019.

33 James Reardon-Anderson, *The Red Star and the Crescent: China and the Middle East*. New York: Oxford University Press, 2018.

34 Muhammad Zulfikar Rakhmat, "China and Bahrain: Undocumented Growing Relations," *Fair Observer*, May 22, 2014, https://www.fairobserver.com/region/middle_east_north_africa/china-and-bahrain-undocumented-growing-relations-66107/.

35 "Celebrating Strong Ties," *Bahrain this Month*, October 1, 2018, https://www.bahrainthismonth.com/magazine/interviews/chinese-ambassador-celebrating-strong-ties.

36 Han Lu, "Bahraini business environment gives it edge," *China Daily*, May 30, 2018, http://www.chinadaily.com.cn/cndy/2018-05/30/content_36295733.htm.

37 "Bahrain to host Mideast's largest Chinese trade expo," *Trade Arabia*, December 25, 2018, http://www.tradearabia.com/news/IND_349105.html.

38 Nyshka Chandran, "Bahrain sees 'growing interest' from Chinese tech firms," *CNBC*, September, 20 2018, https://www.cnbc.com/2018/09/20/bahrain-sees-growing-interest-from-chinese-tech-firms.html.

39 Bernd Debusmann Jr ,"Bahrain's Investcorp makes first foray into China," *Arabian Business*, September 20, 2018, https://www.arabianbusiness.com/banking-finance/404734-wknd-bahrains-investcorp-makes-first-foray-into-china.

40 "A high-level Bahraini delegation is visiting China to further strengthen trade and economic ties," *StartUp Bahrain*, November 12, 2018, https://startupbahrain.com/a-high-level-bahraini-delegation-is-visiting-china-to-further-strengthen-trade-and-economic-tie/.

41 "Bahrain signs eight landmark agreements to deepen economic ties with Shenzhen,"

PR Newswire, November 16, 2018, https://www.prnewswire.com/news-releases/bahrain-signs-eight-landmark-agreements-to-deepen-economic-ties-with-shenzhen-300751963.html.

42 "China's Provincial Economies: Growing Together or Pulling Apart?," *Moody's*, January 2019, https://www.moodysanalytics.com/-/media/article/2019/china-provincial-economies.pdf.

43 "Bahrain signs key business deals with China," *TradeArabia*, November 22, 2018, http://www.tradearabia.com/news/BANK_347879.html.

44 "Bahrain signs more agreements with China as economic ties deepen," *The National*, November 20, 2018, https://www.thenational.ae/business/economy/bahrain-signs-more-agreements-with-china-as-economic-ties-deepen-1.793952.

45 "Bahrain EDB seals strategic agreements with China," *Trade Arabia*, November 20, 2018, http://www.tradearabia.com/news/BANK_347823.html.

46 "Vision and Actions on Jointly Building Silk Road Economic Belt and 21st-Century Maritime Silk Road," *National Development and Reform Commission, Ministry of Foreign Affairs, and Ministry of Commerce of the People's Republic of China*, March 28, 2015, http://en.ndrc.gov.cn/newsrelease/201503/t20150330_669367.html.

47 Sam Bridge, "Gulf forecast to see 81% rise in Chinese tourists by 2022," *Arabian Business*, December 19, 2018, https://www.arabianbusiness.com/travel-hospitality/409972-gulf-forecast-to-see-81-rise-in-chinese-tourists-by-2022.

48 "International tourism, number of arrivals- Bahrain," The *World Bank Group*, 2019, https://data.worldbank.org/indicator/ST.INT.ARVL?locations=BH.

49 Aarti Nagraj, "Bahrain, China sign visa exemption for diplomatic, special passports," *Gulf Business*, October 17, 2018, https://gulfbusiness.com/bahrain-china-sign-visa-exemption-diplomatic-special-passports/.

50 "Arabian Travel Market Series: GCC Source Market China," *Colliers International*, January 2018, http://www.shamalcomms.com/sites/default/files/Colliers%20-%20ATM%20Knowledge%20Partner%20-%20China%20%20-%20English.pdf.

51 "Celebrating Strong Ties," *Bahrain this Month*, October 1, 2018, https://www.bahrainthismonth.com/magazine/interviews/chinese-ambassador-celebrating-strong-ties.

52 "Bahrain takes part in Arab Arts Festival in China," *Arab Today*, September 13, 2014, https://www.arabstoday.net/en/75/bahrain-takes-part-in-arab-arts-festival-in-china.

53 "4th Arabic Arts Festival Opens in City," *Go Chengdu*, July 16, 2018, http://www.gochengdu.cn/news/Highlights/4th-arabic-arts-festival-opens-in-city-a7585.html.

54 "8 more countries set up Confucius institutes or classrooms in 2019," *Xinhua*, December 11, 2019, http://www.xinhuanet.com/english/2019-12/11/c_138623776.htm.

55 Huang Zhiling, "10 new Confucius Institutes lift global total to 548, boosting ties," *China Daily*, December 5, 2018, http://global.chinadaily.com.cn/a/201812/05/WS5c07239da310eff30328f182.html.

56 "Confucius Institute/Classroom," *Confucius Institute Headquarters (Hanban)*, 2020, http://english.hanban.org/node_10971.htm.

57 "The Confucius Institute at University of Bahrain," *University of Bahrain*, 2016, http://www.uob.edu.bh/en/index.php/administration/centers/confucius-institute.

58 "Chinese Government Scholarship Open for Application," *Embassy of the People's Republic of China in the Kingdom of Bahrain*, January 16, 2019,

http://bh.china-embassy.org/eng/xwdt/t1528121.htm.

59 Muhammad Zulfikar Rakhmat, "China and Bahrain: Undocumented Growing Relations," Fair Observer, May 22, 2014, https://www.fairobserver.com/region/middle_east_north_africa/china-and-bahrain-undocumented-growing-relations-66107/.

Bibliography

Al-Masri, Ahmed and Curran, Kevin. *Smart Technologies and Innovation for a Sustainable Future: Proceedings of the 1st American University in the Emirates International Research Conference – Dubai, UAE 2017*. Cham, Switzerland: Springer, 2019.

Alterman, Jon B., and Garver, John. *The Vital Triangle: China, the United States, and the Middle East*. Washington: Center for Strategic and International Studies, 2008.

Alterman, Jon B. "China's Soft Power in the Middle East," in C. Mcgiffert (ed.), *Chinese Soft Power and Its Implications for the United States* (pp. 63–76). Washington, D.C.: Center for Strategic and International Studies, 2009.

Anoushiravan, Ehteshami and Horesh, Niv. *China's Presence in the Middle East: The implications of the One Belt, One Road Initiative*. London; New York: Routledge, Taylor & Francis Group, 2018.

Armijo, Jacqueline. "China and the Gulf: The Social and Cultural Implications of Their Rapidly Developing Economic Ties," In T. Niblock and M. Malik (Eds.), *Asia-Gulf Economic Relations in the 21st Century: The Local to Global Transformation* (pp.141–156). Berlin: Gerlach Press, 2013.

Bin Huwaidin, Mohamed. *China's relations with Arabia and the Gulf, 1949–1999*. London: Routledge, 2011.

Bitzinge, Richard A. "Arms to Go: Chinese Arms Sales to the Third World," *International Security*, 17 (2), 1992, 84–111.

Blanchard, Jean-Marc F., and Flint, Colin. "The Geopolitics of China's Maritime Silk Road Initiative," *Geopolitics*, 22 (2), 2017, 223–225.

Cai, Peter. *Understanding China's Belt and Road Initiative*. Sydney: Lowy Institute for International Policy, 2017.

Calabrese, John. "China and the Persian Gulf: Energy and Security," *Middle East Journal*, 52 (3), 1998, 351–366.

Chaziza, Mordechai. "China's Middle East foreign policy and the Yemen Crisis: Challenges and Implications," *Middle East Review of International Affairs*, 19 (2), 2015, 1–9.

Chaziza, Mordechai. "Comprehensive Strategic Partnership: A New Stage in China-Egypt Relations," *Middle East Review of International Affairs*, 20 (3), 2016, 41–50.

Chaziza, Mordechai. "Sino-Turkish 'Solid Strategic Partnership': China's Dream or a Reality?," *China Report*, 52 (4), 2016, 265–283.

Chaziza, Mordechai. "Israel–China Relations Enter a New Stage: Limited Strategic Hedging," *Contemporary Review of the Middle East*, 5 (1), 2018, 30–45.

Chaziza, Mordechai. "China's Counter-Terrorism Policy in the Middle East," In M. Clarke (ed.), *Terrorism and Counter-Terrorism in China: Domestic and Foreign Policy Dimensions* (pp. 141–156). New York: Oxford University Press, 2018.

Chaziza, Mordechai. "China's Mediation Efforts in the Middle East and North Africa: Constructive Conflict Management," *Strategic Analysis*, 42 (1), 2018, 29–41.

Chaziza, Mordechai. "The Significant Role of Oman in China's Maritime Silk Road Initiative," *Contemporary Review of the Middle East*, 6 (1), 2018, 1–14.

Chaziza, Mordechai. "China's Economic Diplomacy Approach in the Middle East Conflicts," *China Report*, 55(1), 2019, 24–39.

Chaziza, Mordechai. "Six Years After the Arab Spring: China Foreign Policy in the Middle East-North Africa," In C. Çakmak and A. O. Özçelik, (Eds.), *The World Community and Arab Spring* (pp. 185–204). Palgrave Macmillan, Cham, 2019.

Chaziza, Mordechai. *China and the Persian Gulf: The New Silk Road Strategy and Emerging Partnerships*. Great Britain: Sussex Academic Press, 2020.

Chaziza, Mordechai. "China's Relationship with Egypt and Oman: A Strategic Framework for the Implementation of China's Maritime Silk Road Implementation," In M. Clarke, M. Sussex and N. Bisley (Eds.), *The Belt and Road Initiative and the Future of Regional Order in the Indo-Pacific* (pp. 141–157). London: Lexington Books.

Chen, Juan. "Strategic Synergy between Egypt "Vision 2030" and China's "Belt and Road" Initiative," *Outlines of Global Transformations: Politics, Economics, Law*, 11 (5), 2018, 219–235.

Cheng, Joseph Y. S. "China's Relations with the Gulf Cooperation Council States: Multilevel Diplomacy in a Divided Arab World," *China Review*, 16 (1), 2016, 35–64.

Dorsey, James M. *China and the Middle East: Venturing into the maelstrom*. Cham, Switzerland: Palgrave Macmillan, 2019.

Duchâtel, Mathieu, Oliver, Bräuner, and Zhou, Hang. "Protecting China's Overseas Interests: The Slow Shift Away from Non-Interference," *SIPRI, Policy Paper 41*, Stockholm, Sweden: Stockholm International Peace Research Institute, 2014.

Eberling, George, G. *China's Bilateral Relations With Its Principal Oil Suppliers*. Lanham: Lexington, 2017.

Efron Shira, Shatz J. Howard, Chan Arthur, Haskel Emily, Morris J. Lyle and Scobell Andrew. *The Evolving Israel–China Relationship*. RAND Corporation, Santa Monica, Calif, 2019.

Erickson, S. Andrew and Strange, Austin M. *Six Years at Sea . . . and Counting: Gulf of Aden Anti-piracy and China's Maritime Commons Presence*. Washington D.C.: Brookings Institution Press, 2015.

Ehteshami, Anoushiravan and Horesh, Niv. *China's Presence in the Middle East: The Implications of the One Belt, One Road Initiative*. London; New York: Routledge, Taylor & Francis Group, 2018.

Fallon, Theresa. "The New Silk Road: Xi Jinping's Grand Strategy for Eurasia," *American Foreign Policy Interests*, 37 (3), 2015, 140–147.

Fardella, Enrico. "China's Debate on the Middle East and North Africa: A Critical Review," *Mediterranean Quarterly*, 26, (1), 2015, 5–25.

Feng, Chaoling. "Embracing Interdependence: The Dynamics of China and the Middle East," *Policy Briefing*. Doha, Brookings Doha Center, 2015.

Ferdinand, Peter. "Westward ho-the China dream and 'one belt, one road': Chinese foreign policy under Xi Jinping," *International Affairs*, 92 (4), 2016, 941–957.

Fulton, Jonathan. "China's Presence in the Middle East: The Implications of the One Belt, One Road Initiative/The Red Star and the Crescent: China and the Middle East," *The Middle East Journal*, 72 (2), 2018, 341–343.

Fulton, Jonathan and Li-Chen, Sim. *External powers and the Gulf monarchies*. London, Oxon; New York, NY: Routledge, 2019.

Fulton, Jonathan. *China's Relations with the Gulf Monarchies.* Abingdon, Oxon; New York, NY: Routledge, 2019.

Ghafouri, Mahmoud. "China's Policy in the Persian Gulf," *Middle East Policy Council,* 16 (2), 2009, 80–92.

Goh, Evelyn. *Meeting the China Challenge: The United States in Southeast Asian Regional Security Strategies.* Washington: East-West Center, 2005.

Goldstein, Avery. *Rising to the Challenge: China's Grand Strategy and International Security.* Stanford: Stanford University Press, 2005.

Gormley, Dennis M., Erickson, Andrew S., and Yuan, Jingdong. *A Low-Visibility Force Multiplier: Assessing China's Cruise Missile Ambitions.* Washington, DC: NDU Press, 2014.

Gresh, Geoffrey F. "A Vital Maritime Pinch Point: China, the Bab al-Mandeb, and the Middle East," *Asian Journal of Middle Eastern and Islamic Studies,* 11(1), 2017, 37–46.

Han, Zhibin and Chen, Xiaoqian. "Historical Exchanges and Future Cooperation between China and Oman Under the "Belt & Road" Initiative," *International Relations and Diplomacy,* 6 (1), 2018, 1–15.

Hoh, Anchi "China's Belt and Road Initiative in Central Asia and the Middle East," *Digest of Middle East Studies,* 28 (2), 2019, 241–276.

Horesh, Niv. *Toward Well-Oiled Relations? China's Presence in the Middle East Following the Arab Spring.* London: Palgrave Macmillan UK: Imprint: Palgrave Macmillan, 2016.

Huang, Yiping. "Understanding China's Belt & Road Initiative: Motivation, framework and assessment," China Economic Review, 40, 2016, 314–321.

Hudson, Michael and Kirk, Mimi. *Gulf Politics and Economics in a Changing World.* Middle East Institute, Washington DC, 2014.

Jalal, Mohammed N. "The China–Arab States Cooperation Forum: Achievements, Challenges and Prospects," *Journal of Middle Eastern and Islamic Studies (in Asia),* 8 (2), 2014, 1–21.

Kamel, Maha S. "China's Belt and Road Initiative: Implications for the Middle East," *Cambridge Review of International Affairs,* 31 (1), 2018, 76–95.

Kaiser-Cross, Sarah and Mao, Yufeng. "China's Strategy in the Middle East and the Arab World," In J. Eisenman and E. Heginbotham (Eds.), *China Steps Out: Beijing's Major Power Engagement with the Developing World* (pp. 170–192). New York: Routledge, 2018.

Kaplan, Robert D. "Center Stage for the 21st Century: Power Plays in the Indian Ocean," *Foreign Affairs,* 88(2), 2009, 16–33.

Kumaraswamy, P. R., and Quamar, Md. Muddassir. *India's Saudi policy: Bridging the gulf.* Singapore: Palgrave Macmillan, 2019.

Lanteinge, Marc. *Chinese Foreign Policy: An Introduction* London: Routledge, 2013.

Layne, Christopher. "The US–Chinese power shift and the end of the Pax Americana," *International Affairs,* 94 (1), 2018, 89–111.

Len, Christopher. "China's 21st Century Maritime Silk Road Initiative, Energy Security and SLOC Access," *Maritime Affairs: Journal of the National Maritime Foundation of India,* 11(1), 2015, 1–18.

Li, Sharon Li and Ingram, Colin. *Maritime Law and Policy in China.* London: Routledge-Cavendish, 2013.

Liu, Haiquan. "The Security Challenges of the "One Belt, One Road" Initiative and China's Choices," *Croatian International Relation Review,* 23 (78), 2017, 129–147.

Liu, Zhongmin. "Historical evolution of relationship between China and the Gulf Region." *Journal of Middle Eastern and Islamic Studies (in Asia)* 10(1), 2016, 1–25.

Min, Ye. "China and competing cooperation in Asia-Pacific: TPP, RCEP, and the New Silk Road," *Asian Security,* 11 (3), 2015, 206–224.

Miller, Tom. *China's Asian Dream*. London: Zed Books, 2017.

Mo, Chen. "Exploring Economic Relations between China and the GCC States," *Journal of Middle Eastern and Islamic Studies (in Asia)*, 5 (4), 2011, 88–105.

Niblock, Tim and Yang, Guang. *Security dynamics of East Asia in the Gulf region*. Berlin: Gerlach Press, 2014.

Niu, Xinchun and Haibing, Xing. "China's Interest in and Influence Over the Middle East," *Contemporary International Relations*, 24, (1), 2014, 37–58.

Olimat, Muhamad S. *China and the Middle East: From Silk Road to Arab Spring*. London: Routledge, 2013.

Olimat, Muhamad S. *China and the Middle East since World War II: A bilateral approach*. Lanham: Lexington Books, 2014.

Olimat, Muhamad S. *China and the Gulf Cooperation Council Countries: Strategic Partnership in a Changing World*. Maryland: Lexington Books, 2016.

Perez-Des Rosiers, David. "A Comparative Analysis of China's Relations with Lebanon and Syria," *Sociology of Islam*, 7 (2–3), 2019, 189–210.

Qian, Xuewen. "The New Silk Road in West Asia under "the Belt and Road" Initiative," *Journal of Middle Eastern and Islamic Studies (in Asia)*, 10 (1), 2016, 26–55.

Qian, Xuming and Fulton, Jonathan. "China-Gulf Economic Relationship under the "Belt and Road" Initiative, "*Asian Journal of Middle Eastern and Islamic Studies*, 11(3), 2017, 12–21.

Qian, Xuming. "The Belt and Road Initiatives and China-GCC Relations," *International Relations and Diplomacy*, 5(11), 2017, 687–693.

Reardon-Anderson, James. *The Red Star and the Crescent: China and the Middle East*. New York: Oxford University Press, 2018.

Rodrigue Jean-Paul, Comtois Claude, and Slack Brian. *The Geography of Transport Systems*. New York: Routledge, 2013.

Schmierer, Richard J. "The Sultanate of Oman and the Iran Nuclear Deal," *Middle East Policy*, 22 (4), 2015, 113–120.

Scobell, Andrew and Nader Alireza. *China in the Middle East: The Wary Dragon*. Santa Monica, Calif.: RAND, 2016.

Scobell, Andrew. "Why the Middle East matters to China," In A. Ehteshami and N. Horesh (Eds), *China's Presence in the Middle East: The Implications of the One Belt, One Road Initiative* (pp. 9–23). New York: Routledge, 2018.

Çolakoğlu, Selçuk. "Turkey's Perspective on Enhancing Connectivity in Eurasia: Searching for Compatibility between Turkey's Middle Corridor and Korea's Eurasia Initiative," In Jung-Taik Hyun (ed.), *Studies in Comprehensive Regional Strategies Collected Papers* (pp. 543–634). Sejong: KIEP Publishing, 2016.

Sevilla, Henelito A Jr. "China's New Silk Route Initiative: Political and Economic Implications for the Middle East and Southeast Asia," *Journal of Middle Eastern and Islamic Studies (in Asia)*, 11 (1), 83–106.

Shariatinia, Mohsen and Azizi, Hamidreza. "Iran–China Cooperation in the Silk Road Economic Belt: From Strategic Understanding to Operational Understanding," *China & World Economy*, 25, No. (5), 2017, 46–61.

Shichor, Yitzhak. *The Middle East in China's Foreign Policy: 1949–1977*. Cambridge: Cambridge University Press, 1979.

Shichor, Yitzhak. "China's Middle East strategy: In search of wells and power," In L. Dittmer and G. T. Yu (Eds.), *China, the Developing World, and the New Global Dynamic* (pp. 157–175). Boulder and London: Lynne Rienner Publishers, 2010.

Shichor, Yitzhak. "Vision, provision and supervision: the politics of China's OBOR and AIIB and their implications for the Middle East', In A. Ehteshami, N. Horesh (eds.),

China's Presence in the Middle East: Implications for One Belt, One Road Initiative (pp. 38–53). London: Routledge, 2017.

Shichor, Yitzhak. "Gains and Losses: Historical Lessons of China's Middle East Policy for Its OBOR Initiative," *Asian Journal of Middle Eastern and Islamic Studies*, 12 (2), 2018, 127–141.

Struver, Georg. "China's partnership diplomacy: International alignment based on interests of ideology," *The Chinese Journal of International Politics*, 10 (1), (2017), 31–65.

Sun, Degang and Yahia H. Zoubir. "China's Economic Diplomacy Towards the Arab Countries: Challenges Ahead?," *Journal of Contemporary China*, 24 (95), 2015, 903–21.

Tessman, Brock, F. "System structure and state strategy: Adding hedging to the Menu," *Security Studies* 21(2), 2012, 192–231.

Tian, Wenlin. "The belt and road initiative and china's middle east strategy," *West Asia and Africa*, 2, 2016, 127–145.

Valeri, Marc M. *Simmering Unrest and Succession Challenges in Oman*. Washington, DC: Carnegie Endowment for International Peace, 2015.

Wan, Michelle, Lui, Maomin, and Yang, Guang. *China–Middle East Relations: Review And Analysis*. UK: Paths International Ltd, 2012.

Wu, Bingbing. "Strategy and Politics in the Gulf as Seen from China," In B. Wakefield and S. L. Levenstein (Eds), China and the Persian Gulf: Implications for the United States (pp. 10–26).Washington: Woodrow Wilson International Center for Scholars, 2011.

Wu Sike. "Constructing 'One Belt and One Road' to Enhancing China and GCC Cooperation," *Arab World Studies*, 2, 2015, pp. 4–13.

Wu, Sike. "The Strategic Docking between China and Middle East Countries under the "Belt and Road" Framework," *Journal of Middle Eastern and Islamic Studies (in Asia)*, 9 (4), 2015, 1–13.

Xiao Xian. "The 'Belt and Road Initiative' and China–Israeli Relations," *Journal of Middle Eastern and Islamic Studies (in Asia)*, 10 (3), 2016, pp. 1–23.

Yang, Guang. *China-Middle East Relations*. UK: Paths International Ltd, 2013.

Ye, Min. "China and competing for cooperation in Asia-Pacific: TPP, RCEP, and the New Silk Road," *Asian Security*, 11(3), 2015, 206–224.

Yetiv Steven A., and Chunlong Lu, "China, Global Energy, and the Middle East", *Middle East Journal*, 61 (2), 2007, 199–218.

Yetiv Steven A. *Challenged hegemony: The United States, China, and Russia in the Persian Gulf.* Stanford, California: Stanford University Press, 2018.

Yu-Shek Cheng, Joseph. "China's Relations with the Gulf Cooperation Council States: Multilevel Diplomacy in a Divided Arab World," *The China Review*, 16 (1), 2016, 35–64.

Zambelis, Chris. "China and the Quiet Kingdom: An Assessment of China–Oman Relations," *China Brief*, XV (22), 2015, 11–15.

Zhao, Hong. "China's Dilemma on Iran: Between Energy Security and a Responsible Rising Power," *Journal of Contemporary China* 23 (87), 2014, 408–424.

Zhiqiang, Zou. "Sino Turkish Strategic Economic Relationship in New Era," *Alternatives: Turkish Journal of International Relations*, 14 (3), 2015, 13–25.

Zhiqun Zhu. "China–Israel Relations: Past, Present and Prospect," *East Asian Policy*, 11 (4), 2019, 37–45.

Zreik, Mohamad. "China's Involvement in the Syria Crisis and the Implications of its Natural Stance in the War" *Journal of Political Science*, 21 (1), 2019, 56–65.

Index

Printed and bound by CPI Group (UK) Ltd, Croydon, CR0 4YY

23/09/2024

14561512-0001